COVENANT AND WORLD RELIGIONS

THE LITTMAN LIBRARY OF
JEWISH CIVILIZATION

Life Patron
COLETTE LITTMAN

Dedicated to the memory of
LOUIS THOMAS SIDNEY LITTMAN
*who founded the Littman Library for the love of God
and as an act of charity in memory of his father*
JOSEPH AARON LITTMAN
and to the memory of
ROBERT JOSEPH LITTMAN
who continued what his father Louis had begun
יהא זכרם ברוך

*'Get wisdom, get understanding:
Forsake her not and she shall preserve thee'*
PROV. 4:5

*The Littman Library of Jewish Civilization is a registered UK charity
Registered charity no. 1000784*

COVENANT AND WORLD RELIGIONS

■

Irving Greenberg, Jonathan Sacks, and the Quest for Orthodox Pluralism

■

ALON GOSHEN-GOTTSTEIN

London

The Littman Library of Jewish Civilization
in association with Liverpool University Press

2023

The Littman Library of Jewish Civilization
Registered office: 14th Floor, 33 Cavendish Square, London W1G 0PW
in association with Liverpool University Press
4 Cambridge Street, Liverpool L69 7ZU, UK
www.liverpooluniversitypress.co.uk/littman

Managing Editor: Connie Webber

Distributed in North America by
Oxford University Press Inc., 198 Madison Avenue
New York, NY 10016, USA

Catalogue records for this book are available from
the British Library and the Library of Congress

ISBN 978–1–800348–50–9

Publishing co-ordinator: Janet Moth
Copy-editing: Agnes Erdos
Proof-reading: Mark Newby
Indexing: Chris Cecot
Production, design, and typesetting by
Pete Russell, Faringdon, Oxon.

Printed and bound in Great Britain by
TJ Books Limited, Padstow, Cornwall

For

Y E H U D A G E L L M A N

*In appreciation of the sharing we enjoy on so many levels
and in gratitude for the hospitality and welcome
extended by Edie and yourself to Thérèse and myself*

■

Preface

■

THE HISTORY OF THIS BOOK is, in a reversal of common practice, like a Sunday meal turning into a shabbat meal. I am not referring to shabbat and Sunday as respective holy days for the two traditions that will be the focus of our attention. I am referring to the reality in our home, and I believe in many Jewish homes, that Sunday meals are basically constituted by leftovers from shabbat. A meal of leftovers can be quite tasty, especially if the remains of what were three distinct meals are served together. That was, more or less, the initial concept for the book, which was, I have to confess, based on 'leftovers' of other projects. Three distinct figures, each of whom was the focus of independent studies, were to be considered within one book, whose conceptual framework was contemporary Jewish thinkers facing world religions. The three were Abraham Joshua Heschel, Jonathan Sacks, and Irving (Yitz) Greenberg. I had published two essays on Heschel. I had studied Sacks' *The Dignity of Difference* and the differences in the two versions for a paper delivered at Yale University and posted online. I was asked to write an essay about Yitz Greenberg and Christianity. The essay grew and grew beyond what was necessary for that article, and I thought the full study of Greenberg would be the bulk of the present book. Bringing the three into dialogue held the promise of offering important insights into how Jewish thinkers relate to world religions.

As it turns out, the present book is, to maintain the analogy, worthy of a shabbat meal in its own right. As I worked on the project, I became increasingly aware of the depth and extensivity of Jonathan Sacks' work. This fuller awareness was, in part, an outcome of the scholarly quest to speak of Sacks in the fullness of knowledge that any subject deserves; but it was certainly also a response to his death. With the wave of appreciation for him following his passing away came a realization of his importance, of the riches of his thought, and consequently of the need to engage more fully and more deeply with it. As a consequence, the present book no longer focuses only on one important and representative work. It seeks to cover the entire Sacks corpus, extensive and challenging as it is. Owing to the sheer volume of his writing, the analysis of his thought ends up occupying the larger part of this study.

As a consequence of my own fuller discovery of Sacks (I say 'fuller' because I had been a fan for years and years), the book ends up focusing on only two of the three figures I had meant to study at the outset. I make the argument in the introduction for why the two should be studied in tandem, on historical and on conceptual grounds, as well as on the grounds of one of the theses of this book, that Sacks was influenced by Greenberg in his views of other faiths.

The two individuals on whom this book focuses are teachers, but they are also learning partners, theological *ḥavrutas*. As it happens, both are my personal acquaintances: I have enjoyed their friendship and shared with them theological ideas. The relationship is therefore not simply one that grows out of books; it grows out of life situations, themselves expressive of common theological interests. Yitz (as I call him, as do his friends) has been a conversation partner and supporter of my work for decades. Jonathan (as he asked me to call him) was a collaborator in interfaith work, also for decades, as part of the Elijah Board of World Religious Leaders, which I founded and to which he belonged. It is in light of these friendships, no less than in light of purely philosophical or theoretical concerns, that I engage with their writing. A spirit of friendship and familiarity of sorts allows me to show appreciation, but also to criticize as part of advancing a conversation—a conversation grounded in real relationships, not only in the ongoing pursuit of knowledge and wisdom in dialogue.

Throughout, I present and analyse; I explain, but I also engage critically. My method of presentation seeks to bring out the best in the thought of these two teachers but also to advance the field by asking how one might approach the subject matter differently, to my mind in a better way. This might involve taking other positions, broadening one's awareness of positions taken by thinkers in other faiths, or taking up issues and perspectives that were shunned. Whatever it may be, I show profound appreciation for both thinkers, even as I query, dialogue with, and even criticize them.

I must admit, however, that I wish I had had some of the conversations I am having over the pages of this book with the two figures. The need for having conversations with, in addition to analyses of, these individuals whom I have known has led to the inclusion of two appendices, in the form of interviews, that augment the textual studies of Sacks and Greenberg. In the case of Greenberg, I was able to engage him in discussion after my work was completed (Chapter 6). The interview is as much a theological dialogue as it is an interview in the journalistic sense of question and answer, designed to deliver information. It is thus a theological resource in its own right, allowing us to see Greenberg as he articulates his position, in dialogue with my own critique of his thought. In the case of Sacks, as I have already stated, most of this work was undertaken during the year of mourning for him. Consequently, I could not talk with him about these issues. As will become obvious in the course of reading, it may well be that it would have also not been possible to really enter into conversation with him on the issues that concern me as I read his work. While interviewing Sacks was not possible, I did feel the need to hear the voice of his interfaith partners and to gain some perspective on my readings of him. This led to a second interview, with Rowan Williams, former Archbishop of Canterbury, probably Sacks' closest interfaith partner (Chapter 14). Being able to discuss what I saw in his writing and to relate it to what *he* experienced was hugely helpful as it confirmed my understanding and shed a constructive light on how Sacks engaged personally in interfaith relations.

If all this sounds rather personal, then indeed that is one of the lessons that emerges from this book. Theoretical reflection in this domain, indeed in most reflective domains, is not theoretical only. It is deeply personal and conditioned by experiences, relationships, and, in this area of study, by friendships. To study thinkers who engage with other faiths in a constructive and dynamic way is therefore to study not only their ideas, but also their person and their relationships. It is to meet them in their greatness, as well as in their humanity. I am honoured and grateful to have the possibility of complementing the more abstract analyses with these personal interviews.

Friendship and collaboration are also key themes in my relationship with this book's publisher, the Littman Library. Connie Webber was supportive of the project from the get-go. Her encouragement and friendship are now decades old, building on the accumulated achievements of multiple publications at Littman, now home to my ongoing work in the field of Jewish theology of religions. Connie's support and understanding include not only working towards acceptance of the initial project. She was also supportive of the revised concept, and has proven a solid ally in ways too numerous to mention in the present context. I express my fond gratitude to her in a professional as well as personal sense.

This is my second book copy-edited by Agi Erdos. Her philosophical acumen and engaged reading are complemented by her careful attention to every iota of the text. This careful attention is another way of deepening friendship—a kind of academic *ḥavruta* in realizing a common project. Indeed, as this project has advanced so has our friendship, and the subject matter of Judaism and other faiths has opened up important avenues for enriching exchanges.

Janet Moth has been a silent and hidden presence, facilitating completion of the book in a smooth way, away from the limelight. That too is a form of friendship.

And final words of gratitude go to Pete Russell for his creativity, both artistic and theological. Working with Pete is never only a matter of aesthetics. It is where aesthetics and spirituality come together.

The dual themes of professional association and personal friendship are also apt for a description of who Yehuda Gellman, to whom this volume is dedicated, is for me. For years, he has been one of my closest conversation partners, fully sharing in the concerns of the present book. As philosopher, Jewish scholar, and above all spiritual seeker, he has emerged as one of my closest associates, who really understands what I am trying to achieve in my work and who partakes in it and contributes to it regularly. My and Thérèse's friendship with Edie and him is another evocation of the theme of the shabbat meal, mentioned above, that gives such meaning to our life. Whether in the framework of the numerous shabbat meals that we have shared or in the generous lending of their home to us so we can celebrate shabbat in Jerusalem, a bond of friendship has developed that unites shabbat and weekday, human, intellectual, and spiritual concerns—a friendship lived in God's presence, as part of a common spiritual and intellectual quest. May Edie and Yehuda live to see the coming to light of a Judaism that realizes the many spiritual qualities that both Greenberg and Sacks put forth as its true character and ideal.

All the themes of this book coalesce as I think with gratitude of my partner to the journey—Thérèse. Our covenant of marriage is a covenant of friendship, and an important component of that covenant is our common exploration of Judaism and world religions. As the one person who more than any other understands my life mission, she has been an integral part of the meetings, conversations, and reflections that find expression in this book. Our covenantal love finds expression in the very quest to which this volume is dedicated.

Contents

■

Note on Transliteration xiii

Introduction 1

PART I
IRVING (YITZ) GREENBERG
Covenant, Christianity, and World Religions

1. Introducing Irving Greenberg 23
2. Reading Religions: A God's-Eye View 33
3. Confronting the Faith of Christians 45
4. Covenant: A Necessary Cornerstone of Greenberg's Thought? 67
5. Greenberg's Theology: Reception and Evaluation 132
6. Interview with Irving Greenberg 149

PART II
JONATHAN SACKS
Covenant, the Dignity of Difference, and Religious Pluralism

7. Introducing Jonathan Sacks 193
8. Covenant: Structuring Judaism, Structuring Human Relationships 214
9. *The Dignity of Difference* 255
10. Religious Pluralism 299
11. Viewing and Presenting Other Religions 331
12. What Is Dialogue for Sacks? 358

13. The Power of Religious Imagination and
the Legacy of Sacks 386

14. Rowan Williams on Jonathan Sacks 397

PART III

Engaging with Greenberg and Sacks

15. A Comparative Appreciation 411

16. Jewish Theology of Religions: Continuing the
Conversation 425

Bibliography 445

Index 457

Note on Transliteration

■

THE TRANSLITERATION of Hebrew in books published by the Littman Library reflects consideration of the type of books they are, in terms of their content, purpose, and readership. The system adopted therefore reflects a broad, non-specialist approach to transcription rather than the narrower approaches found in the *Encyclopaedia Judaica* or other systems developed for text-based or linguistic studies. The aim has been to reflect the pronunciation prescribed for modern Hebrew rather than the spelling or Hebrew word structure, and to do so using conventions that are generally familiar to the English-speaking reader.

In accordance with this approach, no attempt is made to indicate the distinctions between *alef* and *ayin*, *tet* and *taf*, *kaf* and *kuf*, *sin* and *samekh*, since these are not universally relevant to pronunciation; likewise, the *dagesh* is not indicated except where it affects pronunciation. Following the principle of using conventions familiar to the majority of readers, however, transcriptions that are well established have been retained even when they are not fully consistent with the transliteration system adopted. On similar grounds, the *tsadi*, although generally *ts*, is rendered by 'tz' in such familiar anglicized words as 'barmitzvah'. Likewise, the distinction between *ḥet* and *khaf* has been retained, using *ḥ* for the former and *kh* for the latter; the associated forms are generally familiar to readers, even if the distinction is not always borne out in pronunciation, and for the same reason the final *heh* is indicated too. As in Hebrew, no capital letters are used except that an initial capital has been retained in transliterating titles of published works (for example, *Shulḥan arukh*).

Since no distinction is made in this transliteration system between *alef* and *ayin*, they are both indicated by an apostrophe, but only in intervocalic positions where a failure to do so could lead an English-speaking reader to pronounce the vowel-cluster as a diphthong—as, for example, in *ha'ir*—or otherwise mispronounce the word. An apostrophe is also used, for the same reason, to disambiguate the pronunciation of other English vowel clusters, as for example in *mizbe'aḥ*.

The *sheva na* is indicated by an *e*—*perikat ol*, *reshut*—except, again, when established convention dictates otherwise.

The *yod* is represented by *i* when it occurs as a vowel (*bereshit*), by *y* when it occurs as a consonant (*yesodot*), and by *yi* when it occurs as both (*yisra'el*).

Names have generally been left in their familiar forms, even when this is inconsistent with the overall system.

Introduction

Jewish Theology of Religions Today

Religions reflect on other religions. It is part and parcel of the religious thought of any religion, anywhere, anytime, to consider the status of another religion. This has always been the case. It is natural for believers to understand themselves in relation to others and to evaluate the validity, efficacy, problematics, or any other dimension of another religion, and which in turn reflects upon their own. It matters little whether attitudes to those other religions are positive or negative. The point is that the fullness of religious reflection involves thinking about them. We nowadays refer to such reflection as theology of religions, the theological consideration of a given religion by another.

Judaism has been reflecting on the status of other religions since its foundation. Views have changed, as have the religions that Judaism encountered. Judaism has, over the course of millennia, offered a rich array of possibilities and precedents for viewing other religions.[1] These views continue to serve religious thought today in a variety of ways, at times complex. From this perspective, present-day thinking stands in continuity with a long history of Jewish reflection on other religions.

There is, however, also a novelty in present-day reflection on other faiths. That novelty stems from fundamental changes in attitudes between faiths globally, especially since the time of the Second World War. Overall, we have entered an interreligious age, or at least an age in which co-operation is increasingly replacing competition, acceptance of the other faith is gradually replacing its rejection, and a new paradigm for relations between religions is taking hold, with the goals of peace, social harmony, and global flourishing

[1] For an overview of typical Jewish modalities of relating to other religions, See Brill, *Judaism and Other Religions*. For a representative analysis and examples of the concerns of a Jewish theology of religions, see Goshen-Gottstein and Korn (eds.), *Jewish Theology and World Religions*.

defining new ways in which they relate to each other and view each other. These changes do not mean that older ways of thinking have disappeared. Rather, a gradual process can be recognized, where new thoughts enter, paradigms gradually change, and broader circles are shaped by a new ethos of interreligious understanding and co-operation. All religions at this time give expression to older, often more competitive and exclusive, paradigms alongside the more recent and more accepting, one might say pluralistic, ones, whether of recent or of older vintage. Thinkers and adherents of all religions face a choice regarding the kind of teaching they preach and uphold in relation to other faiths. The choice involves taking up positions and justifying them in theoretical terms, both with regard to adherents and beliefs of other faiths and concerning precedents and patterns found within one's own faith. All this is the stuff and process of theology of religions as it shapes ideas, attitudes, and movements in today's world.

Judaism too takes part in the redrawing of boundaries and attitudes between faiths. It does so during a time of great change within itself. Geographical and demographic changes resulting from the great historical events of the twentieth century, especially the Holocaust and the founding of the State of Israel, are matched by ideological changes pertaining to Jewish denominations and new agendas defining the internal Jewish conversation.

One of the agendas that have come to light as part of broader theoretical shifts during the course of the twentieth century is the attitude to other religions. In practical terms, the question is tackled differently in Israel and in the diaspora. In Israel, Judaism is the majority faith. The incentive for understanding other groups is lower, especially given the polarization within Israeli society and the ongoing struggle against its neighbours, all too often identified by their religious identities. In the diaspora, a more robust interaction with other faiths is found, leading also to greater theoretical engagement in theology of religions. Another fault line in the development of recent Jewish theology of religions is denominational. For many years, as Jewish–Christian relations improved following the Second World War, Orthodoxy was behind other streams of Judaism in its engagement with other faiths. This was in part due to more conservative leanings among the Orthodox and a greater tendency to insularity as a means of self-protection and of upholding religious identity. This tendency found expression also in theoretical terms. While some figures, such as the famed halakhist Rabbi

Moshe Feinstein, forbade any form of interfaith engagement, more 'open' leaders placed their own boundaries on engagement with other religions. Rabbi Joseph B. Soloveitchik is a particularly important voice here. The leader of modern Orthodoxy, he sought to establish a balance between openness and collaboration, on the one hand, and the protection of Jewish religious interests on the other. This led to a position that rejected theological dialogue while approving of collaboration on the social front, in the common living space between Jews and members of other faiths.[2]

The starting point for the entry of the Orthodox into interreligious dialogue, and even more so into the domain of theology of religions, is thus characterized by boundaries and hesitancy. At the same time, it is also characterized by deep care for the tradition and mastery of its details, in ways one often finds lacking among other streams of Judaism. I recall a session I once moderated with several top Jewish thinkers, where the issue of other religions as *avodah zarah*, idolatry, was raised. A leading Conservative (by then post-denominational) head of a rabbinical seminary declared flatly: 'These questions are of no concern to me.' While he did not speak for all non-Orthodox, it is clear that Orthodox thinkers will typically have a heavier theological burden to carry, and more justifying to do, if they seek to advance interfaith relations, recognize other faiths, or put forward a vision of Judaism that validates other religions and is positive towards them.

Putting forth a vision of other faiths is a project that is carried out by individuals who seek to advance thinking within their own tradition or sub-tradition. It is a process that requires more than citing existing sources and positions. It engages the thinkers in theoretical construction, a re-reading of key sources in their tradition, the establishment of new theoretical paradigms, and shaping hearts, minds, and attitudes towards a new, typically more open, orientation towards other faiths and their adherents. It is, accordingly, a work for the few, and as such also for the excellent few who have the capacity, interest, and vision to undertake a reconsideration of Jewish views of other faiths. Typically, this is carried out as part of a broader vision of Judaism, its present-day standing, and of where it can, or should, grow. Such a broader vision is often at odds with common perceptions, seeking as it

---

[2] Rabbi Soloveitchik's ideas were expressed in a famous essay, 'Confrontation', published before the Second Vatican Council. For the essay and responses to it, see 'Rabbi Joseph Soloveitchik on Interreligious Dialogue'. 'Confrontation' still holds great sway for many and remains an official position that guides modern Orthodox participation in interfaith dialogue.

does to advance a form of Judaism that may be seen as higher or more noble, more humanistic, more spiritual. In sum, articulating a Jewish view of other religions is a task for thought leaders.

Among the Orthodox, there have been very few thinkers who have undertaken the task of propounding a contemporary view of other faiths. Most of Orthodoxy does not share in the need for such restatement, which would require that one make room in one's thinking for a series of changes and novel realities. This includes awareness of and participation in the new global paradigm of collaboration between faiths. It also must include knowledge of changes in the way Judaism is viewed by other religions, notably Christianity, and of the theological revolution that may be designated by appeal to its symbol, the Second Vatican Council document *Nostra aetate*. One must be willing to believe in changes in the attitude of the other almost as a condition for willingness to revisit one's own attitudes. At the very least, one must be willing to participate in common social movements that grow out of such changes, even if one insists that they should not lead to theological changes or to changing one's stance towards another faith. One must further recognize a global need for religions to collaborate towards either peaceful coexistence, the common work of addressing global challenges, or the spiritual opportunities that open up through deeper mutual understanding.

Few Orthodox thinkers can be described as 'compliant' with such a vision. Whether owing to Orthodox insularity or because of adherence to limitations on dialogue and engagement with other faiths following the guidelines of Rabbi Soloveitchik, or perhaps as a result of broader avoidance of theological questions,[3] the number of Orthodox thinkers who have advanced theoretical reflection on other faiths can be counted on one hand, if that.[4] Among these are the two rabbis studied in the present work—Irving Greenberg and Jonathan Sacks.

Both of these figures are thought leaders, whose contribution to a Jewish view of other religions should be appreciated in line with a fuller vision of present-day Judaism and its needs. While they both value and cite Rabbi Soloveitchik, Greenberg as his student and Sacks as a great admirer, neither

---

[3] Some consider that it is this very avoidance that led Rabbi Soloveitchik to adopt his position, fearing Jewish inferiority in the framework of a theological conversation.

[4] In more recent years the tides are changing and a new generation of young scholars is helping shift perspectives from within Orthodoxy.

of them is bound by his mandates. Both have engaged not only in theoretical reflection on other religions but also in on-the-ground relations with other religious communities, leaders, and thinkers, each according to his specific profile, spelled out in the present study. Both of them have put forward a theory that has a significant degree of substance, novelty, and consistency, beyond simply citing one or another medieval voice and applying it to current relations with other faiths. In short, both are original thinkers who have sought to restate a vision of Judaism, including a vision of its relations with other faiths.

The comparison between the two figures goes beyond their being thought leaders. Several other individuals might also be described in those terms.[5] Both thinkers have addressed the above issues consistently over the scope of decades and have built a robust body of reflection. They have engaged in scriptural interpretation in line with the concerns of Judaism and other faiths. But most importantly, both of them have undertaken the task by appeal to one of the central categories of Jewish theology—the covenant. I do not know of other thinkers who can be described as bringing together all these elements. This is especially so with regard to the application of 'covenant' to the concerns of a Jewish theology of religions. To think of other faiths in covenantal terms, as part of one's own Jewish theology, is in fact to include the concerns of a Jewish theology of religions in the heart of one's own religious reflection, an expression of the most central and formative category of Jewish self-understanding. A Jewish view of other religions is accordingly considered fundamental to Jewish self-understanding and ultimately to the fulfilment of Judaism's spiritual purpose, or at least its spiritual vision.

All this justifies the common analysis of these two thinkers alongside one another, and the organization of that analysis around the core structuring notion of the covenant. This, then, is the logic that governs the present volume. I study Greenberg and Sacks as they relate to other faiths and put forth a view of other faiths—their own theology of religions—by reflection upon the 'covenant' and its application to the Jewish view of religions. In so doing, I hope to make available the riches of their thought first and foremost to their own 'home' constituencies. Thought leaders are not always followed,

---

[5] I think of Michael Wyschogrod, David Hartman, and possibly David Novak, putting aside issues of denominational identity.

and even when they are, they may be followed for part of their vision, not for its entirety. A systematic exposition of the ideas of these thinkers allows us to appreciate their thought in its fullness. Such exposition, as we shall see, also allows us to foreground their achievements, their comprehensive vision, but also some of the drawbacks and limitations that attach themselves to their outlook. Theological reflection, like all forms of knowledge, is an incremental process, where growth and advancement are attained gradually, through further reflection, critique, and exposition. In presenting these thinkers I hope to contribute to their fuller appreciation, with their complexity, which involves also recognizing their limitations.

Having said that much brings me to a further purpose of this study. Description is half the work, probably a great deal more than half. But beyond description lie analysis, critique, and evaluation. The growth of thought and reflection from generation to generation involves exposing assumptions, querying decisions, and clarifying method. The practice of Jewish theology of religions is young and its method must be questioned as it grows. These thinkers, then, must be appreciated and evaluated not only in terms of the positions they have taken, but also in terms of their method, how far they have gone, and where the application of other methods or other approaches might yield alternative, hopefully even better, outcomes. Thus, in engaging with Sacks and Greenberg I treat them as part of my own ongoing work in the field of Jewish theology of religions.[6] Accordingly, I consider them theological conversation partners. We share concerns and goals. They have done important work. In presenting them and engaging with their thought, I seek not only to make their positions more broadly known, but to advance the very agenda they put forth. My goal is, one might say, qualitative as well as quantitative. In quantitative terms, I would like their thought to be better known, better received, and more fully owned, both by their home communities and by others, within Judaism and beyond. In qualitative terms, I attempt to deepen, improve, and advance the theological conversation within Judaism in the field of theology of religions.

[6] This work has found expression in a series of publications, single as well as group-authored, that has sought to advance the contemporary agenda of a Jewish theology of religions. More than half a dozen titles have appeared to date that serve this quest. See the list of publications in the Wikipedia entry 'Alon Goshen-Gottstein'. The present study should be appreciated as continuing the conversation found in those works. It is a means of tackling these concerns by focusing on two of the most important voices of Orthodoxy over the past decades.

What, then, are the issues that we will tackle as we study these two figures? Broadly speaking we will examine how they viewed other religions. In the case of Greenberg, we will be looking especially at one particular religion—Christianity; in the case of Sacks, we will have a broader view of religious pluralism. The difference is suggestive and representative of greater differences between them, as my analysis will show.

We will also study how their view of other faiths stands in relation to tradition and try to identify how to best understand them in continuity with tradition. At the same time, we will seek to appreciate their novelty and originality, which itself can be viewed in dialogue and in continuity with tradition. We will study not only their positions but also their method, and how they go about relating to other faiths. This, in turn, will lead us to an evaluation of their own interfaith involvement. As will become apparent, there are meaningful differences between them, so much so that one may recognize two very different modalities of engaging with other faiths: the one more personal, relational, and theologically oriented, the other more theoretical and social in its goals. These differences touch upon theoretical issues such as the nature and extent of religious pluralism. They also touch on practical questions such as how deeply and in what ways relations between faiths and their adherents should be practised.

As it turns out, Sacks and Greenberg are as close as they are far apart from each other. They are close in that they share broad common sensibilities with respect to Judaism and other religions. They both advocate relations with other religions. They both offer us a theory for doing so, and, significantly, they both ground these efforts in the concept of the covenant, thereby making a view of other faiths fundamental to Judaism's self-understanding. They also share in the ideal of the centrality of the creation of mankind in the image of God and apply it to the concerns under discussion. They share multiple commonalities either as they read texts or as they apply traditional concepts.

But they also differ significantly in how deeply they are willing to enter into relationship, how much they are willing to gain a religious, as opposed to a human, understanding of the other. They differ, ultimately, in how radical they are willing to be. Better yet, they differ in how they are positioned in relation to their community and how they articulate their message while maintaining their position within the community.

As we consider these two figures, we are invited not only to explore their views but also to reflect on *how* they respond to other faiths and what models for engagement they put before us. In fact, this is where the critical exposition of their thought comes to the fore. Even more than critiquing ideas, I shall explore the viability of different methods, interrogate boundaries and internal breaks as these are found, and ask how necessary, helpful, or damaging they are to the ultimate cause that both thinkers seek to advance.

In light of all this, the programme of the book emerges. My introductory overview is followed by a brief history of the notion of covenant. Given how central covenant is to Sacks' and Greenberg's theology and to the focus of the present study, I begin with a historical review of the category, which will allow us to better appreciate their respective positions and their specific contribution to covenantal thinking.

The first part of the book is devoted to Greenberg. I study his position on Christianity, his views of world religions, and his approach to pluralism. Greenberg builds on the covenant as a means of affirming other faiths, primarily Christianity, and in so doing puts forth novel theological suggestions. I will query and critique these. One important lens for such critique is his reception within the Jewish community—one of the subjects of our conversation in Chapter 6. While Greenberg serves, to me, as a model of how to go about engaging with another faith, the specific theological moves he makes and the way he applies the covenant to other faiths seem to me to be more than his task requires and consequently end up alienating his audience. He can be appreciated between the three foci of deep and sincere engagement, including theological engagement, with the other, daring and original theological suggestions, and a mostly poor reception within the community. Negotiating and calibrating these three dimensions is the exercise undertaken in Part I of the book.

Part II is devoted to Sacks. His corpus is significantly larger than Greenberg's and therefore analysing his work involves a thorough reading of his many books, identifying common motifs as well as the progress of ideas. I seek to identify the unchanging key elements that give his theory of religions its stability, consistency, and potential long-lasting impact. Sacks' approach is open and forthcoming in relation to other faiths, but it is also characterized by deep ambivalence and self-imposed breaks, be they emotional, theological, or practical. Analysing his thought is a process of entering into the core of this complexity—great intellectual achievement and interior breaks and limitations. This reflects on the extent and depth of his involvement with other faiths, his method of their study, his theory of pluralism, and ultimately the value of his interfaith engagement, or rather, different valuations of different forms of interfaith engagement. All this complexity leaves us with the challenge: What are Sacks' actual legacy and testimony in the field of theology of religions and interfaith work? If Greenberg's testimony was unequivocal, limited only by issues of reception, Sacks' testimony, popular as it is in its own way, is significantly complicated, even marred, by his own internal complexities. My exposition of Sacks seeks to bring all these complexities to light. In so doing, it will, I hope, make his thought and deeper vision available to all. His ideas and perspectives are interrogated and presented both for what they have already brought to light and for the potential they still hold, a potential that exceeds what Sacks himself was able to realize.

All this brings me to the final part of this book. Part III draws together the various insights, challenges, and perspectives studied in Parts I and II, with an eye to the future. I begin with a comparative evaluation of the two authors in terms of their theology and method. The comparative appreciation gives us a crisper view of both men, as well as highlighting what I, as someone deeply engaged in this field both theologically and practically, consider to be the optimal manner of advancing the conversation. Accordingly, it is a descriptive comparison, by means of which various points we have studied are drawn together into a composite view. But it is also an evaluative comparison, where, having recognized the different models of interfaith engagement that each of our authors represents, I express my own voice, preference, and method—once again, in dialogue with them both.

The final chapter extends my dialogical process to the theological domain. While greatly appreciative of the theological edifices Sacks and Greenberg have constructed, I am also unconvinced by significant parts of these edifices. Theological thought is a conversation with our teachers, friends, and predecessors. What kind of conversation would I have with the theologies put forth by these two thinkers? In the final part, I seek to restate many of their views in a way that rings truer to me or, to me, has greater integrity either theologically or exegetically. Put differently, their thought has provided us with very significant building blocks. In the final section, I take these building blocks and propose novel ways of combining them, thereby creating a new theological structure. Were it not for their prior work, these building blocks would not be available to me. At the end of the day, and the end of the book, the structure that is proposed by means of these building blocks is entirely my own.

Covenant—A Brief History

During the biblical period, covenant was the most central theological category by means of which Israel's relationship with God was expressed.[7] A widely used political notion of the day, covenant provided, in the context of this exclusive relationship, a framework for identifying the mutual responsibilities of both parties, offered a definition for the relationship, and established God as Israel's God, while they in turn were his people. Israel's history could be recognized in light of faithfulness to the covenant. What went well and what went wrong could be interpreted as blessings and curses related to the covenant, recompense for faithfulness or lack thereof. Of all the peoples of the ancient Near East, Israel alone used this concept to describe its relationship with God, and claimed that it alone had a covenantal relationship with God. The vicissitudes of its history reflected its own adherence to that covenant.

What is most central in the covenant is the establishment of a relationship, a unique relationship, grounded in the Torah and its commandments as the primary framework from within which the covenant is viewed. Israel's history is thus intimately linked to the Torah and its commandments, and these in turn are tied into a narrative and conceptual framework provided by the covenant idea. Israel's history is viewed through a history of covenants, beginning with the patriarchs, continuing with the revelation at Sinai, and extending to moments of covenant renewal in the Torah and in prophetic and later literature. History, in this view, is a process of moving away from and returning to the covenant and therefore of re-establishing the relationship with God time and again, in faithfulness to the original covenant, or its primary articulation, typically understood in the context of

---

[7] This is best captured in Eichrodt, *Theology of the Old Testament*, vol. i. On this seminal work, see Spriggs, *Two Old Testament Theologies*, and Gottwald, 'W. Eichrodt: Theology of the Old Testament'. For a historical overview of the covenant idea and its study, see Nicholson, *God and His People*. It is common in theological circles to refer to Israel as the carrier and subject of the religion of Judaism. Some readers may be more used to talking of 'the Jewish People', but typically the use of this latter term serves historical studies more than theological reflection. In accordance with what is common in theological discourse, I will refer to Israel, rather than the Jewish People.

the revelation at Sinai or the Exodus. Because covenant is marked by possible failure and lack of fidelity, a return and a reaffirmation of it are necessary. The history of covenants is part of the ongoing quest to make Israel conform to God's will in faithfulness to the covenant.

One of the important features of the biblical covenant is that it is not a once-for-all reality. In fact, the Bible tells of multiple covenants, some in the human sphere and some between humanity and God. Covenant is a matter of history. It touches on history, it relates to historical events, and it has a history of its own. This history is crucial to the present book. The two authors whom we will study relate both to covenant as a broad structuring idea of Jewish religion and to specific covenants that form a history. How the different covenants within this history are to be related to each other and what is the scope of affiliation in the covenant are both questions that lie at the heart of their presentation as they consider covenant and its relationship to Israel, on the one hand, and to other religions, on the other.

In thinking of the history of the covenant, we can focus on its earliest stages as expounded in the biblical narrative, or on its history in its entirety. A consideration of the earlier stages of the covenant involves primarily the book of Genesis. While there is no explicit covenant made with the first human, Adam, a covenant is mentioned with reference to Noah in Genesis 9. The next one is that concluded with Abraham, in Genesis 15 and 17, with possible follow-up covenants with the other patriarchs, Isaac and Jacob.[8] A series of suggestive questions presents itself with regards to these covenants. Are they of a kind? What is the relationship between them? What is their actual content and substance?

For most of the history of Jewish reflection, the most important covenant was the one concluded with Israel in Sinai, as described in Exodus 19. It serves as the basis of Israel's religion and provides its primary reference point. That covenant is appreciated in relation to two trajectories, moving forward and moving backwards in time. Moving forward, it is the reference point for additional covenants, such as the one at Arbot Moab or that concluded by Joshua.[9]

Understanding covenant as a serial phenomenon also points us back from Israel's covenant to that with the patriarchs. What is their relationship? Is the earlier one fulfilled in the later one? Is it the basis for upholding the later one, under all circumstances, including at times of violation of the

[8] See Lev. 26: 42.   [9] Deut. 28; Josh. 24.

covenant? That much would seem to be the case in various instances in the Torah.[10]

The serial nature of covenant provides an important hermeneutical challenge as well as a vital point of departure for further theological reflection. It should be stated that nowhere do we find a comprehensive *Jewish* history of the covenant, taking into account the various covenantal moments. Whereas Christian theologians have created multiple constructs that place covenant within a 'covenant history', typically pointing beyond the Old Testament to the New Testament, Jews have never developed anything that approximates a covenantal history. We thus lack a Jewish religious view (as distinct from that of a Jewish scholar in biblical studies) of the history of covenant either from Noah or from Abraham through the entire Hebrew Bible and beyond. We similarly lack an agreed-upon account of the need for multiple covenants from Sinai onwards. A likely understanding of that need is the breaking or violation of an earlier covenant, which is replaced by a later one. Texts such as Jeremiah 31 are explicit about this. Rabbinic sources from the Middle Ages onwards repeatedly appeal to the strategy of making a new covenant where a previous one has failed in order to account for multiple covenants, whether in human relations[11] or in Israel's relationship with God. A new covenant reinstates, extends, and upholds the earlier one, following failure or other problems associated with the earlier covenant.

There are several reasons why we do not find an attempt to develop a systematic Jewish view of the history of covenant. The first is that Jews did not engage in systematic readings of the Bible until very recently, when they were exposed to literary and theological norms that had developed mostly among Christian Bible readers. Rabbinic reading practices were more focused on the smaller exegetical unit than on larger theoretical or theological constructs.

But there is an even more fundamental reason. It is not only that *systematic* did not mean much to post-biblical Judaism. *Covenant* did not mean much to it, or it meant much less than it did to biblical Judaism. In post-biblical Judaism we witness a significant decline in the function and centrality of covenantal thought. The idea did not exercise the same hold over all generations of Jewish faithful as they sought to articulate their relationship with God. Rabbinic Judaism showed far less interest in the term and

---

[10] Lev. 26: 42.   [11] See e.g. *Ḥizkuni* on Gen. 26: 28.

in the concept, having almost abandoned it completely.[12] It is a matter of conjecture as to why that might have been the case. One possibility, and one that I personally favour, refers to the very fragility of the covenant, as just described. The category contained in it its own constant undermining as it was vulnerable to Israel's disobedience and its possible loss of status and special relationship. Later generations, especially following the destruction of the First Temple, would seek to construct Israel's relationship with God on a much firmer foundation. To this end, elements of the covenant were applied independently of the covenantal framework. The relationship with God, obedience to the Torah, the promise of the Land of Israel, the merit of the fathers, reward and punishment—all operated as significant religious motives, but were not tied together in the structure of the covenant. Post-biblical Judaism, in this reading, provides us with substantive continuity with the core messages of biblical Judaism, but without the one central conceptual category that had held it all together for biblical faith.

It is often hard to offer one answer only for a transition as significant as the decline in biblical covenantal thought. Perhaps we need to think of an amalgam of ideas that came together to produce the change. If so, we can consider some other candidates as part of the broader paradigm shift that led away from biblical covenantal faith. One of these could be the rise of faith in the world to come as the site of true and ultimate religious significance. Covenantal thinking, tied as it is to the Land of Israel and to earthly reward and punishment, may not be suitable for capturing such a shift. The rise in the centrality of Torah study may be another dimension. For biblical faith, the Torah was mostly the set of covenantal commandments to be obeyed, not an object of study and contemplation. While in theory Torah could have been viewed as one more covenantal obligation, the fact is that biblical covenantal thought did not afford Torah study such a central role. Perhaps, then, the rise of Torah study launched separate ideals that stood on their own, independently of the covenantal structure, thereby leading to, or further contributing to, the cohesive notion of covenant falling apart and giving way to other means of expressing the centrality of core religious virtues.[13]

[12] See Davies, *The Gospel and the Land*, 107–8; Bonsirven, *Le Judaisme palestinien*, i. 79 ff. Compare Kimelman, 'The Rabbinic Theology of the Physical', 996.

[13] On Torah and the world to come as the two major rabbinic innovations, see Guttman, *The Philosophy of Judaism*, 32–5.

And then there is another theological consideration to take into account. Biblical thought was not fully monotheistic. It was, as some have called it, monolatric or henotheistic. That is, the Bible, in its earlier strata, recognized multiple gods. Israel's god was the greatest, the most powerful, possibly the highest. But for a very long stretch of the history of biblical thought, Israel's God was not the only God, nor was he the only God who could be legitimately worshipped. For some strands of biblical thought, other nations had the right to worship their gods, just as Israel was expected to worship its God.[14] It is only within such a theological matrix that one can understand the emergence of the idea of the covenant.[15] Covenant makes sense as the exclusive relationship that one god makes with one people. This god is not expected to forge similar relationships with other peoples, if for no other reason than that he is not understood, at least not primarily, as either the one and only God or the universal God. Once a more universal sense of God had come to the fore, such a view conflicted with the plain sense of the covenant. Therefore, among the various changes that led to the decline in covenantal thinking, we must also take into account the very understanding of the Divine, its universal relevance, and the position of Israel in relation to the universal God.[16]

We will never be able to suggest with certainty what the one single cause that led to the decline in covenantal thinking was. However, pointing to the process, recognizing how it was embedded in various shifts and developments in rabbinic thought, and seeing the changes as a whole do allow us to recognize how different rabbinic Judaism was from biblical Judaism. This difference is reflected in relation to the appeal to the notion of covenant.

Following the biblical period, the term never regained the currency it had enjoyed in biblical literature. Later Jewish thought systems were either shaped by rabbinic language or formed by various external influences. For them, covenant remained a biblical term that was interpreted in a specific context, rather than the governing logic of the entire religious structure. Covenant lost its centrality as a key structuring concept in post-biblical Jewish thought. Nevertheless, the different components of the biblical cov-

---

[14] See e.g. Gen. 31: 54; Judg. 11: 24.

[15] See Sperling, 'Israel's Religion in the Ancient Near East'.

[16] Reuven Kimelman, accordingly, relates the shift from biblical covenant to the rabbinic sovereignty of God as a formative notion with strong liturgical expressions to changes in the understanding of God. See Kimelman's chapter on the Shema in *The Rhetoric of the Jewish Liturgy*.

enant continued to shape Jewish religious life. In other words, functionally the covenant remained in place, even though conceptually it was no longer evoked as the overarching governing notion of the religious system.[17]

For nearly two millennia, the idea of the covenant lay dormant. Of course, it never fell into disuse, because the Bible kept nourishing religious language, imagination, and practice. In some groups, the centrality of biblical covenantal thinking found direct expression in how the life of the community was structured. We cannot understand the life of the Qumran community without realizing that it had kept alive biblical covenantal thinking, which led to ceremonies such as the annual renewal of the covenant and to the overall structuring of its religious life in covenantal terms. For most of rabbinic Judaism, however, the covenant continued to provide a language that was mostly used in specific contexts, outside the framework of a central governing notion and organizing principle of Judaism's theological world-view. Accordingly, *berit* could be understood as taking an oath,[18] as evaluating some significant mitzvah (commandment),[19] or as a means of God establishing the rules and norms of creation.[20] Later, for the kabbalistic tradition, the term took on other shadings. These could only be assumed once the overall meaning of covenant, *berit*, broke down, making room for other linguistic associations and ritual identifications to emerge. Primary among these was the identification of *berit* with circumcision, the male member, and sexual purity, all understood within the kabbalistic framework of the godhead and corresponding to one particular *sefirah*—Yesod. While it is a valuable thought exercise to weave together the biblical and kabbalistic senses of *berit* in a unified structure,[21] we must first acknowledge the fundamental reality of the breakdown of the comprehensive system of the meaning of *berit*. This breakdown allowed these multiple new emphases to arise, thereby providing theoretical building blocks for a future and altered

---

[17] In this light, one should mention the work of Sanders, *Paul and Palestinian Judaism*. Sanders describes the various forms of Second Temple Judaism in terms of 'covenantal nomism'. A close reading of his important study reveals that most of the sources that express this pattern of the religious life do so without explicit mention of the covenant. This is certainly true of the rabbinic sources he analyses in chapter 1.

[18] *Mekhilta*, 'Shirata', 9, and numerous occurrences in rabbinic literature.

[19] Mishnah *Ned.* 3: 11.

[20] Note the expression *berit keruta* in rabbinic literature, for example BT *RH* 17b, *MK* 18a, *Nid.* 58a, and more.

[21] I explore this in my forthcoming *In God's Presence*, chs. 2 and 8.

covenantal theology, and it made possible theological innovations that were absorbed into the covenantal framework. Thus, while being informed by the fundamental covenantal dynamics, Jewish faith grew, expanded, and deepened in various ways that ultimately aided in the realization of the key covenantal aspirations.

Throughout its history, Israel continued to adhere to the understanding that it existed in a constitutive relationship with God, one which did not fade with time or with political changes. In coping with new realities, new ideas came to the fore. Certain concepts that had played a major role in biblical Israel's religious vocabulary were moved from centre stage to the sidelines. New theological formulations replaced older biblical ones. These offered new theological understanding, suitable for the time and the circumstance of the people as it moved through history and as its spiritual understanding evolved.

A purposeful view of Judaism's evolution seeks to recognize the deepening of spiritual understanding as ideas and institutions came into place through historical failure. Lack of covenantal faithfulness and ensuing shifts in the structure of Jewish religion took away and destroyed some key institutions and ideas. But they also gave rise to new forms of religious life that helped Judaism advance on its spiritual path. For example, the destruction of the Temple gave rise to set prayer. The loss of prophetic guidance was a fundamental loss, but it led to alternative forms of spiritual development, associated with the cultivation and development of Torah knowledge. A further factor, crucial to our present study, was the place of the covenant in the universal vision of Judaism. The relational exclusivity of the covenanting God gave way to a vision of the universal God, who reached out to all of humanity.[22]

A change in the uses of covenant occurred in twentieth-century Jewish thought. Here too we lack a definitive history of how this change came about.[23] Several elements can be suggested. First and foremost is the on-

---

[22] While this can be conceived of also within a covenantal framework, the receding of the covenant to the conceptual background allows a more universal face of the Divine to come to the fore.

[23] The point can be illustrated with reference to Eugene Borowitz, one of the noted covenant theologians, who, by his own admission, introduced the term 'covenantal theology' to Jewish theological discourse. As Kavka, 'The Perils of Covenant Theology', notes, Borowitz, on the one hand, claims to have introduced covenant into contemporary Jewish theology, but he also discovers earlier parallels in the Protestant theology, or federal theology, of

going testimony of the Bible itself. As long as the Bible is read, one cannot ignore the significance of the idea of the covenant. The reader is exposed to it and therefore it will eventually assert itself and speak out, over and against any changes that may have led to its relegation to the backstage of Jewish thought.

Then there are the various readers of the Bible, not all Jewish. Certain Protestant groups have been mindful of the centrality of the covenant idea since the Reformation.[24] It has accordingly surfaced in Christian theologies of the Bible and among noted Christian theologians.[25] These could then impact Jewish readers who were current with contemporary theological developments.[26]

A return to the biblical legacy is also part of Jewish modernity, especially in conjunction with the return to the Land of Israel. The Land of Israel is central to covenantal thinking. The decline in covenantal thought went hand in hand with physical removal from the Land and the overall lower place it occupied in specific configurations of Judaism.[27] If one seeks to recover a robust sense of the Land, biblical covenantal resources are primary.[28]

A third trajectory may also be proposed. Jewish thinkers in post-Holocaust America spent much time reflecting on the meaning of Jewish particularity and election.[29] The issue was of obvious importance both from the perspective of concerns for maintaining Jewish identity and survival and as a new focus that would shift attention away from a Holocaust orientation

American Puritans. A partial discussion of sources of twentieth-century Jewish covenantal thought is found in Cooper, *Contemporary Covenantal Thought*, 47–58. Cooper does not consider Christian influences, nor earlier Jewish figures such as Rabbi Hayim Hirschensohn and his covenantal-political thought.

[24] As I learned from Professor Christian Chalamet, Zwingli is probably the fountainhead of a movement that continues in various forms, through 'federal theology' and up to theologians such as Karl Barth and the various expressions of Christianity that he influenced.

[25] Notably Walter Eichrodt. The idea also receives prominent attention in the theology of Karl Barth.

[26] One of these is Rabbi Soloveitchik, who influenced both authors studied in this book. On Soloveitchik and Barth, see Schwartz, *From Phenomenology to Existentialism: The Philosophy of Rabbi Joseph B. Soloveitchik*, 319–63; Singer and Sokol, 'Joseph Soloveitchik: Lonely Man of Faith', 240–1.

[27] See Goshen-Gottstein, 'The Covenant with the Fathers' (Heb.); id., 'The Land of Israel in the Economy of Rabbinic Thought', (Heb.).

[28] Seen from this perspective, it is striking how small a role, if at all, the covenant and its realization played in the formative stages of Zionist ideology, including religious Zionism.

[29] See Eisen, *The Chosen People in America*.

that impacted much of post-war Jewish thought. We thus note a rise in interest in election, and with it in the notion of covenant, among Jewish thinkers since the 1970s.

The combination of the various factors here suggested, as well as others that I may not have taken note of, led to 'covenant' becoming a major structuring category of Jewish religious thought in the latter part of the twentieth century, especially among English-speaking thinkers and theologians. Furthermore, the covenant became a major category within Jewish–Christian relations, in ways that had not been seen in the two millennia of their shared history.[30]

The 'return' of covenantal thinking is not a simple return to a biblical world-view. That would be impossible, given the history and development of Jewish thought. Rather, it is an integration of emphases and characteristics of Jewish thought, as it developed over millennia, into a restatement of Judaism in the light of the covenant. This restatement features elements that are new or that were never articulated with as much clarity as their recent iterations provide. Covenant is founded upon free will and human initiative and choice. Already the biblical covenant is characterized by a sense of reciprocity in terms of obligations. That reciprocity takes on fuller expression in later thought. Human responsibility and initiative complement divine initiative and grace. When this complementarity is extended to its fullness, we come to a further dimension of how covenant is understood. Beyond reciprocity lie synergy, co-creation, power-sharing within a common space inhabited by God and Israel, a matrix wherein the spiritual life and reality itself are born jointly between the two covenantal partners.[31]

This brief history provides us with the context within which to appreciate the two figures to whom this study is dedicated. Both Greenberg and Sacks partake in what may be called Jewish covenantal revival, in terms of the return to covenant as a central structuring idea of Jewish faith. They both share the broader tendency that characterizes many thinkers in the second half of the twentieth century to present covenant as a major category that informs Jewish self-understanding, and possibly even offers a definition of what Judaism itself is. Both of them are aware of the place that

[30] Two volumes of Jewish–Christian dialogue are organized around this theme. See Korn and Pawlikowski (eds.), *Two Faiths, One Covenant?* and Jenson and Korn, *Covenant and Hope: Christian and Jewish Reflections.*

[31] On covenant, reciprocity, and power-sharing, see Elazar, 'The Political Theory of Covenant'.

covenant has gained in recent theory, be it political theory, biblical studies, or contemporary theology, though they do not necessarily draw on the same modern or contemporary sources. Both of them cast the message of Judaism to the world in terms of the covenant. While that may not seem such a novelty, in fact it is. During the entire eclipse in covenantal thinking over the stretch of millennia, we do not find the concept as part of an account of the meaning of Judaism and its purpose among classical thinkers.

If one of the gains or benefits in the eclipse of the covenant was the rise of universality in Judaism's vision, both thinkers make the striking move of including that universal vision within their understanding of covenant. This is without precedent, nor is it obvious from biblical sources. It requires an act of theological creativity to cast Judaism's message in relation to the world at large in covenantal terms. The common constructive exercise is all the more pronounced when covenantal thinking addresses not simply humanity, but other religions. Greenberg and Sacks are the first to appeal to covenantal thinking as a means of addressing Judaism's relations with world religions. This, I believe, is unique to them, both within Orthodoxy and among other Jewish covenantal thinkers. It also highlights one of the questions of this study, namely, the relationship and likely dependence that exists between these two thinkers.

How Greenberg and Sacks use covenant echoes many of the later developments in the term. However, where we note their originality is in their use of the biblical sources. I mentioned earlier the covenant being a serial phenomenon and the need to account for the multiple successive covenants found in the biblical narrative. While we lack a comprehensive Jewish or rabbinic narrative of covenant, and while neither of these authors provides one, they do grapple with questions that had not been part of the agenda of classical Jewish authors. Specifically, the history of covenant in Genesis and whether it might be considered a universal category relating to all of humanity or whether it designates Israel's particular relationship with God are questions that lie at the heart of their reflections. Both authors thus engage in parallel, and often related, readings of the same biblical sources in service of the same theological challenge: to find the place of Judaism among world religions and to identify its message to the world at large. These uses are novel in the history of Jewish covenantal reflection and justify the detailed study of both thinkers as well as of the likely relationship between their theoretical and hermeneutical work.

Let me make the statement even more clearly. If I were asked to name a third author whose interests overlap with those of Greenberg and Sacks, I could not. Not only is there not another Orthodox thinker who has tackled these issues in this way, I am not aware of any other Jewish author who has devoted attention to this precise configuration of the covenant, its challenges and promises. The combination of reading Genesis, considering its relationship to Israel's covenant, tying it in with Israel's mission to the world, and putting all these in the service of a Jewish vision of other faiths and a statement of the relationship between Jewish particularity and universality is unique to these two authors. While other authors have tackled some of these ideas, Sacks and Greenberg are the only ones who have put forth a comprehensive vision of what covenant is, how it defines the message of Judaism and its view of other faiths, and how key biblical sources are to be understood in service of this vision. They thus form a group of their own, both by way of denominational affiliation and by way of theoretical and hermeneutical interests. This increases, of course, the likelihood of influence of one on the other as these ideas come together and find expression in their writings.

Let us then embark on an in-depth study of these authors in order to identify how each of them relates to the covenant, its biblical foundations, and above all to the relationship between Judaism and other religions as seen through the lens of the covenant.

PART I

IRVING (YITZ) GREENBERG
COVENANT, CHRISTIANITY, AND WORLD RELIGIONS

CHAPTER ONE

Introducing Irving Greenberg

R ABBI IRVING GREENBERG is, I would submit, far and away the most engaged contemporary Jewish thinker to have thought through the meaning of Christianity for present-day Judaism and to have put forth a carefully constructed notion of their relationship. He is not the most prolific author, nor is he the greatest expert on the historical relationship between the two faith communities at various points in time and place over the past two millennia. But he is arguably the thinker, certainly the Orthodox Jewish thinker, who has thought hardest and deepest about the meaning of this relationship. For Greenberg, the question of Jewish–Christian relations goes well beyond formulating a halakhic ruling or a community policy. It is also more than a theological challenge that has to be overcome. It is, rather, a deep personal quest to come to terms with another religion and its spiritual message, and to gain a higher vision of the purpose of that religion's existence and of what kind of relationship Judaism and Christianity should enjoy.

Greenberg's thought is constructed from several building blocks, by means of which he wrestles with these issues in essay after essay over the scope of several decades. Thankfully, his major contributions have been assembled in one volume, which makes it possible for readers to follow the evolution of his thought and to watch his deep personal engagement as it unfolds over time.[1] One of the greatest assets of this collection of essays is the introductory piece, which contextualizes the different essays in his own life process.[2] This autobiographical, reflective piece allows us to view Greenberg the man behind Greenberg the theologian. It is a must read not

---

[1] Greenberg, *For the Sake of Heaven and Earth*.
[2] The essay is entitled 'On the Road to a New Encounter between Judaism and Christianity'.

only for understanding the background to his own thinking, but also for the lessons it teaches us about how to do theology, particularly theology that concerns relations between religions. One encounters the pains, struggles, aspirations, attempts, and above all the deep engagement and creative spirit of a theologian who has engaged with Christianity consistently over a life-time,[3] seeking to come to terms with that religion and its significance for a sensitive and thoughtful Jewish thinker.

Personal Background

Key to Greenberg's process is the fact that Christianity is not encountered as a theoretical construct or a historical reality. It is encountered through deep and committed personal relationships. It is fair to state that, were it not for the power of such personal relationships and their hold on his con-science, his theological reflections would have never advanced as far as they have. As he tells the story, while he has enjoyed many friendships, one in par-ticular, that of Alice and Roy Eckardt, whom he describes as soulmates, had a commanding power over him.[4] At crucial points, when needing to articu-late his own theological position in relation to the community to which he belonged, he would ask himself: What would Roy and Alice do?[5] I believe this is not an incidental detail. The power of close spiritual friendship serves as a catalyst for new theological thought, by virtue of personal example, moral command, and a significant other that redefines whom one is responsible to. We thus begin with one important lesson gleaned from Rabbi Greenberg's path and what it might mean to someone engaging in theology of religions —this field cannot be approached from the comfort of one's study. It involves relationships, new role models, new commanding presences that frame one's sense of responsibility. And with all these comes keen struggle that ultimately leads to theological creativity. I am hard pressed to identify an-other contemporary Jewish thinker[6] who comes to the task of exploring

[3] Or, perhaps better, over half a lifetime, considering the centrality of studying the Holo-caust in his theological writing, which does not depend on the Jewish–Christian work.

[4] It is worth noting that Greenberg's formative friendships are with Christians, not with Muslims or members of other faiths. As a consequence, his theological work is developed in dialogue with Christianity, his most significant other, and only by extension and gradually, over time, applied to Islam and possibly to other faiths.

[5] This is also the title of a brief essay in which he describes his process and the place the Eckardts occupied in it. It appears in Peace, Rose, and Mobley (eds.), *My Neighbor's Faith*.

[6] A. J. Heschel was a pathbreaker in establishing a Jewish attitude to other religions. See

another religion with the same intense personal charge, grounded in commanding and defining relationships.[7] We may well consider this one significant source of the theological wealth of Greenberg's thought.[8]

Greenberg's personal relationships are but one dimension of what we must take into account when thinking of the background to his work. As he states, it is the study of the Holocaust that launched him into Jewish–Christian dialogue, through which he hoped to address the conditions that led to the Holocaust and tackle the root cause—the Christian teaching on Judaism.[9] While I see his Jewish theology of Christianity as standing independently of his work on the Holocaust, the latter provides the background and motivation for his engagement in this area of work.[10] There are two perspectives through which the Holocaust leads to Greenberg's Jewish–Christian work. The first goes back to the power of witness of those formative Christian friendships. When Greenberg encountered the prophetic voices of Christians who were willing to critique their own religion following the Holocaust, this served for him as a means of appreciating the moral grandeur that Christianity has the potential to lead to.[11] The point is broader than the testimony of a handful of individuals. The paroxysm of Christian post-Holocaust self-criticism is a healing sign of life and of remarkable spiritual and religious renewal. 'A faith that shows such a deep capacity for repentance

Goshen-Gottstein, 'No Religion Is an Island'. Heschel, however, is not a contemporary author. More importantly, while he suggests fundamental reasons for positive engagement with other faiths, he never undertakes a close and detailed study of any of them. This is precisely what Greenberg does.

[7] Greenberg's latest book, still in manuscript, is entitled *The Triumph of Life: A Narrative Theology of Judaism*. There are many references in this book to other religions. However, while he applies to them the insights gained from the field of Jewish–Christian relations, the discussion lacks the depth of listening to another religion that characterized his earlier work. It also lacks his previous sensitivity and resorts to broad generalizations and polemics; see pp. 226–7 in the manuscript. It is not based on an attempt to engage in deep listening and understanding, and is not grounded in the same kind of commanding personal relationships; see e.g. p. 141. As a consequence, Greenberg's prophetic voice ends up preaching to religions, rather than trying to understand them fully and to accommodate them theologically.

[8] On the role of friendship across religions in enhancing understanding of the other, see Goshen-Gottstein, 'Conclusion: Friendship Across Religions'.

[9] For a brief description of this motivation, see 'What Would Roy and Alice Do?', 16.

[10] The discussion of Greenberg's views in Krell, *Intersecting Pathways*, 133–5, largely contextualizes his Jewish–Christian work in the context of his Holocaust theology. There is no need for me to revisit the ground covered by Krell.

[11] 'What Would Roy and Alice Do?', 15.

demonstrates its capacity to be a vehicle of love.'[12] Greenberg is a post-Vatican II dialogue partner who has internalized changes in the Catholic and other churches. His work engages with Christian documents,[13] but more significantly has drawn on the spirit of an entire movement of Christian self-examination.

There is also a moral lesson to be drawn from the Holocaust. The search for a more affirmative model of Christianity is based at the very least on the realization that 'if we take the other's spiritual life less seriously, we run the great risk of taking the biological life less seriously, too.'[14] 'A new theology is ethically necessary.'[15] Hence, Greenberg seeks more than tolerance. He seeks affirmation of the fullness of the faith claims of the other.[16] This is a radical demand that in many ways departs from the history of Jewish views of other religions. Such views, when they were not completely dismissive and derogatory,[17] acknowledged other religions *in part*. They were seen either as sufficiently adequate morally and theologically, or as fulfilling in part the greater vision and ultimate historical mandate of Judaism.[18] The moral lesson leads Greenberg to legitimate the Christian faith. This is a breakthrough in terms of theological method. He distinguishes himself from Buber, who could only recognize Christianity in terms of the Judaism he loved. Instead, Greenberg endeavours to affirm Christian self-understanding. This, as we shall see, is one of the hallmarks of his theological method.

Greenberg is a theologian who is sensitive to the great moments in history and factors them into his theological task and method. He goes as far as

---

[12] Greenberg, *For the Sake of Heaven and Earth*, 193.   [13] See ibid. 124–8.

[14] Ibid. 145.   [15] Ibid. 174.   [16] Ibid. 146.

[17] For an overview of the history and typology of Jewish views of other religions, see Goshen-Gottstein, *Same God, Other god*.

[18] Maimonides' stance on Christianity and Islam is a classic case in point. See *Mishneh torah*, 'Laws of Kings', 11: 4. The same is also true of Rabbi Jacob Emden's views, which are in and of themselves some of the most advanced and positive views of Christianity, and which have been the subject of an important essay by Greenberg's wife; see Blu Greenberg, 'Rabbi Jacob Emden'. Greenberg engages in an analysis of Maimonides (*For the Sake of Heaven and Earth*, 226–9). It is interesting, especially given his wife's research, that there is no reference to Emden in his study. He likely felt that Emden's views, while accommodating, were not adequately pluralist. Indeed, Emden is fully an inclusivist, applying the Noahide commandments to his understanding of Christianity and not going beyond such application. In any event, for all their historical and theological significance, neither of these figures, nor any other traditional source I am aware of, sets an expectation as high as the one set here by Greenberg—affirmation of the fullness of the faith claims of the other.

to speak of the revelational dimensions of the formative experiences of this generation: the Holocaust on the one hand, and the founding of the State of Israel on the other.[19] In examining the conditions that allow him to reconsider his view of Christianity, we must also take into account the new historical situation of Judaism following the founding of the State of Israel. 'The security of its own confirmation; the restoration of the land, the covenantal sign, releases Judaism to ponder anew the significance of Christianity.'[20]

There is one final point to be made in presenting the background to Greenberg's theology. One misses out on an important dimension if one does not realize that Greenberg's own thinking is informed by a continuous exchange with some of the most important voices in Jewish–Christian dialogue and the Christian theology of Judaism. As Mark Krell has shown, Greenberg's theology must be appreciated against the background of the theological work of his Christian conversation partners, especially the Eckardts and Paul van Buren.[21] It may well be that he has engaged in theological dialogue with Christians for longer and in a more sustained way than any other Jewish personality, ultimately shaping his own theology of both Judaism and Christianity. Absent this recognition, we will not understand adequately the efforts he makes to consider Christianity in terms of one or two covenants—and, even more importantly, in terms of the People of Israel. Greenberg is thus a theologian of the dialogue. It was dialogue that led him to a new theology of Christianity, and dialogue has also been for him the matrix from within which his own thinking has evolved and reached its maturity.

Theological Method

I have already referred to the novelty of the theological attempt to fully validate another religion, on its own terms and in view of its self-understanding. An appraisal of Greenberg's theological contribution requires us to not only refer to the positions he takes on specific issues, but also to consider his theological method and how it sets new standards in terms of a Jewish theology of other religions. Let us move into an exploration of his method, in view of his stated goal of full affirmation of Christianity.

Greenberg is willing to examine issues such as the Crucifixion, the Incarnation, and Jesus' messianic status as part of his attempt to validate Christian

---

[19]   *For the Sake of Heaven and Earth*, 15, 114. See also p. 139.
[20]   Ibid. 138. See further Krell, *Intersecting Pathways*, 113.
[21]   Krell, *Intersecting Pathways*, 120–3.

self-understanding. Interestingly, the Trinity seems to fall beyond the scope of his efforts.[22] Needless to say, he does not recognize any of these theological positions as true in the sense that the faithful might proclaim. He nevertheless seeks to view these faith claims as valid and as somehow consonant with the faith foundations of Judaism. To do this, he evokes a notion of models or depth structures. Accordingly, even if the Incarnation is contrary to some biblical principles, the notion itself is operating out of classic biblical modes.[23] Biblical faith provides a frame of reference that defines the grammar common to both traditions, even if what they say may seem contradictory.[24] A depth theology or a comparative theology therefore serves as a means of affirming Christianity as a whole and the possible legitimacy of its particulars.

A central notion in Greenberg's attempt to validate Christianity is appeal to Christian experience. If Christians have experienced something significant, we must try to accommodate their feeling and self-understanding within a Jewish framework, without necessarily subscribing to the truth of such claims. This is a very fine line to walk, but Greenberg is able to apply this strategy in some important contexts. He is willing to validate the Christian experience of spiritual regeneration through faith in Jesus as a messianic figure who forgives sins and launches a new reality.[25] The beauty of his approach is that, rather than affirming the truth claim of that faith experience, he is content to validate solely the experience, but only as relevant to those who have had it. Jews, by contrast, at the time of Jesus and in later generations, had a different experience. They did not, through Jesus, undergo the deliverance they had been awaiting. Christian experience is therefore only relevant for Christians, and has no claim on Jews.[26]

Other expressions of this approach are found in Greenberg's validating the Christian experience of the Resurrection, which he says should be

[22] Is this a function of deep-seated Jewish attitudes to idolatry or is it that one theologian cannot cover all bases? Significantly, the one time that Greenberg injects his own preference into Christian theological debates, rather than accepting Christianity on its own terms, is his discussion of the divine status of Jesus; see For the Sake of Heaven and Earth, 92, 232. I find this disturbing in some ways and not fully in keeping with Greenberg's own theological approach. It would seem, in this discussion, that affirmation of the same God would be contingent on adopting certain non-classical views of the Christian godhead. This is in marked contrast to the tone and method that governs most of his work. It may be a later development, reflected in essays written in the late 1990s and published from 2000 onwards, or an expression of theologizing that does not meet his own standards.   [23] Ibid. 232.
[24] Ibid. 43.   [25] Ibid. 64.   [26] Ibid. 65.

viewed as an expression of God's closeness, following the biblical claim that God is close to all.[27] He goes as far as asserting that 'Christianity's birth is a triumph of human fidelity in the face of tragedy that was rewarded with such powerful religious experiences as to enable the steadfast to know God's presence in the midst of the faith community'.[28] Christians' experience of election is valid: they have experienced God's love, which singles out the beloved and transforms and revivifies life.[29]

Greenberg's willingness to go to the heart of Christian religious experience and accommodate it from a Jewish perspective is a deeply empathetic approach. He is thus able to state that 'The Kingdom of God is within you' is a true statement while recognizing the ways in which its application has tended to move into a spiritualized realm, ignoring concrete reality.[30] This empathetic view of Christianity, based on his recognition of the validity of the experience of Christians, leads him to acknowledge the faithfulness of the early Jesus-believers, whose response to Jesus' death was an expression of Jewish faithfulness in the ongoing quest for the messiah.[31] For Greenberg, the way he deals with issues such as the Incarnation, to be discussed further below, 'allows faithful Jews to respect the distinctive theological claims of Christianity—and not just the models and values that Jews and Christians hold in common'.[32]

The hermeneutical move of validating Christian experience finds its counterpart in theologizing that is equally informed by a sense of positive-mindedness and caring towards Christians and Christianity. One notable moment is Greenberg's claim that working for the well-being of Christians is in fact a fulfilment of the core principle of *imitatio dei*. Of God it is said, 'I will be with him in time of trouble' (Ps. 91: 15).[33] Similarly, when we offer help to persecuted Christians we are following in God's ways. This is a small instance of the theological creativity shown by Greenberg, which informs not only details such as this, but the entire structure of his theological thinking in relation to Christianity.

Let me move on to other aspects of Greenberg's methodology. His writing is surprisingly sparing in footnotes and quotation of sources. It seems

---

[27] Ibid. 66–7.   [28] Ibid. 66.   [29] Ibid. 233.   [30] Ibid. 79.   [31] Ibid. 149.
[32] 'The Relationship of Judaism and Christianity', 204.
[33] This verse plays a surprisingly important role in Greenberg's theological thinking and is for him one of the founding principles of the covenant. See *For the Sake of Heaven and Earth*, 25, 100, 189.

he is much more concerned to articulate what matters most, which is the theological stakes of his position and the larger theological view. The reader may therefore not realize how much reading has gone into shaping his views. Greenberg's thought is deeply situated in contemporary research and theology. His own discussion of key issues reflects contemporary Christian discussions, especially on questions of the covenant and the status of Christians in relation to the People of Israel.[34] Along the way, we learn how much of contemporary research on the historical Jesus and the study of the New Testament Greenberg has ingested.[35] While he only gets into an analysis of *Nostra aetate* on one occasion, it is clear that he is much informed about current Church statements and documents.[36]

Greenberg's theologizing involves him in a review of Jewish and Christian history and beliefs. As we shall see below, he is more than capable of criticizing Christianity, not simply for historical wrongdoings but for various theological or attitudinal imbalances when contrasted with Judaism. A kind of comparative theology of ideas, grounded in a historical view of the two traditions, takes up significant attention. That Greenberg is able to review both religions from a high vantage point and to evaluate their respective strengths and weaknesses is in itself uncommon. That he contextualizes his criticism of Christianity within such a broad comparative vision is even more unusual. And that he seeks to accomplish all this in a fair-minded way is a unique characteristic of his approach. Rather than using criticism —including the criticism of Christian wrongdoing to Jews—to invalidate Christianity, he seeks to offer a balanced view of strengths and weaknesses within a framework that includes both Judaism and Christianity.[37] It is therefore no surprise that time and again we encounter the expression 'to be fair', a sign of his core approach.[38]

One final point on method concerns Greenberg's use of Jewish sources. Reading through his essays, one is struck by how much he refers to the kabbalah as a source of structuring thought and providing conceptual building blocks. This fact is particularly striking when we consider that he is not especially versed in kabbalah and does not strongly identify with either the kabbalistic or the hasidic tradition. One possible way of understanding this phenomenon is that the kabbalah allows him to make meaningful and novel theological moves. It is suggestive of certain sensibilities and possibilities,

[34] *For the Sake of Heaven and Earth*, 99.   [35] Ibid. 222.
[36] Ibid. 127–9.   [37] Ibid. 79.   [38] See e.g. ibid. 72, 80.

and these come in handy when reflecting on Christianity. It is not altogether impossible that a kabbalistic approach is in some ways closer to the pattern of thinking of Christianity, or at least allows one to view Christianity from a framework that opens up dialogue, or empathy or understanding.[39] However, a likelier explanation is that Greenberg does not really work through kabbalistic materials so much as he appeals to them on the basis of how they have become embedded in broader Jewish thought and culture. Let us look at some examples.

Greenberg asserts that going through exile without losing one's self constitutes *imitatio dei* (note the appeal to the concept yet again) of the highest order—an explanation based on kabbalistic understanding.[40] One of the cornerstones of his theology, and a foundation for his comparison of the respective evolutions of Christianity and Judaism, concerns the question of human and divine activity. As a religion evolves, so God recedes as primary actor, making room for human action. This movement too is appreciated in the light of a kabbalistic notion, *tsimtsum* (divine self-contraction for purposes of making space for an autonomous creation).[41] It is noteworthy that as a non-kabbalist, Greenberg does not apply the concept in its original cosmological context, but rather in a new relational context, wherein the presence and activities of one of the covenant partners are intentionally reduced as an expression of *tsimtsum*.[42] His application of this kabbalistic idea is based on it having taken broader hold in contemporary Jewish and philosophical thought, making it more pliable and adaptable to changing theological needs.[43]

The same is true for the kabbalistic concept of *tikun olam* (the work of reparation and restoration of a fallen or imperfect world). This notion plays a central role in understanding the purpose of the covenant and therefore of both Judaism and Christianity.[44] Here too we note a removal from the

[39] On the relationship between kabbalistic and Christian patterns of thought, see Goshen-Gottstein, 'The Triune and the Decaune God'.

[40] Greenberg, *For the Sake of Heaven and Earth*, 84.   [41] See ibid. 52 and 98.

[42] The same is true of David Hartman. See Cooper, *Contemporary Covenantal Thought*, 89–96.

[43] It also goes back to its use by his teacher, Rabbi Soloveitchik. See Cooper, *Contemporary Covenantal Thought*, 102–4.

[44] Freedman, *Living in the Image of God*, 47. The notion appears repeatedly throughout Greenberg's corpus. It is particularly prominent in his new book, *The Triumph of Life*. It is also applied to the relations between religions; see *Triumph of Life*, 643 ('The Case for Pluralism').

original kabbalistic context and a new social and theological application as part of contemporary thought.[45] Greenberg participates in this broader tendency.[46]

The intuitive appeal to the mystical tradition leads Greenberg at one point to affirm that historically mystics of both religions influenced each other across faith lines.[47] This is a very hard claim to substantiate. While there have been discussions of Christian influences on the kabbalah,[48] and while forms of Christian kabbalah have emerged, Jewish and Christian mystics, unlike their philosophical counterparts, had remarkably little contact with or influence upon each other. It seems that Greenberg manifests here an openness to the mystic dimension, which he colours in light of his own positive reading of Jewish–Christian history. This openness is noteworthy, even if the historical terms in which he casts it may be disputed.

Finally, Greenberg's own remove from the actual study of kabbalah finds expression in his description and criticism of it as similar to eastern religions in that it seeks release from this world.[49] This description, and the resultant distinction between kabbalah and covenant, trivializes the former as a historical movement and its own strong sense of history. It can only be made by an author whose knowledge of kabbalah is second-hand. Thus, while kabbalah does provide some of Greenberg's building blocks, it does so not on the basis of his own familiarity with kabbalistic sources but rather on account of how kabbalah has become embedded in contemporary Jewish thought. When it comes to actual references to and appreciation of the kabbalistic movement, we encounter some off-key statements that betray his insufficient first-hand acquaintance with this literature.

[45] See Fine, '"Tikkun": A Lurianic Motive in Contemporary Jewish Thought'. See further Rosenthal, '*Tikkun Ha-Olam:* The Metamorphosis of a Concept'.

[46] Greenberg, 'Modern Orthodoxy and the Road Not Taken', 52 refers to the building blocks of tradition from which his theology is constructed. This is a good characterization of his overall method, where existing building blocks of wider theological discourse serve to construct a new theological edifice. See also my interview with Greenberg in Ch. 6 below.

[47] *For the Sake of Heaven and Earth*, 81.

[48] See Liebes, 'Christian Influences in the Zohar' (Heb.).

[49] *For the Sake of Heaven and Earth*, 189.

CHAPTER TWO

Reading Religions: A God's-Eye View

Judaism and Christianity: Historical and Comparative Evaluations

Greenberg seeks to evaluate Christianity from a Jewish perspective; this involves him in a reading of the other faith that is not divorced from his reading of Judaism. The two traditions are viewed in tandem as large monoliths, beyond the distinctions of individual schools and many historical moments. The act of reading the two simultaneously is an important one: it raises our vision to a high vantage point from which they can be seen in their entirety, and it allows us to appreciate both traditions from a kind of neutral perspective—if you will, from God's perspective. Greenberg can thus focus on what is good and true in both, without engaging in the type of polemics that recognizes one at the expense of the other.[1] Moreover, this method enables him to affirm Jewish continuity and the maintenance of Jewish identity, *sans* Christianity. When both traditions are read in tandem, the self-standing of Judaism comes across more clearly, including its refusal to accept the Christian faith. The respective historical contributions and ultimate mission of the two can also be seen from this high vantage point. Finally, a broad comparison of the history and faith of both traditions also provides a possible point from which to critique specific developments in each. Greenberg thus comes across as a thinker who is not only inclusive in his view of another religion but also capable of rising above the instinctive identification with his religious tradition at the exclusion of another. He is a big thinker who strives to see the whole, inclusive of both traditions, as if from God's viewpoint, in service of the ultimate evolution of all faith communities. Let us now consider the various expressions of this broad perspective and high vantage point from which he views both Judaism and Christianity.

[1] This is not to say that his writing is totally devoid of polemics. See e.g. *For the Sake of Heaven and Earth*, 122 for a lovely argument against supersession in light of God's love.

We begin with a view of history. A crucial point to which Greenberg returns time and again in his writings is the status of Judaism and Christianity at the time of the latter's birth. If one is to validate Christianity for Christians, one must also be able to account for why it is not appropriate for Jews. Specifically, one must revisit the age-old charge that Christians have levelled at Jews—their refusal to accept the Christian faith. Greenberg constructs a view of history that has a certain purpose and evolution, and then measures both religions in relation to this view. His overarching understanding of the growth of religion is that of a move from greater dependence on God to greater human autonomy and empowerment, wherein God recedes, if you will, contracts his presence, while the human partner grows in responsibility and autonomy. He offers a reading of Jewish history based on such a view. Broadly speaking, Jews were moving into phase two, a more advanced stage of their religious life, while Christians were entering with full force phase one. The two religious communities were thus at different points in their respective evolution. While it made sense for new publics to enter into relationship with the God of Israel through the newly launched religion, it would have been out of place for Jews to go backwards, so to speak, given the growth and development they had already undergone within their own religion. Thus, 'even as Christians responded to their great religious experiences by proclaiming a New Covenant, Jews responded to their extraordinary flowering by affirming a *renewal* of the covenant'.[2]

This is a major expression of Greenberg's all-encompassing view of both traditions and their historical evolution. Its details, as concerns the stages of the evolution of Judaism, are, however, less than universally agreed upon. It is easy enough to recognize when Christians had their great religious experience and felt called into a covenant. But when exactly did Jews affirm a renewed covenant? There really is no historical moment that corresponds fully to the description here found. As we have seen in Chapter 1, covenant language does not reflect the thought of the rabbis, and so we seek in vain rabbinic proclamations of a renewed covenant. Even those texts and events that are made to speak to such a view would span a fairly large period in time. At one extreme, Greenberg appeals to a talmudic reference to Purim, putting us in pre-Second Temple Judaism.[3] In another context, he speaks of Judaism's response to the destruction of the Temple and the ensuing emphasis on human responsibility.[4] More than anything, what we encounter

[2] *For the Sake of Heaven and Earth*, 156, 223. [3] Ibid. 124. [4] Ibid. 221.

through this historical recounting is a description of how rabbinic Judaism, as represented in its canonical works, operates. Post-prophetic Jewish literature and the role that the sages and their creativity play in it, along with the flourishing of Judaism and its literature following the destruction of the Second Temple, are retroactively cast into a moment that is imagined or portrayed in terms of covenantal renewal. Such a description has more to do with the phenomenology of religion than with any particular historical moment or movement. It would seem, then, that the comparison between where Judaism and Christianity were in their evolution, while put in historical terms, is actually a phenomenological evaluation, based on the theological criteria that Greenberg brings to bear. In fact, this highlights his method of high vantage-point evaluation, which is, at the end of the day, a way of making a theological claim. He does not describe history but rather offers a historiosophy, a value-laden approach to the presentation of history, based on his theological premises. Put differently, what Greenberg describes in narrative terms is in fact a metanarrative, which he constructs for the purposes of the simultaneous evaluation and presentation of both Judaism and Christianity.[5]

This allows us to take note of other instances in which Greenberg offers a comparative perspective that is indebted to his own theological views and religious phenomenology. Let us consider some original formulations of what is common to Judaism and Christianity. The essential teaching of the new faith is 'Creation made new and perfected through covenantal actions of God and humanity'.[6] In another context, he proposes a broader definition of the commonalities between the two communities:

Both Judaism and Christianity dream of total transformation while remaining willing to accept the finitude and limitations of humans and go one step at a time. Both groups persist in preaching their messages despite their difficulties and historical suffering. And despite the terrible history of their relationship, each has witnessed to God and the human covenantal mission in its own way. For what often seems an eternity, both have hoped and waited, and both have transmitted the message and worked for the final redemption.[7]

The categories by means of which the religions are described are very

---

[5] From this perspective, Greenberg can not only describe the respective situation of both traditions but also offer an evaluation that ultimately works in Judaism's favour. Rabbinic religion, from the perspective of this religious metanarrative, is thus 'a more mature mode of religion'; see ibid. 156.   [6] Ibid. 71.   [7] Ibid. 169.

different from common descriptions of the two faiths—belief in God, Scripture, prophecy, providence, and so on. Instead, Greenberg develops his own descriptive categories, which highlight, on the one hand, the encounter between human and divine as these jointly seek to transform historical reality, and, on the other, the similar patterns of traversing history in that quest. The human covenantal mission is a central notion here. It is the idea of partnership between God and humans towards the perfection, transformation, and redemption of the created order. Both faith communities share in this covenantal mission. In fact, the commonality between them can be summarized by reference to this shared mission. The 'grammar of biblical covenant' allows Greenberg to speak of the coexistence of Judaism and Christianity as 'partner religions'.[8]

Interestingly, Greenberg does not spend much time on the pastime of historians and theologians—tracing origins and influences. It is clear that one tradition grew from the other and carries over its deep logic. This is seen as a blessed and divinely intended development. There is, therefore, little need to engage in the game of comparisons and parallels that is often played against a view of contrasts and a chasm that divides the faiths. Occasionally, though, Greenberg too refers to Jewish tradition as the source for the evolution of a particular Christian belief. He offers his own original account of the Christian faith in Jesus as the Son of God:

As Christians brought the message of hope to Hellenized gentiles, the new audience heard the proclamation about Jesus, the son of God, bringing them closer to God. According to the Jewish tradition, metaphorically, all people are the children of God. The newcomers understood the message in a more literal way. They accepted with gratitude the news that God sought to close the gap between humanity and the Divine by crossing over and sharing human experience in the flesh.[9]

There is something accommodating in this description. Rather than polemicize over Jesus' sonship, let alone his incarnation, Greenberg highlights common biblical foundations. Christians indeed took biblical tradition beyond the faith of Israel, but they did so in continuity—metaphor became reality.[10] Where others might cry foul and proclaim Christian faith idolatrous, Greenberg is satisfied in understanding how it had evolved from its

[8] *For the Sake of Heaven and Earth* 43.   [9] Ibid. 72.
[10] I am hard pressed to justify Greenberg's description of sonship as a trait of all peoples. Biblically and rabbinically, sonship is associated with Israel. See Goshen-Gottstein, 'God and

Jewish roots.[11] Clearly, he does not consider this issue to be as momentous as polemicists and theologians of old did. What matters most is the common covenantal vocation of the two faith communities, and not the differences in their faith affirmations. This is an important theological position, which undercuts a long history of bitter polemics, preferring a recognized common ground to disagreement over details of faith. As I suggest below, Greenberg's approach has precedent in Jewish views of Christianity, even if the particular construct he offers is novel.

The ability to acknowledge differences is crucial to Greenberg's portrayal of the two faiths. Difference does not translate to lack of legitimacy or even to the superiority of one faith over the other, even if at certain points he does not hide his preference for the Jewish view and approach, which he does consider superior. But this need not affect questions of legitimacy and mutual recognition. Accordingly, Greenberg goes beyond the affirmation of differences and their legitimacy to develop a theory of pluralism and mutual complementarity that is based precisely on these differences.

There is a difference in sexual values, as Christianity operates out of the model of Jesus as the fruit of a virgin birth and as the perfect, untainted sacrifice. Christianity valorizes purified, sacrificial religious activity. Its saints are saintly. Priests and nuns devote their lives to Christ and practise celibacy, poverty, and service. Jews operate off the model of the patriarchs and biblical heroes, who were exemplary but flawed. Rabbinic religion valorizes the sanctification of everyday activities instead of extraordinary acts that distinguish leaders from the rank and file.[12] A different spiritual profile, we can already expect, need not translate to legitimate and illegitimate, let alone good or bad, religion. Only someone who is cognizant of common rabbinic descriptions of Christianity in contrast to Judaism will realize how radically Greenberg departs from the views and descriptions of many of his colleagues. The differences are real, but they do not carry with them the negative pronouncement that other observers project on them.

What allows Greenberg to be content with a description of differences is the recognition that there is a need for multiple covenanted communities because they all require correction, and it is only by the existence of multiple

Israel as Father and Son' (Heb.). In this discussion, Greenberg sidesteps the mountains of literature devoted to the roots of faith in Jesus' divine sonship. He offers instead an irenic, but somewhat simplistic, view of its genealogy.

[11] *For the Sake of Heaven and Earth*, 223.   [12] Ibid. 77.

communities that such correction can be attained. Moreover, distinctions are never as extreme as they may appear. While the differences described above remain, one also recognizes opposite trends within Judaism itself. One must thus consider the broader economies of the religions. There is a game of major and minor that is played out between them, as distinct from right and wrong, true and false. Similar themes may be found in both religions; it is only the emphases that vary. The price of antagonism between the two is the loss of opportunity for mutual enrichment and inspiration as similar themes are configured variously within the respective economies. In an ideal relationship, both faith communities serve as correctives to one another and allow an interchange that rebalances one's models following the encounter with the other.[13]

The description of alternative emphases sets the stage for a genuine pluralism through which Christianity is accepted. The reasoning that Greenberg provides, however, would seem to go beyond a Jewish view of Christianity. The notion of related ideas finding shifting emphases can be equally applied to Judaism and other religions, certainly to Islam, and probably to all religions. The method espoused by Greenberg thus lays the foundations for a broader Jewish pluralism beyond its immediate application to Christianity.

There is an important consequence to this approach. A polemical and oppositional view of Christianity will tend to highlight differences, and therefore to focus on some ideas at the expense of others. The more irenic and pluralistic view espoused by Greenberg allows one to recognize shifts in emphases without seeking to make polemical gain through such recognition. The understanding that the two religions share a common pool of ideas and that it is only the relative emphasis within the overall economy that is altered leads us to a different approach to both of them. Rather than identifying certain ideas as Jewish and others as Christians, one recognizes that ideas have been shifting through the ages, in part as a consequence of the antagonism between the faiths. Accordingly, we may engage in the act of reconstruction of values. The antagonism, associated with the separation between Judaism and Christianity, led to the muting of certain ideals within the former. Notions such as grace, love, and the pathos of divine suffering, all covenantal themes, were relegated to the background as Judaism sought to set its identity over and against Christianity.[14] Considering shifting eco-

---

[13] *For the Sake of Heaven and Earth*, 77.

[14] Ibid. 223. While Greenberg nowhere quotes the work of Daniel Boyarin, the essay here

nomies of ideas as a reflection of the situation of competition between the faiths allows us to reclaim lost parts of the tradition that had hitherto been identified with Christianity. A more dynamic view of the respective theologies in their historical development over the centuries, mirroring one another, allows one today to adopt a new posture of recognizing the other while re-owning ideals and parts of one's own tradition. One may argue whether this is best described as a fruit of interreligious dialogue or whether it is really a reclaiming of self on the basis of a revised view of the other. Either way, the pluralistic approach by means of which Greenberg accommodates Christianity and its history of faith has potential for the spiritual enrichment of Judaism. 'Once the triumphalism stops, one discovers that the very themes one dismissed in the other are present in one's own repertoire.'[15]

An Invitation to Pluralism

Recounting the metanarrative requires a vantage point that is more elevated than the position of someone who is exclusively identified with his tradition and its history. For the theologian, there is only one way of imagining such a position—the attempt to insert oneself in, or raise oneself up to, the mind of God. God, in this understanding, is greater than particular religions, and works through their multiplicity. In other words, an appeal to God's view of things serves as the ground for a pluralistic approach to religions. Greenberg's theology purports to offer just such a God's-eye perspective.

Even if at first sight there is something presumptuous about this posturing, upon further reflection every theological position is an imagined act of speaking from God's perspective. There is nothing more presumptuous about considering God's view from a pluralist perspective than there is about considering it from the exclusivist's world-view. If anything, the attempt to offer a broader theory that would encompass more data within the unfolding of a divine mind and a divine plan is truer to the nature of God, which by definition should be as all-encompassing as possible. One might thus recommend Greenberg's view precisely because he seeks a higher perspective, grounded in a God's-eye view of religions. Greenberg is aware of the difficulties associated with adopting such a perspective.

analysed was written after Boyarin's work was published. It is likely that it impacted Greenberg's work, even if he does not cite it or offer detailed proof for his own description.

[15] Ibid. 182.

[My] account attempts to break out of the ethnocentric parameters and conflict-ridden historical context within which the two faiths have primarily related over the past two millennia. I am tempted to say that the perspective of the narrative is theocentric. That is to say, it seeks to look at the patterns of interaction from the vantage point of an imagined divine intention to bring into being two covenantal communities working side by side for *tikun olam*. Of course, one cannot write from a truly theocentric perspective; in the end, we are human and not God . . . Nevertheless, much of sacred Scripture seeks to lift our gaze up to the mountains and beyond.[16]

It is interesting to note who Greenberg is in dialogue with as he views both Christianity and Judaism from God's perspective.

Yet even Paul, who led the charge in turning to the gentiles and who brilliantly interpreted the rootedness of Christianity in Judaism, could not fathom the fullness of the divine pluralism . . . Paul found it hard to affirm that the divine plan included two independent channels of redemption, operating side by side.[17]

We are led to conclude, then, that Greenberg is able to see more clearly into God's mind and intention in recognizing the two faiths as complementary revelations, linked within the same covenantal structure, than Paul was as he struggled to understand his religious experience. This may not be as extreme a statement as it may sound initially. After all, Paul was at pains to make sense of the nascent religion just as it was forming, and sought to articulate whom it was intended for. Greenberg has the advantage of 2,000 years of history to guide him to an understanding that is informed by the realities of that history as it has unfolded. One may therefore reasonably attribute such unfolding to divine intention. What Greenberg may lack in the direct experience that Paul had he more than makes up for through the testimony of history.

More than anything else, seeing from God's perspective allows Greenberg to affirm that both Judaism and Christianity are willed by God.

God intended that Judaism and Christianity both work for the perfection of the world (the Kingdom of God). Together, both religions do greater justice to the dialectical tensions of covenant than either religion can do alone.[18]

In the history of Jewish engagement with Christianity there have been some positive moments of appreciation.[19] I believe, however, that a descrip-

---

[16] *For the Sake of Heaven and Earth*, 49.   [17] Ibid. 73.   [18] Ibid. 226.
[19] Notably R. Jacob Emden, mentioned above. Another important voice that fully vali-

tion of Christianity as intended from God's perspective is a novel theological articulation.[20] Christianity is not chosen, any more than Judaism is, to reveal a truth or even offer a teaching. The key to its election is the work of perfecting the world, *tikun olam*. In Greenberg's theology this is the core message and purpose of religion, as it fits within a structure that begins with Creation and moves towards redemption through the collaborative work of perfection, undertaken jointly by humans and by God, understood as a covenantal partnership.

There are several arguments that justify a God-based validation of Christianity. The above passage explains the divine intention in having both religions work for the common cause through the dynamics of the covenant. Covenant assumes a balance of responsibility and action between humans and God. In the process, there is a possibility of the human covenantal partner getting things wrong, or at least off key. The existence of multiple covenantal communities functions as a corrective to the errors that could creep in if God's redemptive work were carried out through the agency of only one human partner, one covenant community. Thus, multiple religions are needed in order to offset errors in how humans go about their covenantal tasks: they are a means of divine correction of flawed human partners.

There are other reasons for recognizing Christianity as divinely intended, and these relate to the choice of target audience.

Judaism's focus on family as the context for *berit* is constructive; pursued one-sidedly it can lead to tribalism and amoral familialism. The religion needs to be corrected by a faith that breaks out of the family model and explores the power of a universal, self-defined belief group. Rabbinic Judaism brings humans more powerfully into participation in the covenant; but it needs a counterpart religion to explore the element of grace and transcendence in a more central way. In this

dates Christianity is that of Franz Rosenzweig. For an overview of his views, see Krell, *Intersecting Pathways*, ch. 1. Not every assertion of the validity of Christianity is expressed in terms of a God's-eye view. (See, however, Krell's discussion, p. 36, which might be construed in this way.) Conversely, a God's-eye view can be applied even when Christianity is deemed only partially valid, as is the case in Maimonides, discussed by Greenberg in *For the Sake of Heaven and Earth*, 226–8. Greenberg is, to the best of my knowledge, the only author to fully affirm the validity of Christianity while adopting a God's-eye view.

[20] Theologians who recognize multiple revelations would in effect arrive at such a view. See Brill, *Judaism and Other Religions*, 111–12. Greenberg, however, arrives at this view without appeal to the notion of divine revelation, and herein lies the novelty of his approach. On revelation as part of his construction of religions, see the interview in Ch. 6 below.

perspective, Jewish covenant peoplehood and Christian faith community are both validated. Both models are a necessary expression of the plenitude of divine love and of the comprehensiveness and range of human roles in the covenant.[21]

The question of intended audience is thus clear. Jews can recognize that Christianity is a means of God reaching out to gentiles.[22] The just-noted distinction between a faith community and a family is important for understanding why it was necessary to create a second covenantal community and why inclusion in Israel was not the chosen divine strategy. 'Entering this new faith removed the risk that, in joining the covenant of Israel, they would be deemed second-class citizens in the Israelite partnership because they were not genetic descendants of the original stock.'[23] Sadly, this insightful suggestion says much about Jewish mentality, then and now, as Greenberg knows only too well from his practice of rabbinic leadership.

The attempt to see things from a God's-eye view is at the root of genuine pluralism, as one endeavours to see oneself and the other as God sees them.

Each partner affirms that its truth/faith/system alone cannot fulfill God's dreams. The world needs the contribution that the other religion can make for the sake of achieving wholeness and perfection for all.[24]

The formulation is somewhat less prophetic than speaking for God. Still, the attempt to consider oneself in the light of God's dreams leads, of necessity, to humility and to making room for the other religion. By this reasoning, it is only the totality of all religions that stands the chance of realizing God's dreams for humanity.[25]

The high vantage point that characterizes Greenberg's writing is not limited to offering an irenic theory of religious pluralism. It also allows him to evaluate history and to both affirm and criticize historical developments in the history of Christianity. On the one hand, it enables him to validate the faithfulness of Jesus' early followers as they recognized the messiah in Jesus. But it also allows him to speak of their hermeneutical error. Pushing the

---

[21] *For the Sake of Heaven and Earth*, 226.   [22] Ibid. 68.

[23] Ibid. The Vatican document 'The Gifts and the Calling of God are Irrevocable' makes the same suggestion, justifying why there was a need for Christianity, given certain Jewish sensibilities. See sects. 27, 35. The argument can be traced to Cardinal Walter Kasper. See Gregerman, 'Superiority without Supersessionism'.

[24] *For the Sake of Heaven and Earth*, 43, 263.

[25] Greenberg develops this notion in the framework of a Jewish view of Christianity. Its significance extends to other religions as well, as the evolution of his own thought suggests.

long-awaited redemption beyond the boundaries of history as a response to Jesus' crucifixion is seen by Greenberg as an error. That judgement generated a fundamental continuing problem for Christianity, the temptation to trivialize the reality of this world and its suffering.[26]

Greenberg's metanarrative allows him to offer counsel to Christians also in the theological domain.

As a Jewish theologian, I suggest that Christianity also cannot be untouched by the [Holocaust]. At the least, I believe that Christianity will have to enter its second stage. If we follow the rabbis' model, this stage will be marked by greater 'worldliness' in holiness. The role of the laity would shift from being relatively passive observers in a sacramental religion to full (or fuller) participation.[27]

His view of history suggests a definite pattern, and this pattern allows him to issue an invitation to Christians in a post-Holocaust world, suggesting shifts and processes of growth that are internal to the religion. Few Jewish theologians, if any, can speak in this way to another religion. Tellingly, these words, authored decades ago, in 1986, correspond to many of the changes that we have seen in the Christian, specifically Catholic, world since they were first articulated.

It takes a lot of courage to recommend certain internal movements and processes in another religion. The appreciation of laity and the need for greater democratization within religion are repeated in a later essay, with specific reference to changes brought about by Vatican II. Such democratization and the related emergence of certain charismatic forms of Christianity parallel movements within Judaism.[28] Greenberg thus offers a prophetic reading and evaluation of both religions in as even-handed a manner as possible, drawing on his own broader vision anchored in the attempt to gain a theocentric perspective on the unfolding of the two faiths.

It is perhaps worth noting that the theocentric perspective from which Greenberg speaks equips him for engagement not only with other religions but also with processes of modernity, including secularism.

Perhaps one can again conceptualize the religious significance of the modern age from a 'theocentric' perspective and assume that Judaism and Christianity were jointly and severally intended to serve as role models in the unfolding divine plan to perfect the world. From this vantage point, one may argue that modernity

---

[26] 'The Relationship of Judaism and Christianity', 198.
[27] Ibid. 210.   [28] For the Sake of Heaven and Earth, 91.

uplifted humanity's godlike capacities . . . In the divine will, modern civilization was intended to liberate human capacity to the fullest, making otiose the God of the gaps, the Omnipotent One worshiped by human beings out of fear, need, intent to bribe, and other unworthy motives.[29]

The God's-eye perspective of Judaism and Christianity provides a segue to broader reflection, which includes reference to contemporary phenomena and to modernity's contribution to the spiritual evolution of mankind.

[29] *For the Sake of Heaven and Earth*, 87.

CHAPTER THREE

Confronting the Faith of Christians

Greenberg's Jewish Precedents

The reader who encounters Greenberg's views on Christianity for the first time may be astounded by his originality. To those only superficially familiar with Jewish tradition, his perspective seems to be so different from standard Jewish polemics and views as to be non-representative. However, that is not the case. Greenberg is deeply formed by his tradition and, were it not for certain rabbinic precedents, he would have had a much harder time making his case. Let us consider his views in light of these precedents.

A polemical approach to another religion seizes upon disagreements, viewed as errors, in order to discredit the other religion. The Jewish history of engagement with Christianity is replete with philosophical and scriptural articulations of the errors of Christian faith. This has been a powerful defence tool in preserving Jewish identity, as well as in keeping the purity of Jewish faith against what was seen as possible corruption by false ideas. Greenberg operates from a non-polemical, non-exclusivist perspective. This conditions his attitude to Christianity. As we have seen, he has a remarkable capacity to contain theological disagreement, even possible error, without it turning into an invalidation of Christianity. Underlying this attitude is a very particular approach that was developed long before Greenberg and to which he makes conscious appeal. One major rabbinic voice of the Middle Ages articulated a view of Christianity that has a remarkably high tolerance level for theological error. I refer to Rabbi Menahem Meiri (1249–1310). Let me begin by citing one representative passage from Meiri's work.[1]

Nevertheless, nations that are bound by the ways of religion and believe in His (blessed be He) existence, His Unity, and His power, even though they are in error

---

[1] I have presented Meiri's views at length in my *Same God, Other god*, ch. 10.

concerning some matters according to our faith, the rules discussed above do not apply to them.[2]

According to Meiri, once the basics of proper religious faith are established, we need not be unduly concerned with details. To the extent that this passage does refer to Christianity, and it would seem it does, this means that the Trinity is one such detail. Meiri would be willing to recognize Christians as monotheists, and to disregard the theological error of the Trinity as a detail that one can forgive or overlook as part of the overall assessment of Christianity. Accordingly, the Trinity, the Incarnation, and even the claim that Jesus is the messiah do not detract from the legitimacy of Christianity as a valid religion, certainly for its non-Jewish followers.[3] When Greenberg approaches various Christian beliefs from an accommodating stance, unconcerned with their theological correctness or propriety, he is in fact following in the footsteps of Meiri.

This reliance on Meiri is not reconstructed; it is explicit in Greenberg's writing.[4] Therefore, he can say the following of the Trinity:

From a Jewish perspective, one hopes that the growing Christian emphasis on Jesus as the path to the Father rather than on Jesus as God incarnate may yet win out as a more proper understanding. If it does not, then one may argue that Christianity is wrong on this understanding. But a single error, even on a major point, does not destroy the overall legitimacy of Christianity's covenantal way. Implicit in pluralism is the recognition that there are limits in my truth that leave room for others. Such limits may include the acknowledgement that erroneous doctrines do not necessarily delegitimize the faith that incorporates them.[5]

As we shall see later in this chapter, Greenberg is capable of showing positive appreciation toward the faith of Christians in the incarnation of Jesus. This, nevertheless, does not come at the expense of absolving Christian faith from error. In the first instance, Greenberg states his own theo-

---

[2] *Beit habeḥirah* on *Git. 62a*.

[3] Meiri's views may actually be more extreme and include cases of Jews following Christianity. See Berger, 'Jews, Gentiles and the Modern Egalitarian Ethos', 101.

[4] See *For the Sake of Heaven and Earth*, 68, 93, notes. Greenberg is aware of the seminal essay on Meiri by Moshe Halbertal, '"Ones Possessed of Religion"'. As he states: 'Meiri's willingness to apply the halakhic guidelines to behavior by bringing Christians inside the mutual obligation universe is based on his philosophic analysis of the various religions' status; this aspect of his approach is particularly important as precedent.'

[5] *For the Sake of Heaven and Earth*, 232.

logical sensibilities, which are very much in line with classical Jewish belief. Accordingly, he allows himself to prefer certain Christologies over others.[6] Recognizing that Christians may not theologize to his liking, he is ready to declare them wrong, at the same time adding that error is not necessarily that big a deal. This view is grounded not only in precedents such as Meiri but also in a broader theory of pluralism, which, as we shall see, is divinely sanctioned. Making room for others includes making room for their errors. And, conversely, as part of a broader theory of pluralism, it also includes the possibility that one's own faith contains error. Ultimately, this too is not such a big deal.

Following Meiri does not mean that there are no criteria on the basis of which a religion is rejected or deemed idolatrous. The criteria are simply different. For Meiri, moral behaviour provides the proof for true religion. Religions of old lacked a moral code; valid religions have one, which Meiri sees as grounded in knowledge of the Divine. The test of true religion is thus not in its theological teachings, but in its moral character. Greenberg very much follows Meiri in this.

Far be it from me as a committed Jew to dictate to God or to other faith communities what religious signals should be given or how they should be heard in those communities—unless they have evil consequences for others.[7]

As we shall see, Greenberg deems Christianity to be valid or false on the basis of whether it teaches compassion and goodness or whether it leads to triumphalism and persecution.[8] The true test of a religion is in its actions, not in its teachings. This translates to Greenberg's view of idolatry.

Idolatry is as idolatry does. If Christianity comes dealing death or spreading contempt that encourages others to degrade and kill Jews, then it is idolatrous, that is the faith of death. But if Christianity repents and comes bearing love and affirmation of the spiritual and physical life of Israel, then blessed be all who come in the name of the Lord.[9]

I do not know of any other rabbinically informed author who has internalized Meiri's ethos so deeply. Idolatry is completely redefined. Greenberg

---

[6] See also ibid. 92, where theologies and Christologies such as Bonhoeffer's are preferred, making it easier to affirm the same God in Judaism and Christianity.
[7] 'Judaism and Christianity: Covenants of Redemption', 158.
[8] See *For the Sake of Heaven and Earth*, 180.
[9] Ibid. 68, citing in the note Meiri's teachings.

takes the case beyond morals. He reframes the meaning of idolatry by offering a broader theory—does the religion support death through its bad moral
teaching, or does it affirm life? This he does in line with his overarching
view of what religion is about. Religions fit into the fundamental scheme of
meaning where the impulse of life governs the movement from Creation
to redemption and places special charge upon humans to act accordingly.
A total world-view concerning the meaning of religion therefore frames
anew the moral intuition of Meiri and allows Greenberg to speak of Christianity not as a block, a fixed entity that requires ruling concerning its idolatrous status, but as a dynamic entity whose value shifts according to its
teaching and specifically in dependence on how it relates to Jews.[10]

The view of idolatry in terms of life and death makes particular sense in
the light of twentieth-century history and flows from Greenberg's theological engagement with the Holocaust.

In the twentieth century, human power, worshiped, metamorphosed into a life-
consuming absolute. This is the archetype of idolatry—a human, finite power
breaks out of its limit, is turned into a pseudo-absolute, and becomes the source
of death, instead of life. The ultimate expression of this moral religious cancer
was the Holocaust, and not only because of its all-out infliction of death. The
Shoah was the fruit of unlimited human freedom and power.[11]

Two strands of thought come together with great elegance. On the one
hand, idolatry is defined in moral terms, proceeding from Meiri's core definition and recast in terms of life and death as the ultimate moral parameters.[12]
But Meiri's views, seen on their own, fail to account for why moral failure is
idolatrous rather than simply morally faulty. Greenberg provides an accounting for this, which I believe goes to the heart of Meiri's thought, even though
it was never articulated with such clarity by Meiri himself. Idolatry exalts
human power at the expense of the Divine.[13] Inasmuch as acting on behalf of

[10] In my *Same God, Other god*, I move the discussion from the typical view that sees religions as large units to a more dynamic model that allows for multiple views and perspectives
with reference to every religion. I am therefore very much in sympathy with Greenberg's
dynamic application of the notion of idolatry, and in particular with the depth of understanding of Meiri's position that grounds this view.

[11] *For the Sake of Heaven and Earth*, 88.

[12] On one occasion Greenberg offers an alternative framing for idolatry—a faith with no
redeeming spiritual value. See ibid. 80. This too can be understood in the light of Meiri.
However, Greenberg does not really develop the possibility beyond this passing suggestion.

[13] See further ibid. 171: 'Any assumption of divine power raises the possibility of idolatry,
the risk of making partial human power absolute and using it without limit.'

the Divine will yield life-affirming and morally upright behaviour, affirmation of the human self, devoid of its divine anchoring, is capable of turning idolatrous, generating a culture of death. This, I submit, is one of the most profound contemporary articulations of the meaning of idolatry, drawing simultaneously on classical Jewish sources and recent historical experience, and illuminating classical Jewish understanding in the light of the later experience.

What this means, then, is that rather than being concerned about Christianity, or at least the positive manifestations of Christianity that Greenberg engages with, as idolatry, we ought to consider historical movements such as Nazism, and various other twentieth-century ideologies that have served humanity a potion of death, in light of the category of idolatry. This is surely a hugely valuable insight that casts new light on a fundamental Jewish category, even as it extends and offers a frame of understanding for a prominent voice in Jewish legal history.

But perhaps more than any specific doctrine or formulation, Meiri is important for Greenberg because he is in many ways one of the pre-eminent and most prestigious Jewish pluralists.[14] We have seen and will continue to note how central pluralism as a world-view is for Greenberg. The relationship between the two figures is more than the older, historical foundation validating the contemporary thinker. The relationship is, rather, reciprocal. If Meiri provides a foundation and justification for such pluralism, Greenberg provides the deeper reasoning and accounting for why such pluralism might be willed by God. The structure of Greenberg's thought and his affirmation of Christianity as part of a covenantal reality can help make sense of Meiri's pluralism through a theory of multiple covenants. Such covenants go to the heart of the relationship with God and emphasize the centrality of the core religious structure and world-view, over and against belief in particulars of doctrine and the possibility of theological error. Thus, when Greenberg writes, 'Once it is understood that the two religions are intended to function side by side, those changes that differentiate them from each other must be judged as differing tactical steps taken to reach out to the world',[15] he is in fact offering a theory by means of which to make sense of Meiri. Why is it that other religions are valid and must be respected, given the conditions set by Meiri? Because they fit into a divine plan and fulfil a divine

---

[14] On Meiri as a religious pluralist, see my 'Concluding Reflections', 325–7.

[15] *For the Sake of Heaven and Earth*, 99.

mandate. The accommodation of particular Christian faith tenets that we shall study presently can be evaluated positively as a tactical means of achieving the required end. Meiri himself simply ignored the divergences of faith and theological error, preferring instead to highlight commonalities. Greenberg can advance the thought pattern established by Meiri by accounting also for difference, diversity, and even error. These are, or can be seen as, strategic adaptations of the divine plan to other audiences, who require such theological adaptations, taking into account their collective psychology, culture, and orientation, in order to enter into the fuller, and fundamentally more important, divine plan, described by Greenberg as the covenant.[16]

While Greenberg is clearly and consciously indebted to Meiri, the latter is not his only reference point within the theological resources of halakhah and Jewish thought. There is a recurring theme, itself an expression of a kind of pluralism, by means of which he accommodates the particulars of Christian faith. For Meiri, errors in faith are to be overlooked. Greenberg's suggestion for accommodating them is based on the notion of multiple audiences —different aspects of a broader divine plan for different parts of humanity. The argument from different audiences is one that has deep roots in halakhah. It is one of the fundamental strategies for tackling the challenge of idolatry posed by Christian faith. By distinguishing between different audiences, the halakhah applies to them different strictures. In this view, the norms of monotheism that apply to Jews do not apply to non-Jews, for whom a softer monotheism is suitable and of whom lighter demands are made. This view is commonly known as the permissibility of *shituf*, worship by association with other beings.[17] One way of describing Greenberg's theological position is to say that upon a 'Meiri' foundation he superimposes a '*shituf* view', by means of which he makes sense of theological divergence, as suitable for non-Jews. There are several statements that relate to Christianity in terms of its intended audience, rather than in terms of its absolute truth.

---

[16] One should note, however, that reference to Meiri, explicitly or by way of extending his assumptions, does not require adopting a covenantal view of either Judaism or Christianity. Meiri developed an entire theology of religions without appeal to the covenant and Greenberg could extend his thought in a similar manner. The point is of significance in view of the discussion below, where I question the need for or effectiveness of constructing a view of other faiths around the category of covenant. Reliance on Meiri suggests there are various theological tools in Greenberg's arsenal and that he has taken significant theological steps irrespective of how one evaluates his application of the covenant.

[17] Chs. 8 and 9 of *Same God, Other god* are devoted to the analysis of this legal construct.

In contrasting rabbinic religion with Christianity, we hear Greenberg's preferences, as well as the grounds for his accommodation: 'I consider the Rabbinic to be a more mature mode of religion. However, I would also affirm that the sacramental mode (Christianity) is most appropriate for Gentiles.'[18] A kind of audience-based theology thus accounts for his willingness to recognize and appreciate Christian theological particularity. Similarly, in describing how gentiles were drawn to the covenantal path of Christianity, Greenberg recognizes that

A universal Lord would distance the new believers from this Godhead that was a far more cosmic and transcendent Other than that with which they were familiar. It thus became essential—and appropriate—that a strong mediating presence enable the new relationship with the gentiles. This is precisely what Christianity preached and offered in the new religion.[19]

Once again, Greenberg offers a historical theory and context to explain an old halakhic position. The permissibility of *shituf* makes sense if we consider the divine strategy for bringing other parts of humanity into a covenantal relationship.[20] The approach must be tailored to their temperament and previous religious experience. This, in turn, necessitates and legitimates a mediating presence, that of Jesus. Religious truth is not a universal. It can be accommodated to different audiences, primarily distinguishing Jews from non-Jews. This becomes a means of validating Christianity, without compromising Judaism.

Revisiting Contested Issues

Greenberg goes beyond the generalities of a pluralistic theory or even of a broad acceptance of Christianity. As part of his making sense and developing a theory for a Jewish accommodation of Christianity, he engages with some of its fundamental and most hallowed faith articles. The issues he tackles have been the focus of Jewish polemic and the basis of rejection, at times even of mockery, for millennia. It is therefore a significant break-

---

[18] *For the Sake of Heaven and Earth*, 156.   [19] Ibid. 69.

[20] I have noted above how acceptance and rejection of faith in Jesus are, for Greenberg, the outcome of different communities hearing different messages (see *For the Sake of Heaven and Earth*, 68–9). This argument extends into the experiential domain the multiplicity of approaches made possible by the *shituf* construct, which recognizes, on the legal level, that different criteria apply to different communities.

through for a Jewish theologian to be prepared to engage in detail with the tenets of a religion that until yesterday was a rival.

There are three faith principles of Christianity that are addressed in the framework of his discussion: faith in Jesus as messiah, the Incarnation, and the Crucifixion, though the last receives much less attention than the former two. Let us review where the novelty in Greenberg's approach lies in relation to each of these foci of faith.

Jesus as Messiah

The messianic status of Jesus is possibly the biggest stumbling block in Jewish–Christian relations as far as Jewish recognition of Christian faith is concerned. At the heart of the divide is the question of whether Jesus was the messiah awaited by Israel. This has obvious implications for whether Jews should have recognized Jesus and whether they should accept him today. The question lies at the heart of Christian missionary efforts to this day, though it must be made clear that none of Greenberg's conversation partners, or their denominations, engage in missionary work towards Jews.

We have seen that Greenberg adopts a hermeneutic of empathy, wherein he seeks to understand the religious reality and experience of early Christians and to validate it. This hermeneutic also informs his approach to the messiahship of Jesus. The question for him is not one that can be answered with a yes or no, true or false. Rather, it should be addressed from the perspective of the faith and experience of the respective communities. Each of the faith communities responded differently to the same events and to the existence—if you will, coming—of Jesus. Both responses are legitimate, and make sense within the historical and experiential framework of the respective faith community. Greenberg's task is therefore not to argue that Jesus is not messiah, or that he could be. Rather, it is first and foremost to validate Christian experience. In the second instance, he attempts to translate this validation into classical Jewish terms that do not compromise the traditional Jewish position, which refused to recognize Jesus as messiah.

Greenberg goes about making the argument by shifting the focus from the person of Jesus to the very fact that a claim for messiahship is being made. He appeals to the vitality, and therefore to the continuing emergence, of messianic movements within Judaism. The discourse shifts, then, from the Jesus movement to what may be called messianic phenomenology in the course of Jewish history. The vitality of Judaism, he argues, is expressed in its ability to generate messianic movements.

The test of Judaism's vitality is that it will continue to generate further movements toward Messianic redemption. As long as Judaism generates Messiahs, one can be certain that it is alive. When Judaism stops generating Messiahs, it is no longer faithful to its own tradition. That does not mean that every Messiah is the final one or even a true one. It does mean that the Messianic impulse is a fundamental test of Judaism's own integrity. In that sense, Christianity is not a mere deviation or misunderstanding; it is an organic outgrowth of Judaism itself.[21]

These words rely on an important phenomenon in the course of Jewish history. Messiahship is claimed time and again, though in fact no single individual has been recognized as *the* messiah, at least not by all of Israel. Jesus must therefore be seen in the framework of the broader workings of Jewish history and the place that messianic expectation holds within it. If messianic aspiration is a constant of Jewish history, claims for Jesus' messiahship are simply one more case of such a claim being made, in and of itself no more harmful or problematic than other cases. And, the implied argument continues, if we can come to terms with other instances of messianic ascription that did not justify itself, we should be able to extend the same accommodating attitude to claims of Jesus' messiahship. Moreover, in a funny way there is something healthy in the ascription of messianic title to an individual. It is not a deviation but rather a sign of spiritual vitality and authenticity. Seen from the perspective of Jewish history and the history of messianic movements, Christianity's messianic claims may thus be considered normative, an organic outgrowth of Judaism, all the while bypassing any discussion of their truth value.

Just how 'Jewish' the recognition of someone as messiah is emerges from the following passage:

Like good, faithful Jews, the early Jewish followers of Jesus were looking for the Messiah, particularly in a difficult century. Lo! and behold! in Jesus' life they recognized his arrival. To recognize that the Messiah has arrived, and to respond, is a very faithful response on the part of a Jew. Therefore, a Jew does not initially forfeit the state of faithfulness by recognizing someone as Messiah—even if he or she has erred.[22]

The process, then, is more important than its content. It is the faithful response that counts rather than the specific identification of the messianic

---

[21] *For the Sake of Heaven and Earth*, 175.   [22] Ibid. 149.

figure. And therefore even the mistaken identification of Jesus as messiah is profoundly Jewish. Greenberg goes further and makes the point that error in the identity of the messiah is not some fundamental error in faith. He has much of Jewish history to back this claim. And in our own times, he is surely aware of the most recent iteration of Jewish faith in a deceased messiah, in the person of the late Rabbi Menachem Mendel Schneerson of Lubavitch.[23] By switching the focus of attention from Jesus to the religious response that belief in him represents, and by contextualizing such response within the history of Jewish messianism, Greenberg is able to lay the foundations for a novel approach to the Jewish view of Christian messianic claims.

Greenberg's attitude to Christian messianism does not stop with an appreciation of the overall intentionality and expression of faith. In seeking to provide a positive framework for appreciating Christian messianic claims, he puts forth a novel, daring, and easily misunderstood suggestion. Aware of the long history of messianic claimants and of the fact that such claims, in and of themselves, do not lead to the delegitimization of the claimant or his followers (to date there have been no women claimants), Greenberg proposes a new category by means of which to describe the messiahship of Jesus. There are two variations to the proposal, and, despite the different ring, they seek to achieve the same goal. Both address the Christian understanding of Jesus as messiah in a respectful and accommodating way, while at the same time upholding the Jewish refusal to recognize Jesus as Israel's messiah. The first way of speaking of Jesus in this context is as 'would-be Messiah'.[24] Such a description refers to the self-understanding of either Jesus

---

[23] This would not have been the case in 1986, when Greenberg's essay was first published. In terms of fidelity to Jewish history and its great currents, I believe his forgiving and accommodating stance towards errors in messianic identity is much truer than the attempt to castigate Lubavitch messianism in light of the history of Jewish objection to Jesus' messiahship, as argued by David Berger in *The Rebbe, the Messiah, and the Scandal of Orthodox Indifference*. Note Greenberg's striking statement: 'I once wrote that I was ashamed of the fact that, in this generation, there was not at least a false Messiah. A false Messiah would show that the Jews were truly living up to their vocation, which is to hope and expect the Messiah, particularly in such tragic times. If one hopes for the Messiah and a false one shows up—well, it is regrettable but at least one has tried. Not to generate even a false Messiah is a sign that people are complacent; they have either lost hope or do not care' (*For the Sake of Heaven and Earth*, 149). It is worth noting in this context that the State of Israel does not seem to have messianic overtones, at least not in terms of the present discussion, which focuses on the messiah as a person. Greenberg approaches it more in terms of responsibility than in terms of fulfilment of messianic expectations. See his discussion ibid. 159–61.

[24] See *For the Sake of Heaven and Earth*, 149, an essay dating from as early as 1986.

or his followers. It suggests potentiality, and at the same time also signals that the potential was not fulfilled, at least not according to Jewish standards. A description of 'would-be messiah' is consonant with the classical halakhic formulation of Maimonides concerning the testing and verification of a true messiah.[25] It has been employed in very recent times with reference to the Lubavitcher Rebbe.[26] Greenberg's view of Jesus as would-be redeemer is particularly irenic:

the two communities owe special help to each other. One feels special rejoicing in the achievement of fellow citizens. Therefore, Jews who always yearned for a universal redeemer and who accept little of Jesus' message should nevertheless appreciate Jesus' service as a spiritual messiah to gentiles; he is not a false messiah, but a would-be redeemer for the nations.[27]

If Christianity is the means of fulfilling the latent universalism of Judaism, Jesus must be valued positively. It is not fully clear what the 'would-be' status of Jesus for gentiles is. 'Would-be' suggests potentiality, and such potentiality hinges on the criteria for messianic work. If Christians apply different criteria to the messiah than those of Israel, then in fact they have redefined what messiah is and argued for Jesus' successful fulfilment of the expectations. If so, his status is no longer that of a 'would-be' messiah. In line with Greenberg's pluralistic approach and his recognition of multiple covenants, we should expect multiple definitions of messianic work, and an affirmation of their suitability for the respective faith communities. To speak of Jesus as a would-be messiah is to apply Jewish criteria to his status as messiah, while upholding the benefits that he brought to those who have faith in him. Greenberg seems to not be able to go all the way. His attempt at a positive evaluation of Jesus as messiah for non-Jews falls short of a full acceptance of such claims, in terms suitable for non-Jews. All the

[25] See *Mishneh torah*, 'Laws of Kings', 11: 4.
[26] Significantly, while the Rebbe was alive, Chabad teaching emphasized his messianic potential on the basis of the above ruling of Maimonides. In an utter reversal of this logic, most of his followers continue to uphold his messianic status despite the failure to meet the criteria cited in his lifetime, thereby making his case all the more similar to that of Jesus. Greenberg's later reference to messianism consciously links the cases of Jesus and the Lubavitcher Rebbe. See *For the Sake of Heaven and Earth*, 48.
[27] Ibid. 100. In terms of the evolution of Greenberg's thought, this represents a late stage in his thinking and the quote grows out of his later views of Judaism and Christianity as one people, to be explored below. This piece was authored after the Lubavitcher Rebbe passed away. While growing out of his views of one people, the statement can stand on its own.

positive outcomes of Jesus' work are viewed through a Jewish lens, which provides the criteria for messianic legitimacy, leaving Jesus as would-be messiah, while rejoicing in his achievements and in how a deep Jewish universal vision is fulfilled through him.

There is a second formulation by means of which Greenberg seeks to affirm the Christian view of Jesus. This is to speak of him as a failed messiah.

> The general Jewish position has been that Jesus was a false Messiah. Why? Would it not be more precise to say that a false Messiah is one who teaches the wrong values and who turns sin into holiness? A more accurate description from the Jewish perspective would be that Jesus was not a 'false' but a 'failed' Messiah. He has not finished the job but his work is not in vain.[28]

The claim that Jesus was a false messiah grows out of a view of the messiah as a zero-sum game, assuming there is only one redeemer and that therefore Jesus either is or is not it. Greenberg stretches the category and makes it more elastic. A failed messiah, in this reading, refers to someone who has participated in the messianic process and has advanced it, but has not completed it. One might almost have said Jesus was part-messiah, or, more readily, that he played a part in the messianic process, thereby removing the focus from his person to the process in which he participated.[29] With the focus on Jesus as person, the best Greenberg can do is to acknowledge him as 'failed'. The failure may not be the result of his person, but simply indicates that the process has not come to its end.

Once again, the criterion is Jewish. If the view were fully pluralist, one could have imagined multiple messiahs for multiple purposes and multiple communities. At one point, in fact, Greenberg does experiment with such an idea, appealing to the notion of messiah son of Joseph, a rabbinic tradition that recognizes at least two messianic figures—the son of Joseph and the son of David.

> This concept of a 'failed' but true Messiah is found in a rabbinic tradition of the Messiah ben Joseph. The Messiah ben David (son of David) is the one who brings the final restoration. In the Messiah ben Joseph's idea, you have a Messiah who comes and fails, indeed is put to death, but this Messiah paves the way for the final redemption.[30]

---

[28] *For the Sake of Heaven and Earth*, 177.
[29] On the messiah as person and process, see Goshen-Gottstein, *In God's Presence*, ch. 8.
[30] *For the Sake of Heaven and Earth*, 153.

To speak of Jesus as messiah son of Joseph is to affirm his messianic status by identification with a messianic figure who is different from the ultimate figure to which Jews look. It is, nevertheless, a powerful means of recognizing Jesus as a messiah (not *the* messiah) from a Jewish perspective. The notion of failure is, for Greenberg, a characteristic of many Jewish heroes, and therefore not something to be ashamed of. Moses, Jeremiah, and many of the great Jewish heroes were 'failures'.[31] Therefore, Jesus is viewed in continuity with Israel's great ones. One may augment Greenberg's reading further by recognizing that the status of the messiah son of Joseph, or a failed messiah, is itself a title that allows us to relate to a long list of messianic claimants.

The distinction between false and failed messiahs is a reading of history that is not divorced from the history of Jewish–Christian relations. In an interesting note to a previously quoted passage,[32] Greenberg makes the distinction hinge on how Christians treat Jews. When Jews are persecuted, hated, and degraded in Jesus' name, then in fact it turns out he is a false messiah. By contrast, the term 'failed messiah' points to the benefits of love and consolation brought to hundreds of millions in Christianity's name. It is obvious that tying messianic achievement and status to the moral dimension of how Jesus' followers act towards Jews introduces a category that is extraneous to the discussion. This is an indication of the fine line that Greenberg has to walk, both within his community and in relation to Christians. He cannot ignore the history and he is not oblivious to the criticism levelled by Jews against Christianity and what it has done to Jews in Jesus' name. At the same time, he cannot overlook all the good that Christianity brought to the world, similarly in Jesus' name. While these differing perspectives can be acknowledged independently of messianic titles, Greenberg struggles with how to speak of Jesus as messiah also in view of the moral consequences and the historical relations between Jews and Christians. Whether this is germane to his core argument or not—a fact witnessed by the relegation of this argument to a footnote—it gives us a peek into the workings and struggles of his mind and heart as he seeks to be faithful to his community and its history as well as to the reality he encounters in Christianity.

The notion of a failed messiah is meant to construct a positive view of Jesus as messiah. As argued, it does so from an exclusively Jewish ground, rather than moving towards a more pluralistic notion of messiah. In viewing

---

[31] Ibid. 153.   [32] Ibid. 177.

Jesus from a Jewish perspective of messianism, one wonders how successful this attempt is.[33] Greenberg himself acknowledges that this suggestion is one that has been readily misunderstood. 'Failed' messiah is not a classical Jewish category, and therefore would not have much resonance with a Jewish audience. As for Christians, it is hard to imagine them settling happily for faith in a failed messiah, even if the term is loaded in the most positive way by Greenberg.[34] I have heard similar criticism from Jewish colleagues.[35] While still not fully pluralistic, the parallel formulation of would-be messiah ultimately serves Greenberg's interests better than the notion of a failed one.

While the consideration of the messianic status of Jesus is obviously a central concern for Jewish–Christian relations, from another perspective it is not, or should not be, a major deterrent to the advancement of relations. At the end of the day, what counts is not how the past is viewed, as much as the proper orientation for the future. Greenberg shares with many other Jewish thinkers a practical emphasis that is oriented towards the future, rather than the past.

Let us side-by-side, then, bring the Messiah instead of arguing whether it is the first or second coming. Instead of the fighting and the belittling and the denying that delays the coming, let there be mutual activity and love that hastens it.[36]

Note, he is not saying, as some often do, that rather than debating the first coming, we should focus on the second coming. The point is that the emphasis should not be upon the debates on coming, but rather upon common action. Such common action is itself a means of hastening the coming of the messiah. This is, of course, a Jewish view of how to relate to redemp-

---

[33] See also Shapiro, 'Modern Orthodoxy and Religious Truth', 130–1; Kogan, *Opening the Covenant*, 148. The point is brought up forcefully in David Berger's review of Greenberg's book. See Berger, 'Covenants, Messiahs, and Religious Boundaries'.

[34] One could make the argument that faith in the messiah gave way to faith in the Son of God, thereby making Jesus' status as messiah secondary. If so, reference to him as a failed messiah may not undermine Christian faith as much. Still, for the faithful, this is a very counterintuitive way to speak of the subject of their faith. See *For the Sake of Heaven and Earth*, 32.

[35] At a recent gathering, where I mentioned Greenberg's work, Deborah Weissman, a foremost teacher and activist in Jewish–Christian relations and former president of the International Council of Christians and Jews, shared a conversation she had had with Greenberg, where she expressed admiration for his overall theological oeuvre, with the major exception of the concept of a failed messiah, which she considered a failed idea.

[36] *For the Sake of Heaven and Earth*, 197.

tion. While the typical Christian attitude is one of awaiting, within Judaism, especially within the kabbalistic school, we find a much more active approach, wherein our actions provide the conditions and circumstances for the coming of the messiah. The kabbalistic world-view of *tikun olam*, which initially saw ritual activity as a means of hastening messianic redemption, has been adapted by contemporary Jewish thought to good actions meant to heal the world.[37] Greenberg extends this approach as an invitation to both Jews and Christians to engage in common actions for the ultimate common good, the coming of the messiah.

In the most recent iteration of his thought, Greenberg bases the call to common action on the Jewish view that Christian claims of the world having been redeemed are false, standing that view on its head and turning it into a call for collaboration:

Jews now have to understand that their triumphant assertion that the Messiah has not come is not a victory for Judaism. There can be no complacency about the fact that the world was not redeemed—as claimed by Jesus' followers—for this flawed reality bred evil forces that threatened Jewry's very existence. Thus Judaism needs to reach out to every movement that hopes to bring the Messiah, jointly working to temper the absolutist, utopian elements in this commitment, while seeking to attain redemption as soon as possible.[38]

Moving away from a model of competition between the religions, Greenberg considers the need for redeeming the world a common need for both faiths. In this context, he does not even leave room for the belief of Christians that they have experienced redemption or for the power of their subjective testimony spilling over into objective, historical reality. Likely, the forces of evil in the world make it hard to uphold such a Christian view. More urgent is the task of attaining redemption. There is a messianic urgency in Greenberg's writing that cuts across the divide between faiths and which translates into an invitation to work together to heal the world and to transcend those portions of our religions that are obstacles to its eventual, and speedy, healing.[39]

---

[37] See Fine, '"Tikkun": A Lurianic Motive in Contemporary Jewish Thought'.

[38] *For the Sake of Heaven and Earth*, 91.

[39] In the interview in Chapter 6, the urgency of the messianic dimension in Greenberg's thought comes to light, both in the choice of presenting *tikun olam* as a central theological notion, but also more broadly, as it informs his entire theological project.

The Incarnation

A second focal point of Christian faith to which Greenberg devotes his attention in a movement of accommodation is the incarnation of Jesus. Theologically, this is a much more challenging view to affirm. If messianic faith is
a constant in Judaism and a history of failed messiahs provides the backdrop
for a re-evaluation of Jesus as messiah, the Incarnation would seem to be a
much harder concept to justify in Jewish terms. It is, after all, a claim the
likes of which are not made with reference to other figures in the history of
Judaism. It stands at the heart of the theological divide between the faiths,
touching on concerns as central as the view of Christianity as idolatry.[40] It
therefore requires much theological will and ingenuity to affirm the validity
and legitimacy of faith in Jesus' incarnation for Christians.

There are two strategies one can identify in Greenberg's writing. One is
to focus on the religious experience of the early Christians and legitimate it.
The other is to consider the Incarnation an extension of the faith of Israel,
even if it crosses a line that the Jewish tradition would not cross. The depth
structure of biblical faith is accordingly deemed more important than the
particular boundaries and theological positions that have served for centuries as demarcations distinguishing one faith from another.

Let us consider the reference to the faith of Christian believers, returning to a passage we have already touched upon.

As Christians brought the message of hope to Hellenized gentiles, the new audience heard the proclamation about Jesus, the son of God, bringing them closer to
God. According to the Jewish tradition, metaphorically, all people are the children
of God. The newcomers understood the message in a more literal way. They
accepted with gratitude the news that God sought to close the gap between
humanity and the Divine by crossing over and sharing human experience in the
flesh. God sharing human experience was an established Jewish idea, but the conclusion that this identification took the form of Divine Incarnation, literally, was
ultimately deemed by Jews to be in conflict with the monotheistic idea . . . Historically, Judaism rejected what it saw as the divinization of a man. Many Jewish
sages rated the Trinitarian teachings as idolatry or, at best, as the dilution of the
monotheistic principle. Yet the Trinity represents Christianity's effort to honor
the Jewish normative understanding of God's oneness . . . (To be fair, one should

---

[40] Note that even authors who are willing to come to terms with the Trinity have a hard
time justifying the Incarnation. See Goshen-Gottstein, 'Judaism and Incarnational Theologies', 242–3.

add that it is also trying to be faithful to its religious experience with the One God it worships.)[41]

Greenberg cannot affirm Christian faith in the Incarnation or in the Trinity. But he can affirm the religious experience of believers and their efforts to keep their faith somehow tied to its Jewish roots. It is the gentile Christians who take the Jewish teaching of divine sonship and make it literal, an expression of God sharing human experience in the flesh. And it is in the nature of their religious experience that Christians recognize in the one God also the presence of Jesus, who is himself experienced as divine. Greenberg does not acknowledge either the validity of Christian faith or its normativity from the perspective of the history of Jewish views. He does, however, defend the integrity and authenticity of the intention of the Christian faithful, both in recognizing Jesus as God and in seeking to contain such recognition within the bounds of classical Jewish monotheism. This defence suggests that somehow, ultimately, intention is more significant than the eventual theological stance taken by Christians. Christian religious experience is self-validating at least in terms of legitimation for upholding positions that are foreign to Jewish theology. We note an interesting primacy of religious experience over and against doctrinal correctness. One cannot divorce such an approach from contemporary modern and postmodern sensibilities, which privilege subjectivity and individual, or collective, experience over 'truth' conceived in a hard and fast way. From this perspective, then, understanding how Christians got to where they got and appreciating the depth of their religious experience should be the grounds for accepting and respecting them, even while maintaining distance with reference to their actual beliefs.

The above passage makes reference to one sense in which Christian faith in the Incarnation has biblical roots. It considers the biblical notion of sonship to have been extended from a metaphor to reality, and from all people (or perhaps all Jews) to the one unique Son of God. This move is repeated in several different ways in an attempt to ground even the seemingly idolatrous faith in the Incarnation in a Jewish way of thinking.

Christianity is a commentary on the original Exodus, in which the later event— the Christ event—is a manifest, 'Biblically' miraculous event—God becoming incarnate and self-validating through miracles. Obviously, many Jews will argue

---

[41] *For the Sake of Heaven and Earth*, 72.

that closing the Biblically-portrayed gap between the human and the Divine, between the real and the ideal, by Incarnation, is idolatrous or at least against the grain of the Biblical way. But even if Incarnation is contradictory to some Biblical principles, the model itself is operating out of classic Biblical modes—the need to achieve redemption, the desire to close the gap between the human and the Divine which includes Divine initiatives, etc. Thus, a faithful Jew can affirm that Incarnation is improbable and violative of other given Biblical principles and that it is unnecessary in light of the continuing care of the Jewish people; yet such a Divine gesture is not destructive of the original covenant if it was a Divine act intended for the salvation of the Gentiles and 'broadcast' to them rather than to the Jews. This . . . allows faithful Jews to respect the distinctive theological claims of Christianity—and not just the models and values which Jews and Christians hold in common.[42]

The goal is stated in the final sentence—respecting Christianity in its distinctiveness and theological particularity. Several strategies combine here. One is the biblical grounding of the Incarnation as an extension of the Exodus story. The combination of miraculous action and closing the gap between human and divine, itself a biblical movement, brings the Incarnation into the realm of the possible. Significantly, Greenberg does not reject the actual claim out of hand. It is improbable, but not impossible. And the claim is made further possible, at least theologically if not metaphysically, when its intended audience is gentiles.

In another discussion, Greenberg makes a similar effort to accommodate faith in the Incarnation:

Judaism denied the occurrence of divine incarnation; it needed to be authentic to its own religious life. This tempted it to overlook the genuinely Jewish dimension of this Christian attempt to close the gap between the human and the Divine. Even while rejecting the model, should Jews not recognize that it grows out of the tormenting persistence of a great distance between the divinely sought perfection and the human condition? One can conceive of a divine pathos that sent not only words across the gap but life and body itself. I say this not as a Jew who accepts this claim, but as one who has come to see that it is not for me to prescribe to God how God communicates to others.[43]

Greenberg does not depart from the Jewish refusal to recognize the Incarnation, but he significantly weakens opposition to the idea. He can speak of

---

[42] 'The Relationship of Judaism and Christianity', 206. The text was slightly toned down in *For the Sake of Heaven and Earth*.   [43] *For the Sake of Heaven and Earth*, 180.

'the genuinely Jewish dimension' of this belief. Jews are called on to be empathetic to the religious sensibilities and causes that generated it, assuming that somehow understanding its motivation and genealogy compensates for significant substantive differences with it. Greenberg appeals to the religious imagination, envisaging divine pathos going one step beyond speech as the bridge of the human–divine chasm. Finally, he remains open to the theoretical possibility of such an occurrence. The problem with the Incarnation is not its metaphysical impossibility, as classical Jewish polemicists might claim. Rather, it is a matter of belief not shared. Greenberg takes a big step in leaving it to God to decide how to communicate with others, without imposing his own faith's constrictions on God's actions.

There are, however, constrictions of another nature, and I have already noted these in an earlier reference. Immediately following this passage, Greenberg states:

Our task is to find ways for humans to hear God. We should measure religions by the criterion of how people act after they hear the word in community. If the Incarnation and Resurrection of Jesus lead to Christian triumphalism, to persecution, and idolatry, then Christianity proves itself to be false. If it leads to deeper compassion and understanding and a grasp of the human realities and human needs, and motivated covenantal action, then it validates itself as a channel of the Divine.[44]

This is a hugely important quote. It may be the core of Greenberg's theory of religious pluralism. What matters in religion is not the faith one upholds, but how it translates into action in the life of the community. What makes the Incarnation, as well as the Resurrection, and in theory any other aspect of the Christian faith, valid or not is not the actual content of faith, but how it is lived in the community. The reason why Greenberg is willing to affirm the biblical roots of the Incarnation is not that this is a good or valid application of biblical principles. Rather, the truth value of the faith claim is proven by the life that Christians lead. Basically, because he has come to know Christians whose faith inspired them to compassion and to taking what he calls covenantal action in response to human needs, this leads him to validate their faith. Having validated Christianity in terms of its fruit, he can then make the additional moves of grounding it in biblical precedent and practising humility or agnosticism as to how God might communicate with other communities. The reverse is true as well. Triumphalism and persecution

[44] Ibid.

provide testimony to the falsity of faith rather than theological correctness.[45]

One final discussion suggests that Judaism and Christianity apply the same biblical principles, but through alternative strategies for achieving the same end:

Whereas Jewish tradition affirms that the final goals can be attained under the leadership of a human avant-garde, Christianity adds the claim that God became the human model that leads humans into the final state. Thus Christianity also concedes that only a human model can bring out the fullness of humanity. Once the triumphalist distortion is removed, Christians can begin to recognize the Incarnation model is profoundly Jewish, albeit rejected by Judaism. Jews can begin to recognize that the Incarnation concept should not be dismissed as some bizarre import from Hellenistic culture but viewed as an extension of the use of human exemplars to evoke maximum covenantal behavior. It is not that Jews and Christians will accept each other's views on this issue, but they can come to realize that both positions grow out of strategies for achieving the goals of the covenant held in common.[46]

It is a marvellous way of minimizing theological differences to speak of them as alternative strategies. A strategy is an interim step taken towards some ultimate goal. Judaism and Christianity, in this view, share the same story and participate in the same covenantal processes. This fundamental identity overrides all those differences that, throughout the centuries, have been highlighted as the means of differentiating one religion from the other. In Greenberg's view, we should not be looking at the details of faith, but at the broader participation in the common covenantal structure, or even in the common covenant. Details are then to be subsumed under this fundamental similarity, which outweighs all other differences. At the end of the day, details are no more than alternative strategies for fulfilling common covenantal aspirations. Faith in the Incarnation, in this reading, is simply a strategy that takes the biblical belief in following a human leader and identifies this human leader with God himself.[47] But the model is Jewish and not

[45] I am hard pressed to account for 'idolatry' in the above quote. Idolatry is not a moral category, and certainly does not relate to the Christian treatment of Jews. It is thus out of place in the present discussion. Reference to it in this context is begging the question around which this paragraph is constructed, namely whether belief in the Incarnation is idolatrous.

[46] *For the Sake of Heaven and Earth*, 166.

[47] In a later formulation, Greenberg suggests Jews need not insist on the relevance of the truth of their historical experience to another faith community. 'It is sufficient for Jews to

Hellenistic, inasmuch as it echoes the fundamentals of Jewish faith and seeks to realize the biblical covenantal model.[48]

The Crucifixion

The Crucifixion poses much less of a theological challenge than the articles of Christian faith covered above. After all, it is a fact and is not in and of itself one that is contested between Jews and Christians. Whereas with reference to messiahship and the Incarnation, Greenberg spoke to his Jewish audience in an attempt to make it more accepting of Christian faith, with reference to the Crucifixion he addresses a Christian audience and engages it in the question of meaning.

I have argued elsewhere that the true lesson of the Crucifixion had been misunderstood by Christians because of their past triumphalism. In the light of the Holocaust, one would argue that the true lesson of the Crucifixion is that if God in person came down to earth in human flesh and was put on the cross and crucified, then God would be broken. God would be so exhausted by the agony that God would end up losing faith, and saying, 'My God, my God, why have you forsaken me?' If God could not survive the cross, then surely no human can be expected to. So the overwhelming call for both religions is to stop the Crucifixion, not to glorify it.[49]

It takes very deep engagement in dialogue with another religion to tell its believers what the meaning of their fundamental religious symbol is and what is the lesson to be drawn from a formative religious moment. Perhaps it is the high vantage point that characterizes Greenberg's writing that allows him to propose to Christians a totally new meaning of the Crucifixion. The explicit reference to the Holocaust provides the context for such a daring statement, and serves as the moral justification for telling Christians what the Crucifixion really means, or at least what it ought to mean today. It is not a sign of love, a great offering, a redeeming sacrifice. It is a teaching of how deep humanly inflicted suffering can operate. It can operate even on God's self, causing God himself to lose faith. The Crucifixion is God going to the extreme in order to show us how not to act towards one another.

affirm that they have no interest in restricting God's choice of tactics and method of revelation' (ibid. 67).

[48] Greenberg affirms the continuity of the two faiths despite Hellenic elements in Christianity. Contrast this with Sacks' discussion below, Ch. 11.

[49] *For the Sake of Heaven and Earth*, 158.

It is a moral lesson that we must learn, and all religious communities need to learn this lesson, whether they affirm their faith in the saving power of the cross or not.

The Crucifixion also provides us with a view of another side of Greenberg's approach to Christianity. He is as capable of criticizing it as he is of being empathetic and accommodating.

The narrowing of its messages that grew out of its unconditional rejection of Judaism penalized Christianity itself in no small measure. The focus on Crucifixion strengthened ascetic tendencies and devalued the spiritual significance of pleasure. The model of self-abnegating sacrifice as the key relationship to God generated fideism, sometimes at the expense of reason; it also nurtured the self-image of a powerless human, dependent on a mediator, unable to help himself or play a fully dignified role in the covenant.[50]

This is powerful criticism of Christianity. But it does not seek to devalue it as much as to view it from the perspective of checks and balances, provided, in Greenberg's view, by the existence of multiple covenantal communities. From the perspective of a true pluralism, one can ask whether all that has transpired as a consequence of key Christian symbols and moments of faith has been beneficial. Gone from this passage is the appeal to the faith of Christians or a deeper drive by means of which their belief can be justified, experientially or biblically. Instead, Greenberg considers how symbols and beliefs can distort a spiritual path. Implicit in this criticism is the view of Judaism's alternative choices as superior to those made by Christians in light of the cross. Here, as in other instances, Greenberg is less concerned with the truth or falsity of a belief than with its impact and fruits in the lives of believers. The ultimate question is what the Crucifixion means and what it leads to. Some of the consequences of faith in the Resurrection are undesired, especially when weighed against Greenberg's ultimate standard of humans taking their dignified place as partners in a covenantal relationship with God.[51]

[50] *For the Sake of Heaven and Earth*, 224.

[51] This passage dates from 2000. I therefore suspect that this critical note is part of a later Greenberg. Some of his later writing lacks the clarity and particular orientation that is typical of his earlier writings. The question of lack of clarity and rigour is one of the main points of criticism raised in David Berger's review, 'Covenants, Messiahs, and Religious Boundaries', 66–78.

CHAPTER FOUR

Covenant: A Necessary Cornerstone of Greenberg's Thought?

T HE FOLLOWING CHAPTER is the longest and most complex part of the presentation of Greenberg's views on Christianity and other religions. We are already aware of the centrality of the covenant to his theological thinking and of how that concept serves as a bridge and a means of validating other religions. Had covenant functioned in Greenberg's thought only as a broad and general category, we could have appreciated the work it does and its theological utility. However, it is the subject of significant attention in Greenberg's theologizing and is dealt with in detail. Not only are we presented with the concept; we are introduced to an entire range of biblical covenants, which become categories of theological thinking and tools for developing a view of the religious other. An elaborate theoretical construct emerges in dialogue with biblical texts and as their relevance for Jewish, Christian, and other readers is revealed.

The more elaborate and the more biblical the discussion becomes, the greater the theological stakes as well as the chance for misunderstanding and disagreement, and consequently also for Greenberg's message to not be well received. Therefore, it is not possible to simply present his ideas on the covenant and its relevance to relations between religions in the same descriptive manner that has served our discussion up to this point. A presentation of the variety of biblical covenants and the thick associations of 'covenant' for a Jewish theology of religions must go hand in hand with a critical examination of Greenberg's ideas: their coherence, their viability, and the likelihood of their reception by the audiences that are addressed. Such critical engagement does not seek to argue with nor to disprove the theological constructs. But it does seek to clarify their meaning, the stakes at hand, and the theological price that is being paid for various assertions. In short, good theology requires proper theological engagement and it is in this spirit that I will scrutinize Greenberg's use of the covenant in Jewish–Christian and other contexts, and its multiple dimensions.

There are several reasons why these ideas must be analysed critically. The first relates to the likelihood of reception. Religious communities draw their patterns of thinking from Scripture and it is by appeal to Scripture that arguments are made within and across traditions. A covenantal approach to inter-religious relations is fundamentally a scriptural approach. It draws upon and further expands a scriptural category. As already stated, Greenberg's use of the notion in a Jewish–Christian context is based on a sequence of biblical covenants, which he casts into structures of meaning through which Jews and Christians can address each other and reach understanding. The entire process is informed, then, by scriptural reading and its application to a novel theological challenge. How central is the act of reading, scriptural exegesis, to this process? To what extent does the outcome of the process, and therefore its eventual reception by religious communities, depend on good, proper, or acceptable readings of Scripture? Can good theology be constructed on problematic or disputed scriptural foundations?

One might argue that *all* theology, to some extent or another, engages in bad exegesis. Within Judaism, entire world-views were constructed upon biblical foundations, often uprooting their original intent and supplanting it with alternative meanings. From a Jewish perspective, and one acknowledges the point can be made reciprocally, the very project of a Christian reading of Hebrew Scriptures is based on bad or wrong exegesis. Why then make a fuss about proper biblical readings? Is not every theology an act of co-opting Scripture and its message to novel theological perspectives that serve the needs of the day? The answer is: yes and no.

Two important distinctions must be made that set the kind of theologizing and scriptural justification that Greenberg engages in in a different context than millennia of Jewish and Christian appeal to Scripture, which often overrides Scripture's message with novel religious understandings. The first distinction relates to the novel situation of doing theology *simultaneously* for Jews and Christians (and others). Underlying Greenberg's interreligious theological project is the question of audience. Is he writing for Jews or for Christians? I believe the proper answer is that he is writing for the Jewish–Christian *situation*. In other words, he is offering a vision that is relevant to the coming together in dialogue, and in the quest for mutual understanding, of certain open and dialogically minded Jews and Christians. These seek new understanding for their relationship, new theological paradigms, and accordingly they require a new approach to Scripture. It is thus a unique moment involving scriptural exegesis across religious communities, with audiences engaged on both sides of the divide. But it is precisely the uniqueness of this situation that raises the question of how Scripture is approached. If both Jews and Christians are to relate to a novel, scripturally based, vision, then the scriptural grounding must be transparent and solid enough to speak to both traditions. Moreover, it must meet the critical standards that apply in both. Just as good theology grows on biblical foundations and then expands them to construct novel theological edifices, so too such a new theological construct must make sense first in terms of biblical exegesis and only on the basis of that in terms of its internal theological coherence.

This brings us to the second contextual question. Most of the participants in the Jewish–Christian dialogue have assimilated to a significant degree certain norms of how Scripture is read. This includes some historical awareness (putting aside the not irrelevant issue of biblical source criticism), literary analysis, and an approach to the biblical text that is informed by its plain sense and historical meaning, as distinct from many of the things the Bible has meant for later readers. So, in addition to having to read the biblical text in a way that can speak to two religious communities, the challenge of developing a kind of Jewish–Christian theology, inasmuch as this is what a theology that serves the needs of the dialogue really does, also requires reading patterns that will sit well with contemporary, critically informed readers. In short, for a theological construct to pass muster, it must look good enough at face value to serve a present-day theological agenda and must withstand critical objections stemming from a plain-sense reading of the biblical text. A big question therefore arises in the case where one can demonstrate that the actual meaning of Scripture is at odds with a suggested theological construct. Even if at first view and according to a common view a certain reading is upheld, we face the challenge of falsification in the hypothetical case where this common view can be shown to be wrong. Would this undermine the entire theological construct?

I have entered into these abstract considerations because it seems to me that they are germane to an evaluation of Greenberg's application of the covenant in a Jewish–Christian context. By raising these points I offer early indication of one of the biggest concerns I have with Greenberg's theology —it is not based on sound biblical foundations. This concern takes on various expressions. One could disagree with individual readings. That, of course, is an occupational hazard of the theologian and one that has always loomed large over any theological reading. More significantly, a reading may not go down well with parts of the intended audience, for failure to meet the canons of reading that are common in the given community. Throughout what follows, I will come back to this point. It is, in my mind, a serious concern that undermines much of Greenberg's elaborate presentation of the covenant in a Jewish–Christian context. Finally, a reading may not simply not go down well; it may be considered wrong or out of place. Such a concern will be raised in relation to how Greenberg attributes meaning to the Noahide covenant. If the objection to this reading turns out to be valid, does this undermine the entire theological construct? In our case: would we be led to drop reference to the covenant as a category that serves the interreligious situation on the basis of readings, and alternative readings, of Scripture?

Greenberg uses covenant as part of his engagement with contemporary Jewish concerns, but also in dialogue with Christian thinkers. For this reason, we must ask what, if any, relationship there ought to be between the biblical foundations of covenantal thought and how he casts the concept. Perhaps, were it not for his Christian interlocutors, the question might be less urgent. But his Christian audience likely maintains even more of an interest in the biblical roots of the idea than Greenberg's Jewish conversation partners. We must therefore consider to what extent, at the end of the day, the covenant propounded by Greenberg, and by means of which he propagates a pluralistic world-view, is recognizable to his biblically minded conversation partners. The same question must also be asked in relation to his Jewish audience. Are they able to recognize the idea of covenant as expounded by him, both in terms of its biblical sources and in terms of the actual applications he offers? If one is pleased with how he constructs the category and how it relates to biblical precedents, there will be no need, of course, for any revision of his theological language. If, however, the reception of his usage, either in the Jewish or in the Christian community, is not problem-free, we must ask whether his view of Christianity can be stated independently of the covenantal language in which it is cast. This is one major concern that I have about Greenberg's thick use of the covenant, grounded as it is in a series of biblical readings.

There is a second, related concern. In order to make a point regarding the covenant as it figures in the discourse of Jews and Christians and in their relations, constructs are developed that have to sit well not only exegetically but also theologically with both sides. The challenge of speaking simultaneously to two faith communities is that one must relate not only to the biblical sources, but also to what they mean to each. In this context we come up against a further difficulty. At least with reference to one major point, but potentially with reference to his entire application of the covenant, Greenberg thinks as a Jew and extends this thinking to his Christian conversation partners. But does the Christian conversation partner really fit into the proposed pattern? The question will become relevant when we consider the inclusion of Christians in the Sinai covenant, something that Greenberg goes to extraordinary lengths to do. Appreciating the importance of this move, as we will, in terms of what it seeks to achieve for Jewish–Christian relations, we must ask whether Christians *have* or *want* to be included in the Sinai covenant. The answer is not unequivocally positive, once again raising the question of how a biblical-theological construct will sit with a part of its intended audience.

A complication of a different kind arises as Greenberg tries to make the covenant work in the service of contemporary Jewish–Christian relations. The thrust of his thought is pluralist. His ambition is to confer equal spiritual value, not to mention validity, on two religions, and more. However, as we shall see in the following discussion, advancing a pluralist agenda by appeal to Israel's particular covenant(s) ends up compromising pluralism. The process of endowing other religions with greater value by incorporating them into ideals that are strictly Israel's unique domain moves Greenberg's thought from pluralism to what is typically considered inclusivism, in other words, regarding the other as valid on one's own terms and by means of categories of signification that are specific to one's own tradition, instead of the full appreciation of the other on his own terms. This potential philosophical difficulty is due also to the attempt to construct a contemporary theological statement by appeal to classical biblical sources.

All this leads to the larger question that informs the present chapter. To what extent does Greenberg really need covenant as a foundation for his pluralistic interreligious thinking? Granted, it is an important category in his own theology and in how he constructs message and meaning for contemporary Jewry. But must this importance extend also to the interreligious situation?

I argue that all that Greenberg seeks to achieve can be achieved without appeal to covenantal language. For me, the use of that language and particularly how he applies it may generate more confusion than clarity, and may raise more questions than it solves. The thrust of his goodwill and the moves he makes could stand on their own, independently of their covenantal garb. Engaging with Greenberg's covenantal expositions is an opportunity to hear his core message and to examine the language and conceptual context he adopts. It is also a moment to query the relationship between message and theological language.

The Covenant in Greenberg's Thought

There are three primary moments or dimensions that define the scope of human history—Creation, covenant, and redemption.[1] A different way of capturing the same structure is to emphasize the image of God as the starting point of the journey and to see the work of redemption as a special human capacity.[2] Creation provides the starting point. Redemption is the final point. What transpires in between, suggests Greenberg, is covenant. To understand covenant, we need to introduce another concept, *tikun olam*, the healing or repair of the world. Creation is imperfect and requires human action to bring it to its fulfilment, its redemption. Humans are entrusted with this task, and *tikun olam* describes human involvement in it. *Tikun olam* is identified with covenant because it points to the actors in the drama. The world is created by God, but its perfection requires the collaboration of humans and the Divine. In fact, the human partner becomes increasingly important as the history of the covenant unfolds. For Greenberg, covenant functions as a category for empowering humans to play their role in a divine drama. The focus of the drama is the battle between life and death. The basic drive is for life. This life-affirming approach entails the human responsibility to act accordingly, which, for Greenberg, is the meaning of covenant.[3]

True to biblical sources, Greenberg's teaching is not made up of abstract truths, but of a narrative. He speaks of a master narrative, and Creation, covenant, and redemption are three stories that fit into that framework.[4] Covenant is, accordingly, in the service of creation. Here Greenberg presents assumptions for how the covenant proceeds. Significantly, these assumptions, while biblically founded, are not classically associated with the coven-

---

[1] *For the Sake of Heaven and Earth*, 40, 101.

[2] Ibid. 187–8, 213–14.   [3] Ibid. 43, 55–6, 162, 186.   [4] 'Covenantal Pluralism', 425.

ant; it is Greenberg's theological creativity that connects them.[5] The first is that God is with us in our troubles. In the broken reality in which we live, God reaches out, often initiates, often helps; but humans must respond and take full responsibility. This premise is founded on a brilliant reading of Psalm 91: 15, a *locus classicus* for acknowledging God's compassion and presence with the suffering person. Hasidic literature affirms that even in times of darkness and suffering, God has not abandoned us.[6] Greenberg gives the biblical text a special twist. God is with us in the same sense that the biblical commandment requires us to help someone who needs to lift his fallen burden—only if he helps carry it himself. A verse typically used to justify divine compassion and aid is thus turned into a statement of collaboration and a condition: aid requires human participation. A second premise is that human models must be found for this work. This is what Israel, the covenanted community, is all about. The work of perfecting humanity requires the recognition and acceptance of particularity and of the distinctiveness of identities. Finally, the perfection process takes place at a human pace, because it involves human actors. It is a long historical haul that is the subject of this master narrative; it cannot be rushed.

Israel's covenant is a model of human responsibility and collaboration with God in the lengthy historical process of perfecting the world. The genius of the covenant, in this reading, is that it affirms particularity and makes room for each group to engage in this task in its unique way.[7]

One suggestive way by means of which Greenberg captures what he means by covenant is to speak of the dream. Both Judaism and Christianity promise a vision of perfection that appears far from present reality. 'The covenant is the pledge to work to realize the dream.'[8] The classical foci of the covenant, including revelation, faithfulness, and attachment to God, are quite secondary in this scheme. Greenberg doesn't seem to include the sabbath, circumcision, or any of the things that give the Jewish covenant its specificity. In fact, it never serves as something particular. It is a partnership to work in the world for goals, but it is not Israel's special covenantal relationship. While there is partnership, the category does not describe a relationship. Covenant does not serve as the basis for a relationship of love

---

[5] Ibid. 428.

[6] See *Ba'al shem tov al hatorah*, 'Beshalaḥ', 23; *Torat hamagid*, 'Ki Tisa', s.v. *ki lo*; *No'am elimelekh*, 'Vayeshev', s.v. *eleh toledot*, and dozens of references throughout the literature. For Greenberg's use of the verse from Psalms in its traditional sense, see *For the Sake of Heaven and Earth*, 100.   [7] *For the Sake of Heaven and Earth*, 191.   [8] Ibid. 163.

and intimacy. It is instrumentalized to doing good in the world, but not to having a relationship with God. What matters most in Greenberg's scheme is how covenant functions as a historical category, spanning from Creation to redemption and drawing on human action in the process of perfecting the world. This abstraction, the distillation of the core of the master narrative, allows an approach that transcends the particularity of Judaism and its covenanted life, and enables Greenberg to speak of the concept as a broader human category that is relevant for all religions.

With this understanding of the covenant, we realize that in fact what Greenberg has in mind when speaking of it is a notion of human responsibility, which is in turn related to the divine–human partnership.

This is the ultimate logic of covenant: If God wants humans to grow to a final perfection, then the ultimate logic of covenant is for humans to take full responsibility . . . the human is like God, but is ultimately called by God to be the partner.[9]

The notion of partnership is central to Greenberg's view of the covenant. He distinguishes between biblical and rabbinic articulations, where the latter deepen covenantal reflection by referring explicitly to 'partnership' to describe what covenant means.[10] A close reading of Greenberg suggests that he has advanced the covenantal model significantly. He not only incorporates a sense of partnership in the covenantal model; what he does is to redefine covenant in light of partnership and to make partnership the primary reality, with covenant as its expression, rather than the reverse.

The concept of partnership implies joint and parallel efforts and mutual obligations. This is one of the revolutionary insights of Israelite religion. The covenant mechanism is intended by its Initiator to give over a sense of stability and dignity to humans and to make them feel that God is deeply and equally involved with them.[11]

It is the concept of human–divine partnership that is primary and covenant is a mechanism for conveying that ideal. Further lessons are derived from this concerning the nature of the covenant:

One of the most profound teachings of covenant is that you cannot separate the

---

[9] *For the Sake of Heaven and Earth*, 159.
[10] 'The Relationship of Judaism and Christianity', 203. Regrettably, this statement is not substantiated and I am actually not sure what he has in mind when referring to rabbinic literature.   [11] *For the Sake of Heaven and Earth*, 214.

ends from the means. The ends are human freedom, dignity, and human value. These goals cannot be realized by coercion on the part of either humans or God. Therefore, *brit* implies that God will not force us.[12]

If it is all about partnership, then the autonomous status and free will of the partner will be primary, offering a teaching on human dignity and freedom.[13]

Covenant and History

Because covenant is about partnership, it is about the empowerment of the human person within the divine–human relationship. Such empowerment, much like the covenant itself, is a process. Covenant is not static. It is, rather, a process of growing responsibility within the covenantal framework. Greenberg speaks of an insight that opens for him a theological door: the idea that the covenant was by its very nature intended to unfold in stages.[14] The stages are not, as often conceived within a Jewish–Christian matrix, the move from one faith to the other. Rather, they are the growing autonomy and responsibility of the human partner in the covenant. The ability to tell the story of an unfolding covenant wherein greater human responsibility ensues results from a reading of Jewish history that contrasts biblical and rabbinic Judaism. It is therefore a model that grows out of a Jewish framework, significantly different from how a Christian might present the unfolding of covenant history. Accordingly, Greenberg can speak of the rabbinic phase as a renewal of the covenant.[15] This is not a renewal in the biblical sense of reaffirmation of covenantal commitments after they have been broken by Israel. Rather, by renewal, as we have seen, Greenberg refers to entering a higher stage of the covenant that entails greater human responsibility, and wherein God's active role is decreased.

Covenant governs God's relationship with Israel, and, more broadly in Greenberg's thought, God's relationship with humanity. While it involves particular stipulations and commandments that require following and faithfulness, its dynamics, as described by Greenberg, are not those of faithfulness and lack thereof. Its true dynamics are rooted in the power-sharing between God and Israel (humans). Covenant defines partnership and partnership,

---

[12] *Living in the Image of God*, 63.

[13] Free will is part of the covenant, even if not defined as partnership. This is implicit in the urging, the warning, and the entire biblical battle for the fulfilment of the covenant. The rabbis also affirm this; see *Mekhilta*, 'Baḥodesh', 5.

[14] *For the Sake of Heaven and Earth*, 29.   [15] Ibid. 65, 191.

in turn, hinges on an allocation of power and responsibility. Accordingly, unpacking the concept of covenant leads us to issues of the autonomy of human free will and how the human will relates to the divine will. Human empowerment and the freedom of choice emerge as even more fundamental than any of the covenantal stipulations that would be obeyed by means of submission of the human to the divine will. In fact, submission does not seem to hold the key to the covenant's effectiveness. It is not in submission that it achieves its purpose, but in the flowering and full manifestation of the human will. Only by means of such full and autonomous manifestation is the covenantal goal of partnership attained.[16]

For Greenberg, covenant functions as a means of interpreting history. However, that interpretation is not carried out by means of the biblical scheme of reward and punishment in relation to obedience to the covenant. Rather, covenant itself has its own internal story, which offers a reading of Jewish history. It is the story of moving from one phase of the covenant to the other, characterized by greater freedom, autonomy, and responsibility of the human partner.

The covenant, as understood in classical sources, has a distinct starting point, located variously with Abraham or at Sinai. Its recasting in the space between Creation and *tikun* suggests an alternative grounding in creation. All of history is its process of realization and fulfilment. Even though the first historical covenant is the one made with Noah, conceptually covenant is grounded in creation itself. This is, in fact, an outcome of Greenberg's identification of covenant and *tikun*. Unlike covenant, which has a distinct starting point narrated in Scripture, *tikun* as a kabbalistic category reaches back to creation itself, and to the need for its rectification following a prior catastrophe within the Divine. *Tikun*, in the kabbalistic reading, is not a his-

---

[16] I am grateful to Tanya White for making me realize the extent to which covenant as a category serves as the means of exploring the boundaries of human autonomy in Greenberg's thought. As she suggests to me, this is in fact a modern development that owes its existence to Kant and the quest for the affirmation of the self as moral legislator. White suggests this is a common feature of all modern Jewish covenantal thinkers. Indeed, this emerges clearly from Cooper, *Contemporary Covenantal Thought*. While his study is devoted to the thought of Borowitz and Hartman, Greenberg's theology and its close resemblance to that of both figures, and especially to that of David Hartman, comes up time and again in his discussions. Empowerment, autonomy, responsibility, and partnership emerge as the defining elements of a covenantal theology that is common to all three thinkers. As Cooper notes (p. 232), this emphasis comes at the exclusion of a view of covenant as contract, as having legal dimensions, and in certain cases even as a category that is centred around relationship. See Cooper, *Contemporary Covenantal Thought*, 189.

torical category per se, even if it informs the entire working out of history, its task and significance. It is, for the kabbalists, history working out the healing of a flawed creation. By identifying covenant and *tikun*, and further-more by grounding their meaning in the image of God, Greenberg shifts 'covenant' to two concepts, both of which relate to creation rather than to history. This may also hold the key to how the covenant can function as a key to all human activity and to all religions. Had it been grounded in his-tory, it might have been exclusive to the people whose story it defines. By basing it in creation, through association with the image of God and the rectification of *tikun*, he opens it up to a universality that recognizes in it the grammar of all religious life.

All this indicates how differently covenant as a category functions com-pared to the classical biblical covenant. Biblical covenant served as the legal category by means of which God's relationship with Israel was defined. In Greenberg's writing nothing is left of this legal dimension. Rather, covenant serves as a hermeneutical concept by means of which history is interpreted and humans are called to rise to a higher vision of their contribution to the ultimate end of perfecting creation. Covenant is a lens through which to view history, even more than it is a lens through which to define relation-ships. As a hermeneutical category, not only can it interpret Jewish experi-ence, but it can also serve as a means of evaluating Christian experience, as well as that of other religions. There is a divine calling to become more active in the unfolding of the covenantal way. The Christian dismissal of Judaism as legalism could cause Christians to fail to hear this calling.[17] Ulti-mately, covenant is a modus operandi of the human–Divine relationship, and its stages, as understood by Greenberg, allow him to view and appre-ciate, as well as to criticize, religions in terms of their coherence with the universal covenantal model. Covenant is not a Jewish particularity. It is, so to speak, the universal code of how humans are to live in partnership with God. Judaism equips Greenberg to identify this code. Its application is uni-versal and extends to Christianity as well as to other religions.

Covenant and Pluralism

In biblical literature, Israel alone has a covenant with God. No other nation has one, either with its god or with the God of Israel.[18] It is therefore quite a

[17] *For the Sake of Heaven and Earth*, 179.
[18] There are instances of the language of election applied to other nations, such as the

stretch to consider covenant as the basis of a pluralism by means of which other religions are validated. But this is exactly what Greenberg does. The focus and understanding of covenant shift. Through this shift, it becomes possible to extend the covenant to other religions. The most important theological shift that has occurred in this regard, as early as the prophetic literature, is the recognition of the universality of God. There are no other gods, as in the biblical view, which could accept the possibility of one nation having a relationship with its god, while another was committed to another god. There is only one God. Consequently, limiting the covenant to one people became a challenge. As the covenantal idea was not present in most of Jewish history, the question of a covenant with other people, let alone religions, did not arise. Even thinkers such as Maimonides, who downplayed the centrality of the notion of Israel's election,[19] did not consider it. The question is therefore new, and so is the sensibility that seeks to extend the covenant to other religions, grounded as it is in the novel circumstances that drive Greenberg in this direction.

For Greenberg, Israel's covenant is a model rather than an exclusive relationship. It is meant to show the way for others to follow suit in the work of *tikun olam*. Grounded in the story of Creation, or the image of God, and pointing to ultimate redemption, this covenantal world-view focuses on what it means to be human, rather than what it means to be Israel. It cuts across religious difference and provides a basis for religious pluralism.

Biblical covenant suggested an exclusive relationship with God. Greenberg revises this sense of particularity:

The elected people of Israel . . . are co-workers with other humans in the process of perfection, because the divine covenantal love is not exhausted with any one people . . . others can give their witness and their model as well. That is also the genius of the covenant; it enables us to affirm the particularity of each group, to make room for other groups to give their witness and exemplify their particular way, as well.[20]

In this reading, the uniqueness of each covenant is not to be understood in

famous verse in Isa. 19: 25. Greenberg cites some of these (ibid. 57). While he does not refer to them as covenants, his wording effectively suggests that they are equivalent to covenants: 'Abraham's covenant . . . is but one in a series of divine initiatives to redeem suffering humanity.'

[19] Kellner, *Maimonides on Judaism and the Jewish People*.
[20] *For the Sake of Heaven and Earth*, 191.

terms of an exclusive relationship with God. In fact, a particular covenant need not be concluded by God in a personal way.[21] Every covenantal relationship is suited to the particularity of the group or faith that enters into that relationship with God.[22] It is important to recognize that covenant as such does not require being part of the biblical story. Greenberg has abstracted it from its biblical moorings so that it is relevant not only to Christianity, or even Islam, which share the vocabulary or the story or Scripture itself. The beauty of this move is that it removes covenant-speak from the historically competitive relationship between the three religions. In this model, they no longer need to fight over the question of who is heir to the covenant.[23] The notion is largely extracted from the Abrahamic heritage and decontextualized in relation to almost all specific biblical covenants. Accordingly, all religions can be covenantal. 'Covenant' and 'covenantal' would then be qualitative dimensions of what it means to be religious and how any religion points to a divine–human partnership for improving and redeeming the world.

This unlimited partnership of the divine and the human is the ultimate dimension of religious calling in both traditions . . . Both religions teach that the people of Israel, the covenantal people (however each faith defines that) are pledged not only to work but to teach and to model how to be human to the rest of humanity.[24]

The discussion focuses on Judaism and Christianity and therefore articulates Greenberg's understanding of the covenant in relation to them. It may also be the case that the two religions share this covenantal positioning because of their common scripture and even because of the dispute over the heritage of the true Israel. Still, a closer look suggests that in fact the structure of Greenberg's thought makes this passage relevant to all religions. Unlimited partnership is the ultimate dimension of what it means to be religious, in any religion. Judaism and Christianity may, to use Greenberg's phrase,

---

[21] Taken to the extreme, this way of thinking could consider Buddhism or other atheistic religions as covenantal by virtue of their service to the common good and by force of recognition of being Israel's co-workers. Affirmation of divine covenantal love is the higher vision that Israel brings to its view of other religions, but which need not inform the actions and motivations of other co-workers for *tikun olam*.

[22] In *The Triumph of Life*, 208, Greenberg expounds in greater detail the ideas he has already developed regarding why one needs covenantal particularity. It is instrumental in addressing and accommodating the emotional and cultural characteristics of different peoples.

[23] In this spirit, see *For the Sake of Heaven and Earth*, 102.   [24] Ibid. 164.

model this for others, but the calling is universal and apparently the fullness of the religious life will only manifest when all religions follow suit.

This is an important statement, but in many ways also a problematic one. It points to a fundamental tension that informs Greenberg's universalizing of the covenant. Let us consider who is addressed in this statement. It is granted that the other religion that Greenberg has in mind is Christianity. Others are simply 'humanity', not particular religions. What, then, does this statement mean for other faiths? It seems that Judaism was the avant-garde of a divine approach to partnership with humans, teaching and modelling covenantal partnership for humanity. Christianity followed suit. Eventually all religions, or all humanity, will join in the covenantal enterprise. Indeed, in his later writings, Greenberg does make an explicit move towards incorporating Islam and possibly other religions into the covenantal framework.[25]

If we speak of modelling, and if we refer to the process of partnership with God for the embetterment of the world as 'covenant', we remain close to Israel's historical covenant, now extended to others. This is a highly Judaeo-centric view. Christianity is grafted, by its own faith acclamation, onto the Jewish heart of the divine–human drama. However, as we have just seen, 'the genius of the covenant' is that it enables us to affirm the particularity of every group. The proof text cited by Greenberg is telling: the Philistines were brought out of Caphtor and the Arameans from Kir, just as Israel was brought out of Egypt.[26] Does the realization of the full genius of the covenant require Israel as a role model? The verse from Amos does not assume that the Philistines have either a covenant or covenantal potential on account of Israel. If so, covenant is a universal dimension of religion. What need, then, is there for modelling to other religions? We encounter here a fundamental tension. Is covenant tied to biblical roots and a common story or has it become a broader category that transcends the common story?

Let us spell out the meaning of these two options. The first option considers covenant and covenantal relationship as standing in some way in direct, conscious relationship to the covenants of Israel in Judaism and

---

[25] *For the Sake of Heaven and Earth*, 94, 232.

[26] Amos 9: 7. See *For the Sake of Heaven and Earth*, 191. The verse from Amos is sandwiched between the claim that God's love is not exhausted with one people and the description of the covenant as a means of recognizing the particularity of each group. I read it in relation to both claims, though it is possible that Greenberg intends a less extreme reading. If so, covenant would show greater dependence on Israel as a teacher, model, and instrument for humanity's realization of a covenantal vocation.

Christianity. In that case, we fall short of full pluralism. Rather, what we call pluralism is an extension of Israel's covenant in concentric circles that will always refer to the original. The discussion below of Christianity's status as Abrahamic covenant and as part of the people of Israel would accord with this possibility. The alternative is a phenomenology of religions. There is a dimension to religions in which they all collaborate with God and that dimension is designated as covenantal. If so, one would have to justify this claim not on theological grounds but on the basis of the empirical study of other religions.

This is a very challenging issue to navigate, primarily because it has not been fully worked out in Greenberg's theology. His discussion suffers from a double limitation, which inhibits the full development of the conceptual potential of 'covenantal' as a dimension of religion. In the first instance, he is so engaged with his Christian interlocutors as to not have thought through the implications of such modelling for other religions. Only his later writings make allowance for a broader application of the covenant, but even here the thinking does not extend significantly beyond Islam. The second limitation relates to his attempt to maintain some association and continuity with the Scripture common to Christians and Jews. While this might not inhibit in principle the application of 'covenantal' to other religions, it does tend to keep the discussion limited to religions that share the same scriptures, thereby implying that other religions are not covenantal until they have learned the required lessons from Judaism and Christianity.

This raises the question of what is necessary for a religion to be covenantal if the term is used phenomenologically rather than theologically. Let us grant that faith in God is a minimum requirement.[27] Once that is admitted, is it not the case that every religion brings its faithful into some kind of relationship with God and that such a relationship inevitably assumes an interplay between the human and the Divine in the framework of religion? And is it not the case that all religions in some way seek to do good in the world? Must the work of *tikun olam* use that language or any other language that is specific to the Jewish tradition? What then are other religions lacking that would make them covenantal? Must they be conscious of biblical covenantal history and concepts? Are they covenantal only if they conceive of themselves in such terms, or is 'covenantal' a depth dimension of every religion?

I am not sure the tension described here has been fully resolved in

---

[27] As noted above, even this minimal assumption may not be necessary.

Greenberg's thinking, largely as a consequence of how his thought has taken shape within the matrix of Jewish–Christian relations. This gives us pause to consider whether his overall message would be better served without covenantal language. Nevertheless, the thrust of his thinking does point to full pluralism, which means approaching covenant as a dimension of religion rather than a specific theological heritage. In the following passage we find a pluralism, described by means of the covenant, beyond the Jewish and Christian contexts to which most of his work is devoted.

Both [Judaism and Christianity] in renewal may yet apply this insight not just to each other but to religions not yet worked into this dialogue. Humans are called in this generation to renew the covenant—a renewal which will demand openness to each other, learning from each other, and a respect for the distinctiveness of the ongoing validity of each other. Such openness puts no religious claim beyond possibility but places the completion of total redemption at the center of the agenda.[28]

While the starting point of Greenberg's discussion is Jews and Christians, it is clear that the covenantal vision includes 'religions not yet worked into this dialogue'. In other words, the limitations are placed by the context of the Jewish–Christian dialogue of the 1970s and 1980s, and not by the inherent theological workings of the covenantal category. In principle all religions have something to learn from each other, and their distinctiveness and validity are recognized. Once again, questions of truth are sidestepped, moving from the realm of the polemical 'impossible' to the realm of the more humble and dialogical 'not beyond possibility'. Truth claims are not the focus. The focus is the completion of total redemption. That should be a common concern for all religions, affirming their respective covenantal realities—and, one might add, affirming them as parts of a broader covenant of humanity with God.

In the more than thirty-five years since this essay was written much has changed in the landscape of interreligious dialogue. Today's reality is no longer limited to Jews and Christians, or even to Abrahamic faiths. Much of the focus of the collaborative work of religions is to heal the earth and to heal humanity of the wounds of violence and hatred. Religious teachers and their communities convene across faith boundaries to collaborate for the common good. It would seem to me that under these circumstances, Green-

---

[28] 'The Relationship of Judaism and Christianity', 211.

berg's covenantal approach is at the very least a Jewish language by means of which to affirm the validity of such processes. It may even be more than that, inasmuch as such language turns out to be inspiring and meaningful to members of other faith traditions. What he describes in the above paragraph is in fact what has been taking place since these words were written. His thought opens up to the broader interreligious possibilities that lie beyond the focus of Jewish and Christian dialogue, from within which they were framed.

Greenberg's Covenant and Its Biblical Roots

There would be no reason to use covenant as the overriding frame for defining Israel's relations with God and expanding that usage to include other religions, were it not for the biblical foundations of the concept. Granted, Greenberg's usage reflects the currency of the notion in contemporary American Jewish theology and is not born of unmediated engagement with biblical sources. Still, these continue to echo through the various uses. One of the tests of the usefulness of the category is how it relates to its biblical antecedents. The greater the remove, the more one wonders whether one really needs the category and whether Greenberg's message might be conveyed by other means. No less important, appeal to a biblical category provides a common ground with Christians, who are the primary conversation partners throughout Greenberg's reflections. It is much easier, or at least was at the time he wrote, to speak to them of covenant than it is to speak to them of *tikun olam*.

This makes the question of Greenberg's usage as compared with biblical usage one of the tests of how well his ideas can be received, in both the Jewish and the Christian communities. Conversely, such a comparison will reveal how much of a private language he has developed—one which can only be used following his specific definitions, in which case it will be of interest only to a limited circle. In the present section, I would like to make some observations relating and contrasting Greenberg's use of the covenant to biblical usage, beyond the points already raised above.

Let me begin by reiterating that Greenberg situates the covenant between the poles of Creation and redemption. Is such a positioning biblical? One fact comes to mind immediately: there is no tie between covenant and the biblical story of Creation. Significantly, there is no covenant made with Adam.[29] If the idea is tied so deeply to Creation, the Bible fails to tell us so.[30] As for redemption, the question is what we mean by it. One of the concerns of covenant is its violation, leading to eventual exile. Return from exile is interpreted biblically in terms of re-establishment of the covenant.[31] However, the redemption that Greenberg has in mind is much broader than Israel's gathering back in its land. It is a cosmic redemption and repair of the broken world order. Again, there are some biblical hints of a new world order being established in covenantal terms.[32] However, on the whole, covenant is a static idea. It describes Israel's state of being with God. Its dynamism hinges on faithfulness and lack thereof. Even the re-establishment of a new order depends on issues of and the conditions required for making a successful and obedient relationship permanent.[33]

Whereas the dynamic of faithfulness places Israel's behaviour at the centre, the dynamic of a new world order—in nature, in society, and in the human heart—which establishes the ultimate covenant, depends on God. Thus, to the extent that the covenant's dynamic includes changes in nature or in human nature, these are the actions of God, intended to finally achieve what was desired in the first instance in the establishment of a covenant with Israel. At the end of the day, this not only does not depend on human freedom, but actually undermines it. For biblical authors, God's despairing of human nature leads him to eventually take charge and do himself what humans were not able to achieve, creating a new heart and bringing about the conditions in which the covenant is fulfilled. Thus, for Jeremiah the ultimate resolution of the conflict regarding covenantal faithfulness is the removal of free will.[34] This is the new covenant he envisions. Compare this with the lessons Greenberg draws, as we have already seen:

[29] Of course this has not prevented the emergence of Christian reform 'federal' theology, which ties the two concepts together. On this, see Williamson, *Sealed with an Oath*; Dumbrell, *Covenant and Creation*.

[30] I would argue that the same holds true for the association of the image of God and covenant. However, the Noahide covenant does prohibit killing because man was made in the image of God (Gen. 9: 6). This at least provides a source for connecting the two ideas. Someone might try to close the gap between Noah and Adam, and to ground covenant in the renewed creation. Such a potential argument pushes the textual evidence and its interpretation too far, and in any event is never made by Greenberg.

[31] This is implicit in the covenantal logic of Deuteronomy 30. Ezek. 36: 24–8 uses the covenant formula, which defines God's relation to Israel as that of God to people.

[32] See Hos. 2: 20.   [33] Hos. 2; Jer. 31.

[34] In *For the Sake of Heaven and Earth*, 30, Greenberg presents himself as following through

One of the most profound teachings of covenant is that you cannot separate the ends from the means. The ends are human freedom, dignity and human value. These goals cannot be realized by coercion on the part of either humans or God. Therefore, *brit* implies that God will not force us.[35]

And yet this is precisely what Jeremiah and other prophets arrive at—God has no choice but to bring about a changed reality in which human freedom will no longer feature. Refashioning human nature is a divine and graceful way of coercing humans to conform to God's will and design.[36]

As a consequence of Greenberg's novel usage, neither commandments nor faithfulness play a role in his view of the covenant. It is about the human partner who may have been commanded, much more than about the commandments themselves and their successful fulfilment.

This also accounts for an important difference with reference to the notion of renewing the covenant. The biblical notion of covenant renewal is related to the possibility of the covenant's breach and annulment. The best case in point is the making of a second covenant at Sinai, following the violation of the original one by making the golden calf.[37] Similarly, the future refashioning of the covenant, as envisioned by Israel's prophets, is a response to a reality of infidelity. The biblical dynamics of obedience and re-establishment of the relationship play no role in Greenberg's theologizing. This is particularly interesting in view of his dialogue with Christians. For Christians, the validity of Israel's covenant and what Israel's status is in relation to God are key sites in their view of Judaism. Christian history itself is understood in continuity with Israel's covenant history,[38] and one theological

on Jeremiah's teaching. I believe the opposite is the case. Jeremiah speaks of man being given a new heart by means of which to follow God, not freedom to act out of love and internalized vision. True, gone is the intimidating fear of punishment, but the biblical alternative too has no room in Greenberg's scheme.

[35] *Living in the Image of God*, 63.

[36] See Goshen-Gottstein, 'The New Covenant'. Some modern commentators understand the oracle in a less radical way, suggesting instead a spiritual opening, without the transformation of human nature. See McKane, *A Critical and Exegetical Commentary on Jeremiah*, 826.

[37] Exod. 34.

[38] A recent representative articulation of the Christian view is found in the Vatican document 'The Gifts and the Calling of God are Irrevocable'. An entire section is devoted to consideration of the relationship between the Jewish and Christian covenants on biblical grounds, at times leading to some astonishing biblical acrobatics to get to the point. See the reference to the covenant with Noah in sect. 32. This is only the most recent expression of the long-standing tendency to ground any covenant talk in biblical precedent. It would seem the very appeal to covenant would be meaningless absent such grounding.

current considers Christianity to have inherited Israel's covenant as a new covenant following an earlier failure, and thus a renewal of the original.[39] All this is absent from Greenberg's construct. This leads one to wonder whether, given the charge on the breach and re-establishment of the covenant, and given how Judaism and Christianity were contextualized in terms of old and new covenants, he did not make a conscious attempt to disengage from such conversations and to construct the idea of covenant independently of them, and by extension independently of the dynamics of its biblical foundations.

In any event, Greenberg casts covenant renewal in a completely new light. To renew the covenant is not to return to its observance in faithfulness following a falling away from it. Rather, it is to advance to a higher degree of its fulfilment. As the covenant captures the dynamics of the partnership between man and God, the stages of religious growth, which in this case mean greater human autonomy and responsibility, are seen as the renewal of covenant. The language is the same as biblical language. The intention is completely novel.

This difference in relation to faithfulness as the goal of the covenant translates to the following lesson drawn by Greenberg, and which I consider to be at odds with the biblical logic of covenant:

We act out of weakness to retain the otherness of others because we are afraid we cannot survive choice. Is not the ultimate message of the covenant that God wants us to exercise choice? Models of faith are what we have to gain from each other. Those models invoke our own deepest possibilities.[40]

I am in total sympathy with the sensibilities and views expressed in this statement. I fully concur that we can be inspired by models of faith of other religions to discover our own deepest possibilities. I believe this is the deeper meaning of the practice of interreligious dialogue. But in response to the rhetorical question as to whether this is not the ultimate message of the covenant, I am forced to reply negatively, if by covenant we refer to the biblical covenant as described in the Hebrew Scriptures. The point of covenant is not choice; it is faithfulness. Biblical covenant is, in fact, a motivator for developing barriers and preventing contact with others as a means of protecting identity and loyalty to the covenant.[41] One may legitimately argue that there is a difference between other gods and other faiths that turn to the

---

[39] See Heb. 8: 7–13.
[40] 'Judaism and Christianity', 27; revised version in *For the Sake of Heaven and Earth*, 183.
[41] See Exod. 23: 32.

same God. One may argue that dialogue, collaboration, and mutual inspiration are required by contemporary reality and reflect God's will for today. But at least to the extent that this allows us to recognize how different Greenberg's use of the covenant is from classical biblical usage, we see here another expression of his original, and non-biblical, usage.

Let me note another teaching on covenant that Greenberg articulates, and which also, to my mind, is not a feature of biblical teaching:

There is another powerful dynamic in the concept of *brit*. The covenant idea teaches that, ultimately, humans are not alone. Still, God is not blatantly manifest in the world, but must be discovered. God is not self-evidently present, but must be sought out behind—and within—the veil of reality. This hiddenness reflects not God's lack of concern, but the way in which the Divine, lovingly, acting pedagogically as a great teacher, tries to evoke constantly increasing levels of human participation and human responsibility in the process of *tikkun olam*.[42]

Greenberg takes the point further and speaks of increasing hiddenness as humans become more capable and powerful; he refers to this in terms of divine self-contraction, *tsimtsum*. Within a few lines we find reference to two important kabbalistic notions, both of which are coherent with Greenberg's teaching. They provide him with the theological arsenal needed to make his point. However, all this is ascribed by Greenberg not only to the idea of covenant but to its biblical foundations.[43] It seems to me that this view of the biblical covenant would be unrecognizable to the biblical authors. If there is anything about the biblical notion of covenant, it is that God is a real relational partner, real enough to be party to a legal construct that serves other parts of society in their day-to-day relations. The covenant assumes divine presence, not absence. This is substantiated by biblical stories of miracles, by signs of God's presence, by the close relationship that biblical covenanters enjoy with God, by the blessings of the covenant, captured in terms of divine presence and intimacy,[44] and by the grounding of covenant in the overall sense of closeness and familiarity that the relevant biblical literature expresses in relation to God. I think nothing could be farther from biblical reality than the description of covenant as somehow straddling divine inaccessibility or absence. Because biblical covenantal thinking is so centred on divine presence, it must also account for absence and God's turning his

[42] *Living in the Image of God*, 47.
[43] Note the text immediately following this quote: 'Biblically, the fact that God is not fully revealed . . .'
[44] See Lev. 26: 11–12.

face away.[45] This, however, is undertaken within the covenantal dynamics and particularly within a covenantal theory of retribution. For Greenberg, by contrast, divine hiddenness is not a punishment but an expression of the growth, maturity, and attainment of full autonomy of the human covenantal partner.[46]

If anything, we might view the loss of immediacy of divine presence as one of the causes of decline in Jewish covenantal thinking, to be added to the list of factors we have already considered. If so, hiddenness is what led Jewish thought *away* from the covenant; it is not a core teaching of the covenant itself.

Let me note one more interesting divergence. The covenant is a hermeneutic framework for interpreting history. It is accompanied by blessings and curses, which are an inseparable part of the ancient Near Eastern covenant structure. In biblical thought, calamities are understood in light of the covenant, and therefore as signs of its violation. Biblical authors have no difficulty coming to terms with calamity, as the conceptual framework for understanding them is provided by the covenant. Against this background, consider Greenberg's assertion:

The challenge of renewal—or death of the mission—is greatest when a crisis or disaster tests the credibility of the *brit*. This challenges the Jewish people to respond again.

In the course of history, particular crises have arisen and affected the Jewish experience of God. These are the moments of catastrophe that undermine the confidence that Jews have that the world will be saved. When these major disasters occur, they seem to strike at the whole structure of faith. 'Does God really care?' 'Are we still the chosen people?' 'Is the hope of redemption still alive?' These questions were asked during crises in previous eras of Jewish history.[47]

It takes a great distance from biblical faith to stand the theological concerns on their head in such a way. For biblical thought there is a ready-made response to catastrophe—violation of the covenant. The issue is not whether God cares, but how we have acted. The reasons for moving away from a bib-

---

[45] See Deut. 31: 17–18.

[46] One cannot divorce this view of the covenant from Greenberg's Holocaust theology. The Holocaust raises the greatest challenge to the sense of divine presence and therefore redefines the parameters of the covenant. See Krell, *Intersecting Pathways*, 103. More broadly, Greenberg sees his own pluralism as the antidote to the wrongs of the Holocaust. See Greenberg, 'Theology after the Shoah'.   [47] *Living in the Image of God*, 53.

lically based theodicy may be understandable, and certainly a theologian who has spent so much energy thinking of the Holocaust cannot be expected to affirm covenantal theodicy in the face of the most recent catastrophe. Still, to present this as a challenge to the covenant is an indication that the term is being used in ways that would be unrecognizable to those who employed it in the first instance.

One final note on Greenberg's understanding of covenant actually takes us back to biblical uses of the idea and suggests important continuity. As I have already noted, covenant is central to biblical theology of the Land of Israel. In much Jewish–Christian discussion of the covenant, the subject of the Land is omitted, for either theological or political reasons. Greenberg is very sensitive to the status of the Land of Israel and the State of Israel. He considers the founding of the state, like the Holocaust, to be a revelational event.[48] Therefore, it is important to note that he includes reference to the Land as he develops his idea of covenant.[49]

Redemption will take place through humans who are rooted in the natural order. The people of God seek roots in their land, grow attached to their own homeland, identify with particular heroes, relate to a particular family and create a particular community. Thus redemption takes place within the matrix of human history.[50]

For the Bible, the promise of land was an inextricable part of the divine promises and of the special relationship formed with Israel. Greenberg has expanded the notion of covenant to include others. But this does not lead him to abandon the relationship to the land. This is revisited through the lens of particularity. Because covenant works through particularity, part of that is also the particularity of land. As a consequence of this, homeland becomes a feature of the covenant in its universal expression:

The covenant model suggests that all peoples should have a homeland where their right to exist is self-evident and unquestioned . . . In the act of election, God asks the beloved to set up and lead the way for humanity by making the promised land a microcosm of perfection, a land in which economic equality, righteousness, justice and equal treatment before the law will be the lot of everyone.[51]

Land has been universalized in a double fashion. The right to a homeland

---

[48] *For the Sake of Heaven and Earth*, 136. See further pp. 130 and 159.
[49] This fact has been criticized by Kogan, *Opening the Covenant*, 146.
[50] *For the Sake of Heaven and Earth*, 165.   [51] Ibid. 219.

is universal, grounded in the universality of the covenant model. The particular land of Israel also has universal attributes, as it is a model land and model society for others. One imagines that Greenberg seeks to not only contextualize biblical Israel's land and promise in the framework of his broader universal unfolding but also to quietly allude to the present State of Israel with a prophetic voice, conditioned by the broad universal horizons of his covenantal theology.

Let us move on to a consideration of how biblical covenants are worked into his pluralistic use of the term, and in particular how Christianity is accommodated within the new theological articulation, which both draws on biblical resources and stands beyond them.

The Covenant with Noah

There are two clusters of biblical texts that are particularly significant in Greenberg's construction of a notion of covenant. The first is Genesis 9— the covenant made with Noah following the flood. The other describes God's covenant first with Abraham and then with Israel at Sinai. Closer attention to his use of these two key sets of texts is important for an appreciation of what covenant means for him as well as for understanding how he goes about adapting biblical material to present-day realities of relations between religions. Let us begin by looking at his uses of Genesis 9. By way of introduction, it behoves us to make some observations on the biblical text before noting Greenberg's applications of it. The passage reads:

And God blessed Noah and his sons, and said unto them: 'Be fruitful, and multiply, and replenish the earth. And the fear of you and the dread of you shall be upon every beast of the earth, and upon every fowl of the air, and upon all wherewith the ground teemeth, and upon all the fishes of the sea: into your hand are they delivered. Every moving thing that liveth shall be for food for you; as the green herb have I given you all. Only flesh with the life thereof, which is the blood thereof, shall ye not eat. And surely your blood of your lives will I require; at the hand of every beast will I require it; and at the hand of man, even at the hand of every man's brother, will I require the life of man. Whoso sheddeth man's blood, by man shall his blood be shed; for in the image of God made He man. And you, be ye fruitful, and multiply; swarm in the earth, and multiply therein.'

And God spoke unto Noah, and to his sons with him, saying: 'As for Me, behold, I establish My covenant with you, and with your seed after you; and with every living creature that is with you, the fowl, the cattle, and every beast of the earth with you; of all that go out of the ark, even every beast of the earth. And I will establish My covenant with you; neither shall all flesh be cut off any more by the waters of the flood; neither shall there any more be a flood to destroy the earth.' And God said: 'This is the token of the covenant which I make between Me and you and every living creature that is with you, for perpetual generations: I have set My bow in the cloud, and it shall be for a token of a covenant between Me and the earth. And it shall come to pass, when I bring clouds over the earth, and the bow is seen in the cloud, that I will remember My covenant, which is between Me and you and every living creature of all flesh; and the waters shall no more become a flood to destroy all flesh. And the bow shall be in the cloud; and I will look upon it, that I may remember the everlasting covenant between God and every living creature of all flesh that is upon the earth.'[52]

This text is the earliest mention of covenant in the entire Torah.[53] Significantly, there is no covenant made with Adam. However, rabbinic tradition collapses the historical gap between Noah and Adam and claims that the commandments presented in verses 1–7, the first paragraph of the above quote, applied to Adam, with the exception of the prohibition of verse 4, which forbids the eating of the flesh of a living animal—something that could not have applied to him, as he was forbidden to eat any kind of meat. The commandments in the first paragraph are part of a set of laws referred to in rabbinic tradition as the seven Noahide commandments.[54] They form the basis of a universal moral code that the rabbis see as pertaining to all of humanity. This code, according to the rabbis, goes back to Adam, and is called Noahide because its recipients are the children of Noah—a rabbinic expression referring to non-Jews—but it does not date from Noah's time. The Noahide commandments are the foundation of a Jewish view of other religions, inasmuch as other religions are evaluated on the basis of whether they are compliant with the Noahide code, and are thereby granted legitimacy, or not, in terms of Jewish law. The Noahide commandments reflect classical rabbinic views, and we cannot appreciate the originality of Greenberg's reading of Genesis 9, or his application of this text to the notion of covenant, without recognizing the rabbinic framing of the passage. Significantly, when the rabbis appeal to this text, they do so without any reference

[52] Gen. 9: 1–16, Jewish Publication Society translation.
[53] This should be qualified by reference to Gen. 6: 18. The possible relationship between these verses is explored in Goshen-Gottstein, 'Genesis 9, Noah's Covenants and Jewish Theology of Religions'.   [54] See Novak, *The Image of the Non-Jew in Judaism*.

to the notion of covenant. To understand Greenberg's use of it, then, we must consider how the rabbinic view is integrated into a covenantal conceptual framework. This is only possible by means of relating the set of commandments listed in verses 1–7 to what follows immediately.

Verses 8–16 introduce the notion of covenant. The passage raises a hermeneutical challenge: what is the relationship between the first and second paragraphs? The notion of covenant appears only in the second paragraph, beginning with 'As for me'. What does this opening suggest? Is it the other side of a covenantal commitment, or is God making a promise, under the rubric of covenant, independently of the commandments of the earlier verses, which are not, in this reading, part of the covenant?[55] Both perspectives may be upheld. It is indeed a covenant with God, and, like all biblical covenants with God, it is also related in some way to commandment and obligation.[56] Nevertheless, there is not full reciprocity here between two commitments, one human and one divine, or between the opening 'as for me' and the earlier part. This is not because the earlier part is divorced from the covenant. Rather, the scope of the covenant shifts in the second part of the chapter. This second part, wherein God makes his covenantal promise, addresses not only Noah or humanity. It is a covenant 'with you, and with your seed after you; and with every living creature that is with you, the fowl, the cattle, and every beast of the earth with you'. It would be meaningless to consider a covenant of mutual obligation between God and non-humans. It is, however, quite meaningful to consider a one-sided divine promise that encompasses not only humans but all creatures, a promise never again to destroy the world. In this reading, then, the covenant with Noah is somewhat of a misnomer. It is not a covenant properly speaking with him, nor is the heart of the covenant to be found in the prohibitions listed in the first paragraph. It is

[55] Jewish and Christian scholars are divided, largely along faith lines, with regard to the parameters of the covenant story in Genesis 9. Jews tend to see the entire chapter as part of the covenant, thereby linking the earlier section involving commandments to the covenant, even if the relationship is not one of covenantal stipulations. See the review of literature in Goshen-Gottstein, 'Genesis 9, Noah's Covenants and Jewish Theology of Religions'. While it is legitimate to read some reciprocity into the two-part structure of Genesis 9, one must also take stock of the fact that the term *berit* appears only in the second part of the chapter and not in relation to the commandments stated in the first part. See Barr, 'Reflections on the Covenant with Noah', 19. On the question of unilateral versus reciprocal obligations with reference to this particular covenant, see pp. 11–13.

[56] I have suggested that this is a constitutive feature of biblical covenants with God, regardless of other ways in which they may be classified. See *In God's Presence*, ch. 2.

actually a divine promise to all creation, represented by Noah. Noah, then, is not the personal covenantal partner but the figurehead, the point person, of a more encompassing divine promise that begins with him and extends to all living creatures.[57]

According to this reading, the history of relational covenants in the Bible begins with Abraham. Were covenant the fundamental structuring principle of human relations with the Divine or the concept by means of which the meaning of what it is to be human is explicated, we ought to have found it already with reference to Adam. And were it grounded in Creation per se, as the human response to and continuation of the originary divine creative activity, it should have antedated Noah. Biblical covenant as a category of divine–human reciprocal relationship only begins with the Abrahamic covenant, and then extends through a series of biblical covenants that include Sinai and many others.

Greenberg makes something else, quite distinctive, out of these biblical foundations. Some of his ideas, as noted, may be attributed to the rabbinic reading of Genesis 9 and to the notion of the Noahide *commandments*, which are identified by him as the Noahide *covenant*. But even acknowledging his dependence on rabbinic tradition, it is clear that he has crafted the biblical material into a novel conceptual structure. His creativity ought to be appreciated and admired in and of itself. At the same time, stretching biblical sources as he does raises the question of how this reading will hold when examined by biblically minded readers.[58]

Let us look at some of the formulations of the Noahide covenant as offered by Greenberg:

[57] My analysis of Genesis 9 suggests it is an altogether different form of covenant, quite distinct from the one with Abraham and later covenants concluded with the Jewish people. It is a covenant of no harm, rather than one intended to establish a relationship. Note, however, that this reading does not preclude deriving broader moral and universal lessons that are applicable for today. As I suggest in this essay, the content of the Noahide commandments, which Greenberg identifies with the Noahide covenant, can similarly be grafted upon the reading of the chapter as a covenant of no harm. It cannot, however, serve as a foundation for the religious life, as Greenberg would wish.

[58] Jews and Christians may respond differently to this structure. Jews, having moved away from the covenant and highlighting the Noahide commandments, might be more receptive. Christians would likely respond in light of biblical scholarship, in which case they will find it difficult to accommodate these ideas. Alternatively, they might respond directly to Greenberg's theological creativity.

The fundamental and universal biblical statement is that God wants creation (the world as it is now) to be redeemed. Out of love for humanity, God imposes self-limits and calls humans to be partners in the process of *tikkun olam*. God commits to uphold the laws of nature that allow humans to live constructive, dignified lives within the framework of a stable, dependable, natural order. Humans pledge to live in harmony with the rhythms of the universe—that is, God's plan—to increase life and improve nature and society to fully sustain the value of life, especially human life with its fundamental dignities. This is the universal covenant with all humanity, biblically called the covenant of Noah. This covenant is never superseded. Every religion that accepts these values and goals derives its legitimacy directly, its direct access to God and its partnership with the Deity from this covenant open to all people, all the time.[59]

This is possibly the most succinct summary of Greenberg's covenantal theology as it relates to Noah's covenant. It is a beautiful and inspiring statement. It describes the redemption of creation and grounds it in covenant. Covenant is built on divine self-limitation and partnership with humans. There is a reciprocity in this structure. God commits—humans pledge. God commits to uphold a law that offers dignified living. Humans pledge to increase life and improve nature and society to sustain the value of life, especially human life. Some of these elements are traceable to Genesis 9, under discussion; some not. The divine promise to uphold the rhythms of the universe is a correct rendition of the biblical promise; the framework of meaning of these laws—living dignified, constructive lives—is provided by Greenberg. The commandments of Genesis 9 are stretched significantly in order to link them to the pledge to increase life and to improve nature and society to sustain life, especially human life.[60] If we consider that, for Greenberg, they may also include the fuller set of Noahide commandments, not spelled out in the biblical text, the reading takes on greater credibility, though it still remains a stretch when read against the biblical text.[61] The emphasis on the value of life as such, beyond human life, is certainly an import. It is hard to load the pro-

---

[59] *For the Sake of Heaven and Earth*, 43.

[60] This becomes all the more evident if one considers the essentially 'negative' quality of the Noahide covenant and its related commandments, seeking to limit destruction, not to provide a positive foundation for life. See Goshen-Gottstein, 'Genesis 9, Noah's Covenants and Jewish Theology of Religions'.

[61] See also *Living in the Image of God*, 50, for a rephrasing of the content of the Noahide covenant that stretches the biblical text significantly: 'Some of the covenantal obligations are to treat every human being as equal: to act as if the other is my brother, my sister, my child, for whom I feel responsible.'

hibition of eating an unslaughtered animal with so much meaning. While the sense of reciprocity and mutual commitment may be justified by a juxtaposition of the two parts of chapter 9, the notions of divine self-limitation and the partnership between humans and God with the aim of redeeming creation are certainly absent from the text. All in all, Greenberg has created a novel construct. We recognize elements of the biblical narrative in it, but in fact these are no more than points of contact between his theological construct and the biblical (and rabbinic) sources. What we have here, then, is a highly creative and original construct that appeals to biblical language and sources while making a completely novel statement.

In terms of function, this construct is highly significant. It does more than link Creation and redemption or ground the value of the human person, created in God's image, in a covenantal moment. Beyond these achievements, it provides a common universal frame of relationship with God, which applies potentially to all religions. All religions are, in the first instance, expressions of the Noahide covenant, inasmuch as it provides the basic framework for mutuality and partnership in the common task of redeeming the world. Accordingly, all particular religious relationships are derivative of the Noahide covenant. The importance of this construct is, further, that it serves as the basic instrument for a Jewish theology of religions, validating all religions that accept these values and goals.

Greenberg has here developed a foundation for a Jewish theology of other religions that is far broader than the Noahide commandments. His Noahide covenant is to a large extent an alternative to those commandments.[62] If accepted, it is a significant theological foundation for Judaism's engagement with other religions. It is important to recognize that, in this view, *all* religions, Judaism included, would be derivative of, a second layer placed upon, the foundational Noahide covenant.

The Jewish covenant is best located as a subpartnership of the Noahide *brit* . . . Christianity and Islam should be recognized and respected as covenantal religions working with God, inspiring humanity to *tikkun olam*. Other religions are less

[62] This is made explicit on p. 56, where he ascribes to the covenant with Noah more than what is normally ascribed to the Noahide commandments. There have been other attempts to suggest alternatives to the Noahide commandments—ones that bear some relationship to them and may draw from them, while nevertheless creating a novel conceptual framework. Meiri's categorization of nations bound by ways of religion is one important such attempt. See Halbertal, '"Ones Possessed of Religion"', and my own discussions of Meiri in *Same God, Other God*, ch. 3.

covenantal in their formal theological thinking, but they nonetheless have dignified roles to play in this world transformation.[63]

Structurally, there is no advantage to Judaism over other religions. All are
sub-partnerships of the Noahide covenant and such covenantal status need
not, apparently, be based upon conscious knowledge of the partnership, of
divine revelation, or of the Noahide covenant itself. Greenberg does not say
that Christianity and Islam conceive of themselves as covenantal religions.
They are recognized by him as such on functional grounds, because in fact
what they do fits within his paradigm, which measures covenant by the yardstick of *tikun olam*. In terms of the logic of this paragraph, the preferential
status afforded to Christianity and Islam over and against other religions is
a little bewildering. Do not other faiths also contribute to the elevation of
humans, society, and nature? Certainly all major faith traditions do. One
would be hard pressed to identify a religion that goes out and out against
these values. If covenantal status is a consequence of the functioning of a
religion rather than its theology, why limit the covenant to Christianity and
Islam? Why do other religions only have 'dignified roles' and why should
they be considered less than covenantal? We come back to the questions
raised above regarding the tension between the common appeal to covenant, especially as this grows out of biblical foundations, and the phenomenology of partnership with God that would confer a covenantal status on all
religions.

Once again, the context within which Greenberg's ideas were formed is
crucial for understanding the different potential formulations. These ideas
were first developed with reference to Christianity and drew upon the facts
that the notion of covenant had much theological currency and that it provided a common ground between Jews and Christians. The evolution of
Greenberg's thought involves a detachment from biblical roots, allowing
him to present covenant on phenomenological grounds, in terms of what
religions do, rather than their theologies, what they teach. This detachment
is eventually matched by the broadening of horizons in the dialogue of religions. An idea that was initially formulated in the framework of Jewish–
Christian dialogue is extended to the most important next partner in line,
Islam.[64]

[63] *Living in the Image of God*, 51.
[64] Compare the formulation in 'Covenantal Pluralism', 426, which mentions only Christianity.

Greenberg's later view, expressed in the new essay prepared for *For the Sake of Heaven and Earth*, features Islam alongside Christianity and broadens the parameters of his earlier reflection. He has never engaged with other religions. He is aware of the general need to include all faiths as dialogue between them advances in the twenty-first century. This recognition finds expression in the concluding statement in the above quote. Indeed, other religions are less covenantal in their formal theological thinking, but what of it? After all, Greenberg has shifted the grounds from theology to action. Either he still holds on to common theological foundations that provide common ground to the three Abrahamic faiths—despite all their differences, there is common recognition of the notion of covenant—or he has simply not gone far enough or systematically enough to incorporate other faiths in his thinking. This leads him to speak of them as having dignified roles to play in world transformation, when in fact the structure of his thought should have led to a stronger, and more explicitly covenantal, appreciation of these religions. Once again, it seems that theology is less at the heart of the limited recognition, and that Greenberg's approach to other religions simply needs to catch up with his view of Christianity.

As stated, his later formulations expand the understandings that were conceived in relation to Christianity and extend them to other religions. This expansion is evident in a new essay in *For the Sake of Heaven and Earth*:

The universality of the Noahide covenant does mean, however, that henceforth every religion that works to repair the world—and thus advance the triumph of life—is a valid expression of this divine pact with humanity. Every religion that nurtures the quantity and quality of life (especially if it upholds the dignity and value of life in the image of God) derives its authority and its eternal validity from this divine commitment.[65]

Greenberg's latest book, *The Triumph of Life*, expands the reference not only to other religions not previously engaged, but also to other streams of the religions he has previously explored, such as Eastern Orthodox Christianity and Shia Islam. Over the course of nearly sixty years, the fundamental principles are applied to an increasingly broader scope of faiths, affirming the universal applicability of his covenantal understanding.

The different articulations of the meaning of the Noahide covenant and its theological potential in addressing other religions vary in terms of their

---

[65] *For the Sake of Heaven and Earth*, 57.

closeness to the biblical message. Some formulations seem to me, at least, to have moved quite far:

Genesis teaches us that God has given up neither the Divine vision of a perfect creation nor the Divine love for humans. Rather, God has decided to work with full respect for human capacity and limitation all the way to the final perfection. In essence, the covenantal concept is a Divine pledge not to force humans to be free.[66] The first covenant, the Noahide covenant, is made with all humanity. The paradigm of covenant reveals that God does not prefer the obedience of a perfect robot . . . God has such love for humanity that God wants humans to do the right thing out of their freedom and dignity. God is not going to force good behavior. This means that God accepts the human right to sin . . . the Noahide covenant expresses a primary turning point in the religious history of the universe. God commits not to coercively intervene in history, but to allow humans to become partners in making the world perfect. (Actually, the Noahide is a covenant with all living creatures. That is reaffirmed in Hosea, Ch. 2, where he speaks of a messianic renewal of the *brit* [covenant] with humans and with all life.) All are pledged to work for the triumph of life, to strive for the perfection of the world. The Noahide covenant is made with *all* of humanity because God is the God of all humans.[67]

These words are taken from a transcript of interviews with Greenberg that make up a book-length publication. It is possible, therefore, that there are theological nuances in this wording that fall short of giving perfect expression to his thought. Nevertheless, the broad outline is clear. Covenant is about freedom, boundary, partnership. The key to the Noahide covenant is affirming human free will. One seeks in vain biblical justification for this construct. Tellingly, what was the divine promise not to interfere with nature and to preserve its rhythms has become, in this quote, a promise not to intervene in history. This is a big stretch, and I believe it is reflective of how far Greenberg has stretched the category.

With covenant doing the work assigned to it now by Greenberg, it becomes even harder to make sense of its universality extending to all creatures. This is the only passage in which Greenberg is explicit about the Noahide covenant not being limited to humans.[68] Its universality is in fact

[66] I wonder if there is not an error in this formulation. I believe the intention of the text is better captured by the addition '[but to allow them] to be free'.

[67] *Living in the Image of God*, 49.

[68] See also 'Covenantal Pluralism', 426, where he refers to every sentient being. This wording is not carried over into the book version of the essay.

cosmic. As stated above, such a cosmic perspective makes sense in the framework of a divine promise, but not in the framework of a covenant that defines mutual obligations, let alone one that emphasizes human freedom in the face of the Divine. What are we to make of the covenant extending to all living beings? Even if we push this to messianic times, what is the intent? Will all animals of the field be engaged in the future in the work of *tikun olam*, just as humans are today? One would have to affirm such a conviction by postponing the application of the covenant to non-humans to messianic times, while maintaining their presence in the covenant.[69] Greenberg seems to acknowledge the challenge, but never spells out how he resolves it. I doubt that he would own a messianic involvement of non-humans in *tikun olam*. This would seem to provide one further instance of how far he has moved from his biblical foundations.

All in all, Greenberg's reflection on the covenant grows out of his reflection on human–divine relations, rather than out of an attempt to restate biblical premises in a contemporary context. As these reflections advance, certain features are highlighted that in turn make it easier to validate other religions. Unfortunately, they also make it hard to discern the contours of the biblical covenant in his theology.

Israel's Particular Covenants: Abraham and Sinai

The Noahide covenant provides the foundations for any religion, certainly for those that accept a covenantal way of thinking and relate to the biblical story, which leads to their self-understanding as being in a covenantal relationship or partnership with God. According to this construct, all religions would be species of the genus covenant, as defined in the Noahide covenant. This would grant them all equal value and dignity, at least in terms of the basic relational parameters of the covenant. While we might legitimately expect variety in the accomplishments and charges of individual relationships, all share the same relational structure, and therefore have potentially equal value or possibility for contributing to the world through divine–human partnership.

Given this structure, the covenant with Abraham would be but one of any number of possible relationships that can be classified as covenantal.

---

[69] If the wording in the previous note is taken literally, then animals are called to act as humans should under the covenant today. I doubt he really means it.

Moses concludes a covenant at Sinai that pertains to the Jewish people, as do other biblical figures. This pattern of thinking could have been extended to founders of other religions. One could have imagined Greenberg's line of reasoning extending to Jesus as the one who concludes a covenant with God on behalf of Christians, and to Muhammad as the one who does so on behalf of Muslims. Such an approach would be in keeping with the foundations of his theological thinking and could be justified by appeal to some scriptural sources of the other traditions. Whatever covenant means for Christians, as expressed in the narrative of the Eucharist,[70] this could have been taken as suggestive of Jesus' role in concluding a new covenant, geared at new audiences, on the basis of the Noahide covenant. The Quran's frequent reference to covenant might have similarly served to portray Muhammad as concluding a covenant for the followers of Islam, or the people of Arabia, as one may wish to make the point. As noted, if covenant is a functional category, it may not even require specific covenant-making, and therefore may extend to founders of other religions and to their faith traditions whether or not they conceive of themselves in such terms. Consequently, any religion might provide particularity to the covenantal structure established for all humanity through the Noahide covenant.

I think that Greenberg's views would be far simpler to accept and might have in fact had much broader reception had he followed the course suggested by the important role he ascribes to the Noahide covenant. 'Covenant' would have then functioned as an important concept in a Jewish theology of religions, allowing for recognition of the parallel value of potentially all other faiths, without entering into outright competition over the biblical story and its later application, or what might be called the biblical inheritance. However, Greenberg seems to have gone beyond the attempt to develop a contemporary matrix based on biblical foundations for recognizing other religions. Because his theology was formulated in close dialogue with Christian conversation partners, he has found himself responding to a Christian understanding of the biblical story and the biblical covenant. Eager to accommodate his Christian conversation partners, he has moved Jewish–Christian relations to the much more charged and complicated ground of the covenant with Abraham. The following section explores Greenberg's application of the Abrahamic covenant to other faiths and struggles with the question of its consistency with his own thought

[70] Luke 22: 20; 1 Cor. 11: 25.

structure, as well as with the possibilities of broader reception by a Jewish audience.

The starting point for my discussion is Greenberg's willingness to accept the self-understanding of Christianity as a factor in a Jewish view of Christianity. As we know from his discussion of matters such as the Incarnation and the Resurrection, he can readily distinguish between how Christians view a given topic and how far he is willing to go as a Jewish thinker in affirming their claims, beyond recognizing their validity for Christian self-understanding. In essence, the entire problematic of the discussion of Abraham's covenant, the Sinai covenant, and the view of Christians as part of the People of Israel can be boiled down to the following question: Where does one draw the line between Christian self-understanding and the ways in which a Jewish theology can or should accommodate such understanding? All of Greenberg's ideas scrutinized below are informed by his willingness to uphold or integrate or take seriously the Christian view and to legitimate it from a Jewish perspective. Had he treated Christian views regarding Christian membership in specifically Jewish covenants or in the peoplehood of Israel in the same way in which he treated Christian claims regarding the Incarnation, there would have been no need for some of the theological and scriptural gymnastics that he is forced into. Somehow the option of accepting Christian claims as expressions of the legitimate Christian experience, but nevertheless as having no particular claim on Jewish faith, was not exercised. This in turn leads Greenberg to make assertions that he is aware are hard for his Jewish co-religionists to hear. It also lands him in some significant internal contradictions with reference to his own presentation of the Noahide covenant as the fundamental covenant that governs or provides the foundation for all later ones. As a consequence, his discussion dances between the affirmation of Christianity in terms of the Noahide covenant and recognition of its validity as an Abrahamic and even a Sinaitic covenant. To me, the fact that he recognizes as valid for Christians the later, specifically Jewish, covenants undermines the coherence of his theological presentation. While this could, in theory, be justified as a second layer placed upon the Noahide covenant, in fact it weakens that reliance and introduces contradiction into his thought, weakening its overall impact and potential reception.

I believe the theological tension between seeing Christianity in terms of the Noahide covenant, as suggested by Greenberg's fundamental structure, and his following consideration of it in relation to the Abrahamic story and covenant stems from an effort to recognize the special relationship between Judaism and Christianity. Since all religions are, or can be, part of the Noahide covenant, there is no way of using that concept to express a sense of the unique relationship between Judaism and Christianity. Many Jewish thinkers might be satisfied to develop a structure that accommodates Christianity, without taking the additional step of affirming a special bond. The very idea of such a bond is more of a Christian need than a Jewish one, and it reflects Christianity's sense of dependence upon and continuity with Judaism.[71] A Jewish theology of religions does not necessarily need to affirm a sense of a special relationship and may see Christianity occupying the same status as Islam, and possibly other religions.[72] Greenberg, however, seeks to portray the relationship with Christianity as a special one.

Greenberg never engages in a sustained defence of why this would be and why Christianity ought to be afforded any status beyond that provided by the Noahide covenant. I think this is largely an outcome of the depth of personal relations, the depth of his involvement with the internal Christian theological conversation, and the attempt to reciprocate in Jewish theological terms the kind of openness shown by his own conversation partners.[73] Because the position grows within the matrix of Jewish–Christian relations—personal and theological—it is formulated initially with reference to Christianity, and is only secondarily expanded to Islam. I believe there is no necessity in theological terms to enter the complicated territory into which Greenberg enters. What we have before us is a lot of theological will, motivated by the personal context in which his conversations have taken place. This has driven him to adopt a position that recognizes a special relationship with Christianity and consequently recognizes it as related to the People of Israel and to covenants that are considered particular to the Jewish people.

[71] See Goshen-Gottstein, 'A Special Relationship?', 12–15. The issue of *Current Dialogue* in which this essay appears features multiple brief contributions on the question, 'Is there a Special Relationship between Christianity and Judaism?'

[72] Most Jewish thinkers who have reflected on the matter have indeed taken this broader view and not offered a special status to Christianity. Franz Rosenzweig is a notable exception.

[73] Shapiro, 'Modern Orthodoxy and Religious Truth', 144, describes Soloveitchik's concern that a theological quid pro quo could enter the arena of interfaith relations as a consequence of theological dialogue. Shapiro asserts that this is exactly what Greenberg is doing. While acknowledging the point, one must also consider the more particular nuance of a theological position taking shape within *personal* relational matrixes that take on a moral and commanding presence. See Thatamanil, *The Immanent Divine*, xii.

Absent this personal dimension—the sympathy to internal Christian theological claims, the excess of theological will—all the discussion that follows would not take place. In my tracing of the layering of this theology, I would consider the second layer an addition to his core insights and one that could potentially be removed without undermining the more foundational layers, outlined above. I will, accordingly, present the writings in which he extends the Jewish story and covenant to Christianity, and possibly to Islam, while also noting the difficulties and inconsistencies they generate within his theological thinking.

Before hearing Greenberg's own voice, I would like to raise one final consideration, as this touches upon relating the Abrahamic covenant to other religions. Greenberg is not the only thinker to entertain this possibility, though he is a prominent spokesperson for this option and others are indebted to him.[74] Michael Kogan has developed a Jewish theology of Christianity that centres around the notion of opening the covenant to Christians.[75] Kogan believes that he and Greenberg hold similar views.[76] I am not sure that it is correct to describe Greenberg's views in terms of 'opening the covenant'.[77] Despite including Christians in the Abrahamic covenant, or even in the Sinaitic one, and even despite the claim that we are dealing with one people, Greenberg also underlines the distinctness of the religions and the divine purpose that requires each to be independent of the other. The idea of the two religious communities providing correctives to each other would not be possible if Christians were simply grafted on to Judaism and if Christianity were viewed simply as a case of opening the covenant. Indeed, the notion of opening *the* covenant assumes there is *a* covenant that is presently opened in order to allow others to participate in it, or, differently put, that is being expanded in terms of membership. In this view, one is dealing essentially with one covenant and what changes is its membership. By contrast, it seems to me that even when Greenberg seeks to accommodate Christian self-understanding and to make Christians part of Israel's covenant, purposeful distinctness, grounded in the divine vision, is always maintained. It is not that the covenant is simply opened to others. Rather, a new covenant emerges,

---

[74] Eugene Korn raises similar theological possibilities in his 'The People of Israel, Christianity and the Covenantal Responsibility to History'.   [75] Kogan, *Opening the Covenant*.

[76] This emerges as an underlying message of his discussion, ibid. 143–54.

[77] See, however, the complications around this question in Greenberg, *For the Sake of Heaven and Earth*, 38.

a sub-covenant grounded in the initial one, of which it partakes while also complementing it. This is Christianity. The same pattern that applied to the Noahide covenant applies to Israel's more particular covenants. Recognition of the other and maintenance of Israel's particular covenantal identity take place simultaneously.[78]

Let us then move to Greenberg's own voice. We begin with the most factual basis:

Both Judaism and a new religion, born out of its body, organized to witness to the nations about a loving God; each brought instruction as to how to lead the good life. Both Judaism and its nascent offspring—sometimes united and sometimes clashing as bitter rivals—brought a powerful message to the gentiles.[79]

This is a very appreciative and accommodating view of Christianity in terms of its contribution to the world. It is placed on a par with rabbinic Judaism, and their messages are fundamentally the same. That the history between the two faith communities was not always harmonious does not detract from the view of the two religions as performing a similar historical task. In the framework of this appreciative view of Christianity, Greenberg refers to it having been born out of Judaism. This is a factual description, but it also legitimates recognition of Christianity's message as commensurate and even identical with that of Judaism. In all this, a positive valuation of Christianity is expressed, but it remains a historical appreciation and does not lead to a theological declaration of Christianity's special covenantal status. A new religion could be born out of the body of Israel, out of the body of Abraham, without necessarily expanding thereby the covenant of Abraham. Here, I fear, Greenberg conflates Abrahamic progeny, or being born from the body of Israel, with the theological claims that are associated with it. Had this new religion born of Israel's body simply been one more expression of the Noahide covenant, his theology would be more readily received. As some of his following formulations suggest, Greenberg takes the historical fact and ascribes to it theological value, in line with Christian self-understanding:

[O]ne can make the following declaration about Christianity from a Jewish perspective. Both religions grow out of Abraham's covenant and out of the Exodus. The Exodus, as understood by the Hebrew prophets, is an event that points

---

[78] For a biblical precedent for the notion of expanding the covenant, see Goshen-Gottstein, 'Isa. 56: 1–8: Expanding the Covenant'.   [79] *For the Sake of Heaven and Earth*, 64.

beyond itself to future, expanded redemptions . . . Christianity is a divinely inspired attempt to bring the covenant of *tikkun olam* to a wider circle of gentiles. God intended that Judaism and Christianity both work for the perfection of the world.[80]

Here Christians share in the particular covenant of Abraham, as well as in a fundamental Jewish narrative, which is then extended in other ways deemed legitimate by Christianity. But what covenant is thereby enacted? Here we encounter two distinct voices in Greenberg's writing:

[J]ews can retrospectively say that the new expression of the Abrahamic covenant was designed to reach out to gentiles. The Christian approach opened up the partnership and offered membership in a people fundamentally defined by faith rather than birth . . . the two arms of outreach were complementary; the gentiles were joining another sub-partnership, another iteration of the Noahide covenant. Entering this new faith removed the risk that, in joining the covenant of Israel, they would be deemed second-class citizens of the partnership because they were not genetic descendants of the original stock.[81]

This is an insightful accounting for why a different covenant was required. Christians could not be part of the original Jewish covenant because Jewish self-understanding is too closely tied to ethnicity. Throughout history converts have often been considered second-class citizens. Therefore, Christianity needed to become independent. But under what rubric? This quote offers us two answers. The first is the Abrahamic covenant. Christianity is not only an expression of it,[82] but also offers membership in the people of Israel, as we shall see further below. By contrast, the latter part of the quote refers to an 'iteration of the Noahide covenant'. Of course, one may see the two as successive theological stages, both of which apply to Christianity. But in terms of strict method, what need is there for both? In purely covenantal terms, what does the Abrahamic covenant add to the Noahide one? I believe all that is added pertains to the realm of self-understanding, narrative, and how the factual birth of Christianity from Judaism might translate into theological terms. But in terms of referring to Christianity in a covenantal framework, this has been adequately provided by the Noahide covenant.

If one seeks to justify why another religion would be viewed as compliant with or fulfilling the Noahide covenant, the task is clear, given the definitions for that covenant provided above. However, if one seeks to define

---

[80] Ibid. 264.   [81] Ibid. 68.
[82] See ibid. 71: 'the new wave of the Abrahamic covenant'.

what makes a religion part of the Abrahamic covenant, one would need to define the criteria by means of which a religion is more than a Noahide covenant, and therefore part of the Abrahamic one. I do not think Greenberg has provided these criteria. He has, to be sure, taught us what Judaism and Christianity have in common and what message they bring to the world. But that message is fundamentally that of the Noahide covenant. His discussion fails to include a rationale or a justification for when another religion might be recognized by Judaism as Abrahamic in a covenantal sense.[83]

One reason offered by Greenberg for the inclusion of gentiles in the Abrahamic covenant is covenantal pluralism:

We need no monopoly of divine revelation or presence . . . why should the original covenant, the older of the two covenants, be refuted by the birth of a new *avant garde* . . . ? Far more likely, far more covenantal, far more loving is the possibility that this was the divine resort to covenantal pluralism so as to reach more human beings in human fashion through human communities.[84]

The argument, then, is that there is covenantal pluralism within the Abrahamic covenant. But this, in terms of systematic thinking, may actually undermine Greenberg's argument. We know already that covenantal pluralism is a feature of the Noahide covenant, and a fundamental feature at that.[85] Because each covenant is distinct and suitable to the particular community that manifests the covenant, covenantal pluralism is attained by means of the Noahide covenant. To refer to the Abrahamic covenant is in some sense to limit this pluralism. After all, rather than Christians concluding the covenant of Jesus, or the covenant of the nations, they are now incorporated into an extended Abrahamic covenant, thereby making them less unique, less distinct, a part of Israel. Covenantal pluralism is thus undermined, rather than strengthened, by broadening the Abrahamic covenant to include Christians (and Muslims) instead of relying on the covenant designed to achieve such pluralistic affirmation—the Noahide one.

The tension is further heightened as Greenberg ups the ante by incor-

---

[83] The problem is broader. It applies to all contemporary efforts at describing Judaism, Christianity, and Islam as Abrahamic and the lack of clear criteria for such appellation. See Goshen-Gottstein, 'Abraham and "Abrahamic Religions" in Contemporary Interreligious Discourse'; Levenson, *Inheriting Abraham: The Legacy of the Patriarch*. Greenberg's argument is a more pointed case of the subjectivity or the loose criteria that are applied toward the theological recognition of another religion.

[84] *For the Sake of Heaven and Earth*, 194–5.   [85] Ibid. 213–14; see further p. 196.

porating Christianity not only within the Abrahamic covenant, but also within that at Sinai.

Judaism and Christianity share the conviction that the covenant with Abraham, Sarah and their descendants is foundational. It is the starting point of our journey. Both affirm the authenticity and authority of the Sinaitic covenant that transformed Abraham's way of God into the way of life of a people.[86]

The description goes on with Jewish Christianity being born within the body of the Jewish people, suggesting further continuity. It would seem, then, that Christianity is in some significant way tied into the Sinai covenant, no less than the covenant with Abraham. This is a problematic claim. Obviously more is meant by it than the factual recognition that a covenant was concluded at Sinai. And more should be meant by it than Christian recognition that Sinai is binding for Jews. The paragraph seeks to establish covenantal commonality, which is extended from Abraham to Sinai. The point emerges also in Greenberg's reflections on his earlier writings. He notes where he stopped short of affirming 'that God actively willed the opening of Sinai's revelation and covenant to the gentiles through the formation of a new religion'.[87] But this is precisely where his later thought leads him; or, as he states elsewhere, Christianity is a 'crystallization of the Mosaic tradition'.[88]

What does such a claim mean? To incorporate Christianity into Judaism is an inclusivist move. Christianity does not only give expression to the fundamental Noahide, or even the Abrahamic, covenant. It actually draws from the Sinai covenant. Our willingness to affirm this is part of the legitimation we must afford Christianity. But then that makes Christianity part of 'us' and decreases its fully autonomous status. I do not believe the shift from a more pluralist reliance on a Noahide covenant to a more inclusivist application of a Sinaitic identity to Christianity is intended to decrease the pluralist value of Greenberg's theology. But it can easily do so, inasmuch as the historical argument of Christianity being born of Judaism's flesh now takes on theological value, making it an extension of Judaism.

There are more fundamental problems with this position. Greenberg himself acknowledges that his views may not be well received in the Jewish community, which leads him to not draw out their full potential, for fear of 'another inquisition at the hands of my community'.[89] I am not at all convinced that the Christian community would agree to being described

---

[86] Ibid. 191.   [87] Ibid. 38.   [88] Ibid. 79.   [89] Ibid. 82.

as a crystallization of the Mosaic covenant. Christian self-understanding harks back to Abraham and to a large extent bypasses Sinai as a formative moment.[90] Sinai, ever since Paul, represents what is problematic with Judaism and what needs to be avoided. Neither Jews nor Christians would, on the face of it, be comfortable with this description. What does Greenberg mean, then, by extending the Sinaitic covenant to Christianity? At one point he offers the following definition:

In their separate faith, Christians are nurtured by the mother's milk of Sinai's covenant and Mosaic teachings. Admittedly, Christians often interpret Hebrew Scripture differently. They reinterpret theology and spiritualize or negate various injunctions of Israelite law in light of their own religious experiences, and practice fewer elements of the Torah than do Jews. Still, they attribute a once and ongoing (albeit not equivalent) holiness to the foundational texts of the Jewish traditions. In the final analysis, Christians seek to realize the broadest biblical promises— spiritual, relational and material blessings—and build the fully redeemed world for which Judaism stands. Christian witness confirms the validity of Judaism's testimony as well.[91]

Christians, I am sure, would be reluctant to think of themselves as nurtured by Sinai's mother's milk. Perhaps this is a factual, rather than theological, statement. The continuation of the passage suggests that much. It ultimately relies on the fact that Christians have adopted the Hebrew Scripture into their canon. But it is hard to argue from this fact while divorcing the argument from the actual hermeneutics of Christian biblical interpretation. Whether they allegorize or ignore the contents of the Sinai covenant, or relegate them to the category of what was relevant once for Jews, it is hard to argue for Christian continuity with the Mosaic covenant on the basis of the incorporation of the Torah in their Scriptures. The same holds true for the enduring significance of the ten commandments for Christians. While these are indeed very significant for teaching and preaching, they do not make Sinai a focal point of Christian identity or covenant.[92]

The final sentence may be read in one of two ways. If it is a repetition of the argument, then the problems that applied to it apply here as well. Perhaps

---

[90] See the classic discussion in Gal. 4: 21–31.   [91] *For the Sake of Heaven and Earth*, 99.

[92] This recognition was first corroborated by a broad search of Christian sources and later confirmed by an exchange with David Ford. Christoph Chalamet similarly points, in personal communication, to the centrality of the ten commandments in reformed churches. This, however, does not translate into conscious attachment to the Sinai covenant.

Christians' witness confirming the validity of Judaism's testimony should be understood in the light of Vatican II's and similar affirmations of the enduring validity of Judaism. But if so, we cannot learn anything from such affirmation concerning Christianity's own self-understanding, or for that matter concerning a phenomenologically grounded justification of Christianity in Mosaic terms. It would seem, then, that the main drive behind the presentation of Christianity in both Abrahamic and Mosaic terms is the desire to acknowledge a special relationship between Judaism and Christianity. That Christians seek to partake of the blessings of the Jewish covenants does not make them part of those covenants. At the end of the day, the continuation of the discussion on the same page points to what, in terms of Greenberg's own theology, is the most sound theological foundation for commonality: 'both come to fulfil one covenant—the Noahide'.[93]

Actually, awareness of Christian self-understanding, as recorded by Greenberg, should have led to an affirmation of Christianity's independence, not to it being classified as an aspect of either the Abrahamic or Sinaitic covenants:

The gentile Christians came to understand that the newness that Jesus and his disciples experienced was not a renewal of spirit within a tradition but a radically new covenant. Because Jesus' initial followers were so deeply grounded in the original covenant, they were motivated to reinterpret those inherited symbols and messages as having foreshadowed their experience.[94]

This passage brings out the notion of a 'radically new covenant'. It is hard to present a radically new covenant as being in continuity with all aspects of the Jewish covenant—Abrahamic and Sinaitic—as Greenberg describes. Rather, Christianity's continuing appeal to inherited symbols which they completely reinterpret should be seen in light of their cultural situatedness, rather than as an attempt to remain faithful in some way to the original covenant. The argument from a Christian reinterpretation of Hebrew Scriptures based on the life, crucifixion, and resurrection of Jesus, which Greenberg offers, cannot validate covenantal continuity within the Sinaitic covenant. It seems to confuse the factual use of Jewish texts with the theological construct through which one ought to interpret Christianity. Continuing interpretation of Hebrew Scriptures does not make Christianity part of the Sinaitic covenant. One would have to debate whether Christian self-understanding

---

[93] *For the Sake of Heaven and Earth*, 99.   [94] Ibid. 72.

could achieve this goal, but the point is moot because of the lack of such self-understanding in Christianity. From a theological perspective, all we can affirm, then, if we apply more rigorous standards to Greenberg's constructs, is that the 'radically new covenant' is a further expression of the Noahide one, regardless of the texts it interprets and recognizes as part of its canon.

At several points in his discussion, Greenberg reverts to the Noahide covenant after addressing the Abrahamic or Sinaitic covenant.[95] Greenberg seems satisfied to recognize two layers in the covenant and to see the later one as an unfolding of the earlier one, and to include Christianity and Judaism in both.

In rethinking the relationship of Judaism and Christianity, much of the theological speculation has focused on whether the two religions represent two covenants or one. It is time to suggest that both come to fulfill one covenant—the Noahide. In their further development, both religions grow out of one and the same covenant, the Abrahamic / Sinaitic, but by the will of God they have branched into two parallel covenants to reach out to humanity in all its diversity of culture and religious needs. Nevertheless, the members of the two faith communities remain part of one people, the people of Israel.[96]

The context for this passage is ongoing Christian theological speculation on how Christianity should be viewed through a covenantal lens—as the same covenant as that of Judaism or as a separate one. While Greenberg is aware of this discussion and makes his contribution to it, his answer is drawn from his own theological construct, with no relation to the Christian discussion.[97] This allows him to reconcile the two views. They are both one and two distinct covenants. They are part of the one Noahide covenant. They also grow out of the Abrahamic / Sinaitic covenant, but they have branched into two parallel covenants. One therefore understands that not only the Noahide but also the Abrahamic one, and even the Sinaitic, can have separate sub-covenants under it.

I find the suggestion of sub-covenants much harder to accept with reference to the Sinaitic, even Abrahamic, covenants than with reference to the Noahide one, as defined by Greenberg. The penultimate sentence in this

---

[95] See e.g. *For the Sake of Heaven and Earth*, 93.   [96] Ibid. 99.

[97] Krell, *Intersecting Pathways*, 172 n. 97, notes that Greenberg seems to vacillate between a one-covenant and a two-covenant model throughout his career in writing on this subject. For the most recent Catholic insistence on a one-covenant model, see 'The Gifts and the Calling of God are Irrevocable', sect. 39.

quote offers a further reason for objecting to this classification. The reason for affirming two parallel covenants under the Abrahamic and Sinaitic covenants is in order to reach out to humanity in all its diversity. But this assumes that Christianity is the only faith that reaches out beyond Judaism. This formulation ignores the role of Islam, or of other faiths, in playing out covenantal dynamics independently of conscious adoption of the Abrahamic or Sinaitic covenants. It is framed with Christianity in view. But if it is part of a broader Jewish theology of religions, it must put forth a concept that is applicable to other religions. It is next to impossible to regard Islam as Sinaitic; at best it would be classified as Abrahamic. If the purpose of multiple covenants is to tailor and adapt the core divine covenantal imperatives to different communities, why should some of these take place as sub-covenants of Sinai, others as sub-covenants of Abraham (if we were to classify Islam that way), and still others only as sub-covenants of Noah?

I believe the key to why we find ourselves struggling with these contradictions is to be found in the last sentence. The covenants are distinct, even if they are both founded upon the Sinaitic covenant; but the people are one. The notion of the common peoplehood of Israel suggests what motivates Greenberg's theology. It is the interest to affirm a special relationship and more—a common peoplehood as an expression of that special relationship. The claim that Jews and Christians not only share in a common covenant but are one people is an important argument within Greenberg's theology; we now turn to this argument and examine it more closely.

Jews and Christians (and Muslims): One People

In considering the emergence and value of a given theological position, it is helpful to take into account the theological will that underlies it. Greenberg's theological will is informed by a desire to afford a special status to Christianity and thereby to affirm a special relationship with it. The understanding of that special relationship grows out of Christianity's own view of its relationship with Judaism. Greenberg seeks to reciprocate and to make such an affirmation on Jewish grounds. His aim is to develop a model that will

affirm the profound inner relationship between [Judaism and Christianity], and to recognize and admit how much closer they are to each other than either has been able to say, without denying the other. Up to now, the affirmation that the two religions are internally close was made by Christians who claimed that Christianity grows organically out of Judaism in the *course* of superseding Judaism . . . To the extent that there were Jews willing to see Christianity as a valid religion, they also tended to stress the differences, in order to protect Judaism. This model will seek to reduce the gaps without denying the authenticity of the other.[98]

The 'common covenant', be it Noahide, Abrahamic, or Sinaitic, is one way of affirming commonality. However, the core structure of the Noahide covenant does not provide for the special relationship that Greenberg seeks to establish. It is here that appeal to the notion of one family or one people comes in.

The two self-described peoples of Israel must come to grips with the fact that they are both the children of Abraham—albeit they attain this status in different ways. The patriarch and Sarah were both promised that they would become the ancestors of many nations and that this development would be a blessing to the world.[99]

The argument is twofold. It relies on Christian self-understanding and considers it valid. This understanding is, in turn, grounded in the very biblical foundations that Christians use in recognizing their own tradition as an extension of the Abrahamic promises and blessings. Strikingly, Greenberg is willing to adopt the Christian reading as a way of justifying why Christian self-understanding should lead to a view of the two religions constituting one family and one people.

The family model complements, and to a certain extent supplants, the model of covenant. If the latter describes multiple relationships formed in parallel in relation to God, family—understood as spiritual family, shared vision, mission, and blessing—creates a relationship not only between the covenanters and the covenanting God but also between the members of the different covenants. While the point is made in theological terms, in fact not much is gained theologically beyond whatever was already established by reference to common covenantal foundations. If the covenant regulates the

---

[98] 'The Relationship of Judaism and Christianity', 193. The statement is featured here with reference to Greenberg's overall motivation. It antedates the attempt, described in this section, to apply the notion of one people.

[99] *For the Sake of Heaven and Earth*, 94. I skip here an argument recognizing this as referring to Christianity and not only to Islam, in view of the promise being made to Sarah and not only to Abraham. Implicit in this is the recognition of Islam as sharing the same status as Christianity in relation to Judaism. This will be explored further below.

relationship with God, the family metaphor strengthens relations between those considered to be part of one family. The gain is thus made in the domain of human relations, in the feelings cultivated between different religious communities.

The argument for a familial connection can be seen as the pinnacle of the covenantal reality that informs both religions. It seems, however, that it can also function in the reverse, highlighting how these notions are independent of each other, or at least can be presented without the one depending on the other.

While the new relationship between Judaism and Christianity may start with Jewish affirmation of a familial connection to Christians, it should lead Jews and Christians alike to recognize the common roots as well as the joint and parallel missions of the two religions. In their separate faith, Christians are nurtured by the mother's milk of Sinai's covenant and Mosaic teachings.[100]

The familial connections provide a foundation for the recognition of the parallel paths. Yet these are informed, as we note once more, not by the universal Noahide covenant, nor even the Abrahamic, but by the one made at Sinai. One can perhaps understand how the recognition of Christians as part of one family would go hand in hand with recognizing their affiliation with the Sinai covenant. Both are movements of inclusion and attempts to grant equal or similar status to Christians. In terms of the unfolding of the theological argument, however, we encounter two distinct moves that do not require one another. One could affirm sharing in the Abrahamic blessing, even belonging to the Abrahamic family, without parallel appeal to a covenantal understanding.

The entire discussion of one people or one family places before us, yet again, the problem of biblical sources and how they are made to address the theological task at hand. Greenberg's theological will exceeds the capacity of the sources to sustain his argument. This is as true of biblical proof texts as it is of argumentation from Jewish practice. Beginning with the latter, he makes the point that Judaism recognizes conversion, and is, in other words, not ethnically or genetically limited. He understands conversion as joining the family whose mission it is to teach.[101] This leads him to suggest that Judaism should similarly factor in some understanding of the billions of gentiles who joined in the covenantal mission en masse. Once those members

[100] Ibid. 99.   [101] Ibid. 94.

of the family stop denying the legitimacy of Israel, their conscious member-ship in Abraham's family should be integrated in some way.

Greenberg draws an analogy between a ceremony whose very purpose is to define identity and to establish procedures and boundaries for the per-son entering Judaism and historical processes that lack any parallel process or mechanism. The point seems to be that one can change or become part of the greater whole of a new family. To some extent, such a process should be extended by Jews to Christians, despite history and on condition that Chris-tians, in turn, also affirm such a familial closeness. The argument is forced inasmuch as it appeals to structures of boundary-making in order to weaken such boundaries and to recognize, on a theoretical yet significant level, a new entity, beyond what the formal boundaries would have permitted. It is, in some way, an attempt to extract a principle from the law, almost allegoriz-ing the law, in order to arrive at a principle that transcends the boundaries of the law, all in order to make a theological point. Perhaps it is best to simply recognize this as an expression of Greenberg's theological will, which leads him to great interpretative freedom and creativity.

The problem of biblical witness is encountered in Greenberg's attempt to provide precedent for the notion of one family. The reunion of Jacob and Esau following a lengthy separation, as recounted in Genesis 33, is read as a sign of brothers overcoming estrangement. 'Could this not happen now between adopted siblings?'[102] Yet the biblical Esau never becomes Israel, even when brotherhood is affirmed, or a common Abrahamic heritage is recog-nized. When Greenberg speaks of 'when Jacob and his brother become Israel',[103] he is in fact inventing a biblical tale in service of his theological con-struct, rather than developing his theology around biblical precedents.[104]

The need for moving from viewing Christians as members of a common covenant to seeing them and Jews as one people is in some ways a necessary

---

[102] Ibid. 97. The passage from Genesis has been read with scepticism for most of the his-tory of Jewish interpretation. One notable rabbinic commentator, Rabbi Berlin, the Netsiv of Volozhin, reads the embrace as a coming together that prefigures a future coming together of Jacob and Esau, when Esau will recognize the seed of Israel and Israel will recog-nize Esau as brother. While the Netsiv does not speak of Christianity explicitly, the identifi-cation of Esau and Christianity is common enough. This passage provides a helpful pointer in recognizing the theological sources of the Orthodox rabbinic statement, to be discussed below.   [103] *For the Sake of Heaven and Earth*, 102.

[104] I have noted the challenges in how the biblical texts comport with Greenberg's theo-logical structures throughout his application of the covenant. The problems with the use of proof texts in the discussion of one people may, however, reflect other issues associated with

outcome of some of the theological moves made by Greenberg. In the first instance, covenant provided the common ground between Jews and Christians. However, Greenberg's definition of the covenant is so broad, especially in view of the broad scope of the universal Noahide covenant, that some other means of affirming a special relationship with Christianity must be sought.

Personally, I believe that world religions such as Islam and noncovenantal faiths such as Buddhism and forms of Hinduism should be recognized as movements legitimately striving to fulfill the universal divine covenant with humanity. However, only Christians (although possibly also Muslims) may be deemed to be members of the people Israel, even as they practice differing religions than Jewry does.[105]

This expression of a later Greenberg shows awareness of the broader interfaith reality as it impacts his thinking, formulated initially with reference to Christianity only. Opening up what he had previously made available to Christians in their relationship with Israel forces him to articulate alternative means of asserting the particularity of the Jewish–Christian relationship.

The following statement may expand the application of 'people of Israel' still further, possibly extending it beyond the Abrahamic faiths:

In my usage here, 'the people of Israel' refers not to Israelis alone or to Jews only but to all who affirm that God has made a valid covenant with Abraham and his descendants, all who take up the covenantal task of world redemption so the covenant can be fulfilled, for that is the purpose of making the covenant. That is to say, Christians also—and, indeed, Muslims too—are recognized as Abraham's cherished children, at least when they purge themselves of supersessionist claims and hatred of Jews.[106]

This definition leaves some wiggle room. It refers primarily to Christians but also to Muslims. But if the definition of peoplehood is that one claims a valid covenant with Abraham and takes up the work of world redemption, in theory this could be extended beyond Christianity and Islam. On the other hand, the definition does relate to the status of being Abraham's

a later stage of Greenberg's thinking. The move from covenant to one people characterizes a later Greenberg. I find the argumentation of this later stage less crisp and theologically less precise than the earlier discussions of covenant. This spills over into the imprecise use of biblical proof texts as well.

[105] *For the Sake of Heaven and Earth*, 233.   [106] Ibid. 185.

cherished children. Presumably, the affirmation of the covenant with Abraham and his descendants is made from the perspective of a descendant, rather than of a member of another faith who is willing to acknowledge the criteria suggested by Greenberg. The argument goes a step further. Both covenant and sharing in the Abrahamic heritage could be recognized without conferring the status of Israel. Greenberg collapses these terms and suggests that the criteria for covenant, along with the recognition of spiritual descendancy from Abraham, lead to an expansion of the definition of 'people of Israel', on which Christians, Muslims, and perhaps even others may be grafted.[107]

It should be noted that the status of 'people of Israel' is not conferred upon the religions exclusively on the basis of their faith and action—faith in Abrahamic promises and covenantal actions. Because of the history of supersessionism and in an attempt to ensure that the original meaning of 'people of Israel' is not lost, Greenberg makes the status of the term conditional on purging hatred of Jews and supersessionism. The moral brakes and the relational context serve an important function but they also make it extremely hard to assess a religion. In fact, one is forced to move away from a blanket view of a religion and to consider sections of it, or individuals. Members of another faith may share the same views. Some would be included in the people of Israel while others would be excluded.[108] The criterion would be how they relate to the original people of Israel. Needless to say, a shifting definition is one that religious communities will have a hard time adopting. The moral strings attached to the application of 'people of Israel' constitute one further impediment to a broad reception of this expanded sense of Israel by either Jews or Christians and Muslims.

This is not the only possible objection. Some of the responses to Greenberg's work focus on the difficulties inherent in his challenging suggestion. Krister Stendhal, a leading Christian voice in Jewish–Christian theological engagement and in purifying the theological roots of Christianity from anti-Judaism, is quite uncomfortable with these ideas.

---

[107] Greenberg recaps this argument on p. 40. Another contemporary thinker who has made a similar move is Arthur Green. See Green, *Radical Judaism: Rethinking God and Tradition*, 139. In a related vein, see Kellner, 'Steven Schwarzschild, Moses Maimonides, and "Jewish Non-Jews"'.

[108] An assessment of a religion that is centred on individuals or on groups on the basis of their belief may make more sense than a global evaluation of a religion. As I have already noted, this is the direction I recommend for viewing Hinduism in *Same God, Other god*.

I am hauntingly reminded of the way we Christians have claimed to be Israel. To loosen the word 'Israel' from its Jewish moorings was the decisive move toward Christian supersessionism, the bane of Jewish–Christian relations. And I wonder if the best way to overcome that invidious construct is by substituting a kind of successionism.[109]

David Sandmel, critiquing Greenberg from a Jewish perspective, goes to the heart of Greenberg's motive, what I call his theological will: 'Does the recognition on the part of some Christians that we Jews continue to be Israel in covenant with God require that, in turn, we must acknowledge the legitimacy of the church's claim to identify with the name "Israel"?' Sandmel is open to considering the meaning for Jews of the fact that some Christians affirm God's continuing covenant with the Jews while claiming to be in covenant with that same God. This is a theological challenge that should be taken up. The idea of one people is, however, for Sandmel, not the appropriate response. Fidelity to Jewish tradition precludes recognition as Israel of those who do not meet Israel's definitional criteria.[110]

There is a tension that runs deep in Greenberg's thought. At times he is a genuine pluralist. At others, his thought is better described as inclusivist, wherein other faiths, especially Christianity, are incorporated into Israel and understood along Jewish lines. The construct of a covenant with Noah has the potential for genuine pluralism, albeit based upon a construct that is Jewish. Given that that construct does not define Judaism itself, it is ultimately a means of creating a pluralist position. As the argument becomes more pointed, Greenberg moves increasingly towards inclusivism. Understanding Christianity in terms of the more particular covenant of Abraham, and even more so of Sinai, makes Christianity part of Judaism. In terms of how systematic Greenberg is, it seems there is a tension between the affirmation of one peoplehood and his view of the covenant in the context of Judaism and Christianity. From his vantage point 2,000 years later, he can claim that even Paul 'could not fathom the fullness of divine pluralism. Paul found it hard to affirm that the divine plan included two independent channels of redemption.'[111] Positing two independent channels is indeed pluralism. But when Christianity is considered part of the people of Israel, is this pluralism surrendered for the sake of the gains of unity, special relationship, and reciprocity? While one could, in theory, argue for two covenantal tracks within one people of God, it seems the pluralist thrust loses much

[109] *For the Sake of Heaven and Earth*, 266.   [110] Ibid.   [111] Ibid. 73.

of its power once the argument for one people is made.[112] That Christianity is viewed not only as Abrahamic but even as somehow an extension of Sinai further underscores the point.

The affirmation of one people is motivated by respect and a quest for reciprocity. But it ends up creating the mirror image of some of the fundamental problems that have informed Jewish–Christian relations since their foundation, as Krister Stendahl points out. The Christians' claim to be Israel is taken to the extreme and they are reincorporated in Israel. In fact, Greenberg has been said to strip Christians of their own self-proclaimed identity.[113] Christians, states R. Kendall Soulen, cannot be completely satisfied with Greenberg's view of Christianity as only a 'spin-off' of the Jewish covenant with God.[114] Ultimately, it has been argued, he ends up subordinating Christianity within a Jewish framework. In so doing, he appears to be guilty of what he has accused Buber of, namely viewing positively a Christianity that is suspiciously like the Judaism he loves.[115]

Greenberg's discussion moves from covenant to peoplehood. It is interesting to consider how he conceives of this in light of Christian reflection, with which he has engaged in dialogue for decades. The following passage, which we have already seen when discussing the different covenants, captures the complexity of his position:

In rethinking the relationship of Judaism and Christianity, much of the theological speculation has focused on whether the two religions represent two covenants or one. It is time to suggest that both come to fulfill one covenant—the Noahide. In their further development, both religions grow out of one and the same covenant, the Abrahamic / Sinaitic, but by the will of God they have branched into

---

[112] For Greenberg, the difficulty is encountered in the form of messianic Jews. One cannot be Jewish and Christian at once (*For the Sake of Heaven and Earth*, 98). He insists on the distinctiveness of the two covenantal communities as an expression of the will of God, a decision that was made during the first four centuries of the Common Era. This is a good indication of the tension, which is to a certain extent unresolved, between the pull to pluralism offered by the notion of multiple covenants and the inclusivist tendency of the notion of one people, which runs the risk of crossing boundaries and confusing identities. Greenberg has no problem stating that Christians are also Israel. His difficulty arises only when one attempts to make the reverse case, thereby blurring Jewish identity. It would seem the problem is more a matter of the boundaries he considers sacred than of constraints placed by the categories that he has developed.

[113] The point is made with reference to Greenberg's understanding of Christian symbols such as the cross (see Krell, *Intersecting Pathways*, 128). But it can also be applied to how covenant and peoplehood are extended to Christians.

[114] See Soulen, 'Israel and the Church', 169.   [115] Ibid.

two parallel covenants to reach out to humanity in all its diversity of culture and religious need. Nevertheless, the members of the two faith communities remain part of one people, the people of Israel, the people that wrestle with God and humans to bring them closer to each other.[116]

This is one of the most recent statements by Greenberg and as such provides us with a view of his later thought. He is aware of the question of one or two covenants as a subject of discussion in Christian thought. In some instances, his writings, quoted above, point in the direction of two covenants.[117] But what we see here is a series of moves aimed at upholding a sense of unity while still affirming distinctiveness and difference within the covenants. The first move is the statement that both fulfil one covenant: the two fulfil the one. This is repeated in the recognition that both grow out of the one Abrahamic/Sinaitic covenant, which has branched into two parallel covenants. In brief, Greenberg upholds a view of two covenants while maintaining their fundamental unity. This recognition is juxtaposed with the category of 'people'. Even in the diversity of covenants, we find only one people of Israel. Unity wins, affirming multiple covenants that are really one.

I would like to conclude this discussion by noting a parallel discussion that took place several years ago, after Greenberg's work was published, and which suggests another way of the covenant and peoplehood playing out. Because Greenberg is explicit about the Christian view of covenants as a background to his own reflection, it is worth contrasting his ideas with some recent theological statements by the Catholic Church and Catholic theologians. At the end of 2015, the Pontifical Commission for Religious Relations with the Jews issued a document in honour of the fiftieth anniversary of the publication of *Nostra aetate*. The document, to which I have already referred, is called 'The Gifts and the Calling of God are Irrevocable'. It is explicit about one covenant and rejects a view of Judaism and Christianity as constituting two. It also employs the language of peoplehood within this context of the proclaimed unity of the covenant. In the document we find several references to the People of God. This is what both Israel and the Church are recognized to be.

A more recent Christian iteration of the very same thematic with which Greenberg grapples suggests that there are other ways of using peoplehood, and which do not involve reference to the 'people of Israel'. Some of the

---

[116] *For the Sake of Heaven and Earth*, 99.   [117] Krell, *Intersecting Pathways*, 172 n. 97.

objections raised above may disappear when the quest for unity is expressed by appeal to the 'people of God'. The same document uses another expression—the people of the covenant.[118] Again, there is something less radical, and therefore both less offensive and less likely to be contested, in describing Israel as the people of the covenant. Christians may be described as either people of the covenant or people of the new covenant. Either way, the expression would convey the sense of continuity without entering the millennia-old, fraught territory of the usage of the term 'people of Israel'.

From Greenberg's perspective, would anything be lost if he articulated his intuition using this alternative formulation? I believe not. Perhaps he would lose the ability to draw upon certain biblical narratives. However, as I have suggested, the proof offered by those narratives is less than fully convincing.

Perhaps, then, we ought to restate Greenberg's insight by moving from covenant to peoplehood, but without, at the same time, touching the name 'Israel'. It seems to me this is a fruitful way to continue addressing his ideas and the theological impulses they serve. It opens up a new hermeneutical and theological horizon. And it does so while allowing us to sidestep the difficulties that are inevitably evoked by the suggestion that Jews, Christians, and maybe Muslims are all part of the people of Israel.

Covenant and Other Religions: An Evaluation

It is time to draw together the various perspectives relating to the covenant and to assess the need for and usefulness of thinking of Jewish–Christian relations, and more broadly of a Jewish theology of religions, in terms of the covenant. Greenberg has undoubtedly developed a highly original covenant theology that serves the needs of the new reality of Jewish–Christian relations and of interfaith relations more broadly. It is original, inspiring, and often moving. However, it is fraught with difficulties, as I have indicated throughout the analysis. I will not mention these difficulties again. Instead, I'd like to list several purposes that are achieved by means of a covenantal approach to other religions. These allow us to grasp the usefulness of the category, as well as many of the more detailed discussions offered by Greenberg. It also allows us to focus in more specific ways on the need, or lack thereof, for addressing other religions through the lens of the covenant. If, as

[118] Pope John Paul II coined the expression.

I have suggested, Greenberg's theology of religions could potentially be better served without appeal to that concept, we need to break this argument down according to the different ends that it achieves. Here, then, is the 'work' that reference to the covenant in Jewish–Christian and interfaith relations could accomplish.

1. Legitimation and Validation

The validation of other religions is the primary concern of a Jewish theology of religions.[119] A review of the issues at stake and of the major Jewish approaches to other religions suggests that the main question for Jewish authors is the legitimacy and validity of other religions. When one religion views others, the lens through which it sees is particular to it and suggestive of its main concerns. For example, in Christian theology of religions, the central question is the status of other faiths as effective means of salvation for their believers.[120] This is a distinctly Christian perspective, not shared by Judaism. Similarly, the distinctly Jewish perspective on other religions focuses on their very legitimacy: Is another religion valid, one might almost say 'kosher'? Greenberg achieves the goal of validation by establishing his own novel criteria for what makes another faith valid. These include the life-affirming orientation that a religion takes and how it guides its believers into positive, covenantal collaboration with God for doing good in the world, *tikun olam*. Greenberg thus offers a new criterion and a new lens by means of which to confer legitimacy upon other religions.

However, when considering the challenges that accompany his use of the covenant, one may also ask whether he could not obtain the same result without reliance on that concept. I will suggest below that everything that a covenantal perspective achieves by way of validating another religion can indeed be achieved by other elements of Greenberg's thought, even if these are not brought together under the rubric of covenant. Furthermore, as we have seen, the moral, socially positive perspective on religions and how they uphold ordered societies, and which can be understood as a means of advancing positivity and the common good, is found already in Meiri. Greenberg is aware of this precedent and cites it. It is, therefore, not the covenant in and of itself that confers legitimacy. Rather, once a religion is recognized as legitimate, one can readily view it in covenantal terms, as

---

[119] See Goshen-Gottstein, 'Jewish Theology of Religions'.
[120] The concern is universal and is summarized in Hick, *A Christian Theology of Religions*.

Greenberg does. Similarly, one can view it positively, using Greenberg's very arguments, without these being cast in terms of the covenant.

2. Recognition of Spiritual Value

Beyond legitimacy, one can think of other religions in terms of respect and spiritual admiration. One can form relationships with members of the other religions. One can learn from them in a mutual process of sharing a spiritual vision. All these elements are found in Greenberg's view of other religions and they lend it a depth that far exceeds the common Jewish approach, which is limited to concerns of validity. Validity does not mean that the other religion has something to teach us, nor that it should be a partner in spiritual processes. The foundations of Greenberg's relations with members of other faiths provide precisely this particular depth dimension, and he repeatedly signals that this is a fundamental feature of relations between religions. His covenantal theology is therefore also an instrument for cultivating such deep respect and appreciation.

This is an important element of Greenberg's theology of religions and one can see how it is related to a view of other religions as covenantal. But let us revisit the relationship between spiritual appreciation and covenant. It is not because they are covenantal that other faiths are deserving of our deep respect. It is the reverse. Because they are recognized as spiritually rich, as expressive of a genuine relationship with God, ultimately as points at which God touches humanity, they are considered covenantal partners. If so, what Greenberg brings to the interfaith table is a quality of respect, engagement, listening, appreciation, and more that is significantly above average. This conditions his relationships with members of other faiths. He himself accounts for it in numerous ways as his arguments unfold, but the covenantal status of those religions should not be seen as the cause of their special standing. It is, at most, Greenberg's personal way of translating to the maximum his spiritual appreciation for other religions.

3. A Sense of Common Mission and Participation in *Tikun Olam*

An important dimension of Greenberg's covenantal partnership is his view of religions as sharing in the broader mission of advancing humanity and all beings on the journey between Creation and redemption—a journey entrusted to humans in partnership with God, and consequently one on which religions travel together. This succinct description of one important dimension of the covenant was articulated without appeal to the word 'covenant'. This is an indication that the ideal stands on its own and does not require a covenantal view in order to be justified. As I will argue presently, this is the core of Greenberg's theology of religions. That he casts it in covenantal terms certainly adds colour to it and brings it in line with his broader theology and its driving category. However, when we reflect on the price paid for relating to other religions in terms of covenant and on the difficulties such a perspective could meet, we might decide to acknowledge this partnership for the good on its own terms, independently of the language of covenant.

4. Expressing a Special Relationship

As we have seen, Greenberg seeks to affirm a special relationship between Judaism and Christianity. Here covenantal language becomes more essential to the claim, in view of ongoing debates as to how covenant applies to the two religions: whether one or two covenants are involved, and, more specifically, what the covenant is through which Jews and Christians share a special relationship. Greenberg has repeatedly upped the ante on the covenant as the main means of affirming that special relationship: he has moved from the Noahide covenant to the Abrahamic, the Sinaitic, and eventually to a notion of one people, all in the interest of affirming a special relationship. As the notion of one people suggests, one can make the argument for a special relationship in ways other than by appeal to the covenant. The difficulties described above in the application of the more particular dimensions of Israel's covenant to others are also a drawback to making the case for a special relationship by means of the covenant.

Covenant and a Jewish Theology of Religions

The final consideration for the use of covenant is never stated explicitly by Greenberg. I think it is an important perspective deserving of attention and which in some ways compensates for the various difficulties associated with the use of the term in his view. Point 1, and to a certain extent point 2, focused on the evaluation of another faith—the process in which it is assessed and appreciated and various criteria are offered for cultivating the best possible view of that religion. As I have just argued, covenant is an outcome of the application of other criteria, not a criterion of evaluation in and of itself. Now, let us adopt the opposite perspective. Instead of defining our goal as evaluating and validating another religion, what if the argument proceeded from identifying an internal Jewish vision or drive, which would, in turn, furnish a view of other faiths? Here covenant takes on unique and exclusive significance. While never stated, I believe in a deep way this has been a factor that informs and may have even shaped Greenberg's thinking. Let me explain.

Greenberg is a covenantal thinker, who organizes his entire religious world-view around that concept. It is not simply a strategy, like Meiri's definition of morally ordered religions, or like the reference of the *Tosafot* to *shituf*. Covenant has a prior theological existence in Greenberg's spiritual universe. In the interreligious situation he draws upon a category that is foundational to his thinking rather than searching for some alternative notion that could do the work. His application of the covenant to other faiths is thus a way of remaining deeply faithful to a formative category that shapes his thought, while seeking out its deepest potential in relation to others. I reconstruct the process as follows. Covenant is a foundational Jewish vision. Its validity is expressed in the work it does within Jewish reflection and through what it makes possible in a Jew's relation to other faiths.[121] That the covenant can be extended to other religions, which then become covenantal partners with Judaism, is part of unpacking this key theological concept. It is not other religions that are validated by means of the covenant; it is the covenant itself that is validated because it can be opened to accommodate other religions. This becomes a means of affirming its centrality, its power, its theological vitality. In this, Greenberg points us in a novel direction: rather than the concern for validity and legitimacy articulated above in point 1, his covenantal approach suggests what might be another way of conceiving of an internal Jewish approach to other religions. In this line of reasoning, if Christianity's core question is how other religions can effect salvation, the concern of Judaism, à la Greenberg, is how other religions can manifest a (common) covenantal reality.

This suggestion is important, very important. It helps us account for the extraordinary efforts Greenberg makes to describe other religions in covenantal terms. The price he is forced to pay is for a good cause. He may well be aware of the questionable hermeneutics or the conceptual contradictions. But these may be necessary for realizing a profound drive that goes to the

---

[121] Greenberg's work in the field of theology following the Holocaust is also accomplished by means of this category; Krell, *Intersecting Pathways*, 103 ff.

core of Judaism and its vision. The fullness of that vision is brought to fruition in relation to other religions, as this points to their common covenantal reality.

Greenberg then develops a master narrative of all religions as they conform to a spiritual-historical drive that has its roots in Israel and that extends to the world at large through all religions, and especially those closest to Israel. The name of this drive and the name of this process is covenant.

I find myself gaining sympathy for Greenberg's efforts and the lengths that he goes to in order to develop a covenantal view of other religions as the stakes rise and the problems are redefined. Nevertheless, the process of reading other religions through a covenantal lens remains fraught with challenges that may not justify it. Let me add to those listed above also the following fundamental concern that arises from Greenberg's work. The process of affirming other religions is undertaken by means of the category of covenant, whereby he seeks to validate potentially all religions, and certainly Christianity and Islam. Importing a category by means of which another religion is viewed narrows the perspective on that religion and forces upon it a frame of interpretation that is often foreign to it.[122] Greenberg strives to open up horizons in the relations between religions, but he does so by means of a term that is the epitome of a particular language of a particular community. Granted, he recasts it in new ways. However, the very usage of a concept as particular as the covenant is in itself a means of forcing a structure that is potentially foreign to other religions and interpreting them in terms of Judaism. Would it not be preferable to simply speak of religions as givens? Could their positive value not be appreciated in terms of the good they do in the world, without forcing such a positive appreciation into too narrow a theological category? This is, after all, the road taken by Meiri, who provides some of the theoretical justification for Greenberg's own work. And could religion itself, following biblical precedent, not be taken simply as a natural and appropriate part of human life in God's presence, without imposing upon it a category by means of which it must be accounted for?[123]

[122] A case in point is the Jewish attempt to interpret Hinduism in terms of revelation. See Goshen-Gottstein, *The Jewish Encounter with Hinduism*, 198–9, and contrast it with the discussion in ch. 9 of that volume.

[123] There are various ways of making the argument that religion is natural to life and to human society and a positive expression of these. The book of Genesis' openness to other religions, while affirming what is particular about Judaism, is one possible precedent. See Kaufmann, *The Religion of Israel*, 222.

All this leads us to consider whether Greenberg's theological goals could not be met without appeal to the covenant. The reader, or the believer, will ultimately have to decide what price he or she is willing to pay for upholding a covenantal view of other religions and which of the purposes spelled out above is served by it. In order to make an 'informed' choice in this matter, let us consider how Greenberg's core argument could be pitched without reference to the covenant.

I would like to suggest that everything that Greenberg seeks to achieve in his Jewish–Christian theology and in cultivating a Jewish approach to other religions can be attained without 'covenant'. Restating his views in this way will allow his originality and creativity to stand out, unhampered by the internal tensions generated by the appeal to covenant. Inasmuch as the very notion of 'partnership' is a later expansion upon the biblical usage of covenant, applying this notion without relying on a biblical covenant may also resonate better with readers for whom continuity with biblical usage is a guiding theological principle.

There are several key definitions of covenant used by Greenberg that deliver what he requires for a view of other religions, and which can stand on their own, irrespective of the term 'covenant'.

This unlimited partnership of the Divine and the human is the ultimate dimension of religious calling in both religions . . . both religions teach that the people of Israel, the covenantal people (however each faith defines that), are pledged not only to work but to teach and to model how to be human to the rest of humanity.[124]

As we have seen above, responsibility is one of the key factors of the covenant and of the unfolding history of covenant in Greenberg's view, and in the light of which the biblical notion of covenant is recast. But if he recasts the biblical notion, could we not speak of partnership and responsibility directly, without having to redefine the covenant in order to convey these ideals?

One of the reasons why covenant could be eliminated as a conceptual foundation is that, to a large extent, its contours have been redrawn in light of another concept, also current in late twentieth-century American Jewish theology—*tikun olam*. 'The basic idea behind covenant is *tikkun olam*.'[125]

---

[124] *For the Sake of Heaven and Earth*, 164.   [125] *Living in the Image of God*, 62.

If so, one asks, doesn't directly using *tikun olam* allow us to say all that needs to be said by way of partnership, without involving covenantal language and the complications it brings with it?

The same holds true for another kabbalistic concept—*tsimtsum*. Let us consider the following paragraph, entitled 'Covenant—The Process of Tikun Olam'.

Bound by divine self-limitation through the laws of nature and intertwined in the matrix of a reliable reality, God further renounced power. God entered into covenant (partnership) with people in order to engage humanity in its own liberation. The Lord promised not to complete the redemption by coercion or divine force majeure. This was a remarkable act of love and respect, for in giving humans an indispensable role in perfecting the world, God accepted the inescapable outcome: a considerably longer duration for the process of *tikkun olam* (repairing the world) . . . In effect, God took on boundless suffering to enable human beings to grow into dignified and responsible partners in perfecting the world.[126]

This paragraph would be unrecognizable to a biblical author informed by the biblical notion of covenant. The dynamics of that covenant consisted of faithfulness, lapse in faithfulness, and the re-establishment of the covenant relationship, as reflected in Israel's history. These dynamics have here given way to those of cosmic redemption and of historical processes, which extend far beyond the range of the biblical covenant, have a historical and even cosmic dimension, and, most importantly for Greenberg, also include other faiths in this redefined covenant. While this view would not resonate with biblical authors, kabbalists would recognize it, even if they do not call it covenant, but rather relate to it through the dual notions of *tikun olam* and *tsimtsum*.[127] With covenant now recast as partnership, the core ideas are really the later kabbalistic ones and not the earlier biblical notion. In fact, covenant has now lost the definition it had for biblical authors—the relationship between God and Israel. Much of what makes the covenant particular— love of God, adherence and attachment to him, faithfulness, Torah study, and the range of emotions that are captured by faithfulness to the covenant —no longer has its rightful place in a category that signals partnership and cosmic responsibility. That relationship has now been recast as a respon-

[126] *For the Sake of Heaven and Earth*, 55.
[127] Actually, kabbalists may also not recognize it. As Lawrence Fine's essay teaches us, Greenberg's use of *tikun olam* grows out of kabbalistic sources but does not properly represent them.

sibility, shared by others, to work for *tikun olam*. Covenant is instrumental-ized to doing good in the world.[128]

Once covenant is identified with *tikun olam*, there is no need to stick to the historical sequencing of biblical covenants.[129] Even though covenantal history begins with Noah, the dual kabbalistic concepts of *tsimtsum* and *tikun olam* hark back to Creation and therefore apply to Adam and hence to all humanity.[130] If humanity is enjoined, from its very creation, to parti-cipate in *tikun olam*, this can stand without any need for the later Noahide covenant.[131]

The identification of *tikun olam* and covenant brings about a remove from the biblical meaning of the term. It allows Greenberg to extend the covenant to all religions, even those that are not aware of it as a historical concept, let alone as a way of structuring their relationship with God.[132] Could this not have been achieved equally well by appeal to the notion of 'repairing the world', *tikun olam*, which lies at the heart of this definition?

Greenberg seeks to reach out to all religions, but also beyond religion, to secularists. His vision of collaborating for the improvement of the world includes even those without religion.[133] This works very well for *tikun olam*. The currency the term has gained in general circles is proof of that. It does not really work for covenant.

The suggestion that covenant may be superfluous to Greenberg's core message may draw further support from other ways in which he develops

[128] I ask myself whether such a move does not ultimately reveal Greenberg's ideological moorings in the nineteenth-century *musar* movement. Current primarily in Lithuanian ye-shivas, the likes of which Greenberg attended, *musar* (lit. ethics) emphasized practical out-comes and perfecting human personality and human relations. Had his spirituality been shaped by hasidic literature and its emphases on intimacy and relationship with God, would covenant have been pitched in the same way?

[129] This sequencing is all the more problematic from the perspective of the reading of Genesis and its history of covenants, as I propose in 'Genesis 9, Noah's Covenants and Jewish Theology of Religions'.

[130] See Krister Stendahl's response to Greenberg, where he suggests a human oneness that precedes any covenant, based on the common humanity of the image of God. *For the Sake of Heaven and Earth*, 266.

[131] As already noted, there is some confusion regarding the association of the Noahide commandments and Noah himself. Rabbinically, the seven Noahide commandments were given to Adam (that is, six of the seven). This forms a bridge between the commandments given to *benei no'aḥ*, the sons of Noah, in other words humanity, and Adam.

[132] We recall the citation from *For the Sake of Heaven and Earth*, 57 (see p. 97 above).

[133] Ibid. 101.

his pluralist ideal. If covenant runs the risk of becoming inclusivist, rather than truly pluralist, as I have suggested, there are other mechanisms suggested by Greenberg that would allow us to cultivate full pluralism in relation to Christianity as well as other religions. One of these has already been alluded to—the image of God. This notion has the capacity to generate a pluralist view, grounded in an appeal to the Divine that extends beyond Judaism.

This is a special part of the mission of this generation: to renew revelation, to continue the covenantal way, to discover each other. At least let these two religions model the truth that the love of God leads to the total discovery of the image of God in the other, or to its distortion or elimination. If committed and believing Christians and Jews can discover the image of God in each other, if they can uncover and affirm each one's proper role in the overall divine strategy of redemption, surely the inspiration of this example would bring the kingdom of God that much closer for everyone.[134]

While the passage refers to 'the covenantal way', in fact it could equally well have omitted it. The key notions are love of God, image of God, and the revelatory power of mutual discovery grounded in the image of God.[135] Encounter has a kind of revelatory, possibly even commanding, reality. Mutual discovery is the discovery of God in each other. Such revelation is the source of inspiration for others. It is worth noting that 'image of God' stands completely independently of covenantal thinking. Biblically they are never associated, nor, to the best of my knowledge, in any other significant foundational source. Intuitively, the range of 'image of God' is far wider than that of the covenant. It applies to all men and women, though applying it to a religion is a stretch, or at least a secondary application. But this extension is not more far-reaching than the extension of biblical covenantal thinking to other religions. While Greenberg, especially in his later writings, is open to extending the covenant, in theory, to all religions, there still seems to be something more universal in the application of 'image of God' than in the application of 'covenant'—the latter will always retain its ties with the foundational biblical context of the special covenant with Israel.[136]

[134] Ibid. 183–4.
[135] For Greenberg, the Holocaust and the founding of the State of Israel are revelatory moments. Appreciation of another religion can be included in this broader openness to ongoing revelation.
[136] We recall the cautionary note sounded by Krister Stendahl on this point and his own preference for the image of God as the central category (n. 130 above).

Once the door is opened to a direct recognition of the other and of the other's role in God's plan, new ways of recognition and validation are found. One such way is recognition of the sincerity and the religious life of the other. At one point Greenberg speaks of the need of the two faiths, Judaism and Christianity, for other faiths, for they alone cannot accomplish the work of redemption. 'Once they admit this truth, they can respect other faiths as well. Then wherever people call out in the name of the Lord, there God will come and bless them all.'[137] We find here a very direct way of validating other religions, on grounds that are universally recognized and do not draw on a particular Jewish, or Jewish–Christian, construct, let alone on its most recent recasting. Rather, the believer's direct appeal to God establishes a relationship through which God can be known in any other religion. Within this short phrase is contained an entire theologoumenon that provides the foundation for a genuine pluralism that does not require a biblical category as the basis for a common religious vision for humanity.

Finally, we come across a reasoning that is fully pluralistic, grounded in revelation, independent of covenant, and which extends further the logic of a sincere call to God.

Jews must develop the ability to recognize the full implications of the truth that the Lord has many messengers. While it is true that Jews have always believed that there is salvation for the individual outside of Judaism, this generality does not do justice to the full spiritual dignity of others who, after all, live their lives in religious communities, and not just as individuals.[138]

This passage combines two powerful arguments for pluralism. The first assumes multiple revelations, or multiple messengers. This notion, which has lived on the margins of Jewish theology, especially in authors from the Muslim diaspora such as Nathanel Al Fayumi,[139] moves here to the centre. Pluralism either requires or makes credible the claim that God has many messengers and that neither access to him or to his path, nor the ability to receive his word is limited to Jews. This theoretical foundation for pluralism is matched by an empirical-phenomenological argument. An unbiased view of the lives of the faithful of other religions would lead one to appreciate the full dignity of others and of the life afforded by religion as practised in the communal reality of other faith traditions. This argument can be

---

[137] *For the Sake of Heaven and Earth*, 101.
[138] Ibid. 175.   [139] See Brill, *Judaism and Other Religions*, 111–12.

taken as a theological echo of Meiri's position described above. Recognition of the same God by means of attention to the faithful establishes the validity of the other religions in line with Meiri's views, without having to rely on the notion of the covenant.

Tying all these elements together, it seems one can indeed formulate Greenberg's interreligious theology by other means, without making it dependent on covenant. The reader will choose what gains are made by appeal to the covenant and how essential the notion is to Greenberg's theological views of other faiths. I believe his thought is best served by appreciating the deeper impulses that inform it and by highlighting the originality of his views, the structures he establishes, and the moves he makes. All this can be done to a large extent without reliance on covenant. It made sense for Greenberg's theology to be centred around that concept given the intellectual history of the preceding decades. Perhaps it is less of a need today. Perhaps we can receive from him and extract from his teachings all that he seeks to convey without fully buying into the particular form his thought takes in dialogue with the notion of covenant.

That Greenberg's key ideas can be stated without appeal to the covenant emerges from a review of his latest book, *The Triumph of Life*. The book is not concerned, as its major focus, with a Jewish view of Christianity and other religions. However, various key ideas that are representative of his theology are featured in it. We find, for example, several descriptions of the purpose and function of other religions, a function that in earlier works is described in covenantal terms, without invoking that category.[140]

---

[140] See p. 28 ('God's Capabilities and the Image of God') and p. 601 ('The Status of Gentiles') in the manuscript. Only once in this work, on p. 208 ('Human Emotions'), does he relate to how particularity expands from the Noahide covenant. The idea of all religions being sub-covenants of the Noahide one is absent in this book.

CHAPTER FIVE

Greenberg's Theology: Reception and Evaluation

S OME OF THE PROBLEMS surrounding Greenberg's work have already come to light. Others will be listed presently. These problems are interesting from a theoretical perspective, but they take on greater urgency when we consider the reception of Greenberg's interreligious theology. If his theology does not have an echo, the problems we identify may play an important role in this. In the present chapter, I would like to outline what I think is the biggest challenge that emerges from Greenberg's project of legitimating Christianity as well as other religions. It seems to me this challenge is closely related to the reception history of his ideas—in other words, to how his work has been or can be accepted by Jews, Christians, and others.

I have described the tension between pluralism and inclusivism as running through the different dimensions of Greenberg's view of the covenant. This tension characterizes much of his approach to Christianity, not only to the covenant. On the one hand, we find in his writing an honest attempt to validate and accept on their own terms other faiths, notably Christianity. In this he is a pluralist, allowing the different religions to stand on their own, facing God and collaborating with each other. And yet, much of what he does is an appreciation of Christianity in terms that are Jewish. All too often, Christians will not recognize themselves in the form of Christianity that is being validated by Greenberg. Reading Christianity in Jewish terms runs the risk of seeing it as simply a branch of Judaism, or of not recognizing it duly as a self-standing religion.

This brings us back to the fundamental question of who Greenberg's audience is. Is his theology meant for Jews or for Christians? I have already raised this question above and suggested that Greenberg writes for the Jewish–Christian *situation*. Greenberg seeks to serve the relationship and the encounter, seen, so to speak, from above, reminding us of the God's-eye view that he seeks to capture. While he may serve the relationship, we cannot avoid asking: Whom does he have in mind as his primary readers—Jews or Christians? In reading Greenberg, it seems he tries to relate to both communities, even though his primary audience is Jewish. This may be how some of the tensions in his thought arose in the first instance.

Would a Jewish audience respond better to an inclusivist approach or to a pluralist one? There is, perhaps, an intuition wherein one prefers to adopt an inclusivist approach to the other.[1] In principle, it is less extreme in the recognition of the other, who is afforded legitimacy on one's own terms and as somehow coming under the rubrics of one's own tradition. Greenberg's inclusivism may, however, go too far for his Jewish audience. He has given Christians, and possibly Muslims, a share in the covenants of Abraham and Sinai. He has gone so far as to consider them part of the people of Israel. These ideas have, in my view, little chance of being broadly accepted. Indeed, overall, there is not much echo of Greenberg's theology on these issues even in wider theological circles, engaged in relations between the faiths.[2]

The Noahide covenant has its own problems of reception, especially in how it relates to biblical material. At the same time, it affords more of a sense of pluralism, wherein all religions and all revelations operate under one theological umbrella. It is a pluralism based on a category that is Jewish, but because it is biblical, it can be equally well said to be Christian.

For Christians the problem is possibly more pronounced. Greenberg makes a breakthrough in relation to Christianity. He moves beyond a general pluralism that affirms other religions in principle, as found, for example, in Meiri, to an attempt to read, understand, and uphold the particulars of the Christian faith. This is a pluralism that respects the particularity of the other, beyond the abstracted general being and principle of the other. In this, he is probably the most advanced Jewish thinker with reference to Christianity. Greenberg thus finds a way of validating Christians—yet it remains a *Jewish* way and therefore can be criticized for falling short of a fully pluralist view. It would seem that genuine or full pluralism requires validating or appreciating the other on his own terms, and several Christian

---

[1] It must also be recognized that the Christian view of Judaism is not pluralist, but rather inclusivist. The point comes across clearly in the recent Vatican document, 'The Gifts and the Calling of God are Irrevocable', sects. 37, 40. While the enduring validity of Judaism is upheld, it is ultimately Jesus' salvific work that is operative also in Judaism.

[2] See Krell, *Intersecting Pathways*, 130, for further reference to Greenberg's reception.

authors have made the point that Greenberg's pluralism fails in this regard as he casts them in a Jewish light. Greenberg did set out to develop an appreciation for Christianity on its own terms, unlike Buber's, which was based on what he found to be common between the two faiths. But, as some have noted, he ended up repeating Buber's overall orientation.[3]

Let us consider Greenberg's view of fundamental Christian ideas and symbols. What I described above as novel and daring approaches to core Christian symbols—the cross, the Resurrection—are not necessarily perceived that way by Christian interlocutors. Or let us recall one of the hallmarks of Greenberg's theological novelty—the view of Jesus as failed messiah. On Jewish grounds this is a breakthrough notion, original, and one that could generate respect towards the focal point of Christianity. But how can a Christian appreciate this concept? We are best off assuming that Greenberg was not thinking of his Christian reader and had his attention turned to how the Jewish reader might be aided in advancing in his views of Christianity.

Greenberg's good will and theological audacity should not be minimized. But when a Jew tells Christians what their symbols mean, is this dialogue at its best or is this a form of interreligious colonialism?[4] I think the question cannot easily be resolved. It can be alternately viewed as one or the other. I personally consider it a high point of sophisticated and nuanced dialogue, a sign of true exchange and sharing, but some Christians have reacted differently. At the root is the tension of an inclusivist versus a pluralist approach to the other faith.

Mark Krell has noted that Greenberg has not succeeded in presenting a truly decentred Jewish–Christian framework, where both parties are equidistant from God.[5] There could be two reasons for why this is so. The first is that Greenberg thinks like a Jew and therefore casts Christianity in Jewish terms. A picture is drawn up consequently that subordinates it to Judaism, whether with regard to key concepts and beliefs or in terms of the covenantal framework.[6] The other possibility, and one that I favour, is that

[3] Krell, *Intersecting Pathways*, 129.

[4] As Krell states (ibid. 128), while Greenberg is sympathetic to Christian concerns, his portrayal of Jewish–Christian relations still provides the impression of a subordinate Christian role in a Jewish framework.   [5] Ibid. 130.

[6] See also the comment by Kogan, *Opening the Covenant*, 151, regarding Greenberg's theological one-upmanship.

Greenberg had set out to develop a truly pluralist framework that affords Christianity its full autonomous value. However, his main instrument for achieving this end was a rereading of the meaning of covenant. Because biblically this category is so closely intertwined with a Jewish perspective, the place allotted to Christianity is inevitably defined within a Jewish framework. Involuntarily, the pluralist impulse and desire are limited, and theological concepts are framed within an inclusivist context.

The tensions under discussion are more complex than recognizing the other on his own terms or on one's own. The matter is made far more complicated with reference to Christianity (which it is not in relation to Islam) because Christianity itself claims to be part of Israel's story and even to constitute Israel. Thus, to really appreciate Christianity on its own terms one cannot simply take up a pluralist perspective. One must validate Christianity's own sense of being included in a Jewish narrative or theological framework, while doing so not from the internal Christian perspective. The pluralist urge therefore hits up against internal Christian 'reverse inclusivism' (the claim to be part of Israel and its story), which it must either override with a general pluralism, such as that provided by Meiri, or present an alternative to, such as the efforts marshalled by Greenberg. Put differently, given their complex relations and the different claims made by Judaism and Christianity in relation to one another, it may be impossible to come forth with a position that would be acceptable to both Jews and Christians, because the argument for inclusion is itself a complicated part of the Jewish–Christian history and relationship. Greenberg's challenge is therefore the same as that of Christian theology, which seeks to assert itself and its own validity alongside the enduring validity of Judaism, after having renounced a supersessionist view wherein it stands in lieu of Judaism. For Christian theology this is the biggest conundrum, and one that has not been successfully resolved.[7] It may be that neither Greenberg, nor any other Jewish theologian, can successfully resolve the tension of affirming Christianity on its own terms while at the same time viewing it in Jewish terms. Christianity's own terms are in some way deeply Jewish.[8] It may be that the attempt made by Greenberg is as good an effort as can be made.

[7] The recent Vatican document 'The Gifts and the Calling of God are Irrevocable' (sects. 36–7) leaves this theological conundrum in the domain of mystery.
[8] This does not necessarily apply to all details of the views of both religions. Greenberg could, in theory, view certain symbols in ways that are less Jewish.

The preceding discussion considered the theoretical challenges to Green-berg's perspectives on Judaism and Christianity. What of their actual recep-tion? How has he been received by either Christians or Jews? Perhaps one should note, before attempting a response, that the reception of a theologian is very hard to monitor. We are dealing with a rarefied discussion taking place among a narrow group of specialists, theologians who show a special interest in Jewish–Christian or interreligious relations. This is not a group of individuals who simply subscribe to the theology of any given person. Knowledge, discourse, and reflection are an accumulation of the efforts of many individuals, who visit and revisit key questions from changing per-spectives. Each contribution adds something to the sum total of the pro-cess, and it is extremely rare, perhaps non-existent, for the views of someone to be simply received wholesale. It is against the nature of theological pro-cesses and it is not appropriate to the audience that engages with these ideas.

To illustrate the point, let us draw a comparison with Franz Rosenzweig, another Jewish theoretician of Jewish–Christian relations. What can we say of his reception history? If there is anything to learn from it, it is that every theoretical articulation becomes a resource and a reference, rather than a position that receives full acceptance, in toto. Rosenzweig's work is known in narrow circles of specialists, an approach among many, a rich treasure of the spirit, a sign of goodwill, a vision of hope. If Rosenzweig were to review his own reception, would he be satisfied?

The fact is, however, that Greenberg does feel a sense of not having been well received. He has expressed this personally.[9] Others have written about this with reference to Jewish–Christian relations.[10] It is part of a broader phe-nomenon of feeling that the path that he has described has not been walked by others, as the title of a recent collection of studies devoted to his thought suggests.[11] What are the mechanisms by means of which we might consider the positive dimensions of his reception, offsetting this basically negative assessment? I would like to list three such mechanisms.

Following this reflection on what constitutes reception in the field of Jewish–Christian theology and the sense of frustration that is almost endemic to it, one recognizes that any attempt, regardless of its details and

---

[9]   The point comes up, inter alia, in the interview featured in Ch. 6.

[10] Krell, *Intersecting Pathways*, 130.

[11] Ferziger, Freud-Kandel, and Bayme (eds.), *Yitz Greenberg and Modern Orthodoxy: The Road Not Taken.*

suggestions, is already an accomplishment. People know that Rosenzweig articulated a theory of Judaism and its relations with Christianity. They may have the broadest sense of it and be far from any particular knowledge. Yet the very fact that it exists is in itself a landmark, a point of reference that serves the purposes of goodwill and an inspiration for further study. This is certainly the case with Greenberg as well. It's not necessarily what he says or how he says it. What's important is the very fact that he has made a major contribution and is known in this capacity.

A second approach is the one suggested above. Greenberg's key insights may stand but can be stripped of some of their particularity and unique flavour. Identifying the deep structures and the ways in which theological goodwill has been extended is a meaningful example for the future and a valuable resource for the present. I hope to have helped in reducing some of Greenberg's ideas to their bare essentials through the critique and recasting offered above.

For all the self-doubting and external querying, one cannot claim his work has not had an impact. Some thinkers are so deeply impacted by Greenberg's approach, consciously or unconsciously, that their thought may be considered an extension of his, even if it has undergone nuancing and change in details.[12] Furthermore, if impact and reception are not full, they nevertheless do take place partially or in ways that recast the original with an eye to its improved reception. Rather than asking how Greenberg's entire thought approach has been received, we might be on the lookout for the marks that he has left upon broader discourse.[13] Key ideas, combinations of motifs, snippets of insight all have a life of their own and can function independently of the full complex of thought within which they were couched. This has probably been a significant channel for disseminating Greenberg's ideas, even if he is not fully aware of it. To illustrate the point, at the time of writing these lines, I received, in the context of preparing another publication, a written contribution by the patriarch of the Jerusalem Latin Church, a figure of great symbolic significance, a serious practitioner

[12] I consider Eugene Korn's appeal to the covenant to belong in this category.

[13] A classical way of spreading ideas is, of course, through students and disciples, not only through writing. In latter years, there have been increasing opportunities for Greenberg to assume the role of teacher, not only of thinker. This began with Yeshivat Chovevei Torah, as he testifies in our dialogue in Chapter 6 below. His recent appointment as teacher at Yeshivat Hadar and in particular his relationship with Shai Held provide a channel of continuity and modelling.

of Jewish–Christian dialogue, and a man learned in both Jewish and Christian terms. Patriarch Pizzaballa, in an essay devoted to Abraham Joshua Heschel, inserted a quote from Greenberg concerning God's suffering and how this is to be appreciated as a lesson that Jews must absorb, despite what seems a Christian message.[14] This tells me that Greenberg is being read. Different readers will pick and choose what strikes them and what is helpful to their theological cause. This is one expression of selective use.

There are two additional ways in which Greenberg's teachings have been recast and partially applied by others. The first is the Jewish Orthodox Statement on Christianity (2015), which I study below. In brief, key ideas of Greenberg's theology made it into a public statement that was signed by dozens of rabbis and has been disseminated throughout the Christian world as a significant resource of Jewish–Christian relations. Should we minimize the significance of such dissemination?

Actually, the subject at hand is not the reception of ideas and their validity. It is how theologians go about the business of spreading their ideas. Reception may require other means of dissemination than the theological books that Greenberg has written or the present volume, which is a response to his own efforts. Broad dissemination requires adaptation to the appropriate medium. There is perhaps no greater wizard of Jewish learning, who mastered the art of adapting content to form and who had unprecedented success in broad dissemination of key, and oftentimes complex, ideas than the other hero of this book, Rabbi Jonathan Sacks. Here too, we should not be asking whether all of Sacks' ideas have found a receptive audience. The point is that a significant corpus of key ideas has been made broadly available using a variety of media and formats. Reception is as much about the message as about the method. I say this not only as a way of finding another argument to lighten the burden of non-reception and to underline the significance of the Orthodox Statement. Beyond this, Sacks is himself one of the key disseminators of Greenberg's theology. This is a novel and daring claim and I will explore it at length in another part of the present book. If this thesis is borne out, then the question of Greenberg's legacy should be considered not simply in itself but as part of a broader view of the dissemination of ideas, the means of contextualizing and recontextualizing

---

[14] The essay on Abraham Joshua Heschel appears in *Interreligious Heroes*. I asked Patriarch Pizzaballa to remove the quote from Greenberg due to the space constraints of the very short article, which is focused on Heschel.

them, and of identifying the carriers who have the ability to deliver complex messages to broad audiences, often in an unsuspecting way. This is certainly cause for optimism in terms of reception history.

Philosophers and theologians may debate and nuance their arguments, as the present conversation does. But at the end of the day ideas travel, have a life of their own, and add up to an impact that is cumulative over a lifetime and beyond, where a person's vision and legacy help shape the mind and spirit of others.

With these encouraging words, I would like to now turn to one of the means of disseminating Greenberg's thought. Let us pay close attention to how some of his key ideas are reflected in the Orthodox Statement.

The Orthodox Statement on Christianity

On the occasion of commemorating the fiftieth anniversary of *Nostra aetate* in 2015, a group of Orthodox rabbis issued a statement on Christianity. In the English-speaking world, this was the first ever such statement to come from Orthodox rabbis.[15] It was drafted by a group of rabbis, and Greenberg was not its initiator, though he was an inspiration and a point of reference. Having been involved in the initiative myself, I can testify to the major role that he played in formulating this statement. He was the most respected theological voice to have been consulted along the way.[16] When one considers the final statement, one realizes how much it is indebted to Greenberg's theology. I would therefore like to review this document in light of all that we have learnt of Greenberg's view of Christianity. We will see where it is indebted to him, and where it goes beyond his previous work. The statement is one vehicle by means of which his ideas have received broader dissemination and recognition within the Jewish community. To a certain extent, all signatories ended up affirming his brand of a Jewish view of Christianity.[17]

[15] One important document that is often overlooked in the history of Jewish–Christian statements is that of the rabbis of France in 1968. See Touati et al., 'Le Christianisme dans la théologie juive'. This statement can also be described as Orthodox, having been issued by the central Orthodox rabbinic organization of France.

[16] The other major voice was Rabbi Shlomo Riskin, who nevertheless does not have the same theological gravitas as Greenberg does in this domain.

[17] Some, as I know all too well, signed the statement because they believed in its general purpose, rather than in its details. Still, in the public view, this is a way of affirming and disseminating Greenberg's theology.

I present the statement in its entirety below. I have **emphasized** those parts that can be traced back in some way to Greenberg's thought, thereby providing a graphic illustration of the prominence of his theology in the document.

To Do the Will of Our Father in Heaven
Toward a Partnership between Jews and Christians

After nearly two millennia of mutual hostility and alienation, we Orthodox Rabbis who lead communities, institutions and seminaries in Israel, the United States and Europe recognize the historic opportunity now before us. We seek to do **the will of our Father in Heaven** by accepting the hand offered to us by our Christian brothers and sisters. Jews and Christians must work together as partners to address the moral challenges of our era.

1. **The Shoah** ended 70 years ago. It was the warped climax to centuries of disrespect, oppression and rejection of Jews and the consequent enmity that developed between Jews and Christians. In retrospect it is clear that the failure to break through this contempt and engage in constructive dialogue for the good of humankind weakened resistance to evil forces of anti-Semitism that engulfed the world in murder and genocide.

2. **We recognize that since the Second Vatican Council the official teachings of the Catholic Church about Judaism have changed fundamentally and irrevocably.** The promulgation of Nostra Aetate fifty years ago started the process of reconciliation between our two communities. Nostra Aetate and the later official Church documents it inspired unequivocally reject any form of anti-Semitism, affirm the eternal Covenant between G-d and the Jewish people, reject deicide and stress the unique relationship between Christians and Jews, who were called 'our elder brothers' by Pope John Paul II and 'our fathers in faith' by Pope Benedict XVI. On this basis, Catholics and other Christian officials started an honest dialogue with Jews that has grown during the last five decades. We appreciate the Church's affirmation of Israel's unique place in sacred history and the ultimate world redemption. Today Jews have experienced sincere love and respect from many Christians that have been expressed in many dialogue initiatives, meetings and conferences around the world.

3. As did **Maimonides** and Yehudah Halevi,[1][18] we acknowledge that the emergence of Christianity in human history is neither an accident nor an error, **but the willed divine outcome and gift to the nations. In separating Judaism and Christianity, G-d willed a separation between partners with significant theological differences, not a separation between enemies.** Rabbi Jacob Emden wrote that 'Jesus brought a double goodness to the world. On the one hand he strengthened the Torah of Moses majestically . . . and not one of our Sages spoke out more emphatically concerning the immutability of the Torah. On the other hand he removed idols from the nations and obligated them in the seven commandments of Noah so that they would not behave like animals of the field, and instilled them firmly with moral traits . . . Christians are congregations that work for the sake of heaven who are destined to endure, whose intent is for the sake of heaven and whose reward will not be denied.'[2][19] Rabbi Samson Raphael Hirsch taught us that Christians 'have accepted the Jewish Bible of the Old Testament as a book of Divine revelation. They profess their belief in the G-d of Heaven and Earth as proclaimed in the Bible and they acknowledge the sovereignty of Divine Providence.'[3][20] Now that the Catholic Church has acknowledged the eternal Covenant between G-d and Israel, we Jews can acknowledge the ongoing constructive validity of Christianity **as our partner in world redemption, without any fear that this will be exploited for missionary purposes.** As stated by the Chief Rabbinate of Israel's Bilateral Commission with the Holy See under the leadership of Rabbi Shear Yashuv Cohen, 'We are no longer enemies, but unequivocal partners in articulating the essential moral values for the survival and welfare of humanity.'[4][21] **Neither of us can achieve G-d's mission in this world alone.**

4. Both Jews and Christians have a common covenantal mission to perfect the world under the sovereignty of the Almighty, so that all humanity will call on His name and abominations will be removed from the earth. We understand the hesitation of both sides to affirm this truth and we call on

---

[18] The note cues of the original statement are here preserved, and their content is incorporated in the notes below. Note 1 of the statement is: *Mishneh torah*, 'Laws of Kings', 11: 4 (uncensored edition); *Kuzari*, 4: 22.   [19] *Seder olam rabah*, 35–7; *Sefer hashimush*, 15–17.

[20] 'Principles of Education', *Talmudic Judaism and Society*, 225–7.

[21] Fourth meeting of the Bilateral Commission of the Chief Rabbinate of Israel and the Holy See's Commission for Religious Relations with Jewry, Grottaferrata, Italy (19 Oct. 2004).

our communities to overcome these fears in order to establish a relationship of trust and respect. Rabbi Hirsch also taught that the Talmud puts Christians 'with regard to the duties between man and man on exactly the same level as Jews. They have a claim to the benefit of all the duties not only of justice but also of active human brotherly love.' In the past relations between Christians and Jews were often seen through the adversarial relationship of Esau and Jacob, **yet Rabbi Naftali Zvi Berliner (Netziv) already understood at the end of the 19th century that Jews and Christians are destined by G-d to be loving partners: 'In the future when the children of Esau are moved by pure spirit to recognize the people of Israel and their virtues, then we will also be moved to recognize that Esau is our brother.'[5]**[22]

5. We Jews and Christians have more in common than what divides us: the ethical monotheism of Abraham; the relationship with the One Creator of Heaven and Earth, Who loves and cares for all of us; Jewish Sacred Scriptures; a belief in a binding tradition; and the values of life, family, compassionate righteousness, justice, inalienable freedom, universal love and ultimate world peace. Rabbi Moses Rivkis (Be'er Hagoleh) confirms this and wrote that 'the Sages made reference only to the idolator of their day who did not believe in the creation of the world, the Exodus, G-d's miraculous deeds and the divinely given law. In contrast, the people among whom we are scattered believe in all these essentials of religion.'[6][23]

6. Our partnership in no way minimizes the ongoing differences between the two communities and two religions. **We believe that G-d employs many messengers to reveal His truth, while we affirm the fundamental ethical obligations that all people have before G-d that Judaism has always taught through the universal Noahide covenant.**

7. In imitating G-d, Jews and Christians must offer models of service, unconditional love and holiness. We are all created in G-d's Holy Image, and Jews and Christians will remain dedicated to the Covenant by playing an active role together in redeeming the world.

A review of the **emphasized** sections shows what a strong influence Greenberg's ideas had on shaping the statement. To be sure, the text incorporates other influences; however, many of these are in the form of precedents

[22] Commentary on Gen. 33: 4.   [23] Gloss on *Shulḥan arukh*, 'Ḥoshen mishpat', 425: 5.

and sources that justify the contemporary position. Rather than articulate a theological stance towards Christianity, they provide justification for the present efforts. When this is taken into account, the constructive role of Greenberg's theology is seen in even clearer relief. Many of the points that are **emphasized** have already been noted in my discussion, but not all. It has not been possible to cover all the details of Greenberg's rich contribution on Christianity. The statement opens a window onto some additional ones.

The document is called 'To do the Will of Our Father in Heaven'. The reference to God's will in the framework of a revision of Jewish–Christian relations is repeated several times in Greenberg's writings.[24] It is worth noting, however, that his writings simply talk about the will of God. The phrase 'our Father in Heaven' is obviously a reference to the common person of God the Father as what binds Jews and Christians together.[25] While there is no discussion of the particulars of the Godhead, other than multiple mentions of Christian monotheism in section 5, the use of the phrase 'Father in Heaven' is clearly a contextual decision to choose the most appropriate designation for God in a Jewish document discussing Christianity.

Section 1 refers to mutual hostility and alienation. This point has drawn the ire of some readers, who feel that an equivalence has been created between Jews and Christians in terms of hostility, when in fact Jews, for the most part, have been on the receiving end of Christian hostility. One notes that Greenberg also refers to a reciprocity of hostility in his writings.[26]

Section 2 begins with a reference to the Shoah (Holocaust). One can readily understand that a statement on revised Christian teachings on Judaism would also take into account the history that led to *Nostra aetate* and the prominent place of the Holocaust in this history. Still, once one recognizes the centrality of Greenberg's theological contribution to the statement, one cannot ignore the fact that he started his career as a theologian reflecting long and hard on the Holocaust and that it is such reflection that eventually pushed him into the field of Jewish–Christian relations.[27] The statement follows a similar trajectory.

[24] *For the Sake of Heaven and Earth*, 98. See also Greenberg, 'Covenantal Pluralism', 135.

[25] On the figure of God the father between Christians and Jews, see Goshen-Gottstein, 'God the Father in Rabbinic Judaism and Christianity'.

[26] Or at least of implicit hostility: 'each faith at the other's throat' (*For the Sake of Heaven and Earth*, 101).

[27] On this, see his autobiographical essay, 'On the Road to a New Encounter between Judaism and Christianity', 4–9.

Section 3 mentions Maimonides. It is interesting to contrast this reference to Greenberg's discussion elsewhere, where he describes Maimonides
as suggesting that Christianity's success brings Judaism's end goals closer.[28]
Christians advance an outcome on which Judaism has staked its credibility
and truth. This is a very fair rendition of Maimonides' text in *Mishneh torah*.[29]
It omits his derogatory words on Christianity, while highlighting his views
of the beneficial long-term service rendered by it. The statement continues,
as if still citing Maimonides, that in separating Judaism and Christianity,
God willed a separation between partners with significant theological differences. None of this is actually stated by Maimonides. He only refers to
the thoughts of God, which remain hidden in relation to Jesus' teaching and
its subsequent harm to Jews. There is a significant distinction between this
affirmation and the claim that the Christian faith is God's will.

The same is certainly true of the following claim, that God willed a
separation between partners. This latter assertion is essential Greenberg
theology: the dual appeal to God's will—that Christianity should exist as
an independent faith and that it should form a partnership with Judaism
—is part of his God's-eye view. It is not, however, to be found in Maimonides. It is, rather, an extended reading of the Maimonidean passage that
pushes the text past its limits. Given the strong Greenbergian resonances
of this formulation, I imagine it originated with him and not another author
(in any event, Greenberg vetted the text and had the final say). Why then
the more radical formulation than what we find in Maimonides? I believe
the statement seeks to justify these moves to the Orthodox Jewish community by citing precedents and authorities. Indeed, it is fairly heavy on
such citations, much more so than Greenberg's own writings. It seems that
in an attempt to convince rabbis or Jewish readers, the statement pushes
Maimonides past what he says, recasting him in line with Greenberg's own
theology. While one can understand this attempt not only in terms of the
result it is meant to achieve but also in terms of how certain seed ideas of
Maimonides are extended through the higher principle of divine will, it is
ultimately not a felicitous move with respect to the potential for reception

---

[28] Greenberg, 'On the Road to a New Encounter between Judaism and Christianity', 99.

[29] 'Laws of Kings', 11: 4 in uncensored editions. According to Shapiro, 'Modern Orthodoxy and Religious Truth', 131, the difference between Greenberg and Maimonides lies in the
former's belief that there is an actual covenant with Christianity. I have suggested that
Greenberg's application of the concept of covenant does not depend on concluding one.

of this text. Indeed, it has been criticized for misrepresenting some of the sources it cites.[30]

Recognition and validation of the changes in Catholic teaching regarding Judaism is a foundation of Greenberg's writing on Christianity. He refers to it throughout and, as noted above, even analyses several Vatican documents in detail.

Putting aside the question of proper referencing, the description of Judaism and Christianity as partners goes to the heart of Greenberg's theology. The partnership is for the sake of the redemption of the world. Greenberg offers a trajectory of history moving from Creation, through redemptive covenantal work, to redemption. The multiple covenants, specifically Judaism and Christianity, move along the same axis. In speaking of a partnership for the sake of redemption, the statement thus echoes a fundamental insight of Greenberg's. Similarly, the claim that 'Neither of us can achieve G-d's mission in this world alone' is an important contribution of his. Not only does he assert that Christianity is God's will; he argues that there is a need for both these communities, because otherwise the work of redemption could not be carried out successfully. In other words, both communities need each other in order to achieve God's mission.

It is not superfluous to note the concern in Greenberg's writings about missionary activities carried out by Christians. Partnership should not be a cause for such activity. We watch him opening up to Christianity, all the while concerned that this openness not be misinterpreted by missionaries. In fact, his openness is conditioned on the Christian legitimation of Judaism and the renouncement of all attempts to proselytize.

Section 4 continues the same theological thrust in referring to a common covenantal mission to perfect the world. Where this statement moves beyond section 3 is in referring to the partnership between Jews and Christians as covenantal. Note, nowhere does it say that Jews and Christians have a covenant between them. This has never been suggested by Greenberg. Rather, the reference to the common covenantal mission to perfect the world draws upon his view of both traditions as expressions of a covenant. We cannot understand this statement except through the lens of Greenberg's theology. 'Covenantal' could be a way of describing partnership, as we are aware of Greenberg's understanding of the covenant in such terms.

---

[30] Berger, 'Vatican II at 50', claims, with reference to the citation from Maimonides, that 'there is something disingenuous about citing only half the position'.

It could also mean a specific covenant. If so, what specific covenant is
referred to: the Noahide, the Abrahamic, or the Sinaitic? The text could support any of the readings, and we find all of them in Greenberg's teachings.
Clearly, this is where a public statement, authored by a group and intended
for broad signature and dissemination, cannot develop ideas as specific as
those found in Greenberg's writings. Suffice it to say that there is a common covenantal mission. Most readers would not grasp the intention, which
must remain out of reach without its context in Greenberg's thought.

One of the texts cited in section 4 is the commentary of Rabbi Naftali
Tsevi Berlin (Netsiv) on Jacob and Esau. This very text and this very argument were used in Greenberg's own discussion, as we saw earlier.[31]

Section 6 is the most explicitly pluralist. It refers to God's many messengers. I have noted this motif in Greenberg's writings. Is Jesus one such
messenger? Likely. The point is never made explicit. One notes a tension
between revealing the truth by means of these messengers and the ethical
obligations taught by Judaism through the universal Noahide covenant.
Most readers will not notice that the Noahide commandments have been
replaced by the Noahide covenant. Readers of the present book will be
aware of how central the latter is for Greenberg, and how he has subsumed
in it the Noahide commandments.

What is the relation between the many messengers and the Jewish
teaching of fundamental ethical obligations? The two are tied together with
'while'. This is a very rich theological moment that affirms the validity of
Christianity while couching its value in a Jewish concept, that of the Noahide
commandments, here presented as a covenant. What do the messengers
teach? The same content as the Noahide covenant? Do they teach a different
kind of truth? Do they provide the theological superstructure for the universal Noahide covenant? Where does the heart of the argument lie—in the first
or the second statement? Might the notion of multiple messengers and the
appeal to truth serve the need of Christians to recognize themselves in this
statement? It seems that here the text duplicates a fundamental tension
found in Greenberg's work. One part of the sentence sounds a pluralist
note; the other an inclusivist one. Tying them together with 'while' does not
really resolve the theological tension. It remains unclear whether the text
is making the argument one way or the other. Perhaps the tension in this
passage is the result of different intended audiences. Christians must hear

[31] See above, Ch. 4 at n. 102.

the validation of their truth and messenger. Jews must validate Christianity through the category that has always served Jewish thinkers—the Noahide commandments. And thus, both arguments are presented alongside one another, mirroring some of the deeper and unresolved tensions in Greenberg's own theology.

The final section echoes some important notions found in Greenberg's work. It begins with the idea of the imitation of God.[32] Imitation offers a model. For whom? Again, we encounter a key Greenbergian notion. The vista opens up beyond Judaism and Christianity, effectively addressing the challenge of how to situate their relationship within the broader framework of world religions. The answer is that both religions, jointly, offer a model for others. The notion of God's image is another important idea introduced here, and one which Greenberg uses repeatedly. The range of influence expands beyond the two faiths to all others, all who share in the divine image. Whereas Judaism and Christianity are spoken of as partners in God's covenantal plan, others are called to follow their example by appeal to the idea of the image of God. All this is fully in keeping with Greenberg's views, or at the very least it provides a new iteration of key ideas found throughout his work.

After this broader application of the image of God principle, the concluding point returns once again to the covenant as the common domain of Jews and Christians. Reviewing the uses of 'covenant' in the statement, one may well argue that this is the climax of the document. It begins with the underlying reason for the changed attitude to Christianity: Christian affirmation of the enduring validity of the Jewish covenant with God, as repeated in points 2 and 3. The Jewish covenant thus provides the entry point into covenantal language, and its validity is twice repeated. In section 3 we have a reference to a covenantal mission, with the word in an adjectival form whose precise meaning remains vague. Section 6 introduces the Noahide covenant, suggesting that not only Jews but also Christians (among others) have a covenant. Section 7 seems to tie it all together by reference to 'the Covenant'. It seems that 'the Covenant' is larger than any of the particular covenants, and describes the fundamental mode of relating to God in assuming responsibility for perfecting the world, a mode shared by Jews and Christians. Reviewing the unfolding of references to the concept highlights how central

---

[32] On this see *For the Sake of Heaven and Earth*, 171, 210.

it is and how it provides the frame for delivering the theological message, in light of which not only is Christianity affirmed, but Jewish–Christian relations are redefined along covenantal lines.

It is hard to exaggerate the importance of Greenberg's theology to this statement. It is threaded on the lead string of the covenant. Judaism and Christianity are cast in partnership along the lines of his understanding. All statements as to the nature of Jewish–Christian relations, other than quotes from earlier sources, are rooted in his theology. Most of the sources introduced to align the statement with well-known Jewish views on Christianity come from another editorial hand and at times conflict with Greenberg's own core views.[33] Nevertheless, even some of the citations of earlier sources could be understood in line with how he has reread them.[34]

There is a dialectic here. In one way the statement serves as an important vehicle for disseminating Greenberg's ideas. But precisely because these do not necessarily communicate fully and effectively without a fuller appreciation of his theology, it may be that the statement falls short of transforming hearts and minds. Its close dependence on Greenberg's theology may be the source of its theological creativity but it may also draw the boundaries of Greenberg's reach. It is hard to imagine how a reader could grasp the full significance of this statement without prior knowledge of Greenberg's thought. Until his theology is more broadly accepted, the statement cannot do its work in full. And yet it is a marvellous instrument for making Greenberg's thoughts, categories, and formulations a household matter, at least in rabbinic households.

[33] See also the interview with Greenberg in Ch. 6.

[34] For Greenberg's creative reworking and building upon Maimonides' statement on Jesus and Christianity, see *For the Sake of Heaven and Earth*, 226–9.

CHAPTER SIX

Interview with Irving Greenberg

Introduction

ALON GOSHEN-GOTTSTEIN: Yitz, I'm grateful to you for making time for this interview. As you know, I am writing an extensive piece on your approach to other religions. It is part of a forthcoming book in which I discuss Jonathan Sacks and yourself and your views of other religions. The project actually is an outgrowth of the essay I wrote for the volume *A Torah Giant*,[1] celebrating your work. I was very moved when you wrote to me that my essay in that volume, discussing your views of Christianity, was the best piece that had ever been written on the subject. In fact, that emboldened me to request this interview, having now completed the entire manuscript on your work.

Reception of Greenberg's Jewish–Christian work

IRVING (YITZ) GREENBERG: The good news is that your treatment of my writing on Christianity is the best. The bad news is: that standard is set at a low bar. Very little has been written on the subject and most of it is polemical and of low level. Authors were not trying to understand what I was attempting to develop. That led to accusations of my being a closet Christian, whatever. Well, let me just say, in general, one of the regrettable truths about my career and my life is its reception in the community. The American Jewish community wasn't much into theology. And professionally, most of the work I did was programme administration and not theology. So the theology writing has been relatively neglected. And so I guess most of the time I was talking to myself.

I don't mean to take back my compliment. Your piece was written at a very high level and was very intellectually perceptive. Still there has been next to nothing substantial written about my Jewish theology of

[1] Goshen-Gottstein, 'Genius Theologian, Lonely Theologian'.

Christianity on the Jewish side. Even in the theology of the Holocaust, there was very little written of significance in relation to my work. Steve Katz wrote, I thought, the best serious essay after 'Voluntary Covenant',[2] which included a fairly substantial critique. And I thanked him. I've always felt that the capacity or the significance of the thinker has relatively little to do with the thinker's own work. It really all depends on the *talmidim* [students] and on what people make of it. So in a way I was quite sad that there was nobody doing serious work on it because I felt that meant that I'm talking to a wall.

AGG: In terms of evaluations, there have been several evaluations of your work. Mark Krell wrote about it.

IYG: That's true. I shouldn't allow myself too much self-pity. Yes, he wrote a good, intelligent book. But that's one book. When was that written?

AGG: In 2003. I was just looking at it.

IYG: So that means that for forty years no one paid attention—or if they did pay attention, they didn't address it seriously. I don't want to complain. I believed that this was an important issue. I worked at it, and stayed with it for six decades—with or without reception.

AGG: So you feel there's been no echo to your work in this field?

IYG: Very little. You tell me otherwise.

AGG: Well, I'll tell you because it's actually part of my project, which focuses on you and Sacks and your views of covenant and world religions. One part of my discussion of your thought is devoted to the question of reception. I've had the feeling that you are carrying a pessimistic burden in terms of the reception of your work. I picked that up in some of your writings. Yet I see various people who do echo your work, with or without referencing it. I hope this is of some comfort to you. I think Eugene Korn very much carries your way of thinking. I don't know if you're aware of that or not.

IYG: Yes. We are in regular contact and exchange.

AGG: Okay. Then there is the Orthodox Statement, which we'll get to later, and which is a way of carrying over your ideas.

[2] Greenberg, 'Voluntary Covenant'; and see S. T. Katz, 'Voluntary Covenant'.

IYG: Fair enough, but that statement appeared fifty-five years after I started.

AGG: One of your ideas is taking a God's-eye view of things, is that right? From a God's-eye view, forty years is nothing. If somebody even gets to the age . . . You're not even 90, what are you complaining about? So, you know, if you're seeing in your lifetime . . .

IYG: I'm not complaining, I'm just trying to be realistic about what effect my approach had—and didn't have. Let me speak from my perspective. I started in the Jewish–Christian dialogue in the 1960s. In the sixties, I was still semi-respectable in the RCA [Rabbinical Council of America] and the Orthodox establishment. As a matter of fact, when I was in graduate school in Boston, I was quite friendly with the Rav [Rabbi Joseph B. Soloveitchik]. After his 'Confrontation' essay was published in the late 1960s, the establishment set up this massive Jewish–Christian dialogue event. The Ford Foundation funded it. In order to get Soloveitchik's approval and for the Orthodox to come, they turned the programme over to him, meaning that he vetted the planned programme. And the truth is, in the name of not having theological dialogue he ripped the programme to shreds. All along, the RCA and the official leadership said his message in 'Confrontation' is that Jews and Christians can't have theological dialogue. So how come they agreed to this dialogue? They said, well, we'll make it all . . .

AGG: Practical, social.

IYG: On civic problems and social justice, etc. In doing so, they eviscerated the programme, removing a lot of the substance. Now, I was not invited through the RCA because their position was that theology discussion was *treif* [not kosher] and wrong. I was invited because the Christian planners knew of my work and valued it. At the last minute, the New York Times published a front-page story asserting that this dialogue is a turning point in Jewish–Christian relations. Well, of course, the religious Orthodox right went crazy. At the last minute, because of the publicity, the Rav repudiated the conference. He said, 'I'm not going to go.'

AGG: Oh, the article came out before the event, not after?

IYG: Just before the event. In response, he said: 'I'm not going.' The RCA then announced: 'We're not participating.'

My theory all along was that Rabbi Soloveitchik wanted to permit dialogue but he was intimidated by the opposition from the right. I argued that 'Confrontation' was a Marrano piece of writing.[3] To the right he said: 'I have forbidden (theological) dialogue.' To the public and the left he said: 'I have permitted (social justice) dialogue.'

Then [Rabbi Israel] Izzy Miller called me. He was the vice president of Yeshiva University and Soloveitchik's hands-on manager of the issue. Miller called me and said: 'You know, we're not going to the Boston conference.' I said, 'I'm sorry to hear that.' Miller: 'We don't think you should go either. I hear that you're going; you shouldn't go. You'll be violating the Rav's instructions. You're going against the community. If you go, you will be sorry. You're going to be held accountable.' I said to him: 'Izzy, look: (1) I'm not going by your RCA invitation and I still intend to go. I think theological dialogue is a valuable and important process. (2) Your excuse for backing out is that the Rav said it's *osur* [forbidden]. But you and I know damn well that he can't take pressure. If you had gotten out in front of him and said: "We're going and we intend to go, that's our decision", he would have backed you. Instead, you want to put him out there so he should take all the arrows— and he yielded. (That was the RCA showing cowardice all along, in every other area, when they confronted the haredim as well.) It's unfair, you're putting the guy up there to take arrows which he shouldn't have to, at his age anyway.' In the end, I went. What could they do to punish me? But that was the tone of the thing. And throughout the 1970s, and 1980s, and 1990s, when they got into official dialogues, they would never designate or use me, because from their point of view my theological dialogue was not respectable. It was not legitimate.

The Orthodox Statement

IYG: When you ask me how I judge my influence, the RCA exclusion and similar marginalization led me to this conclusion.

What happened with the Orthodox Rabbinic Statement? This came fifty years later, mind you. The answer is that I gave a talk on the

[3] Marrano is the term for Jews who secretly kept their Jewish identity after converting formally to Christianity. It designates a hidden opinion that is different from the one publicly stated.

relationship of Judaism and Christianity for a Catholic international conference sponsored by the Neocatechumenal Way, two years in a row. They brought many Orthodox rabbis in from all over the world. Following the second conference, Rabbi Josh Ahrens responded that we (Orthodox rabbis) who have positive attitudes toward Christianity should put out a statement. At that point I was overwhelmed with other obligations. I said that I can't do it. Ahrens said: 'If you want to issue such a declaration, I'd certainly be happy to draft a statement.' Then he asked Eugene Korn, who said he also would do it. The most important development, from my point of view, was that Eugene was working for Rabbi Shlomo Riskin's Center for Jewish–Christian Understanding and Cooperation at the time. He said, 'I think I can get Riskin to sign a statement.'

In order to make this statement acceptable to Riskin and rabbis like him, some of the more radical thoughts were not included. In addition, they brought in a lot of traditional sources to support the statement.

AGG: And those sources in many ways go against your logic. In fact, if you look at the depth of your thinking, and you look at the sources they cite, the sources, in a sense, downgrade the key messages.

IYG: I would accept your critique. Years before, I said about positive liberal Jewish religious approaches to Christianity, 'Basically, what they're saying is that Christianity is a great religion, because it's so Jewish. It's too bad it got spoiled by Christian elements, meaning Paul and Hellenistic elements, etc.' Over the years, I concluded that God was asking us to do something much more serious, which is work at a pluralism that takes the other religion seriously in its own terms, in its distinctive beliefs. This is what I've been trying to do ever since.

From my point of view, when they wrote the statement, I was happy to compromise and put anything that Riskin and the others wanted to put in there to give them cover. I felt this is the first time the opponents will not be able to dismiss the statement, saying it's only Greenberg. They'll have to deal with the fact that it's Riskin, who is a very much more established and respected figure in the official Orthodox community, and there will be other rabbis who sign. So, from my point of view, as I said, on the one hand, there was dilution and soft pedalling, but it was worth it. Of course, afterward David Berger, the official RCA expert on Christianity and dialogue, published a review of the statement saying that he detected my sinister influence. It's funny because, as I said, I did my best to be invisible. Still, I did have some influence on that statement. I'm not denying it.

To summarize, in terms of the Orthodox community, I felt that there was little following, very little impact, very little understanding. I regret this because I think the Orthodox can make a major contribution to the dialogue. The paradox being they *did*. I refer to two Orthodox people whom I was friendly with and who helped by making important contributions to the dialogue (certainly, they were an important part of keeping me satisfied emotionally during those years of isolation): Michael Wyschogrod and David Hartman. Both of them became important figures in Jewish–Christian theological dialogue.

Wyschogrod was in before me. He did his Ph.D. on Protestant theology, absolutely independently of me. He was there emotionally and intellectually for me. We could talk and he would make comments. You may have seen his review of 'Cloud of Smoke',[4] which is probably the most important or influential essay that I ever published. He is very critical.

But his was a good critique, meaning he took my views seriously. He understood what I was saying, and he disagreed. As against . . . well, before the RCA heresy trial, the Orthodox Union *Jewish Action* magazine published this article that said that I have accepted Christian claims, that I really believe Jesus is the messiah, claims which simply garbled what I said in order to delegitimate my views. So I think it's a fairly accurate description that, in terms of the official community, in terms of the mainstream, I was sidelined, not heard and not listened to.

AGG: So with fifty years' hindsight, how do you see it? Do you feel that things are better than they were fifty years ago?

IYG: Well, to the extent that there are some Orthodox rabbis who have evolved a positive attitude, yes.

AGG: Just saying positive attitude to Christianity or adopting your theology —which of the two?

[4] See Greenberg, 'Cloud of Smoke', and Wyschogrod, Review of Irving Greenberg, *Auschwitz: Beginning of a New Era?*

IYG: I'm not sure if anybody has adopted my theology, although you're right; people like Eugene Korn are practising parts of it. Furthermore, Rabbi Sirat and others who have signed the statement are very respectable people.[5] I'm not saying they took my ideas; rather, they developed a positive appreciation for Christianity and a much greater respect.

AGG: I'd like to distinguish between two notions. One is positive views of Christianity; the other is adopting positive views 'Greenberg-style'. You seem to be unhappy on both counts. In other words, you're unhappy with the fact that there was negativity before, and, all the more so, that your own position wasn't taken seriously. My question is, to what extent do we have people who are 'Greenberg', that is, who have embraced your views concerning Christianity?

IYG: I haven't done a survey. I don't know the extent of acceptance, but my approach is certainly not broadly affirmed in the Orthodox community.

AGG: But what about the Christians? You mentioned earlier that the Christians had invited you to this conference, not the Jews. Do you feel your ideas have been better received on the Christian side than on the Jewish side?

IYG: Yes and no. Certainly, they took me seriously: they invited me. They questioned me, they talked to me, they argued with me, they accepted some ideas. That's a much higher level of respect and of interest than not only being ignored but effectively being put in *ḥerem* [social exclusion].

AGG: Here's a little anecdote. For a project entitled *Interreligious Heroes* that I am editing, I recently received a contribution from the new patriarch of Jerusalem, Archbishop Pierbattista Pizzaballa. He's an Italian, very learned in Judaism. He wrote a piece on [Abraham Joshua] Heschel.[6] And in this piece on Heschel, he quotes you at length. In other words, you can see the penetration of your own thinking into contemporary Christian thinkers on Judaism.

[5] Rabbi René Sirat is former chief rabbi of France and former UNESCO Chair for Mutual Knowledge of Religions of the Book at the Institut Universitaire Européen Rachi in Troyes.
[6] Pizzaballa, 'Abraham Joshua Heschel'.

IYG: I do believe that it was *retson hashem*, God's will, that Christianity should develop out of Judaism, separate from it in order not to destroy it, and bring the Torah's covenant to the world. From my point of view, I really believe that. So it was a privilege, or an opportunity, to write that or to argue that, whether the Orthodox—or the Christians —would accept it or not. The other way I dealt with the lack of acceptance—all cowards do that—was to say, maybe I'm a little ahead of my time, so the next generation will accept my views. We'll just have to be patient. I would appreciate it if acceptance came in my lifetime, but I'm not counting on it.

I'll give you a good example of the reverse. On the haredi [ultra-Orthodox]–modern Orthodox front, the same thing happened: some gradual growth in understanding and acceptance. But here there was much more vigorous, much more active development. I had really mentally given up on influencing the modern Orthodox community because the establishment moving to the right successfully excluded my voice from the internal discussion—not just me personally, but my voice. *Tradition* did not run a review of any of my writings on Christianity, by my recollection. References to me were hostile. The *rashei yeshivah* [rabbinic leaders] of Yeshiva University tried very hard that the school should not invite me to speak and they got their way. Suddenly, I woke up in the 1990s to find that there was a serious community of followers. It started with my wife Blu, so I can't say it was totally new. But suddenly there was a whole group: Rabbi Avi Weiss started Yeshivat Chovevei Torah [YCT] to train open Orthodox rabbis,[7] and then Yeshivat Maharat to ordain women. These people were very, very much in tune with my ideas, which in many cases influenced them. As I said to Blu, it's like getting a second life. I sort of felt I was not going to have any serious following in the Orthodox community in my lifetime. I hoped that in the next generation I would—because I still believed that Orthodoxy had to go that way to be relevant to the Jewish people as a whole. Yet in the 1990s they showed up. I was delighted, of course. YCT to me was like a restoration. But that happened in the internal Orthodox community. An equivalent didn't happen in the Jewish–Christian dialogue, at least not yet. The Jewish–Christian issues

---

[7] For Rabbi Avi Weiss's concept of open Orthodoxy, see the Wikipedia entry 'Open Orthodoxy'.

are not as interesting for others. CLAL was an organization whose whole purpose was internal Jewish dialogue. They weren't against my interfaith work, but they weren't particularly interested. I never had a board meeting where they asked me to report what I'm doing with Jewish–Christian dialogue. Nor did they circulate my articles there like they would circulate my holiday booklets. Again, not that they were hostile, they just had other priorities.

AGG: So you're saying that even with YCT and their openness to you, even that only touched the Jewish–Christian thing marginally?

IYG: Correct. Because, in general, Christianity is a very marginal phenomenon in Orthodox lives.

AGG: I want to go back to just conclude the question of impact. One of the theses that I'm gradually coming to is that one of the channels of influence of Greenberg is actually Jonathan Sacks. Have you ever thought about that?

IYG: After he died, somebody said to me, you know that he was really influenced by you . . . I have to make a major confession. I did not read either my peers or my competitors to the extent that I should have. Unfortunately, I was not an academic. I had a tremendous load of administration and fundraising, not to mention teaching and other responsibilities. So, the truth is, I skimmed. Regarding Jonathan Sacks, I confess, I read some articles. I read some of his *divrei torah* [weekly Torah portion commentaries], but not most of his major works. I was not aware of influencing him—or not.

Daniel Goodman, a student at YCT, went on to write a Ph.D. thesis at JTS [Jewish Theological Seminary], and he's writing on Hartman, Sacks, and myself, in relation to Soloveitchik. Some years ago he came to me and said he was reading Sacks. To give this context, I myself had said to him orally that Sacks basically knew I was right, i.e. he recognized the legitimacy of my positions even if he didn't agree. But politically he made a decision not to defend my views publicly, not to include me in official Orthodox conversations—wanting to avoid criticism or pressure from the right. I deeply regret this. This decision [not to contest the delegitimization of the Orthodox left] really hurt modern Orthodoxy. In the end, the centrist Orthodox leadership lost the control of community policies to the right. Be that as it may, I said this to

Daniel, I tried not to take it personally. He made a political decision. He was the chief rabbi, with institutional considerations that I did not have. So I'm sorry, but that's the way the ball bounced . . . Goodman said to me: 'I'm reading his writings, and I think you're wrong. I think he really disagreed with you, much more than you acknowledged.'

I didn't read Sacks' work carefully. He had written much more specific critique or rejection of this idea or that idea of mine. But I hadn't read it, so I didn't know it. My esteem for him as a thinker was not determined by his attitude toward my views. Let me put it this way. This is what I liked about him: I felt, here's a person with a modern consciousness, reading what I consider to be a humane, affirmative, religious view of life into the tradition. I've been trying to do the same thing myself. How can I quarrel with him? So I felt, basically, this religious approach is something I'm in favour of. I'm positive about his writings overall, but I didn't read him enough to realize the extent of influence or to identify where he disagreed with me more.

AGG: One last thing regarding influence and impact. As part of my analysis, I took the Orthodox statement on Christianity and I underlined wherever I think the statement reflects Greenberg. Please look at the underlined sections of the Orthodox statement and consider them as Greenbergian motifs.

IYG: [after reviewing] Fair enough. I think it's fair to say that those elements, at least in part, are furthered by my participation. Correct.

AGG: And that also shows you where the other stuff is coming from, which is not Greenbergian. All the stuff from [Jacob] Emden and Be'er Hagolah,[8] one thing and another. That's all the non-Greenberg, which shows the committee work.[9]

IYG: They said, and honestly felt, that they needed to cover this public statement—and I said, well, be my guest.

---

[8] The *Be'er hagolah* is a seventeenth-century commentary on the *Shulḥan arukh*, the foundational code of Jewish law, composed by Rabbi Moses Rivkes. Greenberg is referring to the ruling of Rabbi Rivkes regarding the status of contemporary Christians not being idolaters. See *Be'er hagolah* on *Shulḥan arukh*, 'Oraḥ Ḥayim', 15b and 'Ḥoshen mishpat', 425.

[9] In other words, this is a positive view of Christianity but not one that grows out of Greenberg's theological work.

AGG: In terms of reception, of the possibility for reception, was it the overall openness, or is it specific theories that have been the problem? Put differently: for the sake of improved reception, is there anything that, with the hindsight of fifty years, you would redo or renounce in your thinking in order to make it more accessible and acceptable? If you had to say it all over, are there things that you wouldn't say now?

IYG: I think there were some things that were politically very damaging, no question. If I had known how they'd be used—there were things I said that lent themselves to be used to describe me as a closet Christian— I would have said them more carefully.

AGG: What I see from listening to you is that, in the best and nicest possible way, but also in a way that makes you pay a price, you're very naive. You know, we just celebrated Pesach. Someone said to me that every person has all four sons in him.[10] Usually one thinks of you as the *ḥakham*, the wise son, but in fact you're very much a *tam* [naive, simpleton]. In other words, you go back with great simplicity, naivete, sharing your truth, not always aware of how it's going to be received, and even your *ḥokhmah* [wisdom] you put out there with *temimut* [naivety]. I actually think that's a beautiful quality, but it's the quality that got you in trouble. Because the recording doesn't capture your head nod, let me put it in words.

You have not been calculating in your sharing, in relation to how the audience could receive it, by your own admission. With reference to Jewish–Christian reflections, is there *anywhere* where you think your writing was calculated to take into account, or was toned down in view of, audience considerations?

IYG: Not much, because I didn't think it was being read by the Orthodox community for the most part. You're right. I was naive. I took on more fights than I should have. Now I tell my students, pick your fights because you can't fight every issue, or you're going to lose. But I didn't act that way in relation to Jewish–Christian matters. This acknowledgement makes it sound like, *nebakh* [Yid. poor thing], I did not cover myself prudently. From my point of view, and I should have said that,

---

[10] A reflection based on a celebrated passage in the Passover Haggadah where four sons ask about the Exodus from Egypt; they are described respectively as wise, wicked, naive, and the one who does not know how to ask.

a big factor is that I was working at CLAL, which was a pluralist environment. And I felt I had a lot of support and a lot of respect and a lot of feedback, constructive feedback, from a whole range of people, including about 25 per cent of CLAL's supporters and activists, who were Orthodox. Otherwise, I don't think I could have stood up or been as outspoken. And the same holds true for the Jewish–Christian materials I felt I had a very serious response from the Christians and any Jew who was into this in a serious way.

AGG: So basically you became the Jewish theologian for the Christians.

IYG: The truth is that Jewish–Christian dialogue remained marginal throughout my life, even though I believe and participate in it very deeply.

AGG: Okay, but still, in the context of Jewish–Christian dialogue, what you're saying is that, in fact, you became the Jewish theologian for the Christians. Because the Jews weren't listening to you. Basically, your audience was more the Christians, which is really why you've got better reception there. And to a large extent, if I asked the question: Who is your audience for your Jewish–Christian work? then the answer is that your primary audience really is Christian and not Jewish.

IYG: It could be. However, let me enter one general demurral to your last words. I wrote from within the Jewish tradition. I believe that someday my view of Christianity and of God's use of this religion to bring the nations of the world to God and to work for *tikun olam* [repair of the world] will become the accepted view inside Judaism. Also, that my idea that Hashem [God] intended these two faiths to separate—but to work as partners not enemies—will be realized in history. In the short run, then, my views have achieved more currency among Christians. In the long run, I consider these writings to be Jewish theology which will be incorporated into the continuing Jewish covenantal tradition.

AGG: Now, this is an important recognition. So, in fact, this younger generation and the Orthodox Statement are ways of starting to move it more to the Jewish world. In fact, maybe that's what needs to happen. Maybe your reception is better with the Christians because obviously they're happy with a rabbi, especially one who's considered Orthodox, affirming them. And now it's time to see how some of these ideas can penetrate the Jewish world better. Well, maybe my book will make some small contribution towards at least asking some of these questions.

On Covenant and Jewish–Christian Relations

AGG: Michael Kogan develops this notion of opening the covenant.[11] And I'd like to ask whether that describes your views as well. I'm not sure it does. Do you feel comfortable saying that that was the time for opening the covenant and that Christianity was a form of opening the covenant? Or maybe 'opening' isn't the best way to describe your views?

IYG: That language is an interesting question. As I say, I think Christianity was meant to be, and *was*, a way of bringing some of the central ideas of the covenant to the non-Jews. That having been said, I didn't want to give it a monopoly. In other words, here I should turn the table and talk about you [AGG]. With all due respect to my work in the Jewish–Christian dialogue, you have to look at history here. I got into this field because of the Shoah. In my judgement, looking back now, the deeper issue for all of us was developing a positive attitude to other religions, not just Christianity; to talk in each other's presence in ways that respect the other—all the things you are trying to do. This is one of the main missions, because otherwise religions cancel each other out and they undercut each other's influence. All religions, including my own, grew up with self-validating attitudes that denigrated or undercut or misrepresented or stereotyped the other religions. And that backfired and was devastating to our credibility when we came out into the open society. Thanks to saturation with media—and geographic propinquity —suddenly everybody was seeing everybody else. And everybody's views were being seen first-hand, not just through inherited stereotypes. At that point, religious people lost a lot of credibility. One of the central challenges of this culture is: can you develop not just your religion, but also any value systems that are not, in the end, based on this internal–external or inner–other distinction for their credibility? This is a central issue and an ongoing challenge for all religions. To the extent that religions and religious value systems didn't open up, they really suffered loss of credibility in the whole society. That is why I consider your work (and the Elijah Institute), trying to engage many religions with each other, to be so important.

[11] See Kogan, *Opening the Covenant*.

AGG: Okay, I'm definitely committed. This is part of my life's work. But going back to the question of opening the covenant.

IYG: Your contribution is broader. I just didn't have time, energy, or the ability to pursue all the other religions. And it's one of the things I admired about your work. I thought that's an important issue for all religions, not just for Judaism.

AGG: Yes, this is my work. So now going back to opening the covenant, are you comfortable with that? Or would you prefer to describe your approach differently, or as distinct from his?

IYG: Well, in *The Jewish Way*, in the chapter on Shavuot as the *ḥag haberit*, the feast of the covenant, I said there, describing the covenant: it's an open covenant, meaning not just those who are there at the time, but it's open so people can come later and join.[12] So I'm using the word 'open' in a different sense than he [i.e. Kogan] is using it. But 'opening the covenant' is not an unreasonable language. But from my point of view, I would prefer to say it the other way. That Hashem brought at least some part of this *berit* to non-Jews through Christianity. Christianity is part of Judaism's contribution to the world, in my judgement.

AGG: So what that means, then, is not opening up our covenant. To give it full value, it's not opening our covenant, it's creating a separate covenant.

IYG: It's a fair point, except that it's so closely related, it seems to me; it's like you're talking to a cousin, you're not talking to a stranger.

AGG: I prefer to describe your work as expanding the covenant, because if you say 'opening the covenant', then they come into where we are. 'Expanding it' suggests it's going somewhere else, and in the process it becomes something else.

IYG: I like that.

AGG: That's why I'm not comfortable with the 'opening the covenant' metaphor, and I don't feel it's the best description of your work.

IYG: Like I said before, the thinker's influence is much greater if you have

---

[12] For Shavuot, see Lev. 23: 15–22. The biblical festival is commonly celebrated as the time of Israel receiving the Torah at Sinai. See Greenberg, *The Jewish Way*, 66.

important students. I mean, Plato made Socrates much more influential. I feel the same way here. In other words, from my point of view,
once the word of God is put out there, other people can take it, be
inseminated by it, even if it's not necessarily what I had in mind. But it's
there, and it's part of my contribution, even if I didn't want to say it
that way. I'd say, the same way here in general; I think it's one of the
paradoxes that justify the dialogue. I say, the truth is, who would take
Judaism seriously today? It's 14 million people; it's trivial; it's a rounding
error in the Chinese census. The reason they've taken us so seriously,
and they think we're an important religion, is because of Christianity.

It's very hard to admit that, because Christians abused us and
denigrated Judaism for millennia. Yet after the dialogue taught me the
strengths and contributions of Christianity, I was doubly appreciative of
that faith. For one, Christianity made Judaism important in people's
eyes—albeit often in negative ways. Secondly, the people that I've met in
the dialogue, they were really trying to stop the abuse and stop the history of the supersessionism. And really go to where we, I think, should
have gone in the first place—that is, to two parallel, closely related
covenantal communities trying to bring the world to God's kingdom.

AGG: Part of this question of expanding the covenant really touches a further
theological dimension. I refer here to the notion of revelation. I believe
you consider Christianity to be not only a covenant, but also a revelation. But what is the moment of revelation? Is it Jesus' coming and
Jesus' teaching? Is it Christianity coming to the world? Or, maybe, since
for you covenant is a structure, Christianity is a covenant, but not
necessarily a revelation. I've been trying to get my mind around this.

IYG: You're a better theologian than me. I haven't thought about that. The
truth is I have danced around the topic of revelation a lot . . .

AGG: Marc Shapiro, in the book that came out of the Oxford seminar,[13] argues
that you claim Christianity is a revelation. And I read that and I hummed
and hawed: does Greenberg say that or doesn't he? I really want to
know: what is it that Greenberg thinks, or thought, or will think?

IYG: First, you have to tell me what is revelation.

[13] Shapiro, 'Modern Orthodoxy and Religious Truth'.

AGG: Revelation is some way in which a divine message is sent into the world. It is an intentional, new or updated, way of God expressing a message that takes shape through a messenger and through a path and through a community. So one can look at it and say: this has been revealed to us in some way. So it's something parallel to what we consider to be the revelation at Sinai. Of course, Christians don't have a moment of revelation. For them Jesus himself is the revelation. But there's still a dimension of something new being revealed into the world, as opposed to claiming Christians are just behaving in a certain way and therefore fit our covenantal structure.

IYG: I have to think it through. I don't have a quick answer. But it seems to me there is a revelation here simply in the sense that . . . what's the Jewish revelation by God? That the material, physical dimension of existence does not exhaust reality. That there are whole major dimensions of existence that are not measurable and touchable, but are real and maybe more real. That's Judaism's revelation. So to the extent that Christianity brings that message to the rest of the world, it's a revelation.

AGG: But we're talking about an intentional act of God, rather than the retroactive consequences of the fact that people teach a certain thing. You're moving it to the teaching, as opposed to an event. Is there some event in Christianity that makes it a revelation, even if in different terms? Let us recall that revelation was part of the common stock of Jewish–Christian–Muslim conversations, and all shared in the notion of a revealed religion. So, within this covenantal structure, is there room to talk about Christianity as a revealed religion?

IYG: I have to think about it.

AGG: You said that you yourself danced around that question?

IYG: Well, for another reason, because I felt the more literal versions of revelation are very questionable, and very subject to refutation, particularly with Bible criticism and the strong evidence that revelation is not spoken at one time, in one place, in one voice. And so I'd like to fudge that topic a little bit. Because I don't really have a good sense of the precise meaning of revelation, I haven't thought it through. By revelation I think what we're claiming is that, in some way, we're in contact with this transcendent force, which is giving us a message. To that extent, that's the closest I've come to, because when you get any more specific than that, suddenly the questions arise: So God spoke literally? I don't think so, etc. Still, Judaism has been a medium through which the word of God has been brought to humans. Christianity also can legitimately make this claim.

AGG: So then how could Christianity *not* be a revelation, if the definition is so vague?

IYG: Well, I'm saying, if it's vague enough, you could say now that Christianity is revelation.

AGG: But that would then apply to all religions.

IYG: Right, Islam certainly claims to be revealed.

AGG: No, but they would claim to be revealed in the sense that you deny. The point is you have to affirm an alternative sense in which something of the transcendent comes through and shapes our life. So that's what you subscribe to. But then, why would we want to make Christianity or Islam part of the Abrahamic or even the Sinaitic covenant, even if they're close enough to us? If they *are* a distinct revelation, they don't need to be part of our revelation.

IYG: One of my main moves theologically is that I'm saying that, since Judaism makes historical claims, it sort of meets the test of refutability (i.e. it can succeed—or fail—in history). As I try to deal with that whole question, all religions—in order to be credible—truly should be subject to refutation. I'm saying, that is what *yahadut* said (i.e. the messianic denouement) and this is what the covenant is about. We're going to transform the world. Achieving that transformation of the world into a paradise—or not—that's the real test of our truth.

Of course, Steve Katz correctly called me out and said: in the meantime, world repair hasn't happened.[14] Yet Jews still believe in messianism. Right? So, he said, the religion is not really refutable because if its promises do not come true, they still believe in it. To which I say: the final *tikun* will happen in the future. So I'm saying that Judaism was not just teaching about God. It was putting its truth on the line to be validated (or refuted) by the actual development of human history.

[14] S. T. Katz, 'The Issue of Confirmation and Disconfirmation'.

As Torah-true Jews, we're not just giving you ideas, we're giving you a promise of a world that's going to change in certain ways. And we're staking our credibility, this will happen.

AGG: And this itself is a revelation, because Christians are picking up the idea and bringing it to the world; they are acting on it, transforming the world on it, right? So why does Christianity need to be part of the Sinai revelation? Why can it not have received the message and be working like Judaism? It's a parallel phenomenon. Why does it have to be part of our covenant?

IYG: I have no problem with that formulation, but it's not what happened in history. You have to deal with reality. It grew in Judaism, and a lot of these ideas could only make sense if you drew on their background in Judaism. And Christianity took a lot of Jewish ideas with it when it separated. Take its central teaching of resurrection and its message. It seems to me that the concept of resurrection is so deep in the Jewish tradition—including that it will occur universally in messianic time —that you can't ignore that the concept is taken over and made central in Christianity (even if Jews contest whether Jesus actually was resurrected and/or reject that he fulfilled the messianic promises/ prophecies of the Hebrew prophets.)

AGG: But in terms of our evaluation of it, isn't there a historical evaluation and a theological evaluation? Historically they may have grown from us, but our appreciation of their revelation can be independent of our appreciation of ours and therefore a parallel covenant rather than *part* of our covenant. You're collapsing the historical and the theological evaluation.

IYG: You're right, partly because the two interact to shape the faith: the revelation and witness are the product of the interaction of religion and history. And since both religions are trying for an historical outcome, the historical events play a part in the religious or theological claims and their persuasiveness.

I've written pretty much saying that I'm not sure whether to use the language of one covenant or two covenants in relating Judaism and Christianity. I have been back and forth on this question. I think that it's important; if you try to say that the two are part of one covenant, it's important to say that each covenantal community is independent. Each has value in its own right. Christianity is not just validated because it's proclaiming some good Jewish ideas out there. That's how I would put it. Let me add that part of my theology is, any religion that contributes to *tikun olam* or creates a *tselem elokim* by that fact has a claim to validity and truth.

AGG: Yes, but that's a Noahide covenant, not the Abrahamic or the Sinaitic. In your structure, Noah provides that.

IYG: Fair enough. I'm saying the Jewish is only a sub-covenant of the Noahide.

AGG: That the Jewish covenant is a sub-covenant of the Noahide, and there-fore each one is independent, that's fine. The problem begins when you want to make Christianity not only part of the Noahide, but also part of the Abrahamic or Sinaitic covenant.

IYG: Well, that's because of the history.

AGG: But in theory, if you distinguish the historical claims of the other and the theological valuation of yourself, then you can do away with the whole move. I actually think that it's much easier; also in terms of going back to the reception of your ideas, it'll be much easier for this idea to be accepted if it's independent. In other words, if Judaism as well as other religions are part of the Noahide covenant, and Christian-ity has validity as part of the Noahide, it's much easier to accept than to say that they are part of one people and they're part of not only the Abrahamic but also the Sinaitic covenant. In other words, you're giving so much to them that it will make it hard for the audience to receive and I don't know that you really need to do so.

IYG: You may be right. Allow me a side comment. I'm a self-trained theo-logian, and, as I've described, have had very little intelligent critique. It turns out, a whole area, like revelation, I haven't thought through care-fully. That's my weakness. So I'm happy to hear somebody, i.e. you, who can maybe help me think through these questions, or at least draw my attention to what I haven't thought through myself. On one or two covenants, I am answering hesitantly or laconically because I am still torn between the two approaches. I am attracted to the two-covenant theory because of the substantial differences and conflicts in theology

Interview with Irving Greenberg

and to protect the integrity of each faith. I am attracted to the one-covenant theory by the unique congruence of core message and vision —but am worried that the religion of the few will get 'drowned' in the sheer masses of Christianity.

AGG: So you're not only *tam* [naive], you're also an *anav* [humble person].

IYG: No, no. I'm not being an *anav* at all. My personal temperament—I consider this to be one of my better features—is that I don't dig in. I'm willing to listen. And people come and sometimes they'll argue, and I will respond, you're right. They'll say, you said this, but I think it's really A+C or D. And I'll think about it and conclude that they were right. In other words, I've never felt that I have to defend this initial formulation as the last word. In general, my feeling on all theology is that it's at best a partial and flawed and intrinsically distorted analysis, because it comes from inside me, and every individual carries a partial and inevitably 'distorted' picture of the whole world.

AGG: But that applies to everyone.

IYG: Correct. So I'm saying, given that fact, when I write something, I feel I'm not dug in. This piece is not *torah misinai* [revealed truth that is immutable]. I have changed my thinking many times. Not so much because I kept seeking, but because other people or actions or suggestions came that really convinced me there was more to the matter.

AGG: Let me be more extreme. I think you can make the whole argument for validating other religions without the notion of covenant at all. In fact, that's one of the theses I argue in my discussion. We just discussed Noahide versus Abrahamic and Sinaitic covenants. But I think we can just do without covenant altogether. If the key definition is *tikun olam*, plus *tselem elokim*, plus measurable contribution to the world, why do we need to complicate everything with covenant?

IYG: Because I think covenant is a key religious concept. Believing that God enters into covenant or partnership leads to a much more respectful attitude toward, and role for, the human partner and offers a much more balanced picture in relation to God. Otherwise, in history (and forget for a moment about the intrinsic theological issues), one discovers that God, for much of history, and for most people, is approached in an infantilizing manner: God is going to save me; God's going to perfect the world; God is going to do the magic for me. Probably the majority of religious people are very much on that wavelength. The other widespread alternative is that God is so amazing and so unbelievable that I'm a *gornisht*, I'm a nothing, everyone else is a nothing. The other positive dimension about partnership is that it captures the strength of God's connection, meaning, you know, *imo anokhi betsarah* ['I am with him in suffering', Ps. 91: 15]; *gam ki elekh begei tsalmavet* ['though I walk in the valley of the shadow of death [you are with me]', Ps. 23: 4], *lulei toratekha sha'ashu'ai* ['were it not for your Torah being my delight [I would have been lost in my neediness]', Ps. 119: 92]. Covenant gives you all these good advantages and it takes away the negative of infantilizing.

AGG: Can't you say partnership without saying covenant? Because by saying covenant, you're drawing on a set of biblical associations. And, in fact, you're using the term differently than the Bible uses it, which means you're creating a problem between your usage and biblical usage, and therefore further issues in the acceptability. Why not say partnership without covenant?

IYG: I've never thought of that, partly because I translate covenant as partnership. Now, you say it's not what the Tanakh [Hebrew Bible] means. But my articulation is clearly the expansion of the usage in the Torah. The spectrum of meaning of the word 'covenant' includes this extended version of what is partnership. From my point of view, I grew up with that language of covenant. It shaped my thinking. And so it was a natural thing to expand the concept while keeping it.

AGG: That's understandable. But one of the things that I struggle with is that you could have said all of this without using the word 'covenant' once. In fact, I would want to put to you that now in the new book,[15] there are several formulations that I found in there that describe how religions operate. And you give all the elements without the use of the word 'covenant', which to me is very nice proof. He can say it without covenant. All the elements are there: partnership, *tselem elokim*, *tikun olam*, it's all in there without covenant.

IYG: Well, except that the covenant is a big part of the book, including the

---

[15] Greenberg, *Triumph of Life*.

thesis that humans mature in the covenant. And that comes back to humans in the image of God. In other words, this covenant method enabled people to grow into full *tselem elokim*, as against just taking orders from a divine ruler. Obedience is not to be trivialized, but in many cases simple obedience leads to a level of less than full responsibility. And also, the point is that because of the partnership, you really grow into the *tselem elokim*, you're really equal. I have this citation of the Rav [Soloveitchik] which I always love to use. He has, in *Lonely Man of Faith*, concerning partnership, a description of how the partner feels, and he mentions three things. (1) Full recognition of the rights of the other; (2) mutual responsibility; and (3) equality.[16] And he was so nervous about that last word that he put quotation marks around equality. But to me that's exactly the point. If a *tselem elokim* is equal, it's because God has given them a mechanism [i.e. covenant] that doesn't make them feel unequal, even though they are unequal. Here's an infinite power, and he is a finite person. But in the covenant at least they are made equal.

Sources of Greenberg's Thought

AGG: So covenant as partnership goes back to the Rav? I wasn't aware of that.

IYG: I would say he's the first person who taught the idea to me in meaningful ways. The first important source other than the Tanakh [Bible]. I studied Tanakh with my father, who was a big *talmid ḥakham* [scholar] and he gave over this idea as important. Those ideas of covenant are certainly in the Tanakh. Then the Rav articulated this concept, and many other facts that I knew, into rich theological concepts. I mentioned this impact of the Rav in *The Jewish Way*. That was his single major contribution to my personal development. I knew a lot of these facts of Judaism and it never occurred to . . .

AGG: That covenant is partnership?

IYG: No, that there are patterns. They are not just behaviours; they're patterns, they're meanings. There are patterns of meaning there, worldviews. They're not just behaviours.

---

[16] Soloveitchik, *The Lonely Man of Faith*.

AGG: What is 'they'? The mitzvot [commandments]?

IYG: The mitzvot—all of the *halakhot* [laws]—are part of the system and they have a shape, or a world-view shape, to them. It blew my mind. I never thought about it because I knew a lot of these individual ideas. But they were atomistic, albeit positive, ideas. They weren't part of a systematic conception of an attitude to life. So I would say he's probably the first person who talked particularly about covenant, although he didn't teach it as a separate topic. He taught it in his *shiurim* [classes, talks] or in his classes on the *parashat hashavua* [weekly Torah portion].

AGG: It was in his *shiurim*? I wasn't aware of that. Has this come out?

IYG: The truth is, most of his halakhic *shiurim* are just pure halakhah. It's like two separate worlds.

AGG: But you're saying in *parashat hashavua shiurim* he brought it in.

IYG: He did. You know, in Boston, he did classes on the *parashat hashavua* every Saturday night. Plus other times when he would give [a talk on] just the *parashah* or some equivalent texts from Torah or from Tanakh. So those were very influential on me. Because again, as I said, I had never seen these ideas articulated. (Incidentally, many of these ideas have been published in the Toras HoRav Foundation series, edited by Wolowelsky, Helfgott, etc.[17])

   I was very lucky. I became the rabbi of the Young Israel [synagogue] of Brookline. His sister Ann Gerber was a member; we became very close. She was like a second mother to me. And it was a tremendous break. She brought me into his house. And he was willing and gave me really a lot of personal time and conversation about these issues.

AGG: So your whole covenantal thinking draws from the centrality of covenant to his ongoing teaching?

IYG: It certainly planted a seed, and it didn't stop. My thinking has changed over fifty years. For then I met David Hartman—I give him a lot of credit. First of all, he was on to covenant also, very much thinking about it. Secondly, I didn't spend so much time and I didn't really read them as much as I should have, but I heard (that was good enough for

---

[17] See the torashorav.org website.

me) that a group of Reform rabbis, particularly [Eugene] Borowitz, were interested in covenant. As I said, this is one of my strengths, to recognize patterns. If I read a little bit more, and heard a little more in the conversation, in the end, I could figure out mentally: if he said this or this, that's a B, then he must be implying F, G, and Q. And so each of those experiences deepened my understanding of the covenant.

AGG: So here are the possible sources of covenantal thinking. First of all, the Rav . . .

IYG: I think the main sources are the Tanakh and Talmud. So I still think that it started as a child by studying these texts with my father. That would be the first step. Then a second step into a more articulate notion of covenant as a concept would be the Rav. I would give him the initial credit.

AGG: And the relevant material in the Rav's teachings is *torah shebe'al peh* [oral teachings], stuff that we can't read. In other words, beyond what there is in *Kol dodi dofek* and *Ish ha'emunah*,[18] there is a world of covenantal thinking that you were exposed to through your teaching career.

IYG: Correct.

AGG: Wow, this is major, this is a very significant piece of information for me. And its main characteristic, you're saying . . .

IYG: The main characteristic is the Rav's version, which is that it's a community. In other words, you and God, or you and your partner with God, it's a covenantal community.

AGG: You and God make a community together, you mean?

IYG: That's what the covenant is—you enter into community with the partner.

AGG: Okay, you enter into community with God. Not that the community makes the covenant with God, but you make the community with God.

IYG: Correct. God is a member.

---

[18] See Soloveitchik, *Kol Dodi Dofek*, and id., *The Lonely Man of Faith*.

AGG: So, the main thing was community. What other characteristics of covenant can you relate back to the Rav?

IYG: It's hard to remember who I relate what to. The whole idea of a dynamic relationship. It's not just talking to each other, it's a relationship. The fact that halakhah or all the mitzvot are really covenantal behaviours. When the Rav communicated to Herschel Schachter [head of the yeshiva at Yeshiva University and an opponent of Greenberg], he said this is a legal system, and it's purely objective. And there's a whole side of him that says that. But what he communicated to me—there was a whole side of him there—was that, on the contrary, these are behaviours not purely based on legal precedent, or legal thinking, but they expressed the dynamics of the relationship.

AGG: Amazing. So here are the possible sources of covenantal thinking. The Rav, Hartman's influence, Borowitz, and then, finally, Paul van Buren.[19] Can you make any order in all these?

IYG: Paul van Buren came really much later. By then most of the ideas were formulated. That's number one. Number two, let me come back to an even earlier influence. One other Christian influence—not so much on covenant, but in taking Christianity seriously as a religion—is Niebuhr. In college, I was first exposed to all these religious challenges—history, change, conflicts of science and religion, philosophy. I never took any such courses before. When I took them, they posed questions that were really shocking. I was looking for some help. How do you deal with these questions? And the truth is that most of the modern Orthodox theology books were on the primitive, apologetical level. So I couldn't get a satisfactory answer there. Somehow, someone called my attention to the neo-Protestants.

AGG: Which Niebuhr?

IYG: Reinhold. I came across Reinhold in the college years. He (and other neo-Orthodox Protestants that I came across) was tremendously helpful, both in terms of how you could still believe in Scripture seriously, though not literally, and, of course, [in terms of] the tension between ideals and realities, which is a very central part of my thinking. You're

---

[19] Paul van Buren (1924–88) was a Protestant theologian who developed a Christian theology of Judaism, affirming its covenant.

trying to realize ideals in the real world and the conflict between them. I don't recall anymore how much Niebuhr talks about covenant but I certainly recall his treatment of reconciling ideas/ideals and reality. Certainly, I think, in terms of conceptual religious understanding, he made a very important contribution to me at a critical moment in my religious development.

AGG: And how central was Borowitz? It sounds like you weren't deeply immersed in Borowitz, but only in passing.

IYG: Correct. The fact that he was working in this area gave me hope that this is a good area to work in, so to speak. I would say that was his main contribution to me.

AGG: I was trying to figure out to what extent you're indebted to Borowitz. So instead of spending too much time reading about it, I have your testimony that, in fact, it's more moral support than actual substantive influence.

IYG: I read a little bit, but not much. Borowitz said: here's an idea that can guide behaviour. By the way, that was one of the things in which I was very disappointed in Borowitz. He did not translate covenant into observance. In other words, Jakob Petuchowski had much more influence on me personally, because he was a *talmid ḥakham* [talmudic scholar].[20] And we talked about halakhah. I remember a transforming conversation, back in the 1960s. The first year together in Canada (we brought Orthodox, Conservative, and Reform rabbis together for a week of study and conversation), Jakob and I went for a long walk. We got into a conversation about *gitin* [the process of Jewish ritual divorce and some of the contemporary moral challenges it engenders]. To me that was transformative. The whole idea of how halakhah develops, that it can have flaws, that it can be corrected, should be corrected. I felt that was a very positive influence. And I give Petuchowski a lot of credit for showing me a model that you could do this. Gene Borowitz was not that active in our group meetings in Canada. He came once, while Petuchowski came just about every year. So, with Gene, when we did meet and talk, it was a good experience and a positive influence

---

[20] Jakob Petuchowski (1925–91) was a scholar of rabbinics and Jewish liturgy at the Reform Hebrew Union College in Cincinnati.

for pluralism. But again, I was very disappointed that he did not translate his thinking into any notion of observance.

To me it's critical that all the mitzvot should be seen as covenantal
actions. In other words, actions and life behaviours that are reshaped
to maximize the choice of life and / or minimize the elements of death
or reduction of life quality in them. The mitzvot are also responses to
historical events and guides to behaviour and policies that advance
tikun olam.

AGG: So of all covenantal thinkers, the most important was Soloveitchik,
who profiled relationship, the grounding of mitzvot in a pattern that's
covenantal and that's dynamic, and which empowers the human person in responsibility. That was your key takeaway from Soloveitchik.
And that crafted your notion of covenant, which then you went ahead
and extended in the Jewish–Christian context. Is this a correct summary?

IYG: Fair enough.

AGG: This is so important for me to understand. Because I've been racking
my brains around this whole centrality of covenant: He doesn't need
covenant. Where on earth did he get covenant from? Why is he talking
about it so much? Where are his building blocks coming from? I'm
struggling with the extent to which I need to go historical on this or just
to go look at the whole thing synoptically. I find this very interesting
and very helpful. Let me ask you something else. What about the
notion of *tikun* [repair]? Do you get this primarily from Fackenheim or
also from other sources?[21]

IYG: As for my stress on *tikun olam*, I think I got it mainly from a reaction to
the Shoah. That's what I think. In my new book I stress that while
Judaism is a utopian vision of creating a paradise on earth, the concrete,
practical, gradualist method of covenant saves it from runaway ideological utopianism. In my judgement, covenant is the Jewish method of
tikun olam. This method saved Judaism from turning its utopianism into
oppressive, anti-human behaviours. In most of the great redemptive
movements of the past two centuries, the means / methods defeated
the ends. I believe that covenant is a pedagogical device—designed to

[21] See Fackenheim, *To Mend the World*.

correspond to the then state of human consciousness and culture—whereby God educates humanity and nurtures it to full maturation. The Jewish covenant is renewed/reconceptualized in a major way three times—each time the partners' roles are reshaped as to each one's authority and activity, which also transforms (that is, upgrades) the quality of the relationship. The biblical concept is foundational and eternal but the covenant morphs substantially in the course of Jewish history.

AGG: But why does *tikun* specifically emerge as a reaction to the Shoah? It seems someone had articulated the idea and you picked it up.

IYG: The answer is: you're immersed in death and destruction and suffering, and all that sort of stuff. And at some point, and it may be in part defensively—because a lot of the criticism of Emil [Fackenheim] was that his religion is all about destruction and death, whereas my Jewish life was all about daily living—I lived at the other extreme. Ninety per cent of my observant life had nothing to do with the Shoah, so I didn't feel I was totally focused by religion on death, to not give Hitler a posthumous victory. I thought those statements of Fackenheim were extraordinary, but I didn't feel that they expressed *my* feelings about what this religion is about. But I was convicted as being one of the theologians of the Holocaust who are teaching that Judaism is all focused on death and suffering. So it was partly a defensive reaction to that. It's partly my own life, my own family. My wife was much more upbeat, much more affirming.

AGG: Well, you have to get the notion from somewhere. Where do you take it from? Look, today it has currency. In the 1960s it didn't have currency. So where do you get it from?

IYG: I said, it was partly a reaction to the Holocaust, partly it's there.

AGG: That's what it serves. But it doesn't say where you're taking it from.

IYG: The messianic stuff is all in the Tanakh.

AGG: But not the language of *tikun*. The language of *tikun* is kabbalistic. Greenberg is not a kabbalist. Where does Greenberg get the language of *tikun* to apply it to his definition of what ultimately Judaism was all about?

IYG: That's a fair point, you're right. I'm not a kabbalist. Maybe it's *Zeitgeist*; I'm not sure.

AGG: What is the likelihood of your having picked it up from Fackenheim?

IYG: It's hard to say.

AGG: When did you start talking about *tikun*?

IYG: I think probably more in the 1980s. If you review my thought in stages, for the first ten, fifteen, or twenty years, I was really paralysed between Shoah and Israel, or between, you know, destruction and renewal. 'Voluntary Covenant' was written in 1982–3. That means, starting in the eighties, I began to think much more of moving forward. So I'd say around that time is when I started talking about *tikun*. Now, in the nineties and 2000s, when *tikun olam* became sort of a slogan, my line was, yes, it's a slogan, and it's a good contemporary liberal viewpoint. But I prefer to say: this is a contemporary reformulation of messianism. Of course, messianism goes back a long way. I always had a very strong messianic dimension. At the beginning of my thinking on the Shoah, my reaction was that the only thing that could restore some religious balance would be to match the destruction of this magnitude with some messianic breakthrough counterweight. It wouldn't be enough just to make a better world. You'd have to really have improvement of a messianic scope.

AGG: I'm really even more curious about where you get *tikun* from. I think Fackenheim put *To Mend the World* out before the 1980s.

IYG: Yes, he did.

AGG: So, in all likelihood, you probably picked it up from him, but gave it, maybe, a different depth.

IYG: Possibly. Emil Fackenheim was a world-class philosopher whom I came to love for his passionate Jewish heart and *neshamah* [soul]. In critiquing modernity and liberating Judaism and Jewry from its dominance, he inspired and influenced my thinking greatly. When it came to the Shoah and responses to it as well as revelation in historical events, most of the influence went the other way (from me to him).

AGG: What about *tsimtsum*? Another kabbalistic idea that you use much. Where do you get it from?

IYG: Well, because I've tried to . . . as I shifted to a conscious notion of changing roles in the covenant with God, I had to come up with some explanation. How did that happen?

AGG: What do you mean, changing roles? Within the history of covenant?

IYG: Yes. *Tsimtsum* was the only language I saw around me. And I didn't read much. But again, I can recognize patterns. And so the idea of *tikun* hit me immediately—and later, the idea of *tsimtsum*.

AGG: In other words, with the exception of covenant, which seems to have been deeply ingrained from home plus Soloveitchik plus conversations with Hartman, plus some impact from Borowitz, the other ideas were in the air, you found them useful, you picked them up, you ran with them, you crafted them.

IYG: You're talking about *tikun*?

AGG: I'm talking about *tikun, tsimtsum*. And, to a certain degree, the centrality of being in the image of God [*tselem elokim*]. In other words, these ideas are all out there.

IYG: The image of God—that goes back to the 1960s. And the truth is, it goes back to the 1950s or earlier, including the impact of the *musarniks*[22] on me—even if they didn't use the specific formulation of the words *tselem elokim*. Although it's based on the Mishnah,[23] I really felt that it was a personal ḥidush [innovation] to claim that it's right there in the Mishnah—the infinite value, quality, and uniqueness of the human person.

AGG: So covenant and *tselem elokim* emerged during the same period. *Tikun* and *tsimtsum* came up later. And both of them came up because they were in the air? Not a source, nor a school. They were in the air, you picked them up. You're not even sure where you picked them up from—you used them. They spoke to you.

IYG: Correct, I did not have a teacher who specifically developed these teachings.

[22] See p. 128 n. 128 above.
[23] Greenberg is referring to Mishnah *San.* 4: 5, where the value of the human person is expounded.

AGG: Returning to *tikun olam*, you were saying that you reclaimed it as messianism in the 1990s, when it became more current. You're saying that when people started to talk *tikun olam*, you affirmed its messianic value more, as opposed to just social action. And where is this spelled out?

IYG: I didn't publish that much in the nineties. It's in the new book. It's probably also in *Living in the Image of God*, which is this set of conversations with Shalom Friedman. So again, the front piece is a story about the messiah. It's a joke—the punchline of which is that waiting for the messiah may not pay much but it's a steady job.

AGG: Are there other building blocks in your thinking that I'm missing?

IYG: By the way, Hartman and I, after he went to Israel, had many wonderful conversations and disagreements. Because all the messianism in Israel, you know, involves out-of-control people like Gush Emunim.[24] So he came to the conclusion that you have to repudiate messianism because it's poison. And I would come and talk to him. And he'd say: 'You're messianist because for an American it has no consequences. It sounds like a noble idea, but I'm telling you, in the real world it's poison.' So we went through this for years and years, and I wouldn't budge. The only concession I made was to refer to *covenantal* messianism, which is messianism with limits, a messianism that understands that humans must be responsible—not act recklessly as if the end of days is coming and God and / or a messianic redeemer will cover all our excesses.

AGG: Are there any ideas as part of your toolkit, theological toolkit, that you've discovered in Orthodoxy, as opposed to picking them up in the air, and which you're introducing to the conversation? Because one of the things that I was struck by is: Well, he's using the terms that everybody's using. Can't he bring in something original? For example, *imo anokhi betsarah* ['I am with him in suffering', Ps. 91: 15] I don't think other people are pushing that and you've pushed that. I think that's a simple idea of yours, maybe growing out of your work in the Holocaust, which I don't see other people pushing as much.

IYG: Well, the combination of divine *tsimtsum* and coming closer, which I stress, has eluded many people. Readers had a lot of trouble grasping

---

[24] A right-wing settler movement with messianic overtones.

this combination when it first appeared in 'Voluntary Covenant'. Most people categorized *tsimtsum* as a form of *hester panim* [divine conceal-ment]. It's not. *Hester panim* says that God is not visible because the Lord is distancing from humanity, whereas I use *tsimtsum* to describe God making God's self less visible (and toning down the visibility and intensity of divine energy) in order to come closer. God is voluntarily self-limiting to call humans to a higher level of activity. Hashem is enabling rather than withdrawing or hiding to punish us for our fail-ures, or humanity for its bad behaviour.

AGG: There's a hasidic parable about the father who stops supporting the lit-tle child so he can learn to walk on his own. In a sense, he removes the support, but it's all about helping the child advance.

IYG: People missed that. I'm saying, even as God is giving up control, God is coming closer and sharing human fate more intensely. The divine influ-ence, therefore, in many ways is even greater after the *tsimtsum*. It's like the difference between humans responding because they are taking orders, as against being deeply related and acting willingly the way they feel that God is asking them to act. People do the mitzvah not because it is an order, but because they feel they want to live up to God's expec-tations out of the depth of the relationship. Like I always felt I wanted to imitate the *musarniks*, or I wanted to imitate my father. These emo-tional bonds are very powerful forces, much more powerful than if somebody gave me an order. In my interpretation I play down God's commanding voice (and/or rewards and punishments). Instead, I focus on love of God and love of the good as the driving forces for religious behaviour.

On Theological Method

AGG: Kogan points out that there's a tension in your thinking, and I've noticed this as well.[25] There's a tension between, on the one hand, try-ing to accommodate Christians and accept them on their own terms, and then, on the other hand, seeing them from a Jewish perspective and even affirming the superiority of the Jewish side. And there's an inter-esting tension between accommodation and affirmation of the Jewish side. Do you recognize this as an issue in your thinking?

[25] See above, p. 134 n. 6.

IYG: It really has to do with how you understand pluralism. I've said all along pluralism doesn't mean that you don't make judgements. In fact, pluralism doesn't mean you give up the idea of absolute principles or rules. Pluralism is an absolute 'ism' that knows its own limitations. So you admit either you don't have the whole truth, even though what you have you believe is the real truth, or you admit that your faith doesn't cover everybody or was not meant to cover everybody. When you affirm a religion, you're affirming it *on balance*. You're not affirming everything about it. You're affirming on balance. This leaves room, in my judgement, for specific disagreements with the other, or for being able to say: I think Judaism is superior on this and I think Christianity is superior on this. So I don't feel it's a contradiction in my thinking. In fact, what I argue in one of the articles that I've published since then is that that's the point of a partnership between our two faiths. These are both religions, but they're so close that frequently they're acting out two pieces of one dialectic. For example: the collective, biologically born into the community [Judaism], and the individualist, spiritual member of the community [Christianity]. These single positions are polar versions of what's really a dialectical situation. I think, in the Torah and in the healthiest parts of the tradition, there is a holding together of dialectical positions already.

So this is the point of partnership. Since you can't dance at all weddings, you can't have a strong individualist focus without neglecting somewhat the collective and vice versa. So each religion should focus a little more on its best speciality, but, and this is where the partnership comes in, check with each other and look back and see where I went too far here, and where we can balance better internally. So, at the end, the two religions won't come out in the same place, but they'll come out with a balance on these dialectical positions (obedience versus autonomy, individual versus collective, universal versus particular, etc.).

I've often critiqued that Christianity is too self-effacing and too demanding, over-focused on Crucifixion. I have suggested that its ethic should be more affirmative, more accepting of normal self-expression and self-interest. Then I had this experience in Sri Lanka, where this Christian community came out of Norway. The head of the community had been the leading television anchor in Norway. He decided to give up fame and fortune because he wanted to follow Jesus. He and his followers went off to the backwoods of Colombo, Sri Lanka, in order to take care of brain-damaged children. And there is no patient less responsive. Nothing could be more time-consuming than giving care to brain-damaged children, and in return for very little appreciation. I was extraordinarily moved by the community's behaviour and self-sacrifice. Then I realized that they were acting this way because they have this Christian tradition of taking up the cross. In other words, all the Christian virtues that I had critiqued were the source of this amazing reality. So again, Judaism could be strengthened by exposure to the dialectic of commitment even as Christianity could and should rebalance toward greater legitimacy for self-expression and self-fulfilment. So I feel that there's room for criticism from both sides toward the other. In other words, Jews, even religious Jews, don't necessarily demand the level of sacrifice that Christians demand. That is both a strength and a weakness.

AGG: Friendship. You recount the centrality of meeting the Eckardts and then other people as the key to your transformation.[26] Now I want to ask a follow-up question. I have a sense, which is perfectly understandable, that when you met the Eckardts, these were strong friendships. I think the same holds true for Paul van Buren.

IYG: Correct. But van Buren came later. And I have to add the personal side of that. It wasn't just the friendship with the Eckardts. I was just extremely moved by their model. I saw them expressing a prophetic strength, a self-critique of Christianity. And I didn't see leaders in my tradition, or my people, showing anything like that level of intense repentance—all the more impressive in that their response was driven by the Shoah. So it wasn't just the friendship; it was that they took a white hot, passionate, prophetic position vis-à-vis their own religion because of their response to the Shoah. That was very moving to me.

AGG: Now these formative friendships occurred in the 1970s. But my sense is that, probably for a significant period of time, maybe even decades, even though you've been active in the field, you haven't maintained the same kind of generative, commanding, transformative friendships. That's my impression. Is that correct or not?

[26] See above, p. 24.

IYG: That's probably correct. I stayed with those friends, but I didn't keep making new friends.

AGG: And the reason for that is circumstance or personality?

IYG: Mostly circumstance, but I don't know. I neglected my social life in general, because of the various career demands.

AGG: Well, I'll tell you one thing about myself. There are many differences between us. One of them is that you're a very successful fundraiser. And I'm a very failed fundraiser. My wife Therese says that though I'm not a fundraiser, I'm a friend-raiser. What happens is that when I go fundraising, I make new friends. So I'm constantly making new friends. And I have just come to accept the fact that my work is very often an opportunity to grow a network of friends, and some of them are deep, significant new friends. Recently, I'm delighted that I made my first really meaningful Bahai friendship that is totally mind-opening. And I always say: is this the end? No. Now there's new Mormon friends on the horizon. So new groups and new friends. I think, for me, that's a source of my staying interreligiously young. Reading your new book (and this is going to sound like a criticism, quite possibly, because it is, so I apologize for putting it that way), I get the feeling that what you have been writing recently about other religions, to put it positively, takes the lessons you've learned from Jewish–Christian relations, and tries to export them to other arenas. But it doesn't grow from the same depth of engagement that you had with Christianity. And consequently, it just lacks the depth of solidarity, appreciation, capacity to see and interpret. When I read your descriptions of Hinduism and Buddhism and Shia Islam and Eastern Orthodoxy, it sounds like a Jew talking about other religions, not like Greenberg, who makes a new path through personal relationships.

IYG: That's very possible, but again, I don't remember that I wrote much on other religions in the new book. I thought I had written very little.

AGG: There's enough in there. I combed the book looking for references to other religions. It's not major, but what strikes me is that the new material is more expansive in the scope of religions related to and less deep in terms of what it brings to the conversation.

IYG: It may well be, but this book was consciously meant to be about Judaism and not about other religions. And I may have given specific examples which come across as judgemental on the other religions, therefore your comments/criticism may well be correct. Darren Kleinberg complained about this point. In fact, he read some of the chapters, and he got me to tone the writing down. He read some of the things I wrote about Buddhism. He said that he felt I'm not sympathetic enough.

AGG: That's another way of saying what I'm saying.

IYG: It's probably a fair criticism, but again, the difference is that I wasn't writing about those religions or Jewish relations with those religions. I was using those specific examples to contrast to certain Jewish ideas. Still, I agree that part of the reason for less sympathetic treatment was the absence of an encounter. The emotional impact of meeting people was transformative. Their ideas were much more penetrating because I liked the people and because I felt close to them or I was impressed by them personally.

AGG: I mentioned to you that I would describe you as a seeker. Why do I think you are a seeker? You may not think you're a seeker. In my view, someone who's able to question, re-question, reposition, rethink, search for the truth, be open to change, be open to other people, is by definition a seeker. You may not feel that you're lost. In other words, you may use the term 'seeker' differently.

IYG: I thought 'seeker' meant that somehow you haven't found something you're looking for, and therefore you keep looking.

AGG: No, seeker, in the way I use it, is someone who may have found, but he's always seeking deeper and trying to go more into it, and trying to get the fuller understanding of things. He's not satisfied staying with where he is. A *doresh hashem* [seeker of God] is someone who's always on a spiritual quest for more and more and more.

IYG: That's a fair point. I give a lot of the credit in my thinking to the impact of other people. I would think about this in two ways. One is the students. They were lay students, both at CLAL and at Wexner.[27] They

[27] The Wexner Heritage Program provides American Jewish volunteer leaders with an intensive learning programme to expand their vision and deepen their knowledge. For more information, see the Wexner Foundation website.

were lay students, but they took me very seriously. And they responded. So every time I taught an interpretation of Judaism, I felt I saw—or learned—new things I hadn't seen before.

AGG: That's not the same. Every teacher goes through that.

IYG: Because each time I taught it, I was trying to make it clearer. I saw things from year to year that I hadn't seen before.

AGG: No, but I'm talking about your willingness to revise your whole thinking, to open up new avenues, to question everything, to struggle to say this better, to try in the process to become a better person. To try to know that better. That's the seeker.

IYG: Fair enough, I accept that. But I think the students' responses—the fact that they listened and the fact that they responded—also reshaped my thinking.

THÉRÈSE GG [who is also participating]: But it is a consequence. Because you are a seeker, you can hear what the students say, and query yourself.

IYG: I feel this is one of my redeeming qualities. I listen to other people even when they disagree.

AGG: That's why it's so hard for you that you were ignored.

IYG: Fair enough.

AGG: Where do you get this from psychologically? Where do you get the capacity and the need to hear and be heard? Where does it come from?

IYG: No idea. Everybody has the desire to hear and to be heard.

AGG: No, it's not universal. Many people go through life without being heard, when they have nothing to say, and they don't make a point of hearing others. It's not universal. Were you always that way?

IYG: I haven't thought about it. If that is the measure, I went through periods of great interest and enthusiasm in a field or a thinker, and then went on. Even before I became a theologian, I remember I went through a whole period of interest in psychoanalysis. There was another period when I was a big fan of Erich Fromm.

AGG: I'd like to ask the final methodological question of the interview. I hinted at this before, but I want to bring this question up again. When a Jew speaks—and we're hearing now that actually your primary audience for your Jewish–Christian work is Christians, only secondarily Jews, because Jews are not interested in the field and are caught up in their own issues—so, when a Jew speaks to Christians and uses biblical language and biblical categories, you would expect it somehow fits well with current biblical hermeneutics. When there's too great a gap between the theology and the plain sense or notions that can be historically, literally applied to the Bible, it makes the reception much harder, and the notions lose credibility. I've asked myself to what extent, on various occasions, especially in relation to covenant, your usages fail to come over because they no longer correspond to biblical usages. Now, you said earlier, okay, but it's an extension of it. But I want to ask a more fundamental question. And here there may be a difference between how a Jew thinks and how a Christian thinks. For Christians, I think, ultimately will use the ability to go back to the Bible and to apply the biblical theology to a contemporary theology as a yardstick, as part of the method that stays faithful to Bible. Jews don't work that way because of *torah shebe'al peh* [the oral tradition], and therefore we can develop ideas in whole other ways. What importance, if any, do you ascribe to staying rooted in a biblical message and faithful to the biblical usage of categories that you use?

IYG: I'm not sure what you mean by being faithful to it. You can't forget, I studied the Tanakh as a fundamentalist meaning at the yeshiva, with my parents, my father. So you read *peshat* [seeking the plain meaning of the text].

AGG: You read *peshat*, which is Rashi, which may not always be *peshat*.

IYG: The theology wasn't fundamentalist, but the reading was. And so, as I grew and I developed these other ideas, I took my (mis)understanding of the Bible with me.

AGG: What happens—and this is something that I struggle with as I work through your materials—if I come to a point of saying: Greenberg's ideas don't make sense in relation to how the biblical text should be read? It doesn't work that way. Would that be a problem? It would probably be for the Christians. Is it a problem for you that you use biblical verses, terms, categories in ways that don't really fit with the use of the Bible itself?

IYG: Let me just say this, because I have thought about the expansion of biblical ideas in a different way. My answer is that I think this is what the
Sages, the *torah shebe'al peh* [oral tradition], taught me.

AGG: Exactly. So this is a Jewish thing.

IYG: Literally, the word of God has multiple levels of meaning. That's one of
the things that shows that it's the word of God. If it only had one level
of meaning, it would die with the particular location where it originated, and in the culture in which it was originally spoken. I think that I
learned the many layers of meaning from the Sages. They uncovered
many layers of meaning in the Torah text. (Remember that Rabbi
Akiva taught new meaning in halakhah to Moses from Sinai—which
Moses did not understand.[28]) I felt I was carrying on that same tradition. Do I have a different priority? Or a different set of values than previous commentators in many of these cases? The answer is yes. But
I feel the biblical words are legitimately applied or interpreted this way.

AGG: And for me, this is going to be one of the issues I'm struggling with,
namely, the application of the term 'covenant'. To what extent does
it have to relate to the biblical usage itself? I think especially of the
acceptability for a Christian audience. What happens when the notions
don't really reflect their understanding in the Bible? Can the ideas really
communicate successfully?

IYG: I'll be happy to see a case in point. I think that is part of the Jewish,
rabbinic, way of doing business. And I also think it's correct, that the
Sages were right in saying that the biblical words have multiple meanings. So it's not that they invented the additional meanings and then
tricked us into believing that these were uncovered [not created]. These
meanings are there—waiting to be uncovered and applied in different
ways in different eras.

AGG: I'll give you a good example on which I've worked recently. I've just
written this essay relating to the covenant with Noah in Genesis 9.[29]
I begin the essay by reviewing you, Levenson, Sacks, various other
people. They're using Genesis 9 to create a tension between universalism and particularism, and thereby addressing the question of Judaism

---

[28] BT *Men*. 29b.

[29] See Goshen-Gottstein, 'Genesis 9, Noah's Covenants and Jewish Theology of Religions'.

and other religions. You yourself have developed this in a very particular way. My analysis points me in the direction that the Noahide covenant is not about relationship. It's a covenant of 'no harm'. There are two kinds of covenant and this is, I think, my ḥidush [novel idea]. The Bible knows of two kinds of covenant. One covenant is relational; one is a no-harm covenant. A no-harm covenant means I won't harm you, you won't harm me, that's a kind of passive (*shev ve'al ta'aseh*) relationship, as opposed to a positive relationship. Consequently, the covenant is not really a covenant with Noah, it's a covenant with creation. Noah is standing in for creation. God promises not to harm and humanity in turn is also commanded not to harm God. And that's why you don't kill, because to kill is to harm the *tselem elokim*. This is how you establish reciprocity: you don't destroy us, we don't destroy you. If my reading is correct, then basically much that has been said regarding Genesis 9 falls away. This relates also to you. So this is a good hypothetical case. Of course, you can say: very nice, but I want to stick to my commentary. However, assuming that we agreed that this is not the correct reading, and the covenant is not about establishing a relationship, then religion cannot ground itself in Genesis 9, nor can the seven Noahide commandments. So the whole edifice crumbles. How would you deal with such a challenge? For me, this is part of the reason I say let's just do away with covenant, let's just talk about the substance. But I'm asking methodologically; you built your argument on a certain reading, which then is upended.

IYG: Well, because you made the defining issue relationship. And I would say that the defining issue should be *tikun olam*, which is, in the end, what the Torah is leading us towards. In saying *peru urevu umilu et ha'arets* [procreate and fill the earth] in establishing the Noahide covenant, God is pointing toward filling the world with life, which is what *tikun olam* is about.[30] The continuity of my commentary way down to the present moment, I think, matches your claim that this is not the original intent.

---

[30] Support for Greenberg's reading might be found in a discussion of Genesis 9 by James Barr. Barr lists the contents of Genesis 9 so that they add up not to a code of morality but to a view of life and subsistence. The overall concern of the passage is for the subsistence of life: how to make life, how to nourish, protect, and respect it. Ensuring life may go beyond a no-harm approach. It also defines reciprocity in the sense of reciprocal affirmation and generation of life. See Barr, 'Reflections on the Covenant with Noah', 16.

AGG: But that assumes that Genesis 9 is one unit, and that the first part of the chapter, verses 1–8, is part of the covenant, and then God in the second part gives also his covenant. If, on the other hand, the covenant is God's promise not to destroy, the earlier part of the chapter may not be, strictly speaking, a covenant. The term appears multiple times in the second part of the chapter, but never in the earlier part.

IYG: To me, the other main point of covenant is that this is a maturation point for God. God voluntarily gives up the power to coerce—a catastrophic punishing flood is coercion, using overwhelming force to press humankind into submission. Giving up coercion is the main transformation point of covenant in general. God says I'm accepting human limitations and I'm going to work with them.

AGG: Okay. At the end of the day, basically the answer is alternative readings. It's not one correct reading; there are alternative readings. That's really what it boils down to. Every reader highlights something else.

Conclusion

AGG: By way of conclusion, for me, it's been, first of all, a great privilege to have had this time together. Secondly, it helped me get some clarity on some specific issues.

IYG: I feel it's a privilege. I'm not sure what the word is. Maybe it's an honour that is grace, ḥen, to have someone who is a serious theologian read the ideas and deal with them. I also feel that your other work is very important. It's important because, I think, in the end religions will have to move positively together if they want to retain their credibility.

AGG: Let me conclude with a personal appreciation of something that emerged from this interview. I'm very messianic and my consciousness is highly messianic. And not in the way that Hartman was worried about its politicization. So I'm very, very, very happy when you tell me that, beyond everything else, you have this strong messianic dimension that informs your thinking. So not only are you a brother, seeking to reach out to the world, to affirm others, and to articulate a Judaism that is for the world, but all this is also informed by a messianic quest. There's a lot of information in today's conversation, but the spiritually revelatory part of today's conversation, for me, is this affirmation of your strong messianic consciousness. I wouldn't have known that. And for me, this is what drives me. But my messianic consciousness, you see how I apply it—very differently than other people. Which means, in a deep way, both of us are applying the messianic drive and in similar ways. Well, that's a great, great, great discovery of spiritual kinship. No? How many people can I say that about? All joking aside, this is a big, big thing. And to say that that's shaping everything you do in your quest for Judaism, and the correct Judaism, and open Judaism, and transformative Judaism and human growth—what you're saying is that the battery that's ultimately driving your whole enterprise is a messianic quest—that's a huge statement.

IYG: I do believe that.

PART II

JONATHAN SACKS

COVENANT, THE DIGNITY OF DIFFERENCE, AND RELIGIOUS PLURALISM

CHAPTER SEVEN

Introducing Jonathan Sacks

J ONATHAN SACKS is arguably the most important Orthodox Jewish thinker and spokesperson of the twenty-first century, possibly also of the latter part of the twentieth century and possibly of all branches of Judaism. It is still hard to speak of Sacks in the past tense, following his recent death, which sent shock waves throughout the Jewish world as well as in broader circles in Britain and worldwide. The deep sense of loss, captured in the public domain and in the blogosphere, is testimony to his reach and popularity. He brought a combination of gifts to his public ministry and these account for his unique voice and the extent of its reach.

Sacks had an astounding ability to master large bodies of knowledge and to acquire a broad overview of significant issues of public concern. His academic training in philosophy equipped him with precision of thought, extensive knowledge of social and political thought, and above all with the skills needed to integrate new research, scholarship, and knowledge in a variety of contemporary disciplines. What this means, then, is that he was able to address the burning issues of the day not only through well-known religious positions, but also through nuanced engagement with contemporary philosophical and social sources. To these he brought a very particular range of Jewish learning. While broadly learned in a classical Jewish Orthodox curriculum, Sacks carved out a special niche in his teaching and preaching with close and careful readings of the Hebrew Bible, especially the Torah. He was an original exegete who brought to the task of reading the Torah a combination of skills not usually employed by other rabbis. This included, in addition to familiarity with traditional interpretations, awareness of key concerns of biblical scholarship, but especially a literary eye that uncovered new meanings in biblical narrative. When these were put to use in the dialogue of Torah wisdom and broader social, political, and religious questions, a new Torah teaching emerged, by means of which present-day challenges were addressed. Sacks was unique among Jewish scholars and thinkers, of all denominations, in his ability to create this particular form of conversation between Torah wisdom and contemporary concerns, and unique also in society at large, among those seeking the wisdom and input of religious voices.

This special positioning bore precious fruit thanks to a further gift of his. Sacks had outstanding communication skills. Both in writing and orally, he was able to convey often complex ideas to broad audiences in an attractive manner and in a popular way. As a result, he became not only Britain's, or even Orthodoxy's, most prominent spokesperson in the conversation of Judaism and the world at large. It is fair to claim that he was the most articulate and original spokesperson over the course of several decades, during which he shared Jewish wisdom with a globalized world in need of direction and meaning. His position as original and creative communicator was enhanced by his position as the most representative Jewish figurehead in the English-speaking world. Given that the United States does not have an institution of chief rabbinate, and that Israel's chief rabbinate has had little to offer to the English-speaking world—and, regrettably, precious little vision or wisdom to offer to the world at large—Sacks emerged as the great star of Judaism, serving both the Jewish world and broader society.[1] Colleagues in the European rabbinate with whom I have spoken were aware of his unique gifts and special standing amongst them, as were various bodies of civil society in the UK and internationally.

It is not only that Sacks was well positioned given his standing as chief rabbi of the UK; he also had a good mediatic sense. His ideas were spread via a series of books, averaging about one a year. But they were also disseminated through weekly Torah teachings that were widely distributed. More importantly, he had regular appearances on national media in the UK. In addition to being a highly sought-after voice, he also had regular programmes on radio and television and annual special programmes that he directed, where issues such as morality and broader social concerns were raised. In other words, in addition to all his other gifts, Sacks was also the most high-profile Jewish religious leader of any denomination in his day.

[1] Sacks' gifts and eventual star status were not a guarantee of a problem-free tenure as chief rabbi when it came to the internal concerns of the Jewish community. See Persoff, *Another Way, Another Time*. None of this diminishes his present evaluation as the most important Jewish voice in the global conversations of the past decades.

While, to make the comparison, rabbis in Israel may have had a high profile due to their range of oversight in matters of public affairs, Sacks had a far greater profile internationally not because of his office, but because of the wisdom and message he bore. His office, then, served as an ideal platform for the particular message and voice that was Jonathan Sacks. His retirement from the role of chief rabbi in 2013 did not impact his ability to contribute in the ways described. The afterglow of his previous position, but even more importantly his continuing engagement in Torah wisdom, with its particular contours as expounded in his exegesis, and in the concerns of the world at large, found ongoing expression in his teachings, publications, and public engagements. His most recent book, *Morality*, was published just months before his death, at the height of the global coronavirus pandemic.

My interest in Sacks is due, in part, to his importance as a thinker and a representative voice of Jewry. He has a lot to say about the concerns of the present book, which reflect my ongoing engagement over several decades of work in this field. In fact, some of this work involved Sacks himself, with whom I enjoyed a friendly and collaborative relationship. He joined the Elijah Board of World Religious Leaders, which I founded in 2003. He took part in meetings in person and contributed in writing to publications, as well as in video to an important international campaign on friendship across religions.[2] He was, then, a partner in common work. That work included religious leaders and communities, but, more importantly—and in line with the concerns of the present book—it also focused on a Jewish view of other religions and on how Judaism saw itself among world religions. Sacks represents one of the most important Orthodox contributions to the contemporary discussion of Judaism and world religions. Both in his capacity as chief rabbi and in his various engagements following his departure from that seat, he was a prominent actor and thinker in the encounter between religions. His originality, his reach within the Jewish and general community, and, above all, the fact that he had devoted much time and attention to a Jewish message that speaks to the world at large, to other religions, and to relations between religions, all make him a voice with which one must reckon. Better yet—his is a voice of inspiration and vision that has the capacity to shape future Jewish (Orthodox) as well as non-Jewish views of other religions. It is with this profound appreciation for the person

---

[2] See his short video 'Make Friends' on YouTube.

and teaching of Rabbi Sacks that the present enquiry into his view of other religions is being conducted.

Sacks' Writings: A Methodological Note

The common approach to studying Sacks is to cite a book or two of his and to highlight key ideas or the contribution of the said work. In the field of relations between religions, the most famous of his writings is *The Dignity of Difference: How to Avoid the Clash of Civilizations*.[3] This volume is deservedly famous. It is a first-rate book that features original and important ideas on the relations between religions in the broader context of a theory of how to deal with the challenges of globalization. It was written for a wide readership and has justly earned him acclaim. Another reason for its fame is that it became the subject of much internal Jewish controversy owing to the ideas it expresses.[4] For some Jewish readers, Sacks had gone too far in legitimating other religions or in putting Judaism on a par with them. The details of this controversy and the ensuing revision of the book, which led to the existence of two versions, will be studied below. For now, it is enough to recognize this as Sacks' most famous book when it comes to relations between religions. However, citing *The Dignity of Difference* alone, or any other of his published volumes, will not allow us to gain the fuller view needed for an appreciation of Sacks in the interreligious field. In order to understand his message and his particular contribution to this area, we must study his method as it finds expression across his corpus of published works. This method can be characterized by two complementary observations:

Sacks resorts to a number of fixed tropes that are repeated throughout his oeuvre. While he has published voluminously—his publications are reminiscent of the Babylonian Talmud—the extent of copying material in multiple contexts, both themes and entire chapters, leads to a significant discrepancy between the gross and net scope of his publication. While in certain cases such repetitions are no more than just that, in others the new context redefines motifs, bringing out new insights. He returns time and again to his stock themes and applies them to new contexts and new challenges as his thinking evolves. What this means for the student of Sacks, then, is that it is not enough to consider one formulation of an idea. His key

---

[3] All citations, unless otherwise stated, are from the first edition.

[4] Shapiro, 'Of Books and Bans'; Persoff, *Another Way, Another Time*, 171–86.

ideas are ideally studied across his corpus, in the various iterations they take, yielding nuances of understanding, like a diamond whose beauty is appreciated from multiple angles and perspectives as it is held up to the light.

While there is some overlap in the themes of Sacks' books, each of them tackles a specific problem. Accordingly, the key themes that characterize his contribution as a thinker are worked out variously in relation to each of the problems he tackles. In order to gain a picture of Sacks as a thinker, and especially of his approach to other religions, we need to view his oeuvre in its entirety. While the key motifs remain stable, their varying application in the different contexts leads to changes in their meaning, to which we must pay attention. It may also account for tensions and conflicts between Sacks' statements. More importantly, the very positioning of Judaism and its relations with other religions shifts across his books as a result of the different problems he tackles, with different audiences in mind. While his earlier books are written for a Jewish audience and are characterized by careful academic scholarship, mostly within the field of Jewish philosophy and Jewish studies, the later writings are meant for a wider audience. Accordingly, they are less academic and draw less on Jewish studies. Instead, they rely on Sacks' broad control of general social and political thought as it is brought into conversation with key Jewish ideas and ideals, especially as these emerge from his biblical readings. All this, then, must be taken into account as we seek to gain a fuller picture of Sacks' contribution to a Jewish view of other religions and of his understanding of relations with them.

In light of this methodological introduction, I will now offer two schematic overviews. The first is a survey of Sacks' main ideas pertaining to the concerns of the present study. The second is a brief review of those parts of his corpus that are relevant to the present project. Once these two introductory presentations are in place, we can engage in a more detailed and critical analysis of the major themes that define Jonathan Sacks' contribution to a view of Jewish relations with other religions.

The Key Ideas

In the pages that follow I list the main building blocks by means of which Sacks constructs his view of other religions. I offer these here in a rudimentary and skeletal form as each of these ideas will be dealt with at length in the ensuing discussion. The purpose of this conceptual overview is to suggest how these key ideas cohere into a comprehensive view of Judaism and world religions.

A Covenantal Perspective

Covenant is the major conceptual basis upon which Sacks' entire religious world-view is founded. He is possibly the most covenantal of all modern and contemporary religious thinkers. This is certainly true in the Orthodox camp, where Sacks is responsible for introducing covenant as a key religious concept to communities and in contexts where the idea had not previously taken hold. Given its centrality to his thinking, it is no surprise that other religions too are seen from a covenantal perspective. There are several elements that contribute to his covenantal approach to other faiths.

1. The view that other religions, too, are covenantal, paralleling Judaism's covenant.

2. The view that other religions partake of a foundational covenant that antedates Judaism's particular covenant.

3. The application of a biblically based dichotomy between the covenant with Noah and that with Abraham or at Sinai to the dichotomy of Judaism and other religions.

4. The idea of a global covenant of solidarity, also referred to as a covenant of hope, as a blueprint for ideal global and civic relations, either as an expression of or independently of the Noahide covenant.

5. The application of a distinction, initially formulated by Rabbi Joseph B. Soloveitchik, between two kinds of covenant—one of fate and the other of destiny. This internal distinction, which is a topos that characterizes Sacks' covenantal thinking, is applied also beyond Judaism, to relations with other religions.

This brief overview suggests Sacks' rich application of the idea of covenant. It also allows us to anticipate that his use of the term in the domain of Jewish relations with world religions could involve conflicting positions or shifting nuances. These are appreciated as his writings are studied diachronically. The changes may also be related to the controversy surrounding *The Dignity of Difference*. We thus recognize covenant as a major building block of Sacks' religious and interreligious theology, while at the same time bearing in mind the multiple, and potentially conflicting, applications of this central category.

The Universal and the Particular

One of the hallmarks of Sacks' interreligious theology is the turn from the universal to the particular. It is fully appropriate that the volume devoted to him in the series of contemporary Jewish philosophers is entitled *Universalizing Particularity*.[5] It is one of Sacks' central contributions to battle a view of universalism as a 'one truth fits all' approach, whether this is cast in terms of religion or in terms of ideology, and to prefer instead a view that privileges the particular. Along with this shift in emphasis comes the shift from truth to relationship, and the shift in the approach to God from idea or ideal to person. The affirmation of the value of the particular over the universal has implications for a view of other religions in two distinct and potentially conflicting ways.

First, each religion is seen as valid in its particularity (provided certain preliminary conditions have been met). Judaism's claim of its own special value, as an instance of the particular, is matched by the validity afforded to other religions. We can see how the idea of multiple covenants, of one type or another, interacts with the idea of multiple particularities and their value.

Second, the privileging of the particular over the universal entails a criticism of certain religions, notably Christianity and Islam. Alongside a major emphasis in Sacks' thought on the validity and value of other religions, we thus also encounter a strong polemic against the world's two largest faiths, and with which Judaism has had the longest relationship. The criticism, it will be noted, is not undertaken as part of an ongoing and classical religious polemic, but as part of the quest for the affirmation of the value of the particular, which is itself related to one of Sacks' principal aims in engaging with other religions—the reduction of religiously based violence, the advancement of a civic and global accord between religions, and their beneficial contribution to society at large. Nevertheless, as part of this quest, he does engage in a polemic against these two global faith traditions. This is not the only instance in which Sacks' goals as a thinker drawing on Jewish sources and applying them for the welfare of all of society lead him to polemicize against Christianity or Islam.

Sacks' efforts to characterize other religions from what he regards as the representative Jewish position lead to contradictory approaches to them. These contradictions are best appreciated when one realizes that Sacks does

---

[5] Tirosh-Samuelson and Hughes (eds.), *Jonathan Sacks: Universalizing Particularity*.

not set out to establish a definitive position vis-à-vis any religion. Rather, his goal is to harness religion, and particularly a Jewish view, in the service of global well-being and social peace. This leads him to apply differing and even conflicting approaches to other faiths. The unifying element in his thought is not his view of other religions as a whole or individually, but the fundamental approach of applying a religious message to social, civic, and global issues. Sacks, then, is a faith leader who harnesses religious wisdom for the well-being of society, local and global, rather than a theologian who is concerned, in the abstract and theological sense, with the status, value, and validity of other faiths.[6]

The Dignity of Difference

The title of one of Sacks' most famous books captures something essential about his outlook on life in general, but also on religions specifically. The dignity of difference is a powerful driver for respect between religions as each upholds its difference and is respected for this, rather than only for a common core, spiritual or ethical. The notion of difference stands in obvious relationship to the idea of the particular. Affirming particularity also means affirming difference, which in turn leads to the positive valuation of difference as an ideal. Rather than the uniformity of the universal, we encounter the beauty and value of the particular, and with it the call to uphold the dignity of difference. The ideas are close, and serve effectively as alternative ways of stating the same notion. Nevertheless, we take note of the specific formulation recognizing the dignity of difference. The idea translates more clearly in terms of its social implications than the more philosophically oriented dichotomy of universal and particular. A social and ethical principle of respect for otherness can more readily be formulated with reference to difference than in relation to particularity. It is also worth referring to the term 'dignity of difference' inasmuch as it has become associated with Sacks and is a hallmark of his social and philosophical vision. It bears his stamp, more so than the dichotomy of universal/particular. Finally, 'dignity of difference' also serves as a code for the storm generated within the Jewish community by the publication of *The Dignity of Difference*. This storm marks one of the important points in Sacks' public career as chief rabbi and highlights the tension between the different facets of his service—facing inwards, towards the com-

[6] An alternative approach is to reconcile contradictions, seeking to establish philosophical consistency in Sacks' thought. See Lebens, 'One God, One Truth'.

munity, and outwards, towards society and the world at large. This controversy and how it has impacted his teaching and its shifting formulations is
one of the themes to be discussed below.

Upholding Pluralism

The cluster of ideas that is emerging from the previous points leads us to consider one further dimension of Sacks' view of religions—the idea of pluralism. Upholding particularity and affirming difference are readily translated
to religious pluralism. Indeed, in many ways Sacks is a thinker who advocates
religious pluralism. However, the extent of such pluralism must be queried.
As we shall see, Sacks draws a distinction between internal and external
pluralism, legitimating only the latter. Upon closer scrutiny, though, one
may pose the question whether the distinction can really be upheld. In large
measure, this depends on what it is we mean by pluralism and how extensive
Sacks' pluralism really is. One might say that the more other religions are
viewed in fully covenantal terms, equal to Israel's covenant, the fuller the
pluralism. If we find less than full affirmation of other religions' covenantal
status in some articulations of his thought, we may query the depth of his
pluralism. Probing the depth of his pluralism is actually necessitated by the
question of what pluralism means for Sacks and what its implications are.
This in turn hinges on how he views the relations with other religions and
their members, as opposed to a more theoretical view of the very existence
of other religions. The fuller the engagement and the more reciprocal it is,
the more the pluralist vision comes to expression. The more detached the
view in terms of concrete encounter and reciprocal exchange, the more formal, perhaps even shallow, is the pluralism. If, as I shall immediately note,
Sacks' interest in the teachings and message of other religions is fairly limited, we may query the extent of his pluralism, and whether his positive and
affirmative view of other religions is best described as pluralism; perhaps it
might be better captured in other terms. The different versions of *The Dignity
of Difference* and shifts in the emphases of Sacks' views in relation to other
religions further raise the question of whether he is best described as a pluralist thinker and whether this designation holds true throughout his corpus.

Engagement and Relationships

All previous points relate to theoretical constructs and considerations that
inform the view of other religions. What can we say of Sacks' actual involve-

ment with their leaders, communities, texts, teachings, and wisdom, and how does this tie in with the theoretical perspectives noted above? Several factors must be taken into account:

1. Sacks' relationships with religious leaders and the interfaith initiatives in which he engages.

2. His strategy for interfaith relations; he places a strong emphasis on a 'side-by-side' approach, where diverse religious communities engage in joint action for the common good.

3. The above strategy as contrasted with engagement in the more classical forms of dialogue and encounter that can be characterized as 'face to face'. This leads us to consider Sacks' actual views on the value of interfaith dialogue. As we shall see, his attitude ranges from ambivalent to negative, though in some contexts he also offers positive and idealized support for dialogue work. Once again, we face the challenge of reconciling conflicting statements and orientations. And once again, it is likely that the resolution of conflicting approaches is a function of context, rather than an outcome of change or evolution in his thinking. Sacks is a contextual thinker and has a gift for adapting message to context. As a result, his messages are not uniform and contain contradictions, or at least conflicting orientations.

4. The question of Sacks' attitude to other religions in a concrete, as opposed to theoretical, manner. This is linked not only to his understanding of action and encounter but also to how he views other religions and how they are featured in his writing. We have already taken note of the fact that Christianity and Islam are not always presented in a positive light. Identifying circumstances when religions are viewed positively and, conversely, when they are criticized is essential to understanding how Sacks functions in relation to other faiths. The key is, once again, contextual. The context shifts as different issues are tackled in his various writings and as his interests change over several decades.

Qualified Openness

The sum total of Sacks' attitudes to other religions—how these are portrayed and the parameters within which he views them—leads to an attempt to offer an overall evaluation of how he engages with other religions. Sacks represents a qualified openness to other faiths. The hermeneutical challenge is to determine wherein lies the qualification and what are its causes.

At the one extreme, Sacks is a marvellous theoretician who extols the value of respect, dignity, and appreciating diversity and difference. He offers some of the most inspiring formulations for how relations between religions and their members ought to be conducted and can provide a robust theory for sustained interfaith engagement on all levels—spiritual, theological, social, moral, civic, and more. At the other extreme, one discovers significant gaps between Sacks the theoretician and the ideals he envisions and the realities he imagines and Sacks the practitioner, whose activities, positions, and actual dealings with other religions are significantly narrower in scope than the breadth of vision and imagination to which he opens his readers. This, then, is the conundrum of Sacks on world religions. How does one reconcile some of the most imaginative, open, and accommodating views of other religions with a practice that severely limits the actual scope of engagement with them and their wisdom?

I can see two possible explanations for the gap between Sacks the theoretician and Sacks the practitioner. The first is ideological, the second is personal. According to the first, he enters the domain of interfaith relations in line with certain restraints that are common within Orthodoxy and which are associated with guidelines set forth by Rabbi J. B. Soloveitchik.[7] Soloveitchik was an important influence upon Sacks and played a formative role in his spiritual biography as well as Jewish intellectual formation. According to this line of reasoning, Sacks is a master rhetorician who is capable of extolling the virtues of interfaith relations while in fact engaging in them on a limited basis on *ideological* grounds. Even if in many ways he has gone beyond the theoretical perspectives that are shared by other Orthodox rabbis, his actual engagement and his personal practices are defined by certain Orthodox conventions. In this reading, Sacks presents us with a juggling act in which conflicting tendencies are reconciled in a fine equilibrium between theoretical openness and practical control on the extent of interfaith engagement.

There is a second possibility, and this is the alternative I prefer. The issue is personal and not ideological. No matter how pioneering or brilliant one may be, there are personality limits that shape one's practice and place limits upon his or her reach and range of experience. In this reading, Sacks the

[7] See Soloveitchik, 'Confrontation'.

theoretician is possessed of an imaginative power that exceeds the capacities or tendencies of Sacks the person. While Sacks the theoretician can construct wonderful palaces with words and ideas, Sacks the person is not made and has no desire to dwell in these very palaces.[8] But if this is a matter of personality, it allows us to appreciate him in a new way. If Sacks the person is not inclined to deep interfaith engagement, what power of imagination comes to expression in his thought, formulated almost in opposition to his own personal tendencies! Surely this is a sign of greatness and rising above one's personal limitations. More significantly, if the reason for the discrepancy between Sacks the theoretician and Sacks the person is ideological, then in fact he is inviting us to follow suit and to practise interfaith relations as he did, in a more circumscribed manner, guided by a side-by-side ethos, putting aside concerns of authentic spiritual sharing and deeply engaged interreligious friendships. If, however, he has created palaces in which those who are inclined to pursue such deeper engagement may dwell, then we need to follow his theory rather than his personal example. A study of Sacks on world religions is an introduction to greatness, imagination, creativity, and inspiration. But it also requires a willingness to consider the personal limitations of our subject. Rather than demeaning his view, it allows us to recognize greatness over against personal limitations and liberates Sacks' followers from those limitations. Those who follow in his footsteps can, accordingly, go farther than he did, and they can do so in his light.

A Review of Sources

In view of the above description of how Sacks' corpus is constructed and how his creativity finds expression in shifting contexts, facing multiple challenges, it is helpful to review those of his writings that I have used in the present analysis, and in which he treats other religions or provides foundations for how they should be seen. My descriptions include the genre of the given book, its intended audience, and above all the problematic that Sacks

---

[8] I owe this way of describing the situation to the former Archbishop of Canterbury, Rowan Williams, who, of all major faith leaders of other religions, was probably closest to Sacks. Chapter 14 is an interview I conducted with Williams, and in which I explore the relationship between Sacks the theoretician and Sacks the person, and, in particular, Sacks as friend and as interreligious friend. Williams confirmed hunches that emerged in the course of studying Sacks and allowed me to finally settle on the personal, rather than the ideological, reading as a reason for the limitations in Sacks' interfaith involvement.

sets out to deal with. Most of his writing is characterized by a 'book per problem' policy. Accordingly, it will be useful to identify the problem he addresses in each book as the framework within which his specific thoughts are articulated and within which his views of other religions are stated.

1. *Tradition in an Untraditional Age.* This book is subtitled *Essays on Modern Jewish Thought.* It is the earliest of the works studied, dating from 1990, before his tenure as chief rabbi. Academic in style and intended for a Jewish and a primarily academic audience, it is a collection of essays on various topics and lacks one single focus. In this book we also find a dedicated discussion of Jewish–Christian and more broadly interfaith relations.

2. *Crisis and Covenant: Jewish Thought after the Holocaust* is, again, scholarly and oriented towards a Jewish audience. It reviews the state of Jewish thought and the multiple challenges facing it. Published in 1992, it suggests the centrality of covenant to Sacks' thought. There are several important points that emerge from this book. One is the extent of Sacks' familiarity with the work of Irving Greenberg. This detailed familiarity is, of course, relevant to an evaluation of the relationship between the two authors, to which I turn in a later chapter. One also sees how much Sacks is indebted to Soloveitchik and how he applies the distinction between the two types of covenant—of fate and of destiny. Most importantly for our purposes, his reading of the story of the Tower of Babel, which forms the foundation of his approach to particularity and difference as expounded in *The Dignity of Difference,* is first articulated here. As noted, time and again Sacks reuses materials he has developed if he deems them useful to the agenda at hand. We can see that the ideas that were so central, and so controversial, in his discussion in *The Dignity of Difference* had already been formulated more than a decade earlier and did not elicit any objection then. One of his important analogies for religious pluralism, the linguistic analogy, wherein multiple languages are part and parcel of our normal reality as established by God, is presented here.

3. *One People? Tradition, Modernity and Jewish Unity* was published in 1993, and, as Sacks notes,[9] was completed before he took up his position as chief rabbi. This book is devoted to one problem—the unity of the Jewish people, given the existence of multiple denominations. My personal favourite, it is a

---

[9] In an interview with Hava Tirosh-Samuelson, in Tirosh-Samuelson and Hughes (eds.), *Jonathan Sacks: Universalizing Particularity*, 125.

visionary masterpiece of engaged scholarship that strikes a balance between erudition and expansion of horizons. While his entire corpus can be characterized by these three 'E's, to me, as a Jewish academic, this book offers a particularly stunning coming together of these factors. While other faiths are not at the heart of the discussion, it shows Sacks' awareness of issues of pluralism and its alternatives as framed by theologians of religions, notably John Hick,[10] using the concepts of exclusivism and inclusivism.[11] Sacks redefines the terms in original ways.[12] Most importantly, he makes the claim, which he repeats in various contexts, that Judaism is internally inclusive and externally pluralistic. In other words, internal pluralism undermines Judaism, which leads him to prefer a view that is inclusive of the reality of various denominational Judaisms, without affording them the theoretical legitimacy that pluralism, as espoused for example by Greenberg, would. Other religions, however, are appreciated in light of a pluralistic ideal, in line with the emphases on covenant, difference, and particularity with which we are already familiar.[13] For our purposes, it is important to note the distinction between internal inclusivism and external pluralism. This juxtaposition raises the question of what Sacks means when describing his approach to other faiths as pluralism and how extensive his pluralism really is.

4. *Faith in the Future* is a 1995 collection of short essays and addresses delivered on various occasions. It is popular, intended for multiple audiences, and lacks one consistent problematic. One essay in this collection, 'The Interfaith Imperative', is important to our discussion of Sacks' views on interfaith relations.

5. *Radical Then, Radical Now,* or, in its American title, *A Letter in the Scroll,* is a kind of general introduction to Judaism, expressing key ideas of Sacks' philosophy. Dated 2001, it is particularly noteworthy for the extensivity of its covenantal thinking. The presentation of Judaism and its covenantal moorings includes comparisons with various other religions. All of Sacks' key ideas in relation to other religions are expressed here. These include the divinely ordained multiplicity of religions, the centrality of the human

---

[10] See *One People?*, 141.

[11] See *Tradition in an Untraditional Age,* 177. For an application of these categories to a Jewish theology of religion, see Brill, *Judaism and Other Religions,* who expands the typology further.   [12] See *One People?*, 142. See further the section title on p. 214.

[13] On the challenges of inclusivism as a modality of relating to denominational Judaism and on Sacks' difficulty in fully adopting inclusivism, see Persoff, *Another Way, Another Time.*

person as the image of God, acceptance of the stranger, and the need for respect for others. At the same time, Judaism is juxtaposed with other faiths and its uniqueness, and implicit superiority, are affirmed. In addition to the distinction between Judaism and Christianity and Islam noted above, we also find references to other religions, ancient and new, and one is struck by their superficial presentation. They are boiled down to a representative and often stereotypical idea, as contrasted with the extensive and nuanced discussion of Judaism. One of the issues that occupies Sacks' attention already in this book is the problem of religious violence. He considers the particularity of Judaism an antidote to religious violence, given its affirmation of the legitimacy of particularity and difference, thereby undermining the appeal to violence by totalitarian religious systems that uphold one truth and one path only.

6. *The Dignity of Difference.* These concerns are reiterated in *The Dignity of Difference: How to Avoid the Clash of Civilizations*, which appeared a year later. Sacks based most of his argument on his reading of the biblical narrative, which, in terms of Jewish argumentation, is a very weak and ultimately unacceptable form of making major theological points, especially when these are announced as novel positions reached through the author's own insight in an attempt to address contemporary issues, insights not visible to previous generations.[14] A traditionally minded perspective relies on earlier authorities and does not engage in contemporary innovation, and the mode of making a point is by pointing to precedent, rather than hearing tradition anew. As Sacks' pluralism lacked the internal rigour that his Orthodox interlocutors expected,[15] he was forced to revise the book and to tone down many of his more daring statements.

The *Dignity of Difference* is not written for a Jewish audience. This was part of Sacks' defence when he was charged with heresy and unacceptable religious views.[16] The point is not only one of audience but of overall style. He emerges in this book as a global thinker, who, from the resources of Judaism, addresses the most burning problems of a world facing multiple

[14] See the quote below from p. 19. See further pp. 17 and 48. The adjective 'radical', by which Sacks describes his own efforts, appears only in the original and not in the revised version.
[15] See Shapiro, 'Of Books and Bans'. After stating the problem, Shapiro makes some moves in the direction of offering traditional support for the earlier views of Sacks.
[16] Persoff, *Another Way, Another Time*, 173.

challenges brought about by globalization. The problem of religious violence is only one of the issues tackled in the book. Sacks' covenantal thinking finds multiple expressions as he brings Jewish wisdom and Jewish sources to the conversation with the world at large. Given the revision of this book in response to internal Jewish pressure, we have the possibility of exploring Sacks' thought in detail as he addresses global concerns and as these are nuanced in light of internal Jewish concerns. My discussion will accordingly include a detailed analysis of the differences between the two versions of *The Dignity of Difference*, as well as of the relationship between this book and earlier formulations of the same ideas in previous works.

7. *To Heal a Fractured World* is a 2005 publication that offers a Jewish social ethos for society at large. It combines an internal Jewish presentation of a social vision and its radiation outwards, beyond Judaism. While not academic, it is detailed in its erudition and does not rely on generalities, as some of Sacks' other books do. I would say this work strikes the optimal balance between a vision for the insider and one for the outsider,[17] as well as between popular and scholarly writing. Naturally, covenant plays an important role, both in establishing Jewish society within and in establishing broader human responsibility. As part of a Jewish social vision, the issue of relations between faiths is one important theme that Sacks deals with. Here we find the ideal of *ways of peace* as a justification for charity and deeds of kindness to the other. In a non-utopian world, this is the means of keeping social harmony. In some ways, the book summarizes Sacks' views on religious diversity as stated in *The Dignity of Difference*, but here seen from within a Jewish context.

8. *The Home We Build Together: Recreating Society* is a 2007 book that is one of Sacks' least Jewish books. His voice as chief rabbi is unique in that it allows him to address the limitations of multiculturalism and to suggest a way of cultivating a common social identity for the United Kingdom against the background of religious diversity. The challenge of multiple religions and communities therefore lies at the heart of this volume. However, it is approached not from the perspective of Judaism and its challenges, but from the perspective of British society and how it can advance beyond a model of multiculturalism that has failed to deliver the desired social unity

[17] Sacks describes it as a Jewish book with a message that is relevant to the broader human conversation. See p. 267.

and cohesion. To this end, Sacks draws on many of the ideas found in other works of his. However, rather than offer theological justification for legitimating the other, he puts his ideas forward in a civic context. This is the most civic of his works, and it shows what may be most important for him in the interfaith encounter—its civic benefits. Accordingly, the ideal of side-by-side engagement finds its first full articulation here as a strategy for building a common society across diverse religious communities.

9. *Future Tense* is a 2009 book that is more popular in nature and offers a largely political view of Judaism, religions, Israel, and the nations. It tackles issues relating to the State of Israel, as well as to antisemitism. Some of the themes discussed above appear here, but they are not used in novel ways. The most important messages of the book include a call for the renewal of human solidarity and the avoidance of Jewish insularity. While it does not focus on attitudes to other religions, in fact it lays the foundations for relations with them, inasmuch as it addresses one of the greatest obstacles to interreligious openness—Jewish insularity, defensiveness, and victimhood. Accordingly, Sacks puts forth a vision of sharing Judaism with other religions on an equal footing.

10. *The Great Partnership: God, Science and the Search for Meaning* is a 2011 defence of religion, written against the background of the new atheism. Many of the ideas cited in other works appear again in this new context. We notice that as the years advance, Sacks' writing is less academic, less reliant on the erudition of either the rabbinate or Jewish academia, and, above all, is geared at broader audiences. The challenges this book deals with are not particular to Judaism, as were those of some of the earlier books, such as *Crisis and Covenant*. It is therefore important to realize that Sacks assumes a different voice. He now speaks for religion, rather than for Judaism. In the process a new 'we' emerges: it is either the 'we' of monotheists, specifically Abrahamic monotheism, or of religions more generally. This is a new positioning. It obviously grows out of his work as chief rabbi, representing the Jewish community alongside the religious leaders of other faiths to society at large. If works such as *Radical Then, Radical Now* highlighted the uniqueness of Judaism over against other religions, the later books consider it, primarily along with monotheistic faiths, as part of a common spiritual reality. It is from within this reality that Sacks tackles common challenges. Significantly, the person of Abraham emerges as the figurehead for this new reality.

Seen as a foundation for Jews, Christians, and Muslims, Abraham's image is constructed in contrast with empire, power, and the various forces that religion (monotheism) comes up against and which continue to constitute the social and theological challenges that Sacks' work addresses. Some of these challenges point to imperfections within the religions themselves, primarily the problem of religious violence. This is one of the issues dealt with in this book.[18] Key ideas articulated more than a decade earlier are echoed again, and will find even fuller expression in the next work surveyed.

11. *Not in God's Name* is a 2015 volume devoted exclusively to the problem of religious violence. Most of its key ideas have been enunciated previously, but the positioning is different. Sacks speaks from within an Abrahamic perspective, so to speak, rather than from a typical Jewish one. However, if in the confrontation with the new atheism all religions could be presented as a whole, *Not in God's Name* tackles the problem of violence in God's name that forces a theoretical confrontation between religions. The book is, in fact, much like *The Dignity of Difference*, a response to Islamic terrorism and violence. We recall that within Sacks' corpus we encounter conflicting or complementary moves. Judaism is pitted as unique in comparison with other religions; it is also seen as part and parcel of them and as forming part of a larger whole. Similarly, all Abrahamic faiths are seen as a whole, but Judaism ends up defining the true Abrahamic ideal and vision over against the ideals set forth by other religions and especially other forms of religion, notably Islam, which betray the Abrahamic ideal. The move is complicated and must ultimately be queried. By providing a definition of what constitutes the true Abrahamic heritage, Sacks seeks to undermine from within the negative practices of another religion that shares common Abrahamic foundations.[19] This is a clever but problematic strategy. Judaism, as understood by Sacks, holds the key to defining proper Abrahamic identity and practice. But for this to have any meaning one must assume that other religions share the

[18] Hughes, *Abrahamic Religions*, 12, points out that full-scale 'Abrahamic religions' discourse was created following the attacks of 9/11 as an ecumenical term to promote peaceful relations among the three religions. This is certainly the context within which Sacks transitions to his 'Abrahamic' voice.

[19] One might substitute 'biblical' for 'Jewish', but the point is still made from within a Jewish matrix. Essentially, this is a quest for a neutral or objective Abraham that lies beyond the three traditions and that can therefore impact and correct their respective theologies. For a critique of such a possibility, and more broadly for a critique of the very term 'Abrahamic' in this context, see Levenson, *Inheriting Abraham*, ch. 6, esp. pp. 204–14.

definition of a common Abrahamic monotheism and that they would be willing to reconsider their theological and practical stances on the basis of the new-found understanding of true Abrahamic identity revealed by Sacks. If the first premise is questionable,[20] the second seems highly unlikely. Would so-called jihadists turn away from their practices by reading Sacks? Could his original and creative ideas, largely based on novel exegeses of Genesis, bring about religious transformation within, undermining an entire history of self-understanding in terms of truth and mission, and going against specific interpretations of Islam that beget violent behaviour? If the answer is negative, one must ask who Sacks' imagined audience is. Surely, the ideas are creative and enriching, and provide convincing grounds for the rejection of violence in God's name. But most of these ideas have been articulated previously, and their appeal seems limited to those who share Sacks' world-view and premises. In other words, the book is preaching to the choir. Its brilliance as a theological statement should not be underestimated. However, though pitched at a general audience and cast from within a broader Abrahamic identity, it seems to really only work for an audience that is able to follow Sacks' logic from within, in other words, for a Jewish audience. If *The Dignity of Difference* carried some of the same ideas to a wider readership in a movement of what Sacks calls sharing, the dense Jewish argument, cast within a dual framework of belonging to a broader category of Abrahamic monotheisms while critiquing it from within, is likely to be limited in its impact to those who have already integrated his religious world-view.

12. *Morality* is Sacks' last book, published in 2020, months before his passing away. It is probably the least Jewish of his books. One looks hard for Jewish sources and for the contribution of Jewish ideas to the larger conversation of humanity. While such ideas do exist, they do not define the book. It grows out of Sacks' philosophical studies and his work as an ethicist, broadcaster, and public intellectual in Britain over the course of decades. It sums up the trajectory of the intellectual contribution that is his social and moral thought, carried out as a Jew, but largely independently of Jewish

---

[20] On the problems associated with reference to religions as Abrahamic, see Goshen-Gottstein, 'Abraham and "Abrahamic Religions" in Contemporary Interreligious Discourse'; Hughes, *Abrahamic Religions*. See also ch. 6 of Levenson, *Inheriting Abraham*. For an attempt to validate continuing appeal to the category despite its inherent limitations, see Bakhos, *The Family of Abraham*, Introduction and Conclusion.

sources, let alone a specifically Jewish discourse. The voice is, once again, that of religion, as it addresses moral challenges in society. So much so that religion is no longer limited to Abrahamic monotheism. If Sacks was careful in earlier works to branch out to monotheisms that share something in common with Judaism, in this book we come across instances of positive reference to pagan forms of religion and their social benefits. The social, civic, moral agenda clearly works against Jewish exclusivity or even against the process of sharing specifically Jewish wisdom with society at large. Sacks' oeuvre, it seems, should be understood as taking place between a religious and a social/civic pole. As social ideals are explored for the benefit of society, these are drawn from religion at large, and not from Judaism.

13. *Covenant and Conversation*. To complete this survey, we should mention more popular writings of Sacks. Under this title we find a website that features a vast range of his teachings in various media. It is also the title of a series of books that grew out of weekly Torah homilies delivered by Sacks. A large part of his broad reach within the Jewish community is due to the dissemination of his key ideas in the form of popular, and relatively brief, weekly teachings corresponding to the weekly synagogal readings. For our purposes, we do not find anything novel in these pieces. Their importance lies in echoing the big ideas found in Sacks' books on the level of communal teachings. Almost all the big ideas surveyed above can be found in *Covenant and Conversation*. True, they are more present and more dominant in the books than in the weekly sermons, where they appear only once or twice. But the genre of the discourse may require variety, and in any event it is adequate for our purposes to establish that Sacks did not keep his ideas as theoretical statements for his books, but took the trouble to share them as religious teachings within his community.[21]

The history of Sacks' written contribution shows remarkable elasticity as his voice expands and shifts in different contexts, addressing different audiences,

---

[21] By contrast, there is little that is typically Sacks in his commentaries on Jewish liturgical texts. A review of his commentaries on the siddur, the *maḥzor*, and the Passover Haggadah yields next to nothing in line with the concerns of our study. The only instance I could identify was the reference to universal and particular in his commentary on the Rosh Hashanah service. See his commentary in the *Koren Sacks Rosh Hashana Maḥzor*, 72. It would seem the liturgical texts may not invite engagement with these ideas, and in any event, a commentary on the liturgy may not be the appropriate context for their dissemination.

and representing different configurations of community, a different authorial 'we', at times Jewish, at times much broader. In all this, some key ideas are repeated and reworked time and again, at every turn serving the social, civic, or theological challenge (often all three) at hand. With the shifting context, theoretical challenge, and authorial 'we' come different nuances and different applications of the set of core ideas, described above.

CHAPTER EIGHT

Covenant: Structuring Judaism, Structuring Human Relationships

The Theoretical Context

The covenant occupies an important place in the writing of modern Jewish thinkers of the second half of the twentieth century. Our discussion of Greenberg has presented us with the typical range of concerns that are attached to the covenant in the thought of Eugene Borowitz, David Hartman, and others.[1] The idea serves mainly to affirm human responsibility and autonomy in the framework of a partnership with God. Against such usage, one must recognize the vast scope of Sacks' appeal to the concept throughout his corpus. For him, Judaism is a covenant and this defines its character as a religion. Whereas most modern authors only refer to the covenant in the context of specific theoretical concerns, especially those related to the respective empowerment of the two covenantal partners—God and Israel or the human person—for Sacks it informs the very being of Judaism throughout. As a consequence, he applies the notion not only to the formation of the relationship or to the concerns of human freedom and empowerment, but virtually to all aspects of Jewish life.

Such extensive use is noteworthy in and of itself. It is even more noteworthy when we consider its occurrence within an Orthodox framework. Orthodox thinking tends to be traditional, relying on ideas that have been handed down through generations. Given the decline in covenantal thought described earlier in this book, the fact that the concept plays such a significant role in the writings of an Orthodox author deserves attention. Just how central covenant is to Sacks' thinking emerges from the fact that it serves not only as a framework or definition for Judaism itself, but also as *the* Jewish contribution to broader social thinking and theoretical concerns. It applies to society at large, where the biblical ideal offers a message that humanity

---

[1] These are summarized in Cooper, *Contemporary Covenantal Thought*.

needs. That message is best described as carrying with it religious conno-
tations, while applying the concept beyond strictly religious parameters. All
this makes Sacks' use of the covenant the most extensive among all modern
Jewish thinkers. In fact, given its broad social application, one might even say
it is the broadest understanding of the term by any Jewish thinker, ever.

One can think of three sources that inform Sacks' extensive appeal to
the covenant. First, he is an avid and careful reader of the Hebrew Bible. As
noted already, his teaching within the Jewish community, as well as his contribution to broader conversations in which the Jewish message is articulated, draw heavily on biblical exegesis. Given the centrality of covenant to
the biblical world-view, it is not surprising that Sacks would pick up on the
idea and give it a new shape and novel application.[2]

Sacks is, furthermore, aware of biblical scholarship on the covenant in
its ancient Near Eastern context. Other modern Jewish covenantal thinkers
tend to ignore the historical and scholarly foundations of the biblical concept and often develop the idea on the basis of rabbinic material. Sacks develops his ideas with an understanding of biblical and historical scholarship.
Moreover, he approaches the notion of covenant precisely as delivering a
unique message against the background of ancient empires. Abraham's faith,
the meaning of monotheism, and the particularity of the covenant are all
appreciated against this ancient background; what emerges from this juxtaposition remains relevant till today and is part of Judaism's contemporary
global message. In this way, Sacks brings to the idea of covenant a range of
meanings that is different from what other modern thinkers find in it. In the
same way that the covenant established the vision of Judaism when it was
first framed as a theological notion, it continues to define its special contribution to today's global conversation of religions and society.[3] If, for other
thinkers who appeal to the covenant, the idea serves mainly internal Jewish
concerns touching upon our relationship with God and its boundaries, for
Sacks the very return to biblical foundations ends up, paradoxically, opening
up the notion to broader significance to others. The idea that emerged as
the unique theological approach of Judaism is cast by Sacks as the voice of
Judaism in the global human conversation.

There is a third source that accounts for the centrality of covenant to
Sacks' thinking. The concept was employed in the political tradition of the
Puritans and provided part of the ethos of the foundation of the United

---

[2] Note, for example, his reference to Lev. 26 in *One People?*, 45.   [3] *Future Tense*, 86.

States. It thus has a place in contemporary political tradition. As such, it straddles the realms of the religious and the political and draws its significance not only from hoary biblical antiquity but also from recent political history. This positions it in a special way and contributes significantly to its contemporary appeal. Sacks is therefore able to move between these different dimensions as he develops a vision of Judaism that is founded upon covenant and articulates a Jewish message to society in dialogue with more recent political theory.

These ideas appear in different parts of Sacks' corpus. One convenient way of seeing how they operate is in his more popular synthesis in his weekly Torah teaching. Sacks' commentary on the Torah portion of 'Va'ethanan' is quoted here at length as it provides a comprehensive, popular summary of many of his key ideas.

The effect of Christianity and Islam was to spread the Jewish message—albeit in ways with which Jews could not fully agree—throughout the world. Today these religions represent more than half of the six billion people on the face of the earth. The 'Judaeo-Christian ethic' and the Abrahamic faiths have shaped much of the civilization of the West. The Torah really did become 'your wisdom and understanding in the eyes of the nations'.

I want to examine one example of this influence . . . the politics of covenant.[4]

One notes with interest that the starting point is the recognition of how the idea of covenant has spread via other religions. Rather than the exclusive domain of Israel, it is part of Israel's heritage to humanity and is mediated via other religions in a movement of commonality and sharing.

The book of Devarim/Deuteronomy is the great text of covenantal politics—the idea of a nation linked together in an explicit bond, a foundational text or constitution of mutual responsibility. It is a highly distinctive form of politics. Unlike the politics of power or organic development, it is predicated on the equal dignity and freedom of all its citizens. It involves a narrative—the story of the origins of the people and how they came to join together in collective enterprise to pursue the common good.

One of its most distinctive features is that it is essentially moral. It sees the nation as charged with a mission, a set of values, a destiny and responsibility. The health of the nation is directly related to the degree to which it is true to its voca-

---

[4] 'Va'etchanan (5768)—In the Eyes of the Nations'. On the political appeal of covenant and, in particular, the admiration of the American model, see Sacks, *Radical Then, Radical Now*, ch. 8; *To Heal a Fractured World*, ch. 9; *The Great Partnership*, ch. 7.

tion. John Schaar, writing about the political beliefs of Abraham Lincoln, summarises the idea well:

> We are a nation formed by a covenant, by dedication to a set of principles and by an exchange of promises to uphold and advance certain commitments among ourselves and throughout the world. Those principles and commitments are the core of American identity, the soul of the body politic. They make the American nation unique, and uniquely valuable, among and to the other nations. But the other side of the conception contains a warning very like the warnings spoken by the prophets to Israel: if we fail in our promises to each other, and lose the principles of the covenant, then we lose everything, for they are we.

This serves as a good introduction to the proposition I want to argue here, namely that the single greatest experiment in covenantal politics in modern times has been the United States. From the beginning, its founders saw themselves as the children of Israel of their day, escaping from Egypt (= England) and a cruel Pharaoh (England's kings), across the Red Sea (= the Atlantic) to what George Washington called 'the almost promised land' . . .

What is extraordinary about America is that this deeply theological way of speaking about national purpose did not end (as it did in Britain) with the 17th century. It has continued to this day. One of the least well-known yet sustained commentaries to the book of Deuteronomy is the collected inaugural addresses of American presidents, from George Washington to George W. Bush.

In the first inaugural in 1789, George Washington declared, 'It would be peculiarly improper to omit in this first official act my fervent supplications to that Almighty Being who rules over the universe', and warned that 'the propitious smiles of Heaven can never be expected on a nation that disregards the eternal rules of order and right which Heaven itself has ordained'. In his second inaugural (1805), Thomas Jefferson compared the story of America to the Exodus: 'I shall need, too, the favor of that Being in whose hands we are, who led our fathers, as Israel of old, from their native land and planted them in a country flowing with all the necessaries and comforts of life.' . . .

Succeeding the assassinated Kennedy, Lyndon Baines Johnson spoke of 'the American covenant' in language resonant with undertones of Exodus and Deuteronomy:

> They came here—the exile and the stranger, brave but frightened—to find a place where a man could be his own man. They made a covenant with this land. Conceived in justice, written in liberty, bound in union, it was meant one day to inspire the hopes of all mankind; and it binds us still. If we keep its terms, we shall flourish . . . Under this covenant of justice, liberty and union we have become a nation—prosperous, great and

mighty. And we have kept our freedom. But we have no promise from God that our greatness will endure. We have been allowed by Him to seek greatness with the sweat of our hands and the strength of our spirit.

. . . No other country in the West uses this intensely religious vocabulary. It is particularly striking in view of the fact that the American constitution, in the form of the First Amendment, formally separates religion and state.

It was the great French writer, Alexis de Tocqueville, who in the 1830s, in the course of his classic *Democracy in America*, explained the paradox. There is a separation between religion and state, but not between religion and society. 'Religion in America', he wrote, 'takes no direct part in the government of society, but it must be regarded as the first of their political institutions.' What he meant was that, though it had no power, it had enormous influence. It sustained families. It bound communities together. It prompted people to join voluntary organizations for the promotion of the common good. It was the basis of a shared morality which, precisely because it was upheld by faith, did not have constantly to be enforced by law. 'In France', he noted, 'I had almost always seen the spirit of religion and the spirit of freedom marching in opposite directions. In America I found they were intimately united and that they reigned in common over the same country.'

We owe to Robert Bellah the idea that America has a 'civil religion'—a set of beliefs and a shared faith that underlie its public and political life. A public theology has been part of America's political culture from the very beginning. That public theology is based, as Bellah himself notes, on the Hebrew Bible, above all on the book of Deuteronomy/Devarim. American presidents speak of Divine providence and the sovereignty of God. They refer to covenant and the moral bonds by which societies are sustained. The liberty of which they speak is biblical rather than libertarian: a matter less of rights than responsibilities, not the freedom to do what one likes, but the freedom to do what one ought, thus contributing to the common good. The 'American story' is essentially that which Moses articulated at the end of his life. America is the promised land to which successive generations of immigrants have come to find freedom from oppression . . .

The story of the Hebrew Bible is intensely particularistic. It tells of how one people, long ago, experienced oppression and were led to liberty through a long and arduous journey across the desert. Yet no story has had greater impact on the political development of the West. Moses knew that the events of his time had a significance that went far beyond those days and that people, and that they would eventually become an inspiration to others . . .

It is a disservice to Judaism to see its teachings as meant for Jews alone. Moses knew that God had summoned Israel to be more than just one other nation among the many that have surfaced in the course of history. It was to become an example, a role model, a living tutorial in what it is to construct a society built on the idea of the equal dignity of all as the image, and under the sovereignty, of God. As Paul Johnson put it in his *History of the Jews*:

> It seems to be the role of the Jews to focus and dramatise these common experiences of mankind, and to turn their particular fate into a universal moral.

That is what Moses meant when he said: 'This is your wisdom and understanding in the eyes of the nations.' It was a supreme challenge then. It remains so now.[5]

I believe this rehearsal of ideas that find repeated expression in Sacks' writings captures a fundamental aspect of the centrality of covenant in his thinking. It is central because it is an idea that can be exported and has withstood the test of at least one major political entity—this continues to demonstrate its relevance. Israel's covenant is thus a model to be shared with others, and it is shared in political terms. The idea of covenant as a model has great appeal when we consider the universal God and his covenant-making. As noted in an earlier chapter, the foundations of the idea of covenant may be in a view of God that is less than fully universalistic, or even completely monotheistic. What is the meaning of covenant once a universal and sole God is affirmed? As suggested by Reuven Kimelman, this may be one reason for the historical decline in the centrality of the covenantal idea. Once it is reclaimed and emerges as a central notion in relation to the universalistic God, the question must be posed why God concludes a covenant with one particular people rather than another. Two possible answers may be suggested. The first is that this particular covenant serves as a model for others. If so, Sacks is in fact pointing us to how Israel's model covenant gives rise to other covenantal expressions. While these are more horizontal, community-based, and political, they still owe their existence to Israel's foundational covenant and may therefore be seen as modelled upon it. The alternative answer is that indeed there are multiple covenants. Israel's is a model for other covenants that follow suit as other religions also enjoy their own relationship with God. We will explore this possibility, as it appears in Sacks' writing, below.

A careful reading of the text above reveals a fundamental difference between the biblical definition of covenant and its later application. In the latter, a covenant is made as a human commitment, a mutual engagement, in light of a vision, even in the presence of God. But it is not a direct relation-

[5] 'Va'etchanan (5768)—In the Eyes of the Nations'.

ship with God, as the biblical covenant is. Herein lies an important distinction between different forms of covenant, which we may refer to as horizontal and vertical. Historically covenant was a horizontal relationship between human parties. In the Bible, it is applied vertically to our relationship with God. The later political applications are primarily horizontal, based on a mutual coming together in joint purpose and vision. The horizontal social-political covenant maintains religious traces, just as the human covenants of the Bible did, even though God is not directly present in these covenants. It is interesting to note that Sacks presents the political-horizontal covenant as a latter-day application of Israel's covenant. In fact, even the covenant in Deuteronomy, a prime example of the vertical type, is cast here in moral, social terms, rather than in the more religious terms that are appropriate for a description of the biblical covenant and of which Sacks is well aware. He is able, it seems, to move between these different dimensions—the ancient and the modern, the religious and the political, the vertical and the horizontal, the spiritual and the moral. This flexibility or elasticity in the application of the concept is key to its varying uses, which are, in turn, key to the popularity of the covenant in Sacks' thought. Recognizing its centrality to biblical theology, he relies upon it as heavily as he does not only out of a sense of historical faithfulness or theological discernment. Covenant allows him to construct his world-view on multiple, complementary levels. The religious category is also social, political, and civic. It lays the foundations for building society, in all its dimensions. It holds promise for redefining human relations and makes it possible to deliver a particular Jewish message that impacts all aspects of life. The promise of covenant lies in the potential it has for extensive application. It appeals to Sacks not only because of its religious value but also because it simultaneously holds religious and social values, which allows him to envision a society that is served by both dimensions in its quest for order, meaning, and vision.

Covenant as Relationship

Let us return to the foundational definition of covenant: it is a relationship based on mutual obligations. Basic as this definition appears and true as it is to the biblical foundations of the idea, it is often lost sight of. Modern theologians all too often foreground other ideas in the name of covenant, rather than this basic foundation. For Sacks, it remains a core dimension of the definition,[6] which can be seen as equating covenant with the very definition of Judaism, given how basic it is. Indeed, its centrality to Sacks' thought would lead us to conclude that covenant defines Judaism.[7] The affirmation of a relationship is crucial to the centrality of the covenant. 'At the heart of Judaism is a *relationship*.'[8]

While the covenant forms a relationship with God, it also constitutes the people of Israel as a people, whose members bear mutual responsibility for one another as faithfulness to the covenant emerges as a common duty, carried out through collective interdependence.[9] The theological and political dimensions of the covenant are thus woven into the foundational covenant of Sinai. This enduring association of the theological and political perspectives, as we saw, lies at the heart of Sacks' enchantment with the concept.

The community- or nation-building dimension of covenant is important for Sacks because it allows him to emphasize what is most important in human relationships: their depth and authenticity. He repeatedly contrasts covenants and contracts.

Unlike contracts, which are entered into for the sake of advantage, covenants are moral commitments sustained by loyalty and fidelity, even when they call for sacrifice. They are about you and I coming together to form a 'We'.

A contract is a *transaction*. A covenant is a *relationship*. A contract is about *interests*. A covenant is about *identity*. That is why contracts *benefit*, but covenants *transform*.

A covenant creates a moral community. It binds people together in a bond of mutual responsibility and care.[10]

---

   [6] *Crisis and Covenant*, 1.

   [7] There is an important potential distinction that has not received due attention in the literature. Is Judaism a covenant or does Judaism (or Israel) *have* a covenant? In other words, how deeply engrained is the covenant in the very definition of Judaism? I have not found a discussion that examines the history of covenant and its modern application with the same clarity and directness found in this question. The different theological formulations of modern thinkers can be read as being closer to one or the other position. I am also unable to identify when it became common to think that Judaism *was* a covenant. I have posed the question to several scholars of modern Jewish thought, who also struggled to come up with a clear answer. The question is certainly worthy of further study.

   [8] *Covenant and Conversation*, i. 5.

   [9] *Radical Then, Radical Now*, 113–16; *To Heal a Fractured World*, ch. 9.

   [10] *Morality*, 313. See further *Radical Then, Radical Now*, ch. 8, and *The Dignity of Difference*, 151.

The contrast between contracts and covenants takes on significance as it highlights the horizontal dimension of the latter. As we shall see, this provides a foundation for one important aspect of Sacks' vision for religions today, the global covenant of hope or solidarity.

Covenant, for Sacks, is also the means by which society is built. This contemporary social vision can be presented at a remove from both its theological and its Jewish roots.

We can no longer build national identity on religion or ethnicity or culture. But we can build it on covenant. A covenantal politics would speak of how, as a polity, an economy, and a culture, our fates are bound together. We benefit from each other. And because this is so, we should feel bound to benefit one another. It would speak about the best of our traditions, and how they are a heritage we are charged with honoring and handing on to future generations. It would be warmly inclusive. A nation is enlarged by its new arrivals who carry with them gifts from other places and other traditions. It would acknowledge that, yes, we have differences of opinion and interest, and sometimes that means favoring one side over another. But we will never do so without giving every side a voice and a respectful hearing. The politics of covenant does not demean or ridicule opponents. It honors the process of reasoning together. It gives special concern to those who most need help, and special honor to those who most give help.[11]

Note how covenant, in this passage, is not the export of a Jewish idea to society at large. It is, rather, the intentional coming together of 'our traditions' as a common heritage of society. There is a new 'we' here that is multireligious, and where Judaism fits within a broader ethnic and religious tapestry. It is founded on respect for all and on giving a voice to all. For Sacks, Judaism may have introduced the idea of a covenant that is all-inclusive and that makes room for all, but the idea operates now in a broader societal framework.

One striking fact emerges from the above: Sacks transposes the covenant from the theological to the political, from the vertical to the horizontal, from Israel's particularity to other communities and other contexts. This shift may be considered in terms of modelling. It may be seen as an extension of the idea and as its intended consequence. It may also be seen as part of a gradual evolution in covenantal understanding. In one important dis-

---

[11] *Morality*, 321. See further *The Home We Build Together*, 181, where Sacks affirms that though people may be on opposite sides religiously, they are not civically. They share the same interest in the common good. That is the covenant of citizenship, ultimately an acknowledgement that 'though our faiths may be different, our fate is one'.

cussion, Sacks presents a history of the covenant idea as characterized by a shift from divine to human agency.[12] Initially it is concluded on divine initiative; over time, it is enacted by humans.[13] In a beautiful reading, Sacks considers the famous prophecy in Jeremiah 31 concerning a new covenant being inscribed upon Israel's heart, and explains that it is to be fulfilled through the history of Israel, in which responsibility and initiative gradually shift from the divine to the human partner.[14]

It is this shift from divine to human, from vertical to horizontal, that allows Sacks to relate to the covenant idea in very broad terms. In one important discussion of identity, we come across multiple dimensions of identity as these give expression to multiple dimensions of covenant. From a biblical perspective, covenant is not complex: two parties regulate their relationship by means of it. There may be multiple operative covenants, but each, in and of itself, is simple. Once horizontal aspects are introduced into the notion, complexity enters. If vertically there is only one relationship, and if, with reference to forming a people, there is similarly only one relationship, namely that of the individuals constituting the people, later applications of the idea of covenant as a means of forging and defining relationships with a purposeful orientation, drawing on religious significance and contributing to a common identity broader than the interests of the individuals, yield multiple and overlapping covenants.

To make his point, Sacks stresses the multiplicity of biblical covenants, to which we shall shortly turn. The covenants with Noah and Abraham and that at Sinai correspond to different aspects of identity—universal, individual, national.[15] In a similar vein, Sacks lists different dimensions of identity,

[12] This could also correspond to the move from biblical to rabbinic Judaism. As Sacks describes it, the purpose of rabbinic Judaism and its new institutions was to preserve the covenant. See *One People?*, 45. This description assumes intentionality on the part of the rabbis. One might dispute both assumptions, though the description certainly is valid if one is talking about the outcome of their reframing of Judaism.

[13] This, of course, reminds us of a key thesis of Greenberg, and of his cycles or phases of the covenant. Sacks is familiar with Greenberg's ideas, which he disputes in *Crisis and Covenant*, 127–31. This does not prevent him, however, from positing a similar structure, even though his discussion does not lead to notions of a voluntary covenant or to granting equal status to different denominational streams in Judaism. See *One People?*, 37–8, 136–40.

[14] *To Heal a Fractured World*, 155–9. On interpretations of Jeremiah's prophecy in Jewish sources, see Goshen-Gottstein, 'The New Covenant'.

[15] *The Home We Build Together*, 155. This formulation is unique to this context and is a good example of the creativity shown by Sacks as he recasts ideas in different contexts.

all of which may be considered in covenantal terms. These include, to take his own identity as an example, being a human being; a child of Abraham who finds commonality with Christians and Muslims; and being a Jew. He has other covenantal bonds as well—'to my wife; to my children through covenant of parenthood; to my local community through covenant of neighborliness, and to Britain through covenant of citizenship'.[16] The quote is striking because it introduces covenant to a range of relationships one rarely considers in such terms. This is the first time I have encountered covenants of parenthood, neighbourliness, or citizenship. It seems that for Sacks all relationships can be cast as covenants. Growing out of biblical roots, the category has been transformed. It no longer describes Israel's, or humanity's, obligations or relationship with God, but rather any form of relationship undertaken with the intention of contributing to society in a mutually supportive or even self-sacrificial way. The use of covenant to describe parenthood or citizenship may retain some allusion to its origins in the relationship with God, but it is no more than a faint memory. The term is associated now with voluntary and intentional social relations, in their variety and complexity.

All this is undertaken in service of one of Sacks' key ideas. As he writes:

Covenant generates a politics of complexity because human life is complex. It is utterly opposed to the kind of nationalism or absolutism in which loyalty to the state (or faith, or ideology) is everything and other human loyalties nothing.[17]

A thickly textured approach to covenant is a means of protecting against the superficiality and one-dimensionality of a religious view that would undermine the goals of pluralism, difference, and particularity at the heart of Sacks' religious vision. Covenant, then, is part of a protective mechanism that preserves diversity.

One striking fact that is encountered throughout Sacks' corpus is the adjectival use of covenant. He is not alone in describing relationships or realities as 'covenantal'. He is, however, a master at the adjectival application of the word, expanding the range of such adjectival uses beyond the range of uses of any other Jewish author. In the process, a rich and associative understanding of covenant in relation to Israel, its relationship with God, and the religious life is articulated. Even if new types of covenant are not invented, new formulations of how it interacts with Israel's life are encountered at every turn.

[16] *The Home We Build Together*, 155   [17] Ibid. 156.

Adjectival use includes such terms as 'covenantal morality'[18] and 'covenantal society'.[19] Sacks can speak of 'covenantal history' and 'covenantal community'.[20] Individual acts are also appreciated using covenantal language. Those who choose to make a Jewish affirmation in the late twentieth century, in whatever form, make a covenantal gesture of heroic proportions.[21] Internal Jewish disputes are given a positive pitch with each side embracing another covenantal value.[22] Hard texts are a challenge to the religious imagination and to our capacity to engage in covenantal listening to God's word, as we seek to build a future that will honour the sacred legacy of the past.[23]

The expansion of the covenant, as part of a rhetorical and conceptual expansion, also includes novel types of covenant and their scope. Sacks can thus speak of the Jewish people having reaffirmed, after the Holocaust, its covenant with history, a statement that would be utterly meaningless to a biblical author.[24] Or consider the striking, and somewhat problematic, application of the concept to Nazism and to the lessons we must take from it. 'If the covenant of hate did not distinguish between religious and secular Jews . . . neither can its only possible redemption, the covenant of love.'[25] At a certain point, covenant loses its conceptual moorings, be they vertical or horizontal. It ceases to rely on strict definitions and becomes, for Sacks, a rhetorical device that signals a field of meaning within which he evokes the umbrella concept of covenant, however light the point of contact may be.[26] Sacks is so taken by covenant that he casts and recasts it in service of his theological creativity and oratorical originality.

Noah and Abraham

As an overarching concept, covenant stands independently of the particularity of any of its specific manifestations. At the same time, it draws on precedents and lessons from particular covenants and these are found in the Bible. The Bible, and especially the Torah, provides the foundational frame of reference for understanding the concept. We have already encountered Sacks' reference to a variety of biblical covenants, two or three of which serve as core motifs throughout his oeuvre. The first is the covenant with Noah, the

---

[18] The title of ch. 7 of *Radical Then, Radical Now*.   [19] Ibid. 117.

[20] *One People?*, 52 and 55.   [21] Ibid. 139.   [22] Ibid. 143.

[23] *Not in God's Name*, 232.   [24] *Crisis and Covenant*, 48.   [25] *One People?*, 139–40.

[26] It is also possible to expand the uses of covenant while applying the term with greater precision. Such is the case of the covenant of love. See *Radical Then, Radical Now*, 84.

second is that with Abraham, along with its extension and later working out at Sinai. The key distinction is between universality and particularity, in line with one of the major theses expounded in Sacks' thought. While key factors relating to how the covenant defines Israel's being are learned from the Sinai covenant, it is the distinction between the universal covenant with Noah and the particular ones concluded with Abraham and Israel that is most central to his thinking, as it impacts other religions, and to this we now turn.

We have studied the covenant with Noah in the framework of Greenberg's theology. For him, that covenant is the foundation of all religions, and all religions are further sub-covenants of it, Judaism included. It is thus a crucial component of a Jewish view of other religions, which are appreciated and validated through it. I have also noted the exegetical challenge of considering the covenant with Noah on a par with the one with Abraham. As types of covenant, they are distinct, and there are different ways of capturing their distinctiveness. One way is by noting the one-sidedness of the covenant with Noah, which is a divine initiative, as opposed to those with Abraham and at Sinai, which regulate a reciprocal relationship and its commitments. This involves us in an analysis of Genesis 9,[27] which, as we have seen, lends itself to varying possible interpretations, and we are confronted with the question of how to relate the different parts within one coherent framework. Another possible distinction between the types of covenant is that between, on the one hand, a covenant of no-harm, which is a kind of 'negative' promise analogous to a ceasefire and cessation of hostilities, and, on the other, the full relationship that is made possible by means of a covenant, especially if we consider what Sacks sees as its central metaphor— marriage.[28]

One final point to recall touches on the relationship between the covenant with Noah and the Noahide commandments. There is some confusion around this subject, and both Greenberg and Sacks seem to have played a part in creating it. Noah receives a covenant from God in Genesis 9. The essence of this covenant, made with him on behalf of all living beings, is that God will never again destroy the world. Noah is commanded, in the first part of Genesis 9, not to commit murder. The chapter also includes the permission to eat living beings (which were prohibited to Adam in Genesis 1),

---

[27] On this see Goshen-Gottstein, 'Genesis 9, Noah's Covenants and Jewish Theology of Religions'.   [28] See *Radical Then, Radical Now*, 81–6; *Faith in the Future*, 121.

though not while they are still alive. This is the extent of the commands of Genesis 9. Rabbinic tradition marshals a concept that is to be translated literally as 'seven commandments of the sons of Noah'.[29] It is helpful to offer this literal translation, inasmuch as it highlights the fact that these commandments are not really related to Noah personally, nor necessarily to the commandments that he receives in Genesis 9. However, and it is here that confusion ensues, there is some overlap. The two commandments mentioned in Genesis 9 are included in the rabbinic seven. The common English translation of the term—used by both Greenberg and Sacks—refers, moreover, to these commandments as 'Noahide'; this draws them closer to Noah, and therefore potentially to the covenant made with him.[30] However, the term 'sons of Noah' is not related to him. The reason is not that it refers only

---

[29] BT *San.* 56a.

[30] What I am presenting here as a fundamental error has come to pass in two stages. The first is the identification of the seven Noahide commandments with Genesis 9. The second is the identification of these seven commandments with the covenant with Noah and reference to them as the substance of the Noahide covenant. The first stage in this confusion seems to date back to the first part of the twentieth century. I am unable to trace it to classical rabbinic or medieval sources. Even a figure like Samson Raphael Hirsch, who might have benefited from it in terms of his universalistic views, makes no mention of it in his Torah commentary. However, we note several authors in the first half of the twentieth century who do, and this has crept into scholarly commentaries on the Bible as 'the' rabbinic view. Thus, Benno Jacob assumes that the rabbis view the seven Noahide commandments as deriving from Genesis 9. As he puts it, 'this is of course not really contained in the words of the Bible, but nevertheless in its true spirit'. Similarly, John Skinner's commentary, as part of the ICC project, speaks of the rabbinical theologians who were true to the spirit of the passage when they formulated the idea of the 'noachic commandments'. Other authors of the period seem to have held the view that the rabbis actually derived the commandments from Genesis 9, though no one has demonstrated how this might have occurred. This is the view expressed in the Hertz Torah commentary, and it is later echoed by biblical scholars such as Joseph Blenkinsopp, who sees the Noahide commandments as 'duly interpreted' from Genesis 9, while providing no detail for how such interpretation came about. One possible cause of the identification of the Noahide commandments with Genesis 9 is the express reference to the sons of Noah, or to Noah and his sons, throughout that chapter. The appearance of the same term, *benei no'aḥ*, might lend itself on hermeneutical grounds to justifying the association of Genesis 9 and the seven Noahide commandments (Jacob, *The First Book of the Bible*, 64 may already be alluding to this). Failure by any authority to demonstrate how the Noahide commandments are derived from Genesis 9 goes hand in hand with the earlier rabbinic view that they date back to Adam and not to Noah. Westermann rightly rejects the superimposition of the Noahide commandments on the meaning of Genesis 9. None of the scholars cited associate the Noahide *commandments* with the Noahide covenant. This holds true also for David Novak's later presentation of the seven Noahide commandments. It is only later authors, such as Greenberg and Sacks, who take this additional step,

to the subsequent generation. On the contrary, it refers to all generations of humanity. The term is the rabbinic legal designation for non-Jews, and as far as the rabbis are concerned, it goes back to Adam. Indeed, the seven commandments, in essence, are understood to have been given to Adam, not to Noah.[31] Or rather: six of the seven were given to Adam, and the seventh, about eating animals, was added in the days of Noah.[32] In this sense, they can be seen as foundational to creation[33] and as the law or legal guidance that accompanies God's act of creation or the creation of the human person.

Both Sacks and Greenberg fail to make this distinction in their theological and philosophical discussions.[34] As a consequence, when they refer to the covenant with Noah, they bring to it an understanding that far exceeds the content of the biblical source. First, they see it as reciprocal rather than one-sided. It is understood along the lines of later covenants, expressing

thereby creating a robust covenant that can be put to broader theological use. It is, then, a very recent construct that significantly stretches classical usage, as well as the sense of the biblical passage itself. See Jacob, *The First Book of the Bible*, 64; Skinner, *A Critical and Exegetical Commentary on Genesis*, 169; *Pentateuch and Haftorahs*, ed. Hertz, 33; Westermann, *Genesis: A Commentary*, 469; Blenkinsopp, *Creation, Un-creation, Re-creation*, 148.

[31] This raises, of course, the question of why non-Jews are not called sons of Adam, rather than sons of Noah. I am not familiar with a study devoted to this question. In all likelihood, 'sons of Adam' designates all humans, Israel included, leaving 'sons of Noah' as a designation for non-Jews, even though strictly speaking Israel too should come under this designation, as they too are sons of Noah.

[32] BT *San.* 56a; Maimonides, *Mishneh torah*, 'Laws of Kings', 9: 1.

[33] This would go better with the Hertz commentary's identification of these commandments with natural law than with their origin in the covenant with Noah.

[34] I have received some pushback on this strong claim from an anonymous reader of my essay 'Genesis 9, Noah's Covenants and Jewish Theology of Religions'. It is helpful to make several observations that amount to a response to possible objections to the thesis presented here. BT *Sanhedrin* 56b–57a, after citing the conventional view of the seven commandments being given to Adam, cites a source from *tana deve menasheh* that presents an alternative list of commandments. The Talmud (at the anonymous redactional layer) then seeks to offer exegetical grounding for this list, apparently putting aside the question of whether they had already been given to Adam. While the Talmud offers other prooftexts, it does not rely exclusively on Genesis 9, and many of the prooftexts are antediluvian. This cannot, therefore, provide proof for the existence of an alternative rabbinic view that grounds the Noahide commandments in Genesis 9 or in commands given to Noah. There is no talmudic claim for the reiteration or the reaffirmation to Noah of the commandments given to Adam (such as Mishnah Ḥulin 7: 6 provides for laws given again at Sinai; see also Maimonides' commentary on the Mishnah). The talmudic views in *Sanhedrin* 56a that limit the scope of the commandments given to Adam should be seen as statements of value and religious priority. In any event, they do not rely on Noah to make up the shortfall in commandments.

mutual commitment and having legal content that is much broader than a scriptural reading justifies and is identified with the so-called Noahide commandments.[35] A robust usage of the covenant with Noah emerges and it is this robust usage that both authors apply to the relationship between world religions and Judaism.

Maintaining this reciprocal reading allows Greenberg to fully juxtapose the covenant with Noah, as a foundation of all religions, with the covenant with Abraham. Sacks' application of the covenant with Noah is more complex. While it can refer to world religions, more often it is used for humanity, society at large, and the global universals that are identified as humanity and human rights and are associated with the image of God. If Greenberg's understanding of the covenant with Noah maintains its full verticality, paralleling the later covenants with Abraham and at Sinai, Sacks' interpretation moves increasingly towards the horizontal dimension. In fact, what matters most to Sacks as he applies the notion of covenant to other faiths and communities is the 'no-harm' element, rather than the fullness of covenantal relations. Since he does not make the distinction between these two types, he can comfortably apply the lessons of the covenant with Noah to contemporary social needs while juxtaposing the covenants of Noah and Abraham. This juxtaposition is pitched as a distinction between universal and particular, between humanity and religion, between morality and ethics. Although it retains the potential to address other religions and Judaism's relationship to them, it shows where the heart of Sacks' concern lies—in the creation and shaping of society and in harnessing religious ideals and constructs for the benefit of humanity. The contribution of religion to society and to global well-being emerges as a more central area of interest for Sacks than the more focused and theologically charged question of relations between Judaism and other religions. This is one point that distinguishes his application of the Noahide covenant from Greenberg's. As we shall see throughout,

---

[35] Both authors rely on the work of David Novak and his description of the Noahide covenant. Novak, however, never identifies the Noahide covenant with the Noahide commandments, being well aware of the distinction between biblical and rabbinic sources. That both authors repeat the same 'error' while applying the covenant with Noah to world religions and contrasting it with the covenant with Abraham strongly suggests a dependence between them or a dependence on a third source which would have inspired both. I am not aware of another source that combines all these elements. It therefore seems likely to me that Sacks is indebted to Greenberg on this point, as I argue more fully towards the end of this book.

it is also representative of his broader concerns, in contrast to those of Greenberg.

I have already noted that Sacks is a contextual interpreter, who revisits key sources time and again from multiple angles in light of the context and the message that it requires. It is therefore worth noting, before considering the readings that diverge from the plain biblical sense, how he understands and presents the plain sense of Scripture. In one discussion, he extols the value of forgiveness. To this end, he offers a review of that virtue in Genesis, which he describes as

a drama in five acts, each adding a new dimension to the concept's richness. The first appears early in the Bible. Human beings have become corrupt. The world is 'filled with violence' and God 'regrets that He had made man on earth'. He brings a flood, and only Noah and his family survive. Emerging from the ark, Noah brings an offering to God, who is moved to compassion. 'Never again will I curse the ground because of man, even though every inclination of his heart is evil from childhood.' This determination is made the basis of a covenant whose sign is the rainbow: 'Whenever I bring clouds over the earth and the rainbow appears in the clouds, I will remember My covenant between Me and you and all living creatures of every kind. Never again will the waters become a flood to destroy all life.' This is forgiveness as an act of grace, a unilateral decision on the part of God.[36]

While one may ponder whether God's promise is best described as forgiveness or perhaps might be conceived of in alternative ways, the reading emphasizes the one-sidedness of the covenant as a divine initiative. This is also true of another instance in which Sacks comments on this text. Here he offers a history of the covenant and we have already encountered this history, described as a move from divine to human initiative.[37] Accordingly, the covenant with Noah is the example of a divinely initiated covenant that does not rely on human response. As Sacks correctly observes, it does carry a set of laws,[38] but the human partner is entirely passive. According to Sacks, it is a covenant because it has reciprocal obligations. Self-restraint on the part of God is matched by self-restraint on the part of man, who refrains from killing others. Nevertheless, Noah has no part in the act of covenant-making. No assent is required, no act needed to warrant the gift of grace.

[36] *The Dignity of Difference*, 182.   [37] *To Heal a Fractured World*, 152.
[38] A reading I concur with, though some scholars do not even consider the laws of Genesis 9 a part of the covenant. See my discussion in 'Genesis 9, Noah's Covenants and Jewish Theology of Religions'.

These two sources offer a take on Genesis 9 and the covenant with Noah that is largely at odds with most of Sacks' understanding. While he preserves the element of reciprocal obligations, there is no reciprocity in entering the covenant, which is not really conceived of in terms of relationship. If so, the juxtaposition of the Noahide covenant with later biblical ones is forced. They are, indeed, different realities, non-comparable, sharing at most the basic commonality of reciprocal obligations. Consequently, a larger theoretical, let alone theological, edifice will not find adequate foundations in the covenant with Noah, as read independently of later rabbinic additions and broader theoretical constructs. Yet most of Sacks' numerous references to that covenant go in the opposite direction. As the idea is built up and made increasingly robust, it also gains in significance and is made to address contemporary religious and social concerns.

To understand Sacks' appeal to the covenant with Noah, we must return to the two dimensions that characterize his application of the covenant idea —vertical and horizontal. The covenant with Noah is perhaps the best illustration of the riches and complexities associated with working out these two dimensions. As a covenant with God, it operates first and foremost on the vertical level, whether as a divine initiative or understood in a more reciprocal way. However, the lessons, meaning, and eventually the major application of the covenant with Noah occur on the horizontal level. More than a category that defines the relationship of humanity or religions with God, it provides a foundation for relationships within humanity. In the same way that Israel's foundational covenant was recast in social and political terms, so the covenant with Noah provides the basis for a far-reaching vision that Sacks puts forth to humanity today. That vision is increasingly detached from the covenant with Noah as his thought is further developed from one book to another, and it eventually stands in its own right, or nearly does so. Because Sacks tackles contemporary religious and social changes serially, how he applies the covenant with Noah will change from one book to another. However, the foundations remain constant. Within the fluctuation, we note the move from reference to religions in association with the covenant with Noah to reference to morality in general, independently of specific religious vehicles, to the eventual articulation of ideas previously associated with the covenant with Noah independently of that particular covenant, but still in line with the notion of covenant itself. This is the thought trajectory I will present in the following discussion.

The earliest reference to the covenant with Noah and its application to Sacks' foundational distinction between the universal and the particular is found in *Crisis and Covenant*. It thus antedates the political and contemporary concerns of a post-9/11 world as these are articulated in *The Dignity of Difference*, where they receive their widest exposure.[39] Significantly, these ideas were first expounded prior to Sacks taking office as chief rabbi. In other words, they are an expression of his own philosophical and religious vision, formulated independently of the pressures and needs of bringing a public Jewish voice to the conversation between religions and religious leaders. Let us, then, consider his earliest discussion of the Noahide covenant and how he relates it to religions. Perhaps the most important point to realize, in this early formulation, is that the question of that covenant cannot be divorced from the question of multiple covenants, which are in turn identified with other religions.

Faith, after Babel, is covenantal, and one covenant does not exclude another. Isaac and Jacob are chosen, but Ishmael and Esau are also blessed. God rescues Israel from Egypt, but—He asks through Amos—did He not also bring the Philistines from Caphtor and the Arameans from Kir? Is the God of Israel not also the God of the Ethiopians? There can be truth that is absolute and yet particular. There can be covenants which bind a people without negating the other covenants of other peoples. Because there are many faiths but only one God, we are called on to love the stranger who is unlike ourselves no less than the brother or the neighbour who is like ourselves. To be sure there is a covenant that is universal—for Judaism, the covenant with Noah—which sets the minimum threshold for different peoples to live together in justice and peace. But beyond this lies the intrinsic plurality of human meanings and the distinct integrity of different faith communities. To this truth Judaism, with its code of difference, is an eternal witness.[40]

What I'd like to highlight in this passage, first of all, is that the reference to the covenant with Noah is secondary and almost incidental to the main covenantal argument. That argument is based on a notion of multiple covenants corresponding to particular religions—these covenants express parallel relationships with God, all founded on the principle, so central to Sacks' world-

---

[39] See also the essay entitled 'The Interfaith Imperative', 78–9. In dialogue with Hava Tirosh-Samuelson, Sacks reports that these ideas had been tested out on various religious minorities previously, and were thus ripe for application to the situation that arose following the events of 9/11. See Tirosh-Samuelson and Hughes (eds.), *Jonathan Sacks: Universalizing Particularity*, 123.   [40] *Crisis and Covenant*, 253.

view, of one God—many faiths. Far from being the exclusive privilege of Israel, covenant is part of the DNA, so to speak, of entering a relationship with God. One covenant does not negate the covenants of other people.[41] I imagine Sacks did not envisage God concluding covenants with all faiths, seriatim, in the same manner in which a covenant was concluded at Sinai. Rather, the relationship with God and the affirmation of the particularity of a given religion is cast in terms of covenant.[42] Rather than covenant constituting a relationship, relationship is recast as covenant.[43] This is, in itself, a broadening of the range of meaning of the term, in line with other conceptual expansions that characterize Sacks' use of it. Given the importance that he attaches to the idea, his extension of it to any expression of faith, and apparently independently of active covenant-making, is not surprising. Its importance, then, is not derived solely from its social, horizontal, potential. It is the primary vehicle for connecting God and humanity. In view of the multiple forms of humanity and its social organization, multiple religions, each enjoying its own covenant with God, is almost a natural conclusion.

Against this principled view of covenantal religions, the covenant with Noah is cited as a foundational common ground upon which the particularity of religions grows. Its substance is moral and ethical. While it is not religious in a narrow sense, it does provide the basis for religious particularity. One may say that, in a manner analogous to how the one God engenders many faiths, so the one common moral foundation gives rise to the particularity of multiple faiths. This allows us to also appreciate why a covenant is needed. In this context, covenant is clearly understood in vertical, even if not specifically religious, terms, grounding humanity's ethical behaviour in its relationship with God, of universal scope and moral content.

Two further points are worth mentioning in relation to this paragraph. Nowhere is the notion of the image of God featured. The basis for acceptance of the other is the Noahide covenant, not the idea of man being created

---

[41] Ibid. For a discussion of these ideas in the theoretical context of postmodernism and the relativity of truth, see Feldmann Kaye, *Jewish Theology for a Postmodern Age*, index, s.v. Sacks, and especially pp. 131–4. See also ead., 'Multiple Truths and the Towers of Babel'.

[42] I have suggested the same with regard to Greenberg's use of the term to describe other religions.

[43] I believe it is this that lies at the heart of Sacks' views, rather than a concept of religious truth. Jerome Gellman rejects Sacks' views from the perspective of religious truth. See Gellman, *God's Kindness Has Overwhelmed Us*, 61.

in God's image. This will change as the ideas are nuanced over time.[44] As the image of God gains in prominence, what is validated is not the other religion but the other himself, the person, regardless of particularity of religion, not on account of it.

A second observation worth making relates to how the 'other' is being described. The paragraph speaks of different faiths, each enjoying its own covenantal relationship with God. If the lessons are of acceptance and eventually of love, then one could derive from here the obligation to accept, love, and relate to the member of another religion in terms of the particularity of his or her faith. Multiple covenants, all valid, are seen as the basis for love of the other, not the common Noahide covenant. Sacks, however, fails to take his reasoning to its ultimate conclusion. The diversity of legitimate faiths and covenants translates to the command to love the stranger.[45] Yet it is by virtue of otherness and being a stranger that the stranger is loved, not because of the particularity of his or her faith, which, after all, was the focus of Sacks' argument. In part we might account for this by recalling that the Torah speaks of love of the stranger (actually the sojourner, who might also be understood as a convert), not of the love of a member of another faith. Nevertheless, nothing would have prevented Sacks from applying the biblical command to the context that he had developed, and which could have easily yielded the command to love the member of another faith in the *particularity* of that faith. This, I submit, is no accident. It coheres with a broader pattern in Sacks' relationship to religions. While he provides the wherewithal for a foundational acceptance of religious otherness, he consistently stops short of real engagement with the particularity he has fought so hard to legitimate. He is interested either in legitimating and affirming particularity as an idea or ideal, or in making the important gains that such affirmation would bring to the legitimation of Jewish particularity in a broader context. But whatever such affirmation signals in terms of interest and care for the particularity of a member of another religion is never applied. For reasons I discuss below, Sacks' own marshalling of the ideal of particularity never moves from a generalized, universalized validation to an appreciation of the particular in and of itself.

---

[44] See *Radical Then, Radical Now* (roughly contemporaneous with *The Dignity of Difference*), 90. A further development is the view of all people, despite differences in religion, as children of God. See ibid. 91. The theme is echoed in *The Dignity of Difference*, 195.

[45] The same is true of *The Dignity of Difference*, 207.

Let us consider how these ideas are articulated in *The Dignity of Difference*. Sacks' summary provides a good overview of his argument.

I have argued that if we are to find an idea equal to the challenge of our time it must come from within the great religious traditions themselves. I have tried to articulate one possible form of that idea. It is that the one God, creator of diversity, commands us to honour his creation by respecting diversity. God, the parent of mankind, loves us as a parent loves—each child for what he or she uniquely is. The idea that one God entails one faith, one truth, one covenant, is countered by the story of Babel. That story is preceded by the covenant with Noah and thus with all mankind—the moral basis of a shared humanity, and thus ultimately of universal human rights. But it is followed by an assertion of the dignity of difference—of Abraham and his children who follow their diverging paths to his presence, each valued, each 'chosen', each loved, each blessed by God. Until the great faiths not merely tolerate but find positive value in the diversity of the human condition, we will have wars, and their cost in human lives will continue to rise.[46]

The thrust of the paragraph is the validity of multiple particularities. As in the passage from *Crisis and Covenant*, there is something common that touches all of humanity and remains relevant to present-day concerns as these are expressed in the notion of universal human rights. But what matters most in this argument is the value of parallel particularities, each chosen, blessed, and enjoying a relationship with God, captured, among other ways, in terms of covenant. The ideal is finding positive value in the diversity of the human condition, echoing the guarded affirmation of engaging with diversity, noted above.

This passage is one of the many that was revised in the second edition of *The Dignity of Difference*. It is worth noting the changes:

I have argued that if we are to find an idea equal to the challenge of our time it must come from within the great religious traditions themselves. I have tried to articulate one possible form of that idea. It is that the one God, creator of diversity, commands us to honour his creation by respecting diversity. God, the maker of all, has set his image on the person as such, prior to and independently of our varied cultures and civilizations, thus conferring on human life a dignity and sanctity that transcends our differences. That is the burden of his covenant with Noah and thus with all mankind. It is the moral basis of our shared humanity, and thus ultimately of universal human rights. That is why the later covenant with Abraham and his children does not exclude other paths to salvation. The righteous of all nations—those who honour God and his covenant with man-

[46] Ibid. 200. See also *Radical Then, Radical Now*, 90.

kind—have a share in the world to come. Until the great faiths not merely tolerate but find positive value in the diversity of the human condition, we will have wars, and their cost in human lives will continue to rise.[47]

The changes in the second edition are intended to tone down the idea of full and equal value attached to different religions. The first edition claimed equality on both levels: the covenant with Noah was universal by its very definition, and particular faiths and covenants were on a par with one another. These ideas were deemed too radical by some in Sacks' Jewish constituency, leading to their revision, which recasts them in line with classical views of other religions and Judaism's relations with them. Judaism is no longer on a par with others. Rather than validation of other religions by means of particular covenants, it is the covenant with Noah that confers value on other faiths. The revised Sacks, then, downplays the later covenants, which leads to a significant upgrading of the meaning of the covenant with Noah. While formally still engaged in providing a common moral foundation for all of humanity, in fact it does a lot more. In this recasting, it takes on soteriological value and ends up functioning as a kind of religion, or religion in its essence, even though it does not feature any of the particularities of the religious life beyond moral foundations.[48] It thus serves as a universal religion of sorts, bestowing validity on others. Religions would then be judged and validated in view of their compliance with the Noahide covenant, rather than appreciated in terms of the multiple particularities articulated in the earlier formulations.

As noted above, an important conceptual shift occurs as the covenant with Noah is seen in light of the rabbinic 'Noahide commandments'. This identification adds substance to the covenant, making it more robust, which, in part, allows it to fulfil the functions of a religion in ways that the biblical covenant alone could not. Along with this, we also note the emphasis on the image of God as a central feature of this Noahide covenant. If particular covenants are no longer the means of affirming a relationship with God, and especially if one recognizes that the covenant with Noah has moral but

---

[47] *The Dignity of Difference*, 200 (2nd edn., 2003).

[48] While the Noahide commandments do not provide the fullness of a religion, Sacks is able to recast them in very broad terms. 'The Noahide laws, as understood by Judaism's sages, set out the broad parameters of a decent society: respect for God, human life, the family, property, animal welfare and the rule of law' (*Not in God's Name*, 209). On how the Noahide commandments have been stretched in order to form a fuller notion of religion, see my *In God's Presence*, ch. 3.

not religious content, the idea of man being created in the image of God helps close the gap by providing a more religious, and God-related, reasoning to the moral commandments, common to all of humanity and hence to all religions. All these changes are reflected in the revised text.[49]

These constitute a shared code of humanity prior to and transcending religious difference. According to Maimonides, a non-Jew who keeps these laws because of a belief in the revealed truth of the Mosaic revelation is one of the 'pious of the nations of the world' and has a share in the world to come.[50]

Later works offer adaptations of these ideas that are removed from the juxtaposition of the covenants with Noah and Abraham. The association of the covenant with Noah and religious practices and concerns that appear in both versions of *The Dignity of Difference* give way to other emphases. It is possible that the shift is itself part of the controversy around *The Dignity of Difference*. If Sacks' true intention was to contrast the universal moral foundations with multiple covenantal particularities, and if this emphasis was revised in line with more classical Jewish views of other religions and their valuation, it is possible that he simply cut his losses. What he wanted to say he could no longer say, and what he could say was far less interesting. Hence, the juxtaposition of the two covenants is no longer featured in later works. Alternatively, the dynamic process wherein Sacks adapts a set of sources to varying needs and theses indicates that he has exhausted the concerns of religious pluralism. Later writings feature the same sources in the service of other social issues, often related but nevertheless distinct.[51]

There are two changes in these later books that seem to me significant in terms of how the covenant with Noah is applied. One is the emphasis on the horizontal dimension of that covenant; the other is the potential shift in the context of the Noahide commandments towards creation itself. Both changes show how creative Sacks is in providing new contexts and emphases for his covenantal thinking. They also show how the earlier association of the Noahide covenant with religions or with proper religious concerns has

---

[49] See also *The Dignity of Difference*, 17, where 'can I, a Jew, hear the echoes of God's voice', with reference to the religious other, has been changed to 'can I, a Jew, recognize God's image'.   [50] Ibid. (2nd edn.), 20.

[51] He does offer a succinct version of the thesis of *The Dignity of Difference* and of the two covenants in ch. 4 of *Future Tense*. The message is toned down. Covenant is referred to in relation to the global covenant of solidarity. Other religions have integrity, but they are described neither in terms of truth nor in terms of covenant. The stark juxtaposition of version 1 of *The Dignity of Difference* is never again repeated in Sacks' corpus.

been replaced by other concerns.[52] If, as I have suggested, Sacks' use of the dual structure juxtaposing the covenants with Noah and Abraham reflects Greenberg's influence, the later uses suggest a breaking away from the earlier formative influence and continued independent adaptation of these motifs.[53]

Let us consider first the horizontal understanding of the covenant with Noah, mostly detaching it from its biblical context and its associations with God and his commitments, whether as a one-sided or as a reciprocal engagement. In various places Sacks issues an appeal for a covenant of human solidarity, sometimes also referred to as a covenant of hope. The very description of a covenant of human solidarity indicates horizontal dimensions. The wording similarly suggests a mostly human initiative, paralleling the Puritan political application of the Sinai covenant: 'It is the time to renew that most ancient of biblical institutions, the covenant of human solidarity, made in the days of Noah after the Flood.'[54]

Covenant renewal today would be a human initiative, and the covenant of solidarity similarly has strong horizontal values. Missing from this declaration is an accounting for why the covenant in Noah's days would have been one of solidarity. A likely suggestion relies on its content. If the substance of the Noahide commandments defines their purpose, then Sacks has identified a very smart way of restating the purpose of those six or seven commandments. He offers here a common denominator that provides a framing for them: the various prohibitions, notably that of murder, but other commandments as well, all contribute to human solid-

---

[52] The counterpart to these changes seems to be a redefinition of the significance of Abraham. Rather than a model of particularity, Abraham provides the common denominator for 'Abrahamic monotheisms', which are now viewed as a group. Accordingly, the particularity of Judaism, previously symbolized by Abraham, is appreciated as part of the message of Abraham and of the various religions that look to his person. Rather than universality and particularity, a new dyad emerges—the person and the image of God, as taught by Abrahamic religions, versus empire and its dehumanization. The image of God, previously associated with the covenant with Noah, now features as the message of Abraham. These moves are seen in *The Great Partnership* and in *Not in God's Name*. It is worth stating, against this overview, that in no configuration of his thought does Moses (or Sinai) emerge as the major religious archetype. In this, Greenberg's attempt to incorporate Sinai into his conceptual scheme does greater justice to classical Jewish perspectives.

[53] This doesn't mean that Sacks ceases to point to the juxtaposition. However, it no longer serves to support religious particularity and the covenantal validity of multiple faiths. Instead, it simply illustrates the principle of moving from the universal to the particular. See *Future Tense*, 80.   [54] Ibid. 9–10.

arity.[55] The horizontal dimension of the covenant of human solidarity is a notion to which I shall return in greater detail below.

Moving away from the concerns of affording full dignity and value to other faiths, Sacks uses the same building blocks to make an argument in favour of a double message and double valuation, upholding universality and particularity both. While this message can confer value on the religious other, it serves also as an important corrective to excessive self-interest and loss of a broader perspective that recognizes the values that grow from the common denominator between Jews and humanity, or, if you will, the proper balance between Israel's particularity and ways in which it must continue to uphold its share in broader universality. Here is how these building blocks serve this message, now oriented inwards. Let us hear Sacks' own summary of *Future Tense*:

I have argued, not only in this chapter but throughout the book, that a basic duality runs through Judaism, shaping its view of the world. It honours both the universality of the human condition and the particularity of Jewish faith. So the Torah contains two stories, one from Adam to Noah, the other from Abraham to Moses. It contains two covenants, one with all humanity, the other with the people of Israel. There are two different names of God. There are two manifestations of God, one in creation, the other in revelation. And there are two forms of knowledge, *chokhmah* and Torah. Neither displaces or supersedes the other. To be a Jew is to be both. We are part of humanity and its story, and we are children of Abraham and Sarah and their story.[56]

Note: we are now speaking of a duality within Judaism, rather than of the message of Judaism to the world.[57] The two covenants are mentioned, but as expressions of internal Jewish consciousness. This corresponds to the two names of God, one more universal, one more particular, or, as Sacks points out in other contexts, more relational. This, in turn, corresponds to two forms of knowledge—wisdom, which is creation-based and is shared with all of humanity, and Torah, which is revelation-based and is particular to Israel.

Sacks never makes the connection explicitly, but in fact he has moved Noah's covenant back to creation. There are three ways he could have

[55] While this is a very clever way of presenting the Noahide commandments, it fails to take account of the more purely religious prohibitions of idolatry and cursing God.

[56] *Future Tense*, 226.

[57] An earlier passage in *Future Tense* did speak in those terms; see p. 86.

got there. The first is the grounding of the Noahide commandments in creation, inasmuch as they were given to Adam. This is a path not taken by Sacks, but in fact, unwittingly, he returns to the foundations of the rabbinic view of the Noahide commandments as being independent of the covenant with Noah. The other is to tie the notion of covenant to creation itself, and then to push back the covenant with Noah to an earlier covenant.[58] Again, this path is not consciously taken by Sacks, though in fact he makes it credible in his argument. The Christian reformed view that associates covenant with creation would be very comfortable with the cluster of themes that Sacks ties together.[59] The way he arrives at this series of ideas is by associating the universal, identified with the Noahide covenant, with creation, wisdom, and the universal knowledge of God, going back to Genesis 1. In effect, then, the covenant with Noah is read in the framework of broader universal concerns that remove it from covenantal history and further weaken its relevance to other religions. The idea continues to fascinate him, but now in the context of internal Jewish balances, in light of his juxtaposition of universal and particular. In effect, Sacks has moved the discussion back to what matters most to Jews—the relationship between Creation and revelation, rather than the construct of two covenants, which meant a lot in a view of other religions but means much less when fundamental tensions within Judaism are concerned.

Another configuration of the Noah–Abraham juxtaposition plays out in terms of universal and particular, while sidestepping the concerns of religious pluralism. Instead, the dyad serves as a means of refracting different dimensions of morality, in line with the perspectives of the universal and the particular. Thus we hear in his later book, *Not in God's Name*:

The Noah covenant is the Bible's universal code, the basic infrastructure of a just social order. The Noahide laws, as understood by Judaism's sages, set out the broad parameters of a decent society: respect for God, human life, the family, property, animal welfare and the rule of law. These principles are general, not specific: thin, not thick. They apply to everyone in virtue of the fact that they are in the image of God, therefore worthy of dignity and respect. They are universal rules of what today we would call responsibilities and rights.[60]

[58] See Sarna, *The JPS Torah Commentary: Genesis*, 53, on Gen. 6: 18.
[59] While he is aware of the Puritan political tradition and its appeal to the biblical covenant, I have found no indication of his active use of so-called federal theology, namely the reformed understanding of covenant tradition, recognizing in it the narrative core of the biblical story. See above, p. 17.   [60] *Not in God's Name*, 209.

For Noah's covenant to represent what a decent society is, we require a degree of abstraction beyond the content of the Noahide laws. Sacks provides this in a very creative way. Note, once again, the appeal to the image of God as a central moral principle. These laws achieve dignity and respect. These, however, are far less than the love and particularity of relationship that are enabled by the covenant with Abraham.[61] Let us consider one further juxtaposition of the two covenants.

The covenant with Noah (Gen. 9) uses the word Elokim throughout, while the covenant with Abraham uses the word Hashem (15: 18; 17: 1–2). The Noah covenant expresses the unity of God and the shared dignity and responsibility of humankind. The Abrahamic covenant expresses the particularity of our relationship with God, which has to do with our specific identity, history, language and literature. The result is that in the Bible there is both a morality that applies to everyone, insider and outsider alike, and an ethic, that is, a specific code of conduct that frames relationships within the group. To use the language of contemporary philosophy, morality is thin (abstract, general) while ethics is thick (full of local texture and specificity).[62]

What is most important for Sacks is to maintain the fundamental polarities of universal and particular. This is the concern that drives his thinking. The validation of other religions, especially in terms of covenant, is one specific means of applying these ideas—almost episodic and subject to pressures and potentially unfavourable responses. They do not, however, undermine the core distinction between universal and particular, which is then cast in alternative terms—but these are secondary to the dyad. This being the case, attacks on Sacks' application of the two covenants to the concerns of religious pluralism only touch the secondary expressions of a deeper insight that informs his thinking. Whether they are accepted or recast in other terms, as in the second version of *The Dignity of Difference*, what matters most is the basic distinction, which finds new expressions as Sacks' interests shift in later projects.

A Covenant of Hope and Responsibility

Covenant is an ancient idea, but for Sacks it is also a vital and urgent need of the present. Drawing from the twofold sources of biblical tradition and political theory, he holds up to the world a vision of organizing society,

---

[61] Ibid.   [62] Ibid. 208.

locally and globally, by means of that concept, replacing the older reliance on the social contract.[63] As the idea derives from both sources and as it is put in the service of pressing contemporary needs, its uses are horizontal rather than vertical. The application of covenant to the global and civic situation is a motif that runs throughout Sacks' corpus. As such, it is not relevant to the concerns of the present discussion of religions. There are, however, two perspectives that allow us to consider this important theme also with regard to religions, and in so doing to gain a better sense of Sacks' views of relations between religions.

The first of these has to do with the relationship between the global covenant of hope or solidarity and the covenant with Noah. If, as we have seen, the latter intersects with religious pluralism, then its application to the present call to a global covenant of solidarity would also be relevant to religions. Here, however, it seems that religions are not specifically considered as part of the appeal to the covenant with Noah. First, one must recognize that the call to a new global covenant does not specifically rely on the Noahide covenant.[64] Sacks himself considers the idea of a global covenant to be self-standing and the reference to the covenant with Noah is secondary.

The covenant of human solidarity, which we call the covenant with Noah in Genesis, chapter nine, although it doesn't matter what theological basis you give.[65]

The covenant with Noah after the flood is at best one example of a sense of global responsibility, drawing at the same time from other sources.[66]

The detachment of the global covenant from Noah may be linked to a further shift in Sacks' positioning in relation to world religions. His earlier work pits Judaism against them, offering a vision of particularity that all should uphold, and which is based on the contrast between the covenants of Noah and Abraham. Sacks' later work is carried out less in the name of Judaism and more as a thinker serving humanity and its needs, while continuing to draw from Jewish sources. In the process, he speaks increasingly of Abra-

[63] *The Dignity of Difference*, 205.

[64] A close reading of chapter 11 of *The Dignity of Difference*, where the idea is put forth, shows that only minimal contact is made with the covenant of Noah. The idea largely stands on its own. The covenant with Noah provides grounding and illustration, but is not really the source of the idea. Hence, the associations it has with religions remain irrelevant to this call.   [65] 'Interfaith Relations and the Holocaust'.

[66] *The Dignity of Difference*, 209. In *Morality*, Sacks can speak of this covenant without any reference to the covenant with Noah. See pp. 312–14.

hamic monotheisms and their common testimony.[67] In an attempt to go beyond the particular clothes that the religions wear, he speaks of the core of monotheistic faith as such.[68] In his later writings, Abraham appears as the religious ideal common to Jews, Christians, and Muslims. The original Abrahamic stand against ancient empire is revived in the message that Sacks draws from his biblical reading of the patriarch, and by means of which he seeks to correct other Abrahamic religions and the ways in which they have strayed from the proper faith of Abraham. With this new positioning, the figure that establishes commonality between Sacks' primary conversation partners, though surely not all religions, is Abraham. Rather than serving as the emblem of particularity posited against the universality of Noah, he becomes the focal point of commonality. With this new emphasis, there is less need and less interest in the unifying figure of Noah and his universal covenant.

There is a second sense in which religions enter the conversation on the idea of the global covenant put forth by Sacks, who also notes the contributions of religions to that covenant. Here, he draws on his experience as a religious leader and on the ways in which collaboration between religious leaders provides precedent and example for how such a covenant of solidarity or hope functions. The theme appears in several contexts. The civic or global perspective leads to what seems like a flattening of the religious potential of his vision. The covenant is not made with God; it is made between diverse members of society. The Bible, with its dual vertical/horizontal perspectives, provides the inspiration but does not define the parameters within which the covenant is concluded.

The point is even more striking when it comes to religions and their contribution to the global covenant. Their teachings are to be shared as part of a common human heritage. Religious leaders provide models for positive social behaviour and for the acceptance of and care for the other. But religions never interact with each other in a covenantal way. Given the dual concern with the covenant and relations between religions, one might have expected the idea of a covenant between religions to be one of the high points of Sacks' vision for society today. One could have expected a

---

[67] This shift in orientation is noticed most visibly in *Not in God's Name* and *Morality*. Prior to referring to them in this way, Sacks simply referred to them as 'great' monotheisms. He has certainly imbibed the common designation of these faiths as 'Abrahamic'. See *Another Way*, 86.   [68] *The Great Partnership*, 7.

statement that, whereas in the past religions competed with each other, today they must affirm each other, show respect for each other, and draw on each other's finest resources. To this end, a covenant between them would be concluded, for the benefit of the religions, the faithful, and society at large. But such a statement is nowhere to be found. Despite the centrality and prominence of the covenant in Sacks' thought, it is never applied directly to religions and their relations. He emerges as a social thinker who seeks to deliver a message to society, drawn from religious sources, among others. He is also a religious leader who appreciates the benefits of interreligious collaboration and how it contributes to society at large. However, his *religious* vision stops short of implementing the fullness of covenantal ideals to the relations between religions, and through them to society.

Before analysing some of the relevant texts, we would do well to consider why the idea of covenant is not extended fully to religions. In theory, the ancient biblical prohibition on concluding a covenant with other gods or other religions might cast a shadow on this possibility.[69] However, I doubt this is the case. If Sacks is accepting of the validity of other religions and is willing to collaborate with them for civic and global purposes, and if he has developed an idealized view of religious pluralism, it doesn't seem likely that this ancient prohibition would suddenly be resurrected to provide boundaries to the application of the covenantal ideal to present-day relations between religions. It seems, rather, that once again we have an indication of Sacks' range of interests. As we note at every turn, Sacks is a social thinker who reflects deeply on issues of political and social significance as these relate to religions. The actual encounter between religions, and the potential sharing of ideas this involves, seems to be of less interest to him. Hence, he will invest much in how religions contribute to society. He shows no interest in what religions can contribute to each other.

The following passage urges a covenant and almost suggests the need for one between religions, but never goes so far.

What makes covenant a concept for our time is that it affirms the dignity of difference. The great covenantal relationships—between God and mankind, between man and woman in marriage, between members of a community or citizens of a society—exist because both parties recognize that 'it is not good for man to be alone' ... Covenants exist because we are different and seek to preserve that difference, even as we come together to bring our several gifts to the common good.

---

[69] Exod. 23: 32.

They are brought into being because of the non-zero-sumness of relationship and interaction.

Covenants—because they are relational, not ontological—are inherently pluralistic. I have one kind of relationship with my parents, another with my spouse, others with my children, yet others with friends, neighbours, members of my faith, fellow citizens of my country, and with human beings wherever they suffer and need my help. None of these is exclusive . . . Pluralism is a form of hope, because it is founded in the understanding that precisely because we are different, each of us has something unique to contribute to the shared project of which we are a part. In the short term, our desires and needs may clash; but the very realization that difference is a source of blessing leads us to seek mediation, conflict resolution, conciliation and peace—the peace that is predicated on diversity, not on uniformity.

Covenant tells me that my faith is a form of relationship with God—and that *one relationship does not exclude any other*, any more than parenthood excludes a love for all one's children. Nowhere is this more magnificently set out than in the vision of Isaiah in which the prophet sees a time in which the two great historical enemies of Israel's past—Egypt and Assyria—will one day become God's chosen alongside Israel itself: . . . 'In that day Israel will be the third, along with Egypt and Assyria, a blessing on earth. The Lord Almighty will bless them, saying, "Blessed be Egypt my people, Assyria my handiwork, and Israel my inheritance"' (Isaiah 19: 19–25).[70]

The choice of proof text is striking. Sacks is quoting one of the most 'pluralistic' of biblical prophecies, one that can be read as assigning equal value to other nations in covenantal terms, and by implication to other faiths as well.[71] Significantly, the biblical text affirms the standing of other groups in relation to God, and not only to one another. It too does not speak of relations, let alone covenantal relations, between these different groups. However, once the religious pluralism that emerges from Isaiah's vision is seen within the broader web of covenantal relations that Sacks describes, we must ask ourselves why a covenant between religions could not exist, in parallel with the many other forms of covenant that he presents. Here is a suggestion for how he might have tackled the idea of a covenant between religions. Given the multiple particularities of religions in their respective covenants with God, and given their common foundations in the Noahide

---

[70] *The Dignity of Difference*, 203–4. For Greenberg's use of this prophecy, see *For the Sake of Heaven and Earth*, 205.

[71] On interpretations of this verse, see Goshen-Gottstein, *In God's Presence*, ch. 9 .

covenant, which grounds human responsibility in the relationship with God, we have now grown to the point of discovering within the covenant of Noah a shared covenantal commonality between religions. The covenant with Noah would then not be limited to moral concerns, but would provide the foundation for a solidarity that is based on *religious* identities and their plurality. That covenant would then be a covenant of covenants, going back to the foundation of the covenants of all religions, drawing out their vertical and horizontal significance. Yet this is a path not taken by Sacks, an unfulfilled promise and potential in my view.

The path he does take is that of a covenant of the common contribution of religions and their leaders to society.

It is the time to renew that most ancient of biblical institutions, the covenant of human solidarity, made in the days of Noah after the Flood. Without compromising one iota of Jewish faith or identity, Jews must stand alongside their friends, Christian, Muslim, Buddhist, Hindu, Sikh or secular humanist, in defence of freedom against the enemies of freedom, in affirmation of life against those who worship death and desecrate life.[72]

This show of solidarity is one expression of the movement wherein religions contribute to a broader covenant within society. While that covenant does not occur in the space between the religions, they do contribute to the common space of society.[73] We note once again the purpose for which the religious leaders of different traditions stand alongside one another:

Leaders of the various religions in Britain should be able to come together to create a covenant of their own. It would not be a declaration of faith, for we each have our own faith. It would be, instead, a declaration of collective commitment to the values of citizenship, belonging, respect for diversity, tolerance and the common good.[74]

Faith is excluded from the coming together of religious leaders, let alone a faith-based covenant between them. The purpose of the encounter is civic, affirming the civic values listed at the end of the passage.

At one point Sacks refers to 'a new covenant between the faiths'.[75] But its contents are the good deeds jointly performed, not the common grounding in God and its implications for the mutual flourishing and inspiration

---

[72] *Future Tense*, 10.
[73] This is the logic that informs *The Home We Build Together*. See *Morality*, 320–1.
[74] *The Home We Build Together*, 156.   [75] Ibid. 180.

between religions. If in this work this new covenant is detached from the one with Noah, in another context it is related to it. The lessons of the Noahide covenant are seen in relation to society as a whole. This finds expression in the application of the Jewish ideal of 'ways of peace'. Chapter 9 of *To Heal a Fractured World* explores the sense of global solidarity that emerges from the covenant of Noah. Its scope covers all those ideals that have been put forth by Sacks in *The Dignity of Difference* and other books—a duty to the well-being of ever-widening concentric circles to alleviate suffering. It also includes bringing the heritage of wisdom of specific religions to the public domain. The notion of 'ways of peace' as a social approach is a concrete application of the covenant of solidarity and a contribution of Jewish wisdom to the public domain. It has informed Sacks' view of interreligious relations as being action-driven in a side-by-side collaboration, enhancing respect between faiths.[76]

While it would seem that the category of ways of peace can exist in a purely horizontal manner, describing the relations between people, whether or not it is modelled on the covenant with Noah, I find one moment telling in terms of the coming together of horizontal and vertical dimensions. Sacks refers to the covenant of solidarity and its association with ways of peace with a passing reference to Psalm 91: 15: 'I will be with him in time of trouble.'[77] We recall the significance of this verse for Greenberg's theology.[78] What does it mean in the context of a global covenant of solidarity? There are two possible readings of this all-too-brief allusion. The one is that human solidarity is founded upon the shared reality of suffering, which leads to compassion. The other possible reading is to interpret the verse in its biblical context, where it is God who is suffering along with the human person. The global covenant of solidarity would then be based on the theological foundations of God suffering with us. If so, we have here a possible vertical association of the global covenant, beyond whatever the covenant with Noah brings with it, by way of association with a relationship with God.

Covenants of Fate and Destiny

Sacks is a master of recasting and reframing teachings. A set of basic insights is applied under varying circumstances, to novel situations. As opportunities

---

[76] *The Dignity of Difference*, p. viii, and ch. 15 of *The Home We Build Together*.

[77] *To Heal a Fractured World*, 106.

[78] See Ch. 1 above. Is this another point of contact between the two thinkers?

arise and as these texts are made to address them, new insight is gained by means of this set of teachings. One teaching in particular is cited time and again by Sacks and is central to his covenantal thinking: an idea originating with Rabbi J. B. Soloveitchik.[79] Soloveitchik distinguishes two types of covenant. In Hebrew these are *berit goral* and *berit yi'ud*, the covenant of fate and the covenant of destiny. This duality plays on the dual nature of Jewish identity as peoplehood and religion, and represents the different ways in which contemporary Jews identify themselves with Judaism: either by appeal to Jewish history, especially a lachrymose history, or, conversely, by appeal to Torah, its vision, and the common purpose it provides for the Jewish people. Two moments in the history of biblical Israel serve as convenient anchors for this dyad—the Exodus and Sinai. This is a powerful teaching that allows Soloveitchik to address fundamental challenges that face the Jewish people today regarding its identity.

This idea is cited time and again by Sacks. Most often, it is used in the very same context in which it served Soloveitchik—the struggle for purpose, meaning, and unity within a diverse Jewish people.[80] It is a tool for the critique of Jewish thinkers, including Greenberg, who relate to the state of the Jewish people only from the perspective of fate and not that of destiny / faith.[81] It also allows him to include the non-Orthodox by referring to the covenant of fate, regardless of religious disagreements.[82] Looking at Sacks' teachings on covenant as a whole, one may suggest there are two dyads that shape his outlook in this area. The first is this coupling of fate and destiny; the other is the dyad of the covenant with Noah and its counterpoint—that with Abraham. What happens when these two are superimposed upon one another and brought into conversation? It is here that Soloveitchik's distinction, initially framed within an internal Jewish context, is extended to world religions.

The following text shows Sacks' genius in opening teachings up to new meanings and making them address new audiences and new circumstances. In 2008 he was invited to address the Lambeth Conference, a decennial assembly of bishops of the Anglican community, who gather in London, at Lambeth Palace, seat of the Archbishop of Canterbury. It was the first time

---

[79] Soloveitchik, *Kol Dodi Dofek*, 51–68.

[80] See *Tradition in an Untraditional Age*, 154, where it is used with reference to the Holocaust.

[81] *Crisis and Covenant*, 140.   [82] Ibid. 194. See further *One People?*, 86.

a rabbi was invited to address a global gathering of Anglican bishops, and a sign of the advancement of interfaith relations. Sacks is adept at identifying the message most suitable for the specific audience, which accounts for how teachings are recast in context. The text of his speech at Lambeth Palace is a fascinating example of how a Jewish message can be extended to broader publics and how internal Jewish categories are adapted to that end. Here is the relevant part, on the dual covenants of faith and fate.

Now that we have made this distinction, we can state a proposition of the utmost importance. When we read Genesis and Exodus superficially, it seems as if the covenants of Noah, Abraham and Sinai are the same sort of thing. But now we can see that they are not the same kind of thing at all.

The covenants of Abraham and Sinai are covenants of faith. But the covenant of Noah says nothing about faith. The world had been almost destroyed by a flood. All mankind, all life, with the exception of Noah's Ark, had shared the same fate. Humanity after the Flood was like the Jewish people after the Holocaust. The covenant of Noah is not a covenant of faith but a covenant of fate.

God says: Never again will I destroy the world. But I cannot promise that you will never destroy the world—because I have given you free will. All I can do is teach you how not to destroy the world. How?

The covenant of Noah has three dimensions. First: 'He who sheds the blood of man, by man shall his blood be shed, for in the image of God, He created man.' The first element is the sanctity of human life.

The second: Read Genesis 9 carefully and you will see that five times God insists that the covenant of Noah is not merely with humanity, but with all life on earth. So the second element is the integrity of the created world.

The third lies in the symbol of the covenant, the rainbow, in which the white light of God is refracted into all the colours of the spectrum. The rainbow symbolises what I have called the dignity of difference. The miracle at the heart of monotheism is that unity up there creates diversity down here. These three dimensions define the covenant of fate.

Note that the covenant of fate precedes the covenant of faith, because faith is particular, but fate is universal. That, then, is Genesis 9: the global covenant of human solidarity . . .

All three elements of the global covenant are in danger. The sanctity of human life is being desecrated by terror. The integrity of creation is threatened by environmental catastrophe. Respect for diversity is imperilled by what one writer has called the clash of civilisations. And to repeat—the covenant of fate precedes the covenant of faith. Before we can live *any* faith, we have to live. And we must honour our covenant with future generations that they will inherit a world in which it is possible to live. That is the call of God in our time.

And that is what we began to do last Thursday when we walked side by side: Christians, Jews, Sikhs, Muslims, Hindus, Buddhists, Jains, Zoroastrians and Baha'i. Because though we do not share a faith, we surely share a fate. Whatever our faith or lack of faith, hunger still hurts, disease still strikes, poverty still disfigures, and hate still kills. Few put it better than that great Christian poet, John Donne: 'Every man's death diminishes me, for I am involved in mankind.'

And we, Jews and Christians, who have worked so hard and so effectively at reconciliation, must show the world another way: honouring humanity as God's image, protecting the environment as God's work, respecting diversity as God's will, and keeping the covenant as God's word.

> Too long we have dwelt in the valley of tears.
> Let us walk together towards the mountain of the Lord,
> Side by side,
> Hand in hand,
> bound by a covenant of fate that turns strangers into friends.
> In an age of fear, let us be agents of hope.
> Together let us be a blessing to the world.[83]

This is a remarkable text. Sacks draws on theological resources to create a sense of commonality between Jews and Christians, as well as members of other religions, as they jointly serve the world. The conclusion is poetic and inspirational. It echoes Sacks' 'side-by-side' principle that guides interfaith relations. It includes hope, one of the key motifs in his theology.[84] It applies covenant, the cornerstone of his thought, to the relations between religions, providing the ground for friendship and echoing the key teaching, repeated throughout his corpus, of welcoming and loving the stranger. All this is made possible by employing the covenant of Noah, whereby interreligious relations are cast in light of a common fate, sidestepping all concerns of a common faith or lack thereof. This underscores the concern for the contribution of religion to society and its well-being. Religions, in this reading, have a common task in addressing the world and the challenges of the day. To this end, Sacks revisits the covenant with Noah and finds new meaning in it. If its earlier uses highlighted the divine initiative, in the context of deliver-

---

[83] 'Address by the Chief Rabbi to the Lambeth Conference'.

[84] Two books of his feature 'hope' in their title: *The Politics of Hope* and *From Optimism to Hope*.

ing a message to the leaders of other traditions Sacks stresses exclusively human responsibility, which he connects to the covenant in Genesis 9. Doing so involves a stretch in the meaning of the biblical text, which, as we see here and elsewhere, is pliable in the hands of Sacks the homilist for his pedagogical purposes.

The argument for the sanctity of life is a reasonable lesson to be drawn from Genesis 9, inasmuch as it is related to the obligations placed upon Noah, and humanity, either as part of or in conjunction with the covenant described later in the chapter.[85] The second lesson flows from the fact that the covenant is made with all life, not only with Noah. This does not lead to a reconsideration of whether this covenant really belongs within the covenantal history narrated by Sacks.[86] Rather, it yields one additional message of the covenant—the integrity of the created world. That this integrity is affirmed by divine promise, rather than as part of the injunction that is placed upon all of humanity, as part of this covenant, seems to not matter. The lesson to be derived, from whatever part of the covenant is being exegeted, is what counts. The most original lesson is linked to the symbol of the covenant, the rainbow—it is a means of asserting the dignity of difference against the backdrop of divine unity.[87] Again, it is not the mandate of the covenant but its lesson that is featured, and it is derived here not by expanding or recasting the contents of the text, but by offering a symbolic reading of the sign of the covenant.

Sacks recalls a side-by-side walk of leaders of almost all faiths. The contrast between faith and fate is striking: 'Because though we do not share a faith, we surely share a fate.' This is a powerful way of making the point that religious leaders, as well as those who lack faith, can still find common ground for addressing the pain and needs of humanity. But it also raises a big challenge. Is it true that there is no common ground of faith? An even more extreme version of this assumption is Sacks' statement elsewhere: 'faith divides'.[88] We must query this assumption. Surely Christians, his audience

[85] For the two possible readings, see my essay 'Genesis 9, Noah's Covenants and Jewish Theology of Religions'.

[86] This is the point I make in 'Genesis 9, Noah's Covenants and Jewish Theology of Religions'.

[87] Sacks attributes the idea to Rabbi S. R. Hirsch. See *Future Tense*, 79. An implicit allusion to the multiple colours of the rainbow may also be found in a passage by Rav Kook, cited by Sacks in ch. 11 of *Not in God's Name*, n. 8, as *Orot hakodesh*, iii. 15.

[88] *The Home We Build Together*, 299.

here, are comfortable thinking of the particularity of their faith in covenantal terms. Moreover, they would surely not feel comfortable with the claim that they have no common faith with Jews. After all, theirs is the God of Abraham, Isaac, and Jacob. And most, probably all, religious leaders who undertook the side-by-side walk would similarly argue that their commonalities, including commonality of faith, outweigh their differences. As religious people, there is much that binds these leaders across their diversity.

When the chief rabbi addresses bishops worldwide, is a common humanity the only thing that unites them? The lack of common faith might be stated with greater insistence than need be in view of the conceptual framework of this discourse, pitting faith and fate against each other. Yet one wonders whether a more 'religious' argument, based on common faith, could not be made. Doesn't deep faith unite, rather than divide? And what has become of the multiple covenants that other religions enjoy? Why does Sacks make no room for all that is common, shared, and pointing to the one God who is the goal and quest of all religions?

The answer lies, in part, in the rhetorical unfolding of the speech. Having extended Soloveitchik's teaching to other religions and linked it to the dual covenants of Noah and Abraham, Sacks is almost forced by his own rhetoric to affirm common fate, at the expense of common faith.

There may be, however, a deeper cause, which goes to the heart of Sacks' own spirituality, his approach to religions, and, consequently, his application of the covenantal dyad of Noah/Abraham. Repeatedly, he regards the covenant with Noah as a source of commonality, while the covenant with Abraham represents religious difference. Here we must pay close attention to the juxtaposition that is established. The alternative to commonality may be *particularity* or it may be *difference*. To argue for particularity does not mean to argue for non-comprehensibility, nor for the impossibility of sharing. By contrast, to argue for difference is, in fact, to make a statement that such difference keeps otherness off limits, relevant only to the other, commanding our respect but nevertheless beyond the scope of comprehension or sharing. If we recall, the first text we saw from Sacks' teachings described the covenant as part of the universalized wisdom of Israel. It can be shared and exported. The context there was political, but the idea of covenants being shared with others finds expression in Sacks' thinking also in relation to other religions. The passages from *Crisis and Covenant* and the original framing of *The Dignity of Difference* referred to multiple covenants. If different religions are different covenants, then the very application of the concept of covenant to other religions actually assumes a foundation of commonality, a similarity of structure, and hence something that in essence, even if not in detail, unites them across their diversity. However, the argument for *difference* as a value ultimately undermines this. Passages like the Lambeth speech and others repeatedly assume we have nothing to do with one another's religious particularity, which in fact has become a source of difference.[89] All we can share in is the moral foundation, represented by the covenant with Noah.[90] Actually, the very application of the fate/faith dyad may belie this claim. After all, Sacks is here sharing and universalizing an internal Jewish understanding, applying it to others with no concern for boundaries potentially established by particular covenants. But beyond this, the very claim is problematic and is largely undermined by his own theoretical foundations as spelled out in the earlier texts. And it is not only problematic in terms of its potential reception by audiences who feel more of a commonality with the religious other than Sacks allows for. More importantly, it is belied by religious phenomenology, spirituality, and the proven fact of individuals being able to share their religious particularity across religious differences, beyond the social and moral common ground.

As Sacks' thought evolves, so the possibilities of understanding, and therefore of sharing, particularity decrease and only a common moral ground remains. Close study of his attitude to other religions, and of the nuances that have been articulated at various stages, makes us aware of the barriers that he has set between Judaism and other religions, or between himself and other faiths. Herein lies the crux of the challenge. Is this a reasoned position stemming from a clear sense of a necessary boundary and separation between religions, or is this simply a matter of his own personal

---

[89] See further *To Heal a Fractured World*, 127: 'our faiths are different, profoundly so'. Why is the difference *profound* and why does its profundity outweigh all commonality? Sacks never exposes or explicates his fundamental assumptions. See also *Not in God's Name*, 218.

[90] The point is relevant with reference not only to Christians but to all religions. Consider the following description of what Jews can share with members of other faiths: 'Judaism is a faith and for the first time in history we have a chance to share that faith with others on equal terms, as Christians strive to rediscover the Jewish roots of their own faith, as moderate Muslims seek to understand how religion is compatible with democratic freedoms, and as Hindus and Sikhs turn to Jews for guidance in the delicate art of integration without assimilation' (*Future Tense*, 69). On the face of it, this is an open, outward-facing approach to other religions, in a spirit of sharing. However, closer scrutiny reveals that it is not really faith proper that is shared. What is shared is much closer to fate than it is to faith.

choice, personality, and preference? I will address this question farther along. For the time being, suffice it to note how covenant is extended to other religions and how Sacks does here what he does so well—universalizing particularity[91] and extending the messages of Judaism, framed internally, beyond Judaism.

[91] We recall this is the title of a presentation of Sacks' philosophy: Tirosh-Samuelson and Hughes (eds.), *Jonathan Sacks: Universalizing Particularity*. This phrase captures a fundamental move in Sacks' thought.

CHAPTER NINE

The Dignity of Difference

Sacks and a Jewish Theology of Religions

Sacks' distinction between covenants serves him as an instrument in creating a new position within Judaism towards world religions. In this, he makes an original and significant contribution to the field of Jewish theology of religions. His repeated application of the distinction, as well as his references to Judaism's vision of universality and particularity and how it offers a unique model for religious pluralism appear repeatedly throughout his corpus. The basic view remains the same while nuances and emphases shift in line with the particular project at hand. *The Dignity of Difference* focuses on the view of other religions and as such may be considered his most important and representative statement of a Jewish theology of religions. However, the fact that there are two versions of the book, along with supporting sources published in parallel with the revised edition, adds complexity to this fundamental statement of the Jewish approach to other faiths. Below I examine *The Dignity of Difference* in detail: I tease out the implications of the different versions for a Jewish theology of religions, as well as situating the work in relation to earlier and later iterations of the same key ideas. But before entering into a close discussion of *The Dignity of Difference*, let us consider in more theoretical terms Sacks' contribution to a Jewish theology of religions and situate it both within his own body of thought and within the history of Jewish reflection on other faiths.

While, in my mind, Sacks' contribution to the field is significant, he never describes his efforts in this way. He is aware of the literature; in *One People?* he shows familiarity with one of the most noted Christian theologians of religion, John Hick, and relies on his threefold categorization: exclusivism, inclusivism, and pluralism.[1] While he redefines the meaning of these terms, he does apply them, which allows us to refer to his work, and even to his

---

[1] *One People?*, 141. See also *Tradition in an Untraditional Age*, 175.

description of his own view of other religions, as pluralistic.[2] And yet Sacks never labels his application of multiple covenants to other religions as a Jewish theology of religions. Significantly, the one instance I have identified that comes near to that designation, in *Not in God's Name*, refers to his project as a Jewish *theology of the other*.[3] This, I believe, is a very significant distinction. The project of a Jewish theology of religions is concerned with the status of other religions, their validity, their purpose, and more. While Sacks contributes to this project, as I shall demonstrate, his real interests lie elsewhere—in developing a theory of legitimating and accepting otherness. The religious particularity of the other is less important than the reality of the other; the other religion less significant than the face of the other. And, to a large extent, the image of God in the human person is more significant than the question of the other God and affirming the sameness of his identity and that of the God worshipped by Israel. And so both the achievements and the limitations that characterize Sacks' view of other religions may be attributed to the fact that whatever his contribution is to a Jewish theology of religions, it is a by-product of what for him is a more burning concern— developing a theory of accommodating the other in his or her particularity and difference, or, if one prefers to put it that way, a theory of religious pluralism.

Theology of religions is never conducted in a vacuum. Biblical and rabbinic views of other religions are not divorced from a view of empire. Classical Jewish attitudes to Christianity took shape against the backdrop of common living and the social and financial pressures that Jews had to deal with as a consequence of their view of Christianity as *avodah zarah* (idol worship) or its reverse.[4] Contemporary social circumstances play into present-day discussions of the status of Hinduism as *avodah zarah*.[5] The same holds true for Sacks' views of other religions. These too are formed in a particular social and political framework that shapes his concerns and defines the contours of his thinking. Recognition of the framework within which his thought is formed is relevant to understanding his task and to an assessment of his contribution to a Jewish theology of religions. Sacks is a social thinker who is concerned with society, its well-being, its moral development, and with peaceful relations within it. From the start, even prior to assuming the

---

[2] *One People?*, 119, 143.   [3] p. 27.
[4] The classic study of this is Katz, *Exclusiveness and Tolerance*.
[5] Goshen-Gottstein, *The Jewish Encounter with Hinduism*, ch. 11.

office of chief rabbi, his view of other religions focused on moral issues that religions had to tackle in common and in dialogue.[6] In his capacity as chief rabbi, he contributed to reflections on the building of a common home in the United Kingdom, where different religions must collaborate.[7] As a global Jewish thinker, he sought to advance peace and peaceful relations between religions, challenges that are articulated following the events of 9/11 in *The Dignity of Difference*, and, after more than a decade of further hatred brought about in the name of religion, in *Not in God's Name*. Sacks' concerns are civic, social, political, and international. As such, they are not strictly speaking theological, a fact that will shed light on many of the contradictions, gaps, and unfulfilled expectations that characterize his references to other religions, seen as a whole.

Students have studied Sacks' work from the perspective of his views of other religions, and especially in relation to the problem of religious truth. The differences I shall note in the two versions of *The Dignity of Difference* have therefore assumed great importance, given the shifts that are consequential from the perspective of a Jewish theology of religions. While it is important to analyse those shifts, as we shall, and while Sacks certainly provides some significant, at times ground-breaking, statements regarding Jewish views of other faiths, I believe it is important to consider his discussions in the context of what his true and ultimate concerns are. These, I submit, have more to do with the contribution of religion to society than they do with the understanding of other religions. In this he is completely unlike Greenberg, who is interested in genuine theological engagement with Christianity, and by way of extension with other religions. If, for Sacks, religion— by which I mean the combined efforts of different religions, their leadership, and their communities—is important for what it brings to society, then the view of other religions is similarly conditioned by this perspective, rather than by a more theological, theoretical one. As a consequence, Sacks provides often conflicting responses to the kinds of questions that a Jewish theology of religion might ask. Specifically, the status of other religions as *avodah zarah* and how it relates to his overall acceptance of them is a question that receives conflicting answers in his various writings.[8] One cannot avoid

---

[6] See Sacks, 'Jewish–Christian Dialogue: The Ethical Dimension'.

[7] *The Home We Build Together*.

[8] The question was raised, in relation to *The Dignity of Difference*, by Marc Shapiro; see 'Modern Orthodoxy and Religious Truth', 137; id., 'Of Books and Bans', 12–15.

addressing this issue if one seeks to develop a genuine Jewish perspective on world religions. However, if the purpose is different, the question will be either sidelined or will receive less attention, as is the case with Sacks' references to other religions that might be considered *avodah zarah*. He can comfortably refer in one breath to Christians, Muslims, Hindus, and Zoroastrians, with no concern for the possible theological distinctions that may exist with reference to each group.[9] Because they are all part of society and must all contribute to it positively and harmoniously, a theory is offered that accommodates all and positions Judaism in relation to all of them, as in turn they are positioned in relation to society. Sacks does not tell us how he bridges the gap between a theory of religious pluralism and the classical concerns of a Jewish theology of religions. This is where his interpreters, such as myself, may come forth with suggestions of how he might deal with some of the challenges he had left unsettled. I believe the gap between what interested him and what concerns a Jewish theology of religions can be closed. In the process, Sacks can not only be justified, but his own contribution may be appreciated for how it advances a Jewish theology of religions and how it deepens the understanding of specific positions already taken in the tradition, positions that take on new meaning in light of his oeuvre.

The question of Sacks' views of other religions touches on the issue of whether differences between religions are ideal. To put it in terms of classical Jewish learning, are they *lekhathilah*, intentions set out *ab initio* by the Creator as part of a divine design of an ideal world, or are they *bedi'avad*, ex post facto acceptance of a reality that is faulty, but the only one we have, and therefore a reality we must cope with as best as possible. Whether religious difference is an ideal established by God or some secondary, fallen reality will impact how other religions are seen, accepted, and legitimated. Moreover, the number of religions that are legitimated will be greater if they are seen as part of a divinely willed ordering of human reality and not as the result of human error, or even misguided aspiration towards God.

There are several statements in Sacks' corpus that are relevant to the discussion of religious diversity, *lekhathilah* or *bedi'avad*. One key issue is tracing the roots of that diversity, for which one of the most frequent reference points is the story of the Tower of Babel, discussed in multiple locations.[10]

---

[9] *The Dignity of Difference*, 21; *Not in God's Name*, 9; *Future Tense*, 88.

[10] *Tradition in an Untraditional Age*, 161; *Crisis and Covenant*, ch. 9; *The Dignity of Difference*, 51–2; *Future Tense*, 76–7; *Not in God's Name*, 204–6.

Note, the biblical story speaks of *linguistic*, not *religious*, diversity.[11] Sacks consistently expands the concept to include religion and in the process puts forth one of the central and most powerful analogies for religious diversity—the linguistic analogy.[12] Different religions are like different languages, and their legitimacy is as fundamental and almost as natural as that of languages in their diversity.[13] The linguistic analogy allows us to extend a tolerant view of the other—why should there be an intolerant view of another language?—to the domain of religion. It also allows us to appreciate diversity as something God-given, in the same way that the linguistic diversity reported in the Tower of Babel story was, after all, something enacted by God himself.

There is, however, a profound challenge, even a problem, in relying on the Tower of Babel story as the grounds for diversity. It is a story of human sin or pride, and the enactment of diversity is a measure of divine self-protection, so to speak, against humanity going too far, whatever that means. It is therefore not ideal. The ideal is linguistic (religious) unity and it is the imperfection of mankind that has brought about such diversity. Here we encounter one deeply engrained difficulty in Sacks' view of other religions, and one that shows us where different concerns make a difference to the kind of solution proposed. If the concern is common, harmonious living, then grounding the legitimacy of diversity in the story of the Tower of Babel is adequate. If, on the other hand, the concern is more theological, relating to

[11] Genesis does not really have a distinct notion of religious diversity. Even references to other gods seem to be contained within the overall framework of the view of one God. See Kaufmann, *The Religion of Israel*, 222.

[12] The linguistic analogy typically speaks of the languages by means of which God speaks to us. It can, however, also describe the many languages we use to speak to him. See Sacks, 'Global Covenant: A Jewish Perspective on Globalization', 226. This essay is a summary of the revised *Dignity of Difference*, though this particular argument does not appear in the revised version. It seems this is a further watering down of Sacks' more daring original formulations. This novel emphasis would seem to dispense with a prior requirement for monotheism and recognizing the same God. Humanity may be speaking to God in other languages, even by means of idolatry.

[13] The linguistic analogy is also used internally, to describe different forms of Orthodoxy as dialects of a language. See *One People?*, 92–3. This raises the interesting question of when different religious forms are to be considered languages and when dialects of the same language. On the basis of Sacks' later work, could the different Abrahamic monotheisms be described as dialects of a common Abrahamic language? In even more radical fashion, could the commonalities between religions not justify a view of them as dialects of the common Noahide covenant, rather than as different languages? The possibility of grouping of languages, which Sacks does not consider, offers further potential nuance to this question.

spiritual reality as an ideal, then in fact an inbuilt tension becomes apparent regarding the degree of legitimacy and idealism that can be attached to religious diversity.

The eschatological perspective refracts the question. What is the messianic vision of religious diversity?[14] Two answers are found in Sacks' corpus. The one view considers the legitimation of difference and diversity, including the ensuing legitimation of other religions, as temporary measures belonging to a pre-messianic age.[15] Accordingly, the ideal is not diversity, which, however, is the law for the present, imperfect era. The other view, also found in Sacks' writings, is that religious diversity is a feature of the eschaton.[16] Obviously, the two positions are in conflict and cannot be reconciled. They do not conflict, however, in terms of Sacks' intention for religions and their relations. In both cases, he urges and cares most about peaceful relations between religions today. Whether *lekhatḥilah* or *bedi'avad*, whether following one messianic vision or another—accepting diversity among religions is the will of God for today.

The plot thickens when a third moment in time is introduced into the consideration of religious diversity. From several perspectives, religious diversity is understood as ultimately founded in the order of creation. Complementing the linguistic analogy is the biological one. Diversity is a fact of life, and the diversity of species provides the most common and understandable parallel for recognizing this. Just as God wills the existence of multiple species, so he wills that there should be multiple religions.[17] It is worth noting that grounding religious diversity in creation is not a novel idea in and of

[14] For this question as a measure of a view of other religions, see Goshen-Gottstein, 'Towards a Jewish Theology of World Religions', 10–11.

[15] *To Heal a Fractured World*, ch. 8. Since Sacks includes non-monotheistic religions in his discussion of *darkhei shalom*, he employs an alternative strategy to that of the dual covenants to establish a universal language across religious difference. See p. 105. The difference between the limited acceptance of other religions here and the idealized acceptance of diversity in *The Dignity of Difference* is best explained as a function of conscious reference to pagan religions. This would also confirm that the fuller accommodating voice of *The Dignity of Difference* (probably in both versions) still assumes an understanding of a common God. Where such recognition is absent, the *darkhei shalom* theory serves as a substitute. Granting all this, there may still be a contradiction between Sacks' broader theory of religious difference and his appeal to *darkhei shalom* when he describes the rabbinic view that 'speaks directly to our situation in the religiously and culturally plural liberal democracies of the west' (*To Heal a Fractured World*, 109). If we are speaking of monotheistic religions, then the category is not the appropriate one to apply.

[16] *Future Tense*, 74.   [17] *The Dignity of Difference*, 22, 62, 173.

itself. It is found among Muslim theologians.[18] In this line of reasoning, the broadest affirmation and validation of religious difference should be offered to all. Religious diversity is a part of the created order and thus a clear expression of the will of God.

There is a second, if less direct, way of grounding religious diversity in creation. The cluster of ideas that Sacks advances in relation to realities outside Judaism includes several distinctions that complement the differentiation between the covenants with Noah and Abraham. The biblical story begins with Genesis, where God is known by the name Elohim. This is a universal name for God, shared by all humanity, and which contrasts with the special name known to Israel, the Tetragrammaton, typically referred to by the Jewish faithful as Hashem. Sacks is a proponent of universal knowledge of God alongside the special relationship Israel enjoys. Following this logic, as he himself does,[19] other religions would be related to the name Elohim, while Israel's faith is in Hashem. But that amounts to a grounding of all religious knowledge outside Judaism in creation itself, as the world was created by Elohim.

The same conclusion has to be drawn from the distinction between wisdom and revelation that complements this cluster of associations.[20] There is universal wisdom, which is not the same as the special knowledge that Israel receives through revelation. This wisdom is grounded in creation. Here Sacks carries forth a key recognition of biblical literature regarding the universal status of wisdom, a common heritage of all humanity. Other religions are seen in light of wisdom, and they take on a highly idealized, *lekhathilah* status. This affirms religious diversity and grounds it, once again, in creation, which, of course, has consequences for a Jewish theology of religions beyond the beneficial social consequences of adapting Sacks' understanding to social practice. The more ideal the view of religious diversity, the more Sacks' thought moves to the core of the concerns of a Jewish theology of religions.

It is clear that these different strategies yield different nuances. One of the differences has to do with the relationship between Judaism and other religions. Paradoxically, grounding faith outside Israel in creation creates a distinction, rather than a commonality, between Judaism and other faiths. Judaism enjoys a revelation and knows God by a different name than other

---

[18] Sacks shows no awareness of this fact.

[19] *Not in God's Name*, 207.   [20] See, among other sources, *Future Tense*, 226.

faiths; these, though legitimate, remain different. By contrast, grounding all difference in the Tower of Babel places Judaism on a par with other religions. In fact, the argument for particularity, learned from Abraham's covenant following the Tower of Babel story, is based on universalizing the relational pattern of Judaism as covenant and extending it to all religions.[21] Judaism, in this configuration, is not fundamentally different from other faiths as far as the key structures of the respective covenants with Noah and Abraham are concerned. The content differs, but the covenantal standing of the religions is identical. This difference in nuance reflects a key difference between the various writings of Sacks. In some of his books, Judaism is contrasted with all other religions.[22] The very structure of multiple covenants entails a balance of particularity and universality that is a special feature of Judaism, and Judaism alone.[23] In other writings, especially his later works, Judaism is appreciated as part of a larger cluster of religions, the Abrahamic monotheisms, and key lessons and messages apply to all.[24]

What we see, then, are shifting parameters for appreciating Judaism in relation to other faiths, shifts that amount to internal contradictions if the corpus is read as a whole. To these one might add one further significant difference—the attitude to non-monotheistic religions. As noted, Marc Shapiro has queried the implications of Sacks' theory of religious diversity for a Jewish view of *avodah zarah*.[25] Sacks himself offers different possible gateways for tackling the question. The perspective of *The Dignity of Difference*, and

[21] *The Dignity of Difference*, 56, 60.
[22] This is the case in *Radical Then, Radical Now*, *The Dignity of Difference*, and other, earlier works.
[23] Of course, if this is grounded in the Tower of Babel and the flow of the Genesis narrative into further covenants, there should not be a difference between Judaism and other religions and all should partake equally of this balance. This is also the basis for considering Judaism a model for others. Sacks does not address this challenge. It stems from the dual perspective of analysing, on the one hand, the message of the biblical story, leading to an equality between religions, and, on the other, the depth structure of Judaism compared to other religions, leading to a distinction. Even though the same argument is being made, it will feature Judaism as distinct or identical to others depending on what it is one analyses.
[24] The tendency is found in *Future Tense* and defines the logic of *Not in God's Name*. Its earliest articulation is *The Dignity of Difference*, 208. In his latest book, *Morality*, Sacks speaks not only for monotheistic religions, but for religion as such, as the debate with secular society requires. In this context, he is even willing to include the testimony of pagan traditions in his view of the benefits of religion, thereby placing them and Judaism in the same camp. See p. 290.
[25] The question appears in Shapiro's report on *The Dignity of Difference*, 'Of Books and

especially its grounding of religious difference in creation itself, would make the category of *avodah zarah* superfluous, or at least require some clear response as to how Sacks handles it. One possible answer that is taken up by Sacks in some contexts limits the application of this ideal to observance of the Noahide commandments, in other words the rejection of *avodah zarah*.[26]

The perspective of other works, where religious diversity is seen as *bedi'avad*, a reality of the present world but not an ideal, aids Sacks in confronting *avodah zarah* directly. The rabbinic notion of ways of peace, practices undertaken for the sake of harmony within society between Jews and their non-Jewish neighbours, is expanded into an ideal of interreligious relations and an affirmation of religious diversity.[27] Seen as a feature of premessianic existence, a necessary compromise with a faulty reality, it applies even to pagans and non-monotheists, all for the sake of social harmony.[28]

Another possible gateway might be to appreciate his emphasis on the *image* of God rather than on God himself. It may be that Sacks is less concerned with the problems of idolatry per se and more with human behaviour. Accordingly, idolatry might be defined as a function of moral behaviour rather than of theological nuance. I will suggest this presently, in reading Sacks in light of Meiri. But even before doing so, Sacks might have redefined the notion of idolatry, even if not for halakhic purposes, on the basis of this social and moral emphasis. Accordingly, he states at one point: 'The crimes of religion have one thing in common. They involve making God in our image instead of letting him remake us in his.'[29] There is a direct consequence to this definition. 'Terror is the epitome of idolatry. Its language is force, its principle to kill those with whom you disagree.' What this

Bans'. I do not think that Sacks' argument for the value of difference in other religions requires foregoing the notion of *avodah zarah*, and I doubt he ever intended that.

[26] *One People?*, 119; 'Miketz (5768)—Faith, Universal and Particular'. The answer antedates the changes to *The Dignity of Difference*. Shapiro, 'Modern Orthodoxy and Religious Truth', 142, claims that the meaning of the change to a Noahide foundation to other religions is that Judaism maintains theological veto power in terms of idolatry.

[27] See *To Heal a Fractured World*, ch. 8, and *The Home We Build Together*, 176–9.

[28] The following point is never made by Sacks, but does seem to derive from his thinking. Central to Sacks is the lesson of accepting the stranger, the other. This lesson is learned from our status as strangers in Egypt, which led the Torah to command us to welcome the Egyptians. They were, however, idol worshippers. If so, the welcoming attitude to the other and a key proof text for it are learned from the case of a non-monotheistic religion. See Deut. 23: 8.

[29] *Not in God's Name*, 279. See also *The Dignity of Difference*, 201.

means, then, is that the ultimate measure for idolatry is not God, but how we treat the image of God.[30]

As I believe we recognize by now, it is pointless to try to reconcile these conflicting views. Sacks can pitch his vision of religious harmony as *lekhat-ḥilah* or *bedi'avad*, as applying to monotheists or to non-monotheists, as extending to the eschaton or beyond it. These contradictions could be reconciled by changes in his views over time. More likely, however, is my own approach of reading Sacks contextually. He will put forward the argument that best fits his context, applying the same set of key ideas to various present-day social challenges. His goal, in his various projects, is to provide a religious perspective for these challenges. In the same way that he is not really interested in the theology of other religions, but only in justifying their very existence, it seems he is also not interested in the precise details of a *Jewish* theology of religions and more interested in applying Jewish sources, contradictions and all, to the present-day global need for peace and harmony.

From a traditional perspective, Sacks' innovations must be grounded, or evaluated, in dialogue with classic rabbinic views of other religions. His most central resource is the Bible as read creatively with a contemporary eye. Nevertheless, for his views to gain credence and to better be appreciated, they must stand in relation to rabbinic and halakhic sources as well.[31] To this end, I would like to consider Sacks' views of other religions through the prism of Meiri's thought.[32] We have already seen how Meiri provides the framework, and is also cited as a reference, for Greenberg's attitudes to Christianity. He is also the best classic rabbinic author through whom to appreciate Sacks' work. Moreover, while Meiri offers a view of other reli-

---

[30] There are other definitions of idolatry that could equally help address the present challenge. See, for example, that in *Radical Then, Radical Now*, 102: 'An idolatrous culture is one that sees reality in terms of impersonal forces. A Jewish culture is one that insists on the ultimate reality of the personal.'

[31] The problem of Sacks' reception in a rabbinic milieu is raised by Jotkowitz, 'Universalism and Particularism in the Jewish Tradition', 60–7. It is further highlighted by the problematic reception of *The Dignity of Difference*, which led to its revision and the ensuing attempt to ground his views in classical rabbinic sources, published in a sourcebook in conjunction with the revised edition. See below.

[32] Meiri is cited by Sacks in *One People?*, 143, and *Faith in the Future*, 121. In the former context, it is clear that he is one reference among several and does not necessarily provide the foundation for Sacks' own thinking. It would seem Meiri plays a more central role, consciously, for Greenberg than for Sacks.

gions, he does not explain the fact of religious diversity. Sacks could help account for a Meiri-based view of other religions by providing the theory of religious pluralism for which Meiri has laid the halakhic foundations.

There are two ways of applying Meiri to Sacks' view of other faiths.[33] The first focuses on religions as contributing to the moral order and to the establishment of a law-abiding society. The orientation of this reading is social and moral rather than theological. This coheres beautifully with Sacks' interests. The 'ways of religion' that uphold law and order in society can easily be seen as equivalent to an affirmation of the value and dignity of the human person and to the supreme value attached to the human person as the image of God. Meiri might even point to the kind of reasoning that informs Sacks' theory of religious diversity. For Sacks, the need for a diversity of faiths stems from the diversity of recipients. Ultimately no one civilization encompasses all the spiritual, ethical, and artistic expressions of mankind.[34] Because there are differences in humanity, each nation or religious community either hears God or approaches him in accordance with the particularity of its situation—be it geographical, genetic, psychological, climatological, or other. Meiri himself does not refer to religions. He refers to 'nations bound by the ways of religion', prioritizing people and ethnic identity over religious identity. This might be understood as equivalent to Sacks' emphasis on difference and variety as inherent in creation. Sacks, then, complements Meiri in accounting for why today, more than in previous ages, a Meiri-based view of other faiths makes sense and is a necessary foundation for a Jewish view of religions.

Meiri would also be helpful in resolving the question of non-monotheistic religions and how they fit into Sacks' view of religious diversity. Meiri almost rules out the existence of *avodah zarah* today.[35] His moral criterion leads to the recognition of all, or nearly all, forms of religion we know as compliant with his basic view of religions. Basing a view of religions on their common moral outlook, rather than on differing theological perspectives, even if these touch upon or compromise monotheism, is precisely what Meiri achieves. This, in turn, is refracted by Sacks and the criteria he applies to other religions.

---

[33] For an analysis of Meiri, see Goshen-Gottstein, *Same God, Other god*, ch. 10.

[34] *Dignity of Difference*, 62.

[35] The possibility of *avodah zarah* does remain in theory, and it is likely that the same would hold true for Sacks.

There is a second possible reading of Meiri, according to which a common moral ground points to a common God. In this reading, underlying the broad acceptance of other religions is a 'same God' view of other faiths. God, rather than a shared morality, is what establishes the common ground between them. Sacks' discourse is not primarily a God discourse and he does not take the trouble to analyse respective theologies in the interest of establishing how they point to a common God. However, the covenantal structure he applies to all religions, even if he does so mostly horizontally, does ultimately assume a same-God approach to religious diversity. Key arguments in *The Dignity of Difference* speak of the unity of God and how the one God relates to the different religions, either as they seek him or as they hear his voice. While this is embedded in his thought structure, I would like to cite here one particularly powerful passage where the notion of same God is applied, as part of a critique of religiously based violence, to members of all faiths, monotheistic and non-monotheistic. The argument is put forth tentatively, perhaps because it also extends to non-monotheistic religions. Yet I believe this captures an important dimension that is fundamental to the structure of Sacks' theory of religious pluralism.

What if the God of the Crusaders, the terrorists, the inquisitors, the witch-burners and the jihadists were also the God of their victims? What if one could not, with absolute certainty, rule out that possibility? Humanity lives in that 'what if' and cannot survive without it. For we are finite, but God is infinite. We are limited, but God is unlimited. However perfect our faith, there is something of God that lies beyond, which is known to God but cannot be known to the frail, fallible humanity that is all we are and ever will be, this side of heaven.[36]

Sacks, as we now recognize, is not a theologian of religions, though he makes significant contributions to the field and can be brought into fruitful dialogue with key voices in the history of Jewish appreciation of other faiths. That very fact also accounts for the limitations that are built into his approach. Because he is interested in legitimating other religions for social purposes, he does not relate to them in their particularity. Considering his structure, though, one wonders if it does not point to the possibility of a fuller engagement with other faiths than Sacks himself undertook. The key challenge of a Jewish theology of religions, historically, has been to legitimate other faiths. The starting point has been one of illegitimacy, and dif-

---

[36] *Not in God's Name*, 218.

ferent halakhic and theological perspectives were presented in an effort to afford legitimacy to religions under discussion. Sacks' starting point is the affirmation of legitimacy based on his dual-covenant model. As a consequence, the entire thrust of his teaching holds promise for more extensive and more thoughtful engagement with other religions. In this light, two perspectives for the study of other religions emerge.

The first has to do with the meaning of other religions for oneself. I shall devote an entire chapter to this problem, and will therefore only briefly mention it here. If all religions share in the covenantal structure and especially if all are grounded in creation, does this only serve as a strategy for respect and offering dignity to the other, or does it amount to an invitation to more active engagement and mutual enrichment? The comparison with Greenberg is obvious, but, more fundamentally, this seems to be a challenge inbuilt in Sacks' theoretical structure.

Sacks plays on the themes of unity and diversity as he legitimates the latter, and in turn difference. Unity above generates diversity below.[37] His theory not only accounts for how this diversity is related to the higher unity of the one God, but also affords legitimacy and respect to members of other faiths. But it does not spell out the mission of religions towards one another, nor does it define the tasks and challenges of a theology of religions. Nonetheless, the challenge of unity in diversity seems built into the fabric of his view of religions as a whole. If the story of the emergence of religions, whether *lekhathilah* or *bedi'avad*, is one of translating unity into diversity, shouldn't that story amount to an invitation to recover and recognize that very unity in the relations *between* religions? Should our approach to the other not go beyond respect and dignity and include the quest for recovering the fundamental unity of all religions? An entirely different theological, spiritual, and experiential agenda opens up if we consider the affirmation of unity in diversity to be the goal of religions and their relations.

In appreciating Sacks and his contribution to a Jewish theology of religions, one recognizes a significant distinction between his teachings and the conceptual thrust that has served all of Jewish reflection on other religions in history. This touches on the question of sameness and difference. The unique position which Sacks preaches and its *discontinuity* with the history of Jewish views are best appreciated as one further indication of his true

---

[37] *The Dignity of Difference*, 20, 52, 54.

concerns: a theology of the other or of religious pluralism, rather than a theology of religions.

One of the novelties of Sacks' view is highlighting the value of difference and his call for legitimating it in the religious sphere. Typically, a Jewish theology of religions overlooks difference. Strategies for affording respect to the other usually appeal to commonalities as the foundations for recognition, appreciation, and valuation. Commonality may be moral, theological, or historical, in the sense of a perceived continuity between Judaism and another religion that carries forth its message. In all this, difference is quietly overlooked. One appreciates what one has in common with the other and grants recognition, thereby often resolving practical challenges, and ignores some of the real stuff of religion, which creates division. This is especially true for Meiri, who was willing to overlook significant differences—theological as well as ritual—once a fundamental commonality, be it moral or theological, was affirmed. Sacks, unlike Meiri, makes religious difference the focus of his thought. Like Meiri, however, he never addresses difference in detail.

The following abstraction seems fair—all interreligious relations, dialogue, and above all theological reflection revolve around the axis of similarity and difference, highlighting one or the other according to the perspective one seeks, that is, whether to narrow divides or deepen chasms. As Sacks puts it, 'Humanity lives suspended between the twin facts of commonality and difference.'[38] The dialectic plays out in Sacks' writings in his highlighting of commonality with reference to the covenant with Noah, and of difference in relation to the covenant with Abraham. While he argues for the *value* of difference throughout his corpus, the actual *content* of difference is typically overlooked. This has implications for the extent and depth of appreciation of the other and for how far-reaching engagement with the religious other in his particularity might be. Ultimately, this raises the question of the extent to which a Jewish theology of religions might be grounded in an appreciation of difference, alongside establishing fundamental commonalities.

The Two Versions Compared and Analysed

As we know, within a year of the publication of *The Dignity of Difference*, Sacks was forced to issue a revised edition, in which he retracted, or reframed, many of the daring statements made in the first edition. Conse-

[38] *Not in God's Name*, 218.

quently, in thinking through a Jewish theory of difference, he ends up, against his will, providing us with not one but two such theories. He also put out an essay in which he spells out for a Jewish audience the traditional sources that support his views.[39] This provides further insight into the discussion, so that all in all we have three literary sources for thinking about how to put forth a Jewish view that respects difference. It may not be superfluous to note that, while the essay is supposed to justify Sacks' position, in fact its sources serve as proof at most for his rewritten thesis, but not for the original and more daring views he had advanced. In what follows, I shall compare the two formulations with an eye to identifying his two different strategies. The initial argument to be analysed is that of the original version. By tracking the changes between the original and the later version we can follow the changes in the argument and the alternative justifications he proposes.

Before presenting the argument, it is worth reflecting on changes in the second edition that shed light on the processes that inform Sacks' thinking. Sacks is aware of the radicality and novelty of his argument. He therefore offers, in the first edition, his own understanding and justification for how he has come to hold these original views.

I believe that God is summoning us to a new act of listening, going back to the sources of our faith and hearing in them something we missed before, because we did not face these challenges, this configuration of dilemmas before. In religions of revelation, discoveries are re-discoveries, a discernment of something that was always there but not necessarily audible from where our ancestors stood. God's word is for all time, but our act of listening is of *this* time, and the challenge is to discern within that word, as it speaks to us now, a narrative of hope.[40]

This entire section is absent from the second edition. Sacks' original hermeneutics are based on a dialectic of being present to novel circumstances and hearing God's word anew in light of those circumstances. Significantly, God's word is applied in relation to the Hebrew Bible, not the entire scope of what is traditionally referred to as Torah. Omitting this section suggests

---

[39] The essay is entitled 'A Clash of Civilizations? Judaic Sources on Co-existence'. It was originally published on the website of the Office of the Chief Rabbi (chiefrabbi.org). Curiously, it was never published on Sacks' personal website following his tenure as chief rabbi. A copy of it is available on http://www.scribd.com/doc/20065780/Rabbi-Jonathan-Sacks-Dignity-of-Difference-Sources-in-Traditional-Jewish-Literature.

[40] *The Dignity of Difference*, 19. See further the quote from p. 65, cited below.

a return to a more traditional approach to the issues under discussion, as indeed the following analysis will demonstrate.

To understand Sacks' thesis, it is useful first to spell out the arguments of which it is composed:

A. God is greater than any religion.

B. No religion is in possession of the fullness of truth.[41]

C. God has created or is responsible for the multiplicity of religions. Divinely ordained diversity extends to religions, hence we must respect them all.

He never presents his thesis in such a formal way. Rather, its elements interact with each other in varying permutations. One such permutation is that the goal is statement C, and statements A and B can lead to it independently, as some of the quotes below suggest. Alternatively, his argument may be reconstructed as incorporating all three statements.

The argument for God being greater than religion seems to be required if we want to make room for other faiths. If God's greatness is co-extensive with one religion, there would be no room for any others. Moreover, recognizing God as greater than a religion makes it possible to present God as the goal of our religious quest rather than obedience to a given religion, thereby creating opportunities for learning and inspiration from other traditions.

The question of the relationship between God and religion is of great educational and psychological import. The educational challenges at hand are broader than the philosophical challenge. A different kind of religious psychology and attitude to the other is established if one fully recognizes God's greatness in relation to religion. This would yield a religion that is God-centred rather than Torah-centred. People who are God-centred, it seems, will have a greater inclination to recognize and share with similar-minded individuals from other faith traditions.

This argument implies and is founded upon the second premise: truth belongs to God, not to religion, and therefore no religion may be considered to possess the fullness of truth. Sacks does not explore the possibility of proximate levels of truth and of one religion being more true than the other, in

---

[41] In conceptual terms, the discussion of different religions as parallel covenants would belong here. In what follows, I do not include this particular theologoumenon, which has been analysed above.

whatever respect, while still deficient in relation to celestial or divine truth. This could have been a way of dealing with his critics while maintaining his core thesis. It is, however, a path not taken. Instead, all religions are deemed equally partial and imperfect in relation to divine truth. To the extent that truth is the goal, no religion has a monopoly on it, which therefore leads us to seek God and to respect other faiths.

Because Sacks' aim is to gain respect for otherness, this argument may be sufficient for his cause. If he argued for the need, or even the legitimacy, of receiving from or being inspired by another religion, one could counter his reasoning and suggest that, since no religion is in possession of the fullness of truth, there is no point in learning from the other. One could further assert that one's religion is truer than that of the other. In that case, Sacks' argument may have to be supplemented by one that requires us to go beyond the inherent limitations of our own tradition in search of some aspects of truth found in another religion but not subject to the same limitations.[42] Given that each culture has its own ways and circumstances of placing limitations upon God's truth, this is not implausible.

One might have argued that the dynamic between God's ultimate truth and the varieties of partial and limited truth does not apply to all religions. This is where the third argument comes in. God is responsible for the diversity of religions, which is understood along the lines of natural and human diversity. Just as these are God-given, so are the numerous religions. In this sense, they are all on a par with each other, manifesting the same dynamics of tension between human and divine truth. No one religion is singled out as superior. Not only is Judaism not portrayed as such; its very message includes the value attached to the multiplicity of faiths. One could almost say that Judaism is best because it does not claim it is.

The meaning of the third argument, that all religions are God-given, must be limited by the second argument. All religions are God-given only within the parameters of limited human understanding, which never exhausts the meaning of divine truth. One assumes that some meaningful

---

[42] This would be analogous to the Indian metaphor of the blind men and the elephant. Sacks cites the metaphor in *One People?*, 142, as an expression of a pluralist understanding. He describes himself, or rather Judaism, as pluralist in relation to other religions. Applying this metaphor to his own theology of religions would have great potential, if worked out in detail. For its application as a justification for learning from other religions, see Glick, *Seeking the Divine Presence*, 224. From a more theoretical perspective, see Thatamanil, *Circling the Elephant: A Comparative Theology of Religious Diversity*.

measure of truth is communicated, otherwise why does God bother?[43] Whatever degree of truth does come through is both the basis for a demand of obedience to a given religion for its adherents and a basis for respect by others. If all religions were deemed to be hopelessly beyond the pale of a God-given truth, there would be no reason to respect them. So Sacks ends up walking a very fine line, wherein respect for the other is contingent simultaneously on the successful communication of divine truth within religions and its inherent limitations. One might think that the need to dissociate truth from religion is an internal necessity, a precondition for acknowledging the validity of other religions, while the claim that all religions share, supposedly to the same degree, their God-givenness is the basis for offering them respect. However, to the extent that the argument is made by dual reference to God's transcendence and the consequent inability to reach truth, on the one hand, and on the other to God's successful self-disclosure in multiple religions, there seems to be some degree of contradiction in Sacks' thinking—a tension that requires resolution. The shift from the earlier to the revised formulation of the argument in *The Dignity of Difference* does in fact reduce this tension.

One last point that emerges from an analysis of Sacks' argument, and which may hold the key to resolving the tension just described, is that in fact religion is not necessarily about truth. God may wish to communicate to us ways of life, ways of being in relationship with him, a quality of presence, and so on, without framing this communication in terms of truth. It is noteworthy that in describing the positive values associated with other faiths, Sacks never appeals to the notion of truth. But if indeed their validation is not for their 'truth content', at least not in the sense intended by argument B, then perhaps Sacks has unnecessarily complicated matters by attempting to relativize or contextualize truth in the first place. Perhaps it would have been better to avoid reference to truth and to construct an argument for

---

[43] Sacks is concerned with affirming the plurality of religions in their God-givenness, not with their truth value. Therefore, the lack of absolute truth of any religion serves as a gateway to the affirmation of equal divine disclosure through all religions. Had truth been his focus, he would have had to state that the God-givenness of religions is a guarantee of their truth. He never makes such an argument. They are to be appreciated as moments of encounter with the Divine, rather than as moments of truth. That the God-givenness of a religion need not lead to a view of that religion's teaching as true was already suggested by David Valle, who argued that all religions are God-given, so that there should be religion, even though they are false. See Brill, *Judaism and Other Religions*, 219.

diversity without entering into that problem. Even if his revisions were not intended to resolve this difficulty but stemmed from other, more political or communitarian, concerns, the later version of his book does in fact eliminate the difficulty by no longer addressing the question of religious truth.

Let us now take a closer look at each of these arguments. For each I will cite the relevant quotes from both editions, thereby providing multiple arguments for the same core point, or, as appropriate, demonstrating how certain ideas were relinquished in the second edition. The following extracts show the comparison between the first and second editions.[44] This will allow us to readily juxtapose the two versions, identifying principal changes. I have chosen to keep quotes in their entirety, even where what I have classified as arguments A–C overlap within one passage. This also allows us to appreciate how Sacks ties the different arguments together. I will comment briefly on the various passages, as appropriate.

A. God Is Greater Than Any Religion

PAGE 55

First edition	Second edition
The same applies to religion. The radical transcendence of God in the Hebrew Bible means **nothing more or less than that there is a difference between God and religion. God is universal; religions are particular. Religion is the translation of God into a particular language and thus into the life of a group, nation, a community of faith. In the course of history, God has spoken to mankind in many languages: through Judaism to Jews, Christianity to Christians, Islam to Muslims. Only such a God is truly transcendental—greater not only than the natural universe but also than the spiritual universe articulated in any single faith, any specific language of human sensibility. How could a sacred	So too in the case of religion. The radical transcendence of God in the Hebrew Bible means **that the Infinite lies beyond our finite understanding. God communicates in human language, but there are dimensions of the Divine that must forever elude us. As Jews we believe that God has made a covenant with a singular people, but that does not exclude the possibility of other peoples, cultures and faiths finding their own relationship with God within the shared frame of the Noahide laws. These laws constitute, as it were, the depth grammar of the human experience of the Divine: of what it is to see the world as God's work, and humanity as God's image.** God is

---

[44] I am indebted for about half the references that follow to the prior analysis in Student, 'The Differences of Dignity', although he presents the material using a different format.

> text convey such an idea? It would declare that God is God of all humanity, but no single faith is or should be the faith of all humanity. Only such a narrative would lead us to see the presence of God in people of other faiths. Only such a world-view could reconcile the particularity of cultures with the universality of the human condition.
>
> God of all humanity, but between Babel and the end of days no single faith is the faith of all humanity. Such a narrative would lead us to respect the search for God in people of other faiths and reconcile the particularity of cultures with the universality of the human condition.

This is possibly the most famous quote from *The Dignity of Difference*, and probably the one to land Sacks in the greatest trouble with his traditionally minded rabbinic colleagues. Here, religions, all religions, are presented as translations of God into particular languages. One supposes the need for translation arises from differences in the capacity to hear, following the linguistic metaphor. The primary difference is thus cultural and national. Human diversity requires multiple translations, engendering different religions.

This passage makes a leap from argument A to C, without addressing the question of religious truth. Accordingly, all religions are equally God-given. God speaks through them all. In fact, Sacks applies the traditional language of revelation to all religions.

All this has been done away with in the revised version. God's transcendence is no longer transcendence from the perspective of religions, but from that of human understanding. Sacks no longer speaks for all faiths, offering a neutral vantage point on how they are situated in relation to God.[45] Rather, he now speaks as a Jew and presents the ideal of the Noahide commandments as the basis for legitimating and respecting other religions. The multiplicity of faith traditions is no longer a divinely ordained fact, but a fact of history. It is grounded in humanity's search for God, rather than in God's reaching out to humanity. The particularity of cultures does not lead to divine translation but to multiple expressions of a common human quest for God. And God's transcendence (argument A) no longer leads to the recognition of multiple God-given faiths (argument C). God may be beyond human understanding, but he has chosen to communicate only through one channel.

[45] Such a vantage point would correspond to Greenberg's 'God's-eye view'.

The passage is informed by the linguistic analogy—that God speaks religions as languages. One imagines Sacks assumed that this would allow his statement to be accepted without theological qualms. The objection it met shows the limits of the analogy. At the end of the day, it was evaluated from the traditional perspective that sees revelation as being exclusive to Jews, and Sacks was understood as giving revelatory status to all religions. Here the linguistic analogy failed Sacks, forcing the eventual revision of his daring theological formulation.

PAGE 65

First edition	Second edition
The way I have discovered, having listened to Judaism's sacred texts in the context of the tragedies of the twentieth century and the insecurities of the twenty-first, is that the truth at the beating heart of monotheism is that God **is greater than religion; that He is only partially comprehended by any faith. He is my God, but also your God. He is on my side, but also on your side. He exists not only in my faith, but also in yours.**	The way I have discovered, having listened to Judaism's sacred texts in the context of the tragedies of the twentieth century and the insecurities of the twenty-first, is that the truth at the beating heart of monotheism is that God **transcends the particularities of culture and the limits of human understanding. He is my God but also the God of all mankind, even of those whose customs and way of life are unlike mine.**

In the revision, God no longer transcends religion but culture. It is not that God exists *in* the other's faith, but beyond the difference of customs.

PAGE 60

First edition	Second edition
The God of Israel is larger than the **faith** of Israel.	The God of Israel is larger than the **specific practices** of Israel.

One wonders whether the meaning of the change is that God is *not* larger than Israel's faith. How would one even argue for such a position? And yet, Sacks has toned down in the second version all references to God being larger than Judaism, let alone other religions.

PAGE 60

First edition	Second edition
Only such a God would be truly transcendent—greater not only than the natural universe but also than the	Only such a God would be truly transcendent—greater not only than the natural universe but also than the

spiritual universe capable of being comprehended in any **one** language, any single **faith**.	spiritual universe capable of being comprehended in any **human** language, from any single **point of view**.

Once again, one wonders whether the removal of 'any single faith' from the reference to God's transcendence suggests that God is *not* greater than Judaism. Strictly speaking, argument A could have been upheld, even if Sacks had to retract arguments B and especially C. But as he has tied argument A to C, he seems to have been forced to step back even on what seems a very sensible statement concerning God's transcendence with regard to any religion.[46]

B. No Religion Is in Possession of the Fullness of Truth

PAGES 64-5

First edition	Second edition
In heaven there is truth; on earth there are truths. Therefore, each culture has something to contribute. Each person knows something no one else does.	God, wrote Rabbi Abraham Kook, 'deals kindly with this world by not putting all the talents in one place, in any one man or nation, not in one generation or even one world'. Each culture has something to contribute to the totality of human wisdom.

The original version tied argument B to argument C. Because there is no full access to truth, there is room for cultural diversity. The reworking presents argument C on its own, with cultural, not religious, diversity being an expression of the grace of God, aiding in search of the fullness of wisdom.

PAGE 64

First edition	Second edition
Truth on earth is not, nor can it aspire to be, the whole truth. It is limited, not comprehensive; particular, not universal.	The Divine word comes from heaven but it is interpreted on earth. The Divine light is infinite but to be visible to us it must be refracted through finite understanding. Truth in heaven transcends space and time, but human perception is bounded by space and time.

[46] While the idea has been suppressed in *The Dignity of Difference*, one does find echoes of it in later writings. See *Not in God's Name*, 216.

The contrast between heaven and earth has been changed from full versus partial truth to the divine word and its interpretation, thereby making it an internal Jewish affair rather than a basis for viewing other religions and cultures. Instead of a discussion of full versus partial truth, which would have made room for other religions and their truth value, we now have a discussion of infinite versus contextual truth, pointing to limitations on our (Jewish) understanding of truth, without opening up to the possibility that truth might exist among others.

PAGE 64	
First edition	**Second edition**
Truth on the ground is multiple, partial. Fragments of it lie everywhere. Each person, culture and language has part of it; none has it all.	–

This entire statement has been removed in the second edition. The claim that all truth is fragmentary is no longer sounded. Note that the original statement does not even refer to religions, only to cultures; still the quote has been eliminated.

PAGE 55	
First edition	**Second edition**
This means that **religious truth is** not universal. **What it does *not* mean is that it is relative.**	This means that **though God makes absolute demands of the Jewish people, other than the Noahide laws these demands are** not universal.

While attempting to avoid relativism, Sacks makes a clear statement that truth is not universal. In other words, no one particular religion can be said to offer a teaching that is universally valid. The reworked statement no longer refers to truth, but only to the nature of demands. There are no universal or absolute demands, a fact immediately qualified by reference to the Noahide laws.

C. Multiplicity as God's Will

God has created or is responsible for and wills the multiplicity of religions. Divinely ordained diversity extends to religions; hence we must respect them all.

PAGE 200

First edition	Second edition
God, **the parent of mankind, loves us as a parent loves—each child for what he or she uniquely is. The idea that one God entails one faith, one truth, one covenant is countered by the story of Babel. That story is preceded by** the covenant with Noah and thus with all mankind—the moral basis of a shared humanity, and thus ultimately of universal human rights. **But it is followed by an assertion of the dignity of difference—of** Abraham and his children **who follow their diverging paths to his presence, each valued, each 'chosen', each loved, each blessed by God.**	God, **the maker of all, has set his image on the person as such, prior to and independently of our varied cultures and civilizations, thus conferring on human life a dignity and sanctity that transcends our differences. That is the burden of his** covenant with Noah and thus with all mankind. It is the moral basis of our shared humanity, and thus ultimately of universal human rights. **This is why the later covenant with** Abraham and his children **does not exclude other paths to salvation. The righteous of all nations—those who honour God and his covenant with mankind—have a share in the world to come.**

Sacks offers a novel idea for theologically validating diversity—divine love. This is a fruitful insight that could be developed way beyond the humble intimations in the original version. Is God's love a way of validating our differences after these have occurred? If so, divine love is a strategy of accommodation and could serve as a basis for our own loving behaviour in relation to difference. In fact, we have here an important suggestion. We need to not only accept or respect difference; we must learn to love it.[47] But Sacks' idea may be even more radical. Divine love may precede diversity and find expression in it. If one asks what is the source of diversity in nature, in humanity, and in religion, one might answer it is founded upon divine love. God loves in rich and varied ways, or gives multiple expressions to his power to love, thereby creating or generating realities characterized by their diversity. Tying together creation and love as a basis for diversity thus opens up an entire theological argument that allows us to move from the realm of truth to the realm of love. The next quote lends further support to such a reading. The language of love inspires Sacks to make an even more radical statement, extending the idea of chosenness, typically the unique privilege of Judaism, to other religions. All are chosen in love, highlighting the value of their diversity.

[47] On this, see Kook, *Midot re'ayah*, 'Ahavah', 10.

If indeed Sacks has developed a theology of diversity grounded in love, his retraction of it is a great loss, inasmuch as it has been replaced by much more standard theology. In the revised text, the reference to religious diversity has been removed and we only have cultural diversity. The revised theology features the Noahide covenant, coupled with the notion of the image of God. The latter endows humanity with value and ultimately includes the various forms of spiritual aspiration that find expression in religions. But this is a far cry from respecting diversity as such. The image of God confers value 'prior to and independently of our varied cultures and civilizations'. Because it remains constant, it retains its values regardless of difference, provided the Noahide commandments are observed. One thus has value *despite* difference, not *in* difference. This particular revision backtracks on Sacks' original insights possibly more than the obvious revisions already analysed.

PAGE 56	
First edition	**Second edition**
God no more wants all faiths and cultures to be the same than a loving parent wants his or her children to be the same. That is the conceptual link between love, creation and difference. We serve God, author of diversity, by respecting diversity.	Just as a loving parent is pained by sibling rivalry, so God asks us, his children, not to fight or seek to dominate one another. God, author of diversity, is the unifying presence within diversity.

God may be the author of diversity, but whereas the original version provides a basis for appreciating religious diversity, the revised version presents religion as the grounds for appreciating human diversity, which in turn opens us to the unifying divine presence. From the revised perspective one would gather that God *does* want all to be the same, at least in conformity with Judaism's vision for humanity, not in the true and existent diversity of faith traditions. It is not that diversity is willed by God, but that its negative consequences are contrary to his will. Linking the multiplicity of religions and creation shows how far-reaching Sacks' initial insights were. Just as there is diversity within creation, so also within religion. In the revision we encounter not the ideal of diversity, but rather its harmful consequences. This passage presents us with one of the key challenges for respecting religious difference—the consideration of religious diversity on a par with natural diversity.

PAGES 17-18

First edition	Second edition
Can I, a Jew, **hear the echoes of** God's voice in that of a Hindu or Sikh or Muslim or Christian or in the words of an Eskimo?	Can I, a Jew, **recognize** God's **image in one who is not in my image:** in a Hindu or Sikh or Muslim or Christian or in the words of an Eskimo?

As we saw in the first text, it is no longer God who speaks or whose voice is heard. All references to a language of revelation have been removed,[48] and replaced with the idea of the image of God that we have already encountered. This text places us before an unanswered question in Sacks' revised theology. Is the image of God itself a source of diversity, or is it a constant that is maintained despite diversity? I noted this question above, but here it arises more forcefully. Is it that the divine image is maintained regardless of his 'Hinduness' or is it precisely his 'Hinduness' that brings to light the full potential of the divine image? I have not been successful in locating a quote that would make the latter point explicitly, though the present re-worked text could be stretched that far.[49]

Had we been able to find clear application of the image of God as a basis for creative religious diversity (or if we are willing to stretch the present quote that far), this could have provided an important alternative to the revelation-based theology that Sacks was forced to retract. Rather than a religiously sanctioned diversity based on God speaking, we would have a religious diversity based on human *realization* of its God-given potential, in the image of God. Realization is a very promising term for the present discussion. The image of God provides an ideal framework for presenting God's gifts and the full potential made manifest in the human person and the myriad original contributions and discoveries, in all fields including the religious field, that come from it. Realization is also a term that serves

[48] But see p. 5, where 'Can we hear the voice of God in a language, a sensibility, a culture not our own?' has been kept without alteration. The reason is probably that this passage did not refer to religious but to cultural diversity.

[49] Sacks' collection of texts in support of his *Dignity of Difference* has numerous references to the image of God. But in all of them it is what must be appreciated about the other, not the innate capacity for creativity leading to religious diversity. The quote from the Mishnah commentator, Israel Lipshuts, on p. 48, where acts of scientific creativity and benevolence are linked to the image of God, comes closest, but it is still a far cry from the potential theologoumenon that draws on the image of God as a source of spiritual or religious diversity.

some religious traditions that indeed operate with such a theology, notably Hinduism. If the shift from Sacks' original position to his revised position had been conceived along the lines of a shift from revelation to realization, this could have been a constructive theological approach that upheld the value of diversity, grounding it in a religious value, without appeal to revelation. This remains a promising avenue for endowing diversity with meaning for those who wish to limit revelation to their classical scriptures and exclude others from recognized revelation. But it seems Sacks did not think through the full implications of employing the image of God for his revised theology. I imagine much more time and thought went into the original theology than into its revision, carried out in a short space of time and under public pressure.[50] Still, he has led us to a point where we might take even his revised theology a step further.

PAGES 52–3	
First edition	**Second edition**
Judaism . . . believes in one God but not in one **religion, one culture, one truth**. *The God of Abraham is the God of all mankind, but the faith of Abraham is not the faith of all mankind.*	Judaism . . . believes in one God but not in one **exclusive path to salvation**. *The God of Abraham is the God of all mankind, but **the demands made of the Israelites are not asked** of all mankind.*

References to religious plurality have been removed, as has been the reference to one truth. Truth and religion emerge as coextensive, and concerning both Sacks retracts the statement that there is more than one of them. The change from 'religion' to 'exclusive path to salvation' is more than a change of wording. The former recognizes other religions as equally valid. The latter refers to two paths offered by Judaism, one for Jews and one for non-Jews. Judaism is not an exclusive path to salvation in the sense that it also offers the Noahide teachings, meant for the rest of humanity.

---

[50] From Dayan Binstock of the London Beth Din I have learned that actually *The Dignity of Difference* itself was written in quite a rush, so as to be published in time for the first anniversary of 9/11. As a result, Sacks, or his team, did not incorporate some of the criticism of close associates that might have mitigated the public criticism. Nevertheless, the ideas articulated in *The Dignity of Difference* had been long in the making, as my analysis suggests, even if some of the specific formulations went farther than previous articulations.

First edition	Second edition
The proposition at the heart of monotheism is not what it has traditionally been taken to be: one God, therefore one **faith, one truth, one way**.	The proposition at the heart of monotheism is not what it has traditionally been taken to be: one God, therefore one **path to salvation**.

Following this, 'unity creates diversity' is replaced by 'unity is worshipped in diversity'. This is a very significant change. In the original version, divine unity is the source of religious diversity. It is therefore, a priori, part of a divine ideal. By contrast, the rewording features diversity as a given reality, not an ideal, and certainly not something created by God. Once there is diversity, God in his unity is worshipped in diverse ways.

First edition	Second edition
We encounter God in the face of a stranger. That, I believe, is the Hebrew Bible's single greatest and most counterintuitive contribution to ethics. God creates difference; therefore it is in one-who-is-different that we meet God. Abraham **encounters God when he** invites three strangers into his tent. Jacob **meets God when he** wrestles with an unnamed adversary alone at night.	*God cares about the* stranger, *and so must we*. Abraham invites three strangers into his tent **and discovers that they are angels**. Jacob wrestles with an unnamed adversary alone at night **and thereafter says, 'I have seen God face to face.' Welcoming the stranger, said the sages, is even greater than 'receiving the Divine presence'**.

In the original version, difference is an invitation to encounter. In the re-worked and much-toned-down version, God does not create difference; he cares about it. The implications of this for a theology of dialogue are obvious. The encounter with otherness is no longer an encounter with God; this reduces the potential value, and threat, of dialogue. God is discovered not in the other, but by *caring* for the other. This accords fully with Sacks' views on dialogue, analysed below.

First edition	Second edition
It would be to know that I am a sentence in the story of my people and its faith, but	It would be to know that I am a sentence in the story of my people and its faith, but

that there are other stories, each written by God out of the letters of lives bound together in community, each **bearing the unmistakable trace of his handwriting**.

that there are other stories, each written by God out of the letters of lives bound together in community, each **part of the story of stories that is the narrative of man's search for God and God's call to mankind**.

While the change in this passage seems innocuous, it is one further instance of removing the reference to God's active involvement in creating and valuing diversity. It is not God who is writing our story; it is we humans who search for God, and our search creates our grand narrative. Here is reflected the core issue—is diversity God-given or is it an expression of the human quest for God?

PAGE 21

First edition
The glory of the created world is its astonishing multiplicity, the thousands of different languages spoken by mankind, **the hundreds of faiths,** the proliferation of cultures.

Second edition
The glory of the created world is its astonishing multiplicity, the thousands of different languages spoken by mankind, the proliferation of cultures.

In this passage is a further argument for justifying diversity as a fact of creation and human culture. Religious diversity therefore is a natural extension of biological diversity, and this provides the foundation and justification for its legitimation as God-given. This argument need not rely on a theory of revelation. Even human creativity as something endowed and God-given could provide an adequate foundation for religious diversity. Therefore, in removing the reference to 'the hundreds of faiths', more is sought than to temper the use of revelation in some of the quotes above. What we have in the rewording is a denial of some level of legitimacy of difference. The likely reason for this is that Judaism has engaged in a lengthy battle against other religions, on theological or moral grounds. It is one thing to justify diversity, assuming certain basic moral or theological requirements have been met. It is completely another matter to validate hundreds of faiths. These would have to be the kinds of faith that are typically repudiated as idolatrous. One of the quotes above includes reference to the Eskimo, not only to the Christian or even the Hindu (notably absent is the Buddhist). Affirming the Eskimo religion as one of hundreds of faiths is not simply to discover something we did not see in earlier readings. It is to go against the thrust of most of Jewish history in its attitude to other religions. Sacks' original theology of difference does not seem to require moral foundations and seems to consider diversity a God-given reality, regardless of any moral or religious requirements.[51] By forcing Sacks to adopt a Noahide foundation to his legitimation of diversity, rabbinic critics not only forced him back into the classical mould, but also brought to light the question of how far-reaching the acceptance of difference can be. It may be that a less radical statement can be more readily accounted for than the out-and-out acceptance of all religions, regardless of their teachings. The later formulation, in which human aspiration fills the place that the original theory allotted to divine creativity, may account much better for actual religious diversity, providing it with no less respectable and more plausible grounds. The reworking does not suggest what foundations might legitimate 'hundreds of faiths', and the phrase is simply deleted. But those reworkings where the human quest for God replaces God's voice and creativity could actually provide the foundations for a theory of diversity that is less in conflict with traditional voices and which can therefore accommodate even hundreds of faiths. We should note, however, that, with reference to these hundreds of faiths, it may be easier to legitimate their difference than to see them as equally valid means of bringing mankind into God's presence.

Evaluating Two Strategies

Let us now assess what resources Sacks has provided us with in the two versions of *The Dignity of Difference*. Do both editions present parallel strategies for affirming difference, or does one do so more than the other?

The original version offers various complementary methods for upholding religious diversity as something God-given and valuable. The most far-reaching is to refer to other religions as God-given, instruments through which God speaks and can be recognized. Complementing this revelation-based appreciation is a creation-based approach: God creates diversity. This line of argumentation has various nuances. It refers to God's paternity and uses the metaphor of family as a means of justifying difference. Here Sacks

[51] One possible proof text for such a theological position is Mal. 1: 10, cited by Sacks on p. 60. The same verse is also used by A. J. Heschel in 'No Religion is an Island', 14. This in itself does not suggest Sacks' dependence on Heschel. The biblical text invites such a reading by readers with an interest in validating other faiths.

also introduces the notion of love—a love that is rooted in the divine love for diversity, whose consequence is obviously a call for love across diversity. He refers to the created order and its inherent multiplicity of species, and the social order and its multiplicity of human types. These are extended to the religious realm, and this extension does not seem to be causal. In other words, Sacks does not state that *because* of the multiplicity of human types and natural species, religious diversity is required so as to make religion suitable to different temperaments and types.[52] Rather, he simply seems to be arguing from the analogy—just as there is variety in other domains, so there must be variety in religion as well, and such variety is itself God-given.

It is clear that Sacks has a very important intuition and insight, and he employs a number of strategies to justify it. His thesis is a call to move away from platonic universals to the concreteness of particular individuals, including individual religions. He has made a powerful argument for validating religious difference and provided us with the nuclei for several conceptual trajectories that can be elaborated upon by further reflection and study. Seen as secondary expressions of his fundamental insight, the particular arguments do not have to be immutable; changes to them, such as revising the statements regarding other religions as being revealed or disclosed by God, do not touch upon Sacks' core intuition. I believe this is the reason why he could afford to cave in to pressure and revise *The Dignity of Difference* without fundamentally undermining his main thesis.

This applies also to the question of truth.[53] The first version of *The Dignity of Difference* showed a willingness to sacrifice the value of truth for the sake of affirming difference and plurality. The ideal of difference, which enables the affirmation of particularity, justifies the recognition that truth in all religions, Judaism included, is partial. The revision of this point did not lead to a contrary conclusion, namely that Judaism, or Judaism alone, was in

[52] This argument has been made by various Jewish thinkers, who could provide a pluralist precedent for Sacks' far-reaching theology. The most obvious case is that of Rabbi Nathanel al-Fayumi (eleventh cent.), who offers a theory of multiple revelations, through different religions, suited to the nature and temperaments of different peoples and cultures. See Brill, *Judaism and Other Religions*, 111 ff. This is similar to the Muslim understanding of religious diversity; see Friedman, *Tolerance and Coercion in Islam*, 13–53. A similar understanding emerges from the writings of Abraham Abulafia; see Brill, 216 ff. Moses Mendelssohn's construction of religion invites a similar recognition, even if it focuses on his understanding of Judaism. See Brill, 112 ff.

[53] On *The Dignity of Difference* in terms of the concerns of truth, see Shapiro, 'Modern Orthodoxy and Religious Truth', 134–9.

possession of absolute truth. It simply led to the omission of this particular argument. In terms of Sacks' overall goals, the value of particularity and the dignity of difference could be acknowledged also using the revised version. The nexus of truth and universality is broken, even if some of the more extreme statements that would implicate the Torah have been removed. What this means is that even if truth is not relativized in relation to God, it is seen as secondary to the more central and defining themes of story and relationship. These are primary and they highlight the value of particularity.

Of the various strategies used in the original version, what is left in the revised text? The two main approaches to upholding diversity have been split apart. The creation-based one validates natural, not religious, diversity. The revelation-based strategy affirms Judaism's multiple tracks of revelation —one particular, one universal—but not the plurality of faiths. As a consequence, in the revised version Sacks no longer offers us a means of accommodating religious difference. Rather, different religions are valued for their similarity, on the basis of acceptance of the Noahide covenant.

Does the common Noahide platform serve as a basis for secondary expressions of religious difference, around a common core of revelation? Some readers of Sacks have replied in the negative, considering therefore the revision inadequate in terms of contemporary interreligious needs. Thus, Bishop Richard Harries argues that if there is not a multiplicity of revelations, then people find their way to peaceful coexistence solely through ethics and not the teachings of their religion. If so, Sacks' revisions no longer give religions any role in the world, since there is a difference between recognizing individual gentile morality and recognizing other religions.[54] I think Sacks deserves a more generous reading. For one, it may be that even within the recognized common moral ground there is room for diversity, wherein religions offer a different colouring to a common moral ground. I have already noted such a possibility in a quote from Rav Kook.[55] Sacks himself, in other works, speaks of diverse approaches in different religions to common moral challenges. The diversity between religions may thus express itself in the moral field.[56] Indeed, Alan Brill has made the point that Sacks moves the

[54] R. Harris, 'Jonathan Sacks' *The Dignity of Difference*'.

[55] This quote is found in Sacks' collection of Jewish sources in support of the dignity of difference, 'A Clash of Civilizations?', suggesting he is informed by it, though I am not sure that he has noted Rav Kook's limitations of this argument to the moral context.

[56] See Sacks, 'Jewish–Christian Dialogue: The Ethical Dimension'. See also *The Dignity of Difference*, 82.

Noahide laws from a universal ethic to an appreciation of the diversity of religions by stating that each contributes to the Noahide moral order.[57] Further, according to Brill, Sacks applies the concept in a new way: rather than it being individual it is now within the scope of religions, in their diversity.[58]

My own reading is that the revised Sacks does recognize other religions in their diversity, and not simply as expressions of the Noahide covenant, coloured or transformed by their particularity. Sacks moves in his revision from a model of divinely authored difference to one wherein difference is humanly generated in the quest for God. Complementing the divinely ordained portion of religion—the Noahide commandments—is, thus, the great wealth of human aspiration for God. Provided the Noahide foundations are in place, there is much room for legitimate religious diversity. The following passage, which we have already seen, makes the point clearly:

As Jews we believe that God has made a covenant with a singular people, but that does not exclude the possibility of other peoples, cultures and faiths finding their own relationship with God within the shared frame of the Noahide laws . . . Such a narrative would lead us to respect the search for God in people of other faiths and reconcile the particularity of cultures with the universality of the human condition.[59]

The universality of the human condition is addressed through the common Noahide covenant. The particular faiths are expressions of humanity's search for God. As the quote suggests, this provides a foundation for respect. Of course, it does not provide a basis for regarding another religious tradition as equal. Sacks seems to have moved from pluralism to an inclusivist view of the other. The revised edition steps back from the full respect based on a pluralist view grounded in God's own initiative, to an inclusivist appreciation of other religions based on a common core of moral revelation known from Judaism, as well as on legitimating their struggle and search for the Divine. It is respect, but based on a lower valuation. Returning to Meiri and the theoretical foundations he provides, we may assume Sacks would still refrain from critiquing other faiths and would see them as fully

---

[57] I do not see the point explicitly in Sacks, but it may be inferred from contextualizing Noahide morality within a broader theory of difference.

[58] For both suggestions, see Brill, *Judaism and Other Religions*, 147. The latter suggestion may be supported by the quote on p. 55, depending on how we understand finding one's relationship with God *within* the Noahide covenant. I prefer a stronger reading, as I suggest immediately.   [59] *The Dignity of Difference*, 55.

legitimate, without entering into details of theology and practice. They would be seen as expressions of human aspirations, but validated and respected as such, rather than rejected as they were by earlier Jewish thinkers under the pressures of religious competition.[60] Sacks' recognition of the religious value of the human quest for God should lead him to view positively the differences in worship rather than ignoring them. These would be expressions of the human spirit and its quest for God, and therefore worthy of our respect, and possibly even of study and appreciation. While a God-given plurality might invite greater potential engagement, even by the outsider to a religion, validating another religion in terms of the spiritual aspirations of its faithful does not close the door to the sharing of spiritual inspiration.

Thinking With and Beyond Sacks

The discussions in *The Dignity of Difference* and in its revision are rich theological resources. Rather than limiting ourselves to the positions explicitly taken by Sacks, especially if these are read as walking back his more daring statements, we can revisit his work in both editions in an attempt to identify theological insights that can further enhance an appreciation of the religious other and contribute to a Jewish theology of religions. The following section points out suggestions, statements, and positions alluded to by Sacks, though not always developed fully, and possible ways of taking his thought further. Sacks does not simply present a position on other religions. Rather, he has a key intuition, or several of them, and he seeks various ways of stating them and placing them in relation to tradition, drawing on tradition, even as he advances it. The flourish of his rhetoric delivers his sentiments and intuitions with power and efficacy. It does not always spell out the range of theoretical implications of his views. In what follows, I draw attention to the wealth of possibilities contained in *The Dignity of Difference* as a resource for theological thinking.

Divine Revelation, Human Aspiration

Sacks' original theology relied on two core arguments for diversity: one from revelation and one from Creation. Clearly, the former is more charged. The criticism under which he came was rooted in a long tradition that juxtaposes reason and revelation, human effort and divine initiative. This is the tradition

---

[60] Sacks' revised understanding would accordingly be at odds with the logic of Rabbi Judah Halevi's *Kuzari*.

that dominated Jewish thought in the Middle Ages, and it owes much to the Muslim sensibilities of the day.[61] I believe this dichotomy is highly overrated and is in need of re-evaluation. To begin with, contemporary sensibilities of what revelation means are much broader than a simple understanding of God speaking as though he were a human. How does God speak? How do we hear him? What is the role of the human partner in articulating the divine voice? Closer study of these issues reveals they are not as straightforward as one might think and that there is more than one sense in which to understand revelation.[62] The internal Jewish understanding of the term is much richer and more nuanced than the Muslim paradigm that informs the dichotomy as it has served a Jewish view of other religions. Judaism's core recognition of a dual Torah—a written one based on divine revelation and an oral one that passes through the human agent, making room for creative interpretation and valuing innovation—suggests we cannot adopt a facile model of revelation. And if we recognize divine revelation *through* human creativity, then the decision of whether to recognize similar revelation in other religions does not stem from the very distinction between revelation and human initiative but from our prior views of other religions. In other words, once a more generous or pluralist view of other religions is espoused, there is nothing inherent in our notion of revelation that would preclude the application of the kind of rich understanding that we find within to other expressions of the human spirit. These too can be considered manifestations of God's revelation, in a manner analogous to the oral Torah, albeit without the authoritative stamp of approval provided by Jewish tradition for its internal purposes. Pushing the argument to the limit, the Noahide commandments could correspond to 'revelation', to the written Torah,[63] while human aspiration and realization of God would correspond to the oral Torah. Sacks'

[61] This conceptualization was a key instrument in establishing Jewish views of competing monotheisms. Rabbinic texts never faced such a challenge and therefore never elevated this dichotomy to a foundational distinction. There is room, therefore, to explore whether it does or does not hold true for rabbinic sources.

[62] Many of these issues have had to be rethought in response to the challenges raised by biblical criticism. But the philosophical challenges are broader. As the present discussion suggests, the interreligious context is itself an important factor that invites re-examination of these ideas. See Heschel, *Heavenly Torah as Refracted through the Generations*; Halivni, *Revelation Restored: Divine Writ and Critical Responses*.

[63] This formulation is somewhat ironic in view of the fact that we only know of the Noahide commandments through the oral Torah and they are nowhere expressed in the Torah itself.

revised theology could have therefore been cast in more traditional terms, had he had the theological and political flexibility of thinking through the core notion of revelation.[64]

A recovery of a richer sense of revelation, undermining the facile dichotomy of human and divine, allows us several things. First, in terms of appreciating Sacks' original position, I suspect he never intended full-blown revelation. What he probably intended is something along the lines I am describing here. Under criticism he had to retract it, not having the leeway to develop an alternative theory of revelation, which would have established a new playing ground. Second, such a rich interpretation allows us to over-come the temptation of reading Sacks' revised theology as meaning that other religions are merely human aspiration. God can speak through human aspiration. Finally, it makes it possible to place Judaism and other religions on a par in terms of the complex dynamics of divine and human initiative, at least partially. Even if we do not recognize a full revelation in other religions, a large part of religion, maybe most of it, ultimately shares the same ground, that of the complex and sometimes confusing meeting ground of God and humanity in the human psyche, mind, and inspiration, and in the human ability to listen, interpret, and understand correctly God's mandate. With this common ground comes the possibility of learning and mutual inspiration.[65]

The Image of God

The notion appears multiple times in Sacks' second edition, as well as in the supplementary essay of traditional sources. However, in all these cases, the image of God is used as the ideal of respect, not as the foundational prin-ciple by means of which further ideals, such as religious diversity, might be legitimated. Given the recognition that our religions are discovered and take place in the space between God and humans, it is worth considering the

---

[64] Sacks, of course, does apply this notion internally. For one of many examples, see 'Toldot (5773)—Between Prophecy and Oracle'.

[65] An understanding of multiple revelations could potentially limit learning and inspira-tion. Everyone should stick to their own revelation. Sharing a common ground that passes through common humanity opens this possibility, unless we argue that each religion follows the particularity of its psyche or social condition, in which case inspiration and learning are once again curbed. But it would be difficult to exclude all commonality in the human condi-tion and to assume that our psyches are only expressions of difference. At the very least, the question of common and different human circumstances would stand at the heart of a quest for deeper mutual understanding, in God's light. These issues are explored in detail in a later chapter.

image of God as the ground principle that empowers human spiritual life and the search for God. I have already raised the distinction between revelation and realization, drawing on a terminology current in Eastern traditions. The image of God can provide a basis for realization of the human potential in the quest for the Divine. Indeed, an examination of how the term has been applied in Christianity, particularly in Orthodox Christianity, suggests it is a rich resource that can carry us into the depths and heights of the human reach into the life divine.[66] A serious engagement with the concept would allow us not only to legitimate the principle of difference but to be inspired by the actual manifestations and expressions of the image of God in the teachings and spiritual realities of other religions.

Wisdom: Universal and Particular

Let me move on to other strategies. As I described above, Sacks had put together a reader of Jewish sources on *The Dignity of Difference* in an attempt to deal with criticism from Jewish authorities. Entitled 'A Clash of Civilizations?', this collection is an argument for an open-minded and inclusive mentality. It is certainly not a defence of the original theology. None of the arguments of the first edition appear in it. There is much theoretical overlap with the revisions, and so it must be seen as a supplement to the second edition. Indeed, it is in this context, in defence of the book, that it was composed. But the argument for openness and inclusiveness does not match that of *The Dignity of Difference*, not even in the second edition. Lacking completely is any attempt to validate religious difference, even as an expression of the human quest for God. What the collection presents is an open view of religions and cultures, mostly in response to a typically insular Jewish mentality, but it has none of the originality found in either edition of *The Dignity of Difference*. The argument runs as follows: There are two tracks to respecting others, one religion-based and one wisdom-based. The religious track is historical, recognizing the offshoots of Judaism in Christianity and Islam. It is thus not diversity that is recognized, but rather oneself in the other. Nothing is said of other religions. Complementing this is an acknowledgement of the universality of wisdom—this allows our quest for wisdom to go beyond

---

[66] One notes the relatively marginal place the notion occupies in Jewish thought. See Goshen-Gottstein, 'The Body as Image of God in Rabbinic Literature'. Therefore, this idea too must be constructed, rather than being taken for granted. See my reflections in Ch. 16 below.

the boundaries of Israel, though not necessarily beyond the boundaries of Judaism. There is an argument for diversity, but it is a diversity of people and its purpose is largely to avoid the kinds of corruption that a unified and totalitarian society might engender.[67] It is not a rich diversity and certainly not a religious one. On the face of it, then, the supplementary text does little to enhance Sacks' argument in *The Dignity of Difference*, in either edition. There are, however, also here certain nuclei of ideas that, if developed further, might yield new lines of argumentation in a validation of difference, especially in the spirit of the revised version.[68]

Sacks' presentation is of a universal wisdom to which all have access. Accordingly, we may receive that wisdom from all who have it. At one point, he does refer to particular cultural achievements of specific nations (pp. 42–3). This leads us to query whether wisdom is really as universal as the Jewish philosophers upon whom Sacks bases his argument contend. The universality of wisdom is a heritage of the biblical as well as the medieval period, where indeed it was understood to be identical across cultures, based as it was on Greek philosophy. But those days are over. This is certainly the case in our world, where we must account not only for 'Abrahamic' wisdom but also for that found in all religious traditions. If the dichotomy between revelation and wisdom that Sacks presents (p. 39) is valid, is it really a universal wisdom, or does Wisdom manifest in individual and particular wisdoms? And do these bear any relationship to concrete religions? Religions that are not revelation-based would feel very comfortable with the wisdom foundations of religion. Even competing revelations may be approached in terms of

[67] Significantly, the final chapter of the reader focuses on diversity and antisemitism, suggesting his audience's concerns. There is no reference to antisemitism in either edition of *The Dignity of Difference*. The themes of religious difference and antisemitism do combine in later works, such as *Future Tense* and *Not in God's Name*.

[68] In 'A Clash of Civilizations?', Sacks cites one author more than any other; this is Rabbi Abraham Isaac Kook, the great mystic, philosopher, and creative genius of the early twentieth century. Indeed, the collection opens with a lengthy quote from him, and his teachings are interspersed throughout the reader. There is good reason for this. Rav Kook may be the finest example of a broad, inclusive, loving view of humanity, taking into account all its spiritual movements, and thereby providing validation for others, as well as for otherness itself. Sacks draws on the inspiration of Rav Kook to set much of the mood for his collection, though he does not attempt an analysis of Rav Kook as such. I believe Rav Kook provides us with a more far-reaching view than the tame theology of 'A Clash of Civilizations?' or even the revised version of *The Dignity of Difference*. For initial thoughts on this matter, see Goshen-Gottstein, 'Jewish Theology of Religions'. Reading Sacks and Rav Kook in tandem is a worthwhile exercise, which cannot be undertaken in the present context.

their wisdom content. Wisdom is elusive and we no longer have the same confidence that we possess it as did our ancient and medieval predecessors. But whatever sense we give to it, if we take it seriously (and most Jewish practitioners, as well as teachers, do not), we must consider constructing it in ways that maintain the same balance between universal and particular that we recognize in our own faith and its related wisdom. If so, wisdom may be retrieved as a category by means of which diversity is appreciated. If other religions are more than simply human aspirations for the Divine but expressions of (divine) wisdom through other cultural and religious instruments, the difficulties that Sacks faced with the notion of revelation may be resolved. Wisdom provides us with precisely that middle ground between the human and the Divine that we seek in order to get past the dichotomy of divine revelation and human aspiration. Certainly, a wisdom-based appreciation of religious diversity would also amount to an invitation to study and engage with multiple expressions of divine wisdom.[69]

The Varieties of Difference

The discussion of difference and its validation has been carried out in abstract terms. The tension between the validation of other religions and the endorsement of otherness as such comes to a head when we pose the question: What aspects of difference are to be validated in another religion? The avowed purpose of *The Dignity of Difference*, as well as of later works, is the reduction of violence and the upholding of harmony in society and globally. In order to meet this need, it may be that the legitimation of the very notion of difference is adequate to the theoretical challenge. Still, if instilling respect for another religion is the goal, as it is for Sacks, then one imagines that moving from the 'universal' of difference to 'particular' kinds of difference is a necessary step in instilling authentic appreciation. This becomes even more pressing when it comes to a theology of religions, as one considers different aspects of a religion, rather than the principle of another faith as such. It is relevant also to two discussions that follow—the first one of our understanding of Sacks as a pluralist thinker, and the other relating to the potential implications of the validation of other religions for purposes of mutual learning and sharing of inspiration.

[69] In 1996 I founded the Elijah School for the Study of Wisdom in World Religions (later renamed the Elijah Interfaith Institute). This was precisely its theoretical foundation, reflected in the choice of name.

In exploring different kinds of difference, some may be easier to accept, others harder. The following are four possible areas of difference that should be considered.

Morality

One might, at first, regard the moral domain as common ground rather than as an arena of difference. The centrality that Sacks affords the covenant with Noah as a universal covenant would seem to reinforce such an assumption. Nevertheless Sacks, as well as his sources, also allow for the possibility of moral differences as part of the dignity of difference. He thus points to the variety of views on key contemporary moral issues as expressions of legitimate difference.[70] One of the quotes that he cites from Rav Kook in 'A Clash of Civilizations?' sounds a similar note. Speaking of the moral power in different people, Rav Kook states that 'because that which connects human thought and feeling with the infinite and all-surpassing Divine light must be expressed in a multiplicity of colours, therefore the spiritual paths of every people are different'.[71] The spiritual paths that are interwoven with moral life are viewed as different and spoken of in terms of a multiplicity of colours. Thus, even if morality is one, it may be coloured in accordance with a diversity of nations and collectives.

Theological Diversity

It seems obvious that different religions have different theologies, hold diverging beliefs, and bring varying nuances even to common belief. For Meiri, this doesn't really matter once a common core faith is established. Once we know what matters most, we can overlook what are ultimately details. As suggested, this may be the case for Sacks as well. However, there is something odd about affirming the other's right to develop robust theologies with which we can disagree and then ignoring these, all the while going out of our way to advocate respect for difference. Should a theory that values diversity not assume that details or theological differences are cherished, beyond the right to uphold diverging views?

The domain of theology is where it is possibly hardest for us to validate otherness in its details. It is particularly hard if we attempt to do so by means

---

[70] *The Dignity of Difference*, 82. See, previously, *Tradition in an Untraditonal Age*, 171, 176–7.
[71] *Orot hakodesh*, 3: 15.

of a pluralistic strategy that sees religions as God-given rather than as expressions of the deepest human yearnings. If we do resort to a view that they are in some way God-given or refer back to God, are we to assume that all the diversity of varying theologies is also God-given, beyond the God-givenness of the right or possibility to reason about, imagine, or otherwise conceive the Divine? It is of course much easier if we hold that theological diversity expresses the human capacity to imagine the Divine and to reason about God. It is much easier to recognize the common human need and common human ground from which theological reflection and religious imagination spring and to legitimate what comes forth from them in its diversity as part of similar processes that take place across religions.[72] I doubt that any proponent of diversity as a religious value would seek to justify the particularity of *all* theological doctrine. The same would hold true for the attempt to validate all religions in any sense beyond the basic respect for the right to maintain differing views of God, acknowledging the benefit those faiths bring to their believers and the common psychological and cognitive processes they draw on.[73] Nevertheless, if we uphold the dignity of difference, it does amount to a summons to listen to the depths of reason, inspiration, and aspiration that come to expression in individual theological doctrines.

Ritual Diversity

I consider it very likely that when we think of diversity and difference in religions we implicitly or intuitively think of varying religious practices and rituals. These are the concrete and most visible manifestations of our differences, faith in action. Again, for Meiri, these differences would be ignored. Following Sacks, however, we must ask how to respect rather than ignore them. How do we view the actual practices of another religion in a respectful way, acknowledging the importance of the rituals for the flourishing of members of that religion? The answer may lie in the question. It seems to me it is easier to draw the line connecting religious practice and flourishing, the human benefit of religious practice, than between flourishing and varying faith positions. Once we recognize the beneficial impact of varying practices,

[72] I have applied such an approach in my discussion of religious imagination in the Hindu understanding of gods and images. See *Same God, Other god*, ch. 12.

[73] Claiming that different theological views are helpful and conducive to the flourishing of believers would command our respect for their positive benefits. This would be one way of bracketing truth issues. The Dalai Lama takes this approach in his *Toward a True Kinship of Faiths*.

respect would seem to follow. Here respect would not be simply respect for the right to or need for specific actions but an appreciation of the specific benefits they bring.

Diversity of Agents of Salvation and Teaching

The role of teachers is rarely considered when we think of the stuff of religion, of what counts most, and consequently of some of the important ways in which religions differ. But in fact it is a central aspect of how religions function and of what matters most to believers. People do not simply adhere to teachings; they follow teachers. Some of these teachers are instruments of salvation and many of them play a role in the lives of believers that goes well beyond being instruments of teaching. In many ways, the instrument is part of the message.[74] Surely, this is the case for incarnational understandings of a religious founder, leader, or teacher. But it is also the case for any school that presents its teacher as a mediator of divine presence and a significant or even necessary means for attaining the goals of the religion. We cannot overestimate the importance of great religious figures, and consequently how they shape the religious lives of their communities. The difference between religions is very often a difference that can be expressed also in terms of the difference between the individuals to whom one looks. To follow or believe in Jesus is not the same as to follow Krishna or Swaminarayan. And they are different not only in their teachings, but also in their personalities, their qualities, and all that they bring to the spiritual life, just as any individual is different from another. Here it may be easiest for us to legitimate difference, as religious-spiritual difference is but the extension of a difference that we readily accept—difference between people as people. In the same way that love may be one but is individualized in relation to the object of love, so the spiritual life may be common but it takes on very distinct and different characteristics depending on the individual one follows. And in the same way that what we admire in a loving relationship is not simply the ideal of love incarnate but the particularity of the person, so our admiration for religious difference in great spiritual individuals would be for their particular individuality, not for their being one more example of common universal ideals.

Returning to Sacks, can we suggest what forms of difference he has in mind as he speaks of the dignity of difference? And how does the fourfold break-

---

[74] This allows us to understand the view that *shituf* is permissible to non-Jews. See *Same God, Other god*, chs. 8 and 9.

down presented above allow us to uphold or further query his thinking? It is useful to consider these four types of difference through the lens of revelation, the bane of the critics of the first edition of his book. While Sacks never spells out what kind of difference he has in mind and what it is he is trying to validate, I suspect that, of the four kinds of difference, what really informs his presentation, as it did that of medieval Jewish views of other religions, is that of ritual and way of life. These, as we learn from Rabbi Judah Halevi and others, must be God-given to have full value.[75] But this is not the only meaningful difference. Theology is certainly not God-given. If the classical definition of 'faith seeking understanding' describes theological activity, then all theology is human—and so is the articulation of faith content and dogma. It is impossible to argue that Jewish theologizing or articulation of faith statements is God-given, while that of other religions is merely human initiative. One may be true, the other false, but the dividing line is not that of divine–human authorship. If so, there is much in theological difference that must be appreciated under similar circumstances, making the concern for revelation almost irrelevant.

And what of the difference in the human instruments of religion? It would be impossible to argue, other than on preconceived grounds, that Moses is God-given, while Jesus is simply an expression of human initiative or aspiration. The category of revelation falls flat when it comes to the manifestation of God in humans, or the approach to God through chosen and unique humans.

Moral difference would seem to matter less than other kinds of difference, inasmuch as we recognize a basic common moral ground between religions. And if Brill is correct, and certainly if we hear the voice of Rav Kook on this matter, morality itself is coloured by the community that carries it. It is a hard sell to argue that Jewish morality is uncoloured, and that only other religions colour their morality in particular ways. Here again, the human and the Divine commingle as part of humanity's journey to God and God's participation in that journey.

Even concerning ritual and way of life, where the distinction would be most apparent, it may not withstand closer scrutiny. While the foundation of Jewish law is God-given, its application, development, and expansion

[75] Yet even Halevi recognizes religious value, even if inferior, in human efforts that aim to bring one closer to God. I have suggested above that Sacks should be read in stark opposition to Halevi.

have been given to human interpretation to such an extent as to make the distinction meaningless. And is human consciousness so impenetrable to divine inspiration as to suggest that all forms of ritual and worship are purely human inventions? If we recognize cultural diversity, can we not recognize inspiration and providence as instruments of shaping other religions, without having to appeal to a full-bodied notion of revelation?[76] And, were we to argue from error and imperfection, in other words from inspiration gone awry or from false attribution of inspiration, can we really say our own tradition is infallible?

Reflecting on Sacks in light of this fourfold analysis of religious difference suggests to me that one must move beyond difference as an abstraction. This is necessary if we are to understand religions in the very particularity for which Sacks argues, and if we seek to truly appreciate and respect another religion and its practitioners, beyond a blanket legitimation of their difference. And it is all the more necessary if such appreciation includes not only validation, in line with classical Jewish approaches to other religions, but the kind of real engagement, sharing, and inspiration that is the stuff of genuine relationships and is a need of the hour and a calling of this period in time. Sacks points to the broader global situation and to how it mandates a new listening to God's will.[77] It seems to me that such new listening must go beyond the general approval of difference and particularity and make these the subject of real and detailed spiritual exchange and engagement.

The vision of deeper and more detailed engagement grows in some way out of Sacks' vision, yet is not part of it. In a later chapter I ask why that is so. But before doing so, I would like to raise the question of how to characterize Sacks' views of other religions. Does the work accomplished by *The Dignity of Difference*, in both versions, allow us to consider Sacks a pluralist thinker? This is the subject of the next chapter.

[76] On providence as a category for the appreciation of religious difference, see Schachter-Shalomi and Miles-Yépez, *A Heart Afire*, 32. Schachter-Shalomi applies the category to the difference in human instruments. It may be applied more broadly, as an alternative to revelation.

[77] A similar call is issued by Heschel. Shapiro, 'Modern Orthodoxy and Religious Truth', 137 n. 39, suggests that Sacks is influenced by Heschel, though I do not see the parallels cited by Shapiro as beyond dispute. What both thinkers have in common is the willingness to understand Judaism not only through study but also by means of a new act of spiritual listening, which includes in its scope a breadth of vision and perspective that redefines a Jewish view of other religions. On Heschel, see Goshen-Gottstein, 'No Religion Is an Island'.

CHAPTER TEN

Religious Pluralism

Is Sacks a Pluralist or an Inclusivist?

One of the possible implications of the changes from version 1 to version 2 of *The Dignity of Difference* concerns the approach to other religions that is often referred to as pluralism. Pluralism is typically viewed in a threefold juxtaposition with inclusivism and exclusivism. The three suggest different degrees of openness to other religions, from supposedly full openness, as in the case of pluralism, to its opposite in exclusivism. Common discourse tends to privilege pluralism as a more open form of relating to other religions, and consequently as more supportive of peaceful, tolerant, and mutually enriching relations. Philosophical nuances are often overlooked in the process, and so, from the perspective of socially aware and dialogically minded individuals, to be a pluralist is preferable.[1] It is with this often unstated preference for pluralism in mind that I now turn to a consideration of Sacks' thought.

Is Sacks a religious pluralist? I have already noted that his thought shifts over the course of decades. It also contains contradictions as ideas are articulated in context, in service of a greater vision that remains constant throughout. The question of Sacks the pluralist must be appreciated not only while mindful of the above considerations but also in light of an analysis of what we actually mean by pluralism. Taking all these dimensions into account, the following discussion suggests that, while formally he *is* a pluralist, in substantive terms he is better described as an inclusivist. One possible application of this recognition is that even though the changes between the editions of *The Dignity of Difference* could be understood as a shift from a pluralist to an inclusivist view,[2] in terms of the core message and substance

---

[1] On pluralism in an interreligious context, see Sagi, 'Justifying Interreligious Pluralism'; Jospe, 'Pluralism out of the Sources of Judaism'; and Kellner and Kellner, 'Respectful Disagreement'. See also Korn, 'The God of Abraham, Yitzhak, and Yonatan'.

[2] See Korn, 'The God of Abraham, Yitzhak, and Yonatan', 145.

of his thought the shift is non-consequential and may even be a more accurate reflection of his overall approach to other religions.

Scholars who have studied Sacks' thought consider him a pluralist.[3] In this, he is seen as belonging in the same camp as Heschel and David Hartman, and I might add Irving Greenberg.[4] Others have questioned whether he can really be described as a religious pluralist.[5] The reason for their doubt is that, upon reading Sacks, one gets the impression that he considers Judaism to be in possession of a fuller measure of truth than other faiths.[6] This makes us realize that it is not enough to apply the label 'pluralist' or otherwise to a thinker. We must also establish what is meant by him, or by others, when they apply it. From one perspective, a thinker will emerge as a pluralist, while from another he will be appreciated differently.

How does Sacks describe himself, or rather, how is he to be understood in view of how he describes Judaism? In several places he characterizes Judaism, and by extension himself, as having a pluralist attitude to other religions. This claim is often supported by his reading of the story of the Tower of Babel.[7] As we have seen above, the idea of the covenant and the approach to other religions it enables are inherently pluralist. As Sacks states, one covenant does not negate the covenants of other peoples.[8] Without the notion of multiple covenants and multiple particularities, his essential point concerning the Jewish balance between particularity and universality being the ideal balance cannot be made. The argument from multiple covenants also suggests what Sacks might mean by pluralism: the equal *validity* of all religions—each being relevant, appropriate, legitimate, and consequently valid for its practitioners. As we have seen, this is in keeping with a classical Jewish theology of religions, whose formative question concerns the validity of other faiths. Covenant, then, is a strategy for providing an affirmative

---

[3] This is true of Alan Brill (see *Judaism and Other Religions*, 144–8) as well as of Michael Harris (*Faith Without Fear*, 151).   [4] Brill, *Judaism and Other Religions*, 146.

[5] See Shapiro, 'Modern Orthodoxy and Religious Truth', 139.

[6] This may be illustrated by the conclusion of *The Dignity of Difference*, a book that more than any other supports the view of Sacks the pluralist. Towards the end he offers a parable, related to him by a great hasidic rebbe (the Lubavitcher Rebbe? He is the only living hasidic rebbe cited in Sacks' corpus). According to the parable, Judaism is equivalent to diamonds, other religions to rubies, and both are contrasted with simple pebbles. See p. 209. The view is, on the one hand, appreciative of other religions, yet it reaffirms hierarchy and gradation between them. The exchange is cited previously in *Faith in the Future*, 74.

[7] *Faith in the Future*, 120.   [8] *Crisis and Covenant*, 253.

answer to this question.[9] This approach will be contrasted below with other ways of understanding pluralism, but we can already note one important distinction. Sacks speaks of multiple covenants, not of multiple revelations. He never suggests that all scriptures have the same ontological or spiritual value, with only the intended recipients distinguishing between one scripture or another. Covenant, in the sense of access to God, the relationship with him, and the particularity of a story, endows a given religion with value, and hence dignity, equal to that enjoyed by any other religion, Judaism included. The parallel value is the basis for affording others dignity, leading to peaceful relations and the avoidance of violence. The goals of such pluralism are well captured in the following quote:

Peace is when under God's sacred canopy different nations and faiths make room for one another. No other religion has shared this idea, of a single God with many names, who has set his image on each of us, but with whom we talk, each faith in its own language, each in its own way.[10]

This is the core of Sacks' religious vision, and its various iterations have led to his being considered a pluralist thinker. While pluralism does figure explicitly in his view of other religions, two facts should be added to the overall view.

First, his reference to pluralism in relation to other religions is contrasted with his reference to attitudes to other groups and denominations within Judaism. Here he adopts the following position: Judaism upholds pluralism in its view of those outside, but not in relation to other groups within Judaism.[11] The distinction should be kept in mind as part of the overall evaluation of Sacks as a pluralist thinker. While the distinction is convenient, are the terms 'pluralism' and 'inclusivism' being used in the same way? What are the values that Sacks loads upon the term 'inclusivist' and how might these describe his attitude to other religions? In fact, what he refers to as inclusivism effectively describes his attitude to other religions, despite his calling such an attitude 'pluralism'. The key lies in the clarity of definition and in what is intended in the different contexts when the respective terms are used.

Second, the description of the Jewish attitude to other religions as pluralism occurs in Sacks' earlier work. *The Dignity of Difference*, which could be

---

[9] This is also the concern that informs Greenberg's description of pluralism, which is measured in terms of how much authority and validity we afford other faiths. *For the Sake of Heaven and Earth*, 52.   [10] *Radical Then, Radical Now*, 94.   [11] *One People?*, 119.

read as providing the theoretical grounding for religious pluralism, does not use the term. On the contrary, its message is contrasted with pluralism.[12] Even if we argue that the revisions in the second edition amount to a change in Sacks' theoretical view of other religions, in the book itself this change is not manifested in a decreased usage of pluralism. The term is not central in the first instance. Throughout Sacks' oeuvre, at the heart of his interests lie universality and particularity and the concern for the dignity of difference, not the problem of religious pluralism. Looking at his later works, *Future Tense* and *Not in God's Name*, we see that pluralism does not figure there either, even though some of the ideas that would support a view of Sacks as a religious pluralist are articulated there. What this tells us is that as his thought evolved, he found it was best expressed by means other than the appeal to pluralism. This too allows us to query whether pluralism is the best term to describe his thought.

Let us examine this question through the lens of the two editions of *The Dignity of Difference*. On the face of it, Sacks has sacrificed something funda-mental in his pluralist religious view. Upon closer scrutiny, it seems the sacri-fice is not all that great and may have, in fact, aided in bringing to light a perspective that is truer to his approach to religions.

One way of viewing the difference between the two editions is to classify the earlier position as pluralist and the later as inclusivist. What is radical about Sacks' pluralism, in this reading, is that he grounds it in God, referring to the differences of other religions as God-given, their particularities on a par with the particularity of the Jewish tradition. The first edition would then feature a pluralist understanding because God himself, not any internal religious principle, provides the ground for legitimating all religions. The later edition makes two substantial moves. The first is that it shifts the basis for diversity to human understanding and aspiration. Multiple revelations give way to multiple human understandings. If the earlier statement was open to multiple truths and to religious (as distinct from natural or human) diversity, the later position only recognizes human diversity as the source of differences between cultures, but has no room for religious foundations for the multiplicity of faiths. The original pluralist view seems to consider reli-gious plurality a divine ideal; the later position seems to accept it as human

---

[12] See p. xi. See also p. 204. The reference on p. 203 casts pluralism in terms of difference and the multiple dimensions of human relationships, not in terms of the classical concerns of religious pluralism.

reality. The second change is the prominent place that the Noahide commandments take in defining a baseline by means of which other religions are validated.

While grounding a pluralistic world-view in God rather than in the human person seems more foundational, in theoretical terms I do not think that a humanly grounded pluralism is any less pluralistic for it. These are two distinct strategies for granting equal value to all religions. Some may prefer one over the other, but in terms of theoretical work, they seem equivalent. The Noahide commandments, however, might be considered a retreat from a fully pluralist position. Other religions are legitimated on the basis of a principle that Judaism provides, and are thus made to conform to Judaism and are seen as part of its own vision of proper relations with God. If so, this could be considered an inclusivist view that confers legitimacy by means of a principle of validation that is articulated within one tradition. It may be, then, that the changes indeed represent a retreat from a fully pluralist position to an inclusivist one.

There are various reasons why I consider the distinction to be less meaningful than it seems at first sight. To begin with, the earlier version also validates other religions in terms that are borrowed from within. The notion of God, the idea of a relationship with him, and the expression of that relationship in covenantal terms are elements that may be applied to most, but not all, religions, but which nevertheless rely on internal Jewish categories and criteria. They are, in fact, inclusivist in their own way. This is why placing monotheistic boundaries on the range of religions that are legitimated does not seem to be a retreat from a fuller pluralistic acceptance of others. It is likely that this was intended from the start by Sacks, as some of his earlier formulations indicate,[13] and is not some later limitation placed on his views as a result of controversy and public pressure.

But beyond the question of classification of his earlier and later statements as either pluralist or inclusivist, designations that can be applied to both positions depending on the criteria that are chosen, the distinction may not matter that much to what Sacks seeks to achieve. He never frames his discussion in terms of pluralism. It is only other authors who analyse his views through this prism. The concern for pluralism is part of the discourse of theology of religions. As stated, this is not Sacks' discourse. His aim to

---

[13] See *Radical Then, Radical Now*, 96, where he describes the phenomenon with the wonderful term 'monotheistic religious pluralism'.

contribute to society is part of a religious-social rather than a theological outlook. From that perspective, it matters little if his views are classified as pluralist or inclusivist.[14] The point is that either strategy may affirm the value of difference and allow us to appreciate the proper relationship between universality and particularity. This, and only this, is what interests Sacks. Accordingly, he may be classified in one way or the other. His implicit application of either strategy is instrumental to his true interests.

This fact allows us to account for the later developments in his thought, especially after he retired from his position as chief rabbi. I have followed discussions, in person and on social media, regarding Sacks' 'true' position in relation to other religions and whether he was a pluralist or inclusivist. The argument I have heard was that his pluralist position should have come to light after the pressures of office were removed following his retirement. A look at his later writings, however, suggests the contrary. Rather than being more pluralist, he shows less interest in the questions that were the focus of *The Dignity of Difference*. He no longer speaks of all religions and their respective covenants, but emphasizes instead Abrahamic monotheisms and their proper understanding in an effort to reduce violence in the name of religion. So, rather than returning from inclusivism to pluralism, he has moved from a religious view that includes others to one wherein Judaism is included among others. The reason why the 'true' Sacksian pluralism does not show itself in later works is that, as suggested, pluralism, or any particular position in the domain of theology of religions, is not really a matter of great concern to him. What he seeks to achieve he is able to achieve in any number of ways, regardless of theological nuances.

If, as I suggest, the labels of pluralist and inclusivist are secondary to Sacks' own concerns, then we might do well to move the discussion from the suitability of this or that label to a closer examination of the implications and significance of his views of other religions.[15] Rather than addressing the *theoretical* issue of how Judaism views other religions, we should consider

[14] If I were to coin a term to describe his view, I would call it multi-particularist. This designation suggests it does not fit into the categories associated with John Hick's analysis of the theology of religions.

[15] Eugene Korn expresses regret at Sacks' not having provided the actual philosophical argumentation for his own position. See 'The God of Abraham, Yitzhak, and Yonatan', 145. In part, this allows us to apply his thought to multiple theoretical frameworks. But, more importantly, it further underscores the difference between Sacks' own socially oriented concerns and the more theological interests of many of his readers, including Korn.

the *practical* implications of how other religions are viewed and whether these fit better with one designation or the other. This leads us to the subject of the following chapter, which is the amount of interest Sacks shows in other religions de facto. The thought exercise runs as follows: If the view of another religion is pluralist, then there is a higher likelihood that there is something to learn from that religion. After all, God has revealed himself through it, or responds to humanity as it calls out through it. If it is valued as fully equal, then the implications of such a position in relation to God could be relevant to others: pluralism would then amount to an invitation to share with others and to learn from them. Continuing the thought exercise, inclusivism, by contrast, is built on the view that the other holds ideals and truths that are recognized by, and even emerge from, one's own religion. If so, there is little to learn or receive from the other. Moreover, an inclusivist view cannot uphold the full value of difference, inasmuch as it relies first and foremost on the commonality afforded by the inclusivist principle. One point of difference between a pluralist and an inclusivist would then be whether one shows true interest in the religion of the other and a willingness to engage in reciprocal exchange and enrichment.

The thought exercise is not watertight. One could also argue that pluralism is based not on the riches of divine reality or truth, such as are revealed in the fullness and plurality of nature, but rather on a prior otherness stemming from the national identity of the other and attendant psychological and cultural factors. If so, the significance of a full pluralism would be limited to the recipients or partners in the particular relationship and would not necessarily be of relevance to others. To the extent that the human person and the image of God stand at the centre of the processes of legitimating another religion, one might similarly argue for the particularity of the identity of one group of individuals, thereby excluding the possibility of their religious testimony having any significance for others. Alternatively, the very fact of a common humanity might invite religious sharing and open one up to a fuller pluralism. Or, to make the point in a more extreme fashion, rather than ask how God's message is made to suit the particularity of different peoples, one might ask what particular aspect of the fullness of divine reality comes to expression through such particularity. Each revelation or relationship would then be viewed with an eye to its particular contribution to the sum total of what is known of God and how the totality of humanity knows God, in its diversity, within which the fullness of God's knowledge is grounded. From such a view, every religion contributes to the totality of humanity's knowledge of God. This lends pluralism a depth that makes it more than simply a strategy for validating the existence of another faith. In sum, while the argument could go both ways, it is likelier that fuller and reciprocal engagement and sharing accords with a pluralist approach.[16]

Sacks, as we shall see, shows little to no interest in the workings of other religions. Having afforded them their full validity in terms of particularity and difference, he never takes this interest in practical directions, beyond the common contribution to broader civil and global concerns. This confirms, once again, that pluralism as an ideal does not lie at the heart of his concerns, but rather the legitimation of other religions for the purposes of social and communal harmony. That his views might be described in theoretical terms by some observers as pluralism is of no significance to his thought structure, which might just as easily be appreciated in inclusivist terms.

To illustrate what a fuller pluralism might mean in practical religious rather than civic terms, I would like to point to a nineteenth-century religious figure, Sri Ramakrishna. Ramakrishna is one of modern India's greatest religious personalities, who has served as the spiritual focal point for millions for over 150 years. He can justly be described as a religious pluralist.[17] His argument is that all religions lead to God and carry the exact same value in terms of their ability to bring about spiritual realization. This is based on his own experimentation, having lived for some time as a follower of diverse religions, and having attained the same God-realization in his own subjective and mystical awareness as a result of such serial practice of different faiths.[18] How these claims might be received by practitioners of those faiths is beside the point at the moment. The key point here is the recognition that religious pluralism opens the way not to the theoretical legitimation of the other's right to exist, but to a fuller appreciation of the other religion. Put differently, if all we seek is to uphold a peaceful social order, we may not need a far-reaching theoretical concept such as pluralism, which affords full and equal value in principle to all religions.

Approaching the question from the perspective of different definitions or applications of pluralism, one is struck by the fairly narrow sense in which

[16] This suggestion is certainly borne out in the thought of Greenberg, who is a declared pluralist and who fully engages with the spiritual ideals of another religion.

[17] See Maharaj, *Infinite Paths to Infinite Reality*.

[18] For a summary of Sri Ramakrishna's journey, see Atmapriyananda, 'Sri Ramakrishna'.

Sacks grants value to other faiths. The lesson, and it is no doubt an important one, is limited to refraining from violence and enmity towards the other, once the legitimacy of the other has been established. If the legitimation of difference for the sake of civic peace is all that Sacks has in mind, then indeed there is no need for a fully pluralist view of other religions. This would account for why he never describes himself in such terms.

Once we recognize that for Sacks the question of pluralism versus inclusivism is not the defining issue, we are led to characterize his approach to other religions in terms of the actual stands taken and of how far his thinking about and relations with other religions extend. I would like to propose that, even though Sacks suggests that Judaism's view of other religions is pluralist, he is ultimately best described as an inclusivist. We would do well to pause on the difference between Judaism and Sacks' own approach. He may be right that *Judaism* itself may be pluralist in relation to other religions. He may have provided an underpinning for a fully pluralist appreciation of other faiths. It is possible, however, that he himself only applies a part of Judaism's potential and consequently is best described as an inclusivist, which leaves room for others to realize a fuller potential contained in his understanding of Judaism. Sacks' religious imagination may exceed the lessons and applications he draws from it in practical terms, either for himself or for the community. Thus, to claim that he is an inclusivist doesn't necessarily go against his own description of Judaism as pluralist.

Moreover, as we are coming to recognize, it is not sufficient to use one label or the other. We must state what it is we mean by either designation. It may be that Sacks is applying the label 'pluralist' in order to make a point, while another observer might make the same point and describe Sacks by appeal to the category of 'inclusivist'. I would like to flesh this possibility out.

Even though the distinction between the two approaches is made in several of his writings, the most important place where it is discussed is *One People?*, where inclusivism (in a sense different from how it is used in the discourse of theology of religions) is applied to internal Jewish difference, while difference outside Judaism is described in terms of pluralism. What Sacks means by this different designation is the theoretical justification of multiple perspectives that go to the heart and definition of a religion. There cannot be multiple Judaisms, differing denominational expressions of what is in essence one Judaism. There can be multiple religions. The question is stated in terms of the very validity of the different options.

The final section of the book is entitled 'Inclusivist Imperatives'.[19] I would have called it 'An Ode to the Inclusivist'—it is a portrayal of the character and orientation of the inclusivist as an individual. Inclusivism emerges as a personality type, not simply as a philosophical position. Sacks describes in the most inspiring terms what the approach of the inclusivist is and in so doing provides a basis for affirmation of the good found in other Jewish denominations. Reading this section, which is a poetic and inspirational high point of the book, I am struck by how much of what he describes here as the orientation of 'the inclusivist' is actually the appropriate approach for relations between religions, and how much it characterizes Sacks' own approach.[20] The key elements in this view are finding the good, identifying the positive, and affirming that, rather than what divides. Accordingly, I wonder whether this isn't in fact Sacks' view of other religions and an appropriate perspective for conferring value on the details of other faiths. Recognizing the validity and legitimacy of another religion does not require effort. Once it has been accomplished, by appeal to a particular halakhic or theological authority, there is nothing left to do, according to Sacks, other than to treat the faithful of that religion with respect. The inclusivist, however, has a harder task. He must constantly find the good in a situation that is comprised of good and bad, teachings and practices with which he agrees and those with which he doesn't. He is engaged in an active spiritual and relational quest to uncover some fundamental commonality, despite disagreement. This quest leads to recognizing the value of the teaching, prayer, practices, and transformative processes that other religions offer to their believers. Such recognition is not a wholesale validation; it is the result of a search for the good, for the commonality in difference, and for God's presence in the other religion.

This brings us back to the discussion at the end of the previous chapter—what kind of difference does Sacks actually acknowledge? Does it extend to all domains of religion, or only to some? For the most part, the recognition of another religion, especially by means of describing Judaism's view as pluralist, does no more than establish its right to exist. But what of the real stuff of religion? What about the spiritual life of the faithful, in all its dimensions? Pluralism does not mean the acceptance of everything within

---

[19] *One People?*, 217–28.
[20] See *To Heal a Fractured World*, 102, where Sacks describes certain elements of his view of other religions as inclusivist.

another religion. That would either mean one doesn't care or that one has a very elevated perspective, perhaps a God's-eye view, where everything in a religion is considered positively. This would be akin to affirming diversity in nature: it is not done partially. It is celebrated in its entirety. But here the analogy to natural diversity breaks down. Other religions are not usually validated as a whole. One could, of course, make allowances for imperfections and corruptions within the religion,[21] but the basic view of a full pluralist would be one in which the entirety of the religion, minus a certain amount of error and corruption, would be legitimated. This is a very rare perspective. Greenberg makes some steps in this direction as he seeks to make sense of Christian theological assertions. Ramakrishna does, too, in applying himself to the practices of other religions. For the most part, however, the declaration of the value and validity of another faith, from a pluralist perspective, is rarely more than an affirmation of its right to exist, or of its efficacy in terms of salvation. If so, we are called to consider whether a more nuanced and creative approach to other religions is not called for.

In this alternative view, another religion would not simply be validated. Instead, one would discover the positive principles in it by searching its meaning and considering the benefits it brings to believers and those beyond. A religion would be affirmed not in theory and principle, but in action and in terms of its actual workings. Such recognition is unlikely to be global. It is also unlikely to be detached, a matter for declaration of validity only. This would be the way of the pluralist. By contrast, a fuller engagement with all that comprises religion and the varieties of its particularities and differences calls for an active approach that seeks the good—in Jewish terms, lifts the sparks—and recognizes the working of the Divine in a religion and in the life of its faithful. To recognize the fulfilment of the Noahide commandments would be one strategy for finding the good in another religion, not simply for affirming its validity. To recognize the ways in which God interacts with the faithful of another faith—whether the initiative comes from above or from below—would be another. The claim that God is greater than religion, and therefore provides a common ground to all faiths, is an inclusivist argument. Even the argument for being included in a divine design where there is room for all, whether as part of creation or as part of a post-Babel reality, is still an inclusivist argument. All are included in the divine design, which does not mean that everything about the religions is fully validated or destined to

[21] An allowance that we would have to equally make for Judaism itself.

remain valid eternally, under all circumstances.[22] Another way of applying an inclusivist appreciation would be in relation to the instruments of salvation and the great individuals who have made their spiritual path through a religion. In all these, the other religion is appreciated in its particularity, and not as an abstraction, in line with spiritual ideals known from our religion. The great paradox of Sacks' approach to other faiths is that even though he calls for an acknowledgement of the dignity of difference, he never engages with that difference. He only engages with the principle of difference, based as it is on the fundamental validation of another religion.

Closer examination of what Sacks' thought achieves and what it calls us to do leads me, then, to suggest that as soon as we go beyond the very principle of validity, we must adopt an approach that is better described as inclusivist. It amounts to a spiritual invitation to recognize, appreciate, and celebrate diversity in its particularity. Such celebration would then become the basis for fuller sharing. It would also serve as the basis for discovering the deeper unity between religions. Pluralism assigns equal value despite differences. Inclusivism, in this reading, recognizes the deeper unity that exists despite these differences, as it finds expression at key points in the religious life. Sacks' thought has gone as far as validating the religious other and one principle by means of which unity is affirmed—the human person as the image of God. A fuller engagement with other faiths in their particularity is certain to reveal many more principles that will bring to light a deeper commonality, pointing to the unity of humanity and its religions, which might itself be viewed as the fullness of the image of God.

Sacks has laid important foundations for the appreciation of other religions. Because his discussion focuses on difference, its acceptance, and legitimation, he has not entered the more complex domain of validation of theology, practice, and spiritual path. He has also not engaged in a philosophical discussion of pluralism versus inclusivism, even though he has made some significant statements on this matter. His work invites us to go where he has not gone and to apply the foundations of his thought, what he describes as the message of Judaism, in a fuller way. I submit that the inclusivist approach is our best, most fruitful, and most spiritually active means of achieving this end. It also describes more appropriately Sacks' own attitude to other faiths.

[22] What this would mean, then, is that while all are included in the divine design, not all share fully in divine truth.

Dignity of Difference and Studying Other Religions

We are already aware of the civic purposes of Sacks' theory of religious pluralism and the dignity of difference. His thought has greater potential and promise for the relations between religions than he may have realized. One of the key points for appreciating his approach to religions is the question of mutual sharing, the need for reciprocal knowledge and the issue of whether full relations between religions require engaging with the substance of the faith of the other. My earlier analysis of the different types of difference is helpful in this discussion. In what sense does Sacks affirm difference and particularity, and does he do so in relation to the specifics of other religions, or only in relation to the ideal of particularity? As with other issues raised in my analysis, there are elements in his thought that lead to opposing conclusions. I will present the various factors that lead the reader to regard the study of other religions and exposure to their wisdom either as an important part of Sacks' view of relations between religions or, alternatively, as something that is given a minor role in his thought structure, ignored, and possibly discouraged. As there are indications in both directions, we will, as with other contradictions, need to consider what is the most reasonable way of accounting for these discrepancies.

Sacks is broadly considered a champion of interfaith relations. Hava Tirosh-Samuelson, a savvy and discerning professor of Jewish philosophy, has devoted a volume to him in her series Library of Contemporary Jewish Philosophers.[23] It is worth noting how she perceives Sacks on the basis of *The Dignity of Difference* and other sources that inform my own presentation. According to Tirosh-Samuelson, in this book Sacks makes the bold claim that to face the pressing challenges of our time we need not only the great religious traditions, but a way to bring them into dialogue with one another through their wisdom.[24] Note the emphasis on dialogue *between* the religions.[25] In other words, rather than the alternative emphasis on all religions contributing their respective wisdom for the benefit of society, Sacks, in her understanding, is a proponent of a direct exchange of wisdom in the interest of society's pressing needs. Similarly, she interprets Sacks as teaching that each tradition needs to find positive value in the otherness of the other, not

[23] Tirosh-Samuelson and Hughes (eds.), *Jonathan Sacks: Universalizing Particularity.*

[24] *The Dignity of Difference*, 11.

[25] For a description, in a news report, of Sacks as engaged in interfaith relations, see Lahmanovitch, 'What does the Messiah have in common with Arsenal FC?'

simply tolerate it.[26] Note, Tirosh-Samuelson does not refer to legitimating diversity as a principle, but to the active quest to identify the positive value in that which is particular to another tradition. This would involve a process of mutual study, interrogation, listening, and sharing. In a similar vein, she attributes to Sacks the claim that, since all humans are created in God's image, we must see the beauty and wisdom in faiths not our own.[27] While she can offer references in support of these views, Sacks never develops these flashes of inspiration into more detailed expositions, let alone into a programme. More importantly, he does not exemplify a path that might be attributed uniquely to him, as Tirosh-Samuelson claims. His brilliant formulations are rich with potential. The message she hears may well be the core of his teaching, though it is a message that he, in fact, fails to deliver. This is an interesting gateway to the complexities of Sacks' view of other religions, consisting, as it does, of inspirational and visionary presentations of how religions relate to one another optimally as well as of consistent avoidance of the implications of these very visions for his own theology and practice.

The heart of the issue is the relationship between the universal and the particular, what religions share in common and the differences that set them apart. Sacks has established an important balance between the two, by means of which particularity and difference are appreciated alongside universality and commonality. However, what he has left unresolved is the question of whether we appreciate the other for what is common or for what is different.[28] Granted, he has devised a structure that validates and calls for respect for difference. But is acceptance ultimately contingent on commonality? And if so, is difference tolerated or legitimated, or is it a source of further inspiration and enrichment across the divide established by it? And how do these ideas play out as Sacks' thought develops? It is in dependence on the answer to this question that one can determine whether the dignity afforded to difference is nothing more than an upgrade of tolerance or whether it implies substantial engagement with particularity and at

---

[26] This is the message of *The Dignity of Difference*, as summarized on p. 200.

[27] Based on Sacks, *The Great Partnership*, 77.

[28] This question goes to the core of his construct and therefore cannot be resolved in one passage only. Recognizing that, the identification of that which can be shared with universal wisdom would suggest that it is what is common that is shared, not particularity. Such a statement appears in the context of a Jewish sharing of wisdom with others, rather than of receiving the other's wisdom (*To Heal a Fractured World*, 127), thereby making it even harder to extrapolate an answer from the passage.

least partial validation of the religious other for his or her difference, rather than for what is held in common.

If otherness, actual difference, is not really appreciated, then we are left with a superficial view of the other that makes no room for genuine encounter. While it may suffice for a distant recognition and acceptance, it certainly cannot provide a foundation for real relationships that value the fullness of individuals or communities in their particularity. Superficial encounter cannot deliver the depth of healing that is sought in interreligious relations. Moreover, it seems to fly in the face of the quest for granting the other genuine dignity. How can that dignity be affirmed if one refuses to deeply engage with the other's identity, what matters most to them? Under discussion, then, are the true meaning of appreciating difference and the scope of interfaith engagement.

In Favour of Mutual Learning

The structure of Sacks' thought points to learning and enrichment across religions as the fruit of appreciating particularity and valuing difference. In fact, one might object to the present discussion on the grounds that Sacks is explicit in his call for learning across religions, while never speaking against it in any of his writing, early or late. Such an emphasis is to be found in earlier works that antedate *The Dignity of Difference*. Some of the ideas appear for the first time in *Tradition in an Untraditional Age*, where Sacks posits the tension between the multiplicity of languages engendered by the Tower of Babel incident and the return to the lost harmony in a future when God will make the peoples pure of speech. His conclusion: 'Learning one another's language of faith is one of the ways we reach back before Babel.'[29] And yet, as the essay 'Jewish–Christian Dialogue' unfolds, he moves the discussion from actual engagement to the common moral message that Jews and Christians have to offer society at large. This transition encapsulates the phenomenon described in the present chapter. A potential breadth of theological vision is channelled into ethical and civic concerns to which multiple religions contribute, while avoiding the kind of dialogue envisioned in light of the biblical ideal.

The idea finds other expressions. Consider the following passage from *The Dignity of Difference*:

[29] p. 161.

Each culture has something to contribute. Each person knows something no one else does. The sages said: 'Who is wise? One who learns from all men.' The wisest is not one who knows himself wiser than others; he is one who knows all men have some share of the truth, and is willing to learn from them, for none of us knows all the truth and each of us knows some of it.[30]

Willingness to learn from others is a sign of wisdom. This statement, appearing as part of Sacks' discussion of universal and particular truths, would seem to amount to an invitation to engage in a search for truth or wisdom. In context, this search passes through the study of other religions. This, after all, is the subject of the entire chapter and the thrust of Sacks' argument. The same applies to calls such as the following: 'Can we hear the voice of God in a language, a sensibility, a culture not our own?'[31] He seems to be inviting us to listen to God's voice through the particularity of the other's culture and religion.[32] In this line of reasoning, mutual enrichment is the positive outcome of appreciating difference.[33]

   While the theory is set in place, one must ask whether Sacks exemplifies it. Does he serve as a model of this approach for his readers? Does he engage in any way in the study of other religions? Does he in any way draw from their wisdom? Does his quest for the fullness of truth in any way pass through the study or exploration of other faiths, of key ideas found in them, and of the incarnated wisdom of the lives of holy and wise men? In short, is there any indication that this visionary statement is anything more than a creative literary expression that captures some ideal, yet remains far from implementation in Sacks' own person and teachings? I will devote the following chapter to a closer review of how other religions are featured in his corpus. The short, and to me sad, answer to the questions just posed is negative. Sacks puts forth the idea; he never implements it in this or any other work.[34] In fact, all too often he deflects it by emphasizing the value of parti-

---

[30] p. 65. While the earlier part of this paragraph was revised in the second edition, this quote appears in both editions, even though it refers to the notion of truth and to the fact that our possession of truth is limited.

[31] *The Dignity of Difference*, 5.

[32] Related to this is the recognition that others may respond to God's calling better than we do. This could have led to deeper study and appreciation of others. The argument, however, only goes as far as affirming the *value* of the other. See *Not in God's Name*, 217.

[33] See *The Dignity of Difference*, 23. See also the concluding paragraph on that page.

[34] By way of comparison, he is very comfortable drawing lessons from the religious reality of the United States and its covenantal moorings for how Britain might construct itself anew. This is the thrust of *The Home We Build Together*. The kind of openness to learn from

cularity for the other, rather than highlighting its positive value for the one engaging with the other.[35] This is the mystery, or tension, which we must solve or address as we make sense of Sacks' message regarding relations between religions.

The tension between affirming the value of particularity and difference and failure to engage with religions in their particularity seems built into some of the core arguments of *The Dignity of Difference*, as well as into others of Sacks' books. I have noted two main analogies by means of which religious diversity is validated: the linguistic and the natural. The first sees religions as languages, and we have just seen it, yet again, in the suggestion that studying the other's faith is a return to the state of Eden, prior to the story of the Tower of Babel. Let us consider this analogy more closely. It confers value and validity upon the other's faith. In the same way that the other's language is necessary for their survival and identity, so is their religion. The linguistic analogy does not, in and of itself, invite study. There are, as Sacks notes, 6,000 languages.[36] One can appreciate the value of Kwakiutl or Urdu without such value amounting to an invitation to study those languages. In this view, languages are an ideal metaphor for affirming value while maintaining distance.

And yet, built into this analogy is also the invitation to gain proficiency in and understanding of the other's religion.[37] A polyglot is someone we admire.[38] The command of multiple languages is a sign of culture and education. A person who masters multiple languages has the keys to different forms of wisdom. He is aided in practical ways, ranging from travel and commerce to negotiating the complex realities of an ever more interrelated world. I have yet to encounter a person who is despised for his knowledge of another language. By this logic, we should know another's religion. We may not know all religions, any more than we would gain proficiency in *all* languages. The analogy, as well as reality, suggest this is an impossibility. But our inability to master all languages does not detract from the accomplish-

the example of the other is *never* applied in the field of religion, despite all the potential openings to such an idea found in his writing.

[35] See e.g. *The Dignity of Difference*, 62. Sacks speaks of what Hinduism means to the Hindu, etc. In fact, the greater challenge he must face is what Hinduism means to the *Jew*.

[36] *The Dignity of Difference*, 201. See, among others, the beautiful application in *To Heal a Fractured World*, 106.

[37] See Sacks' own application of this conclusion, *The Dignity of Difference*, 65.

[38] See *Faith in the Future*, 79.

ment of mastering any individual language, let alone several of them. The same would hold true for religions. Thus, built into Sacks' most fundamental metaphor for appreciating religious difference is a tension as to its potential meaning. Does the analogy stop with validation, or should it be extended to the actual study and use of multiple languages?

The biological metaphor is more far-reaching in terms of its practical application. We do not simply celebrate the diversity of life forms. Our concern for diversity and its maintenance is founded on the recognition that creation requires such diversity. A particular fungus or flower species is not appreciated simply because it offers testimony to the glory of the God who creates such diversity, but because it is necessary for general welfare. Everyone can potentially avail themselves of the medicinal or nutritional or other values that are associated with the diverse forms of life. Even as we struggle with the theoretical significance of the mosquito that makes our life miserable, we recognize that all species are there for the greater common good and a huge amount of them are beneficial to us individually. We value natural diversity because all of it has the potential for some form of interaction and impact on some aspect of our lives. It doesn't make sense to make the argument from diversity of life to diversity of religion if all it means is that religious diversity is theoretically legitimate, justifying the very existence of other religions, which are seen as other species. Species do not exist simply for themselves, in isolation from the benefits they bring to other species. All serve all and all benefit all. Taking the analogy to its logical conclusion would lead to a similar view.

The two key metaphors that Sacks employs ought to inspire full or significant engagement with other faiths.[39] Yet he seems to draw on only a part of their potential significance. They are used to legitimate the existence of other religions, while ignoring the question of the meaning of those other religions for one's own faith, or for the life of humanity itself. The potential of Sacks' thought exceeds what he himself makes of it.

Let us now consider another complexity that is built into *The Dignity of Difference*. As argued above, there are two fundamental strategies for affirming difference, and these correspond to the two versions of the book. The

---

[39] There is a third metaphor that he uses, drawing out the potential of a motif found in biblical narrative—the relationship between brothers. See *Not in God's Name*, 153. This metaphor appears also in his earlier writings, and it too points to a fuller relationship, though this is not the meaning that Sacks derives from it.

first version presents a variety that is rooted in God. In its most extreme form, the text speaks of God relating to religions in terms of revelation. It also refers to other religions as the human calling out to God and recognizing God's image. The second edition shifts the grounds for justifying diversity. Against the common background of the Noahide laws, it speaks of human and cultural diversity, grounding that diversity in the human person rather than in God. This is in line with Sacks' major emphasis on humanity being in the image of God as a core message of the Torah and one that also conditions the attitude to different religions. We respect the human person as the image of God, as he is found practising all these religions. Let us now tease out the potential implications of these two strategies for the question of how extensive and detailed the relationship with other religions ought to be. Is the purpose of Sacks' constructs simply to affirm as legitimate the existence of other faiths, or does such affirmation amount to an invitation to engage with them in reciprocal processes of learning and spiritual sharing? There are different ways in which the argument could be made, and they could potentially support one or the other view.

If diversity is truly God-given and has its roots in God, then, *prima facie*, this means that one must engage with the religion of the other. The fullness of God finds expression in the fullness of religious paths. Judaism's challenge, as Sacks states, is not to find God within itself, but to find him in the other.[40] This seems to be the logic of the passages noted above that see study and understanding of the religion of the other as part of an ideal reality and of the quest for the fullness of truth. If God is greater than religion, then in fact one is seeking God and not seeking another religion, even as one delves into another faith. God is sought *through* or *in* religions, and these constitute a means to an end. If we seek the fullness of God, then potentially there is something to receive from every religion. Indeed, there are some quotes that could be read in this light. Thus, when Sacks speaks of all prayers that come from the heart converging in God's infinity, one might reasonably conclude that spiritual fullness requires all religions taking part.[41] This is a striking claim, regardless of how much of it is actually stated by Sacks. If, in the process of asserting the validity of other religions, he suggests that they are all needed to reveal the fullness of God, then in fact he is also suggesting

[40] *Radical Then, Radical Now*, 96.
[41] See *To Heal a Fractured World*, 127. Sacks clearly does not draw that conclusion himself. He prefers to present profound differences as the norm that, apparently, should govern relations on earth.

that no one religion can bring one to the fullness of God. Something will remain beyond one's comprehension and approach, contained in another religion.

One could argue that it does not matter that some aspects of God remain beyond one's religion. If all the different faiths lead one to God, then the key is to reach God and not to reach a comprehensive understanding of or relationship with him. If we recall Ramakrishna, the point of his experience was that all religions lead to the reality of God, not that one must follow all religions in order to have a full knowledge of God in his revealed diversity. Still, this idea is one that we can't fully avoid if we take Sacks' thought to its ultimate conclusion. It is problematic, inasmuch as it conflicts with the fundamental premise of the adequacy of religion, one's own religion, to reveal God to the believer and to bring him or her into the fullness of a relationship with God. Nevertheless, even if involvement in another religion is not a prerequisite for the wholeness of the religious life, it does seem to suggest some additional fullness, in line with the fullness of God, who reveals himself through yet another religion.

We return here to a question alluded to above. Are diverse religions needed because there are multiple recipients, different peoples with different psychological and physiological orientations? If so, while God may be known in all these religions, in fact the multiplicity stems from God's need to reach people in their diversity, rather than from an inherent divine need to give expression to riches that exceed what one religion can manifest. The question of the God-givenness of religious diversity therefore forces us to consider whether the multiple paths are only instruments for communicating to diverse populations or whether in some way they are ends in themselves, as they convey different dimensions of divine reality. While Sacks speaks of the positive value of the diversity of the human condition,[42] it remains unclear to whom this positive value applies. Even if the second option is followed, we need not conclude that one must fully embrace all religions. However, the door is thereby opened to some dimension of borrowing, inspiration, sharing, and study that would be integrated into one's home faith while seeking a fullness of God beyond one's own faith. That such a process may never be practised in the fullest would be akin to the impossibility of learning all languages. Still, as religious languages are learned, or shared, more of the divine fullness is revealed, even to the practitioners of another religion.

[42] *The Dignity of Difference*, 200.

It should be made clear that Sacks never takes these questions up. As Eugene Korn has commented, he fails to provide us with the arguments that would support his views.[43] We are left to explore the significance of his assertions and to fill them out. One could reason that the fact that Sacks only uses his metaphors and his reasoning to validate religious difference and not to encourage sharing and learning across religions might itself suggest the boundaries he saw as appropriate for applying his theoretical foundations in practice. Yet he commends values he does not practise, as I shall show below, which means that his thought has greater potential than his example might suggest.

Let us now consider the potential implications of the alternative method of arguing for diversity, as found in the revised text. The grounds for religious diversity lie in the human person and in humanity's religious aspirations. One might reasonably suggest that the grounding of diversity in God amounts to an invitation to sharing across religions, seeking to discover the riches of God, while basing diversity in the human person or community would limit such engagement. Human diversity requires multiple approaches to God, but these stem only from the inbuilt diversity of the human race. Hence there is no need for one part of humanity to follow in the spiritual ways of another, emerging as they are from this prior diversity. This argument still holds, though, the possibility of inspiration across religions. If we recognize the fullness of humanity in its very diversity, and all the more so if we consider this diversity to be an expression of the ideal of God's image in humanity, then in fact getting to know another spiritual path could be seen as a way of delving more deeply into our humanity. I don't think Sacks ever argues that the common Noahide foundations exhaust our common humanity. If he calls for the dignity of difference, he is in fact urging us to appreciate the other precisely for their particularity. Grounding such particularity in the image of God could lead us to a quest to understand more deeply all that makes us human and with that the depths of human aspirations to God, as they find full expression in religious diversity.

In any event, we should be aware of the fact that it is not the revisions to *The Dignity of Difference* that are the cause of reduced attention to the particularity of the religion of the other. In neither edition does Sacks show any concrete interest in the religious other. His is an argument for the idea of otherness, not for its particularity or for the ways in which it comes to

---

[43] 'God of Abraham, Yitzhak, and Yonatan', 145.

expression. The tension, then, is not between the two versions of his book. Rather, it is between the theoretical potential of his teaching and its more limited application. The fuller potential certainly comes across in the original version of *The Dignity of Difference* but it can also be identified in the revised edition. Sacks enriches our thought, laying theoretical foundations for transformative engagement with the particularity of another religion. What that particularity consists of and how extensive such engagement might be are never explored, for the simple reason that Sacks avoids all translation of his theory into a practice of sharing between religions. Yet it is precisely his not translating his ideals into action that allows us to speculate about not only how the earlier view might be applied but even how the later view, centred around the image of God and the riches of the human person, might still amount to an invitation to discover God in the processes of learning and sharing between religions.

One final important argument emerges from *The Dignity of Difference*. Version 1 includes reference to one God, multiple covenants. This formulation occupies one pole on the axis of possible attitudes to other religions. If we reflect on this formulation, it may well discourage sharing. As far as the notion of covenant in and of itself goes, it might lead us to a view of parallel paths, each for its own recipient. Covenant is a personal relationship. The metaphor for such a relationship is marriage. The recognition of multiple valid marriages between different partners would not lead to an attempt to enter into the intimacy and particularity of any of those marriages. On the contrary, it would be a means of affirmation while keeping safe distance. The problem, of course, lies in the limits of the metaphor. When one God makes multiple covenants, should we emphasize the multiplicity of these, each distinct and self-standing, or do we consider them a means of coming to know better the one God, discovered in multiple relationships?

In terms of a theology of religions, the reference to multiple covenants is similar to the common Indian view of different religions being paths up a mountain, reaching the same mountain top, which, in Sacks' terms, would be the same covenanting God. The metaphor is designed to validate and appreciate other religions. It is not normally intended to invite members of one faith to walk up the mountain on the path of another faith.[44]

---

[44] Sri Ramakrishna's practice is an exception. Moreover, at the end of the day, his exploration of other faiths did not become either his spiritual path or that of his followers. It provided experiential proof for the Indian theory of religions, rather than engendering a new religious practice.

Let us now turn to those conceptual elements in Sacks' thinking that would suggest the opposite of the recommendation to study other religions in an effort to hear God's voice in them.

The Ideal Not Realized

In many statements, Sacks gives a clear indication of the ideal of mutual learning, sharing, and inspiration. These statements push us further to consider the relationship between his theoretical and inspirational sayings and his own practice. His summary of *To Heal a Fractured World* is telling:

This has been a religious book, a Jewish book. Each of us has a contribution to make, whether we are religious or secular, Jewish, Christian or Muslim, whether we represent the great non-Western traditions, or more modern forms of spirituality. All I have aspired to do in this book is to articulate one voice in the conversation, knowing that no human voice can express the totality of wisdom, and that there is none from which we cannot learn.[45]

This paragraph captures perfectly Sacks' view as it has been put forth by Hava Tirosh-Samuelson. His voice is one of many; we must learn from all. But who is this 'we'? Apparently, it does not include Sacks himself, inasmuch as nowhere in his writings does he cite the voice of another religion as an expression of an enriched conversation. He cites philosophers, scholars, and theoreticians, hundreds of them, across a variety of disciplines. Given his enormous erudition and his ability to master entire fields of knowledge, it is striking that the one field of knowledge of which he writes—religious wisdom, as it finds expression across faiths—is never given voice in his writings.[46] Accordingly, the 'we' may be the audience or the world as a whole.

---

[45] p. 267.

[46] In Chapter 14 I understand this fact in light of Sacks' psychology. In communication, Eliot Sacks, Jonathan's brother, raised an additional consideration that is relevant. As he writes to me: 'I am sure you are very familiar with the highly conservative (with a lower case "c") nature of the Anglo-Jewish Orthodox establishment, especially its Bet Din. I'm sure you are also familiar with the history of Anglo-Jewish Orthodoxy and the fact that the last time a leader (or aspiring leader) of Anglo-Jewish Orthodoxy attempted to write about Jewish tradition in an open and questioning way, we had the "Louis Jacobs Affair". Within this institutional context, the idea of a Chief Rabbi being receptive to learning new religious wisdom from a leader of another religion (or indeed being open to reading scholarly, historicist literature on Jewish tradition) is all but unthinkable.'

While I believe Sacks was not really interested in other religions, for their own sake and in terms of their spiritual message, this lack of interest must surely also be seen within the context of the British rabbinate. That Sacks did not show any influence from other faiths prior to

Sacks is a voice in a conversation, but apparently not a voice that is open to receiving other voices.

Sacks describes his work as bringing to a global conversation the particular voice of Judaism. We recall the speech offered at Lambeth Palace, where a distinction made internally between different types of covenant is shared more broadly with all the bishops of the Anglican communion. This is a good example of Sacks' position in relation to others. He is willing to engage. His engagement includes sharing internal Jewish wisdom with others. Yet even when this is understood as joining in a global conversation, reciprocity may be a feature of that conversation, but it does not describe Sacks' own processes. Other religions are appreciated for the good they do. They are not, however, significant conversation partners that have the power to transform and impact his thinking.

The gap between what Sacks knows and could have brought to interfaith engagement and what he actually made of it and how he practised it can be seen when we look at the very idea of encounter. Encounter as a philosophical/human reality is discussed by Sacks in his final book, *Morality*, but he does not include interreligious encounter. For this reason, it is interesting to see how he envisions encounter as an ideal, and how far that vision is from his own practice, as reflected in his books.[47]

Sacks speaks of two prominent Jewish thinkers of the twentieth century who placed interpersonal relationships at the heart of their philosophy of the moral life.

Martin Buber famously contrasted two modes of relationship: I–It and I–Thou. In an I–It relationship, we see the object of experience as something to be analysed, classified, and quantified. My primary question is: To what use can I put this object in front of me? He called this *experience*.

---

having become chief rabbi is accounted for by his brother in terms of his long-term aspiration to become chief rabbi. That he did engage in occasional quoting as part of his later Abrahamic voice does not change the big picture, given the minimal and largely superficial appeal to voices from other religions. It is notable, nonetheless, that this Abrahamic voice was adopted only after he was out of office. Finally, given the institutional context to which Eliot points, one can but marvel at how far Sacks was able to advance an agenda of respect and acceptance of diversity, while upholding certain boundaries, whether imposed from within or from without.

[47] My conversation with former Archbishop Rowan Williams (Ch. 14) suggests that the gap is representative of his actual approach in the formation of interest and friendships across religions.

The other kind of relationship, I–Thou, he called *encounter*. Between us, there is relationship. We are part of the same world. We are capable of transforming one another. An enormous amount of communication in the modern world is done at the level of I–It. That is what makes us feel alienated, part of a primarily impersonal world. But what really matters to us ultimately is the encounter with another 'Thou.' The supreme example is the relationship we call love, and it is at the heart of moral and spiritual life.

Even more powerful is the account of morality given by the French philosopher Emmanuel Levinas. Levinas believed that moral obligation is born at the moment when we encounter what he called 'the face of the other.' His view was that some basic act of recognition takes place when we make eye contact with another human being: here is a person to whom I have duties because he or she is a person, even if, in the biblical phrase, they are an orphan, a widow, or a stranger. In this immediate, pre-reflective encounter, morality is born. 'The face speaks to me and thereby invites me to a relation,' he wrote. 'The face opens the primordial discourse whose first word is obligation.' It is only when we encounter another human being that we begin to communicate and construct a shared world out of the act of communication: 'Meaning is the face of the Other, and all recourse to words takes place already within the primordial face-to-face of language.'

To be fully human, we need direct encounters with other human beings. We have to be in their presence, open to their otherness, alert to their hopes and fears, engaged in the minuet of conversation, the delicate back-and-forth of speaking and listening. That is how relationships are made. That is how we become moral beings. That is how we learn to think as 'We.' This cannot be done electronically.[48]

The text is relevant for us precisely because the problem of relations across religions is not Sacks' concern here. As the final sentences of this quote suggest, he is interested in personal relations in an environment that shifts relations and substitutes electronic communication for genuine encounter.[49] The concerns are moral, not religious in a narrowly defined sense. What are we to make of these quotes when we apply them to relations between religions, as practised and preached by Sacks? Buber's ideas, as set forth here, and those of Levinas, parallel the idea of covenant.[50] They are presented by Sacks in terms of speaking and listening.[51] He never applies Buber's view, however, when he discusses the covenant of hope and the encounter between religions. The answer for why not may be found in the second

[48] *Morality*, 59.   [49] See further ibid. 298.
[50] Note the transition from the end of ch. 3 to the beginning of ch. 4 in *Morality*.
[51] See ibid. 58–9.

passage from Levinas, who speaks of the meaning and language of face to face. What would that mean when extended from the realm of the individual to the relations between religions? Surely it means more than just humanity or otherness. It is therefore interesting to see how Sacks recasts this in the final paragraph in terms of hopes and fears, the minuet of speaking and listening. I believe the face-to-face encounter with the other as other, especially the religious other in his otherness, may be more than Sacks is comfortable with.[52] The idea is therefore channelled as it is, and in the process loses some of its force. In the process, the possibilities for a fuller encounter between religions, in the mutuality of talking *and* listening face to face, are also lost. Sacks' earlier book *Not in God's Name* illustrates the point well. Fears and hopes are central to the book. Talking and listening are largely absent. In their stead, he offers a path that involves creative imagination.

Not in God's Name is Sacks' contribution to the reduction of religiously based violence. One of the resources upon which he draws are biblical stories that serve as paradigms for relationships that must be healed. In the framework of his retelling of the biblical narrative of Joseph and his brothers, he discusses a biblical verb whose meaning conveys estrangement as well as knowledge, opposite experiences communicated by means of the same verb.

The dual meaning of the verb n-k-r gathers into itself the whole force and dramatic conflict of Genesis as a sustained exploration of recognition and estrangement, closeness and distance. It tells us that if only we were to listen closely to the voice of the other, we would find that beneath the skin we are brothers and sisters, members of the human family under the parenthood of God. When others become brothers and conflict is transformed into conciliation, we have begun the journey to society-as-a-family, and the redemptive drama can begin.[53]

It would seem that knowledge of the other is engrained in Sacks' approach to overcoming estrangement and otherness, which involves listening to the voice of the other in an effort to know them. It would seem that

---

[52] Once again, outside the context of interreligious encounter, Sacks is comfortable preaching 'We need to renew those face-to-face encounters with the people not like us, to realize that we can disagree strongly and yet still stay friends. It's in those face-to-face encounters that we discover that the people not like us are just people, like us' (*Morality*, 312). If we recall his preference for side-by-side as opposed to face-to-face dialogue with members of other faiths, the contrast emerges in all its starkness.   [53] *Not in God's Name*, 171–2.

the best antidote to estrangement, then, is mutual knowledge and sharing. And yet this is not the medicine that Sacks prescribes for the illnesses of the day. Instead, he develops a theory of empathy, in which one imagines oneself in the role of the other, cultivating understanding for their circumstances.

It follows that the most profound moralising experience, the only one capable of defeating dualism, is to undergo role reversal. Imagine a Crusader in the Middle Ages, or a German in 1939, discovering that he is a Jew. There can be no more life-changing trial than finding yourself on the other side.[54]

This is certainly very powerful. But what of talking, sharing, and understanding each other? Are there no relational expressions that are more direct? Sacks actually considers this superior to mutual knowledge, arguing that various scenes of violence and genocide occurred under conditions in which one side knew the other, but could not withstand the pressures brought about in times of change and disruption.[55] This is an important rejoinder, but it forces us to ask what we mean by knowing the other. If the healing of relations and of a painful history is the goal, more is required than superficial acquaintance, the likes of what simply living alongside one another might produce. A more concerted and intentional effort is required to hear that inner voice of which Sacks speaks. Yet, while the logic of his thought points in that direction, he posits another path, one that keeps the person within himself, appealing to the imaginative faculty rather than to the reality of encounter with the other. This allows Sacks to affirm the *value* of the other, but not to appreciate them in their particularity. Accordingly, appreciation of the other's religious reality is not part of our appreciation of the other.[56]

The Contraindications

We have seen explicit statements where Sacks calls for mutual learning and deepening knowledge and appreciation of the other. These statements have their own logic and integrity, even if the question arises whether Sacks could serve as a model for the teaching he offers. A second group of texts pointed

---

[54] Ibid. 164.   [55] Ibid. 200.

[56] In comparing the purpose of *The Dignity of Difference* and *Not in God's Name*, one may see in the former an argument for validating the other, while the latter makes an argument for loving the stranger. This helps account for the strategy of identification by imagination. In either case, Sacks' concern is not encounter. *Not in God's Name* could be cast as a call to know the place and the suffering of the stranger. This, however, is different from knowing the particularity and identity of the other.

to where the idea of fuller mutual knowledge might have been expected to appear, given the structure of his thought and statements made by him, but that idea is lacking. The final group of texts further problematizes knowledge of the religious other. The excerpts that follow, while never arguing *against* the ideal, indicate how problematic the idea is in the light of some of his statements. It would seem that in certain respects mutual learning and appreciation are not simply an unfulfilled potential in Sacks' thought. They are either superfluous or unwanted.

Sacks moves from presenting Judaism as unique to drawing lessons from Judaism for the sake of all religions to viewing Judaism as part of a larger group of religions that share common features. *The Dignity of Difference* is the key text for the second group. The sources that precede it roughly correspond to the first, and his later works, beginning with *The Great Partnership*, correspond to the third. Considering this third category, one realizes he has a new agenda, and with it the interest in getting to know the other and sharing knowledge is seriously reduced. So long as religions were viewed individually, one would wish to gain a better understanding of the other, be it for civic or religious purposes. However, once Sacks focuses on 'Abrahamic monotheisms' and related terms, a message is sounded that is not exclusive to Judaism. The constructed group is appreciated in contrast to ancient empires, present-day social forces, and more. In this 'us versus them' approach, the defining unit is no longer one's own religion. One is, to begin with, aligned with other religions. And what one offers is a teaching, a corrective to prevailing tendencies, a solution to the world's problems. From this perspective, listening to one another, deepening understanding, and appreciation are insignificant. Going back to Sacks' linguistic analogy, different religions would not be different languages; at most they would be different dialects of one common language.[57] Typically, one does not bother to study other dialects of one's language.

There is a further, perhaps even more fundamental, cause for lack of interest in the religious reality and particularity of the other. As I have already noted, Sacks' interests are civic. He harnesses religion to address present-day global challenges. Religious violence and tension and the legitimate place of religious and cultural diversity are his concerns. Notable here is *The Home We Build Together*. Time and again, one notes in this book how the encounter across religions and the relationships constructed among religious leaders

---

[57] This is how he describes internal, legitimate Jewish pluralism. See *One People?*, 93, 117.

are important for their civic benefits, for the peace, law, and order they bring to society, not for the spiritual or pedagogic value they might carry in and of themselves. As a result, all appeal to religion plays down the specifically religious potential of an encounter and features its civic benefits instead.[58] When faith leaders gather or appear in public together, rather than recognize the religious dimensions of the encounter and its broader promise, they prioritize the civic elements.[59] The conscious avoidance of the religious dimension is complemented by the recommendation for side-by-side common action that serves society, rather than more direct and dialogical activities that are characterized as face to face. It is possible that all these emphases emerged later, as new challenges presented themselves to the chief rabbi, who had to identify the optimal strategy to serve British society. However, given what we have seen earlier in this chapter, it is more than likely that the internal brakes that Sacks seems to have applied in his own teachings are earlier and they prevented him from applying what his religious imagination led him to conceptualize. As needs and circumstances changed, other approaches to the relations between religions emerged, further downplaying the significance of direct encounter and reciprocal exchange.

This civic agenda and the emphasis on religion's contribution to society pushes to the front the topic of hate-reduction and, with regard to Judaism, antisemitism. Time after time, Sacks describes his relationships with leaders of other faiths. He does so with great poignancy, especially as he relates an interreligious visit to Auschwitz.[60] Yet what he makes of this visit never goes beyond the common commitment to fighting hatred and antisemitism. All the potential that was found in *The Dignity of Difference* has given way to a much flatter message, supported by the testimony and personal experience of collaboration with other faith leaders. An interfaith message is still sounded, but it lacks the depth, or potential depth, of earlier messages in this arena. Using Sacks' terminology, he has moved from covenant as a moment of faith to covenant as a dimension of fate. Religions are no longer bonded in some way by their faith, only by their common fate.[61]

To make sense of this shift, we should recall the tension between verticality and horizontality in Sacks' application of the covenant. Essentially,

---

[58] See, in contrast, Sacks' reference to prayer in *To Heal a Fractured World*, 127.

[59] *The Home We Build Together*, 167.

[60] *Future Tense*, 88; 109. See also Sacks, 'Interfaith Relations and the Holocaust'.

[61] *Future Tense*, 109: 'We share a covenant of fate and human solidarity.' This, as we have seen above, is also one of the messages of the Lambeth address.

over time, covenant became less and less of a religious concept, grounding the vertical dimension within human relations, and increasingly became a horizontal concept, bonding members of society to each other, following the American political tradition. Religious echoes were maintained by continuing appeal to the term. The political applications, in any event, carried such resonance. But the covenant was no longer the biblical covenants discussed in *The Dignity of Difference* and in Sacks' earlier works. Gone was the tension between the covenants of Noah and Abraham. Gone was the tension between universality and particularity. These had given way to a covenant within society that drew more from the political tradition than it did from the Bible, and whose goal was more social and civic than it was religious. Within such a perspective, all that is religious, knowledge-based, and, for that matter, theological is pushed to the side. Horizontality produces solidarity, and that is the key value that Sacks is describing in his relationship with leaders of other faiths. It does not produce a fuller understanding of the other, let alone the transformative effects of such understanding on the self.

Sacks' teaching in this modality creates a new 'we'. It is no longer the 'we' of 'we versus them' that is so characteristic of Jewish thought. It is a new 'we' that consists of other faiths, either narrowly defined as Abrahamic or more broadly defined, as he recalls his encounters and collaborations with a wide range of religions, represented by their leaders in common gatherings and activities.

One of the striking things about this phase of Sacks' thinking, especially as it finds expression in *Not in God's Name*, is that he speaks for the common 'we' but he does so on his own. One would have expected that the attempt to put forth a position common to Judaism, Christianity, and Islam would be sustained by some personal collaboration between himself and two major faith leaders or scholars of those religions. At the very least, he might have consulted them as he crafted this message of the common 'we'. But Sacks interjects himself into the heart of a 'we' that extends beyond Judaism as a single actor. His imagination, especially his exegetical imagination, leads him to make suggestions for what he considers to be the true Abrahamic faith, which would then be relevant to the other Abrahamic faiths. Yet he remains alone in this exercise. Should we have thought that, in this stage of his thought, when he speaks for others and alongside others, a real need for reciprocity, mutuality, consultation, and understanding of the other would

emerge, redefining his approach to religions, we discover ever more powerfully the problematic nature of avoiding direct contact with others when it
comes to articulating theological ideas and ideals. This phase of Sacks'
thought reflects the avoidance of mutual encounter and study in two ways.
Speaking for multiple religions makes mutual knowledge less of a concern.
At the same time, speaking for multiple religions through the lens of one's
own religion further highlights how Sacks is simultaneously open to other
religions while avoiding the fuller contact that could enhance his thought
and bring about the kind of deeper understanding and transformation that
he preached previously.

There is one final point to be made regarding the parameters and boundaries of Sacks' thinking. This part of the chapter has wrestled with the limitations and the unrealized potential of his thought concerning other
religions. What is it that really prevents him from engaging in the way he is
perfectly capable of imagining as he reflects on ideal relations in his earlier
work and in *The Dignity of Difference*? I would like to suggest that at the root
of it is a deeper reservation with regards to theology, religious experience,
and how God is known. The root of Sacks' hesitancy, if we may refer to it
thus, may go to the very foundation of how he knows God and how he
approaches religion, both within Judaism and in relation to the other. If so,
the unfulfilled potential may be accounted for in terms that straddle psychology and epistemology. We might refer to it as his particular spirituality.
He knows God in very particular ways and those ways either preclude or
make it unnecessary to engage with the depth of the religious experience of
the other whom he seeks to affirm. Let us consider the following passage,
which I find very suggestive in this regard.

People within the Abrahamic monotheisms have always known that for most of
us, most of the time, God, more infinite than the universe, older and younger
than time, cannot be known directly. He is known mainly through his effects, and
of these the most important is his effect on human lives. That is what I sensed on
meeting the Lubavitcher Rebbe and Rabbi Soloveitchik. In them it was obvious. It
is why they commanded so much respect within the American Jewish community. But over the years I have learned to find it so much more widely, in communities that care, in the kindness of strangers, in people who touch our lives, perhaps
only momentarily, doing the deed or saying the word that carries us to safety
across the abyss of loneliness or self-doubt.

It is where I find God in Jewish history. There is a grandeur, a nobility, a heroic passion about Jews that does not seem to come naturally to this fractious, quarrelsome, stiff-necked people . . .

But you have to be very narrow indeed not to see beauty and wisdom in faiths other than your own. I have been inspired by seeing Sikhs offering hospitality to the poor in Amritsar, Christians building homes for the homeless throughout the world, Hindus practising *sewa*, compassion to the distressed, by the majestic wisdom of the great Chinese Confucian and Taoist traditions, and the courage of the many Muslims I know who fight the extremists in their own communities. The statement that every human being is in God's image precedes both the universal covenant with Noah in Genesis 9 and the particular covenant with Abraham in Genesis 17, to tell us that our humanity precedes our religious identity, whatever that identity may be.[62]

On the face of it, this is a very open and outgoing quote. It relates not only to Abrahamic religions but also to others. I note especially the reference to Sikhs Sacks had met in Amritsar, a visit I had the honour to facilitate and which had left a deep enough impression upon him to figure here and elsewhere. Yet what this passage reveals to us is that Sacks is neither a mystic nor a philosopher in the old sense. God is not known to him directly, experientially, mystically. He is known to him in and through people. This is as true of the two great Jewish teachers who shaped his life and set him on his path as it is of the many religious leaders and communities he met along the way. In both cases, God is known through the image of God. The human person takes precedence in experiential, and ultimately theoretical, terms over God as direct object of relationship and knowledge. The shift from God to image of God is, in this new insight, not simply a matter of compromising the radical views of *The Dignity of Difference*. It goes to the core of Sacks' spirituality. It is a spirituality that passes through the human person and human relations. While there is certainly room to consider the vertical dimensions that lend the individual his full depth and dignity and to engage with the theological ideals of religions, once we focus on the human person and human relationships, the horizontal dimension seems to take over. From this perspective, the kinds of ideals that Sacks sets forth as worthy of appreciation in members of other religions, ideals that make mutual study and encounter mostly superfluous, make sense, in their own way.

[62] *The Great Partnership*, 93.

CHAPTER ELEVEN

Viewing and Presenting
Other Religions

T HE QUESTION of learning from other faiths and receiving their wisdom should not be considered in the abstract. It is couched in the broader question of how Sacks presents other religions. How does he view them? Whom does he cite? This will tell us what his basic orientation is, and will indicate the degree of his openness and receptivity. His broader, peace-seeking constructs are to a certain extent put to the test in the assessment of how he actually relates to other religions not in theory but in practice.

By way of introduction, one must state once again the startling fact that there is not a single instance of Sacks' thought showing the influence or in-spiration of a figure from another religion. There is no teacher, saint, philos-opher, or even scripture or scriptural citation that impresses one as having had a formative role in his world-view, spirituality, or even in his appreciation for other religions. The kind of admiration shown to his teachers in the philosophical tradition is never found in relation to contemporary religious leaders or models and paragons of earlier periods. To be sure, Sacks ex-presses sincere appreciation for the changes that the Catholic Church and other churches underwent, and especially their attitudes to Judaism. In this he also acknowledges the important role played by figures such as Pope John Paul II.[1] There is certainly a positive recognition of individuals who have contributed to historical movements. Thus, Calvin is valued for advancing a Christianity with a strong work ethic.[2] Sacks is aware, then, of individual fig-ures and their heritage. However, these are viewed more from a historical and less from a religious or spiritual perspective. In terms of the religious life

---

[1] 'Special praise must go to a series of popes: John XXIII, who began the process leading to Vatican II and Nostra Aetate, Paul VI, who completed it, and John Paul II and Benedict XVI, both of whom continued it in their own way' (*Not in God's Name*, 275).

[2] See *Morality*, 285.

and its ideals, the lack of meaningful contact, knowledge, citation, and inspiration is striking. The only positive reference I could find to a Christian thinker is a phrase used by Paul Tillich, providing a concept one could appeal to.[3] To put it in other words, religions, their leaders, and their thinkers are not Sacks' significant others. He has his significant others who impact his thought and who help shape his vision of Judaism. These, however, are not religious figures. They are philosophers and political thinkers. It is my impression that, more than anyone else, Sacks cites Alexis de Tocqueville, a nineteenth-century French diplomat who reported on democracy and religion in America. The connection with religion is significant. But so is the fact that so much is made of the testimony of someone who is not specifically identified as a figure within religion.

An analysis of how Sacks approaches and portrays other religions leads us to uncover two basic modalities in his relationship to them. I identify these modalities as follows:

1. Contrasting Judaism and other religions. In this modality Judaism is set apart and its uniqueness is highlighted, creating a contrast that offers us a window onto how Sacks views other faiths. This modality is found in his earlier writings.

2. Likening Judaism to other religions. This modality can be further divided in two. The first approach sees Judaism within the broader category of all religions, and presents the positive elements of religion in general. Judaism is one of any number of religions that share in the benefits that faith brings. The alternative to religion is society at large, and the discourse takes place from the perspective of religion versus society, or the marketplace, or science, or similar. This perspective will highlight the positive attributes of religions in general, without an attempt to minimize the value of one or another.

The second approach, which is reflected in several of Sacks' works written during the second decade of the twenty-first century, places Judaism within the broader family of Abrahamic faiths or monotheisms. The perspective here is mixed in terms of how Sacks views the other faiths. On the one hand, there is a fundamental commonality that allows him to feature what is common and praiseworthy in this family of faiths. However, positioning Judaism within this context also leads him to point out where other

---

[3] *Future Tense*, 253.

Abrahamic monotheisms have gone wrong, especially in relation to religious violence, and most particularly its Islamist expression. Judaism is thus both a part of this group of religions and a corrective to it on the basis of Sacks' critical analysis.

Seeing Judaism either as apart from or as a part of other religions leads to broad generalizations regarding other religions, as well as to specific references to their teachings. These can be seen as falling into two modalities.

3. Misrepresentation and superficial presentation. Largely paralleling the contrastive modality, we find various presentations of Judaism in comparison with other religions that support its uniqueness. In order to highlight Judaism's singularity, Sacks makes use of descriptions of other religions, offering definitions of their essence and their respective particularity. These descriptions provide us with a glimpse into how he sees other faiths and how problematic the attempt to define another religion by a single term or key feature is.

4. Criticism and polemic. Largely paralleling the reference to Judaism as part of the Abrahamic family of faiths, we find Sacks engaging in analyses of texts and teachings of other religions. The flip side of a lack of positive appreciation for individuals and ideas found in other religions is the criticism of their tenets or structures and Sacks' entry into the territory we could describe as religious polemics. A critical note is sounded in particular regarding the New Testament and the writings of Paul. Of course, the attitude to jihadist Islam is similarly critical. If one considers the big picture of Sacks' treatment of other religions, one realizes that, alongside principled respect for their very existence, his actual references to them or their key texts are, in fact, more critical than appreciative.

While conceptually distinct, the modalities overlap and reinforce each other in various ways. For purposes of our analysis, I will examine them independently, noting instances of Sacks' application of each.

Contrasting Judaism and Other Religions

'No other religion' or 'I know of no other religion' is the oft-repeated phrase that characterizes Sacks' description of Judaism's particularity as compared with all other religions. Regardless of their theoretical validation, the key message is that Judaism is unique and has a particular lesson to teach the world that makes it distinct from other religions, and quite possibly also superior in this regard. This modality is invoked especially when Sacks presents Judaism, as opposed to when he seeks to articulate a theory that legitimates other religions.[4] Referring to Judaism bringing together God and man as partners in the work of creation, he states: 'I know of no other vision that confers on mankind so great a dignity and responsibility.'[5] According to Sacks, the idea of divine–human partnership is an exclusive teaching of Judaism.[6]

With reference to the Jewish view of other religions, he states:

Peace is when under God's sacred canopy different nations and faiths make room for one another. No other religion has shared this idea, of a single God with many names, who has set his image on each of us, but with whom we talk, each faith in its own language, each in its own way.[7]

Sacks presents this form of pluralism as a distinct and unique feature of Judaism. 'Alone among the great religions, it argues that there is one God and many faiths.'[8] But is this description true? As already suggested, Hindu theology of religions can easily be summed up by the slogan 'One God, many names'.[9] Even if theological nuances will distinguish the Jewish and Hindu positions, what Sacks describes as a unique Jewish view, being himself a nearly unique Jewish voice to expound such a view, is in fact the default Hindu view of religions. When he claims that Judaism is unique in this regard, he is not distorting facts. He is, rather, showing us that, for all the extensivity of his knowledge, it does not include knowledge of other religions to a degree that would justify making such generalizations.

Hinduism is not alone. One may well construct a Muslim theology of religions that similarly affirms a 'one God, many religions' view. Clearly at odds with common perceptions of Islam and many of its present-day jihadist perspectives, it is nonetheless a mainstream, and I would argue official, Muslim view of other religions. The strategy is a little different from the

---

[4] Hence its many appearances in *Radical Then, Radical Now*.   [5] Ibid. 82.

[6] For Greenberg, human–divine partnership is fundamental to the notion of covenant and as such applies to all religions, inasmuch as all religions have some association with a covenant through the covenant of Noah.

[7] *Radican Then, Radical Now*, 94. See further p. 88.   [8] Ibid. 96.

[9] This is a commonplace in Hinduism. A typical example is found in 'Many Names—One God'.

Hindu parallel. The Muslim version is 'one God, many prophets'. Reliance on prophecy provides a form of legitimation of other religions, which are understood as having been instituted by divinely sent messengers.[10] This does not necessarily place them on a par with Islam, which is still considered superior,[11] but it does provide a mechanism for validating them.[12] In this regard, the Muslim view is no different from Sacks' own validation of religions, which does not amount to the kind of relativism that would see them all as fundamentally equal.[13]

One might be tempted to regard Christianity as the exception to the rule of universal religious legitimation. However, one must compare equal to equal. Sacks is a constructive thinker who seeks to articulate a contemporary Jewish view of other religions. In so doing, he draws on classical sources. Nevertheless, what he has to say is novel. There is no earlier Jewish authority who has said precisely what he says, even if he presents his view as that of Judaism. Consequently, the proper comparison of his views should be to similar efforts made by Christians to achieve similar validation of other religions. The field of theology of religions as a theoretical discipline, though certainly not as a practice,[14] was born within a Christian theological matrix, and Sacks is aware of some of its representative works.[15] Given that he is engaged in a similar undertaking on the Jewish side, we would expect him to contrast his own efforts with those of Christians who are also striving to create a culture of peace and understanding between religions. This is not, however, what he does. He contrasts his own, what we may call 'advanced', views of other religions with classical Christian views that would be described as exclusivist, notably the statement that outside the Church no

[10] For a historical overview of Muslim views of other faiths, see Waardenburg (ed.), *Muslim Perceptions of Other Religions*.

[11] The problem for Islamic theology is validating religions that came into being after Muhammad's ministry, as Muhammad is considered the seal of the prophets, locking the door to future legitimation of religions by means of his prophetic authority.

[12] There are other Islamic mechanisms. In fact, Islam seems to have a structure of dual covenants that is quite similar to what Sacks has established in the contrast between the covenant of Noah and Abraham. On the covenant of Creation, see Cornell, 'Islam'.

[13] I can't think of any Jewish thinker who could marshal such a position. Even Meiri, though he relies on the category of 'religion' as the common ground for religions, would still consider Judaism superior in some ways, whether in principle or in application.

[14] The practice itself is timeless and is undertaken whenever one religion considers the value and merits of another, or of other religions as a whole.

[15] I have noted his reference to John Hick and through him to the various sources that Hick discusses.

salvation is possible.[16] When this contrast is made, Christianity emerges as exclusivist, while Judaism is pluralist. Sacks is well aware of developments in the Catholic Church as part of the Second Vatican Council and *Nostra aetate*.[17] That document, and reams of theological work undertaken by Catholic as well as other Christian theologians both before and since Vatican II, provide strong parallels to Sacks' own efforts. If I am correct in my argument that he is better seen as an inclusivist than as a pluralist, then in fact he has much common ground with official Catholic teaching for the past half century and more, which advocates an inclusivist view of other religions. To ignore these developments and to characterize Christianity as identical with earlier, exclusivist Christian positions seems a wilful neglect of the facts in the interest of scoring points in favour of Judaism, its uniqueness, and its possible superiority.

There is a larger problem in the juxtaposition of Judaism and other religions. It is impossible to characterize Judaism by means of one position on a given subject. Sacks builds on a Jewish tradition of tolerance, and his sources include Meiri and the historical trajectory of the permissibility of forms of worship that are less demanding in terms of exclusive worship of God for other religions.[18] In his view, Judaism would never engage in missionary activity, let alone aggressive missionizing. This is fine and is largely true when considering Judaism over the past 2,000 years. But what are we to make of Maimonides' application of the notion of holy war to forcefully impose Judaism on other peoples?[19] I do not see a problem in not citing such a view and not relying on it for a characterization of Judaism. But when Judaism and other religions are reduced to a single formula, a single position, and when, on the basis of such a reduction, two religions are contrasted, we risk a superficial view of Judaism, of other religions, and of their similarities, differences, and respective advantages. A more correct balance seems to me to be that proposed by Greenberg, taking into account the complexities of religions. As Greenberg notes, religions have multiple voices and multiple positions. Differences between them are often a matter of shifting emphases, with one religion emphasizing one position, while another

---

[16] See *Future Tense*, 81; *The Great Partnership*, 62–3.   [17] *Not in God's Name*, 96.

[18] On the *shituf* concept and the history of its application, see Goshen-Gottstein, *Same God, Other god*, chs. 8 and 9, as well as ch. 10 on Meiri.

[19] *Mishneh torah*, 'Laws of Kings', 8: 10. On Maimonides' view of holy war, see Blidstein, *Political Concepts in Maimonidean Halakhah* (Heb.), ch. 9.

tends to another. Such a perspective allows us to approach the subject of comparison in a more balanced, and ultimately fairer, manner.[20]

Likening Judaism to Other Religions

Within the Sacks corpus, different books employ diverse strategies in featuring Judaism in comparison with other religions. The quotes in the previous section came from *Radical Then, Radical Now*, a book whose purpose is to present Judaism and its overall message to an internal audience. By contrast, the following section relies on quotes from *The Dignity of Difference*, whose express purpose is to develop a theory of relations between religions. In this context, Judaism appears as part of the broader category of religions.

One of the classic roles of religion has been to preserve a space—physical and metaphysical—immune to the pressures of the market. When we stand before God we do so regardless of what we earn, what we own, what we buy, what we can afford. We do so as beings of ultimate, non-transactional value, here because someone—some force at the heart of being—called us into existence and summoned us to be a blessing. The power of the great world religions is that they are not mere philosophical systems, abstract truths strung together in strictly logical configurations. They are embodied truths, made vividly real in lives, homes, congregations, rituals, narratives, songs and prayers—in covenantal communities whose power is precisely that they are not subject to economic forces. They value people for what they are; they value actions for the ideals that brought them forth; they preserve relationships by endowing them with the charisma of eternity made real in the here-and-now.[21]

Note how all religions are described as covenantal communities, clearly referring to the horizontal and social dimensions of the covenant. Note also how no religion is singled out as occupying some special position when religion as such is contrasted with market forces. Much as in Meiri, the category of 'religion' designates a domain of life and a quality of living best appreciated against the realities outside it.

There are multiple statements of a similar nature. 'The great faiths teach a different kind of wisdom: *reverence* in the face of creation, *responsibility* to

---

[20] A further instance of 'It is the only religion known to me' concerns Judaism being a religion in which human beings talk, argue, and remonstrate with God. 'There is nothing remotely like this in the sacred books of either Christianity or Islam' (*Radical Then, Radical Now*, 96.) This characterization seems, on first appearance, more correct than some of Sacks' other characterizations. However, I would not be surprised if closer study led to toning down the stark comparison.   [21] *The Dignity of Difference*, 158.

future generations, and *restraint* in the knowledge that not everything we can do, should we do.'[22] 'All of the world's great faiths embody a sense of respect for nature.'[23] 'The world faiths are global phenomena whose reach is broader and in some respects deeper than the nation-state. Judaism is one of those voices.'[24]

Complementing this view of 'religion', in which Judaism is but one voice, is another approach, employed in his final book, *Morality*. The message is the same; Judaism exemplifies principles and processes that pertain to all religions. There are, however, two features that distinguish the way this finds expression in this book. The first is that, rather than religions being the main subject matter, they serve as mere illustrations of how a given moral principle is manifested. The second is that religions include not only monotheistic ones, but also those that would be defined as idolatrous. In other words, the category of religion and its usefulness, when considered in the broader context of humanity and its various institutions, includes also religions that one might not fully approve of.[25]

The citizens of Calvin's Geneva so internalized his strict ethic of work, discipline, virtue, and frugality that they were able to achieve exemplary success socially and economically. The intricate and demanding nature of Judaism allowed Jews to preserve their identity in exile and dispersion for two thousand years despite the fact that wherever they found themselves, they were a cultural and religious minority.

Wilson's most spectacular example is of how the Balinese worship of the Goddess of the Waters allowed thousands of rice farmers, spread across hundreds of square miles, to manage the delicate process of sharing limited rainwater as it makes its way down the sides of a volcano, a marvelous feat of social coordination.[26]

The reason Sacks can include also pagan religions in his description of religion is that he is not speaking theologically; he is speaking sociologically. These examples are part of a larger body of data by means of which he illustrates the claim that religion creates community. He is describing how reli-

---

[22] *The Dignity of Difference*, 172.   [23] Ibid. 171.   [24] Ibid. 12.
[25] This takes us back to the question raised by Marc Shapiro with regard to *The Dignity of Difference* and how Sacks' view of other faiths relates to the Jewish concern with idolatry. These later references do not seem to be limited by the acceptance of the Noahide commandments, a criterion posited by Sacks in the revised version of his book. See above, p. 263; also spelled out on pp. 274, 279, 284.   [26] *Morality*, 285.

gion works in society, and how it interacts with other elements of society. Such descriptions do not depend on theological propriety and legitimacy. While the distinction is significant, it does also suggest how central the social theory that Sacks seeks to construct is. Religion is appreciated more for the value of how it contributes to and operates in society, the horizontal dimension, than for its verticality and the veracity of spiritual claims in relation to God. The following quote, while considering the practical-social impact of faith, nevertheless does enter the domain of faith proper.

It is not only the Bible that tells us God sees all we do. Norenzayan makes the point that divine eyes can also be found in representations of Horus in ancient Egypt, Buddha in villages in Tibet and Nepal, Viracocha in the Inca Empire, and many other portrayals of deities. What moves people to act in prosocial ways is not the idea of God as an abstract creative force, but rather the belief that He sees what we do—and not simply the belief but an active reminder of it.[27]

This is an amazing passage. Sacks is describing how people act in 'prosocial' ways. There is a common belief that God sees people and this motivates them to action. Whether what they think of as God is valid in terms of Jewish recognition, as discussed in classical sources and as reflected even in *The Dignity of Difference*, is totally irrelevant. It does not even appear as a consideration in this book. *Morality* is the least Jewish of Sacks' books, meant for a different audience and drawing on other sources. Still, it tells us something fundamental about how he sees religion, what matters most to him, and how, in this context, distinctions between different forms of religion—legitimate and illegitimate from a Jewish or Noahide perspective—play no role.

Let us turn now to a view of Judaism as part of the Abrahamic faiths, what Sacks often refers to as 'Abrahamic monotheisms'. I begin with a passage that shows Sacks' awareness of the present moment and its challenges. What drives him to take some of the positions he has taken is ultimately accounted for by an act of listening to a divine calling.

As for me, I believe that we are being summoned by God to see in the human other a trace of the divine Other. The test—so lamentably failed by the great powers of the twentieth century—is to see the divine presence in the face of a stranger; to heed the cry of those who are disempowered in this age of unprecedented powers; who are hungry and poor and ignorant and uneducated, whose human potential is being denied the chance to be expressed. That is the faith of

[27] Ibid. 290.

Abraham and Sarah, from whom the great faiths, Judaism, Christianity and Islam, trace their spiritual or actual ancestry. That is the faith of one who, though he called himself but dust and ashes, asked of God himself, 'Shall the judge of all the earth not do justice?' We are not gods, but we are summoned by God—to do His work of love and justice and compassion and peace.[28]

What we are called to is a distillation of Sacks' core message through his reading of Judaism for the world—not for Jews alone. Grounded in the person of Abraham, the historical or reconstructed personality, it is the heritage of other faiths, the three faiths that see themselves as born of him, either physically or spiritually. That Sacks should accept the description of Christianity and Islam as related to Abraham is itself a significant achievement. This is not a classical Jewish perspective. An overview of the pedigree of the idea that these three religions share something in common by reference to the figure of Abraham reveals that it is a rather recent notion.[29] Nevertheless, it has taken hold and Sacks is one of the most prominent Jewish voices to validate this intuition. In the process, he is also validating internal Christian and Muslim faith claims that had been rejected by Jews for centuries. During long centuries, Jews have been locked in conflict with members of those two faiths around issues of memory, what really happened to Abraham and his offspring, and the validity of attachment to the person of Abraham on spiritual, even if not biological, grounds.[30] Sacks makes a revolutionary move. In order to uphold the common front that this group of religions must present for the sake of society, he is willing to recognize the internal faith claims of the two 'rival' religions and to consequently see them as members of the same family of religions. This is a striking and novel, I would even say revolutionary, claim. I am not aware of any classical or even modern rabbinic authority who was willing to make such a claim. It will seem less radical if we recognize that the very attribution of the adjective 'Abrahamic' to these three faiths is a development of the past few decades. Sacks is relying on a common perception that has taken hold, internalizing it, and applying it for his particular purpose, in a largely utilitarian manner. He is willing to cast

[28] *The Dignity of Difference*, 208. See further *The Great Partnership*, 205.
[29] It owes much to Louis Massignon and his efforts at the time of the Second Vatican Council.
[30] In previous eras, Abraham was a bone of contention and a source of competition between the religions, not a symbol of their harmony. See Hughes, *Abrahamic Religions*, ch. 2, and Bakhos, *The Family of Abraham*, 217–18.

aside critical consideration of the designation 'Abrahamic' in order to uphold the moral and social lessons that utilizing this designation makes available to him. In fact, he never discusses what makes a religion Abrahamic, what are its minimal requirements, and wherein lies the common denominator that allows the religions to be studied under the same rubric. It seems the increasingly common designation of these religions as Abrahamic is sufficient.

One point should be highlighted. Covenant does not play into the designation of religions as Abrahamic. The 'Abrahamic monotheisms' discourse of the later Sacks has completely cast aside covenant discourse. Abraham does not receive a covenant. He no longer represents particularity. How could he, if three competing particularities trace themselves to him? Nor is covenant part of the bond of the three Abrahamic faiths. But even if historically there was no covenant between these faiths, we might have expected the centrality of the covenant of solidarity to be translated to a hope or a future vision of a covenant that newly binds the three Abrahamic faiths together, owing to the common patriarch and some agreed-upon understanding of his heritage. This could have been a powerful vision, tying together Sacks' key concerns in different periods of his literary creativity. It could have also pointed the way forward, going beyond past disputes to a commonly agreed-upon image of Abraham that would serve as a foundation for a new covenant between the religions. The ideas are inspiring, but they are nowhere to be found in his writings.

How, then, does the appeal to Abrahamic monotheisms function in Sacks' own writing? There are two distinct moves that are made in relation to Abrahamic faiths. The first pertains to the common challenge.

Until we make theological space for the other, people will continue to hate in the name of the God of love, practise cruelty in the name of the God of compassion, wage war in the name of the God of peace, and murder in the name of the God of life. That is the greatest theological challenge of the twenty-first century. It is a challenge for Jews, Christians and Muslims alike, and its epicentre today is in the same, tiny, fateful land to which God summoned Abraham four thousand years ago.[31]

Jews, Christians, and Muslims have a common contemporary moral challenge. Its present-day political context is the Land of Israel, which in turn is linked to the person of Abraham. Religiously inspired violence lies at the

---

[31] *Future Tense*, 87.

heart of Sacks' concerns. While the argument is primarily aimed at certain forms of Islam, it is couched in terms that apply to the Abrahamic faiths in general.

There was clearly a profound love between Abraham and God, and it is this that eventually inspired not only Jews but Christians and Muslims also, in their different ways, to see themselves as his heirs. But all who embrace Abraham must aspire to live like Abraham. Nothing could be more alien to the spirit of Abrahamic monotheism than what is happening today in the name of jihad. Barbarism and brutality, the embrace of terror and the murder of the innocent, the cold, cruel killing of those with whom you disagree, the pursuit of power in the name of empire, and the idea that you can impose truth by force: these are pagan ideas that have no place in the universe of Abraham or Abraham's God. They constitute neither justice nor love. They are a desecration.[32]

The challenge or invitation is common to all faiths. The problem is identified in relation to one particular expression of Abrahamic faith. And the antidote, which lies at the heart of Sacks' approach, takes us to his second move. Having situated all three faiths together, he offers a reading of Judaism, drawn from Jewish sources and relying on a particular Jewish construct that balances universality and particularity, to affirm the true Abrahamic teaching, which serves as a corrective to false and distorted forms of Abrahamic faith. What Sacks calls for is a return to the true Abraham, who is the common spiritual ideal of all three faiths. In the process, Abraham emerges as the supreme religious figure, eclipsing the particularity of Moses for Judaism. Let us recall, in Sacks' earlier work the Noahide commandments provided the universal while Abraham provided a model of the particular, replicated by all religions in their respective ways. Now, Abraham is the source of commonality and the two figures at either end of the chain of covenants are no longer part of the equation that impacts other faiths. Gone is the reference to Noah and gone is the reference to Moses. Abraham alone remains as the focal point of reflection, admiration, and education.

A further example of extending Jewish interpretative practice to other faiths has to do with the hermeneutics of difficult passages.

The sacred literatures of Judaism, Christianity and Islam all contain passages that, read literally, are capable of leading to violence and hate. We may and must reinterpret them.[33]

---

[32] *Not in God's Name*, 216.   [33] Ibid. 231. See also *The Dignity of Difference*, 207.

While it is true that interpretation is an art common to all three faiths, in fact to all faiths that have a written canon, the particular emphasis on interpretation as a key to neutralizing problematic ideas is distinctly Jewish. Having affirmed Judaism's belonging to this family of religions, Sacks is now able to prescribe a Jewish methodology as the desired approach to be consciously undertaken by all faiths.

The approach is inclusivist. While formally Judaism is *included* in this broader family of faiths, in fact, it sets the patterns that are then to be applied to the other religions. Possibly because Abraham, so I believe Sacks would hold, was Jewish, as a Jewish thinker he can extend the outlook associated with his person and with the religious tradition that grew from him to the other faiths that attach themselves to his person and to his memory. These religions are then included in the approach that is typical of Judaism. 'Abrahamic' is defined in terms of Abraham, who, in turn, is defined by the Jewish approach to his person and to religion in general.

The inclusivist approach is made clearer when we realize that, throughout his later works, Sacks speaks for the other religions from this Abrahamic platform, with minimal appeal to the scriptures and authorities of those traditions. The argument could have been put forth in a different way. He could have collaborated with a Muslim and a Christian teacher to uncover the common Abrahamic teachings that support his line of thinking. It is precisely here that the weakness in Sacks' approach comes to light.[34] He speaks for other faiths from the position of what can be described as the authentic reconstructed view of Abraham. This provides him with a powerful tool to criticize other faiths, where they may have gone wrong in relation to his Abrahamic ideal. But it also raises the question of the efficacy of this strategy. Why would Christians and Muslims accept the construct wherein Sacks alone is privileged to know and speak from the heart of the true faith of Abraham? Why should his voice be considered authentic when it comes to how Christians and Muslims view key features of their faith? Some of these concerns are mitigated by Sacks' references to sources from the scriptures of other faiths. I shall deal with these presently. But before going on,

---

[34] From Dayan Ivan Binstock (London Beth Din) I have learned that, prior to authoring *Not in God's Name*, Sacks wrote a book entitled *Making Space*. The book was never published as Sacks' advisors felt that it suffered from certain weaknesses that would impede its positive reception. This part of *Not in God's Name* originates, as I understand, from that earlier manuscript. It may also carry forth a weakness found in the original into the new context. I have been unable to consult a copy of *Making Space*.

I can already make the point that the outsider's view of these sources, let alone their superficial examination based on common and popular knowledge of the faiths, cannot provide an adequate substitute for the authoritative treatment of religious texts by insiders to the tradition. If Sacks is calling upon the faithful of other religions to interpret their hard texts and to do their theological homework, this call should translate to engaging with authentic voices from within those traditions in the re-examination of their religious teachings. Consider what power the same message would have if it were supported by a joint study document produced by the chief rabbi of the UK, the Archbishop of Canterbury, and the grand mufti of Egypt (Mufti Ali Goma has been closely associated with British religious leaders and could have been a third member of the team). The identity of the religious leaders is secondary to the point being made—Sacks speaking for true Abrahamic faiths is problematic and ultimately undermines the success of his efforts. If we seek to account for why this path was not taken, we will have to consider, as we do in the following chapter, his interest in dialogue and in the study of religions.

Speaking for the Abrahamic faiths leads Sacks to make assertions that the other religions would likely not agree with.

That idea, ignored for many of the intervening centuries, remains the simplest definition of the Abrahamic faith. It is not our task to conquer or convert the world or enforce uniformity of belief. It is our task to be a blessing to the world. The use of religion for political ends is not righteousness but idolatry.[35]

In fact, in the name of Abrahamic faith, Sacks is launching a criticism of Christianity and Islam. What makes his criticism both rich and complicated is that it is not issued simply as the criticism of an outsider. It is issued from a perspective of belonging, though this very belonging to the Abrahamic family of faiths is defined on Sacks' terms, which then serves as the basis for criticizing those faiths. This strategy seems even more extreme than inclusivism. Inclusivism affirms the validity of the other faith or recognizes in it ideals found in one's own. What we see here, instead, is the claim that the true meaning of the faith of the other resides with the observer. Sacks, then, holds the key to the true meaning of the other Abrahamic faiths. Some might call this interreligious colonialism. Here is one way in which he describes this approach.

---

[35] *Not in God's Name*, 5.

I am a Jew, but this book is not about Judaism. It is about the monotheism that undergirds all three Abrahamic faiths: Judaism, Christianity and Islam. It usually appears wearing the clothes of one of these faiths. But I have tried to present it as it is in itself, because otherwise we will lose sight of the principle in the details of this faith or that. Jews, Christians and Muslims all believe more than what is set out here, but all three rest on the foundation of faith in a personal God who created the universe in love and who endowed each of us, regardless of class, colour, culture or creed, with the charisma and dignity of his image.[36]

Sacks builds his edifice on a foundational monotheism that undergirds all three faiths. This description protects him from the potential charge of reading the other faiths in light of Judaism. Judaism is potentially in need of the same corrective as Christianity and Islam. However, at the end of the day it is a Jewish interpreter who has excavated the meaning of the foundational monotheism common to all three faiths. While the common foundations cited in this passage seem innocuous enough,[37] the extension of the faith of Abraham to issues of universality and proselytism, cited above, demonstrates the problematics associated with Sacks' method.

When we move from earlier to later works, we realize just how little dialogue really means to Sacks and how superficially it is embedded in his thought. *The Dignity of Difference* addressed the challenges of religious pluralism, and the ways in which religions should recognize and accept one another and desist from mutual hostility. In the process, an opening was created for the study of the other religion and for entry into a mutually enriching process of gaining deeper understanding of one another. While the problem was societal, the perspective allowed the positioning of religions face to face. The later works no longer allow that. If Judaism is viewed as part of a larger group of faiths, the new matrix does not invite a face-to-face approach. The goal is to correct wrong religious teachings in the interest of social harmony. Such correction is not attained by dialogue or mutual knowledge, but by the recovery of a fundamental, authentic Abrahamic religious understanding. From the Jewish perspective, this does not require an

---

[36] *The Great Partnership*, 289.

[37] Even then, it is not clear that all three faiths can really subscribe even to this minimal definition of Abrahamic commonality. Such commonality includes reference to the creation of the human person, or of humanity, in God's image. This is the most central tenet of Sacks' theology and his approach to religion. Yet the status of belief in the idea of man being created in God's image is far from evident in Islam. It is absent in the Qur'an and exists in one *hadith* tradition, whose interpretations vary in accordance with the concerns of anthropomorphism. See Melchert, 'God Created Adam in His Image'.

understanding of the other or study of another religion's teachings in a dialogical manner. Sacks provides for us the teaching and the perspective by
means of which the other religion is to be understood in its full Abrahamic
authenticity, regardless of its concrete historical expressions and teachings.
There is no need for study of the other, nor for mutuality. Having absorbed
Judaism into the new construct of 'Abrahamic monotheisms', it is now Sacks
who holds the keys to its correct interpretation, thereby undermining processes of dialogue and mutual understanding, sharing and examination.

If the goal is not understanding of the other, and if the key to the proper
understanding of the other resides with Sacks' own reading, we should not
be surprised at how religions are criticized. Rather than an attempt to understand them, his position can, at times, devolve into a criticism of texts, individuals, and even key theological tenets. The fact is not as astounding when
we recall that his thought is geared to addressing social problems associated
with religions. Within this framework, there seems to be room also for criticizing other faiths.

Superficial Presentation of Religions

Before examining some of Sacks' criticism of other religions, let us consider
how he describes them, when he does. This question is linked to the two
modalities mentioned above—that which contrasts Judaism with other
faiths and that which identifies it with them. It is particularly relevant to the
contrastive mode. In the following characterization of other faiths, Sacks
seeks to affirm Judaism's particularity.

The concept of a covenantal bond between God and man is revolutionary and has
no parallel in any other system of thought. For the ancients, man was at the
mercy of impersonal forces that had to be placated. For Christianity, he is corrupt,
tainted by an original sin that only the saving grace of God can remove. In Islam,
man is called to absolute submission to God's will. In secular humanism, man is
alone in a universe blind to his hopes and deaf to his prayers . . . But only in
Judaism do we encounter the proposition that, despite their utter disparity, God
and man come together as 'partners in the work of creation'. I know of no other
vision that confers on mankind so great a dignity and responsibility.[38]

Sacks sets out to establish the uniqueness of the concept of covenant and the
relationship with God suggested by it. To that end, he contrasts Jewish faith

[38] *Radical Then, Radical Now*, 82. See further p. 97.

with other religions. Christianity is presented in terms of original sin and the need for divine grace following it; Islam is presented in terms of submission to God. The problem is that no religion can be reduced to one guiding concept. Even if it were, we would still need to interpret that concept and to see what the faithful make of it. Any attempt to reduce another faith to one key tenet will yield the same kind of corruption that Judaism has suffered from for a long time by being portrayed as a 'religion of law', preaching 'eye for an eye' or any number of other simplified characterizations that are no more than a caricature of Jewish faith. Sacks' portrayal of Judaism's unique covenantal understanding ends up offering a caricature of other faiths.

Let us consider the belief in original sin. To begin with, this belief is not universal to all branches of Christianity. It characterizes Western Christianity, not Orthodox faith. Moreover, even if it is held, why is this idea singled out as the defining trait of Christian faith? Why not love? Why not the kingdom of God? Why not repentance? Why not the bridging of the gap between man and God through the Incarnation? Sacks never accounts for why he chooses one tenet over others as the key defining feature of Christianity. In so doing, he falls into the trap of polemical presentation of another faith. He should have known better either from his experience as a Jew on the receiving end of such characterization or, ideally, from basic studies of religions in the present-day academic context. I am not sure such study was ever part of his formation, and herein lies a fundamental problem regarding his relation to Christianity. It is often poorly informed, relying on ancient stereotypes of yesteryear, not current either with Christian theology or with the best practices of how to describe religions.

In his description of Islam, Sacks assumes that Islam being submission means that there is no sharing of responsibility between humans and God. But here too a series of questions opens up. Why do we assume that submission negates partnership? Doesn't Judaism believe in submission to God's will and does such submission, in the case of Judaism, necessarily preclude active collaboration even to the point of arguing and negotiating with God? Is this really an either/or proposition? And how are we to understand the fundamental phenomenological similarity between how Jews and Muslims engage in jurisprudence and legal reasoning? If Sacks were correct, we would expect wildly diverse approaches to the practice of law and ruling. In fact, the methodologies are quite similar.

Finally, how are we to reconcile this portrayal of Judaism as unique and contrasting with other religions with some of the statements of *The Dignity of Difference*, according to which all religions share in the common ground of particularity and covenant? Has Sacks changed his views? It is more likely that ideas are adapted to rhetorical needs and to the particular conceptual need at hand. Accordingly, he casts religions at times as one thing, at times as another. Had he been more concerned with the reality of other religions, he would have taken greater care to engage with them in more detail, and one might even say with greater respect. The starting point for Sacks' theoretical explorations are these early statements, which show that he inherited a polemical tradition that emphasizes Judaism's superiority to other faiths. Perhaps rather than pointing to the weaknesses of this inherited view, we should marvel at how, as his work advanced, he was able to extricate himself from such views and to put forth alternative ones, be they the fundamental, non-polemical appreciation of other religions found in *The Dignity of Difference* or the incorporation of Judaism into a broader view of religions as found in his later works.

Let us consider another instance of misrepresenting another religion. In *Radical Then, Radical Now*, Sacks contrasts Jewish revelation to an entire people to Christianity, where God appears to the Son of God, and to Islam, where he appears to the Prophet.[39] This is an ancient trope. We find it in Rabbi Judah Halevi's *Kuzari* as an argument for affirming the superiority of Judaism over Christianity and Islam.[40] Can this argument really be made in the twenty-first century? It appeals to simple, naive faith, and is a quantitative argument—we had more witnesses than you did to our revelation. But it is based on a literal reading of Scripture and is not immune to a host of critical questions regarding the veracity of the biblical narrative. It is very naive to put this argument forth when the challenges of biblical criticism and other forms of criticism applied to the biblical narrative could easily upset it. Jewish apologists have moved away from this type of historical reasoning and have preferred more psychological, sociological, or phenomenological explanations in support of Judaism's value and particularity. In fact, Sacks has made a great contribution to this in his understanding of the covenant, exemplified in the passage quoted above. Casting the argument in the polemical modality of the Middle Ages does him a disservice. Not only does

[39] *Radical Then, Radical Now*, 113.

[40] *Kuzari*, 1: 25. For a historical review of the 'argument from witnesses', see the Wikipedia entry 'Argument from Witnesses' (Heb.).

it expose the weakness of his point, it also involves him in misreading another tradition. It doesn't take great knowledge of Christianity to know that it should not be presented as analogous to Judaism in terms of its revelational structure. To describe Christianity as God's revelation to Jesus, akin to God's revelation at Sinai to the people of Israel, shows a complete lack of understanding of how Christians perceive their own religion. There is no revelation given to Jesus, whose prophetic status is, in any event, completely secondary to his existential status as Son of God. It is Jesus himself who is the revelation, the Word of God made incarnate. In the process of attempting to argue for Judaism's superiority over Christianity, Sacks has shown a fundamental lack of understanding of the core of Christian faith.

Misrepresentation does not belong only to the contrastive modality. The call for interpretation as fundamental to Abrahamic faiths, which we have seen above, leads Sacks to make some statements regarding the processes of interpretation in Christianity and Islam.

For almost the whole of their histories, Jews, Christians and Muslims have wrestled with the meanings of their scriptures, developing in the process elaborate hermeneutic and jurisprudential systems. Medieval Christianity had its four levels of interpretation: literal, allegorical, moral and eschatological. Islam has its *fiqh*; its four schools of Sunni jurisprudence and their Shia counterparts; its principles of *taqleed*, *itjihad* and *qiyas*. Hard texts need interpreting; without it, they lead to violence. God has given us both the mandate and the responsibility to do just that. We are guardians of his word for the sake of his world.[41]

Ideally the presentation should have been of problematic texts in the respective traditions and of a sample of the ways that the traditions overcame the difficulties inherent in these texts by means of interpretation. This is a project for scholars and is precisely the kind of project that one could have imagined Sacks, or someone on his behalf, undertaking, along with scholars or leaders of another tradition. Instead, he briefly cites information that could have been lifted from any encyclopaedia or Wikipedia article on interpretation in Christianity and Islam. Does the medieval theory of four senses of Scripture help Christianity confront difficult biblical passages? And of what consequence are the different schools of sharia to the present discussion? Other than giving an air of similarity and parallelism to the efforts of scholars in all three religions, we are not told either what the common point is nor how it

[41] *Not in God's Name*, 220.

is applied to the challenge at hand—dealing with difficult, especially violent, texts in the respective traditions. The three principles of Islamic jurisprudence[42] have to do with the degree of autonomous reasoning and applying analogies between old cases and new cases that might arise. The terms could, in theory, be employed in the interpretation of hard texts. But what Sacks has done is to impose a common Jewish concern for the interpretation of hard texts on some of the interpretative methods of other faiths, without demonstrating that these seek to address the very problems that lie at the heart of his argument. Superficial reference to the methods and institutions of another faith establishes the fact that there are processes of interpretation in other religions, nothing more. For the rest, Sacks imposes his agenda, important as it is, on other religions. Surely, those religions too tackle the moral challenges of their scripture. But identifying the means by which this work is done in other systems requires much closer attention to them. Simply establishing the fact that there are mechanisms of interpretation or jurisprudence in other traditions cannot provide the needed foundation for Sacks' claim that there is a commonality in how the three faiths deal with, or ought to deal with, difficult and challenging texts.

Criticism and Polemics

Sacks is a champion of positive relations between religions and of religions jointly contributing to the well-being of society and the world at large. Ideally, or potentially, this would have led him to try to offer a positive and generous reading of other religions in the interest of increasing mutual understanding and appreciation. Greenberg provides a model for that in how he deals with key features of the Christian faith. Such expectation is not met by Sacks. On the contrary, within the framework of his developing the ideas that are characteristic of his views on religion and society, he engages in what is effectively a polemic or unveiled criticism of other religions. There are various expressions of this. One of them goes to the heart of Sacks' attitude to other religions. Let us recall how he describes the balance of universality and particularity that he considers to be Judaism's special message. Judaism is anti-universal: it rejects the idea of one truth, one religion, destined for all mankind. In this, it disagrees with the view of Islam and Christianity. The impossibility of their model of one truth gaining universal

---

[42] One of which is misspelled—it should be *ijtihad*.

acceptance has become clear in present times. The idea is no longer sustainable.[43] Sacks puts forth an alternative model, that of multiple particularities replacing one universality that seeks to gain global ascendance.

He makes a noteworthy contribution to a universal theory of religious pluralism. However, advancing this theory comes at a significant cost to the very acceptance that he marshals. If it has been a fundamental feature of Christianity and Islam to seek universal acceptance, in fact Sacks is arguing that there is a fundamental error or flaw in these faiths. Their teaching is wrong. It is the source of violence associated with religion. It is a teaching that requires revision, and he is suggesting the parameters for such revision.

There is something both courageous and inappropriate about this fundamental move. It is courageous because he goes to the heart of the teaching of other religions, points to areas where a heavy price had been paid, and suggests what adjustments must be made, today more than ever. It is inappropriate inasmuch as the foundation for dialogue with the other should not be the desire to change the other. The fact that Sacks engages other religions in a movement that requires fundamental change is, in and of itself, a sign, or perhaps an outcome, of his not getting involved in *dialogue*, but in some other kind of activity. It is a thinking *about* other religions, a reflection on global needs in light of other religions. But it is carried out in the privacy of his study, not in a real exchange. If indeed the positions that he ascribes to other religions are fundamental to their self-definition, then how helpful is it to tackle, even attack, a fundamental faith tenet as a condition for advancing global peace?

I am not familiar with any Muslim or Christian responses to Sacks' constructive suggestions and to their potential implication for Muslim and Christian theologies. While he has constructed an irenic view of how religions ought to relate to each other, in fact this idea has been a contribution to internal Jewish discourse and to general public discourse. It has not taken hold in theological circles in the other religions. Does this mean that Sacks' vision of dignity and respect can never be realized, if other religions are unwilling to 'compromise' on core traits? Not necessarily. But the path to the desired end must be one that follows the internal developments within religions and not be dictated from the outside. I believe a more dialogical approach that takes into account internal developments within the religions and their own theology of religions would have yielded a solidarity of spirit

[43] Sacks, 'Global Covenant', 227.

between Sacks and like-minded thinkers of other faiths without having to
mount a fundamental critique of other religions.

Part of the problem that emerges from Sacks' model of affirming the
dignity of difference and how it relates to other religions, as well as from his
treatment of the theological causes of religious violence, is that he regards
Christianity and Islam as large blocks and contrasts these with Judaism or
at least the biblical view, which he associates with the faith of Abraham.
Such a perspective is the outsider's view. It pits one religion against another.
The ensuing complexity of acceptance, validation, and criticism may be in-
evitable when dealing with such large units.[44] I believe there is an alternative, and it requires engagement and dialogue with the other religion. In the
process, nuance is introduced, ideas emerge, multiple forms of the religion
come to light, and one is able to connect with the other faith from within.
Such a process requires contact, dialogue, and listening to the voices that
are internal to the tradition. These voices, certainly in the case of Christianity and Islam, will point the way to theological developments that seek to
achieve what Sacks is after without undermining key tenets of the faith.

To take but one significant example, mentioned earlier, Sacks characterizes Christianity as believing that it holds the exclusive key to salvation,
following the well-known maxim that there is no salvation outside the
Church.[45] The text exists. It has been hugely influential in the history of
Christian theology. But it has had a history of interpretation that has largely
neutralized its message and has found internal ways around it in favour of a
pluralistic understanding.[46] Working from within Christianity, preferably in
dialogue with Christian thinkers, would take the argument beyond a generic
view based on one representative phrase, a problem I have already identified
above. It would allow the affirmation of positive theological developments
in Christianity.[47] And it would likely make Sacks' voice one that Christian, or

[44] In some contexts Sacks refers to types of Christianity, rather than to a single monolith.
It is worth noting that whenever he speaks positively of Christianity, he does not do so in
relation to Christianity as a whole, but with reference to one type of Christianity. We have
seen above his remark about Calvinism. Another case is the reference to Puritanism found
in *To Heal a Fractured World*, 133. The good is attributed to a specific form of Christianity; criticism is levelled at Christianity as a whole.   [45] *Future Tense*, 81.

[46] A simplistic view of the phrase is belied by the discussion in *Lumen gentium*, one of the
Vatican II documents. For a history of the interpretation of this phrase from the angle of
contemporary ecumenical and interreligious concerns, see Sesboüé, 'Hors de l'Église pas de
salut'.

[47] Sacks recognizes the enormous revolution in relation to Judaism brought about in the

Muslim, thinkers could more readily assimilate if their religions were not asked to become Judaism, or to return to the faith of Abraham, which they no longer faithfully represent.[48]

Let us move on to another instance of criticism. Actually, as we review Sacks' different books, we realize this is not an instance but a tendency. Time and again, he engages in a polemic with Paul, and through him with the New Testament and eventually with Christianity itself. The fact stands out in view of the realization that not once is there a positive ideal that Sacks recognizes in or integrates from Christianity, let alone the New Testament. At one point, when speaking in the 'Abrahamic' voice, he does acknowledge a fundamental Christian teaching. As he seeks to develop a common ethic for Britain, he states:

A very similar spirit animates the New Testament. Jesus tells his disciples to feed the hungry, give drink to the thirsty, clothe the naked, visit the sick, and give hospitality to the stranger. Between Judaism and Christianity, and between both and Islam, the theology may be different but the ethic is the same.[49]

As Sacks applies his Abrahamic voice, we find other references, possibly more ambivalent towards Jesus' teaching:

The Sermon on the Mount tells us to love our enemies. That is a supremely beautiful idea, but it is not easy. Moses offers a more liveable solution. Help your enemy. You don't have to love him but you do have to assist him.[50]

The reader familiar with Sacks' style will recognize the slight put-down. A characterization of another religion which in Jewish circles has become a caricature is cited. The issue it raises is not really tackled. Parallels with the same idea found in Jewish sources are not cited. It is somehow bracketed by the simultaneous admission of beauty and difficulty, in a rushed move that then gives way to the more liveable solution of *helping* one's enemy, rather

---

Catholic Church. See e.g. *Not in God's Name*, 275. He does not seem to be cognizant, however, of the theological developments that have gone hand in hand with such advances.

[48] Greenberg is, in many respects, the opposite of Sacks on all these issues. Seeking to understand Christianity from within and to be in dialogue with theological developments within Christianity, he develops his theology in response and in dialogue, rather than independently. As noted, this does not preclude his making some of the critical moves that Sacks makes and judging Christianity, on occasion, against Jewish standards. See p. 46. The question of how much room there is for *theological* criticism of the other religion is a weighty one. It is ultimately all a matter of context and balance. See also my interview with Greenberg in Ch. 6.   [49] *The Home We Build Together*, 127.   [50] *Not in God's Name*, 257.

than loving him. Perhaps the two ideas should have been brought into dialogue with one another; perhaps a pedagogy could have been established that moves a person from help to love—we do indeed encounter that among traditional Jewish commentators. What we find, however, is simple acknowledgement of Jesus' teaching, which is quickly outweighed by the preferable Jewish model, now attributed personally to Moses rather than to the Torah.

Contrasting with this relatively benign way of citing Christianity are multiple references to Paul that are critical of him and of the way in which Christianity developed under him.[51] It is a commonplace among Jewish thinkers and historians to draw a distinction between Jesus and Paul. Sacks makes much of this distinction, describing Jesus' Aramaic context as distinct from Paul's Greek background.[52] The faults of Christianity, including its becoming an independent religion, are attributed to Paul, thereby leaving Jesus clear of criticism. While never articulating this view, Sacks follows this pattern in all his references to Christianity. Christianity is criticized and the culprit is Paul.

Sacks' discussion of the problem of science and its relationship to religion in *The Great Partnership* includes an analysis of Greek and Hebrew thought and their differences. It was as a result of the differences between them that the very tension of science and religion occurred. Proper Hebraic thought is free of this tension. It is only with the turning of Judaism towards a Greek mentality, in the form of Christianity developed by Paul, and its further development in the Middle Ages, that the modern tensions of science and religion arose.[53]

The issue of particularity and universality—at the core of Sacks' view of other religions—is also related to Paul. It is Paul who introduced the

---

[51] There is one neutral citation of a phrase in 2 Corinthians (see *Not in God's Name*, 220) in an attempt to provide Christian justification for Sacks' thesis concerning the need for interpretation. It is part of the Abrahamic voice, which, on occasion, seeks support from texts of other religions. Notably, these citations are from classical, I would say trite, sources of another religion—default passages in favour of a position. They do not grow out of a more detailed engagement. See, for example, the citations of Quran 2: 256 and 49: 13, both standard references in discussions between religions, in *Not in God's Name*, 19 and 206. In all these cases, Sacks never quotes Christian or Muslim authorities. Nor does he exhibit even a fraction of the erudition of history, literature, and scholarship that he exhibits in any other field of learning that he engages with. The degree of interest in the scriptures of other traditions as part of his Abrahamic voice only goes as far as citing well-known primary sources, always limited to a verse or two, and never discussed or analysed in detail.

[52] *The Great Partnership*, 59–61.   [53] Ibid., ch. 3; see in particular p. 76.

element of universality to early Christianity, thereby creating the problems associated with its vision of one truth and the various social and relational implications it has.[54] Accordingly, Pauline Christianity is singled out as one of three attempts in history to impose a unified global culture.

There have been three major attempts in history to realise this dream, and it is immensely important to understand why they failed. The first was Pauline Christianity. Paul famously said, 'There is neither Jew nor Gentile, neither slave nor free, nor is there male and female' (NIV, Gal. 3: 28). Historically, Christianity has been the most successful attempt in history to convert the world to a single faith. Today a third of the population of the world is Christian. But nations continued to exist. So did non-monotheistic faiths. Another monotheism arose, Islam with a similar aspiration to win the world to its understanding of the will of God. Within Christianity itself there was schism, first between West and East, then between Catholic and Protestant. Within Islam there were Sunni and Shia. The result was that war did not end. There were crusades, jihads, holy wars and civil strife. These led some people to believe that religion is not a way of curing violence but of intensifying it.[55]

Paul is the figurehead of the very approach that represents failed religious practices and the source of evil associated with religion. His attempt was partially successful—after all, a third of the world is Christian. But it ultimately failed, owing to both internal schism and the rise of Islam. War and violence are the result of this failure. Even if Paul cannot be accused of all that has gone wrong in religion across the span of history, he is certainly the figurehead who has brought much of it about.

The problem of religiously motivated violence is associated by Sacks with the problem of sibling rivalry. This is one of the core theses of *Not in God's Name*. His detailed biblical exegesis follows the theme in Genesis, up to its eventual resolution, as the narrative unfolds. Sibling rivalry continues to inform the relations between Judaism, Christianity, and Islam, and is expressed in their competition, leading to violence. Sacks' proof for Christian sibling rivalry comes, as we maybe now expect, from the writings of Paul. His commentary on Ishmael and Isaac in Galatians[56] is understood in light of Sacks' identification of the destructive effects of sibling rivalry on the relations between religions. It is important to recognize that Sacks points to a Christian source at the root of religious violence. He does not consider what

---

[54] Ibid. 62–3.   [55] *Not in God's Name*, 42–3.
[56] Gal. 4: 21–31. See *Not in God's Name*, 101–5.

resources Christianity may bring to the discussion and how the challenges of religious violence would be tackled from within Christianity. In other words, he does not engage in the study of that faith nor dialogue with it in search of solutions to a problem that all religions face. Rather, he effectively points an accusing finger at Christianity, having identified sibling rivalry as a psycho-religious force that generates violence. In so doing, it is he who determines the boundaries of what to receive and what to incorporate from Christian sources.

A final instance of anti-Pauline polemics is found in a discussion of the difficulties of dealing with guilt and the sense of shortcoming in fulfilling religious obligations. The Jewish answer is *teshuvah*, repentance. This, how-ever, is juxtaposed with Paul's solution, who did away with commandments. Sacks' point could have been made without any reference to Paul. After all, he is writing a commentary on the narrative of Joseph and his brothers. There is no need to bring Paul into the discussion. Yet he does.

How can one live under such a burden of conscience? The answer Paul gave was to construct, in essence, a Judaism without commands: a religion of the soul rather than the body, of faith rather than deeds. The answer given by the Jewish sages, however, was different. To be sure, we sin. Each of us has a *yetser*, an im-pulse to evil, but as God said to Cain, sin 'desires to have you, but you must master it' (Gen. 4: 7). He does not ask for perfection.[57]

As with the reference to Jesus above, the Christian view is cited only to move on to the Jewish response, which, in context, emerges as more appropriate.

If there is one thing that this chapter has demonstrated it is the degree to which Sacks' discussion of other religions is carried out from within his own space, his theoretical constructs, the privacy of his study. It neither addresses the complexity of the religious other, entering into nuance and detail, nor involves actual collaboration or even dialogue with authoritative voices, especially living personalities and religious leaders of other tradi-tions. Although Sacks boasts these relationships, they do not seem to inform his presentation of the religions. While showing appreciation for the fact of their existence and for some of their human and social benefits, when it comes to the core theologies of Christianity and Islam, one sees no sign of Sacks' views having been shaped either by these relationships or by know-ledge that was made available to him through these relationships or through

[57] *Not in God's Name*, 165.

academic study and mastery of knowledge, at which he so excels. This leads us, then, to the subject of our next chapter. Considering the hugely positive support for harmonious relations on the one hand, and, on the other, the relative lack of real contact with significant others, how should we characterize Sacks' relations with others? Specifically, what is his position on dialogue and sharing across religions? This question, which we have already confronted in the discussion of the possibility of learning from other religions, takes on greater urgency in view of the problematic nature of his approach. Our exploration turns next to an assessment of how Sacks viewed encounter and dialogue with other religions and to the complexities inherent in this subject.

CHAPTER TWELVE

What Is Dialogue for Sacks?

T HE COMPLEXITIES we have seen throughout our discussion are channelled conceptually to the question of how Sacks views interreligious
dialogue. It is here that Sacks the person and Sacks the theoretician come
together. So far we have analysed his views on other faiths, pluralism, universalism and particularism, and related topics. Through these analyses we
sought to identify an approach and to ascertain where he breaks new
ground. But we also encountered unfulfilled potential in his thought, a gap
between what it invites and where he actually takes it. There is more to his
thought than how he applies it. We encountered complexities in his views,
where appreciation of positive relations with members of other faiths
appears alongside avoidance of engagement beyond a certain point. Reconciling these differences takes us to the interface between Sacks the person
and Sacks the theoretician. We explore this domain when we deal with the
broader question of his views on dialogue. Thus far we have studied primarily his views on religions, that is, on their legitimacy and their contribution
to and collaboration for the sake of society. We now turn our attention to his
views on dialogue, that is: how he imagines the parameters, scope, and purpose of interfaith relations as such.

I would like to begin this exploration with two references to Sacks' own
engagement in this area. I begin with these personal testimonies because I
have come to the conclusion that the parameters and application of Sacks'
ideas are informed as much by his biography and personality as they are by
purely theoretical concerns. This is likely to be true of any thinker. In this
case, however, the association of these two dimensions is visible and powerful and holds the key to some of the contradictions and limitations that we
find in Sacks' body of thought relating to other religions.

The first of these references is found in a speech he made to the Council
of Christian and Jews, in which he offers his views on interreligious dia-

logue.[1] He places the entire discussion of present-day as well as future inter-faith relations in the context of his own childhood experience, when he attended Christian schools together with his brothers. He describes that reality as follows:

We encountered teachers who valued their religion, and as a result we learned to value our own. We were conscious of our difference, but the difference was respected. Interacting with our teachers and friends we learned that those who are at home in their own faith, who are confident in their beliefs and assured of their own religious heritage, are not threatened by another faith. On the contrary, they are capable of valuing and being enlarged by it. So, at an early age, I learned how the encounter between Christians and Jews can benefit both traditions by teaching us pride in our own heritage, and humility in the face of the other.[2]

This brief paragraph contains some of Sacks' key ideas in a nutshell. And they are presented or projected back as lessons learned in his childhood by dint of being educated, as an Orthodox Jew, in a Christian school. These lessons form the core of Sacks' view of how members of faiths ought to relate to others. It is a mix of respect for the other while taking pride in one's own faith. It is open and respectful and seeks to bring benefits to both parties. But it is not dialogical. It is by living together that these values are inculcated, not by the encounter between religions. It is, therefore, the very opposite of the practice of interreligious dialogue as an intentional coming together to explore, in some significant way, religious identities, differences, commonalities, and challenges. The model that Sacks describes as having imbibed in his childhood and youth is characterized by common being, respect, possibly friendship. It is based on simply being together in common spaces. Religious identities are recognized, even affirmed; they are not actively engaged with. This is a crucial insight into the formative experience of Jonathan Sacks, long before he was tasked with speaking on behalf of British Jewry or Judaism at large on the public scene, alongside religious leaders of other faiths.

Let me share a second story that, I believe, describes Sacks' first inter-faith experience. He narrates it at length, and I will cite most of it, because it too provides us with key insights into how he viewed interfaith dialogue long before his ideas regarding other religions had been formulated, with their particular mixture of openness and receptivity alongside boundaries and constraints.

---

[1] *Faith in the Future*, 74–81.   [2] Ibid. 75.

This is a true story that took place in the 1970s. Rabbi Dr Nahum Rabinovitch, then Principal of Jews College, the rabbinic training seminary in London where I was a student and teacher, was approached by an organisation that had been given an unusual opportunity to engage in interfaith dialogue. A group of African bishops wanted to understand more about Judaism. Would the Principal be willing to send his senior students to engage in such a dialogue, in a chateau in Switzerland?

To my surprise, he agreed. He told me that he was sceptical about Jewish–Christian dialogue in general because he believed that over the centuries the Church had been infected by an antisemitism that was very difficult to overcome. At that time, though, he felt that African Christians were different. They loved Tanakh and its stories. They were at least in principle open to understanding Judaism on its own terms . . .

So we went. It was an unusual group: the semikhah class of Jews College, together with the top class of the yeshiva in Montreux where the late Rabbi Yechiel Weinberg, author of *Seridei Esh* and one of the world's foremost halakhists, had taught. For three days the Jewish group davenned and bentsched with special intensity. We learned Gemarra each day. For the rest of the time we had an unusual, even transformative, encounter with the African bishops, ending with a Hassidic-style tisch during which we shared with the Africans our songs and stories and they taught us theirs. At three in the morning we finished by dancing together. We knew we were different, we knew that there were deep divides between our respective faiths, but we had become friends. Perhaps that is all we should seek. Friends don't have to agree in order to stay friends. And friendships can sometimes help heal the world.[3]

This story is telling on so many levels. Let us begin by noting the initial suspicion. The students had assumed their teacher would not approve of the encounter with the African bishops, and were surprised when he did. This tells us something of their own attitude, as well as how they perceived that of their teacher. Both suggest avoidance of dialogue and encounter. The formalities of why that may be so are probably less important than the orientation, which is at heart psychological more than ideological. The starting position is one of distance and avoidance of dialogue. The fact is that for all of his having studied with Christians throughout his entire formation, including university education, this seems to have been Sacks' first proper and intentional interfaith encounter.

What was strange was the very request for an encounter whose purpose

---

[3] The story is found in his short piece 'The Heroism of Tamar (Vayeshev 5775)'.

was better knowledge of Judaism. Note, it is not better *mutual* understanding, but a unidirectional process of better understanding Judaism. Significantly, some mutuality is found at the end, when 'we shared with the Africans our songs and stories and they taught us theirs'. This seems to still be one degree less than introducing full mutuality to the encounter, whose stated purpose was to learn about Judaism. The outcome was, nonetheless, a degree of mutuality, and friendship. Sacks describes the encounter as transformative, but does not tell us in what way. To call something transformative suggests it brings about some kind of change. Was there attitudinal change towards Christianity on the side of Sacks and his friends? Did a new appreciation of the value of interreligious dialogue set in following this event? In all likelihood, what Sacks really means to say when he refers to 'transformative' is that the encounter was heart-opening. This is, in any event, what he and his colleagues took away from it. Friendship is the outcome of the event and the lesson of the story. They had become friends and this defines for Sacks what one should expect in relations with others. The encounter across religions leads to friendship rather than to a sharing of ideas. Clearly, ideas were shared. That is why the rabbinical students went to the Swiss chateau. But we hear nothing of that. It is incidental to what mattered most, the formation of friendships. Mind you, we are not told of these friendships being long-lasting in any way. One-time friendships based on a one-time positive sharing seems to be the paradigm that emerges from Sacks' first interfaith encounter. In many ways, this echoes his childhood experience. Friendship, respect, appreciation of difference are all attitudes to the other, positive and open attitudes that are the outcome of shared being. We hear nothing of ideas, deeper encounter, spiritual growth, nor even of deeper self-understanding. While some of these ideas figure in descriptions of the purpose of dialogue that we shall presently analyse, the parameters of what is most important for Sacks seem to be contained in these two stories, and with them also the limitations that are characteristic of his approach.

We may also dwell on the reasoning that Rabbi Rabinovitch is reported to have applied. The rabbi was, on the whole, sceptical of interfaith relations. A history of antisemitism provided the ground for such scepticism. His willingness to make an exception and to permit the encounter was based on the view that African bishops were somehow different, inasmuch as they represented a different culture than their European counterparts and were therefore less likely to be tainted by the history of antisemitism. Their interest in studying Judaism would be genuine and trustworthy. Sacks, in the section omitted, suggests his rabbi relied on Maimonides' permission to teach Christians Torah, because they believe in its sanctity and veracity.

The reasoning is well intentioned, but highly problematic. It shows how removed Sacks and his rabbi were, at this point in time, from developments within Christianity. Certainly if these bishops were Catholics, following the landmark declaration of about ten years earlier, *Nostra aetate*, but even if they belonged to the Anglican communion, they were already acting under a different paradigm in terms of their view of Judaism. This is why they sought to learn more about it. Their rabbinic counterparts seem oblivious to the changes inside the Church and reason, at least in retrospect, in light of medieval precedents.[4] They moreover apply a distinction that probably would not hold up to scrutiny, distinguishing bishops from different parts of the world and legitimating the event because the bishops came from Africa. Certainly, if the group was Catholic, one would have to look at Catholic teaching as a whole and not single out African bishops, but in all likelihood this is equally true of Anglican bishops. Be that as it may, in the gap between the eagerness of the Christian leaders to learn about Judaism and the natural reticence and degree of ignorance of the other side that characterized the Jews, a way forward was found. It doesn't seem that Sacks ever closed that gap in terms of knowledge of these bishops and their motivation, let alone becoming more acquainted with their theology and religious world-view. The two groups seem to have met with completely different assumptions and expectations regarding each other. What mattered most, however, was that the Jews could share their religious teaching for the benefit of the bishops. And what mattered most to Sacks is that they all came away as friends.

I believe these stories provide the framework for how Sacks went about the business of interfaith dialogue. They define his attitude not only in the 1970s, but also forty years later. In other words, for all his engagement in relations between religious leaders and for all the complex and rich theories and resources he provided, and by means of which relations between religions could be justified, at heart his vision of interfaith relations never grew

---

[4] Sacks may be, of course, making the point to defend his rabbi against detractors within the Orthodox community by citing Maimonides. A similar dynamic can be recognized in the visits of Catholic hierarchs to Yeshiva University under the leadership of Rabbi Norman Lamm, and the ensuing criticism it received.

beyond those initial parameters that defined his childhood and his yeshiva days. This is a startling observation to make, inasmuch as it suggests that in significant ways Sacks never grew or deepened his experience over the course and as a result of decades of interaction with leaders of other religions. Yet I believe that herein lies the key to the complexities and limitations that inform his views of other religions. If he was not changed or if he did not develop alternative—I would say deeper—models of engagement, perhaps this is because he felt the need to faithfully defend his childhood model. Alternatively, he may have refused or avoided an alternative kind of engagement that might have yielded a different kind of encounter, more personal, more reciprocal, more theological, and, I would add, more truly transformative. Shaped as he was by his childhood experience, this model suited his temperament, psychology, and even his personal limitations. In this suggestion, while availing himself of new opportunities for encounter with other religions, he astutely avoided a certain quality of interreligious interaction. Whether it threatened him, in the ways the story above suggests, or whether he was simply not inclined to it on personal grounds, his engagement expanded in quantitative terms, reached a broader audience, and took on new nuances, but never fully reciprocated the openness of the African bishops. If they showed an interest in learning about Judaism, he nowhere shows an interest in learning about other religions. If they, in all likelihood, brought to the encounter a particular theological baggage and depth of emotional commitment, this was not reciprocated. We might put it as follows. Sacks' entry into the domain of interfaith relations was in the role of a teacher. While he did a lot more than that in his capacity as a chief rabbi who interacted with others, he never really changed that basic modality. He was a teacher to others, with all the protection and boundaries that such a role brings with it. The fact that friendship could be born of what is not a fully reciprocal relationship, or of a relationship that does not show fully reciprocal interest, is itself a major achievement. It is both a tribute to Sacks, who succeeded in advancing in significant ways beyond his natural inclination and starting point, and a potential model for others to follow.

Let us consider, then, some of Sacks' later references to friendship as the fruit of dialogue.[5] In the following excerpt from a live talk, he describes the

---

[5] In 2017 I launched a project of religious leaders supporting the ideals of friendship between religions. It was based on a series of video interviews with major faith leaders, Sacks being the most important among the Jewish voices. I did not realize at the time how

benefits of friendship between religious leaders.

The Archbishop of Canterbury, at the moment—like his predecessors, with whom I worked very closely, George Carey and Rowan Williams—Justin Welby, is actively engaged in trying to do this right now, to bring religious leaders, take them out of the conflict zone, because once you're in the conflict zone, you know, tempers flare. Just take them out, get them not necessarily to agree on anything, but get them to become friends, because sometimes when religious leaders, when Jews and Muslim and Christian leaders come together with a very inflamed population, but they are seen to be standing together, that can send a very powerful message on the street. And sometimes to do that, you have to take time now to create friendships that will be warm enough to be able to use when you need them. It's just taking early action to create this.[6]

Sacks refers to three archbishops of Canterbury with whom he has worked closely. Interestingly, he does not speak of them as friends, nor describe the extent or depth of their relationship. The point is not the relationship itself or its impact on him. It is how good relations between religious leaders can help reduce religious conflict. This is achieved by a show of togetherness that is based on friendship. In fact, this is the very purpose of cultivating friendships with leaders of other faiths. Friendship is approached instrumentally. It is not an end in itself, nor is it a means to any number of possible benefits that would enrich the spiritual lives of participants, especially religious leaders. Rather, it is understood in terms of its symbolic benefits for the community and is cultivated for that purpose.

This understanding informs Sacks' approach to friendship with members of all faiths. In the following two passages, he takes pride in the extent of friendships he has developed as a religious leader. The purpose conforms to what we learned in the previous passage.

In 2008, on the anniversary of Kristallnacht, or close to it, the Archbishop of Canterbury Rowan Williams and I took a group of representatives of all the major faiths in Britain, not just Christian but Muslim, Hindu, Sikh, Buddhist, Jain, Zoroastrian, and Baha'i, to Auschwitz. I can't remember a bonding experience like it. It was profoundly moving. Not only profoundly moving while we were there,

appropriate the topic was to Sacks' own theoretical approach to other faiths. Seeing this clip again, having now spent extensive time studying the subject, I can see how his entire presentation of interfaith relations is here framed as and comes under the banner of friendship. See 'Make Friends'.

[6] 'Rabbi Sacks in discussion with EJ Dionne and Bill Galston'.

but it was profoundly moving when we sat together in Kraków airport and talked through our feelings. So we became very, very bonded together. We'd been friends before, but this really transformed it and gave it greater depth.[7]

Friendship is the foundation, a relational field that existed prior to the reported event by virtue of the common service of these religious leaders. Sacks describes a deepening of it, which he refers to as transformation. It seems the deeper level is attained by opening to an emotional dimension as a result of a powerful shared experience. The deepening does not occur thanks to a new agenda being introduced, or as a result of opening up to each other's spiritual realities. It is the outcome of a shared experience that is emotionally charged, and that very charge then adds experiential depth to the friendship. What purposes such friendship serves and what its limitations are we see in the following quote.[8]

I have spent much time in conversation with leaders of other faiths. I have cherished my friendships with Christian leaders and many others—Hindu, Sikh, Buddhist, Jain, Zoroastrian and Bahai. No less significantly, I have found an instant rapport with the representatives of Islam, not only from Britain but also those from the Middle East. In Britain and the international arena we have worked together, developing relationships that have allowed us—especially in the tense times that have come in the wake of September 11—to dampen anger, fight the flames of local hostilities, and generate, through our shared fears, a sense of solidarity and goodwill.

But I have also been conscious of something left unsaid. Often, when religious leaders meet and talk, the emphasis is on similarities and commonalities, as if the differences between faiths were superficial and trivial. That is not, however, what comes to the fore at times of conflict. It is then that what seem to an outsider to be minor variations take on immense significance, dividing neighbourhoods and turning erstwhile friends into enemies.[9]

As in the first passage above, Sacks asserts that the main benefit of friendship between religious leaders is its pacifying potential in cases of communal conflict.[10] The semantic field here includes conversation (as we shall see, a

---

[7] 'Interfaith Relations and the Holocaust'.

[8] In my interview with Rowan Williams, I raised the question of whether he thought there were any long-lasting effects to that experience, such that would justify describing it as transformative, in a sense other than having had a powerful emotional experience. For this discussion, see Ch. 14 below. [9] *The Dignity of Difference*, 21.

[10] Ibid. viii: 'Friendships with leaders of other faiths have convinced me that religions have a role to play in conflict resolution.'

term that is distinct from dialogue), friendship, solidarity, and goodwill. This semantic field captures effectively how Sacks practises friendship. I believe his definition is fully sincere, but it is at the same time also instrumentalist and focuses on the outward-facing dimensions of friendship, as these relate to communities and their tensions. The entire passage positions friendship, its benefits and its challenges, in the larger context of communal tensions.

Reading Sacks' *Morality*, I was struck by the number of individuals he knows, refers to, and in some way describes as friends. This is true, in fact, of his entire demeanour in his public persona as chief rabbi and Judaism's most popular lecturer. The number of people (myself included) to whom he referred as friends, or whom he treated in a friendly manner, is astounding. But it is this very fact that raises the question of what friendship means.[11] Surely it means something else than deep friendships, transformative in a sense other than emotionally charged. When Sacks refers to other leaders as friends, how deeply does this friendship go? For him the measure of friendship seems to be its ability to stem violence. This is certainly a possible measure, but it is not the only one, nor the most intuitive one. But another kind of friendship—deeper, more intimate, more transformative—would require going to the heart of faith and cultivating a different kind of sharing than that practised by Sacks. Indeed, the final part of the above passage problematizes for us both friendship and dialogue. While affirming the social benefits of friendships with leaders of other religions, Sacks also offers a criticism of the topics of discussion, claiming that, too often, these highlight similarities at the expense of differences. These differences have the potential to turn erstwhile friends into enemies.

This is an important moment in applying Sacks' theory of inter-religious friendship. Faith leaders demonstrate friendship, but something else is needed.[12] He does not explain why the demonstration of friendship is not enough. He states a discomfort with the enterprise of dialogue, which does not recognize the full particularity of religious difference, and goes on to advocate his theory of the dignity of difference. Presumably this theory will provide something that a public demonstration of friendship will not.

But the entire argument is based on a very particular view of dialogue as

[11] For theoretical reflections on friendship and its dimensions, see Goshen-Gottstein, 'Introduction', xxi–lii.

[12] In the passage above, 'But I have also been conscious' starts a new paragraph, which lessens the tension between the ideas.

a superficial show of commonality at the expense of true engagement with the alterity of the religious other. One must, therefore, ask how representative and effective Sacks' concept of dialogue is. Would affirming and applying a fuller practice of dialogue provide another, perhaps more effective, antidote to the problem of religious violence? It seems friendships between religious leaders, good and important as they are, are built on shaky foundations. They seem not to draw upon deeper faith convictions, nor to go to the heart of religious particularity and difference. Seen in this way, the entire theory of the dignity of difference is informed by a very limiting—one might say faulty—view of dialogue. The dual emphasis on the cultivation of friendship and avoidance of deeper dialogue conforms to the formative patterns of Sacks' youth. As he grows and as his relations with other leaders expand, what changes is not his relational foundation or his praxis of encounter. These still seem lacking, and he nowhere seeks to employ alternative paths in dialogue. Instead, he crafts a theoretical response that will contribute to reducing religious violence, bypassing what might seem like the highway, namely fuller engagement. I believe this is informed, more than anything else, by his personal orientation, which in turn seems to be shaped by his formative experiences. But it is also impacted by his limiting view of dialogue and its purposes. It is to this view that we now turn.

Two texts, both brief, offer us a window onto the complexity of Sacks' view of dialogue. The first is the talk to the Council of Christians and Jews cited above and published as an essay in *Faith in the Future*. The other is a text that was published a few years earlier, when Sacks was already chief rabbi. It is his foreword to a collection of essays on Jewish–Christian relations.[13] While both are presentations made to, or along with, supporters and practitioners of interreligious, or more specifically Jewish–Christian, dialogue, there are significant differences in the emphases of the two essays. Only one year separates the publication dates of the books, and even if there is a greater gap in time between the oral presentation and the written version of the talk to the Council of Christians and Jews, I very much doubt that the differences between them are a function of changes brought about by the passage of time.[14] Moreover, as both appeared in the 1990s, long before

---

[13] Fry (ed.), *Christian–Jewish Dialogue*. Sacks' foreword is on pp. x–xiv.

[14] In *Faith in the Future*, 74, we are informed that the talk was delivered in 1989, in other words before he took office as chief rabbi. Perhaps he felt more free to express criticism of the interfaith enterprise before coming into office. But the key ideas in this essay are articu-

the publication of *The Dignity of Difference*, they cannot be seen as in any way expressive of pressures upon Sacks in his public office concerning how he relates to world religions. There are only two ways of reconciling the different nuances in the two texts. One is to assume that Sacks adapts himself to the context. A contextually formulated message could potentially yield different outcomes, even if the audiences in both cases are practitioners of dialogue. A foreword to a book is a place to share and express support. An address to a body that has long been in existence is a place to challenge listeners to further reflection, while showing fundamental support. The differences in nuance may stem from these different contexts and may depend on what message Sacks considered most appropriate. The alternative is that he speaks in multiple voices, which give expression to complexities and even internal contradictions that are part of him. We have seen throughout that, though a champion of interfaith relations, his engagement in this area is not free from complications. This could account for the different emphases in each text. As we have already begun to examine his presentation to the Council of Christians and Jews, let us turn to that piece first.

Sacks opens his talk with a story of the (Lubavitcher?) Rebbe referring to other faiths as precious stones, even if on different grades of preciousness.[15]

The lesson learnt is that if we cherish our own, then we will understand the value of others. We may regard ours as a diamond and another faith as a ruby, but we

---

lated again in later writings, and in fact it provides some of the early iterations of the ideas found in *The Dignity of Difference*. In any event, Sacks seems to have had no hesitation in publishing the talk when he was in office, which suggests he did not see it as incompatible with his views or responsibilities as chief rabbi.

[15] Sacks applies the story to other faiths. How he tells the story gives the impression that the original question had more to do with wisdom in general outside the halls of Torah than with other religions. The passage is quoted verbatim in *The Dignity of Difference*, 208–9, and therefore does not provide further information regarding the exact scope of the original question. Especially if it was posed to the Lubavitcher Rebbe, I doubt that Sacks asked him regarding other religions. Their conversation took place before Sacks took up the rabbinic office and there is no indication that Sacks had any interest in interreligious matters at that time. Moreover, the teaching seems out of character for the Rebbe. I am not aware of any other saying, remotely similar to this one, that relates to other religions. It seems most likely, therefore, that Sacks is applying the Rebbe's saying to another context. Of course, if the unnamed rebbe is another, this analysis would not apply, but we know of no other significant relationship that Sacks had with a hasidic leader that could have yielded this story. Note the application of the Rebbe's words to tolerance as an implication, rather than as the intended message.

know that both are precious stones. But if faith is a mere burden, not only will we not value ours. Neither will we value the faith of someone else.

This lesson conforms to Sacks' grand thesis—if we cherish our own faith, we know the value of others. Having set forth the ideals of respect for the other and affirmation of self, he goes on to assess the current state of interfaith dialogue, offering a historical perspective. He queries the notion of inter-faith from what is essentially a quantitative perspective. How many people still share the vision of 'pride in our heritage' along with 'humility in the face of the other'? Sacks identifies this as the great vision upon which the Council of Christians and Jews was founded. This is actually a problematic claim. The understanding he describes is generic and applies to all religions. The Coun-cil of Christians and Jews was founded on the recognition of a special rela-tionship between Jews and Christians and the need to study its roots and apply its fruits in society. It is a mission that is closer to that of the African bishops cited above. The gap between what Sacks brought to the encounter and what the bishops did is reflected also in his description of the outlook with which he grew up.

Essentially, Sacks argues that the old world order of interfaith, based on simple mutual acceptance and respect, has fallen apart. He shifts seamlessly between his childhood experience and the notion of interfaith, a movement that reached its peak in the 1960s, when 'dialogue' seemed to promise a momentous transformation of relations between religions, launching a new era of understanding. Yet today the future seems more sombre than it did thirty years ago. Voices of tolerance and moderation have become muted. Religion has become a source of conflict and those who reject pluralism are deemed to be more authentic religiously. Sacks ties together what are in fact different historical currents into one vision. The move away from an acceptance of the other that could be taken for granted on social grounds is coupled with a sense of disappointment in the fruits of interfaith dialogue, and these are coupled with a view of religions turning 'to the right' or to more extremist forms. All these, taken together, seem to pronounce a nega-tive view of dialogue in the classical sense.

The reader who follows his argument carefully is led to consider, and may even expect Sacks himself would suggest, a deepening of interfaith engagement. No longer the live and let live of interreligious relations, no longer a comfortable social view, but a deeper, more proactive, more theo-logically informed, more spiritually charged form of interfaith engagement. Rather than a criticism of the interfaith enterprise as such, one would expect a criticism of the forms and practices of interfaith in favour of more engaging and more effective ones. This, however, is not the path taken by Sacks.

He moves on to ask some of the hard questions that still exist, first on the Jewish and then on the Christian side. Sacks' discourse is informed by a rather naive assumption that interfaith dialogue could and should have eliminated all potential conflicts. The rejoinder to his somewhat naive critique seems straightforward. If difficult questions still remain, this does not necessarily reflect on the work that has been undertaken. The remaining challenges in transforming relations are still informed by millennia of negative patterning, including complicated theological residue. For Sacks, however, the questions posed serve as a criticism of the very enterprise of interfaith.

The rise of religious extremism, symbolized by the Salman Rushdie affair, makes Sacks aware of the inadequacy of the former model that informed interfaith relations. Rooted in the Enlightenment, it was part of a society built on rationality and moving toward a universal concept of humanity. But then a religious revival based on hostility, call it fundamentalism, arose. Religion became a battleground globally. A theology that speaks of tolerance is seen as inauthentic compromise. The upshot of it all is that the interfaith imperative needs to be restated.

Clearly, Sacks has not completely retreated from interest in the interfaith domain. The framing is one of going beyond his childhood model and the Enlightenment associations. Something more is needed. Interfaith, as previously practised, seems inadequate. If we follow his reasoning, then we will surely expect to be invited to a new form of interfaith engagement that is not built on the Enlightenment but perhaps on deeper and more authentic religious foundations. We might explore voices of tolerance within religions and their vision of peace as alternatives to the rise of religious extremism, no longer relying on social convention to provide the grounds for interfaith engagement. We might seek to lend deeper religious authenticity to the encounter between faith members. His framing adds up to a call for a deeper, and above all more religiously engaged, practice of interfaith. Yet that is precisely where Sacks does not go. While still supporting the cause, his discourse shifts away from contact, encounter, and engagement and moves in the direction of theory, concepts, and ideas. Significantly, these ideas are now taken from Judaism and made available to all, rather than deriving from all faiths, or attempting to tap into the deeper religious and spiritual resources of all religious traditions.

Sacks does realize the need to take a stand based on classical texts and principles. But these do not lead to engaging with other *religions*. While he asks what impels him as a Jew to 'enter into conversation with men and women of other faiths', in fact his argument takes an important turn. Instead, Sacks speaks of acceptance and love of the stranger, of compassion for the other. The faith of Abraham, as we have learnt time and again in this book, is one that leaves room for others. Faiths, like languages, are not exclusive. *Darkhei shalom* provides a social ecology that asserts that the basic duties I owe to the members of my community I owe to those outside it as well, because we must all be able to live together. It is a concept that is the opposite of a radical and uncompromising reading of faith. And all these propositions are undergirded by the notion of the human person being created in the image of God. We must seek to recognize the sanctity of the one who is not in our image, but who is nonetheless in God's image.

We are familiar with all these ideas, and we have encountered them in their wealth, nuance, as well as some internal contradiction, throughout this book. These are offered by Sacks as the alternative to dialogue. As he writes in the concluding lines of his essay,

I have tried to show in this chapter how a Jew, through his or her commitment to Judaism, is led outward to the realities of a multifaith world. My argument rests on no hidden liberal or modernist premises that could be rejected by a religious extremist.[16]

I believe the shift in terminology from 'interfaith' to 'multifaith' is indicative of an alternative modality to that of interfaith, as described and conceived by Sacks. Concerned with the rise of religious intolerance and extremism, he finds the old model inadequate and searches for what he calls a new interfaith imperative, which is a way to religiously ground an open and tolerant mode of being in a multifaith world. In the process, interfaith is largely cast aside, deemed inadequate.

The flow of this essay's argument largely confirms what has emerged from our analysis of Sacks on religions. It shows us how closely his outlook is tied to his formative experiences and how these in turn point to a very particular and limited approach to interfaith. Interfaith is inadequate because it does not go deep enough, based as it is on liberal assumptions, and it is unable to meet the challenge of rising religious extremism. The problem with

---

[16] *Faith in the Future*, 81.

Sacks' approach is dual. It is not clear, first, that simply putting forth an alternative teaching will be successful in stemming the tide of religious extremism. That would amount to entering a conflict of interpretations and readings of tradition. Second, it is far from clear whether the war of extremism is simply a war of ideas or a competition for finding the best reading of tradition. The phenomenon is more complex sociologically, psychologically, and ideologically. Why would the extremists be moved by the textual readings of the moderates? More is necessary in educational, sociological, and psychological terms than to offer good new readings that boast religious grounding. In any event, the effort, as Sacks understands here, requires multiple contributions from multiple faiths.[17] And to be effective, these would likely require some co-ordination and discussion among those who put forth such new readings, which in turn leads us back to the question of whether what is required is not relinquishing the old interfaith for the sake of a new, textually informed imperative, but a deeper, more spiritual, and more authentic practice of interfaith, the very kind that is absent from Sacks' upbringing and which never became part of his adult practice and vision.

Let us compare all this with Sacks' introduction to the volume dedicated to Christian–Jewish dialogue. The text is terse and much shorter than the previous essay surveyed. Yet it contains some of the most powerful statements in support of dialogue in all its forms. In a historical review that includes antisemitism, Sacks draws a fundamental conclusion:

If the twentieth century has taught us one thing it is that change, the kind of change that makes a difference, that endows our lives with grace and brings the Divine presence into our midst, must take place in the human heart. Political structures alone do not create tolerance and mutual respect. That requires the direct face-to-face encounter with one-who-is-not-like-us, a genuine conversation with otherness. It means that people of different faiths must meet and talk and come to know one another. It is a conversation that often begins with trepidation, but if carried through it brings with it a great discovery, that one who is not in our image is nevertheless in God's image, and that God speaks to us in many languages, traditions and faiths.[18]

The tone and thrust of the passage could not be more different than how Sacks describes dialogue in the previous essay. Earlier in this chapter I noted the term 'transformative' and queried its meaning. The first sentence offers

---

[17] This assumption is largely abandoned in later works, such as *Not in God's Name*.
[18] Foreword to *Christian–Jewish Dialogue*, p. xii.

an excellent description of transformative dialogue. Face-to-face encounter is recommended; how different from its avoidance in later works that advocate side-by-side encounter. Mutual knowledge is the goal. There is a psychological process here and Sacks describes it with empathy and imagination. All this leads to a powerful theological statement, reminiscent of the original message of *The Dignity of Difference*. Putting these elements together one realizes that encounter with the other is ultimately an encounter with God himself, as he speaks to us in another manner. The horizontal opens up to the vertical.

I am struck by the utter dissonance between this passage and most of what we have read in Sacks' name. This passage shows us just how capable Sacks was of imagining an alternative and advocating for it. And yet, though all this is implied in his teaching and though at multiple points his texts potentially open up to it, this is probably the only piece that advances this vision in an unreserved manner.

Contextual reasoning may be the best way of accounting for this passage, and more broadly for the vision of the entire foreword. Sacks is writing a preface to a series of studies that describe the field of Christian–Jewish relations. He acknowledges the range of topics, which includes theological concerns, typically shunned by him, as well as historical and sociological studies. He also acknowledges multiple voices within each of the traditions, something that does not characterize most of his references to other faiths. The encounter process is recommended as an internal struggle of spiritual significance. Its fruit is self-knowledge, a value completely overlooked in Sacks' address to the Council of Christians and Jews. The balance of commonality and difference can only be appreciated through true dialogue.

The beauty of the message offered by Sacks is that there is a path and that seeking it is a joint affair. Recounting a hasidic story, he asserts that even if we do not yet know where we are going, we know where we do not want to go back to. Searching for the path together is ultimately a position that undercuts all the criticism that Sacks levelled at interfaith dialogue in the essay previously cited. No matter how inadequate the past was, including the recent past of imperfect dialogue, the task remains to search for a more adequate path together. Great change is conditioned on our willingness to talk across the boundaries of faith.

There is no reserve in this text, no problem attached to it. The tone is defined by what Sacks considers one of the insights that should inform the common search—hope. Contrasting the tone of hope of this message and the tone of hopelessness regarding traditional dialogue in the face of the rise of religious extremism, we are back to the mystery of understanding Sacks on dialogue. Was he simply seeking a context to put forth his new ideas in the previous essay, while here he was giving honour to the work of others? Did he envision a different audience in each context? However we reconcile these two texts, one thing emerges clearly: Sacks is capable of envisioning a quality of dialogue that is far in excess of what he typically advocates and delivers in his works. Whether by virtue of experience or by power of imagination, his thought readily leads to a robust, profound, and transformative engagement across religions. Regardless of whether he went that far in opening up to his personal experience and whether these aspects appear as central elements of his teaching, Sacks does have the potential to support, justify, and inspire a full-bodied engagement in dialogue across traditions.

Perhaps one should simply present these two models of Sacks on dialogue and recognize their tension. I think, however, that doing him justice and contextualizing his approach requires taking stock of two further key features of his view of dialogue. Both of these contribute to the more limiting view, preventing the potential contained in his teachings from coming to fruition. The two factors are Sacks' conscious understanding of dialogue as such and his attempt to confine it to the moral realm, avoiding fuller spiritual engagement. The two are interrelated, inasmuch as a limiting view of dialogue will lead to a limiting practice. Let us first consider several references to dialogue, from which a very limiting, and to my mind distorted, view emerges, totally at odds with the foreword just studied. Again, the centrality of this view to Sacks' approach to dialogue is a key cause placing brakes upon it and preventing it from delivering the full results he could, at times, envision.

One important aspect of how dialogue is understood, and which can potentially lead to rejecting either that definition or the activity of dialogue itself, is the view that dialogue seeks consensus.[19] Agreement across religious lines is the bane of Sacks' view of relations between religions. Even more than being a champion of interfaith activity, he is a champion of pre-

---

[19] See *Tradition in an Untraditional Age*, 163: 'The value of talking together is not predicated on discovering we have more in common than we thought or arriving at a convergence. The challenge for liberal democracies is not to evolve a moral consensus but allowing different traditions to live together without threatening one another.'

serving difference. Approaching the encounter with other religions from the perspective of a religious minority, and testing his theories on other minorities,[20] he seeks to maintain particularity and difference in the face of the tyranny of universality and the fears of minorities living alongside majorities. In the potential tension between advocating dialogue and advocating respect for difference, Sacks' choice is clear.

That he has a hard time with the concept also emerges from his preference for 'conversation' rather than 'dialogue'. While recognizing and advocating encounter, he nevertheless seeks to avoid or minimize appeal to dialogue because of a negative conception of the activity.

I speak of conversation, not 'dialogue', because dialogue today is associated with formal, staged encounters in which the various sides come with prepared positions. We have a surfeit of dialogues: between faiths, between religion and science, between cultures and between civilisations. Dialogues are rarely genuine encounters.[21]

One assumes that Sacks has sat through enough of these scripted encounters in his position as chief rabbi to have really developed a distaste for them. Recognizing the real need, he therefore moves away from dialogue, with 'conversation' as his suggested alternative.[22]

The following quote from a video interview with Sacks couldn't be clearer in terms of his feelings towards dialogue. It also allows us to tie his approach to a very particular understanding of the term.

On interfaith. I am really and truly not a fan of interfaith dialogue. I'll tell you why. Interfaith dialogue takes place among very liberal-minded people . . . very open-minded people, usually halfway up a mountain, in some benign, beautiful environment, and you sit together for a week in these lovely surroundings, and you work out: 'he's a good guy', 'he's a good guy'; it's terrific. Then you get down to street level, and it disappears faster than the sun does in England. It's high level, and it doesn't really deliver. And therefore I wrote a book about this, called *The Home We Build Together*, and I used two phrases based on the typology of the Rav

---

[20] Hava Tirosh-Samuelson records, in an interview with Sacks, that the ideas of *The Dignity of Difference* were first tested out on other minorities, and, having been well received, they eventually found expression in the book. See Tirosh-Samuelson and Hughes (eds.), *Jonathan Sacks: Universalizing Particularity*, 123.   [21] *Future Tense*, 184.

[22] Note also the name of his popular series of homilies on the Torah, one of his best-selling works, entitled *Covenant and Conversation*. The value of conversation is much larger than the conversation across religions.

[Soloveitchik] in *The Lonely Man of Faith*, which I call face to face and side by side. Interfaith is face to face; we're both talking about what we believe, but side by side is Jews, Christians, Muslims, Hindus, Sikhs working together, at street level, to solve some problem that all those communities face in common; it may be graffiti on the walls, it may be drug dealers on the street . . . What comes out of that? Friendship. And sometimes friendship is what you need, not theological agreement, but simple friendship. So I am in favour of interfaith activity through social action. Side by side is more powerful than face to face.[23]

Sacks is not against improving interfaith relations. He is against what he describes as the practice of dialogue. Several elements combine to form this critical view of the activity. The first is that it is high-level, in other words, it is not suited for the masses. This might account for the discrepancy between his foreword to Helen Fry's *Christian–Jewish Dialogue: A Reader* and most of his expressions elsewhere. There is room for some high-level engagement, and Sacks is able to appreciate it when he sees it. In fact, he is also capable of taking part in it. I can testify that he was a first-rate and fully engaged participant at a high-level interfaith meeting that I organized.[24] He entered wholeheartedly into conversations with the Dalai Lama and other gathered religious leaders, without any of the obstacles that his writings place on interfaith engagement.[25] But then again, this meeting was organized as the very opposite of the staged encounters that Sacks so abhors.

The second reason for his dislike for dialogue is that it 'doesn't deliver'. This brings us back to the lecture to the Council of Christians and Jews. Interfaith should not be assessed on the basis of its potential impact on participants or the growth and transformation it produces in their lives. It should be measured by its social impact and, in Sacks' judgement, it doesn't deliver. Delivery requires another method that is not dialogue, and here his preference for side-by-side service is affirmed once again. So is the outcome—friendship.[26] If friendship is the goal, then it can be attained, and possibly even more successfully, through the side-by-side method, sidestepping all differences and controversies.

[23] Sacks, 'YU and the World of Tomorrow'.
[24] 'Third Meeting of the Elijah Board of World Religious Leaders'.
[25] Rabbi Meir Sendor, who facilitated the discussion group in which he took part, was taken by utter surprise at my report on Sacks' view on dialogue as it emerges from his writings. It in no way reflects his experience of Sacks as a participant in dialogue.
[26] See also Sacks, 'Rabbi Sacks interviewed by Akbar Ahmed on Jewish–Muslim Relations'.

The final reason for his dislike of dialogue is his equating it with theological agreement. Needless to say, it has never been the purpose of interfaith dialogue to reach theological agreement. Sacks' remark is something of a bogus claim. But it helps him in establishing the distinction between his preferred method of side by side and the rejected notion of dialogue, here equated with face to face and the quest for theological agreement.

This leads us, then, to examine in greater detail Sacks' view of face-to-face dialogue. In the same way that his presentation of the purpose of dialogue seems to me distorted, so his presentation of face to face as its fundamental characteristic is also based on a distortion. To appreciate this, we must review how he understands face-to-face dialogue and the philosophical sources upon which he draws.[27] This leads us to his writing on Buber. Sacks devotes a chapter in *The Home We Build Together* to distinguishing face-to-face from side-by-side dialogue.[28] His discussion includes an analysis of Martin Buber's philosophy as part of his critique of the face-to-face approach. The vision that has informed interfaith relations for the past sixty years, he states, is based on Buber's thought.[29] Buber speaks of the immediacy of human encounters at their most intense. All else falls away when two people meet and each is fully open to the other. We cease to be bearers of adjectives and nouns—this race, that faith—and become simply selves, personal presences, singular, unique. Buber, says Sacks, believed that the divine presence lives in such meetings, which he called I and Thou. Thus, when two selves truly meet, the dialogue is a mystical reality, an unscripted encounter in which we cross the abyss separating self from self.

The problem with this description is that Buber never believed that some abstract, disembodied, decontextualized person encounters another, with similar attributes. For Buber, dialogue did not put aside differences, but actually included them. The other was met in his or her particularity.[30] Understood in this way, his I–Thou relationship seeks to achieve the same thing that Sacks' entire programme does—appreciation of the particularity of the other, not simply affirmation of the abstract otherness of the other. If so, face to face is the process of deepening of the appreciation of particularity,

---

[27] At one point, Sacks refers to 'soul to soul' rather than 'face to face'. While this is suggestive, I am not sure there is a substantive distinction here. See 'Make Friends'.

[28] *The Home We Build Together*, ch. 15.   [29] Ibid. 174.

[30] I have consulted with Buber scholar Paul Mendes-Flohr on this point and am making this statement on his authority.

beyond what might otherwise be a superficial view of the other. It is an essential component of the relations between religions, not to be discarded lightly.

Sacks' ambivalence, which leads him to proclaim that he is not a fan of interfaith dialogue, is in part based on a presentation of dialogue as something other than what he seeks to achieve, rather than as the heart of that very quest—affirmation of the particularity of the other. As he describes it, the fruit of dialogue is encountering the other's humanity, not the other's full particularity as a religious personality.

His reservation towards dialogue is also based on the distinction between elitist and popular activity. This leads to the following description of himself in this domain:

It is a lovely program. In one or other form I have been involved in it [dialogue] for years. I mean to detract nothing from its beauty when I say that, none the less, it is an elite pursuit, for it demands a high degree of confidence, knowledge, openness, breadth and generosity of imagination to come face to face with one whose beliefs are radically opposed to those on which you have staked your life. Interfaith dialogue has enormous achievements to its credit. But it tends to take place among the few, in settings far removed from the fault lines and frontlines of conflict. I support it, value it, and practice it. But some sixty years of dialogue have not yielded a world of peace between faiths.[31]

I hear a lot of ambivalence in this passage, beginning with the odd adjective 'lovely'. Interfaith dialogue has enormous achievements but has not really achieved what Sacks implies is its intended goal. He never discusses what the goal is, nor what the achievements are. He never considers how deeper dialogue might advance these and how the practice of dialogue itself might have to advance. Instead, he changes the paradigm. The ambivalence of this statement is not limited to the affirmation of value alongside the claim that its ultimate goal has not been met. It actually goes to the heart of what dialogue is.

By misrepresenting dialogue, basing it on Buber's I–Thou principle, Sacks is in fact making it more rarefied, more out of reach, and ultimately more ineffective than it might otherwise be. On the one hand, he says that he has practised it and supports it. As noted above, I can testify to that, in the sense of dialogue engagement that is anything but trivial. Yet I wonder whether his dislike for interfaith dialogue, which seems as true as his support

---

[31] *The Home We Build Together*, 175.

for it, is not based on his not having gone far enough with it. The argument for a popular and broad-based practice is well taken, and as such provides a complement to the more advanced face-to-face dialogue. At the same time, while Sacks claims he upholds a balance between the two approaches, the music I hear is one that is somewhat dismissive of dialogue. The brief comment in his video interview seems to capture his view, and his presentation of Buber similarly suggests an understanding of face-to-face engagement as something inconsequential, rather than leading to meaningful results. Perhaps had he told us what the achievements were rather than stating that peace has not come, and had he told us what *he* got out of the engagement in dialogue instead of simply referring to it as an activity he endorses, the impression would have been different. In context, his discussion of face-to-face dialogue is heard as a cross between limited approval and a more fundamental rejection. My own suspicion is that this is less about rejecting the ideal of dialogue than about the praxis not having brought Sacks any meaningful or long-lasting benefits. Perhaps had Buber been understood, and practised, in another way, the outcome would have been different.

Sacks' ambivalence is carried further by his description of the programme of dialogue as utopian when compared to the side-by-side paradigm. It requires 'exceptional' capacities for tolerance and mutual understanding. The I-and-Thou dialogue is ultimately a utopia like all others. A more realistic programme is Sacks' side-by-side approach. It seems to me that a popular, broad-based programme for the engagement of communities in relations can be proposed without the conceptual arsenal that Sacks applies, and which ultimately serves to downplay and put down the value of dialogue, theological, face to face.[32]

There is one final issue that relates to Sacks' views on dialogue. His earliest reflection on the subject is found in an essay entitled 'Jewish–Christian Dialogue: The Ethical Dimension'.[33] In it, he defines the purpose of faiths

---

[32] The difficulties I find in Sacks' presentation may stem from his writing procedures. As we have seen, he recycles ideas from one context to another. The distinction between utopian and non-utopian approaches to members of other faiths was articulated previously in relation to the social vision of Judaism, including with reference to pagan faiths. See *To Heal a Fractured World*, 102. In context the ideas are not problematic. Is it their reuse in a discussion of dialogue that ends up contributing to a more extreme anti-dialogue view sounded by Sacks? I consider it quite possible that he did not intend the consequences, and they are a by-product of the above-mentioned recycling of ideas.

[33] *Tradition in an Untraditional Age*, 161–83.

talking to each other as lessening long-standing hostilities, removing barriers to communication, and deepening our own sense of individuality. The
goals are important. They are, on the one hand, social, seeking to advance
peace, and, on the other, conducive to clearer self-understanding.[34] It is
worth stating that nowhere, in any of his writings, does Sacks illustrate how
his, or others', self-understanding has been enhanced as a consequence of
dialogue. For him, this does not seem to be a function of dialogue. Rather,
one's sense of individuality is affirmed, bringing us back to Sacks' childhood
experiences in the context of a Christian school.

Having acknowledged the value of dialogue, Sacks poses the question:
'But when we talk together, of what shall we speak?'[35] The question is odd at
first sight. Why not speak of everything? In fact, he has just cited Zepha-
niah's prophecy and stated that 'learning one another's language of faith is
one of the ways we reach back before Babel'.[36] On his own terms, as he sets
them out, there is no reason to impose a limit on the domain of dialogue,
and faith should be at its heart. Yet he does introduce a limitation and does
pose the question. This may be one more expression of the complexity that
characterizes his approach. He provides the theoretical grounds for a faith
encounter, while limiting its scope in terms of content.

What reason is there for thinking that some areas would be off limits,
or, alternatively, that some provide more fruitful points for conversation?
Reflecting on this question, this is, I believe, a very particular Jewish, or
rather, Orthodox, way of entering dialogue. Rather than exploring a broad
range of areas of potential common interest, the engagement of Orthodox
Jews has been characterized by reservation and the construction of boundaries. Several factors combine to bring about this attitude. They include an
eagerness to keep the particularities of the other faith, and with them the
danger of being exposed to *avodah zarah* (idolatry), at arms' length, and fear
of exposure to another's faith lest it weaken one's own identity. Looking
at this from some distance, the avoidance of certain topics because of fear
really goes against the heart of the activity of dialogue. Indeed, among
Orthodox Jews there has been great resistance to dialogue activity, for reasons of self-protection. The person who more than others set the parameters of how dialogue could be conducted was Rabbi J. B. Soloveitchik.[37]

[34] *Tradition in an Untraditional Age*, 162.   [35] Ibid.   [36] Ibid. 161.
[37] For Soloveitchik's essay and contemporary evaluations of its enduring relevance, see
'Rabbi Joseph Soloveitchik on Interreligious Dialogue'.

Soloveitchik laid down the guideline that theological dialogue should be avoided, while social and moral engagement may be undertaken. This position, established prior to Vatican II, remains the guiding principle for most of English-speaking modern Orthodoxy.

Getting back to Sacks and his question, he makes a very rapid move towards proclaiming ethics, rather than theology, as the ground for dialogue. He never accounts for why this should be the case, and simply relies on the views of Soloveitchik—who is an important figure for him in many ways—as well as another thinker, Eliezer Berkovits. As a consequence of this emphasis, Sacks' discussion of dialogue as such, not only Jewish–Christian dialogue, shifts from interreligious to interhuman concerns, and focuses on the value of the human person, affirmed despite religious differences. This moral angle provides a counterpoint to whatever might emerge from a theological perspective or dialogue. As the argument unfolds, we realize that dialogue is not about the two parties increasing mutual understanding, as Sacks' opening comments might have suggested. An alternative emphasis emerges—the contribution of religion to society. Once again, a certain view of dialogue is presented when Sacks rejects the possibility of reaching a moral consensus through dialogue.[38] Rather, the goal is social and civic; it is to maintain and respect diversity, without different groups threatening one another. Theology remains an area of fear in view of the imagined danger of establishing agreement and consensus on spiritual matters. Still, there is purpose to dialogue, and its benefits are, once again, social. Each community can learn from the other how to build caring communities. The sense of difference that is so central to Sacks' thinking is evoked in his summary.

Dialogue need not be grounded in the belief that, *au fond*, we all share the same faith or the same morality. There is something profoundly moving in such a belief. But there is something equally momentous in the opposite conviction: that our worlds of faith are irreducibly plural yet we have been cast into the same planet, faced with the same questions. Can we live together? Can we learn from one another? Within this vision, much is possible. Much, too, is necessary.[39]

This summary corroborates what we have seen time and again—in the balance between affirming particularity and advocating the value of dialogue,

---

[38] *Tradition in an Untraditional Age*, 163.
[39] Ibid. 179. On the plurality of moralities, see *The Dignity of Difference*, 82. Here Sacks offers concrete examples of what such moral plurality might consist of.

the care for particularity and difference trumps and informs all other concerns. The fear of flattening all differences is the great fear that underlies Sacks' attitude to encounter. Yet, paradoxically, were he to adopt and recommend a more full-bodied approach to dialogue, particularity would emerge with all its force and beauty. Why, then, does he uphold the distinction between theological and ethical and how is this related to his broader views on interreligious dialogue?

It is tempting to say, especially as this is his earliest statement on record, and in it he cites Soloveitchik, that Sacks is simply following the position set forth by Soloveitchik, whom he holds in great esteem. If so, then never has Soloveitchik had a better and more creative representative of his position. The imaginative and literary flare that Sacks brings to his writing, and the many ways in which he engages in interreligious relations in practice with other faith leaders, largely cover up the fundamental reticence to be involved not only in theological dialogue but even in dialogue proper, preferring for the most part to bring the testimony of his Judaism to broader society for the common good. In this reading, at heart, Sacks holds a Soloveitchikian position and this accounts for the ambivalence and complexities in his attitude. At heart, he operates with a heavy set of constraints; in practice, he finds himself deeply immersed in various forms of dialogue and engagement with other faiths. All that we have seen in our analysis of him is the result of juggling these two perspectives.

However, I am far from convinced that this really provides us with the key to the limits and ambivalences that characterize Sacks' attitude to other religions and to dialogue. We have seen how deeply he is influenced by his childhood experience, how much he seeks to affirm the value of the human person, how central arguing for particularity and difference are to his outlook, and how he lays the foundations for a full-bodied engagement between members of different faiths, but fails to follow through in his own person, making the potential of his teaching greater than his personal realization of it. I do not think all this can be reduced to a Soloveitchikian position, brilliantly covered up by literary creativity and public activity. In many ways, Sacks goes beyond Soloveitchik in the extent of his personal involvement and in the many moments in which his imagination captures a reality that is greater than the more limited, socially oriented engagement recommended —or rather, permitted—by Soloveitchik. Were Soloveitchik the guiding force, we could expect Sacks to actually conduct moral dialogue with other

faiths. We could expect an analysis of the relative value of moral positions found in different faiths and the possible advantages of the Jewish
view.[40] Yet he avoids these as much as he avoids theological discussion.
We must therefore suggest a different explanation for the limits of his engagement.

I believe Sacks is not formed around Soloveitchik and his boundaries. He
is formed around Sacks and his boundaries, and Soloveitchik provides a convenient counterpart to these. As we saw from his biographical note, he
enters the domain of faith relations from a particular positioning that is
both social and psychological. This defines the purposes of dialogue: civility
and tolerance. Perhaps it is really an English phenomenon, the aversion to
an engagement that is too personal, too revealing, too intimate; or perhaps
it is simply Sacks' personality make-up, be its causes whatever they may be.
He moves into the domain of dialogue with a combination of intellectual
appreciation for its value, a sense of social urgency, recognition of its benefits, and a series of brakes and limitations that are the consequence of his
fear of dialogue serving as the grounds for consensus and unity. His limitations include restricting the extent of personal, spiritual sharing and even
of deep and sincere engagement. The moments that he describes as transformative turn out to not have had long-lasting impact. His encounters
with faith leaders are characterized by a very particular set of concerns—
civic and social—and consistently show an avoidance of entering the deeper,
more personal and intimate domain of faith itself. Throughout, upholding diversity and difference are more important than reaching that deeper
understanding that dialogue could lead to, symbolized for him in the person
of Buber and his I–Thou theory. Sacks seems to fear that deeper dialogue
would lead to a washing away of differences rather than to illuminating
them more clearly. A dialogue of particularity might give way to an imagined dialogue of neutrality, of a humanity stripped of its particularity. That,
more than anything, is what he fears. But in all this, we must realize that the
drives for and against dialogue are expressions of his psychological profile.

The cause of Sacks' inhibitions is of great consequence for others. Were
he simply carrying out Soloveitchik's mandate, then others would be similarly limited if they sought to be faithful to Sacks' teaching. However, if his
inhibitions are purely personal and psychological, then others can take

[40] For a typical instance of where this might have been relevant, see *The Dignity of Difference*, 82.

from him the visionary and inspirational moments while going beyond his own personal limitations. By power of his religious and human imagination, Sacks, at many points in his oeuvre, has constructed a vision that others can realize. He has built castles in words that others can then inhabit.[41] If, indeed, he entered the field of dialogue with whatever internal limitations he did, then we must admire how far he came in providing a theory and a vision for engagement across religions. What he could see was clearly more than what he could live, and we have the freedom to be inspired by him in the fullest possible way.

Engagement with other religions is an important aspect of Sacks' teaching. I have explored in this chapter the complexities of his understanding of interfaith dialogue and his practice. Perhaps the best indication for his ultimate lack of interest is that he simply moved beyond the concerns of and need for dialogue. His earliest discussion of the subject, in the 1990s, shows his struggle with types, boundaries, and the extent of engagement. His later work, in the first decade of the twenty-first century, led him away from face-to-face dialogue to the more active and practical side-by-side approach to building friendship across religions. The latest stage of his writing seems to have gone beyond dialogue altogether. The second decade saw discussions such as *The Great Partnership* and *Not in God's Name*, where Sacks no longer speaks of dialogue or otherness or even difference, except as these ideas might be recycled in his later books. Instead, he speaks for all religions or all Abrahamic monotheisms, even if the paradigm for these monotheisms comes from Judaism or from Sacks' reconstruction of biblical faith. Whether intentionally or unintentionally, he has, in fact, moved beyond dialogue. There is no longer any need to consider its boundaries and practices, in whatever form, when one is speaking for all faiths. This is indeed a great paradox. Avoidance of dialogue was, in the first instance, meant to protect difference and particularity, even as it was informed by Sacks' personal orientation and leanings. These selfsame leanings eventually led him to move away from dialogue and to adopt a voice by means of which he speaks for all, or a group of, religions. In so doing, he has in fact done the very thing he feared all along. Speaking for Abrahamic monotheisms or for religion as such, he actually speaks from a space of consensus, commonality, and union. Gone is the concern for otherness; a new discourse has set in.

Perhaps Sacks is less threatened by this discourse precisely because it is

---

[41] I owe this image to Rowan Williams. See Ch. 14 below.

he who sets the tone, defines the parameters of the conversation, and casts other religions in terms of an idealized Judaism, in the process offering a criticism of those religions. If he feared all along that Judaism would have to sell out its particularity as a consequence of full-bodied dialogue, he has overcome this fear in the most striking and courageous move. No longer do others, or dialogue itself, set the backdrop against which Judaism has to define itself, preserving its particularity. Instead, it is Judaism, as presented by Sacks, that sets the standard for others to conform to. Fear of dialogue and dialogue itself are now gone. A new reality, trans-religious or trans-Abrahamic, provides a new paradigm, one that apparently is not only not threatening to Sacks but is quite appealing to his orientation and sensibilities. So long as the goal of dialogue was for religions to better understand each other, boundaries had to be erected. Having shifted the ground to religion's contribution to society, as he does already in his earliest essay, he no longer needs to protect or defend Judaism. That contribution can now be carried out on Sacks' own terms, speaking for all faiths. Whether or not his dialogue activity was transformative may be disputed. What is certain is that his journey in relation to other religions and engagement with them, for the sake of the common good, has been transformative.

CHAPTER THIRTEEN

The Power of Religious Imagination and the Legacy of Sacks

I N AN INTERVIEW with Hava Tirosh-Samuelson, Sacks says that he has not written half the books he would have liked to. Specifically, he has not written on the big theological subjects, nor put forward a systematic theology.[1] This is a very interesting admission. In fact, it amounts to a recognition that his work has not been theological and, for that matter, that he is not a theologian. We know by now that he is a social thinker, whose primary concern, when discussing other faiths, is how they relate to society, not what they are in and of themselves. This is why he engages so little with the actual ideas of other faiths and why, somewhat to my surprise, he levels as much criticism against some religious authors as he does.

And yet it takes a comprehensive study of Sacks—a process by means of which one identifies what he has done, what he has omitted, where the gaps in his thinking and writing are, and what his emphases are—to reach this understanding. If one reads the individual book, or the individual teaching, one would not recognize the extent of the positive approach to other religions coupled with the reservations and hesitations that characterize his approach—in other words, his complexities and ambivalences. Part of the reason is that, throughout his corpus, there is indeed an attempt to draw out the positive dimensions of interreligious relations. Against the background of an Orthodox world that largely shuns all contact, Sacks' openness to encounter and relationships is noteworthy—an important and inspiring departure from norms and an invitation to a new model of relations between religions. Moreover, his literary genius is such that, regardless of the limitations placed on the scope and extent of his engagement, what he says is always inspiring and often heart-opening, and therefore opens the reader to new perspectives.

---

[1] Tirosh-Samuelson and Hughes (eds.), *Jonathan Sacks: Universalizing Particularity*, 132.

Let me illustrate this with one random passage, the likes of which can easily be multiplied. In *To Heal a Fractured World*, Sacks makes the following statement: 'There are 6,000 languages spoken today, but only one is truly universal: the language of tears.'[2] No one can deny the poetics and the suggestiveness of this statement. Further reflection leads me to suggest that the 'secret ingredient' that Sacks brings to his reflections on relations with other religions is not simply his literary power. It is the power of imagination. Some of what he may miss out on as a result of his avoidance of certain forms of engagement he makes up for with the help of his imagination. We may even think of his work as the fruit of inspiration, of an inspired imagination.

The role of imagination in relations between religions finds express articulation in Sacks' writing. We recall that the remedy he proposes in *Not in God's Name* for overcoming estrangement is an imaginative one. One must envisage oneself as living the other's experience, identifying with the other by force of one's imagination. It is clearly a powerful technique, possibly practised by Sacks himself. Earlier I queried why one had to engage in exercises of the imagination in lieu of deeper encounter and understanding of the other. But that is not the point at the moment. The fact is that the imagination is enlisted for the sake of cultivating empathy. Sacks couches this in terms of monotheistic religions, suggesting that empathy should be extended to members of other Abrahamic faiths.[3] The limitation does not seem to me essential. The ideas of respect and care for the other are not limited, in Sacks' teachings, to members of monotheistic faiths, and I therefore doubt that he intended to place such limits on the extension of empathy by power of the imagination.

Having recognized the imaginative faculty as a hidden driver of Sacks' thought, it seems to me we may identify other expressions of it throughout his work. One of his key messages is recognizing the image of God in the other, who is not in my image. We may consider this too an application of the religious imagination. One imagines the other in God's light, or perhaps imagines God's presence and image in the other. For the idea to have

---

[2] p. 106.
[3] *Not in God's Name*, 195. One could also understand the reference to Abrahamic faiths as indicative of the problems in religious relations as they grow out of the prevailing situation among those faiths, rather than as setting a boundary as to how far the empathetic imagination can extend.

meaning it must be more than an 'idea', an abstract statement. If it has power, and I believe for Sacks it does have power, it must be complemented by the imagination, which somehow makes it concrete and turns it into a source of inspiration and a moral imperative.

I wonder whether Sacks' entire approach to other religions would not be seen in a new light if we regarded it more in terms of imagination. The controversy surrounding *The Dignity of Difference* took place as a consequence of reading the book against the background of a history of Jewish views of other religions. In that context, Sacks was seen to be making statements that were radical, novel, and not in keeping with tradition. Regardless of how one decides on that matter, we may be missing something fundamental if we only look at his ideas as a further articulation of ideas of a Jewish theology of religions. What if thinking of other faiths as expressions of God talking to other groups or of other groups hearing God's voice is not meant to be a means of validation and affirmation in the classical sense of Jewish attitudes to other religions? I think we can revisit Sacks by positing that in fact he is calling us to an exercise of the imagination. We change our perspectives on the world and on other groups by expanding the range of our imagination. We can imagine a reality that is broader, and in which God speaks, or relates to, or is known by, all. This application of our imagination in a benevolent and open outreach to other faiths allows us to affirm their validity and lay the foundations for a peaceful world. It is not simply the verdict of a Jewish theology of religions that opens the way to the reduction of violence. It is the active cultivation of an attitude of the imagination that then redefines our view of the world and of the other.

Sacks, as we have seen, engages with all, but, paradoxically, with almost no one in the depth of an interreligious encounter.[4] Others, with Buber as the symbolic representative of this path, meet with the real other in the depth of encounter. Sacks does not enter the domain of interfaith relations by dint of a particular formative or transformative relationship. We never hear of one particular Christian or Muslim friend who changed his life. We are never told of an encounter that opened his eyes to a new spiritual reality. There is no significant other in relation to whom his thoughts were formed.[5] What there is is the idea or ideal of the other. That ideal leads Sacks

[4] See the interview with Rowan Williams in Ch. 14 below.
[5] This is very much in contrast to Greenberg, whose entire path was forged under the influence of formative relationships.

to an internal outreach, carried out by means of the imagination, that makes room for the other in the sight and presence of God, recognizing God's image in the other. The exercise does not remain purely internal, inasmuch as it has multiple concrete external expressions. These include his manifold interfaith activities as chief rabbi and popular speaker. They include his recommending side-by-side engagement for communities. However, what drives these is not the power of a deep encounter that leads to an appreciation of the other. They are driven by the religious imagination, extended to others and inspired by God, in the quest for peace and in the service of society.

Sacks studies are, I surmise, in their infancy. As time passes, and as the enormity of his intellectual creativity is recognized, we will see multiple analyses of his thought. The suggestion that the religious imagination is a key factor in appreciating Sacks' spirituality is one that will likely come into clear focus only with future study, across multiple areas. It is not, to the best of my knowledge, an important topic in his explicit reflection, but that does not mean it is not important in understanding Sacks himself. The suggestion applies not only to his view of other faiths or to the history and experience of members of other faiths. I believe it goes to the core of his own spiritual experience. Once the thesis is on the table, multiple statements relating to God and how he is experienced take on new light. Here is one.

I believe in a personal God, because religion in the Abrahamic tradition is the consecration of the personal. It lives in interpersonal relationships: in love and revelation and vulnerability and trust, all those things in which we put our faith when we commit ourselves to one another in a covenantal bond of loyalty and mutuality. Love is what redeems us from the prison cell of the self and all the sickness to which the narcissistic self is prone—from empty pride to deep depression to a sense of nihilism and the abyss.

So in the silence of the soul I listen for the still small voice, which is God's call to each of us to engage in the work of love and creativity, to bring new life into the world, and to care for it and nurture it during its years of vulnerability. And whenever I see people engaged in that work of love, I sense the divine presence brushing us with a touch so gentle you can miss it, and yet know beyond all possibility of doubt that this is what we are called on to live for, to ease the pain of those who suffer and become an agent of hope in the world. That is a meaningful life. That is what life is when lived in the light of God's presence, in answer to his call.[6]

---

[6] *The Great Partnership*, 205.

This passage concludes Sacks' discussion in a chapter entitled 'A Meaningful Life'. It provides us with a rare glimpse into his faith and spiritual horizons. The foundation of this is not in some powerful God experience, let alone a mystical realization, or even a profound cognitive breakthrough. Relationship and love are key. We realize how crucial the covenant is not only to his theory but also to his experience of religion and in his relationship with both God and humanity. God is a still small voice that is heard within. He hears it, as everyone else must, guiding us to do the work of love and creativity. The divine presence is felt whenever he sees people engaging in this work.

This statement describes a refinement of the religious imagination in an act of attuning oneself to a higher reality that, though subtle, is very real for him. Not to be dismissed as 'merely' imagination, it is in fact an opening of normal reality to a subtle calling that transforms life into something higher. It is also the source of hope. In fact, hope itself, a subject to which Sacks devoted two books, is a projection of the imagination. It is not something reasoned. It is something intuited, cultivated, and translated into action, either individual or collective, either scripturally grounded or personally attained. Hope imprints itself on one's consciousness and orients life for the good. What Sacks describes as meaning, and as his foundational religious experience, is not simply love. He does not state, as perhaps a Christian friend might, that in the love of another person he discovers God, whom he recognizes as love itself. That is not his message. Rather, love in relationship joins a broader movement of begetting and sustaining life, ultimately transforming the world in hope. This movement is driven by love, but its orientation is attained by means of the religious imagination.

We now realize why Sacks is so inspired by the sight of Sikhs serving Langar or Hindus performing service. These are human actions that give expression to fundamental drives of love and solidarity in human relations. But they are also where Sacks encounters God—in his relationship with humans, through other religions. Avoiding theology or an intentional 'religious' encounter is seen in a new light once we recognize Sacks' own approach to the spiritual life. It passes through human relations, is inspired by the religious imagination wherein God is found, and extends broadly to all, regardless of their form of religion. Seen in this light, Sacks is not avoiding theological contact à la Soloveitchik; he is practising religion and finding God in others in the same way he does in his own faith. Whatever boundaries are erected are a function of his person, not his ideologies. And whatever he may not be comfortable engaging with directly and consciously, he approaches in alternative ways, by power of his enlightened imagination.

Recognition of the power of imagination as a driver of Sacks' reflection may hold the key to reconciling some of the conflicts we have seen. I would like to propose that Sacks, like other good writers, can write from a place of inspiration or from the gifts of his brilliant and creative mind. He is capable of writing in different voices or modalities. A different tone and a different perspective will accordingly come to expression depending on the quality that he brings to his writing. If we consider the two contrasting voices that were sounded in his introduction to the volume on Jewish–Christian dialogue and in his talk to the Council of Christians and Jews, we may have a key to reconciling the differences without the need to appeal to the different contexts. While not a participant in the exercise of dialogue, Sacks brings to his foreword empathy and appreciation for the project, drawing from the best of his inspired imagination. The talk to the Council of Christians and Jews, by contrast, is an occasion to present his ideas, and he engages in reasoning and consequently in debate with the achievements of the field to date. If we are struck by the impression that there are two Sackses, or two voices of Sacks, that is indeed the case. Recognizing the role of the religious imagination in his creative processes holds the key to better understanding the nature of these two voices.

This leads me to the final reflection, which is in some ways the most challenging—Sacks' legacy in the domain of interfaith relations and of Jewish relations with world religions. It is hard to assess someone's legacy so soon after that person's passing away. It is often the case that great personalities are only appreciated, and their full impact only becomes visible, with the passage of time. Sacks, I believe, is in the process of becoming more and more valued within the Jewish community. The translation of his works into Hebrew not only opens up new audiences; it gives them the potential for the kind of canonical status that is reserved for great works of Jewish thought. With translation into Hebrew, the question also arises how much of Sacks' contribution is unique to his specific British context and how much his legacy in this field will be felt across the Jewish world—and across the religious world as a whole.

In his earliest essay on interfaith relations, Sacks raises the following question:

With whom, as ministers of religion, *do* we share moral problems? Do we share them with society as a whole, or just with other religious people, or just with people of our own religion, or just with people of our own specific denomination, or just with a minority even of our own congregations?[7]

The questions are raised with regard to moral problems, but they apply equally to Sacks' own literary career. The paragraph encapsulates the very challenge facing us. We can't speak of a legacy until we know who the audience is. Sacks' reach was so wide and shifted over time in so many various directions that we cannot exhaust his contribution by honing in on one target group only. His later works spoke of religion in relation to larger social problems. Others will have to reflect on his reception in broader circles, all the more so if those circles involve members of other religions. Many of the passages studied in this book may not have been written with a Jewish audience in mind. This was, after all, his defence when charges were levelled at *The Dignity of Difference*.[8] Yet there are distinct ways in which we can envision his legacy lasting in the Jewish world and in its dealings with world religions. I shall enumerate several.

1. **Normativity.** Catholics have the pope. The gestures he makes, such as the Assisi convening of religious leaders, or other notable encounters held by popes, have great visibility. Jews do not have popes, neither Ashkenazi nor Sephardi, and no figure in Judaism has the kind of visibility that some leaders in other faiths have. Sacks was probably the Jewish leader with the greatest visibility globally, far more than Israeli chief rabbis or any other chief rabbi or Jewish public figure of his era. Visibility, regrettably, is the lot of politicians, not of religious leaders. Because of who he was, the specific network of associations that comes with the British chief rabbinate, his skill in using media and communication, his travels, his publications, and more, Sacks was probably the most visible Jewish religious personality of our time. A large and significant dimension of this visibility was his public engagement alongside leaders of other faiths. The opportunities provided by his context had the end result of making this engagement normative and a central feature of the rabbinate. This is not, in and of itself, something new. But in quantitative terms, and in terms of visibility, Sacks has legitimated interfaith engagement for the Orthodox world to a significant extent.

---

[7] *Tradition in an Untraditional Age*, 165.   [8] Persoff, *Another Way, Another Time*, 173.

2. Legitimating other religions. Jewish legitimation of other faiths has a long record, and some of the positions that are relevant have been cited in this study. Sacks advanced the conversation with new formulations. What will remain of his legacy is in part a question of how much of the original message of *The Dignity of Difference* will be remembered following its revision, and as echoed in small citations in other works. Potentially, he has advanced the discussion of Jewish theology of religions.

3. The covenantal dimension. Sacks grounds the relations between religions in a core concept of Judaism. While in some of his work he employs classical categories that express a less than full-blown appreciation of other religions, such as *darkhei shalom*, some of his thought goes to the core of Jewish faith by exploring relations with other religions through the lens of the covenant. Because Sacks is such a deeply covenantal thinker, applying this category to other religions makes the concern for relations with others a core Jewish concern. Consequently, the dual covenant construct that lies at the heart of his view of other faiths may be seen as not merely a product of social necessity, let alone of economic necessity,[9] but as a theological drive growing out of the core of Jewish faith. He places the question of Judaism and its relations with world religions on the front line of the agenda of faith. Even if he does not engage with that agenda in detail, he has defined the framework and provided the space from within which it is to be explored.

4. A vision for community. Because of the British context, Sacks has been challenged to come up with a concept for how interfaith engagement can contribute to the broader social good. This has led him to develop his side-by-side approach. Whatever challenges this theory poses to a theological or spiritual approach, it is, in fact, the only theory of public interfaith engagement that has been put forward by a Jewish voice, anytime, anywhere. Sacks is quite right that a large part, perhaps even most, of interfaith work has been undertaken by elites. If we seek advances in interfaith relations, a special programme must be set up to that effect. It cannot rely on the trickle-down effect of religious leaders sharing their experiences with their communities.

It is too soon to tell whether the conceptualization of the side-by-side approach will form part of Sacks' interfaith legacy for the Jewish people. I do

---

[9] See Katz, *Exclusiveness and Tolerance*, ch. 3.

not have a handle on how successful it has been, now nearly twenty years after it was conceived in the United Kingdom. The larger question is whether it can work in other places. It is a formula that ultimately depends on religious demographics and the composition of an interfaith society. Sacks drew his inspiration in *The Home We Build Together* from the United States, and it may be that his model could equally be applied there. It might even be applied in other countries. But what of Israel? Can this model be implemented in a situation where Judaism is a majority and other faith communities are largely invisible? Would it work in mixed cities? I am not aware of any attempt to translate Sacks' method intentionally to any other geographical context, and especially not to Israel. It may have potential, but all potential has to be tested to be confirmed.

5. **Contributions to lowering interreligious tensions**. Possibly the biggest motivator that informs Sacks' work with other faiths is the quest for reducing violence in the name of religion. The concerns are broad, and include both antisemitism, a subject that Sacks treats at length in various publications, especially *Future Tense*, and Islamophobia. When we think of interfaith relations, we think also of the social impact of engagement with other religions. If Sacks is taken seriously and read by Jews as well as non-Jews, his work has the potential to make substantial contribution, *scripturally* based and *theologically* justified, to the promotion of peace among religions globally.

6. **Scriptural grounding.** Sacks' genius is noted in his scriptural reading. He has created a corpus of thought that grows out of close biblical readings, with a strong concentration on Genesis, which he explicates in dialogue with contemporary concerns. Key issues of the day are seen through the prism of biblical interpretation. While commentators have always read the present into Scripture, Sacks has created a genre all of his own of detailed, literary scriptural interpretations, understood in their own light, while delivering messages that are relevant for the day. His literary skills as reader and writer, and an uncanny ability to relate biblical narrative to the concerns of the day in ways that are anything but forced or superficial, make the tackling of contemporary social challenges part and parcel of his biblical readings. While other authors may offer here and there a biblical analogy, the force of Sacks' teaching is in its extensive biblical grounding. What this means in terms of the potential acceptance of his interfaith message is that it is now

read in a deeper way, in dialogue with Scripture. Needless to say, this gives it new grounding and greater conviction, and increases the ability of the message to be received.

7. **Religious imagination.** I conclude the list with the main theme of this chapter. I believe the application of the imagination to the religious other may emerge as a central component of Sacks' interfaith legacy. Paradoxically, precisely because it does not require contact, let alone deep engagement, it can be undertaken by all, regardless of social and geographical circumstances. Sacks invites us to not simply read Scripture but to enter into its message more deeply by means of our imagination. He similarly invites us to consider the other with an empathy that can only be evoked by power of the imagination. The field of interreligious relations has been heavily dominated for centuries by concerns of truth, objectivity, rationality, and irrationality. Introducing a discourse that brings into play the imagination in relation to the other is a great novelty. It cuts the ground from under classical religious polemics and asks the participant to cultivate empathy rather than fight for truth. Moreover, given how strained interreligious relations are by the burden of the past and its memories, an appeal to the religious imagination can help shift emphases. If memory leads to focusing on oneself and the pain one has experienced at the hands of the other, the religious imagination opens us up to the reality of the other, and thereby expands our own sense of self and the range of our interests and care. It seems to me that this may actually be Sacks' greatest contribution. We do not yet know how many of his practical suggestions will be implemented, nor how much his theory of the dignity of difference and acceptance of the other will be upheld over time. All these are teachings, concrete ideas, that will either live on or not. But with regard to the imagination, it seems to me that Sacks has opened up a new field within the domain of interfaith relations. Beyond reason, beyond dialogue, beyond common service, he has identified an area where all need to grow and where all can grow, independently of any of the other areas.

Recognizing the importance of the imagination in Sacks' approach, we may revisit many of his teachings and ask ourselves how these may be applied as exercises for the cultivation of a deeper feeling for the religious other, or as ways of enhancing compassion and solidarity. Sacks' theory of dialogue also includes gaining a better understanding of our own self in relation to the other. This is formulated in the earliest stages of his thought and is repeated time and again. Yet we are never told how in fact one understands oneself better as a result of encountering the other. One assumes that dialogue forces one to define more clearly one's own identity. Now, however, we come to the point of imagining another way in which encounter could work, and I surmise that this may have been how it worked for Sacks himself. Encounter with the other involves also imaginative entry into the other's reality. Such imaginative openness is also a way of expanding the self and establishing new parameters within, where self and other can meet. Sacks fights off Buber's I–Thou model, I believe primarily on personal emotional grounds. While he describes himself as partaking in the practice of interfaith dialogue, and while he attributes such practice to the theoretical grounding in Buber's thought, he never once suggests having had such an experience in relation to a member of another faith. I believe Sacks, without having fully articulated it, developed an alternative, one that was more suitable to his personality and which may turn out to have broader appeal. Whatever may have been lacking in direct transformative encounter was made up for by application of the religious imagination to the religious reality of the other. While Sacks would never extend such a practice to the contents of the faith of the other, he would extend it to the person, memory, history, and fullness of the human reality of the other. Whether these boundaries can or should be maintained is a secondary question. For the moment, we should appreciate what encounter meant for Sacks. It was an exposure to the reality of the religious other that engaged the imagination even more than the mind or the spirit. I believe it is this that gave him the drive to continue his involvement in interfaith and it is thanks to this empathetic and humane imagination that many felt close to him, even though he may have avoided a certain kind of deeper engagement. Seen in this light, Sacks' greatest legacy still has to be uncovered, explored for its fuller meaning, and tested for its fruits in the lives of believers, Jewish as well as non-Jewish.

CHAPTER FOURTEEN

Rowan Williams on Jonathan Sacks

ALON GOSHEN-GOTTSTEIN: Thank you for making time for a conversation on friendship across religions. I'd like to explore the topic in two ways: first by asking you to offer some theoretical reflections on the value of cultivating friendships with members—in your case perhaps leaders—of other faiths. I'd then like to look at one particular case in point, concerning your relationship with our common and much-missed friend, Rabbi Jonathan Sacks. Let us begin with the teaching, which will set the tone for how you approach friendship across religions.

ROWAN WILLIAMS: *Firstly,* according to the Christian Scriptures, one of the things that Jesus said to his closest friends the night before he was arrested and executed was that he wasn't going to call them servants any longer, but friends. Because, he said, servants, or indeed slaves, strictly speaking, don't know what their master is doing. The implication is that friends do. A friend knows what another friend is doing. That's to say there's enough understanding between them that their actions, their words, make sense to each other. There's an assumption, a basis of trust and communication, a kind of transparency. It doesn't mean that friends live in each other's pockets. It doesn't mean that I know everything that a friend is doing or thinking. God forbid, you might say. Nonetheless, there is that crucial difference that Jesus underlines between a servile relationship, an instrumental relationship to someone else, and a friendly relationship. So one thing this seems to imply is that if someone is a friend, they're not an *instrument* to me, they're not a means for me to realize *my* agenda, *my* private ideas. They are who they are. And the friendship is a matter of discovering that deep reality that's there and working with the grain of it. I approach my friend without that kind of agenda, without wanting to make them serve my needs only. Of course, a friend serves my needs in the sense that they meet my loneliness. They listen to me sympathetically, I hope. They also challenge me, I hope. But they are who they are. They're not like that because I make them like that. They are there. And that's the first thing that seems to me to be significant about friendship.

The friend is different, the friend is who they are. I seek, in friendship, to be open to that, to explore that with them, to understand better, to let them understand, and perhaps to understand myself more fully in the process. 'Understanding in the process'—that of course means there's a time-taking element to friendship. The kind of friendship I am talking about is one that picks up after ten years' absence, ten years' separation. We know that taking time, allowing a friendship to mature, is part of it. It doesn't all come at once. It takes the time it takes. So friendship is about resigning having any agenda or any instrumentalizing of another.

Secondly, friendship also entails patience, and a particular kind of patience, the kind of patience that assumes that the other person is not actually a threat. So if my friend says something that challenges, shocks, or unsettles me, I need to assume that they're not out to destroy, to rupture, to tear up the relationship. I'm invited to take time to understand that a bit better. But I should not start by assuming the worst. I assume the friend has goodwill as I do. That spending time will take us forward together. So patience goes with an assumption of what the philosophers magnificently call a hermeneutic of charity. That's to say, I interpret the other in the most generous way that I can. Because that's what grows out of friendship. We've learned we can be together, we've learned a degree of trust. So if there are bumps in the road, if there are sudden gaps opening up, they're not the end of the story; they're work to be done.

Thirdly, alongside all that, there's a third dimension, which seems to be just as important. Friends don't spend all their time looking at each other. They don't just gaze into each other's eyes like lovers. Friends do things together and 'look' together. And it seems to me that one of the most life-giving, renewing elements in friendship is those moments of looking together, those shared experiences. It may be a project that's shared together, or it may just be an experience that is shared together. I like, let's say, to go to a sports event, or to the theatre, with a friend, because looking together at something with our different perspectives will enhance the experience for both of us. And that's where, coming back to the question of interreligious friendship, we strike one of the most significant elements. A friend coming from another religious tradition is a friend I trust to be looking in the same direction as I. When I look at their face, I see their face turns towards God, whatever they may understand by that. And part of the task, part of the challenge, and part of the reward of friendship across faiths is to learn something from the face of a friend as it is turned towards God—not to me, but to God. I see in them the reflection of the holy, the reflection of the infinite. I see their attempt to be at home with the mystery. And all I can do with that sight is to wonder and to be grateful. And I pray that the friend sees that in me, and as we then move on to talk about what divides us, or what at the very least creates difference between us, we don't lose sight of that memory, of the friend's face turned God-wards.

'No longer slaves, but friends.' Slaves don't know what's going on. They're ordered around, they're at the mercy of somebody else's will. Friends are who they are together, voluntarily learning, looking, sharing, patiently discovering, making allowances, making something new together, looking together into the mystery.

AGG: With your permission I'd like change gear and move from these theoretical and very inspiring reflections on the nature of friendship to your recollection of one particular friendship. I'm presently writing on Jonathan Sacks. Working through his multiple discussions of interreligious relations has led me to consider the kind of interreligious friendships he enjoyed and how much his own thinking reflects real, lived relationships—or, conversely, the lack thereof. I therefore value the opportunity to discuss this one particular friendship with you. Having both served as the primary clergymen of your respective religions at the same time, and having had numerous occasions to interact, you are uniquely positioned to offer a testimony to Sacks as a friend from another faith. In fact, you are one of the only two or three named friends, or partners, cited by him in his work. So I am particularly grateful for the opportunity to gain perspective on Sacks the person, the friend, from you. In light of this introduction, and in view of your own reflections on what it means to have a friend from another religion, I would like to go to the core of the challenge at hand and pose the following question, in the most direct way: Was Jonathan Sacks really a friend in the full sense that you've described?

RW: Probably not in the fullest sense. No. We spent time together. We shared experiences, certainly. Yet, in terms of friendship, there were shortcomings. Jonathan was actually *not* a person it was easy to know or get close to. He was somebody of such extraordinary fluency. As we say, he'd quarter the field, he would organize. I used to watch him taking notes sometimes, these amazingly detailed notes and tiny hand-writing on long strips of paper. And I would think: I wish I had a mind that was that organized. And sometimes I suppose I had a slight feeling that he, like so many of us, thought he had a solution when he had a formula.

AGG: Please explain the distinction.

RW: I think people who are quite good with words (and I suppose I have to say I speak as one of them) very often think when they've wrapped it up tidily, that that's it. But there's often in situations an unsolved ache and a lack that you have to keep sitting with. And I wasn't always sure that Jonathan had that sense of the unfinished business.

AGG: That's on the intellectual side. But let's get back to the friendship. You spoke of taking time to get to know the other. I've been asking myself, as a consequence of reading his works, if he really had friends, let alone real interfaith friends. The more I read, and the more I see his theology, the more I am stunned by his mind, stunned by his creativity. Yet I also hit up increasingly against a frustration, a feeling that he is not going far enough. There are two ways of understanding why that would be the case. One is theological, and the other is personal. If it's theological, then we have a problem. Whatever his limitations are, if they are theo-logically grounded, then he can only go so far in his service as a teacher to others. However, if it's personal and psychological, then we could bracket his psychology and credit him with the possibility of opening up paths for others to go forward. Consequently, I find myself engaged in a critique of the person in order to save the person's ideas. It's a funny kind of move I end up making, which ostensibly discredits him by highlighting his weakness. But in fact I'm doing just the opposite. He's greater than who he was. Or he had an intuition and a potential that's greater than what he was. He was a man of true greatness. As I mentioned in my obituary, I really feel he's this generation's finest teacher. And yet he had these limitations. So your honesty in response to my query is invaluable. Which is why I'd like to explore the matter further: where did his friendship fall short? And what were the consequences of that for his interfaith engagement?

RW: I think you're absolutely right that he wasn't somebody who had friends, interfaith friends. I'm not sure he had very many Jewish friends.

AGG: I have a friend in Salt Lake City whom I once called in the middle of a convention. He picked up the phone saying: 'I'm here with 11,000 of my closest friends.' [laughter] I wonder if this was not true also of Jonathan. He was everyone's friend, which potentially meant he was no one's friend, in a deeper sense. My reading of him is that he had Elaine and then the rest, that was basically it. What this means, then, is that all his intense engagement was more outward. Though we could see his depth of heart and intuition, as well as his recognition of places where one could go in a relationship, in fact these were not followed through in the context of personal relationships, due to whatever issues were within him that prevented his going forward.

RW: I think when I say he was somebody who sometimes thought he'd found a solution when in fact he had a formula, that is something to do with his uncomfortableness with being vulnerable in lots of settings. And I think, well, the nearest I got to him, I suppose—and it's a very paradoxical way of saying it—is when we went to Auschwitz together. This was also one of the very few occasions where I've seen him really at a loss. And he said: 'I didn't want to come.' But, well . . .

AGG: In other words, he went because he was pushed to by whatever circumstance, but he himself had preferred the safety of not going there.

RW: I think he knew that he wouldn't know what to say. And, well, like the rest of us . . .

AGG: Well, let me read you what he said about that event. He says the following. 'In 2008, on the anniversary of Kristallnacht, or close to it, the Archbishop of Canterbury Rowan Williams and I took a group of representatives of all the major faiths in Britain, not just Christian but

Muslim, Hindu, Sikh, Buddhist, Jain, Zoroastrian and Baha'i, to Ausch-witz. I can't remember a bonding experience like it. It was profoundly moving. Not only profoundly moving while we were there, but it was profoundly moving when we sat together in Kraków airport and talked through our feelings. So we became very, very bonded together. We'd been friends before, but this really transformed it and gave it greater depth.' That testimony doesn't cohere with your own description.

RW: I think it's true that in Kraków airport afterwards, you know, there was a level of rawness about the exchange. Yeah, difficult in a good way. No, I don't think it created lasting deep friendships between any of the group. But it gave us something on that day, for those few hours, that was, I think, significant. It wasn't empty, it wasn't a waste of time. So somewhere in between, I think, not quite that deep friendship was created, nevertheless a bonding did happen.

AGG: Why couldn't it bear fruit for longer? After all, this really fits with what you described as the nature of friendship—being and doing things together. That's also *his* whole ideal, not face to face, but side by side. What could be more side by side than addressing suffering? It tapped into all the elements of how he viewed relationships. Why didn't it go farther in terms of its long-lasting effects? He describes the people there as friends and the experience as having deepened those friend-ships. But if the friends weren't friends to begin with, then maybe the deepening really wasn't all that deep.

RW: I think part of the fact that nothing much further came of it would have been just the structural, the institutional lack of context for us to go on with it. The nearest we've got to follow up was Jonathan and myself meeting with a group of schoolchildren who'd been visiting the camp on the same day. And after a month or so he and I said: Well, we ought to follow up with some of the youngsters. So we invited them for an afternoon. But that was the only real follow-up to it.

AGG: You know what, forget the others. Did the two of you become closer through this experience?

RW: No, I didn't think so.

AGG: Now, that's telling.

RW: I think that there's that photograph of the two of us at the camp, which I always find quite eloquent, in the sense that both of us were sort of looking at the ground and not quite knowing what to do with it. And then there's a measure of shared vulnerability with each other, which probably wasn't present in any other setting that we'd been in. So I don't want to minimize that. But I'm not sure that it took us to a deeper level in some ways. I think it was probably more significant when we shared meals, sabbath eve meals with him, on a couple of occasions. There we got somewhere towards a sort of relaxed, genuine sharing of views. Not monitoring ourselves or being representative.

AGG: Did you have intimate conversations with him? My assumption is that you would have been the most intimate, the closest to an interfaith friend he would have had, by virtue of the amount of time you spent together, and by virtue of the office. On the basis of his writings, I get a sense that the two of you were as close as he got. So my question to you would be, in your various exchanges, did you ever have conversations that were really intimate rather than formal and functional?

RW: Once or twice we talked about the pressure of managing deeply divided communities and what it felt like to be abused from both sides. Because again, a little bit of vulnerability would come through there.

AGG: So the key really is vulnerability, or rather, lack thereof?

RW: Yeah, I think, you know, when the community was so very, very critical about the *Dignity of Difference*—that hurt him, I could see that, and he did talk to me a bit about that. And we would come back occasionally to that, as one of the things we shared. We were managing very diverse, very articulate, and sometimes quite angry, communities, who didn't particularly want to be kept together, who would look to us to exercise an authority we didn't structurally have, which had to be managed in different ways. And I think we both found it pretty draining. So we shared a bit about that. And I guess that was maybe one of the most significant bits of our relationship, when we were able to share that. Not very much, but it was there.

AGG: Did Jonathan ever ask you to pray for him?

RW: No.

AGG: What about spiritual sharing?

RW: Not very much. And it was partly that Jonathan's presentation of what he said was always fantastically illuminating, and transforming, very much at the level of ideas. And if I'd been asked: 'So what do you think makes him tick as a person of faith?' I would say: 'I wouldn't have that much insight.'

AGG: Did he ever seek to understand what makes you tick as a person of faith?

RW: I didn't sense that he wanted to explore that.

AGG: That's completely commensurate with what emerges from the writings. I'll tell you what I see there. I'm struck by the following facts. Jonathan had the image of someone who's engaged in interfaith dialogue. I don't believe he did, certainly not in a wholehearted way. In fact, he's on record for not believing in it. Which means he managed to 'trick' the whole world by virtue of his brilliance. What does it mean that he didn't engage in it? In eloquent, poetic, suggestive, sometimes almost mystical, feeling, he captures the sense of the parallel legitimacy of religions, the parallel covenants, the parallel ways of seeing God, etc., etc. So you would ask yourself: if so, when you come together with someone else, the natural thing is that you'd want to know: how does that person reach God? and learn from them. If this is pluralism, these multiple paths, it invites enrichment, and he talks about how we should be enriched. And yet there isn't a single instance or indication of being enriched by someone from another faith. There isn't a single reference to a deep relationship other than the fact that he did the Respect project with you,[1] which was basically an act of kindness that didn't engage in a deeper way. Or let's make the point another way. The man was an encyclopaedia. What didn't he know? Yet not once does he cite a spiritual authority from another tradition. Mind-boggling. He knew all the philosophers. He knew everything. There's no one in the history of Christianity you found inspiring? There's no one in the history of Islam you found inspiring? The only thing you have in his writings is systemic critique of Pauline Christianity as a fusion of the faith of Jesus and Hellenism, and the problems that creates, leading ultimately to a

---

[1] See *The Dignity of Difference*, p. viii.

critique of Christian exclusivism. You don't even once get the impression that anyone from another religion had made a serious dent in who he was as a person.

RW: That rings a bell. I didn't think he was very interested in Christianity.

AGG: I don't think he was interested in *any* other religion. He found himself in the position ex officio, and with his brilliance, he managed to adapt himself to it and to give, by his sheer brilliance, the impression that he was engaged in interfaith relations. So I face the following challenge. There are amazing statements about the beauty of appreciating someone from another religion. He provides some of the most powerful theoretical constructs that will allow us to move forward in relations between religions. His ideas are creative, original, deep, insightful, poetic. But then there is a body of evidence that totally belies it all, including his own testimony that he doesn't really believe in interfaith dialogue. So, I ask, what is one to make of it all? Two courses open up here. I can take the course that says he's a disciple of Rabbi Soloveitchik and continues his refusal to go theological. Because he's so brilliant, he covers it up. The alternative is that he has deep intuitions. He has a powerful religious imagination. He has the capacity to imagine a religious life that probably exceeds his own capacity to realize. He tells us what that is, but he never lives it and therefore can't model it. I prefer to show him in that weakness, because then his intuitions can be fulfilled by others, rather than showing him as an Orthodox apologist who just tricked the world.

RW: I know. I can't see him as an Orthodox apologist, up to trick. I can see him as somebody who's at unease with his own incompleteness, if you like, or his vulnerability holds him back in some ways.

AGG: So you consider that readiness to open up to the spirituality of another requires a vulnerability he wasn't able to master.

RW: Something of that sort. Yes.

AGG: Because your key term isn't openness, your key term is vulnerability, which is part of the same family, but it's a different emphasis.

RW: It *is* a different emphasis. Because it means an incompleteness that is felt as painful in some way, as a lack. And it consists of the possibility of just being wounded and then entering an encounter, rather than getting through it quickly and safely. I think Jonathan did feel the hurt of rejection and difficulty very much.

AGG: You're sitting at his Shabbat table. He's sharing his ideas. It's a moment for you to touch into this spiritual reality, and potentially to echo that. It is also a moment for him to receive the mirror image and to be enriched by your mirror image. Does that happen?

RW: I don't remember that happening in those terms. No.

AGG: So ultimately what you're saying, if I reframe it, is that Jonathan taught, but didn't share.

RW: Yes, I think one could put it that way.

AGG: Wow. But don't you think that an effective teacher has to be able to share?

RW: Oh, I think so. Yes.

AGG: So to what extent does this really impede his ultimate power to teach? Yet he was able to create the impression that he was sharing. And that probably got him a good long way. And probably most people won't need that depth of sharing.

RW: Yeah. And I think the other thing a teacher does is, in part, to create a world in language that others can come into and make the most of.

AGG: Beautiful.

RW: He does that, doesn't he?

AGG: He builds palaces for others to inhabit.

RW: Yeah, I think I'd sign up to that.

AGG: It's kind of sad, really, to have had all these opportunities. You know, I brought him to India for the third meeting of the Elijah Board of Religious Leaders. It was with the Dalai Lama. He encountered the Sikhs and was moved by their hospitality. Let me tell you that at that meeting he was absolutely a full participant. You wouldn't know that there were these issues. Because when you sit and talk ideas, there's no problem. It's that deeper dimension of engagement where one seems to hit up against blocks. Well, this totally confirms what I take away from the reading. And it also confirms your sense that I'm on the right track, namely, to acknowledge psychological limitations that would in turn allow others to inhabit the palaces he had created.

The issues go deeper. They go to the heart of the religious experience, which in turn conditions one's ability to relate to the religious experience of the other. When Jonathan talks about his experience of God, he effectively says that he doesn't have an experience of God; he only finds the experience of God in the traces of the goodness he sees in others. This goes to the core of religious experience and what can be shared about it. I will bet that if I spoke to you about your religious experience, you would tell me about your relationship with God, how you're experiencing the meaning of Jesus, compassion, humility, suffering, unification, theosis, something within that family that you've made your own. And I'll hear your personal experience there. You won't tell me, I don't know much about God, but I see the traces of God in other people. That's not going to be your answer.

RW: No, no, that's not.

AGG: What this means to me is that if someone describes their spiritual experience that way, they don't really have the tools to enter the religious experience of another. As a consequence of that, there ends up being a kind of devaluation of such sharing. To me, he makes some really poor arguments that involve putting down interfaith dialogue, saying: Well, you know, it's just for the elites and it really hasn't changed the world that much. So let's just do good service in our communities, as if that's what is going to change the world where dialogue has failed. I think behind it all is just the fear of someone who hasn't cultivated a certain part of themselves.

RW: I can recognize that.

AGG: In an essay on another friend of yours, Professor Akbar Ahmed, in the book *Interreligious Heroes* that I edited,[2] you use two phrases that seem relevant here. The first is 'cultivating a genuine philosophic curiosity about yourself and the other'. The second expression is 'philosophic curiosity and animation in reasoning and imagining alike will persuade

---

[2] Williams, 'Professor Akbar Ahmed'.

more and more to follow where his explorations have led'. Doesn't this describe what you found lacking—the philosophical curiosity and the animation and reasoning about the other? Sacks deals with the other and the theory of the other, yet he doesn't show any real curiosity about the other.

RW: I think that's right. And yes, that expresses in different words what I was trying to say in my opening statement when I referred to the face of the other turned towards God. This is a phrase I've often used in this connection. I feel I know it when I see it.

PART III

ENGAGING WITH GREENBERG AND SACKS

CHAPTER FIFTEEN

A Comparative Appreciation

T HROUGHOUT this study we have had numerous occasions to draw attention to parallels, as well as differences, between the two subjects of our analysis. Their image will have by now emerged in the reader's mind with a measure of clarity that allows us to recognize their distinctness. The present chapter attempts two things. The first is a discussion of their relationship and of the possible influence of one of the thinkers on the other, namely Greenberg's influence on Sacks. Regardless of how these suggestions are received, and of far greater importance, is the second task of the chapter—a comparative portrait of the two personalities. Having studied their thought in detail, we may now attempt a profile of both men and of their respective approaches to dialogue across religions. The importance of such comparison is twofold. By contrasting them, we can see each in clearer relief. But more importantly, these two important teachers provide distinct models for how relations between religions should be carried out and what possibilities have been articulated within Orthodoxy for engagement across religions. Bringing them first into contrast and then into dialogue allows us to reflect on the key subjects that engaged their attention and to advance the conversation. This comparative appreciation serves as the foundation for my own theological reflections in dialogue with the two figures. The order of what follows, then, is first an exploration of the direct impact of Greenberg on Sacks, followed by their comparative portrait. Finally, in the concluding chapter, I theologize in dialogue with Greenberg and Sacks in light of what has been put forth in this book and especially in this chapter.

Relational Complexity

Greenberg is the more senior of the thinkers. Sacks is aware of his work, cites it, and engages with it. In *Crisis and Covenant* he discusses Greenberg's theory of the stages of the covenant, and in particular his radical and novel notion

of the voluntary covenant.[1] He is unhappy with Greenberg's views, considering them an expression of secularity. Greenberg seeks to offer a sense of
unity to the Jewish people, despite lapsed observance. Sacks is appreciative
of this effort, but rejects his approach.[2] Contrary to Greenberg, he is not
willing to allow the Holocaust a defining role in Jewish faith. It is not the
Holocaust that has led to changes in Judaism and to its internal divisions
but rather various sociological movements, which have their origins in the
nineteenth century.[3]

What is at stake is the question of the boundaries of Jewish legitimacy.
Greenberg's theology legitimates the different denominations and sees them
as necessary and justified responses to historical events. Sacks cannot accept
such legitimation and therefore rejects Greenberg's views. As Darren Kleinberg states, Sacks sees Greenberg as being beyond Orthodoxy.[4]

The plot thickens when we consider the personal relations between the
two. Sacks the philosopher is appreciative of Greenberg the thinker. We
know that because Sacks invited Greenberg to speak at Marble Arch syna-
gogue, where he was rabbi. But he then rescinded an invitation to Greenberg to speak at a conference on the future of Orthodoxy under pressure
from a faculty member of Yeshiva University.[5] Here we have two perspectives, reflecting a complexity in Sacks' approach to Greenberg. On the one
hand, respect for a thinker and a senior in the field. On the other, establishing distance and not following through on the promise of a relationship.
Greenberg reflects on this incident in *Living in the Image of God*.[6] He understands Sacks as having acted out of political calculations. Such calculations
would be needed because of the reservations within Orthodox circles towards Greenberg, who was seen as having gone too far in his thinking.
Sacks, operating as part of religious officialdom, had to balance his personal
and philosophical interests with communal propriety and risk-taking.
His relationship with Greenberg was the casualty. Greenberg is remarkably
gracious in accepting this reality.

However, more may be at stake than Sacks' standing within the Jewish
community and potential boundary-crossing. The differences apparently go

---

[1] pp. 127–31. See already *Tradition in an Untraditional Age*, 114–15.
[2] *One People?*, 37. See also Tirosh-Samuelson and Hughes (eds.), *Jonathan Sacks: Universalizing Particularity*, 125.   [3] *One People?*, 138. See further p. 8.
[4] Kleinberg, 'For and Against: A Consideration of David Hartman and Jonathan Sacks',
178.   [5] Ibid.   [6] Freedman, *Living in the Image of God*, 150.

to the heart of Sacks' own thought, leading him to take a strong stance contra Greenberg. Ideologically, Greenberg occupies a position that Sacks is strongly opposed to and from which he needs to distance himself.

At the heart of their difference lies the question of internal Jewish pluralism—that is, affirmation of the equal legitimacy of different streams within Judaism. Sacks, as we have learned, is an opponent of this approach, and adopts, instead, a view that he describes as inclusivist, making room for individuals and communities—in other words, accepting them in practice as part of the broader community, while not acknowledging their theoretical and ideological validity. Greenberg, by contrast, is a declared pluralist, not only in relation to other faiths, but also internally. This is one of the theological conclusions he draws from the Holocaust and which is at the heart of his idea that we now live a voluntary covenant with God. Within that voluntariness there is room for many forms of Judaism. This is the crux of the disagreement.

The question is not theoretical. To accept a position that sanctions multiple Judaisms is to cross the line in terms of the politics of Jewish Orthodoxy. Greenberg has been willing to cross that line. Sacks always took care not to do that, so that his voice continues to speak for Orthodoxy. Indeed, where Greenberg underwent rejection and paid a price for his opinions, Sacks' felt need to maintain a representative position was of greater importance, leading to the eventual revision of *The Dignity of Difference*. We can now see why he would feel that he needed to distance himself from Greenberg publicly.

Sacks describes his reservations regarding Greenberg on principled, rather than simply political, grounds. Greenberg undermines the foundations of religious certainty, which makes him worse than Reform.[7] His quest for unity is therefore a secularized quest. Whereas Greenberg applies the same philosophical approach throughout, both within Judaism and in relation to other faiths,[8] Sacks only affirms pluralism towards other faiths, while guarding religious certainty against the relativism of internal pluralism. He is explicit that the view he has presented in *One People?*, and which sets the limits of Jewish pluralism, is intended against views such as Greenberg's.[9]

This background is important for a consideration of the relationship

---

[7] *One People?*, 38.

[8] In his introduction to *Yitz Greenberg and Modern Orthodoxy*, 17, Greenberg describes his movement from Jewish–Christian dialogue to internal pluralism.

[9] Tirosh-Samuelson and Hughes (eds.), *Jonathan Sacks: Universalizing Particularity*, 125.

between Greenberg and Sacks in their views of interreligious pluralism. Both declare themselves to be pluralists. A closer look suggests that key arguments are repeated, raising the possibility that one has influenced the other. The direction of influence would have to be from Greenberg to Sacks, since he published in this area long before Sacks did, and his works were known to Sacks. Given Sacks' familiarity with Greenberg, the possibility that his thought was shaped by the latter's religious pluralism seems very likely. The following discussion will put more flesh on this suggestion. Sacks' overall reluctance to be associated with Greenberg renders this recognition important in two ways. It is important because it raises the possibility that, despite his reservations on other fronts, he was nevertheless deeply influenced by Greenberg in his views of other faiths. Secondly, it is important because it helps us account for the fact the Sacks never cites Greenberg on other faiths. He is basically a very generous author, who is happy to acknowledge his sources and demonstrate the vastness of his erudition. If he fails to cite someone, there must be a reason. If, indeed, Greenberg is a theological *persona non grata*, then Sacks' standing and argument would not gain much by reference to Greenberg. Hence the silence when echoing his ideas.[10]

Reliance

While it is not a common perception that Sacks' views on religions echo those of Greenberg, I am not the first to make the suggestion.[11] One must, however, distinguish between echoes and wholesale adoption. Sacks does not simply carry over Greenberg's ideas. He takes key insights and incorporates them into his own thought structures, making the dependence less intense, and thereby also making the lack of reference more acceptable. We have seen throughout how Sacks casts ideas in new contexts. The same is true for what I suggest is his reliance on Greenberg. A core insight is taken up, internalized, assimilated, made his own, and then applied in various other contexts. While maintaining a resemblance to the original, these remoulded ideas nevertheless stand on their own.

    Before looking at the details of what these two authors share in com-

---

[10] In *Crisis and Covenant* Sacks discusses various thinkers, including non-Orthodox figures such as Eugene Borowitz and Richard L. Rubenstein, with whom he disagrees. The point is not whether a certain thinker is cited. It is, rather, whether Sacks is dependent in important ways on someone whom he rejects on fundamental grounds on a related theme.

[11] See Jotkowitz, 'Universalism and Particularism', 58.

mon, it is useful to identify a common fundamental approach. A classical approach to other religions focuses on truth, which serves as a significant yardstick in pronouncing their status as true or false. Both authors cast aside concerns of truth. To speak of covenant and to ground a view of other religions in a covenantal perspective is to change perspectives from a focus on truth value to the consideration of a religion in narrative terms. Both authors give greater weight to narrative, and to the grounding of the relationship with God in narrative, than they do to abstract questions of religious truth. Perhaps in this they share a postmodern sensibility. More likely, however, is the suggestion that this is an outcome of a common covenantal perspective—a necessary outcome of the theological application of a category that is essentially grounded in narrative.

Let us now consider the key argument common to Greenberg and Sacks.[12] The fundamental structures by means of which they relate to other religions are either very similar or identical. At their heart is the notion of covenant. For religion to be significant, it must be covenantal. Religion as covenant has two distinct expressions, one universal and one particular. The universal expression is exemplified by the covenant with Noah, and the particular by the covenant with Abraham or by its extension at Sinai. The covenant with Noah is not simply the promise not to destroy the world, along with the attendant commandments not to destroy human life. It is, rather, understood in line with the rabbinic concept of the seven Noahide commandments. Thus, the content of the Noahide covenant is the Noahide commandments. These are not understood simply as the moral foundations for humanity but as the foundations of religion. Accordingly, the substance of the Noahide commandments is abstracted into principles that lend it broader religious significance. The entire structure relates not only to Judaism and humanity, but more particularly to Judaism and world religions. The dual covenant and the reading of the covenant with Noah are a basis for recognizing religions in their particularity. In view of this dual structure, a fundamental shift occurs as compared with earlier rabbinic reference to the Noahide commandments. Previously, the Noahide commandments described the moral responsibility of non-Jews, while the covenant

---

[12] There are secondary instances of possible dependence. See the reference to Amos 9: 7, where God rescues others, not only Israel from Egypt. Compare *Not in God's Name*, 210 and *For the Sake of Heaven and Earth*, 57. Both the verse in Amos and the verse in Isaiah, discussed by Sacks, have been employed previously in the same context by Greenberg. Of course, both thinkers may have been impacted by the biblical verses directly.

with Abraham described Jewish faith. In the new reading, both covenants apply *both* to Jews and to members of other religions. The covenant with Abraham is not balanced by a universal code of ethics. It is, instead, the paradigm that all religions follow. All religions find themselves partaking of a dual commitment. On the one hand, they are informed by the universal foundations of the Noahide commandments; on the other, they gain their full identity in the framework of the particular covenant represented and modelled, but by no means limited to, the Abrahamic covenant. The covenant with Abraham is thus not a Jewish prerogative. It is Judaism's lesson of particularity that applies to all faiths. All faiths share in this dual structure.

This entire set of ideas, each building upon the other, is original and unique and not part of inherited tradition.[13] And it appears in the works of both authors. The similarity is too striking to be accidental and too far removed from scriptural evidence to be explained as the 'simple' reading of Scripture. If so, Sacks has taken up the key structure that Greenberg had developed in support of religious pluralism. This does not mean that he has fully copied it, nor that his emphases are identical to Greenberg's. For example, the idea that all religions are sub-covenants of the Noahide one is not found in Sacks. He is not really interested in providing a precise definition for the covenantal status of other religions. His concern is the relationship between universality and particularity and it is that aspect of the larger construct that he amplifies and transforms in his teachings. Because he is more interested in justifying particularity than in defining the covenantal status of other faiths, he can let go or draw less extensively upon that claim as his

---

[13] The only person I have found who has put forth a similar structure is Jon Levenson ('The Universal Horizon of Biblical Particularism', 147–8). I have suggested to Levenson, in communication, that consciously or unconsciously he was inspired by Greenberg. He denies that, claiming that he had not read Greenberg when he began thinking about these issues. To him, matters are so clear that the insight does not require some precise historical origin. I find it striking that such a detailed series of parallels should arise spontaneously between different authors, with no dependence between them. The fact is that these associations did not emerge among earlier interpreters or in social settings other than the English-speaking Orthodox world. If the idea has become commonplace to the point that we cannot trace where Levenson, and by extension also Sacks, may have received it from, it is still worth searching for its earliest occurrence. To me, Greenberg still seems the best candidate as originator of this set of ideas. Note, for example, that David Novak, who shares many ideas with Greenberg, never speaks of the Noahide commandments as the Noahide covenant. See Novak, *The Image of the Non-Jew in Judaism*. This suggests that the idea was not so obvious as to seem apparent to him.

ideas are reworked, first in the revision of *The Dignity of Difference* and then in later books, where the covenantal status of other faiths is downplayed.

There is one further significant parallel between Sacks and Greenberg. Both, at various points, associate covenant and creation by grounding the former in the latter. This too is not a standard view within Jewish theology, and suggests further the dependence of one thinker on the other. Closely related to this is the association of covenant and the image of God. This association is not surprising, given that the covenant with Noah makes explicit reference, one of only two biblical references, to the creation of man in the image of God. For both authors, the image of God is not simply an idea but a governing notion that orients and shapes the covenant and its purposes.[14] While this shared recognition of the centrality of the image of God could have been attained independently, it is closely linked to the concept of the covenant and is therefore likely part of one complex of ideas.

If we follow the suggestion that the basic structure in Sacks' and Greenberg's interreligious theory is one, we may also consider where they differ and where Sacks could be of benefit to Greenberg. Greenberg assumes all religions are sub-covenants of the Noahide one. In theory, that affords all religions equal status. However, he is not content with creating a pluralistic covenantal view of other religions. He goes on to expand Israel's covenant to others, be it Abraham's covenant or the covenant at Sinai, in an attempt to affirm and accommodate Christian self-understanding. I believe this move has worked against him and is one possible cause for his ideas not achieving the broad recognition he deserves. In a sense, his ecumenical good-will has exceeded the strength of its theological foundations, pushing the covenant of particularity into the domain of universality, thereby upsetting the natural 'ecology' of his own dual covenant theory. It seems to me here Sacks holds the factors in better balance. Precisely because he does not seek to make room for a particular religion but to affirm the very dyad of universal and particular, he keeps the balance between the universal/Noahide and particular/Abrahamic covenants in clear focus. One does not encroach upon the other. As a consequence, it is not only that all covenants have a share in the Noahide one, as Greenberg argues, but all covenants are modelled on the Abrahamic one, a point that Greenberg does not make. The Abrahamic covenant is indeed relevant to others, not only to one particular faith, Christianity, which seeks to position itself within the Abrahamic covenant.

[14] See e.g. *The Dignity of Difference*, 172.

It is relevant to *all* faiths that model themselves on the particularity of the Abrahamic covenant and the balance it strikes in relation to the universal Noahide covenant.[15]

That being recognized, it is fascinating to point out that while Sacks' theory keeps Abraham's covenant to the Jews, in his later work he ends up doing something quite similar to what Greenberg has done. Greenberg has given others a share in the covenant of Abraham. As Sacks develops his view of Abrahamic monotheisms and of Judaism being one in a family of religions, in his own way he too affirms that whatever is represented by Abraham is opened up and recognized as valid to members of other faiths. While this is not the covenant of Abraham, it is his faith, and his entire spiritual way of being.[16]

Sacks and Greenberg: A Comparison

Moving on from the possibility of direct influence, let us now gain perspective on both individuals by means of a comparison. Throughout, we have seen how they operate, what their respective emphases are, and ultimately what drives each of them. When various insights combine, a fuller image of the individuals and their differences emerges. Here is what I see as I consider these two thinkers.

I would like to begin with the question of personal relationships, Greenberg's starting point. He makes clear how he is dependent on formative relationships and what role and impact some outstanding individuals have had on him. None of this is found in Sacks. We do not encounter a single interreligious friend, beyond the universal or general friendships that he has established with religious leaders of his league. Greenberg is transformed by the relationships he has, and his entire theology is, to a large extent, an attempt to make sense of the individuals he has met, their spiritual lives, and their impact upon him. Sacks, by contrast, is a theoretician of dialogue and a theoretician of relationships, though relationships per se do not seem to be anywhere near as central for him as they are for Greenberg. Naturally, inas-

---

[15] Application of this dyadic structure is an interpretative move made from the Jewish perspective that is put forth by Sacks. It does not depend on the self-understanding of the different faiths, that is, they need not consciously appeal to either covenant. From this perspective, the differences between the two versions of *The Dignity of Difference* are irrelevant. Both allow Sacks to make the same move.

[16] At times, this too is referred to as covenant. See *Not in God's Name*, 277.

much as a theory of dialogue is not built on specific relational foundations, it may be lacking. Ultimately, Sacks' rejection of a Buberian model of dialogue cannot be divorced from the lack of formative relationships in the development of his interreligious thought.

If Greenberg's thought is the fruit of encounter, Sacks' thought is an answer to the need to formulate a theory of coexistence that will allow different groups to live peacefully alongside one another in one common society, or in the world we share. As a consequence, Sacks' particularity lacks particularity. He develops a theory that makes room for the particular, but other than lists of specific faith leaders with whom he has met or collaborated by virtue of his office, there is no specific other in his thinking. In fact, we have no sign of him engaging in interreligious relations prior to having assumed office.[17] Greenberg thinks through the meaning of one particular relationship—that of Judaism with Christianity. His particularity is particular, so to speak. Sacks does not begin with relationships; he begins with a problem—a global, moral, societal problem that needs to be solved with the help of religious thought. His particularity thus derives from the abstract 'other' rather than from concrete relationships. Put differently, if Sacks is concerned with the problem of 'the other', Greenberg's trajectory is defined by relationships with 'a significant other'.

Here is another way of putting it: Greenberg cultivates personal relations, which leads him to redefine the relations between religions. Sacks explores the need to live with the other, which leads to a theory of interreligious relations. The centrality of the person and his testimony is the key to Greenberg's journey. As he tells the story, it is because of the moral example and spiritual testimony of certain Christians that he enters an exploration of Christianity, the faith that could shape those people. The logic also accounts for his internal Jewish pluralism. Having been inspired by certain individuals, notably Jakob Petuchowski,[18] he is driven to consider how he can validate their Judaism. The fine example is the driver behind new thinking regarding a group that had previously been cast aside. Perhaps this is what the image of God means for Greenberg. The power of religious example and how the spiritual life comes to expression in the life of the person are central to him. This could be a very concrete way of realizing the ideal of the image of God. Significantly, when Sacks speaks of his encounter with

---

[17] Sacks' essay in *Faith in the Future* was written before he took office, but it does not mention any particular relationship.   [18] See Ch. 6 above.

people of other faiths, it is in their good actions and personal character that he knows them to be fine, and it is in the encounter with them that he finds the touch of God.

In terms of the two thinkers representing different spiritual personality types, the following distinction may be true. Sacks is a man of religion. He defends his faith, he is creative with it, he seeks to deliver its message to new audiences, and even to expand that message. One does not get a sense of his own personal transformation in the process as much as the sense that he is a voice, a representative, a teacher of his faith. Greenberg is also a teacher. But he emerges as someone more open to transformation, to changes in his outlook, and more receptive to new encounters, new spiritual and human realities. Put differently, he is a spiritual seeker striving to expand his faith and its boundaries even as he is transformed. Sacks' aim, by contrast, is to furnish his community, his tradition, and the world with the ideas that will help them grow, without implicating himself in the same way. This may be one way in which he is able to toe the line of rabbinic officialdom and to keep his message, even if transformative, within traditional boundaries, or, if the need arises, adaptable to these boundaries. At the end of the day, he does not share the outcomes of a personal process; he offers the teaching the moment and the situation call for.

Greenberg is a theologian. He examines the religious ideas of the other and seeks to understand them from within his theological framework. Sacks is not a theologian. He is a social philosopher, an educator. He builds on Scripture and a traditional body of teachings to deliver a message that will serve society and the common good. If he is not theologically inclined, this could be one explanation for why he never engages with the substance and ideas of other religions. It is simply not his vocation.

All these differences add up to the following characterization. Sacks' goal is interfaith harmony; Greenberg's is interfaith *understanding*. Sacks works towards increasing social harmony and reducing violence in the name of religion. This does not require a deep understanding of the other. It requires developing a teaching that would achieve these ends. Even where he criticizes other faiths, notably their idea of the universality of their own teaching, he does so for the sake of harmony. Interfaith relations are, at the end of the day, instrumental to peace and harmony. Sacks does contribute to the validation of other faiths, but neither the faiths nor their validation are his true concern. Rather, it is the social harmony that ensues after all are recognized as legitimate. His theory of the universal and the particular is a way of making space for everyone, so that there is harmony in the ensemble. He is a theoretician of the *space* of religions, not of their own teachings.

Greenberg is much more interested in understanding the religious other in detail. He seeks to advance a particular relationship and grow in understanding in it. If Sacks' task is social, I do not think the same can be said of Greenberg. His engagement with other religions grows out of a specific historical context, but is not designed to solve a social problem. Understanding and encounter become goals in and of themselves.[19] Understanding also produces growth, something which Greenberg measures in terms of responsibility and autonomy in the framework of the covenant. His vision is thus not static. On the contrary, it is informed by the dynamism of growth. This growth passes through stages of encounter and understanding as faith traditions are transformed in dialogue.

It is not superfluous to mention once again the understanding of interfaith engagement that is characteristic of Rabbi Soloveitchik. Greenberg was his student, and for years a very close student. In addition to having studied with him in New York, they were particularly close when Greenberg served as a rabbi in Boston.[20] Sacks relies much on Soloveitchik, but was never a close student, even if Soloveitchik was one of the personalities who impressed him during his spiritual quest and pointed him the way forward. Greenberg makes a clean break with Soloveitchik on issues of interreligious dialogue. The subject was raised explicitly in their conversations.[21] Greenberg was after a deeper and more personal dialogue than Soloveitchik had recommended. Sacks, by contrast, cites Soloveitchik as providing the guidelines for dialogue. His own avoidance of theological engagement, while it may not be based exclusively on Soloveitchik, conforms with the latter's orientation, whatever its cause. Soloveitchik too is after interfaith harmony. His recommendation for moral engagement across religions and for contributing jointly to society is a kind of vision that prefers harmony over understanding.

Sacks' task is civic. It focuses on the contribution of religions to society. The more this emerges as the focus of his thought, the less need there is for religions to be in close encounter, let alone to explore their respective

---

[19] By way of illustration: whereas Sacks' corpus has multiple references to peace in the context of interfaith relations, there are only two references to peace between Jews and Christians in Greenberg's writing.   [20] See Ch. 6 above.   [21] Ibid.

religious understandings. As we have seen with reference to the idea of the covenant, Sacks' thought is largely horizontal, concerned with welfare within society and with how religions can contribute to society's well-being. Greenberg's approach is much more vertical. He wants to know what it is about the religious experience of others that shapes them. Though the social impact of relations with other faiths matters to him, he is also interested in the religious ideals that drive them and that shape the individuals he encounters.[22]

Both authors can be understood as continuing the classical Jewish practices of theology of religions and advancing a view of other faiths based on the fundamental question of their validity. At the same time, both go beyond this concern for validity, in different ways. Greenberg poses the question of what religion means for its faithful, how it changes their lives, and what value certain teachings have for those who hold them. It is not only the religion that is validated; specific religious teachings, which, from a validity perspective, notably from a Meiri perspective, would have been left unaddressed, are examined for their meaning for and impact on the lives of believers. Because of this emphasis, Greenberg can also ask what we can learn from the faith of the other. He takes the fundamental starting point further within the framework of a particular relationship—that with Christianity—and affords special status to that relationship in covenantal terms. One may therefore say that his processes of validation are relational. Sacks takes the ideas that confer validity and uses them in a social context to solve a social problem. The ideas of a Jewish theology of religions and the building blocks by means of which other religions are validated serve a social theory that is the core of his concerns. Seen in this way, of the two, only Greenberg engages in interreligious dialogue *lishmah* (for its own sake).

In a lecture given at Domus Galilaeae during a gathering of Christians and Jews in 2015, Greenberg put forth his vision for the relations between the two faiths. His vision had four components: taking responsibility for one another, learning together, common projects, and common witness. This is an interesting programme, coming from a veteran of Jewish–Christian relations. Let us consider what parts of this programme correspond to Sacks' vision. Certainly, taking responsibility for one another is a major aspect of

---

[22] Might this difference account for Sacks' willingness to rescind his views under pressure, while Greenberg underwent great tribulations when he refused to step back from his ideas? See Greenberg, 'Modern Orthodoxy and the Road Not Taken', 25–7, 33–6, 39–42.

his interfaith engagement. This is what he has sought to achieve through his relationships with the leaders of other faiths. One notable instance is his attitude to antisemitism, which is based on the recognition that we are not alone and that others can help us in this battle, just as we care for them.[23] The idea of common projects is, of course, Sacks' side-by-side collaboration. Greenberg's common witness is not articulated in this way by Sacks, but it seems to underlie the very fundamental assumption that religions can contribute to society.

The one element that is particular to Greenberg and that Sacks would likely downplay is learning together. Of course, Sacks speaks often enough of learning from each other. His preface to the volume of Jewish–Christian studies shows that he is more than capable of endorsing this ideal. Yet I believe it is not central to him and certainly not in the way it is for Greenberg. Greenberg goes on to explain what he has in mind. It goes to the heart of theological understanding, where the most important issues are tackled. It touches on questions of whether the messiah has arrived, whether redemption has come, and more. He is informed by a subtle view of ideas, requiring balances, being realized through dialectical processes, and ultimately in need of self-correction. There is a need for more than one covenanted community because otherwise ideas will be understood wrongly with the passage of time. Each community provides a means of correcting the other. But this requires dialogue and mutual study. The process is reciprocal. Sacks never suggests a reciprocal process for the growth or self-correction of a faith. His transmission is largely in one direction, his own sharing of his or Judaism's wisdom with others. For Greenberg, issues such as the balance of individual and collective, self-sacrifice and validating one's humanity, the balance of social justice and hope, of spirit and law, are all examples of balances that must be found and for which both communities, and their processes of mutual engagement in the interest of self-correction, are required. While Sacks is the first to admit to the many faults of Judaism, he never conceptualizes the need for multiple religions as a form of mutual self-correction. I believe this mutual self-correction is largely made possible not only by Greenberg's experience but by his primarily theological emphasis.

This goes to the heart of pluralism. For Sacks, pluralism serves the needs of an existing human diversity. Many religions are needed to suit different

---

[23] *Future Tense*, 18.

temperaments. But each religion is kept apart, distinct from the other. Together they jointly sing God's glory. For Greenberg, pluralism is needed for each of the religions. Only thus can their self-correcting purposes be served. It is not only that Christians need Christians or God needs Christians. Jews too need Christians.

The difference in orientation also accounts for one problematic element we saw in Sacks' work. He makes statements regarding other religions that turn out to be misinformed or expressive of stereotypes. Further study of those religions will reveal that, of the little that Sacks says regarding them, a meaningful part, including his core thesis of exclusivist teachings taught by other faiths, is either incorrect or lacking in nuance. His process does not take him through the actual study of other religions. He can talk about them but has never been deeply exposed to them, most of his knowledge being very general or such that a simple online search might reveal. Greenberg has taken time to think deeply about the particularities of the Christian faith. Clearly, he has not explored all forms of Christianity, nor all key faith tenets, but he has created an approach where thinking of another religion requires study and depth of engagement. This approach is important because it cannot be taken for granted; Sacks is the proof for that, and he is representative of broad Jewish conventions that Greenberg seeks to change. Greenberg, I believe, offers proof by example for the need to engage in serious study of another religion as part of theologizing, and even as part of advancing interfaith relations.[24]

---

[24] Greenberg himself doesn't always live up to this standard. His preference for certain Christologies that he considers more compatible with a Jewish view than others is a case in point. At the same time, one must ask at what point the critique of ideas and reservations expressed towards another faith can be given voice within a serious dialogue between religions. On this, see my interview with Greenberg, Ch. 6 above.

CHAPTER SIXTEEN

Jewish Theology of Religions: Continuing the Conversation

T HE PREVIOUS CHAPTER presented us with two close, interrelated, and yet distinct approaches to world religions. Sacks and Greenberg are at the forefront of consistent public engagement with other religions, spanning a range that extends from the official to the academic, from the practical to the reflective, from the human to the theological. Each has made a significant contribution to advancing Jewish relations with other faiths as well as to a Jewish theology of religions. The final chapter in this book is devoted to my own reflections as these emerge in dialogue with and in response to the thought of both teachers. How do I, as a thinker who cares passionately about Jewish relations with and views of world religions, see their teachings? Am I able to embrace one or the other? What would I take from one or the other? Where do I believe we must go beyond what they have offered and how can we build on the foundations laid by them as we advance reflection? I read these two thinkers as new voices that are built on foundations provided by the tradition, and these voices are in turn approached as foundations for further reflection.

I begin by looking at some key concepts that emerge from the work of both authors, and make suggestions for how I think they might best be restated in the service of a Jewish theology of religions. From there I move on to issues of method and attitude—what is the orientation and what are the processes that should be applied as we continue to march on the road to better understanding between religions and better relations between practitioners and theologians of diverse religions?

Covenant

When it comes to concepts, we must begin with covenant, one key idea that is common to both thinkers. It is the major contribution of their thought, and provides the focus of the present book—to develop a Jewish view of other religions upon covenantal foundations. This is also their great innovation—or, as suggested, of Greenberg's thought, which Sacks developed in his own way—and is, it seems to me, of enormous significance from the perspective of how to do Jewish theology. Covenant is central to Jewish thought. It serves as a foundation for Jewish religious life and orients all religious reflection. Extending the covenant to relations between religions means tying this concern to the heart of Jewish theology. Other religions are viewed from that core and not simply through the application of legal constructs that would permit associating with them. A theological concern with other faiths thus emerges as part and parcel of Jewish thought, and not as something on its margins. Other religions are viewed from within Judaism's most formative category and as an outcome of a drive that is inherent to it.

To appreciate the value of the covenant in this particular theological context, we should compare its uses to those of 'truth'. The latter is a classical theme of theology of religions, where all too often one's own faith is identified as truth, while the other's represents falsehood or at best a partial truth. To talk of covenant is to shift attention away from truth. This is made amply clear by Sacks. He has posited covenant, and more broadly narrative, as alternatives to truth, which he identifies as universal, informed by Plato's ghost. To say we have a covenant with God is to affirm a relationship, not an abstract truth. And for this very reason it is possible to portray another religion as having a covenantal relationship with God, thereby sidestepping the problem of religious truth.[1] Covenant is thus fundamentally suited to an accommodating approach that sees other religions as similarly being in relationship with God.

To think of multiple relationships is, in the first instance, to think of multiple relational partners. This leads us to ask who God's relational partner is when it comes to Judaism. Surely, it is not Judaism that has a covenant with God. It is Israel. In fact, herein lies one further distinction between truth and covenant. These two correspond to Judaism and Israel. To speak of Judaism could (though it need not) lead to reflection on its truth value. To speak of Israel keeps our focus on the story of the people. Thus, organizing theology, and theology of religions, around covenant forces us to consider

---

[1] On narrative as an alternative to truth, see Goshen-Gottstein, 'Towards a Jewish Theology of World Religions', 4–5. On the entire problem of religious truth, see id. (ed.), *Religious Truth*.

what the unit of reflection is. Are we giving an account of Judaism, an 'ism' among many other religions, or are we telling the story of the particular relationship of one people to God and of how it has shaped that people's religious life? The distinction has not been adequately made in previous works of theology of religions. I believe it has the possibility of redefining much of the field.[2]

There is a potential concern that describing other religions, and even *all* religions, as Sacks does, as covenants might take away from Israel's uniqueness. The analogy that is often used of covenant as marriage is only partly helpful. The metaphor suggests that in the same way that one's love for one's wife is not diminished by another man's love for his, so we must make room for other faiths and their relationship with God.[3] The problem with this analogy is that we are dealing with the same husband. Applying the metaphor to God means we are portraying him in polygamous terms, affirming the equal validity of all of his marriages. I do not find this an appealing way of addressing the problem of multiple religions and their respective relationships with God. Taking the marriage metaphor further, one realizes that, to a large extent, the institution is greater than those who enter it. Husband and wife are roles that are filled by all couples in the world. From an institutional perspective the roles of husband and wife are more important than the subjective realities of husband and wife and their sense of particularity and uniqueness. There must, therefore, be a better way of relating to the idea of multiple covenants with the one God. If the marriage metaphor cannot successfully carry the burden of multiple covenantal relationships with God, either conceptually or in terms of reasonable appeal to biblical sources, another metaphor should be sought out that could achieve the same goals.

One way in which we may rethink covenant in an interreligious context is not by focusing on the very foundations of the relationship, as the marriage

---

[2] One thinker who is particularly relevant to exploring further this distinction is Rav Kook, whose theology is mostly constructed around Israel, rather than around Judaism. This also impacts his own theology of religions.

[3] Greenberg does not use the metaphor. Sacks does. It is, for him, the fundamental biblical image for the relationship with God. See *Radical Then, Radical Now*, 82 and 86. Sacks also applies the marriage metaphor in relation to the concerns of pluralism and other religions. See *Faith in the Future*, 121. However, these two applications are never juxtaposed. Consequently, the problematic inherent in the marriage metaphor for the covenant, in terms of its meaning for other religions, is never brought to light.

metaphor suggests, but by seeing the multiple covenants as achieving different divine tasks and purposes. The metaphor for this would be God as king and his covenantal partners as the various nations or ministers who fulfil his designs. There are, accordingly, different purposes and parameters for each relationship. God enters into covenant, or forms a bond, for specific purposes, which may differ from one religion to another. We do not know what these purposes are any more than we know why God created the great diversity found in the world, to return to Sacks' biological analogy. However, the variety within religions would, in this understanding, be more than the same message adapted to different audiences. Commonalities between religions attest to the one God and the fundamentals of the covenant. Discrepancies and variations reflect not only the differences between God's relational partners but the very purpose, intention, and goal that God has in mind in forming different relations and different religions.

The Image of God

There is a second notion that is central to the thought of both Greenberg and Sacks, and which is to a large extent identified by them with the covenant and its message—man being created in God's image. We have evoked Meiri in the course of analysing the writings of both Greenberg and Sacks. Meiri provides a theory for validating religions that ensure the moral ordering of society. His theory is developed as part of a philosophical discourse, and does not overtly rely on Jewish sources. Some have suggested that Meiri is simply presenting the Noahide commandments in another form.[4] I find this reading unlikely. However, it seems to me that it is possible to view Meiri in the light of the notion of the image of God, even if his theory was not directly derived from it. A morally ordered society is one that respects the human person as the image of God. That the biblical prohibition on murder, articulated as part of the covenant with Noah in Genesis 9, is justified by appeal to that idea opens up the possibility that the fuller set of proper moral behaviour that Meiri considers to be constitutive of religion can similarly be understood as a guarantor of proper respect for and treatment of the image of God.

The idea of the image of God, to use a shorthand form, in the hands of Greenberg and Sacks, does some of the same work that covenant does.

---

[4] Novak, *The Image of the Non-Jew in Judaism*, 195.

It moves the discussion from absolute truth and its attainment or realization to the human person, in whom the true test and possibly even the purpose of religion lies. I believe the concept has a potential for a Jewish theology of religions that has not yet been tapped. The two thinkers apply it in the sense of the value and dignity of the human person, emphasizing the religious other. Especially in Sacks' writing, concern for the religious other redefines the interreligious arena, replacing the classical emphasis on the particularity of faith and its practices. It seems to me that deepening reflection on the image of God can open up new avenues in the appreciation of religion itself, its teaching and practices.

The image of God is one way of bridging unity and diversity. Sacks cites in several places the talmudic teaching that the image of God is plural.[5] Whereas a human king places the same image on all coins minted in his name, God places his image on every person, yet each one is different. God's image, then, is one, while it is also many. It seems to me that this sense of unity in diversity that the concept makes possible can be extended from the human dimension to religions themselves. Rather than developing a theology of religions whose fruit is the affirmation of the image of God, we may think of the image of God as key to understanding religions and their diversity. Religious experience, and a religion's understanding of the human person and the transformations he undergoes as part of the spiritual life, are all expressions of the image of God. It thus includes not only the common view of the human person but also his spiritual potential, which finds expression in diverse religions, the experiences of believers, and their spiritual processes. Thus, if we take seriously the notion of the image of God, we are called to a deeper appreciation of the religious and spiritual life, rather than turning our attention from the religious to the human domain.

From another angle, we might regard 'flourishing' as the goal of life, and of religion and its teachings. What flourishing means and how religions bring it about can again be understood in relation to the image of God.[6] Religions, in this reading, cultivate and bring to light the fullness of human potential that the image of God means. If we fail to take into account this potential, we are short-changing the very meaning of the image of God concept.

---

[5] See e.g. *Not in God's Name*, 214.

[6] I have explored this in Rav Kook's thought; see Goshen-Gottstein, 'The Theory of Five Forces'.

One important application of a robust understanding of the image of God is considering religious virtuosi—saints, great teachers, mystics, prophets, and individuals whom I have called religious geniuses.[7] These individuals are not simply religious 'types' to be studied sociologically. They are examples of the perfection that religion can lead to and of how, through deeply engaged religious practice, the human person is transformed, realizing fuller aspects of the image of God. If we take seriously that notion, then in fact we are invited to the study of the finest exemplars of the religious life. Complementing the emphasis on the image of God as a category that confers value upon *every* person, regardless of circumstances such as religious difference, is its possible application to the appreciation of those fine exemplars of a humanity that has advanced into profound and elevated relationship with God within the particularity of a given religious tradition. If we recall the uses of the notion of the image of God in the Eastern Christian tradition, to the point of deification, or attaining *theosis*, the process of entry to and union in divinity, we realize how far-reaching its implications are for appreciating religion and its ideals.[8]

Problematizing the Two-Covenant Construct

Greenberg and Sacks share a two-covenant construct. The covenant with Noah is common to all religions and provides the basis for universality. Particularity is attained by means of the later covenants with Abraham and at Sinai. Covenant is thus used to establish a balance between universality and particularity. While Greenberg consistently appeals to both covenants in the context of religions, Sacks, in some works, refers to the one with Noah in religious terms, while in others he highlights the moral dimension. Indeed, the covenant with Noah has more to do with morality than it does with religion. Even though it includes prohibitions on idolatry and blasphemy, it lacks any positive element that would allow it to function as religion in a fuller sense.[9] The classical application of the Noahide commandments as Judaism's message to humanity suffers from this fundamental weakness. It offers a moral vision, but does not provide a religious path. Therefore, to build on it, especially as it is identified by both authors with the rabbinic

[7]   See Goshen-Gottstein, *Religious Genius*.

[8]   See Thunberg, 'The Human Person as Image of God', esp. p. 308.

[9]   On attempts to infuse the Noahide commandments with positive meaning, see Goshen-Gottstein, *In God's Presence*, ch. 3.

Noahide commandments, in fact fails to deliver a proper religious foundation to humanity. The problem is to a certain extent mitigated if all religions
are understood as a balance between their Noahide universal foundation and
the particularity that is analogous to the covenant with Abraham. Nevertheless, both authors, at least at some point in their discussion of the Noahide
covenant, consider it a religiously adequate universal approach. I find that
hard to accept.

There is an additional problem in applying the covenant with Noah as
the basis of all religions. Both Sacks and Greenberg identify the covenant
with the laws of Noah. They read Genesis 9 in relational terms, making it
akin to the later covenants with Abraham and with Israel at Sinai. However,
in my reading of Genesis 9, the Noahide covenant is not one that establishes
a relationship. My analysis leads me to view it in line with a type of biblical
covenant that has not yet been featured in reflections on the application
of the legal category of covenant to relations with God.[10] The Bible knows
of covenants that establish, define, and control relationships. But it also
knows of covenants whose purpose is to avoid aggression, what I have called
'no-harm covenants'. The one in Genesis 9 is a no-harm covenant. At its core
is God's promise never again to bring about a flood. In parallel, though not
as a condition to its validity, God makes demands of humanity, consisting
first and foremost of the prohibition of murder, which is a form of subject-
ing God's image to harm. A reciprocity is created where neither humans
nor God bring harm upon the other. Regardless of the scope of obligations,
it is not a relationship-building covenant. God does not establish a relationship either with Noah or with his descendants, nor with humanity or all
living beings. God makes a commitment toward them never to destroy
them. That commitment cannot be taken as being on a par with the covenant with Abraham, whose very essence is the formation of a relationship.
What all this means is that the reliance on Genesis 9, the covenant with
Noah, cannot be sustained in this reading of the biblical text.

The two-covenant theory is valuable in that it creates a balance, based on
biblical thought, between universality and particularity. But if we do not see
Genesis 9 as delivering the message that Greenberg and Sacks find in it, can
this construct be upheld? Or is there a different way of establishing a two-
point theory that would both uphold the value of other religions and affirm

[10] See Goshen-Gottstein, 'Genesis 9, Noah's Covenants and Jewish Theology of Religions'.

the uniqueness and particularity of Judaism? This brings me to a suggestion that grows from the work of these thinkers and builds upon it, while introducing a significant tweak into their argument.

A Novel Two-Point Construct

If we consider the two ideas that are central to both authors, we can suggest that, rather than establishing a two-covenant theory understood in light of the identification of covenant and its purpose with the image of God, we can combine these two ideas into one construct. Rather than juxtaposing two covenants, we juxtapose the image of God with covenant. The idea of the image of God, once it is understood in the full sense that I attribute to it, provides the foundation for affirming not only the value of the human person but also the vast potentiality of the religious life as it finds expression in all human beings. All religions would, in this view, be understood not in relation to covenant but in relation to creation. We recall that, in fact, both authors have already moved the discussion of covenant from Noah to creation. Greenberg has linked the concept to *tikun*. Sacks has juxtaposed wisdom and Torah as part of considering Judaism and broader culture. A more radical statement, here proposed, would be to see creation itself as the ground of human religious diversity, an idea first suggested by Sacks but now endowed with further meaning. God created humanity with the potential to know him, to be in relationship with him, and to attain spiritual heights and the evolution of the human person by means of religious practice. Religions all draw from this essential human potential, grounded in creation itself and known in the recognition of the human person as being in the image of God. In this understanding, the balance of universality and particularity is already contained within the notion of the image of God itself, in the same way that the one God places his image upon all, yielding diversity in humanity.

Covenant does different work than the image of God. If the latter enables human spiritual advancement, the former establishes a special relationship and a particular purpose or mission. If, for both Sacks and Greenberg, the second dimension of the covenant was its enhancement and further development, I suggest a similar balance can be attained by juxtaposing the image of God and covenant. To claim a special and purposeful relationship with God is something different to affirming human spiritual potential and legitimating its many expressions—relational as well as interior, moral, philosophical, experiential, and more. In the same way that human relationships allow us to fulfil our human potential, so our relationship with God fulfils the spiritual potential contained in the image of God. In this sense, all relationships with God are expressions of the image of God. Covenant takes us beyond the generality of relationship. It may involve a group, rather than individuals, forging a collective for God's purposes in a particular historical reality. It thus builds on religious fulfilment made available through creation itself and channels it, through a special bond with God, for specific historical purposes.

What does this suggest for the relationship between Judaism and other faiths? One possibility is to consider other religions in light of the creation of man in the image of God,[11] and to see Judaism as having a special task, expressed in its covenant. This understanding is perhaps closest to the biblical sense, in that it does not make the particularity of Israel's covenant a model that all religions must follow. Biblically, the relationship with God does not depend on a covenant. Individuals have a relationship with God prior to and independently of covenants. A covenant establishes a special relationship, but it is not a condition for a relationship with God. If we seek to account for the grounds of such a relationship independently of covenant, the image of God presents itself as a possible answer. While relationship does not depend on covenant, neither is covenant necessarily limited to Israel alone, and other relationships of a purposeful nature may be considered in parallel with Israel's covenant.[12]

An alternative would be to assume that complementing human potential is also a dimension of special relationship and purpose. Each religion strikes a balance between the two. Covenant need not mean the same thing or have the same parameters in all religions. They may all exhibit a similar balance between the fundamentals of the human person and his potential and what is made possible by virtue of the particular mission and purpose of the religion. In this view, the image of God and covenant point to two

[11] The same questions that were posed to Greenberg and Sacks by reviewers, such as Shapiro, would then have to be answered, first among which is understanding idolatry. The answer already provided, that idolatry is tantamount to violation of the image of God, would work particularly well. In some way or other, God would have to be kept as the focus, and turning away from God would result in the religion no longer leading to the realization of the potential of the human person made in his image.

[12] Biblical grounding for such an understanding may be found in Isa. 19: 25, a source cited by Greenberg. See also my *In God's Presence*, ch. 9.

constitutive dimensions of the religious life. The image of God gives expression to a person's divinely given potential for God-realization, laying relational foundations, but nevertheless centred in the human person. Covenant stands for that dimension of the religion that actualizes this potential, draws upon it, and channels it to divine purposes. It is, ultimately, centred in God. For a religion to be legitimated and have value, we need not appeal to the covenant. Whether all religions should be regarded as fulfilling a particular part of God's purposeful design is a matter for future consideration, taking into account religious phenomenology and self-understanding and asking how best to feature Israel's particularity in relation to the universal approach to God provided by other religions.

Let me spell out some of the differences in my reading compared to that of Greenberg and Sacks. The first is that for them the notion of the image of God is to be applied to the *other*. It operates in the moral domain, and defines the dignity and value of the other. This reading is justified by Genesis 9, which links the murder prohibition to man's creation in God's image. However, Genesis 1: 26, where the image of God first appears, also invites consideration of the *self* as the image of God. It is an essential definition of the human person. Strikingly, most of traditional reflection has focused on the other, rather than on the self, as the image of God.[13] I think here the Christian understanding of the concept in relation to spiritual perfection provides an important corrective to Jewish uses.[14] This is illustrative of the value of learning with the other that Greenberg underlines as a fundamental aspect of interreligious relations. Seeing how others understand the image of God allows us to explore that dimension within our tradition and to introduce new balances and emphases in how we use it.

A further difference would be captured by returning to the distinction between horizontal and vertical that has served us in this study. How our authors use the notion is horizontal: it defines and guides the relations between humans. My suggestion is that we must recover its vertical dimension, how it points to God and how such pointing provides a gateway to human fulfilment—fulfilment of the image of God by recalling and pointing to God. As a consequence of this understanding, also covenant is seen in a better balance between its horizontal and vertical axes. Though it is

---

[13] This is true already for rabbinic literature. See Goshen-Gottstein, 'The Body as Image of God in Rabbinic Literature', and Lorberbaum, *In God's Image*.

[14] Such uses do occur in medieval Jewish literature.

essentially a vertical notion, defining the human relationship with God, both our authors draw out different aspects of its horizontal significance. This is certainly the case for the covenant with Noah, which is seen by Sacks primarily in horizontal terms. When covenant is understood as responsibility and autonomy (Greenberg), or as an expression of solidarity following the political tradition (Sacks), it loses some of its verticality. Emphasizing the relational element and how it fulfils divine purposes reminds us that the covenant is and must always remain primarily a vertical notion, defining our relationship with God and the processes that such a relationship generates. Its benefits in terms of establishing a community or other horizontal expressions must remain secondary.

There is one specific implication to my suggestion regarding the association of Creation/image of God and covenant. The theological implications of this link concern all religions, and thereby the particularity or special status of so-called Abrahamic faiths is downplayed. Students, scholars, and activists who describe religions have become fond of the designation 'Abrahamic' to describe Judaism, Christianity, and Islam. On conceptual grounds, however, it is a problematic designation.[15] Why should Abraham serve as the most significant and representative feature of these religions? Is there no more significant common denominator? And if Abraham is chosen simply as a matter of convention, then we need to put forth a substantive argument that would privilege these three faiths over others.[16] The suggested balance of the image of God and the covenant could be applied to those faiths, as it could to all others.[17]

[15] See above, Ch. 7, n. 20.

[16] For Greenberg and Sacks, the challenge is not overwhelming. Greenberg is mainly concerned with Christianity. Consequently, 'Abrahamic' is not a major category for him. It is a designation of the covenant with Abraham, and because Greenberg is willing to open it to others, it does take on meaning also with reference to Christians and Muslims. But he does not resort to the conventional reference to these religions as Abrahamic. Sacks offers different testimony in various stages of his writing. *The Dignity of Difference* makes no allowance for any particular group of religions to stand out. His later work, for very specific contextual reasons, moves from a reference to either Judaism or to all religions to adopting an Abrahamic positioning. Sacks' concern in his later writing is to advance a moral theory on religion and violence, and he does so by appeal to the supposedly common figure of Abraham—but he does not touch on questions of theology of religions.

[17] In theory, a view of the dependence of other faiths on Judaism could have implications for a Jewish theology of religions. Religions deemed to have come under or been formed under the influence of Judaism might be seen as occupying a higher rung on the ladder of religious perfection. This was the view of Rav Kook, as articulated, among other places, in

If we consider that all religions occupy a space that is defined by the image of God on the one hand and by covenant on the other, what does that mean in terms of our use of the notion of covenant to describe other faiths? As I have suggested in my discussion of both authors, in order to speak of other religions in covenantal terms we need not assume they have entered into a formal covenantal relationship with God, as Israel is described as having done. Rather, it is a way of describing a special relationship that serves and advances God's designs, endowing a given religion with a particular mission and purpose.

This, then, opens up a new field of investigation. If we argue that all religions strike a balance between actualizing the divine potential of the human person on the one hand and entry into a special and purposeful relationship with God on the other, how does this lead to a recalibration of the discussion of universal and particular? Sacks has suggested one way of associating universality to particularity, in the process arguing for the importance of difference and for the dignity one must afford it. However, the question may have other expressions and we may only discover these when we embark on the detailed study of religious traditions from within. To offer some possible examples: can we speak of human potential as something that has both universal and particular dimensions? Would the particularity attached to the human person apply to national or group characteristics or might it apply to certain individuals who are gifted spiritually in special ways? What can we learn from the particular practices of any given religion about the human person that might be relevant to members of other faiths, and does such learning point to a common universal or rather to traits of particularity that might appear in some cases and be absent in others? What are the multiple particularities of various purposes associated with different religions, beyond their common foundations in human potential and relationship with the Divine? The philosophical distinctions that Sacks has introduced into our discourse are important, rich, and promising, even though he never went as far as applying them to individual religions in the field. How would the study of religions and the approach to them be impacted by the application of Sacks' categories and how might those categories be further refined in view of the concrete data of religions?

Linvukhei hador. However, the category 'Abrahamic' does not provide for such dependence. On the contrary, it seems to go against any sense of the status of Christianity and Islam as being derived from Judaism. Pointing back to Abraham, they enjoy fully parallel status.

Questions arise also as to how the message of multiple covenants, constituting diverse religions, might be stated from the perspective of other faiths. Unless one holds that other faiths must be consciously covenantal, one is led to recognize that whatever one means by 'covenant' will be expressed differently in the language of those religions. If so, then we must be on the lookout for how they portray the balance of universal and particular, placing their own particularity against the backdrop of universal religious realities and aspirations. Sacks has suggested that Christianity and Islam speak of universality, while Judaism speaks of particularity. In truth, Judaism speaks of both, and I believe that closer scrutiny of the other two will similarly reveal language and approaches that strike a balance between the two. The same would hold true for other faiths, each of which will strike its own balance between a universal view of humanity and of religion on the one hand and, on the other, the particularity of its own message, of the relationship it offers with God, and of its mission and purposes. As part of reconfiguring the elements that Greenberg and Sacks have employed as the grammar of a Jewish view of other religions, I would like to suggest that these elements be applied not to the *distinction* between Judaism and other faiths but to the inner workings of faiths, all faiths. Accordingly, we would wish to study how universality and particularity find expression in different religions, as well as the various articulations of what we might call the 'covenantal principle', the source of particularity in Sacks' thought. Adding texture and nuance to this fundamental distinction will allow us to restate Sacks' point in new ways, integrating it into a broader theory of the study of religion and of a theology of religions. If such a course were followed, Judaism might be able to relate not only to the universal expressions of other faiths, the equivalents of the covenant with Noah, but also to expressions of parallel particularities. Rather than such particularities being relevant only for the individual faith, they could become teachings in how particularity itself is lived and how religions can share on both poles—the universal and the particular. More importantly, this would open our horizons to a God's-eye view, to return to Greenberg's phrase, of how diverse religions fulfil divine purposes through their respective covenantal particularities.

Greenberg and Sacks: The Invitation

The reflections just shared, based on the work of the two thinkers, continue the conversation with their ideas, their contribution to the field of a Jewish theology of religions. However, both authors have contributed a lot more than ideas, which one may accept, reject, or partly own. What makes them teachers is that they exemplify attitudes and invite others to follow suit in their pursuit. Whether one accepts one construct or another of theirs seems secondary to buying into their project and developing it further. It is a project of cultivating openness from within Judaism to other faiths and finding the internal criteria and categories by means of which other faiths are validated and become sources of learning, understanding, inspiration, and growth, not only for their own followers but also for those who encounter them—and, in our case, for Judaism and for Jewish thought. This project cannot grow in a vacuum. It relies on certain attitudes and on an orientation the cultivation of which is as important as any particular stance one may take towards other religions. It is also what must be transmitted to others, allowing future engagement to flow from the same internal foundations. Anything else would simply be mimicking an authentic process without the internal resources required to carry it out from within. I would like to now present some of the attitudes and orientations that I see as fundamental to Greenberg, Sacks, and their common project. While there is much that they share in terms of content, in terms of attitude there are some fundamental divides. I have already pointed to these in describing how both individuals develop their approach to other religions. Let me review the relevant attitudes, beginning with Greenberg.

Greenberg serves as a model of respectful listening. His theology is based on taking the other seriously in terms of the positive valuation of the spiritual experience of the other, and even in terms of the particularity of faith and belief of the other. Greenberg listens, learns, and seeks to offer understanding. These processes acknowledge the religious reality of the other, which is understood on its own terms. Greenberg makes a sincere effort, for instance, to understand Christianity on its own terms. Indeed, he prides himself on doing so, in contradistinction to Buber. Even if my analysis has suggested that he did not meet the high bar he had set for himself, the very effort is an important element of the attitude needed for engaging in a Jewish theology of religions. Sacks, it should be noted, is much less of a model of this trait. His avoidance of deep exploration of religious ideas and of what makes for religious particularity means he really has no context in which to apply these qualities. Or perhaps it is the reverse. Perhaps because he has not cultivated these qualities, he also avoids engagement with religious particularity, preferring instead to treat the religious other in terms of a common humanity and its potential contribution to a common society.

Another point relating to attitude has to do with the readings that are offered of the faith and religious life of the other. At heart, Greenberg practises charity and offers charitable interpretations He does not reject, for example, key Christian faith tenets, even if this means going against the grain of thousands of years of Jewish views of Christianity. Instead, he asks what they mean to Christians and considers their benefits to believers, as well as possible ways of accepting them from a Jewish perspective. None of this is found in Sacks, who never enters the field of belief in any detail. In fact, as we have seen, his orientation is often the opposite of charitable, as when he criticizes religions or presents them in ways that make them less than his presentation of Judaism.

This raises the challenging question of whether an open-minded approach toward the religious other must only validate and affirm, or perhaps there is room for criticism. We lack any discussion of this in internal Jewish sources. It would be unwise to assume that one can never criticize another faith. Greenberg's view of religions or covenantal communities serving as mutual corrections for one another would not be possible if dialogue did not also include an element of reservation. Greenberg himself offers us a balance of affirmation of the faith of Christians along with criticism, such as his indication of preference for some Christian theological positions over others. One might consider Sacks too to represent just that kind of a balance. On the one hand he recognizes the fundamental faith reality of Christianity, seeing in it a legitimate expression of Abrahamic monotheism. On the other, he is critical of its universalism. Is that not also a form of balancing two complementary attitudes? It seems to me that working through this question of affirmation/rejection or acceptance/criticism as two complementary modalities is a challenge that requires much further thinking. Both our teachers allow us to enter the question and own it, even if their example does not provide us with convenient formulae and guidelines for its resolution. Perhaps the ideas that have been presented in this study might serve as guidelines for the desired balance. If, for example, the image of God is a controlling idea that provides fundamental validation for another faith, might it also set boundaries or criteria in light of which one could criticize or point to failure in that faith? Failure could take on multiple expressions, from the failure to live up to the tradition's ideals, corresponding to the image of God, to how social realities frustrate the higher spiritual principles, or how internal voices within another tradition are not recognized as part of the ongoing struggle for the realization of those higher ideals.[18] Seen in this light, the possibility for criticism emerges not as one religion viewing another critically, from a position of superiority or of owning a fuller truth, but from within an internal engagement with the tradition. Entering the stream of spiritual aspiration of a tradition, even that of the other, in light of its key ideals positions us in such a way that we can find a balance of affirmation and criticism that mirrors that of the insider.

I have referred, in a previous chapter, to Sacks' use of the religious imagination, and have suggested that even though he does not conceptualize it as a major driver of his own interfaith efforts, in fact it constitutes an important and novel approach to the field. Sacks, however, limits the application of the imagination to the human reality, to the suffering and oppression that the other has undergone. I see no reason to limit it in such a way. We can cultivate an appreciative entry specifically into the religious reality of the other by means of the imagination, for example by entering the faith content of the other. But on an even more basic level, use of the imaginative faculty could involve appreciating what faith, rituals, and the entirety of the religious life mean to the other and the benefit they bring him. This is not always something that can be discerned intellectually, nor can one simply rely on the testimony of the religious other. Deeper appreciation requires some form of access into his reality, and this, I submit, is achieved with the help of the imagination, applied empathetically and appreciatively. What kind of person has been produced? How has the image of God been realized in the person, or in the community of the faithful, through their following a particular religious path? All these ideas require a deeper response than what the mind alone can provide.

There is another important aspect that emerges, especially from Greenberg's experience. A special relationship, a friendship in more than the conventional sense, redefines how one thinks of the other's faith. The act of

[18]   As an example of what I have in mind, I refer to Anantanand Rambachan's *A Hindu Theology of Liberation*. Rambachan interrogates Vedanta philosophy from within and asks how it is not being translated in terms of present-day Hindu realities. While his controlling notion is not the image of God, it is the Hindu equivalent, namely the view of the spiritual absolute and its human counterpart, Brahman and Atman, and how recognizing their systemic centrality ought to be translated to a range of Hindu approaches and practices.

understanding is an act of interpretation, hence the practice of charitable interpretation, empathetic understanding, and more. What often motivates us to take up such a position is a relationship wherein we feel obligated to a person, to his or her testimony, to the way he or she functions as someone to whom our interpretation is beholden. We think differently when we think not only within our own group framework but when we feel the responsibility of thinking with the other, in light of the other, with the other, so to speak, looking over our shoulder.[19] Here, Greenberg's testimony of how he would think in light of the experience of Roy and Alice Eckardt is very significant. The other becomes a commanding presence, a hermeneutical principle in its own right. Here, the path to viewing and understanding another religion passes through key relationships. In the absence of those, one's framework of thinking remains external to the reality of the other.

The last point I would like to raise combines issues of attitude and substance. The question is not only how we do our theology of the other, but also what its purpose is. I have noted that classically, the key question for Jewish theology of religions has been whether other faiths are valid, that is, whether, in God's eyes, as understood in Judaism, they have the right to be. I have reflected on this way of posing the question elsewhere[20] and wish to use this discussion to consider other possible ways of defining the tasks and opportunities of a Jewish theology of religions. In the course of our study, several ideas came up that I would like to explore once again. It may be that the old paradigm of validation was appropriate under the social, spiritual, and theological circumstances of the Middle Ages, when Jews first started articulating the challenges of a Jewish theology of religions and began offering solutions and constructs by means of which it could be further advanced. However, both our authors have taken the discussion beyond those historical foundations. They are both aware that times have changed and today's challenges are different from those of former generations. They both realize that we must find practical ways of advancing relations and theoretical ways of justifying such engagement. And yet, while offering new ways of viewing other faiths, especially with the help of the language of the covenant, the work their theology does remains essentially within the paradigm of validation. Our discussion has suggested other paradigms may be possible.

[19] See Thatamanil, *The Immanent Divine*, p. xii.
[20] See Goshen-Gottstein, 'Jewish Theology of Religions'.

One possible purpose is that of mutual enrichment. Validation may reduce violence and tension and may permit practical collaboration. But more is possible by means of deeper, empathetic, charitable, and imaginative entry into the religious world of the other. With a richer methodology and approach, we may uncover fuller or deeper motivation for engaging with the religious other. Mutual enrichment is one candidate. Here Greenberg, again, emerges as a paragon. In particular, as we have seen, such enrichment passes through processes of common learning. This suggests that understanding, growth, and transformation are goals of the interfaith process and inform what we seek in relation to the other: not only to declare the other legitimate, but to be transformed by them. The earlier goal of validation provided a solution to social problems—be it the ability of the Jewish community to survive in a social reality in which others were the majority, or the more recent efforts of Sacks to validate other faiths for the sake of a common social reality. The alternative emphasis is upon spirituality and growth. It recognizes the other not just in terms of their right to exist, but in terms of the promises of impact, meaning, and growth that are inherent in their faith and are delivered by means of the encounter.

We have another possible way of viewing dialogue and theology of religions. Following reflections on unity and diversity, I raised the possibility that theology of religions may be practised with the goal of recognizing the fundamental unity within religious diversity. This unity extends from the teachings to society, to the cosmos, if you will, and to the person. Engaging with other religions is a quest for deeper unity, in all possible dimensions.[21] A return to the image of God as a principle of spiritually based unity might facilitate the development of a theology of religions whose goal is the affirmation of unity between religions. Religions mirror the fundamental unity of the image of God, refracted through the different traditions.

If religions share in a fundamental unity, then the purpose of their study and of the development of a theology of religions is to raise one to the heights of that unity. It is a transformative process that takes us beyond divisions, historical memory, conflict, and more (never forgetting nor invalidating their testimony) to a higher dimension wherein unity is made manifest.

---

[21] Returning to Rav Kook, I believe this insight lies at the heart of his ideal drive for cultivating relations between religions. These are viewed through the lens of unity. In fact, tensions in his thought may be described as the conflict between this drive for unity and the more classical perspective of validation, as it encounters various obstacles.

Realization of this unity holds the potential for transformation. Every encounter, as we have seen, has that possibility. And yet we have also seen how hard it can be to define in what way an encounter is transformative. What does change mean and who or what is changed? Grounding a view of religions in a vision of unity offers an answer. Transformation occurs as reality— social, historical, human—is appreciated anew in light of a higher vision of unity. To be transformed is to recognize that power of unity and to understand our faith, and that of the other, in its light. If the goal of a theology of religions is to affirm unity in diversity, the goal of encounter, its experiential counterpart, is to return from diversity to that higher unity.

Who is growing? Who is being transformed? Typically, our sights are set on the individual as he or she progresses in the spiritual life. However, if we are reflecting on units as large as religious traditions and approaching them from the perspective of a vision of unity, and if we are engaging in processes of study that lead to spiritual growth, then we may consider another subject for growth and transformation. It is not only the individuals who grow. It is the religious traditions themselves that undergo transformation. Engaging in dialogue is transformative for the tradition, no less than for participants in the activity. Formulating a theology of religions redefines one's understanding of the religious tradition and in the process puts forth potentially higher visions of what it means and how it interacts with others. Sacks and Greenberg belong to a new generation of thinkers who reflect on other faiths and recognize that more is needed today than in the past because of the multiple changes in society and in the world. In presenting novel ideas, they do more than simply reaffirm old truths in new language. They seek to advance tradition itself and the vision of what Judaism has to offer to the world in the course of reflecting on its relations with world religions. Even if the stated purpose is for religions to contribute to the common good, that vision cannot be separated from the recognition that the tradition itself must grow.

Having come this far allows us to conceive of yet another way of approaching religions. If we posit a higher ground and vision of unity and, at the same time, recognize that growth and transformation are matters for the religions themselves, then in fact religions grow together and in interdependent ways. The fullness of the practice of encounter, dialogue, interreligious study, and theology of religions—all these interrelated activities and approaches—is to produce growth and transformation in *all* religions. All religions, in this view, are in need of spiritual growth, and the process of their mutual engagement is one important aspect of their growth. Under-standing how another religion operates, in the highest possible way, allows one to revisit the question of how one's own works, and how they jointly grow through their historical encounters and through their present-day pos-sibilities for sharing and collaboration. This perspective can be summed up under the term co-evolution.[22] There is a driver for growth in all faiths, and their interdependent growth is a matter for co-evolution. Seen in this light, a Jewish theology of religion goes even further than affirming unity. It is an affirmation of the unity that allows all religions to grow in interdependent ways. The purpose of the study of the other's faith, undertaken in this re-ciprocal way, is to suggest how the co-evolutionary process points to a higher reality of unity. Such a perspective redefines what members of differ-ent faiths do when they come together and what the importance of their col-laboration is.

Sacks and Greenberg do not refer to this notion of co-evolution. That does not mean, however, that they have not contributed to it. I believe they have contributed to it in important ways. They have read Judaism, in tan-dem with other religions, in ways that deliver a higher, more unitive, vision for the day. This vision is a source of inspiration for Judaism and for Jews. But it is also relevant to and consciously addresses members of other faiths, seeking to advance *their* understanding. As we have noted, both authors struggle with the question of audience: who is reading them and upon whom they have an impact. Having come this far, a new answer emerges. The audiences are interdependent, as much as the vision and purpose of their activity also are. These thinkers take important steps towards the recog-nition of growth in traditions through novel thoughts, mutual engagement, and mutual study. Whether they have articulated their contribution in this way or not, having explored their thought, its premises, challenges, and possibilities, and having engaged in my own dialogue with them, I would claim that Greenberg and Sacks contribute through their theology of reli-gions and through the view of Judaism that they put forth to the movement of co-evolution that sees Judaism growing, in tandem with world religions, towards a better, more peaceful world, a world informed by the divine vision of unity.

[22] I have devoted a self-reflective essay to this notion, in which I attempt to read my entire work through this lens. The present discussion is one further expression of that. See Goshen-Gottstein, 'Judaism and Interreligious Co-evolution'.

Bibliography

'Argument from Witnesses' [Ti'un ha'ed], Wikipedia.org.

ATMAPRIYANANDA, SWAMI, 'Sri Ramakrishna', in Alon Goshen-Gottstein (ed.), *Interreligious Heroes: Role Models and Spiritual Exemplars for Interfaith Practice* (Eugene, Oreg.: Wipf and Stock, 2021), 39–47.

BAKHOS, CAROL, *The Family of Abraham* (Cambridge, Mass.: Harvard University Press, 2014).

BARR, JAMES, 'Reflections on the Covenant with Noah', in A. Mayes and R. Salters (eds.), *Covenant as Context: Essays in Honour of E. W. Nicholson* (Oxford: Oxford University Press, 2003), 11–22.

BERGER, DAVID, 'Covenants, Messiahs, and Religious Boundaries—Review of "For the Sake of Heaven and Earth: The New Encounter between Judaism and Christianity", by Irving Greenberg', *Tradition*, 39/2 (2005), 69–70.

—— 'Jews, Gentiles and the Modern Egalitarian Ethos: Some Tentative Thoughts', in Marc Stern (ed.), *Formulating Responses in an Egalitarian Age* (Lanham, Md.: Rowman and Littlefield, 2005), 83–108.

—— *The Rebbe, the Messiah, and the Scandal of Orthodox Indifference* (Oxford: Littman Library of Jewish Civilization, 2001).

—— 'Vatican II at 50', *Tablet Magazine* (2015), https://www.tabletmag.com/sections/community/articles/vatican-ii-at-50.

BLENKINSOPP, JOSEPH, *Creation, Un-creation, Re-creation : A Discursive Commentary on Genesis 1–11* (New York: T&T Clark, 2011).

BLIDSTEIN, GERALD J., *Political Concepts in Maimonidean Halakhah* [Ekronot mediniyim bemishnat harambam] (Ramat Gan: Bar Ilan University Press, 1983).

BONSIRVEN, JOSEPH, *Le Judaisme palestinien au temps de Jésus-Christ*, vol. i (Paris: Beauchesne, 1934).

BRILL, ALAN, *Judaism and Other Religions: Models of Understanding* (New York: Palgrave, 2010).

COOPER, SIMON, *Contemporary Covenantal Thought: Interpretations of Covenant in the Thought of David Hartman and Eugene Borowitz* (Boston: Academic Studies Press, 2012).

CORNELL, VINCENT, 'Islam: Epistemological Crisis, Theological Hostility, and the Problem of Difference', in Alon Goshen-Gottstein (ed.), *The Religious Other: Hostility, Hospitality and the Hope of Human Flourishing* (Lanham, Md.: Lexington, 2014), 69–97.

DALAI LAMA, *Toward a True Kinship of Faiths* (New York: Doubleday, 2010).

DAVIES, W. D., *The Gospel and the Land: Early Christianity and Jewish Territorial Doctrine* (Sheffield: JSOT Press, 1994).

The Divine Life Society, 'Many Names—One God', https://www.sivanandaonline.org//?cmd=displayrightsection&section_id=1488&parent=1239&format=hml.

DUMBRELL, W., *Covenant and Creation: A Theology of Old Testament Covenants* (Carlisle: Paternoster, 1984).

EICHRODT, WALTHER, *Theology of the Old Testament*, vol. i (London: SCM, 1961).

EISEN, ARNOLD, *The Chosen People in America: A Study in Jewish Religious Ideology* (Bloomington: Indiana University Press, 1983).

ELAZAR, DANIEL J., 'The Political Theory of Covenant: Biblical Origins and Modern Developments', *Publius*, 10/4 (1980), 3–30.

FACKENHEIM, EMIL L., *To Mend the World: Foundations of Post-Holocaust Jewish Thought* (New York: Schocken Books, 1982).

FELDMANN KAYE, MIRIAM, *Jewish Theology for a Postmodern Age* (London: Littman Library of Jewish Civilization, 2019).

—— 'Multiple Truths and the Towers of Babel: Deconstruction in Jewish Philosophy', *Tradition*, 52/4 (2020), 37–43.

FERZIGER, ADAM, MIRI FREUD-KANDEL, and STEVEN BAYME (eds.), *Yitz Greenberg and Modern Orthodoxy: The Road Not Taken* (Boston: Academic Studies Press, 2019),

FINE, LAWRENCE, '"Tikkun": A Lurianic Motive in Contemporary Jewish Thought', in J. Neusner et al. (eds.), *From Ancient Israel to Modern Judaism: Essays in Honor of Marvin Fox* (Atlanta: Scholars Press, 1989), iv. 35–53.

FREEDMAN, SHALOM, *Living in the Image of God: Jewish Teachings to Perfect the World. Conversations with Rabbi Irving Greenberg as Conducted by Shalom Freedman* (Northvale: Jason Aronson, 1998).

FRIEDMAN, YOHANAN, *Tolerance and Coercion in Islam: Interfaith Relations in the Muslim Tradition* (Cambridge: Cambridge University Press, 2003).

FRY, HELEN (ed.), *Christian–Jewish Dialogue: A Reader* (Exeter: University of Exeter Press, 1996).

GELLMAN, JEROME (YEHUDA), *God's Kindness Has Overwhelmed Us: A Contemporary Doctrine of the Jews as the Chosen People* (Boston: Academic Studies Press, 2013).

'The Gifts and the Calling of God are Irrevocable: A Reflection on Theological Questions Pertaining to Catholic–Jewish Relations on the Occasion of the 50th Anniversary of "Nostra Aetate"' (Vatican: Commission for Religious Relations with the Jews, 2015).

GLICK, YOEL, *Seeking the Divine Presence, Part I: The Three Pillars of a Jewish Spiritual Life* (Bloomington, Ind.: Trafford, 2009).

GOSHEN-GOTTSTEIN, ALON, 'Abraham and "Abrahamic Religions" in Contemporary Interreligious Discourse: Reflections of an Implicated Jewish Bystander', *Studies in Interreligious Dialogue*, 12 (2002), 165–83.

—— 'The Body as Image of God in Rabbinic Literature', *Harvard Theological Review*, 87/2 (1994), 171–95.

—— 'Concluding Reflections', in A. Goshen-Gottstein and E. Korn (eds.), *Jewish Theology and World Religions* (Oxford: Littman Library of Jewish Civilization, 2012), 317–27.

—— 'Conclusion: Friendship Across Religions: An Interreligious Manifesto', in Alon Goshen-Gottstein (ed.), *Friendship Across Religions: Theological Perspectives on Interreligious Friendship* (Lanham, Md.: Lexington, 2015), 219–24.

—— 'The Covenant with the Fathers and the Inheritance of the Land: Between Biblical Theology and Rabbinic Thought' (Heb.), *Da'at*, 35 (1995), 5–28.

—— 'Genesis 9, Noah's Covenants and Jewish Theology of Religions', *Studies in Christian-Jewish Relations*, 18 (2023), 1–26.

—— '"Genius Theologian, Lonely Theologian": Yitz Greenberg on Christianity', in Shmuly Yanklowitz (ed.), *A Torah Giant: The Intellectual Legacy of Rabbi Dr. Irving (Yitz) Greenberg* (Jerusalem: Urim Publishing, 2018), 71–92.

—— 'God and Israel as Father and Son in Tannaitic Literature' (Heb.), Ph.D. diss., Hebrew University of Jerusalem, 1987.

—— 'God the Father in Rabbinic Judaism and Christianity: Transformed Background or Common Ground?', *Journal of Ecumenical Studies*, 38/4 (2001), 470–504.

—— *In God's Presence: A Theological Reintroduction to Judaism* (Minneapolis: Fortress Press, forthcoming).

—— (ed.), *Interreligious Heroes: Role Models and Spiritual Exemplars for Interfaith Practice* (Eugene, Oreg.: Wipf and Stock, 2021).

—— 'Introduction', in Alon Goshen-Gottstein (ed.), *Friendship Across Religions: Theological Perspectives on Interreligious Friendship* (Lanham, Md.: Lexington, 2015), xxi–lii.

—— 'Isa. 56: 1–8: Expanding the Covenant', *Catholic Biblical Quarterly* (forthcoming).

—— *The Jewish Encounter with Hinduism: Wisdom, Spirituality, Identity* (New York: Palgrave, 2016).

—— 'Jewish Theology of Religions', in *The Cambridge Companion to Jewish Theology* (Cambridge: Cambridge University Press, 2020), 344–71.

—— 'Judaism and Incarnational Theologies: Mapping Out the Parameters of Dialogue', *Journal of Ecumenical Studies*, 39/3–4 (2002), 219–57.

—— 'Judaism and Interreligious Co-evolution: A Retrospective Reading', *Contemporary Jewry*, 40/1 (March 2020), 15–35.

—— 'The Land of Israel in the Economy of Rabbinic Thought' (Heb.), *Da'at*, 86 (2018), 211–58.

GOSHEN-GOTTSTEIN, ALON, 'The New Covenant—Jeremiah 31: 30–33 (31: 31–34) in Jewish Interpretation', *Studies in Christian–Jewish Relations*, 15/1 (2020), 1–31.

—— 'No Religion Is an Island: Following the Trail-Blazer', *Shofar*, 26/1 (2007), 72–111; repr. in Harold Kasimow (ed.), *Abraham Joshua Heschel Today* (Eugene, Oreg.: Wipf and Stock, 2020), 60–97.

—— *Religious Genius: Appreciating Inspiring Individuals Across Traditions* (New York: Palgrave, 2017).

—— (ed.), *Religious Truth: Towards a Jewish Theology of Religions* (London: Littman Library of Jewish Civilization, 2020).

—— *Same God, Other god: Judaism, Hinduism and the Problem of Idolatry* (New York: Palgrave, 2016).

—— 'A Special Relationship?', *Current Dialogue*, 58 (2016), 12–15.

—— 'The Theory of Five Forces: Rav Kook on Human Flourishing', in Matthew Croasmun, Zoran Grozdanov, and Ryan McAnnally-Linz (eds.), *Envisioning the Good Life: Essays on God, Christ, and Human Flourishing in Honor of Miroslav Volf* (Eugene, Oreg.: Cascade Books, 2017), 85–102.

—— 'The Triune and the Decaune God: Christianity and Kabbalah as Objects of Jewish Polemics with Special Reference to Meir ben Simeon of Narbonne's Milhemet Mitzvah', in Theo Hettema and Christine Kooi (eds.), *Religious Polemics in Context* (Assen: Royal Van Gorcum, 2004), 165–97.

—— and EUGENE KORN (eds.), *Jewish Theology and World Religions* (Oxford: Littman Library of Jewish Civilization, 2012).

GOTTWALD, NORMAN, 'W. Eichrodt: Theology of the Old Testament', in Robert Laurin (ed.), *Contemporary Old Testament Theologians* (Valley Forge: Judson Press, 1970), 23–62.

GREEN, ARTHUR, *Radical Judaism: Rethinking God and Tradition* (New Haven: Yale University Press, 2010).

GREENBERG, BLU, 'Rabbi Jacob Emden: The Views of an Enlightened Traditionalist on Christianity', *Judaism: A Quarterly Journal of Jewish Life and Thought*, 27/3 (1978), 351–63.

GREENBERG, IRVING, 'Cloud of Smoke, Pillar of Fire: Judaism, Christianity, and Modernity after the Holocaust', in Eva Fleischner (ed.), *Auschwitz: Beginning of a New Era? Reflections on the Holocaust* (New York: Ktav, 1977), 7–55.

—— 'Covenantal Pluralism', *Journal of Ecumenical Studies*, 34/3 (1997), 425–36.

—— *For the Sake of Heaven and Earth: The New Encounter Between Judaism and Christianity* (Philadelphia: Jewish Publication Society, 2004).

—— *The Jewish Way: Living the Holidays* (New York: Summit Books, 1988).

—— 'Judaism and Christianity: Covenants of Redemption', in Tikva Frymer-Kensky et al. (eds.), *Christianity in Jewish Terms* (Boulder, Colo.: Westview, 2000), 141–58.

—— 'Judaism and Christianity: Their Respective Roles in the Divine Strategy of

Redemption', in Eugene Fischer (ed.), *Visions of the Other: Jewish and Christian Theologians Assess the Dialogue* (New York: Paulist Press, 1994).

—— 'Modern Orthodoxy and the Road Not Taken: A Retrospective View', in Adam Ferziger, Miri Freud-Kandel, and Steven Bayme (eds.), *Yitz Greenberg and Modern Orthodoxy: The Road Not Taken* (Boston: Academic Studies Press, 2019), 7–54.

—— 'On the Road to a New Encounter between Judaism and Christianity: A Personal Journey', in I. Greenberg, *For the Sake of Heaven and Earth: The New Encounter Between Judaism and Christianity* (Philadelphia: Jewish Publication Society, 2004), 3–48.

—— 'The Relationship of Judaism and Christianity: Toward a New Organic Model', in Eugene Fisher, James Rudin, and Marc Tanenbaum (eds.), *Twenty Years of Jewish/Catholic Relations* (New York: Paulist Press, 1986), 191–211.

—— 'Theology after the Shoah: The Transformation of the Core Paradigm', *Modern Judaism*, 26/3 (2006), 213–39.

—— *Triumph of Life: A Narrative Theology of Judaism* (forthcoming).

—— 'Voluntary Covenant', *Perspectives* (New York: National Jewish Resource Center, 1982), 27–44.

—— 'What Would Roy and Alice Do? A Reflection on How I Came to Be a Failure through Dialogue, Thank God', in Jennifer Howe Peace, Or N. Rose, and Gregory Mobley (eds.), *My Neighbor's Faith: Stories of Interreligious Encounter, Growth and Transformation* (Maryknoll, NY: Orbis Books, 2012), 11–16.

GREGERMAN, ADAM, 'Superiority without Supersessionism: Walter Kasper, *The Gifts and the Calling of God Are Irrevocable*, and God's Covenant with the Jews', *Theological Studies*, 79 (2018), 36–59.

GUTTMAN, JULIUS, *The Philosophy of Judaism: The History of Jewish Philosophy from Biblical Times to Franz Rosenzweig*, trans. David W. Silverman (Northvale, NJ: Jason Aronson, 1964).

HALBERTAL, MOSHE, '"Ones Possessed of Religion": Religious Tolerance in the Teachings of the Me'iri', *Edah*, 1/1 (2000), 1–25.

HALIVNI, DAVID WEISS, *Revelation Restored: Divine Writ and Critical Responses* (Boulder, Colo.: Westview, 1997).

HARRIS, MICHAEL, *Faith Without Fear: Unresolved Issues in Modern Orthodoxy* (London: Valentine Mitchell, 2016).

HARRIS, RICHARD, 'Jonathan Sacks' *The Dignity of Difference: How to Avoid the Clash of Civilizations*', *Scottish Journal of Theology*, 57/1 (2004), 109–15.

HESCHEL, ABRAHAM J., *Heavenly Torah as Refracted Through the Generations*, trans. Gordon Tucker (New York: Continuum, 2005).

—— 'No Religion Is an Island', in Harold Kasimow and Byron Sherwin (eds.), *No Religion is an Island: Abraham Joshua Heschel and Interreligious Dialogue* (Eugene, Oreg.: Wipf & Stock, 1991), 3–22.

HICK, JOHN, *A Christian Theology of Religions* (London: SCM Press, 1995).

HIRSCH, SAMSON RAPHAEL, *Talmudic Judaism and Society* (New York: Philipp Feldheim, 1884).

HUGHES, AARON, *Abrahamic Religions: On the Uses and Abuses of History* (Oxford: Oxford University Press, 2012).

JACOB, BENNO, *The First Book of the Bible: Genesis*, trans. Ernest Jacob and Walter Jacob (New York: Ktav, 1974).

JENSON, ROBERT, and EUGENE KORN, *Covenant and Hope: Christian and Jewish Reflections* (Grand Rapids: Eerdmans, 2012).

JOSPE, RAPHAEL, 'Pluralism out of the Sources of Judaism: The Quest for Religious Pluralism without Relativism', in Alon Goshen-Gottstein and Eugene Korn (eds.), *Jewish Theology and World Religions* (Oxford: Littman Library of Jewish Civilization, 2012), 87–122.

JOTKOWITZ, ALAN, 'Universalism and Particularism in the Jewish Tradition: The Radical Theology of Rabbi Jonathan Sacks', *Tradition*, 44/3 (2011), 53–67.

KASIMOW, HAROLD, and BYRON L. SHERWIN (eds.), *No Religion Is an Island: Abraham Joshua Heschel and Interreligious Dialogue* (Eugene, Oreg.: Wipf & Stock, 1991).

KATZ, JACOB, *Exclusiveness and Tolerance: Studies in Jewish–Gentile Relations in Medieval and Modern Times* (London: Oxford University Press, 1961).

KATZ, STEVEN T., 'The Issue of Confirmation and Disconfirmation in Jewish Thought after the Shoah', in S. T. Katz (ed.), *The Impact of the Holocaust on Jewish Theology* (New York: New York University Press, 2007), 291–334.

—— '"Voluntary Covenant": Irving Greenberg on Faith After the Holocaust', in Steven T. Katz, *Historicism, the Holocaust, and Zionism: Critical Studies in Modern Jewish Thought and History* (New York: New York University Press, 1992), 225–50.

KAUFMANN, YEHEZKEL, *The Religion of Israel: From its Beginnings to the Babylonian Exile*, trans. Moshe Greenberg (Chicago: Chicago University Press, 1960).

KAVKA, MARTIN, 'The Perils of Covenant Theology: The Case of Eugene Borowitz', *Journal of Jewish Ethics*, 1 (2015), 96–103.

KELLNER, JOLENE S., and MENACHEM KELLNER, 'Respectful Disagreement: A Response to Raphael Jospe', in Alon Goshen-Gottstein and Eugene Korn (eds.), *Jewish Theology and World Religions* (Oxford: Littman Library of Jewish Civilization, 2012), 123–33.

KELLNER, MENACHEM, *Maimonides on Judaism and the Jewish People* (Albany, NY: SUNY Press, 1991).

—— 'Steven Schwarzschild, Moses Maimonides, and "Jewish Non-Jews"', in Görge K. Hasselhoff and Otfried Fraisse (eds.), *Moses Maimonides (1138–1204)—His Religious, Scientific, and Philosophical Wirkungsgeschichte in Different Cultural Contexts* (Würzburg: Ergon, 2004), 587–606.

KIMELMAN, REUVEN, 'The Rabbinic Theology of the Physical: Blessings, Body and Soul, Resurrection, and Covenant and Election', in Steven T. Katz (ed.), *The Cambridge History of Judaism*, iv: *The Late Roman–Rabbinic Period* (Cambridge: Cambridge University Press, 2006), 946–76.

—— *The Rhetoric of the Jewish Liturgy* (London: Littman Library of Jewish Civilization, forthcoming).

KLEINBERG, DARREN, 'For and Against: A Consideration of David Hartman and Jonathan Sacks in Relation to Irving Greenberg', in Shmuly Yanklowitz (ed.), *A Torah Giant: The Intellectual Legacy of Rabbi Dr. Irving (Yitz) Greenberg* (Jerusalem: Urim, 2018), 169–81.

KOGAN, MICHAEL, *Opening the Covenant: A Jewish Theology of Christianity* (Oxford: Oxford University Press, 2008).

KOOK, ABRAHAM ISAAC, *Linvukhei hador* (Jerusalem, 2009).

—— *Midot re'ayah* (Jerusalem: Mosad Harav Kook, 1971).

KORN, EUGENE, 'The God of Abraham, Yitzhak, and Yonatan: Goshen-Gottstein on Heschel, Greenberg, and Sacks', *Contemporary Jewry*, 40/1 (2020), 137–47.

—— 'The People of Israel, Christianity and the Covenantal Responsibility to History', in Robert Jenson and Eugene Korn (eds.), *Covenant and Hope: Christian and Jewish Reflections* (Grand Rapids: Eerdmans, 2012), 145–72.

—— and JOHN T. PAWLIKOWSKI (eds.), *Two Faiths, One Covenant? Jewish and Christian Identity in the Presence of the Other* (Lanham, Md.: Rowman and Littlefield, 2005).

KRELL, MARK, *Intersecting Pathways: Modern Jewish Theologians in Conversation with Christianity* (New York: Oxford University Press, 2003).

LAHMANOVITCH, OMER, 'What does the Messiah have in common with Arsenal FC?' (15 Nov. 2013), https://rabbisacks.org/news/messiah-common-arsenal-fc-israel-hayom/.

LEBENS, SAMUEL, 'One God, One Truth—Rabbi Sacks' Pluralism Reexamined', *Tradition*, 54/2 (2022), 74–100.

LEVENSON, JON, *Inheriting Abraham: The Legacy of the Patriarch in Judaism, Christianity and Islam* (Princeton, NJ: Princeton University Press, 2012).

—— 'The Universal Horizon of Biblical Particularism', in Mark Brett (ed.), *Ethnicity and the Bible* (Leiden: Brill, 1996), 143–69.

LIEBES, YEHUDA, 'Christian Influences in the Zohar' (Heb.), *Jerusalem Studies in Jewish Thought*, 2 (1982), 43–74.

LORBERBAUM, YAIR, *In God's Image: Myth, Theology, and Law in Classical Judaism* (New York: Cambridge University Press, 2015).

MCKANE, WILLIAM, *A Critical and Exegetical Commentary on Jeremiah* (Edinburgh: T&T Clark, 1996).

MAHARAJ, AYON, *Infinite Paths to Infinite Reality: Sri Ramakrishna and Cross-Cultural Philosophy of Religion* (Oxford: Oxford University Press, 2018).

MELCHERT, CHRISTOPHER, 'God Created Adam in His Image', *Journal of Qur'anic Studies*, 13/1 (2011), 113–24.

'Neocathecumenal Way', Wikipedia, https://en.wikipedia.org/wiki/Neocatechumenal_Way.

NICHOLSON, ERNEST, *God and His People: Covenant and Theology in the Old Testament* (Oxford: Clarendon Press, 1986).

NOVAK, DAVID, *The Image of the Non-Jew in Judaism*, 2nd edn. (Oxford: Littman Library of Jewish Civilization, 2011).

'Open Orthodoxy', https://en.wikipedia.org/wiki/Open_Orthodoxy.

PEACE, JENNIFER HOWE, OR N. ROSE, and GREGORY MOBLEY (eds.), *My Neighbor's Faith: Stories of Interreligious Encounter, Growth and Transformation* (Maryknoll, NY: Orbis Books, 2012).

Pentateuch and Haftorahs, ed. J. H. Hertz (London: Soncino Press, 1981).

PERSOFF, MEIR, *Another Way, Another Time: Religious Inclusivism and the Sacks Chief Rabbinate* (Boston: Academic Studies Press, 2010).

PIZZABALLA, PIERBATTISTA, 'Abraham Joshua Heschel', in Alon Goshen-Gottstein (ed.), *Interreligious Heroes: Role Models and Spiritual Exemplars for Interfaith Practice* (Eugene, Oreg.: Wipf and Stock, 2021), 87–91.

'Rabbi Joseph Soloveitchik on Interreligious Dialogue: Forty Years Later' (23 Nov. 2003), https://www.bc.edu/content/dam/files/research_sites/cjl/texts/center/conferences/soloveitchik/.

'Rabbi Sacks in discussion with EJ Dionne and Bill Galston at the Brookings Institution' (20 Nov. 2015), https://rabbisacks.org/rabbi-sacks-in-discussion-with-ej-dionne-and-bill-galston-at-the-brookings-institution/.

RAMBACHAN, ANANTANAND, *A Hindu Theology of Liberation: Not-Two is Not One* (Albany, NY: SUNY Press, 2014).

ROSENTHAL, GILBERT, 'Tikkun Ha-Olam: The Metamorphosis of a Concept', *Journal of Religion*, 85/2 (2005), 214–40.

SACKS, JONATHAN, 'Address by the Chief Rabbi to the Lambeth Conference' (28 July 2008), https://rabbisacks.org/address-by-the-chief-rabbi-to-the-lambeth-conference/.

—— 'A Clash of Civilizations? Judaic Sources on Co-existence in a World of Difference', http://www.scribd.com/doc/20065780/Rabbi-Jonathan-Sacks-Dignity-of-Difference-Sources-in-Traditional-Jewish-Literature.

—— *Covenant and Conversation: A Weekly Reading of the Jewish Bible*, 5 vols. (Jerusalem: Maggid Books, 2009–17).

—— *Crisis and Covenant: Jewish Thought After the Holocaust* (Manchester: Manchester University Press, 1992).

—— *The Dignity of Difference: How to Avoid the Clash of Civilizations* (London: Continuum, 2002; rev. edn. 2003).

—— *Faith in the Future* (London: Darton, Longman & Todd, 1995).

—— *Future Tense* (London: Hodder & Stoughton, 2009).

—— 'Global Covenant: A Jewish Perspective on Globalization', in John Dunning (ed.), *Making Globalization Good: The Moral Challenges of Global Capitalism* (Oxford: Oxford University Press, 2003), 210–31.

—— *The Great Partnership: God, Science and the Search for Meaning* (New York: Schocken Books, 2011).

—— 'The Heroism of Tamar (Vayeshev 5775)' (8 Dec. 2014), https://rabbisacks.org/heroism-tamar-vayeshev-5775/.

—— *The Home We Build Together: Recreating Society* (London: Continuum, 2007).

—— 'The Interfaith Imperative', in J. Sacks, *Faith in the Future* (London: Darton, Longman & Todd, 1995), 74–81.

—— 'Interfaith Relations and the Holocaust', https://rabbisacks.org/holocaust/topic9/.

—— 'Jewish–Christian Dialogue: The Ethical Dimension', in J. Sacks, *Tradition in an Untraditional Age: Essays on Modern Jewish Thought* (London: Valentine Mitchell, 1990), 161–81.

—— *Koren Sacks Rosh Hashana Maḥzor* (Jerusalem: Koren Publishers, 2011).

—— 'Make Friends' (8 June 2020), https://www.youtube.com/watch?v=ocd-mqilkpA.

—— 'Miketz (5768)—Faith, Universal and Particular' (8 Dec. 2007), https://rabbisacks.org/covenant-conversation-5768-miketz-faith-universal-and-particular/.

—— *Morality: Restoring the Common Good in Divided Times* (New York: Basic Books, 2020).

—— *Not in God's Name: Confronting Religious Violence* (London: Hodder & Stoughton, 2015).

—— *One People? Tradition, Modernity, and Jewish Unity* (Oxford: Littman Library of Jewish Civilization, 1993).

—— *The Politics of Hope* (London: Jonathan Cape, 1997).

—— 'Rabbi Sacks interviewed by Akbar Ahmed on Jewish–Muslim Relations' (16 Nov. 2015), https://rabbisacks.org/rabbi-sacks-interviewed-by-akbar-ahmed-on-jewish-muslim-relations/.

—— *Radical Then, Radical Now: The Legacy of the World's Oldest Religion* (London: HarperCollins, 2000).

—— *To Heal a Fractured World: The Ethics of Responsibility* (New York: Schocken Books, 2005).

—— 'Toldot (5773)—Between Prophecy and Oracle' (12 Nov. 2012), https://rabbisacks.org/covenant-conversation-toldot-between-prophecy-and-oracle/.

—— *Tradition in an Untraditional Age: Essays on Modern Jewish Thought* (London: Valentine Mitchell, 1990).

SACKS, JONATHAN, 'Va'etchanan (5768)—In the Eyes of the Nations' (16 Aug. 2008), https://rabbisacks.org/covenant-conversation-5768-vaetchanan-in-the-eyes-of-the-nations/.

—— 'YU and the World of Tomorrow—Rabbi Sacks Speaks to Rabbi Ari Lamm' (30 Oct. 2017), https://rabbisacks.org/yu-world-tomorrow-rabbi-sacks-speaks-rabbi-ari-lamm/.

SAGI, AVI, 'Justifying Interreligious Pluralism', in Alon Goshen-Gottstein and Eugene Korn (eds.), *Jewish Theology and World Religions* (Oxford: Littman Library of Jewish Civilization, 2012), 61–86.

SANDERS, E. P., *Paul and Palestinian Judaism: A Comparison of Patterns of Religion* (London: SCM Press, 1977).

SARNA, NAHUM, *The JPS Torah Commentary: Genesis* (Philadelphia: Jewish Publication Society, 1989).

SCHACHTER-SHALOMI, ZALMAN, and NETANEL MILES-YEPEZ, *A Heart Afire: Stories and Teachings of the Early Hasidic Masters* (Philadelphia: Jewish Publication Society, 2009).

SCHWARTZ, DOV, *From Phenomenology to Existentialism: The Philosophy of Rabbi Joseph B. Soloveitchik* (Leiden: Brill, 2013).

SESBOÜÉ, BERNARD, *'Hors de l'Église pas de salut': Histoire d'une formule et problèmes d'interprétation* (Paris: Desclée de Brouwer, 2004).

SHAPIRO, MARC, 'Modern Orthodoxy and Religious Truth', in Adam Ferziger, Miri Freud-Kandel, and Steven Bayme (eds.), *Yitz Greenberg and Modern Orthodoxy: The Road Not Taken* (Boston: Academic Studies Press, 2019), 129–45.

—— 'Of Books and Bans', *Edah*, 3/2 (2003), 2–16.

SINGER, DAVID, and MOSHE SOKOL, 'Joseph Soloveitchik: Lonely Man of Faith', *Modern Judaism*, 2/3 (1982), 227–72.

SKINNER, JOHN, *A Critical and Exegetical Commentary on Genesis* (Edinburgh: T&T Clark, 1994).

SOLOVEITCHIK, JOSEPH B., 'Confrontation', Tradition, 6/2 (1964), 5–29.

—— *Kol Dodi Dofek: Listen—My Beloved Knocks*, trans. David Gordon (New York: Yeshiva University, 2006).

—— *The Lonely Man of Faith*, 2nd edn. (Jerusalem: Maggid Books, 2018).

SOULEN, R. KENDALL, 'Israel and the Church: A Christian Response to Irving Greenberg's Covenantal Pluralism', in Tikva Frymer-Kensky et al. (eds.), *Christianity in Jewish Terms* (Boulder, Colo.: Westview, 2000), 167–74.

SPERLING, DAVID, 'Israel's Religion in the Ancient Near East', in Arthur Green (ed.), *Jewish Spirituality* (London: Routledge & Kegan Paul, 1986), i. 5–31.

SPRIGGS, D. G., *Two Old Testament Theologies* (London: SCM Press, 1974).

STUDENT, GIL, 'The Differences of Dignity' (25 Oct. 2007), https://www.torah-musings.com/2007/10/differences-of-dignity/.

THATAMANIL, JOHN, *Circling the Elephant: A Comparative Theology of Religious Diversity* (New York: Fordham University Press, 2020).

—— *The Immanent Divine: God, Creation and the Human Predicament* (Minneapolis: Fortress Press, 2006).

'Third Meeting of the Elijah Board of World Religious Leaders' (Nov. 2007), https://elijah-interfaith.org/meetings-of-the-ebwrl/third-meeting-of-the-elijah-board-of-world-religious-leaders.

THUNBERG, LARS, 'The Human Person as Image of God, I. Eastern Christianity', in Bernard McGinn, John Meyerdorff, and Jean Leclercq (eds.), *Christian Spirituality, i: Origins to the Twelfth Century* (New York: Crossroad, 1987), 291–312.

TIROSH-SAMUELSON, HAVA, and ARTHUR W. HUGHES (eds.), *Jonathan Sacks: Universalizing Particularity* (Leiden: Brill, 2013).

TOUATI, CHARLES, et al., 'Le Christianisme dans la théologie juive', *Revue des Études Juives*, 160 (2001), 495–7; Eng. trans.: 'Christianity in Jewish Theology', trans. Katherine E. Wolff, https://www.bc.edu/content/dam/files/research_sites/cjl/texts/cjrelations/resources/documents/jewish/France1973.htm.

WAARDENBURG, JACQUES (ed.), *Muslim Perceptions of Other Religions: A Historical Survey* (Oxford: Oxford University Press, 1999).

WESTERMANN, CLAUS, *Genesis: A Commentary*, trans. John Scullion (Minneapolis: Augsburg, 1985).

WILLIAMS, ROWAN, 'Professor Akbar Ahmed', in Alon Goshen-Gottstein (ed.), *Interreligious Heroes: Role Models and Spiritual Exemplars for Interfaith Practice* (Eugene, Oreg.: Wipf and Stock, 2021), 263–8.

WILLIAMSON, PAUL, *Sealed with an Oath: Covenant in God's Unfolding Purpose* (Downers Grove, Ill.: IVP, 2007).

WYSCHOGROD, MICHAEL, Review of Irving Greenberg, *Auschwitz: Beginning of a New Era? Reflections on the Holocaust*, *Tradition*, 17/1 (Fall 1977), 63–78.

Index

∎

A

Abraham:
  Abrahamic faiths 115, 133, 341–3, 345,
    352–3, 371
  Christianity and 117
  covenant and 11--12, 76, 90, 93, 99–100,
    104–8, 116, 198, 223–4, 261, 262, 415–16,
    430–1
  monotheism and 142, 341
  Noahide covenant and 225–6, 229,
    240–3, 248–9, 268, 415–18
  Sacks on 209, 223, 235, 237–9, 249, 252,
    278, 281–2, 330, 340
  spiritual descendants of 115–16
  universal/particular and 240–1
absence, divine 87
absolute principles 181
abstract truth 72, 337, 426
abyss 329, 377, 389
accommodation, theological 25n., 26n.,
    28–9, 36, 39, 46, 50–4, 60, 180
action:
  common action for good 58–9, 202
  covenant and 35, 40–1, 62–3, 72, 74, 84,
    175
  faith and 116
  human 31, 72, 74
  idolatry and 47
Adam:
  covenant and 11, 84, 91, 93, 239
  eating of living beings 226
  Noahide commandments and 128n.,
    227n., 228, 240
  tikun olam and 128
Africa, Christian bishops in 360–3, 369
Ahmed, Akbar 407

Ahrens, Rabbi Josh 153
Al Fayumi, Rabbi Nathanel 130, 285n.
America, *see* United States
Amos 80, 232, 415
ancient Near East 10, 88, 215
Anglican Church 248–9, 322, 362
antisemitism 209, 292n., 327, 360–1, 372,
    394, 423
Assyria 245
Auschwitz 327, 364, 401–2
authenticity:
  Abrahamic teachings and 343–6
  Christian faith and 61
  difference and 293
  human relationships and 221
  interfaith and 372
  Judaism and 62, 112
  messiahship and 53
  Sinaitic covenant and 107
  spiritual sharing and 204
  tolerance and 370
  traditional religious views and 369–70
authority:
  Islam and 335n.
  Noahide commandments and 227n.
  Orthodox Jewish tradition and 144
  pluralism and 301n.
  religion and 97
  Sinaitic covenant and 107
autonomy:
  covenant and 75–6, 86, 88, 421, 435
  growth of religion and 34
  human partnership with God and 214
avodah zarah 3, 256–8, 262–3, 265, 380
  see also idolatry

B

Babel, Tower of:
    as analogy for religious pluralism 205, 300
    diversity and 235, 258–9, 274, 278
    faith after 232
    Judaism and 262
    mutual learning and 313, 315, 380
Baha'i 250, 364–5, 402
Barr, James 188n.
Barth, Karl 17n.
beauty, in difference 200, 312, 330, 405
beliefs:
    Christian 54, 64, 66, 347
    Jewish–Christian relations and 30, 36, 41, 46–7, 61, 134, 141–2
    political 217–18
    religious diversity and 2, 63, 116n., 294, 339, 438
Berger, David 54n., 58n., 66n., 145n., 153
berit 15, 41, 92n., 162
    berit goral vs. *berit yi'ud* 248
    see also *brit*; fate
Berliner, Rabbi Naftali Zvi 142
Bible:
    biblical faith 28, 60
    biblical witness 114
    Christianity and 12, 28–9, 37, 63–6, 108, 112, 141, 186–7
    covenant and 243, 328, 431; 'grammar of biblical covenant' 36; Greenberg on 67–72, 169; history of 10–20; human covenants 219–20; Puritanism and 240n.; relational covenants 93; religion and 81
    covenant with Abraham 99–100
    covenant with Noah 90–9
    creation and 84
    criticism 69, 164
    forgiveness and 230
    God and 29
    Greenberg and 72–81, 83–90
    Hebrew Bible 12, 193, 215, 218, 269
    Incarnation and 61–3
    monotheism and 14
    promise of land in 89–90
    Sacks' works and 264, 273, 282
    as source for theological study 71
    see also Exodus
biological life:
    diversity and 260, 283, 316
    Sacks' reading of Judaism and 340, 428
    spiritual life and 26
bishops:
    African 360–4, 369
    Anglican 248–9, 322
Blenkinsopp, Joseph 227n.
blessings:
    Christianity and 108–9
    covenant and 10, 87–8
    difference as source of 245
    family model and 112–13
    religion and 337, 344
Borowitz, Eugene 16n., 76n., 172–4, 178, 214, 414n.
brit 75, 85, 87–8, 95, 98
    see also *berit*; fate
Britain/United Kingdom:
    America and 217
    citizenship and 224
    covenant and 246
    identity and 208, 246
    interfaith engagement in 394
    interreligious relations in 327, 344, 359, 364–5, 401
    Judaism and 321n., 359
    religious diversity in 208, 257
    Sacks and 193–4, 217, 246, 353, 391–3
brothers:
    Jacob and Esau (biblical narrative) 114
    Joseph and brothers (biblical narrative) 324, 356
    Judaism and Christianity as 140, 142
Buber, Martin 26, 118, 134, 322–3, 377–9, 383, 388, 396, 419, 438

Buddhism 79, 183–4, 246, 250, 283, 339, 364–5, 402

C
calling:
  divine 77, 339
  religious 79–80, 126
  see also 'Gifts and the Calling of God are Irrevocable'
Calvin, John 331, 338
Calvinism 352n.
Catholic Church:
  Greenberg's writings on 26, 43
  Judaism and 119, 141, 145, 153
  Nostra aetate 4, 30, 119, 139–40, 143, 331n., 336, 362
  one–covenant model and 110n.
  Pauline Christianity and 355
  Sacks' writings on 331, 353n.
  Vatican Council II 26, 140, 336
  see also Christianity; 'Gifts and the Calling of God are Irrevocable'; popes; Trinity; Vatican
Chalamet, Christian 17n.
Chalet, Christoph 108n.
charity 208, 398, 439, 441–2
chief rabbinate 141, 194, 392
childhood 230
chosen status, religion and 41–2, 278
Christ, *see* Jesus
Christianity:
  African bishops 360–3, 369
  authenticity and 61
  beliefs 54, 64, 66, 347
  Bible and 12, 28–9, 37, 63–6, 108, 112, 141, 186–7
  birth of 105
  blessings and 108–9
  commandments and 108, 141
  covenant and 12, 17–18, 72–3, 75, 77, 85–6, 89, 100–10, 240
  Crucifixion and 65–6
  death and 29, 47, 250

denominations 52
divinity and 347
faithfulness and 29, 42
Greenberg on 7–8, 45–51, 173, 181–3, 350
Holocaust and 25–6, 43, 65, 143
hope and 36, 54n., 58–60
idolatry and 50, 60, 63
Incarnation and 60–5
inclusivism and 107, 343
intention and 61
interpretation of Hebrew Scripture 108–9
Jesus and 52–9, 100
kabbalah and 31–2
legitimation and validation of other religions 121
Maimonides on 26n., 41n., 141, 144, 362
medieval 349
messianism and 42, 46
monotheism and 60–1, 142–3, 439
morality and 57, 65–6, 141
Moses and 108–9, 113
nations and 141, 160, 355
Orthodox Statement on 138–48, 150–60
particularity 51, 62
Pauline 355–6, 404
philosophy and 45
pluralism and 40–4, 79–83, 129, 132–5
polemics and 37–8, 149
redemption and 105, 117
reform theology 84n., 108n., 240
Sacks on 351–6, 362, 367, 379–81
sacrifice and 37, 65–6, 182
salvation and 62, 124, 336, 352
sin and 347
supersessionism 117, 163
theology of religion 121, 256, 335–6
tikun olam and 41, 105
Torah and 108, 362
transcendence and 51
universalism and 55
see also Catholic Church; Jesus; Protestantism

Christianity and Judaism:
  commonalities 35–6, 109, 250
  compared 31, 33–9, 96–7
  covenant and 73, 105
  following Second World War 2
  God and 42
  Greenberg on 123, 130–2, 161–70
  in Orthodox Statement on Christianity
    140–5
  Sacks on 372–3, 391
  Second Vatican Council and 4
  theology 111–20
Christologies 47, 424n.
citizenship 42, 105, 216, 222n., 224, 246
civic issues 151, 198, 200
  covenant and 242–4, 246
  diversity and 381
  religion and 326–8, 383, 421
  Sacks on 209, 213–14, 307, 311
civilization:
  difference and 265
  divinity and 44
  Judaeo–Christian ethic and 216
CLAL (National Jewish Center for
    Learning and Leadership) 157, 160,
    184
co-evolution of religions 444
coexistence 4, 36, 286, 419
Cohen, Rabbi Shear Yashuv 141
commandments:
  berit and 15
  Christianity and 108, 141
  covenant and 10, 13, 75, 92, 146–7
  faith and 75, 85
  see also Noahide commandments
commonalities:
  Abraham as source of 342, 345n.
  between Greenberg and Sacks 7
  between Judaism and Christianity
    35–6, 109, 250
  covenantal commonality 107, 112, 246,
    252–3
  reciprocal obligations and 231

competition, between religions 1, 39, 59,
    288, 355
'Confrontation' (Soloveitchik) 3n., 151–2
consciousness 176, 189–90, 239, 298, 390
Contemporary Covenantal Thought
    (Cooper) 17n., 76n.
Cooper, Simon 17n., 76n.
Council of Christians and Jews 358,
    367–9, 373, 376, 391
covenant:
  action and 35, 40–1, 62–3, 72, 74, 84, 175
  biblical covenant, grammar of 36
  biblical roots of 83–90
  contract vs. 221
  creation and 74, 76–8, 83–4, 417, 432–3
  as divine initiative 223, 226, 230–1, 250
  as expression of special relationship
    and 123
  of fate and destiny 247–54
  genius of the covenant 73, 78, 80
  in Greenberg's thought 72–5
  history and 75–8
  history of 10–20
  of hope and responsibility 241–7
  horizontal aspect of 220, 223–5, 237–9,
    266, 327–8, 337, 339
  Israel and 99–111
  Jewish theology of religions and 123–31
  legitimation and validation 121–2
  Noah and Abraham in relation to
    225–41
  Noahide 90–9
  other religions and 120–3
  pluralism and 77–83
  reciprocal obligations in 92n., 230–1
  recognition of spiritual value and 122
  as relationship 220–5
  renewal of 10, 15, 34–5, 75, 82, 85–6, 98,
    176, 238, 246
  theoretical context of 214–20
  tikun olam and 122–3
  verticality of 229, 327, 339, 435
  voluntary 223n., 412–13

with all living creatures 91–3, 98, 230
  with Noah 90–9
Covenant and Conversation (Sacks) 212
creation:
  berit and 15
  Christianity and 35
  covenant and 74, 76–8, 83–4, 417, 432–3
  diversity and 235, 263, 267, 278–9, 273,
    284, 286, 316
  divine–human partnership and 334
  Greenberg on 93–5
  importance to human history 72
  Noahide commandments and 228, 237,
    239–40
  redemption and 41, 48, 122, 145
  religious difference and 260–1, 309, 346
  revelation and 239, 288
  tikun olam and 128
  tsimtsum and 31
creativity:
  divine 284
  literary 341, 382
  theological 19, 24, 29, 73, 148, 225
credibility 88, 94, 144, 161, 186, 189
Crisis and Covenant (Sacks) 205, 209, 232,
  235, 252, 411, 414n.
Crucifixion 27, 43, 52, 65–6, 109, 181
culture:
  American 218
  covenant and 222
  of death 49
  diversity and 110, 119, 302, 345
  God's truth and 271
  Hellenistic 64
  language and 315
  particularity of 274–5, 287
  religion and 50, 274–9, 281, 283
  wisdom and 291–2, 314, 432
curiosity 407–8

D
Dalai Lama 295n., 376, 406
darkhei shalom 260n., 371, 393

de Tocqueville, Alexis 218, 332
death:
  Christianity and 29, 47, 250
  covenant and 72, 88, 175
  idolatry and 48–9
  Judaism and 176
  messianism and 56
  in Psalm 23: 4 169
debate, theological 28n., 123, 262n.
declaration of faith 246
denominations:
  affiliation and 20
  Christianity and 52
  Judaism and 2–3, 194, 205–6, 301, 307–8,
    412
dialogue, Sacks and:
  approach to 362–3, 367–70
  commonality and 366–7
  ethics and 381–2
  evolving view of 372
  extremism and 370–2
  feelings towards 375–80
  first interfaith experience 359–62
  friendships with religious leaders
    363–6
  interreligious relationships and 382–5
  overview 358–9
  see also Sacks, Rabbi Jonathan
diaspora:
  Jewish 2
  Muslim 130
'dignity of difference' 249, 251, 310, 366–7
Dignity of Difference, The (Sacks):
  agents of salvation and teaching in
    296–8
  comparison of two versions 268–88,
    319–20
  controversy about 196, 198, 200, 237,
    388
  covenant in 237, 241, 244, 247, 252–3,
    327–8
  Crisis and Covenant and 205, 232
  God and religion in 273–6

Dignity of Difference (cont.):
  Image of God in 290–1
  Jewish theology of religions and
    255–68
  morality in 294
  multiplicity as God's will in 277–84
  Not in God's Name and 210–11
  overview 200–1, 207–8
  particularity in 235, 315
  pluralism and 299, 301–2, 304, 345
  religion and truth in 276–7
  religious diversity and 208, 326, 329–30,
    337, 348
  revelation vs. human aspiration in
    288–90
  ritual diversity in 295–6
  study of other religions and 311–13
  theological diversity in 294–5
  varieties of difference in 293–8
  wisdom in 291–3
  see also Sacks, Rabbi Jonathan
disagreement, between faiths 37, 45, 181,
  248, 308
discourse:
  Abrahamic monotheisms 341
  covenant and 70–1, 212
  internal vs. public 351
  interreligious 252, 384
  pluralism and 299, 303
  religious imagination and 395
diversity:
  of agents of salvation and teaching
    296–8
  of covenants 119
  of culture 110, 119
  God and 271
  of human condition 235–6, 318–19
  morality and 294
  in nature 278, 309, 316
  religious 208, 234, 258–66, 279–87, 293,
    315–19, 432, 442
  ritual 295–6
  theological 294–5

divinity:
  Christianity and 347
  covenant and 18, 72–82, 92–9, 108, 111,
    170, 230, 251, 427
  dialogue and 377
  diversity and 258–9, 270, 277, 285, 287,
    295, 297–8, 318
  divine creativity 93, 284
  divine design 258, 309
  divine hiddenness 88
  divine–human partnership 334–5
  divine image 147, 280, 291
  divine initiative 18, 223, 226, 230–1, 250,
    288
  divine love 42, 98, 278–9, 285
  divine presence 87–8, 279, 282, 296, 339,
    372, 377, 389–90
  divine truth 271–2, 277, 310n.
  divine unity 251, 282
  divine will 144
  Greenberg on 31, 36, 72–82, 85, 87–8,
    103, 126
  hester panim and 180
  idolatry and 47–51
  image of God and 434
  Incarnation and 60–3
  Jewish–Christian relations and 141–2,
    147
  Meiri on 47–8
  morality and 294
  pluralism and 39–44, 47, 117, 129, 302,
    305
  relationship with 434–6
  religious diversity and 206, 258
  revelation and 164, 288–90
  Sacks on 223, 258–9, 273, 276, 339
  suffering and 38
  tsimtsum and 127, 179–80
  understanding of 14
  wisdom and 293
divorce 174
Donne, John 250
dream, covenant and 73

E

Eastern Orthodox Christianity 97
Eckhardt, Roy and Alice 24, 27, 182, 441
Egypt 80, 159n., 217, 232, 245, 263, 339, 344, 415n.
Eichrodt, Walther 10n., 17n.
election 17–18, 29, 41, 77n., 78, 89
Elijah Board of World Religious Leaders 195, 406
Elijah Interfaith Institute 161, 293n.
Elohim 261
Emden, Rabbi Jacob 26n., 40n., 141, 158
empathy 31, 52, 325, 373, 387, 391, 395
empire 210, 215, 238, 243, 256, 326, 339, 342
English-speakers 18, 139, 194, 381, 416n.
Enlightenment 370
environment, as God's creation 249–50
error (theological) 45–6, 49–50
erudition 206, 208–9, 321, 354, 414
Esau (biblical figure) 114, 142, 146, 232
Eskimo 280, 283
ethics:
    covenant and 142, 146, 233, 416
    dialogue and 381
    difference and 200
    Hebrew Bible and 282
    morality and 241
    mutual learning and 313
    religious difference and 286
evil 59, 140, 230, 355–6
evolution of religion 16, 31, 33–6
exclusivism 39, 45, 206, 255, 299, 335–6, 405, 424
exegesis 68–9, 195, 215, 355
exile:
    America and 217
    Greenberg on 31, 84
    identity and 338
Exodus:
    America and 217
    Christianity and 61, 104
    covenant and 249
    Incarnation and 62

Israel and 248
    revelation at Sinai 11
extremism 330, 369–72, 374

F

Fackenheim, Emil 175–7
failure:
    covenant and 11–12, 86
    evolution of Judaism and 16
    messianism and 56–7
    moral 48
    religion and 355, 439
Faith in the Future (Sacks) 206, 367
faithfulness:
    covenant and 10–11, 16, 73, 75, 85–6, 127, 221
    Greenberg's assessment of Christianity and 29, 42
    messianism and 53
    redemption and 84
family:
    covenant and 112–14, 240
    Judaism's focus on 41–2
    as metaphor 284, 324
    see also parenthood
fate:
    covenant and 198, 205, 247–53, 327
    religious diversity and 222
    see also *berit*; *brit*
federal theology 16n., 17n., 84n., 240n.
forgiveness 230
freedom:
    covenant and 76, 98–9, 216
    God and 142
    humanity and 48, 75, 85, 214
    religious diversity and 246
    United States and 218
friendship:
    Greenberg on 24–5, 182, 440
    interreligious 195, 204, 250, 397–9
    Sacks on 360–1, 363–7, 376, 418
    Williams on 397–402
Fry, Helen 367

Future Tense (Sacks) 209, 239, 262n., 302,
    394

G
gentiles:
  covenant and 51
  God and 42
  Greenberg on 104–7, 109, 113
  Hellenized 36, 60n.
  Jesus and 55
  messianism and 61–2
  morality and 286
  Paul and 40, 355
'Gifts and the Calling of God are
    Irrevocable' (Vatican document)
    42n., 85n., 119, 133n.
globalization 196, 208, 259n.
God:
  Christianity and 29, 46–7, 49, 51
  covenant and 10–20, 72–99, 245–52
  creation and 228, 230
  Crucifixion and 65–6
  family and 112–13
  Greenberg on 168–70, 179–80
  hope and 389–90
  idolatry and 263–4
  Incarnation and 60–4
  interpretation of God's law 297–8
  Islam and 273, 280, 345
  Israel and 99–100, 118–20, 214
  Jesus and 46
  Jewish–Christian relations and 105, 107,
    110, 112–13, 115–17, 134, 143–5, 156
  messianism and 179
  multiplicity and 277–84
  Noahide covenant and 188–9, 226
  in Orthodox Statement on Christianity
    143–7
  other religions and 121–2, 128–31, 256–
    61, 263–6
  otherness and 282, 372
  pluralism and 39–44, 49
  religion and 31, 33–6, 270–6

  revelation and 164
  Sacks on 218–25, 230–41
  tikun olam and 127–8, 160
  violence done in God's name 210–11
  word of God 163, 165, 187, 349
  see also divinity; image of God
Goodman, Daniel 15–58
goodness 47, 407
goodwill 72, 136–7, 365–6, 398, 417
Goshen-Gottstein, Alon 6n., 25n., 36n.,
  92n.
grace 18, 38, 41, 85, 189, 230, 276, 346–7,
  372
Great Partnership, The (Sacks) 209–10, 238,
  326, 354, 384
Greek cultural influences, religion and
  354
Greek philosophy 292
Greenberg, Blu 26n., 156
Greenberg, Rabbi Irving:
  avoidance of polemics 33, 36
  on Catholic Church 26, 43
  on Christianity 7–8, 45–51, 173, 181–3,
    350
  comparison to Sacks 5, 267, 418–24
  on covenant 67–72, 161–70
  on divinity 31, 36, 72–82, 85, 87–8, 103,
    126
  on exile 31, 84
  on friendship 24–5, 182, 440
  on gentiles 104–7, 109, 113
  God's-eye view of religions 39–42, 133,
    144, 151
  on idolatry 47–8, 433n.
  on image of God 419
  on inclusivism 71, 117, 118n., 133–8, 146
  introduction to 23–4
  on Islam 24n., 38, 79–80, 115–16, 120,
    435n.
  on Jesus 30, 36–7, 51, 134, 146, 154, 166
  on kabbalah 30–2, 87, 176–7
  Maimonides and 144

Meiri's influence on 48–50, 121, 125, 131, 428
on messianism 29, 42, 55, 60, 134, 154, 423
on monotheism 143
Orthodox Judaism and 151–60, 173, 412–13
Orthodox Statement on Christianity and 139–48, 152–60
on particularity 78–9, 199
on partnership 168–70, 181
personal background 24–7
on pluralism 37–9, 63, 132–5, 146, 181, 413–14, 417, 424
reception of his work 132–9, 149–60
on redemption 40–2, 129–30
Sacks and 411–24
on Scripture 79, 81, 420
Soloveitchik and 151–2, 157, 175, 178, 421
sources of his thoughts 170–80
study of Holocaust 25–7, 43, 48, 88–9, 129n., 150, 176, 179, 413
theological method 27–32, 180–9
on theology of religions 24, 122–3, 438
on *tikun olam* 40, 87, 99, 122–3, 160, 167–9, 175, 177, 179, 188
on Torah 156, 168–9, 171
on truth 146–7, 167–8, 181
view of history 40–3, 145

H

halakhah 23, 46, 50–1, 55, 171, 173–4, 187, 263–5, 267, 308
Halevi, Rabbi Judah 141, 297, 348
harmony:
    covenant and 94
    mutual learning and 313
    religious diversity and 1, 208, 263–4, 420–1
    Sacks on 264, 293, 306, 313, 345
Harries, Bishop Richard 286
Hartman, David 76n., 154, 157, 171, 173, 178–9, 189, 214, 300

hasidic tradition 30, 73, 128, 180, 300n., 368n., 373
hatred 82, 115–16, 257, 327
hermeneutics:
    Christianity and 29, 108, 186
    covenant and 12, 19–20, 88, 120
    of difficult passages 342
    friendship and 398
    Genesis 9 and 92
    Greenberg and 42, 52, 77, 124
    Sacks and 203, 269, 349
heroes:
    failure and 57
    Judaism and 37
    redemption and 89
Heschel, Rabbi Abraham Joshua (A. J.) 24n., 25n., 138, 155, 284n., 298n., 300
Hick, John 206, 255, 304n., 335n.
Hinduism:
    as *avodah zarah* 256
    Greenberg on 115
    image of God and 280, 295n.
    interfaith relations and 364–5, 376, 402
    Judaism and 125n., 183, 246, 250, 253n.
    Sacks on 258, 280–1, 283, 315n., 330, 390
    theology of religions 334–5
Hirsch, Samson Raphael 227n.
history:
    Christianity and 85
    covenant and 75–8, 93, 98, 221n., 223, 225, 230, 240, 251
    Greenberg's view of 40–3, 126–8, 145
    human history 72
    of Jewish–Christian relations 26, 30, 32–9, 45, 104, 135, 140–1
    Judaism and 88–9, 329–30
    messianism and 52–7, 60
    religion and 165–6
    twentieth-century 48, 143, 216
History of the Jews (Johnson) 219
holiness 43, 56, 108, 142
Holocaust:
    Christianity and 43, 65, 143

Holocaust (*cont.*):
  the divine and 88
  Greenberg's study of 25–7, 43, 48, 88–9,
    129n., 150, 176, 179, 413
  impact on Judaism 2
  moral lesson drawn from 26
  post-Holocaust view of election 17
  Sacks on 205, 225, 249, 412
  see also Shoah
Home We Build Together, The (Sacks)
    208–9, 222n., 326–7, 375, 377, 394
homeland 89
honouring:
  the covenant 250
  God's creation 235
  the past 225
hope:
  Christianity and 36, 54n., 59–60
  covenant and 198, 222, 238, 241–54, 323,
    341
  God and 389–90
  humanity and 422
  in Rosenzweig's work 136
  Sacks on 323–4, 346, 374
human nature 84–5
humility 42, 63, 359, 369, 407

I
idolatry:
  Christianity and 50, 60, 63
  Greenberg's view of 47–8, 433n.
  language and 259n.
  morality and 48, 263–4
  Noahide commandments and 239n.,
    430
  other religions as 3, 28n., 338n.
  traditional Jewish understanding of 49
  using religion for political ends as 344
  see also *avodah zarah*
image of God:
  covenant and 77–8, 84n., 147, 170, 236,
    240–1, 417, 428–30
  creation of mankind and 7, 233–4,
    237, 371
  discovery of God's image 129, 372
  diversity and 387, 439–40, 442
  in Genesis 9 90
  Greenberg on 419
  humanity and 72, 207, 229, 310, 317
  idolatry and 263–4
  particularity and 319
  pluralism and 129
  religion and 97, 330
  religious diversity and 265, 305
  Sacks on 279–81, 290–1, 320
  theology of religion and 256, 442
  tselem elokim 178
  two-covenant theory and 432–6
  see also God
imitatio dei 29, 31
Incarnation 27–9, 36, 46, 52, 60–5, 101, 347
inclusivism:
  Christianity and 107
  covenant and 129, 222
  Emden and 26
  Greenberg on 71, 117, 118n., 146
  Judaism and 118n., 206
  pluralism and 129, 132–5, 206
  reverse inclusivism 135
  Sacks on 255, 287, 291, 299, 301–10, 336,
    343–4, 413
India, religion and 306, 320
  see also Hinduism
individualism 181, 296, 380
inspiration:
  Bible and 243
  difference and 293, 295
  interfaith relations and 38, 87, 246, 270,
    288, 298, 319, 331
  revelation and 129, 290
insularity 2, 4, 209
intention:
  Christianity and 61
  covenant and 224
  divine 40–1
  revelation and 164

interfaith relations:
  banning of 3
  community and 393–4
  covenant and 120–3
  difference and 313, 327
  engagement and 201–2
  qualified openness and 202–4
  Sacks and 205–6, 209, 249–50, 311, 322,
    359–63, 368
  value of 9
  see also dialogue, Sacks and
interpretation:
  Abrahamic faiths and 346, 349–50
  covenant and 76
  God's law and 297–8
  religious diversity and 211, 343, 441
  of Scripture 5, 108–9, 226, 394
interreligious engagement, *see* interfaith
    relations
Interreligious Heroes (Goshen-Gottstein)
    155, 407
Intersecting Pathways (Krell) 25n., 41n.,
    110n., 118n.
intimacy 74, 87, 128n., 320, 366, 383
Islam:
  Abraham and 210, 224, 243, 343
  covenant and 100, 106, 133, 246
  diversity and 261, 285n.
  extremism and 330
  God and 273, 280, 345
  Greenberg's theological work and
    24n., 38, 79–80, 115–16, 120, 435n.
  interfaith communities and 120, 250,
    340, 364, 376, 402
  interpretation of scriptures 349
  Jewish pluralism and 38
  Maimonides on 26n.
  relationship between religion and
    democratic freedom 253n.
  revelation and 164, 289
  Sacks on 258, 340–3, 347, 351, 353
  submission and 347
  theology of religions 334–5
  see also Muhammad; Shia Islam

J
Jacob, Benno 227n.
Jainism 250, 364–5, 402
Jefferson, Thomas 217
Jeremiah (biblical figure) 57, 84–5
Jeremiah, book of 12, 223
Jerusalem 137, 155
Jesus:
  as agent of salvation 296
  covenant and 100, 106
  Crucifixion 65–6
  early Christianity and 29, 42–3
  Greenberg's study of 30, 36–7, 51, 134,
    146, 154, 166
  Incarnation and 60–5
  Judaism and 141, 144
  as messianic figure 27–8, 46, 52–9
  morality and 297
  Resurrection 28, 63, 66, 101, 109, 134
  revelation and 349
  Sacks on 353–4
  as Son of God 36, 60–1, 348–9
  Williams on 397
  see also Christianity;
    messiah/messianism
Jewish Action magazine 154
Johnson, Lyndon Baines 217
Johnson, Paul 219
Joseph (biblical figure) 324, 356
Joseph (father of Jesus) 56–7
Judaism:
  authenticity and 62, 112
  biological life and 340, 428
  Catholic Church and 119, 141, 145, 153
  compared to other religions 206, 210,
    333, 337
  death and 176
  denominations 2–3, 194, 205–6, 301,
    307–8, 412
  family and 41–2
  heroes and 37
  inclusivity and 118n., 206
  morality and 219

Judaism (*cont.*):
Moses and 218–19
particularity and 17, 20, 199, 238, 255, 262, 300, 333
Paul and 117, 153
philosophy and 197, 292, 311, 413
pluralism and 334, 336, 419
polemics and 51, 63
politics and 209, 413
rabbinic vs. biblical 14, 223n.
theology of religions: Christianity and 95, 102, 120–1; covenant and 123–31; interfaith relations and 100, 111, 422; legitimation and 121; Noahide covenant and 95, 100; Sacks and 255–68, 300, 388, 393
Tower of Babel and 262
see also Christianity and Judaism; Holocaust; Orthodox Judaism; Torah
jurisprudence 347, 349–50
justice:
covenant and 89, 217
religion and 40, 142
social justice 151–2, 423

K
kabbalah:
berit and 15
Christianity and 31–2
covenant and 87, 128
Greenberg's references to 30–2, 87, 176–7
tikun olam and 59, 76–7, 127–8, 176
tsimtsum and 127, 177
Kasper, Cardinal Walter 42
Kennedy, John F. 217
Kogan, Michael 103, 161–2, 180
Kook, Rabbi Abraham Isaac 25n., 276, 286, 292n., 294, 297, 427n., 435n., 442n.
Korn, Eugene 153
Krell, Mark 25n., 27, 41n., 118n., 134, 150
Kristallnacht, anniversary of 364, 401
Kuzari (Halevi) 288n., 348

L
Lambeth Conference 248–9, 253, 322
land:
American identity and 217–18
Land of Israel 13, 17, 89–90, 341
as part of covenant 27
redemption and 84
leadership:
Orthodox 157
rabbinic 42, 141, 151
lekhathilah 258, 260–1, 264, 267
Letter in the Scroll, A (Sacks), see *Radical Then, Radical Now*
Levenson, Jon 187, 210n., 211n., 416n.
Levinas, Emmanuel 323–4
Lincoln, Abraham 217
linguistic analogy 205, 259–60, 315, 326
Living in the Image of God (Freedman) 3n., 179, 412
Lonely Man of Faith, The (Soloveitchik) 170, 376
Lubavitcher Rebbe 55, 300n., 329, 368
Lumen gentium (Vatican II document) 352n.

M
Maimonides, Moses:
Greenberg and 144
Israel's election and 78
messianism and 55
on Mishnah 228n.
on non-Jews 237
on notion of holy war 336
view of Christianity 26n., 41n., 141, 144, 362
marriage, as metaphor for covenant 226, 244, 320, 427
Massignon, Louis 340n.
medieval Christianity 349
see also Christianity
medieval sources 5, 227n.
medieval wisdom 292–3
Meiri, Rabbi Menahem:
diversity and 294–5

on idolatry 48
influence on Greenberg's works 48–50,
  121, 125, 131, 428
on religion 45–8, 124, 133, 135, 287, 294,
  422
Sacks and 263–5, 268, 336, 418
Mendelssohn, Moses 285n.
Mendes-Flohr, Paul 377n.
messiah / messianism:
  Christianity and 42, 46
  Crucifixion and 65
  Greenberg on 29, 42, 60, 134, 154, 423
  Incarnation and 60
  Jesus as 52–9
'Modern Orthodoxy and Religious Truth'
  (Shapiro) 58n., 102n., 144n., 263n.,
  298n.
'Modern Orthodoxy and the Road Not
  Taken' (Greenberg) 32n.
modernity 17, 43–4, 177
monotheism:
  Abrahamic 209–12, 215, 238, 243, 262,
    326, 329, 339, 341–2
  Christianity and 60–1, 142–3, 439
  covenant and 219, 249
  Greenberg on 143
  linguistic analogy 259
  non-monotheists 263–6
  norms of 50
  pluralism and 303
  Sacks on 282, 304, 418; darkhei shalom
    and 260n.; in The Great Partnership
    209; language and 259n.; religious
    diversity and 332–3, 338, 345–6, 384,
    387
morality:
  book of Deuteronomy and 216, 220
  Christianity and 57, 65–6, 141
  commonality and 268
  community impact on 297
  covenant and 221, 231, 233, 235–7, 246,
    253

covenantal 225, 430
de Tocqueville on 218
difference and 286–7, 294, 297
Emden on 141
familialism and 41
as foundation of religions 283–4
Genesis 9 and 93n., 188n.
God and 241
idolatry and 48, 64n.
Judaism and 219
Meiri on 47–9, 124
Noahide commandments and 91
'people of Israel' and 116
Sacks' view of 256–7, 263, 265–6
shared morality 266, 381
universal vs. particular and 240
Morality (Sacks) 194–5, 211–12, 262n.,
  322–3, 338–9, 366
Moses:
  Abraham and 342
  America and 218
  Christianity and 108–9, 113
  covenant and 100, 107–8, 239
  Jesus and 57, 141, 354
  Judaism and 218–19
  word of God and 187
Muhammad (Prophet) 100, 335n.
  see also Islam
Muslim, see Islam
mutual discovery 129
mutual learning 293, 313–21, 325–6
mystical tradition 32, 306, 430
  see also kabbalah

N
nations:
  Christianity and 141, 160, 355
  covenant and 14, 106, 245, 428
  diversity and 294
  pluralism and 301
  religion and 45, 95n.
nature, covenant and 94, 98
Netsiv of Volozhin 114n., 146

Niebuhr, Reinhold 173–4

Noahide commandments 26, 91–5, 128n.,
    188, 226–9, 236–8, 240, 263, 274, 279,
    287

Nostra aetate (Vatican II document) 4, 30,
    119, 139–40, 143, 331n., 336, 362
    see also Catholic Church

Not in God's Name (Sacks):
    Abraham's message and 238n.
    Dignity of Difference and 325n.
    interfaith relations and 324, 384, 387
    Jewish theology of religions and
        256–7
    Noahide covenant and 240
    overview 210–11
    pluralism and 302
    religion and 243n., 354n., 355
    unpublished works and 434n.
    'we' and 328

Novak, David 227n., 229n., 416n.

O

obedience 13, 76, 85, 98, 170, 181, 270, 272

obligations:
    covenant and 18, 99, 220, 224, 230–1,
        251, 431
    ethical 146
    partnership and 74, 142
    reciprocal 231
    religious 356

observance 86, 174–5, 263, 412

One People? (Sacks) 205–6, 255, 271n., 307,
    413

original sin, *see* sin

Orthodox Judaism:
    covenant and 214
    evolution of 2
    Greenberg and 151–60, 173, 412–13
    interreligious dialogue and 3–4, 380–1,
        392
    Jewish Orthodox Statement on
        Christianity 138–48, 150–60
    Sacks and 193–5, 203, 359, 386, 413

otherness:
    covenant and 86
    dignity of difference and 200, 252, 311,
        313
    God and 282, 372
    humanity and 323–4
    identity and 305
    Kook on 292n.
    religious 234
    Sacks on 256, 271, 319, 377, 384
    theological diversity 294
    validating difference and 293

P

pagan religions 212, 260n., 262n., 263, 338,
    342, 379n.
    see also religion

parenthood 224, 235, 245, 324

particularism 187, 218, 358

particularity:
    Christian 51, 62
    commonality and 243, 252
    covenant and 80, 89, 100, 215, 225, 241,
        301, 348, 415, 430–9
    dialogue and 377–8, 381–5
    difference and 252–6, 285–7, 295, 298,
        305–6, 310–15, 319–20, 325, 366–7, 375
    Greenberg on 78–9, 199
    humanity and 73–4
    of Jewish–Christian relationship 115
    Judaism and 17, 20, 199, 238, 255, 262,
        300, 333
    pluralism and 133, 201
    religion and 233–4, 416–18, 429–30
    Sacks on 201, 205–7, 222, 242, 266, 274,
        342, 346, 419
    universality and 199–200, 226, 239, 255,
        262, 302, 304, 328, 350, 354–5

partnership:
    covenant and 36, 41, 74–7, 79–80, 86,
        94–6, 98, 122–3, 126–7
    divine–human 74–5, 79–80, 99, 214, 334
    Greenberg on 168–70, 181

Jewish–Christian relationship and 42, 73, 105, 140–5
patience, friendship and 398
patriarchy 10–11, 37, 112, 137, 155, 243, 341
Paul (apostle):
    anti-Pauline polemics 355–6
    Greenberg on 40
    influence on Christianity 355, 404
    Judaism and 117, 153
    Sacks on 333, 353–5
    Sinai and 108
peace:
    covenant and 232, 245, 301
    diversity and 307
    as goal of interreligious cooperation 1, 4, 142, 200, 208, 394
    pluralism and 301
    Sacks on 257, 267, 307, 331, 334–5, 340–1, 351, 370, 378–80, 388–9
    'ways of peace' 247, 263
peoplehood 42, 101, 111, 115, 117–20, 248
persecution 29, 47, 63
Petuchowski, Jakob 174, 419
phenomenology:
    messianic 52
    of partnership with God 96
    of religion 35, 81, 253, 434
philosophy:
    Christianity and 45
    dialogue and 377
    Dignity of Difference and 200
    inclusivism and 308
    Judaism and 197, 292, 311, 413
    kabbalah and 31–2
    morality and 322–3
    Sacks' background in 193, 211, 232, 331–2, 412
    wisdom and 292
Pizzaballa, Pierbattista, Archbishop 138, 155
pluralism:
    Christianity and 132–5
    covenant and 46, 77–83, 106–7, 129–30, 224, 244–5

dignity of difference and 311–13
Greenberg on 153, 175, 181, 413–14, 417, 424; covenant and 70–1; development of theory 37–9, 51, 63; Holocaust and 88n.; inclusivism and 117, 132–5, 146; Meiri's influence on 47, 49–50; messianism and 55; religious symbolism and 66
    invitation to 39–44
    Judaism and 334, 336, 419
    Meiri and 265
    messianism and 57–8
    mutual learning and 313–30
    rejection of 369
    Sacks on 205–7, 237, 413–14, 423; development of theory 255–6, 258, 266, 268, 345, 351; idealized view of 244; inclusivism and 287, 298–310; Meiri's influence on 265; Noah-Abraham covenants and 240–2; theological diversity and 294; upholding of 201; validation of religions and 293
    upholding 201
polemics:
    in discussion of Christianity 37–8, 149
    Greenberg's avoidance of 33, 36
    in Jewish religious writings 51, 63
    in Sacks' writings 199, 333, 347–8, 350–7
politics:
    covenant and 10, 215–22, 224, 238, 241, 328
    Judaism and 209, 413
    messianism and 189
    morality and 341
    in relationship between Greenberg and Sacks 157–8
    religion and 344
    theology of religions and 256–7, 290
popes:
    Benedict XVI 140, 331n.
    John XXIII 331n.
    John Paul II 120n., 140, 331

popes (*cont.*):
Paul VI 331n.
religious normativity and 392
see also Catholic Church
prayer 16, 308, 317, 337, 346
promised land 217–18
promises:
Abrahamic 112, 116
Christianity and biblical promises 108
covenant and 13, 92–4, 127, 188–9, 220, 230, 415, 431
divine promise 98–9, 251
Israel and 89–90
messianism and 165–6
Protestantism 16n., 17, 154, 173, 355
see also Christianity
providence 36, 141, 218, 298
psychology:
dialogue and 360
difference and 50, 265, 400
interfaith relations and 372–3, 383
pluralism and 305
religion and 270, 295, 318, 329
punishment 13, 76, 88, 152, 180, 189
Purim 34

R
Rabbinical Council of America (RCA) 151–2, 154
rabbis:
covenant and 12, 19, 215, 227–8
Judaism and 14–15
Orthodox 203
religious diversity and 263–4, 284, 361–2
theology and 227n., 231
see also Noahide commandments
Radical Then, Radical Now (Sacks) 206–7, 209, 337, 348
rainbow, as symbol of covenant 230, 249, 251
Ramakrishna, Sri 306, 309, 318
redemption:
Christian theology and 105, 117
covenant and 36, 72, 74, 78, 83–4, 88–9, 94, 129, 225
creation and 94–5, 122
Greenberg on 40–2, 129–30
human–divine relationship and 62, 129
Jesus and 55–6
Jewish–Christian partnership and 141, 145
messianic 53, 56, 59
peoplehood and 115
religion and 35, 40, 48
tikun olam and 59
total redemption 82
tsimtsum and 127
Reform rabbis 172, 174
reform theology (Christian) 84n., 108n., 240
Reformation, the 17
relational complexity 411–14
relativism 277, 335, 413
religion:
authority and 97
autonomy and 34
blessings and 337, 344
chosen status and 41–2, 278
civic issues and 326–8, 383, 421
co-evolution of 444
complexity of 336, 352, 356–7
culture and 50, 274–9, 281, 283
evolution of 16, 31, 33–6
failure and 355, 439
Greek influence on 354
history and 165–6
idolatry and 3, 28n., 338n., 344
image of God and 97, 330
India and 306, 322
justice and 40, 142
Meiri on 45–8, 124, 133, 135, 287, 294, 422
nations and 45, 95n.
particularity and 233–4, 416–18, 429–30
phenomenology of 35, 81, 253, 434
pluralism and 39–44
politics and 344

redemption and 35, 40, 48
salvation and 121, 130
society and 218–20, 250, 311, 327–8, 332,
339–40, 350, 358, 381–2, 385–6
teachers and 296, 359–60
see also Christianity; Hinduism; Islam;
Judaism; pagan religions; theology
of religions
repentance 25, 182, 347, 356
responsibility, covenant and 18, 34, 41,
72–6, 126–7, 216, 221, 241–7
resurrection (Christian concept of) 28,
63, 66, 101, 109, 134, 166
see also Christianity; Jesus
revelation:
creation and 239, 288
divinity and 164, 288–90
human aspiration vs. 288–90
inspiration and 129, 290
intention and 164
Islam and 164, 289
Jesus and 349
at Sinai 11
transcendence and 164–5
wisdom and 261
rights:
covenant and 170, 218, 240
human rights 229, 235, 278
Riskin, Rabbi Shlomo 139n., 153
ritual diversity 295–6
rituals 15, 59, 174, 268, 297
Rivkis, Rabbi Moses 142
Rosenzweig, Franz 41n., 102n., 136–7
Rushdie, Salman 370

S
Sacks, Rabbi Jonathan:
background 193–6
comparison of versions of *The Dignity
of Difference* 268–88
comparison to Greenberg 5, 267,
418–24
complexity in work of 312, 316, 358, 363,
367–8, 382, 384
contributions to lowering
interreligious tensions 394
on covenantal dimension 393
covenantal perspective 198
criticism and polemics 350–7
on dignity of difference 200–1
on divine revelation and human
aspiration 288–90
engagement and relationships 201–2
Greenberg and 411–24
on image of God 290–1
Jewish theology of religions and
255–69
legacy 386–92
on legitimating other religions 392
likening Judaism to other religions
337–46
methodological note on writings
196–7
mutual learning and 313–30
on normativity 392–3
on pluralism vs. inclusivism 299–310
qualified openness 202–4
religious imagination 395–6
review of sources 204–13
scriptural grounding 394–5
study of other religions 311–13, 331–7
on superficial presentation of religions
346–50
on universal and particular 199–200,
291–2
upholding of pluralism 201
on varieties of difference 293–8
vision for community 393–4
on wisdom 291–2
see also dialogue, Sacks and; *Dignity of
Difference*
sacrifice:
Christian belief and 37, 65–6, 182
covenant and 221
self-sacrifice 182, 423
Sages 35, 60, 141–2, 187, 236n., 240, 314, 356
salvation:
agents of 296

salvation (*cont.*):
  Christianity and 62, 124, 336, 352
  covenant and 235
  Incarnation and 62
  inclusivity and 309–10
  Sacks on 278, 281–2
  validation of other religions and 121,
    130
Sanders, E. P. 15n.
Sandmel, David 117
Schaar, John 217
Schneerson, Rabbi Menachem Mendel
    of Lubavitch 54–5, 300n., 329, 368
Scripture:
  approach to 68–70
  belief in 173
  Christian interpretation of Hebrew
    Scripture 108–9
  Christian Scripture 397
  connection to the divine and 40
  covenant and 68, 76, 79, 86
  Greenberg on 79, 81, 420
  Judaeo–Christian faith and 36, 142
  Sacks on 230, 301, 331, 343, 348–50, 394–5,
    418
secularism 43, 128, 225, 262n., 346, 412–13
service to others 37, 79n., 142, 200
sexuality 15, 37
Shapiro, Marc 102n., 144n., 163, 262,
    298n., 338n., 433n.
Shia Islam 97, 183, 349, 355
  see also Islam
shituf 50–1, 124, 296n., 336n.
Shoah 48, 140, 143, 161, 175–7, 182
  see also Holocaust
Sikhism 246, 250, 253, 280, 330, 364–5, 376,
    390, 402, 406
sin 56, 98, 259, 356
  original 346–7
Skinner, John 227n.
society:
  covenant and 94, 214–16, 222, 225, 229,
    240–1, 243–4, 246–7

difference and 293
  as family 324
  interreligious relations and 161, 263,
    265, 370, 394
  Israeli 2, 84, 90
  morality and 212
  religion and 218–20, 250, 311, 327–8, 332,
    339–40, 350, 358, 381–2, 385–6
  Sacks' work as service to 194, 199–201,
    256–8
solidarity:
  friendship and 365–6
  global covenant of 198, 222, 237n.,
    242–3, 247, 435
  horizontality and 328
  at human level 209, 238–9, 390
  in Jewish–Christian relations 183
  religious identity and 246, 341
Soloveitchik, Rabbi Joseph B.:
  'Confrontation' 3n., 151
  covenant and 198, 248
  Greenberg and 151–2, 157, 175, 178, 421
  importance to modern Orthodoxy
    3–4
  on interfaith relations 102
  on partnership 170
  Sacks and 203, 205, 248, 252, 329, 376,
    380–3, 390
sonship, Jesus and:
  as Son of God 36–7, 58n., 60–1, 348–9
  as son of Joseph 56–7
  see also Jesus
spirituality:
  Greenberg and 128n.
  Sacks and 252–3, 321, 329–31, 389, 442
Statement on Christianity, *see* Orthodox
    Judaism: Jewish Orthodox
    Statement on Christianity
Stendahl, Krister 118, 128n., 129n.
supersessionism:
  Christian 117, 163
  Greenberg on 33n., 115–17
  history of 116

T

Talmud:
  covenant and 142, 172
  Genesis 9 and 228n.
  image of God and 429
  reference to Purim 34
tana deve menasheh 228n.
Tanakh (Hebrew Bible) 169–72, 176, 186,
  360
  see also Torah
teachers:
  covenant and 87
  interfaith 82
  religion and 296, 359–60
  sharing and 406
  theological thought and 9
  wisdom and 293
Temple, destruction of 13, 16, 34–5
tenets:
  of Christianity 50, 52
  religious difference and 333, 346–7, 352
theology of the other 256, 268, 441
theology of religions:
  Christianity and 121, 256
  covenant and 67, 95, 100, 320, 426–7
  current state of 1–10
  diversity and 442–3
  Greenberg on 24, 122–3, 438
  Hinduism and 334
  image of God and 429
  Islam and 334
  Judaism and 123–31, 255–68; and
    Christianity 102, 111; and interfaith
    relations 120–1, 300, 388, 393, 422; and
    Noahide covenant 95, 100
  Meiri and 50n.
  pluralism and 303–4, 307
  religious difference and 293, 351
  Sacks on 255–68, 288, 437–8
  as theoretical discipline 335
theosis 407, 430
  see also divinity

tikun olam:
  Christianity and 41, 105
  contemporary adaptation of 59
  covenant and 72, 78, 79n., 81, 83, 126–8
  explained 31
  Greenberg on 40, 87, 99, 122–3, 160,
    167–9, 175, 177, 179, 188
  Noahide covenant and 94–6
  validation of other religions and 121
Tillich, Paul 332
Tirosh-Samuelson, Hava 232n., 253n.,
  311–12, 321, 375n., 386
To Heal a Fractured World (Sacks) 208, 247,
  260n., 321, 387
tolerance:
  dialogue and 379, 383
  dignity and 312
  intolerance and extremism 371–2
  religious difference and 26, 246, 369–70
  Sacks on 336, 368n., 379
Torah:
  Christianity and 108, 362
  community and 181
  covenant and 10, 12–13, 91, 127, 156, 188,
    225, 234, 239, 248
  dual nature of 289
  faithfulness and 127
  Greenberg on 156, 168–9, 171
  Jesus and 141, 354
  Judaism and 16
  Noahide commandments and 227n.
  Sacks on 193–5, 212, 216, 269–70, 286,
    317, 432
  torah misinai 168
  torah shebe'al peh 172, 186–7
Tradition in an Untraditional Age (Sacks)
  205, 313
transcendence:
  Christianity and 51
  God and 273–6, 278
  rabbinic Judaism and 41
  revelation and 164–5
  truth and 272

Trinity, the 28, 46, 60–1
 see also Catholic Church; God
triumphalism 39, 47, 63–5
truth:
 absolute 50, 232, 272, 286, 429
 covenant and 426
 faith and 41–2, 63, 66
 God and 270–4
 Greenberg on 146–7, 167–8, 181
 inclusivism and 305
 intended audience and 50–1
 interfaith relations and 82, 129–30,
  141–2, 146–7, 281, 317, 337, 395, 415, 440
 Maimonides on 144, 237
 messianism and 53, 165
 Noahide covenant and 146, 167
 pluralism and 181, 300, 305
 Sacks on 211, 232, 235, 257, 276–8
 torah misinai 168
 universal vs. particular 199, 285–6, 350,
  437
 wisdom and 314
tselem elokim 167–70, 178, 188
tsimtsum 31, 87, 127–8, 177–80
two-covenant construct 430–7
 see also covenant

U
United Kingdom, *see* Britain
United States:
 covenantal politics and 217, 314n.
 interfaith engagement in 394
 Jewish theological community in 17,
  83, 126, 149, 329
 lack of chief rabbinate 194
 national identity and 217–18, 332
 Orthodox rabbis in 140
universalism:
 Christianity and 55
 covenant and 219
 particularism and 187, 199
 Sacks' view of 199, 358, 439

V
Van Buren, Paul 27, 173, 182

Vatican 42, 85, 133, 135, 145n.
 Vatican II 3n., 4, 26, 43, 109, 140, 331n.,
  336, 340n., 381
 see also Catholic Church; popes
violence, religious 207–8, 210, 326, 333,
 352, 355–6, 367
'Voluntary Covenant' (Greenberg) 150,
 177, 180

W
Washington, George 217
Weiss, Rabbi Avi 156
Welby, Justin, Archbishop of Canterbury
 364
Williams, Rowan, former Archbishop of
 Canterbury 204n., 322n., 401
wisdom:
 covenant and 240, 252
 hokhmah 159
 interfaith relations and 203, 247, 311–12,
  330–1, 337
 knowledge and 239
 revelation and 261
 Sacks and 194–5, 200, 276, 321, 432
 sharing of Jewish wisdom 208, 212,
  322, 423
 Torah and 193–5, 216
 truth and 314
 universal vs. particular 291–3
 willingness to learn from others and
  314–15
women:
 messianism and 54
 mutual discovery and 129
 as rabbis 156
Wyschogrod, Michael 5n., 154

Y
Yeshivat Chovevei Torah (YCT) 137n.,
 156–7

Z
Zoroastrianism 250, 258, 364–5, 402
Zwingli, Ulrich 17n.